SEA-BED ENERGY AND MINERALS:
THE INTERNATIONAL LEGAL REGIME

Volume 2
SEA-BED MINING

Sea-bed Energy and Minerals

Volume 2

SEA-BED ENERGY AND MINERALS: THE INTERNATIONAL LEGAL REGIME

Volume 2
SEA-BED MINING

by

E. D. BROWN

*Professor of International Law in the University of Wales;
Director of Centre for Marine Law and Policy, Cardiff*

MARTINUS NIJHOFF PUBLISHERS
THE HAGUE / BOSTON / LONDON

Library of Congress Cataloging-in-Publication Data

ISBN 90-411-1540-4

Published by Kluwer Law International,
P.O. Box 85889, 2508 CN The Hague, The Netherlands.

Sold and distributed in North, Central and South America
by Kluwer Law International,
675 Massachusetts Avenue, Cambridge, MA 02139, U.S.A.

In all other countries, sold and distributed
by Kluwer Law International, Distribution Centre,
P.O. Box 322, 3300 AH Dordrecht, The Netherlands.

Printed on acid-free paper

All Rights Reserved
© 2001 Kluwer Law International
Kluwer Law International incorporates the publishing programmes of
Graham & Trotman Ltd, Kluwer Law and Taxation Publishers,
and Martinus Nijhoff Publishers.

No part of the material protected by this copyright notice may be reproduced or
utilized in any form or by any means, electronic or mechanical,
including photocopying, recording or by any information storage and
retrieval system, without written permission from the copyright owner.

Printed in the Netherlands.

Table of Contents

PREFACE	xxvii
TABLE OF CASES	xxix
TABLE OF UN AND UNCLOS RESOLUTIONS	xxxi
TABLE OF STATUTES AND OTHER MUNICIPAL INSTRUMENTS	xxxv
TABLE OF TREATIES AND INTERNATIONAL REGULATIONS	xxxvii
TABLE OF THE MINING CODE	liii
TABLES AND FIGURES	lix
ABBREVIATIONS	lxi

Part 1

INTRODUCTION

CHAPTER 1

	Introduction	3
I	THE SCOPE OF VOLUME 2	3
II	THE STATUS OF THE UN CONVENTION	6
	1. Entry into force and transitional arrangements	6
	1.1 Entry into force	6
	1.2 Provisional application of Implementation Agreement and interim budgetary arrangements	9
	2. Breakthrough to universality? Current status	11

v

vi

CHAPTER 2

The common heritage of mankind as a fundamental principle:
ideology or reality?　　　　14

I INTRODUCTION: FUNDAMENTAL PRINCIPLES IN
    CONFLICT　　　　14
    1. Freedom of the seas versus sovereignty: the classical
        conflict　　　　14
    2. Freedom of the seas versus common heritage of mankind:
        a modern conflict　　　　15

II THE FREEDOM OF THE HIGH SEAS VERSUS THE
     COMMON HERITAGE OF MANKIND: THE CONFLICT
     IN HISTORICAL PERSPECTIVE　　　　17
     1. The pre-1967 debate　　　　17
     2. The freedom of the high seas　　　　18
         2.1 Essential character of the principle　　　　18
         2.2 Was there a prohibitory rule?　　　　19
         2.3 Tentative conclusion　　　　22

III THE EFFECT OF DEVELOPMENTS AFTER 1967　　　　22
     1. The Maltese initiative　　　　22
     2. General Assembly resolutions　　　　23
         2.1 The legal effect of General Assembly resolutions　　　　24
         2.2 The Moratorium Resolution　　　　27
         2.3 The Declaration of Principles Resolution　　　　28
     3. The Charter of Economic Rights and Duties of States,
         1974　　　　32
     4. The UNCTAD Resolution of 17 September 1978　　　　33
     5. Group of 77 statements　　　　33
         5.1 Letter dated 23 April 1979 from the Group of Legal
              Experts on the Question of Unilateral Legislation to
              the Chairman of the Group of 77　　　　34
         5.2 Speech of Chairman of Group of 77, 15 September
              1978　　　　38
         5.3 Condemnation of Provisional Understanding　　　　39
         5.4 Towards a *modus vivendi*　　　　39
         5.5 The significance of the 'practice' of the Group of 77　　　　40
     6. Practice of the industrialised States　　　　41
     7. The UN Convention on the Law of the Sea, 1982　　　　45

IV CONCLUSIONS　　　　45

vii

Part 2

THE UNITED NATIONS REGIME OF SEA-BED MINING

CHAPTER 3

The UN Convention regime of sea-bed mining:
I. The principles of the regime   49

I   THE FUNDAMENTAL PRINCIPLE: THE COMMON
     HERITAGE OF MANKIND   49
  1. Ideological milieu – the significance of the Preamble   50
  2. Scope of the common heritage of mankind *ratione loci*   52
  3. Scope of the common heritage of mankind *ratione
      materiae*   53
  4. Scope of the common heritage of mankind *ratione
      temporis*: limited scope   for amendment   54
  5. Scope of the common heritage of mankind *ratione
      personae*   56
        5.1   Does the Convention create obligations for States
              and other entities not parties to it?   56
        5.2   What entities have the capacity to become parties to
              the Convention?   59
              5.2.1   States   59
              5.2.2   Self-governing associated States and
                      territories enjoying full internal self-
                      government   59
              5.2.3   International organisations   60
              5.2.4   National liberation movements   62
              5.2.5   Peoples of non-self-governing territories,
                      territories under colonial domination and
                      territories sovereignty over which is
                      disputed   64
        5.3   Who are the intended beneficiaries of the common
              heritage of mankind?   65
              5.3.1   States Parties to the Convention   66
              5.3.2   States not parties to the Convention   66
              5.3.3   Self-governing associated States and
                      territories enjoying full internal self-
                      government   66

viii

	5.3.4 National liberation movements	67
	5.3.5 People of non-self-governing territories, territories under colonial domination and territories sovereignty over which is disputed	67
	5.3.6 The *travaux préparatoires*	68
	5.3.7 Distribution of the benefit of mankind	70

II   LEGAL STATUS OF THE AREA AND ITS RESOURCES   72

III   GENERAL CONDUCT OF STATES; USE FOR PEACEFUL PURPOSES; NON-DISCRIMINATION   73

IV   BENEFIT OF MANKIND   75

V   RESPONSIBILITY TO ENSURE COMPLIANCE AND LIABILITY FOR DAMAGE   75
1. State responsibility   75
2. Responsibility of international organisations   77

VI   RIGHTS AND LEGITIMATE INTERESTS OF COASTAL STATES   78

VII   MARINE SCIENTIFIC RESEARCH   79

VIII   TRANSFER OF TECHNOLOGY   81
1. The principle stated   81
2. Mechanisms for transfer of technology   82

IX   PROTECTION OF THE MARINE ENVIRONMENT   84

X   PROTECTION OF HUMAN LIFE   85

XI   ACCOMMODATION OF ACTIVITIES IN THE AREA AND IN THE MARINE ENVIRONMENT   86

XII   PARTICIPATION OF DEVELOPING STATES IN ACTIVITIES IN THE AREA   88

XIII   ARCHAEOLOGICAL AND HISTORICAL OBJECTS   92

ix

CHAPTER 4

The UN Convention regime of sea-bed mining:
II. The basic regime for the development
of the resources of the Area 96

I 'POLICIES RELATING TO ACTIVITIES IN THE AREA':
UN CONVENTION, ARTICLE 150 100

II NON-DISCRIMINATION BY THE AUTHORITY:
UN CONVENTION, ARTICLE 152 104

III TITLE TO MINERALS: UN CONVENTION, ANNEX III,
ARTICLE 1 104

IV PROSPECTING: UN CONVENTION, ANNEX III, ARTICLE
2 AND MINING CODE, PART II 104
 1. Prospecting defined 104
 2. UN Convention, Annex III, Article 2 104
 3. The Mining Code, Part II 105
  Regulation 2: Prospecting 105
  Regulation 3: Notification of prospecting 106
  Regulation 4: Consideration of notifications 106
  Regulation 5: Prospectors' annual reports 107
  Regulation 6: Confidentiality of data and information from
  prospecting in annual report 108
  Regulation 7: Notification of incidents causing serious
  harm to the marine environment 109
  Regulation 8: Objects of an archaeological or historical
  nature 109

V THE SYSTEM OF EXPLORATION AND EXPLOITATION:
WHO MAY EXPLORE AND EXPLOIT THE RESOURCES
OF THE AREA; PLANS OF WORK: UN CONVENTION,
ARTICLE 153 AND ANNEX III, ARTICLES 3-6, AS
MODIFIED BY THE IMPLEMENTATION AGREEMENT 109
 1. Article 153: the background 109
 2. Rôle of Authority 112
 3. Who may carry out activities? 113
  3.1 Article 4 of Annex III - qualifications of applicants
   for contracts 113
  3.2 Article 5 of Annex III - transfer of technology 116

	4. Plans of work	117
	4.1 Article 3 of Annex III - applications for plans of work	117
	4.2 Article 6 of Annex III - approval of plans of work submitted by applicants	118
	5. Security of tenure for contractors	123

VI PRODUCTION POLICIES: UN CONVENTION, ARTICLE 151 AND IMPLEMENTATION AGREEMENT, ANNEX, SECTION 6 — 123

1. Unfair economic practices - UN Convention, Article 151(8) and Section 6 of Annex to the Implementation Agreement — 125
2. Economic assistance to developing countries - UN Convention, Article 151(10) and Section 6 of Annex to the Implementation Agreement — 127

VII RESERVATION OF SITES (THE 'BANKING' SYSTEM): RIGHTS, OBLIGATIONS AND OPPORTUNITIES OF OPERATORS OTHER THAN THE ENTERPRISE IN RELATION TO RESERVED SITES: ANNEX III, ARTICLES 8, 9 AND 11 AND IMPLEMENTATION AGREEMENT, ANNEX, SECTION 1(10) — 131

VIII FINANCIAL TERMS OF CONTRACTS: UN CONVENTION, ANNEX III, ARTICLE 13 AND IMPLEMENTATION AGREEMENT, ANNEX, SECTION 8 — 134

1. The objectives of the financial terms of contracts: UN Convention, Annex III, Article 13(1) — 136
2. Types of payment envisaged: UN Convention, Annex III, Article 13(2)-(10) and the Implementation Agreement, Annex, Section 8(1) and (3) — 137
   2.1 The system of payments under the Implementation Agreement: the Implementation Agreement, Annex, Section 8 — 137
   2.1.1 An application fee: UN Convention, Annex III, Article 13(2) and the Implementation Agreement, Annex, Section 8(3) — 138
   2.1.2 An annual fixed fee: Implementation Agreement, Annex, Section 8(1)(d) — 138
   2.1.3 Royalty system or combined royalty/profit-sharing system: Implementation Agreement, Annex, Section 8(1)(c) — 139

	3. Accounting and audit	140
	4. Currency of payments or payments in kind	140
	5. Disputes over financial terms of contracts	140
IX	TRANSFER OF DATA: UN CONVENTION, ANNEX III, ARTICLE 14	140
X	TRAINING PROGRAMMES: UN CONVENTION, ANNEX III, ARTICLE 15	142
XI	EXCLUSIVE RIGHT TO EXPLORE AND EXPLOIT: UN CONVENTION, ANNEX III, ARTICLE 16	142
XII	RULES, REGULATIONS AND PROCEDURES OF THE AUTHORITY: UN CONVENTION, ANNEX III, ARTICLE 17	142
XIII	PENALTIES: UN CONVENTION, ANNEX III, ARTICLE 18	143
XIV	'RESPONSIBILITY OR LIABILITY': UN CONVENTION, ANNEX III, ARTICLE 22	144
	1. The liability of the contractor	144
	2. The liability of the Authority	145
	2.1 Liability for disclosure of industrial secrets	146
XV	REVISION OF CONTRACT: UN CONVENTION, ANNEX III, ARTICLE 19	147
XVI	TRANSFER OF RIGHTS AND OBLIGATIONS: UN CONVENTION, ANNEX III, ARTICLE 20	148
XVII	APPLICABLE LAW: UN CONVENTION, ANNEX III, ARTICLE 21	148
XVIII	RESOURCES OF THE AREA OTHER THAN POLYMETALLIC NODULES	149

xii

CHAPTER 5

The UN Convention regime of sea-bed mining
III. The Mining Code: exploration 152

I THE APPLICATION FOR A PLAN OF WORK FOR
EXPLORATION 153
1. Who may make an application for a plan of work for
exploration 153
   1.1 The general position 153
   1.2 Applications by registered pioneer investors 153
2. The content of the application 154
   2.1 The form of the application 154
      • Information on the applicant 154
      • Information on the area under application 154
      • Financial and technical information 154
      • The plan of work for exploration 155
      • Undertakings 155
      • Previous contracts 155
      • Attachments 155
   2.2 Who submits the application 155
   2.3 Requirement of certificate of sponsorship 155
   2.4 The financial and technical capabilities of the
applicant 155
   2.5 Previous contracts with the Authority 156
   2.6 Undertakings 156
   2.7 'Total area covered by the application' and 'Data
and information to be submitted before the
designation of a reserved area' 156
   2.8 Applications for approval of plans of work with
respect to a reserved area 156
   2.9 Data and information to be submitted for approval
of the plan of work for exploration 158
3. Fee for applications 159
4. Processing of applications 160
   4.1 Receipt, acknowledgment and safe custody of
applications 160
   4.2 Consideration of applications by the Legal and
Technical Commission 160
      4.2.1 When is an application considered? 160
      4.2.2 Criteria to be considered by the Commission 161
         4.2.2.1 Criteria relating to the applicant 161
         4.2.2.2 Criteria relating to the proposed
plan of work 161

xiii

| | | 4.2.2.3 | Grounds for not recommending approval | 162 |

4.2.2.3 Grounds for not recommending approval 162
4.2.2.4 Commission recommendation to Council 163
4.2.3 Procedure for pioneer investor applications 164
4.3 Consideration and approval by the Council of plans of work 164

II THE CONTRACT FOR EXPLORATION 165
1. The contract 165
1.1 The form of the contract 165
1.2 Parties to the contract 166
1.3 Scope of contract *ratione materiae* 166
1.4 Non-discrimination as compared with registered pioneer investors 166
1.5 Contractor's priority for exploitation 167
1.6 Size of area, renunciation and relinquishment 167
1.7 Duration of contracts 170
1.8 Training 173
1.9 Security of tenure and contractor's exclusive right to explore 174
1.9.1 Security of tenure 174
1.9.2 Contractor's exclusive right to explore 175
1.9.3 Periodic review of the programme of work 175
1.9.4 Suspension and termination of contracts 176
1.9.5 Revision of contracts 178
1.10 Responsibility and liability 179
1.10.1 Liability of the contractor for damage 179
1.10.2 Liability of the Authority for damage 181

III PROTECTION AND PRESERVATION OF THE MARINE ENVIRONMENT 182

IV CONFIDENTIALITY OF DATA AND INFORMATION 182
1. What constitutes confidential data and information 183
2. Limitations on use by Authority of confidential data and information 183
3. Period of confidentiality 184
4. Procedures to ensure confidentiality 184
5. Standard contractual clause on confidentiality 186

V SETTLEMENT OF DISPUTES 186

xiv

CHAPTER 6

The UN Convention regime of sea-bed mining:
IV. The pioneer investor scheme   187

I   ORIGINS AND RAISON D'ETRE   187

II   THE ORIGINAL PIONEER INVESTOR SCHEME   190
     1.   Registration as a pioneer investor   190
          1.1   Three categories of pioneer investor   190
          1.2   Applications for registration of pioneer investors   193
          1.3   Allocation of pioneer areas   193
          1.4   Financial arrangements   193
          1.5   Assistance to the Enterprise   194
     2.   Approval of plans of work   194
     3.   Production Authorisations   195

III THE DEVELOPMENT AND ADAPTATION OF THE
     PIONEER INVESTOR SCHEME   195
     1.   The Preparatory Commission: responsibilities, organs,
          rules and procedures   195
     2.   The preparation of the rules for the implementation of the
          pioneer investor scheme: the Preparatory Commission's
          1984 session   196
     3.   The obligation to avoid overlapping areas: the original
          provisions of Resolution II   196
     4.   State practice 1982-84 and the Provisional Understanding
          of 3 August 1984   199
          4.1 The abortive MOU negotiations   199
          4.2   The Agreement concerning Interim Arrangements
                relating to Polymetallic Nodules of the Deep Sea
                Bed, 1982   200
          4.3   Soviet and Indian applications to the Preparatory
                Commission and responses thereto 1983-84   200
          4.4   Provisional Understanding of 3 August 1984 and its
                relation to Resolution II   207
          4.5   State practice 1982-1984: summing up   213
     5.   The Understanding on Resolution of Conflicts Among
          Applicants for Registration as Pioneer Investors of 31
          August 1984   213
          5.1   Principal features of Understanding   214
          5.2   Status of the Understanding   216
          5.3   Autumn 1985: impasse   220
     6.   The Arusha Understanding of 7 February 1986 and the
          New York Understanding of 5 September 1986   221

	6.1	Principal ingredients of Understandings	221
	6.2	General Committee and Group of Technical Experts	223
	6.3	Confidentiality of data and information	224
7.	The 'Midnight Agreement' of 14 August 1987		226
	7.1	Registration of Indian pioneer investor	226
	7.2	The 'Midnight Agreement' network	226
	7.3	Registration of French, Japanese and Soviet pioneer investors	228
8.	The Understanding on Pioneer Investors' Obligations of 30 August 1990		229
9.	The Chinese pioneer investor application, 1990-91		230
10.	Application by East European States and Cuba, 1991		231
11.	Application by the Republic of Korea, 1994		232

IV	THE 1994 IMPLEMENTATION AGREEMENT AND THE PIONEER INVESTOR SCHEME		232
	1.	Plans of work of registered pioneer investors: provisions of the Implementation Agreement and the Mining Code	233
		1.1 The timing of applications and duration of plans of work	233
		1.2 Who may submit applications for approval of plans of work?	234
		1.3 The content of the application	236
		1.4 Fee	236
		1.5 The procedure for processing an application	237
		1.6 Related designation of reserved areas for the Authority	238
	2.	Approval of plans of work of registered pioneer investors: progress report	238
	3.	Monitoring fulfilment of obligations by registered pioneer investors and their certifying States: from the Preparatory Commission to the Authority	240

CHAPTER 7

The UN Convention regime of sea-bed mining:
V. The UN regime versus the reciprocating States regime:
a compromise solution   244

| I | INTRODUCTION | 244 |

xvi

II	THE RECIPROCATING STATES REGIME AND THE UN CONVENTION REGIME COMPARED	246

1. Reasons for and legal basis of 'interim' legislation and relationship to principle of common heritage of mankind embodied in UN Convention   246
    1.1   Common heritage doctrine versus unilateralism   248
    1.2   The scope of the interim regime *ratione temporis*   249
    1.3   The scope of the interim regime *ratione personae*   249
         1.3.1   Who could apply for a licence under the Reciprocating States Regime   251
         1.3.2   Benefits of operating under a Reciprocating State's licence   252
    1.4   Reservation of sites ('site-banking')   256
    1.5   Anti-monopoly and diligence provisions   257
    1.6   Protection of land-based mineral producers   260
    1.7   Financial provisions and the Fund   261
         1.7.1 Levies   261
         1.7.2 International revenue-sharing funds   263
    1.8   Transfer of technology   266
    1.9   Other important provisions of the UN regime   267

III	THE CO-ORDINATION OF THE LEGISLATION OF THE RECIPROCATING STATES	268

1. The Agreement Concerning Interim Arrangements Relating to Polymetallic Nodules of the Deep Sea Bed, 1982   268
    1.1   Scope of Agreement *ratione personae*   268
    1.2   Scope of Agreement *ratione temporis*   269
    1.3   Scope of Agreement *ratione materiae*   269
    1.4   Identification and resolution of conflicts   269
    1.5   Compatibility of Agreement with UN regime   270
2. The Provisional Understanding Regarding Deep Sea-bed Matters, 1984   271
    2.1   Scope of Provisional Understanding *ratione personae*   271
    2.2   Scope of Provisional Understanding *ratione temporis*   271
    2.3   Scope of Provisional Understanding *ratione materiae*   271
         2.3.1 Prohibition of conflicting authorisations or registrations   271
         2.3.2 Co-ordination of national legislation and prescription of operating standards   272
             Applications requirements   272
             Standards   273

			No exploitation before 1988	274
			Notification and consultation	274
			Confidentiality	275
			Dispute settlement	275
	2.4		Compatibility of Provisional Understanding with UN Regime	275

IV THE INCOMPATIBILITY OF THE TWO REGIMES — 275

1. The differences between the two regimes — 275
2. A denial of the common heritage principle? — 277

V MODUS VIVENDI BETWEEN THE TWO REGIMES — 278

1. Scope of modus vivendi *rationae personae* — 283
   - 1.1 The New York Understanding of 5 September 1986 — 283
   - 1.2 The Midnight Agreement of 14 August 1987 on the Resolution of Practical Problems with Respect to Deep Sea-Bed Mining Areas with Related Exchanges of Notes — 283
   - 1.3 Memorandum of Understanding on the Avoidance of Overlaps and Conflict Relating to Deep Sea-Bed Areas between China and Seven Potential Applicant States of 22 February 1991 — 284
   - 1.4 Declarations by Eastern European States, 1991 — 284
   - 1.5 Declarations by Korea, 1994 — 285
2. Scope of modus vivendi *ratione materiae* — 285
   - 2.1 The New York Understanding of 5 September 1986 — 285
   - 2.2 The Midnight Agreement of 14 August 1987 and Related Exchanges of Notes — 285
   - 2.3 Memorandum of Understanding between China and Seven Potential Applicant States of 22 February 1991 — 285
   - 2.4 Declaration by Eastern European States, 1991 — 286
   - 2.5 Declaration by Korea, 1994 — 287
3. Scope of modus vivendi *ratione temporis* — 287

VI THE IMPACT OF THE IMPLEMENTATION AGREEMENT ON THE RECIPROCATING STATES REGIME — 289 xviii

CHAPTER 8

The UN Convention regime of sea-bed mining:
VI. The institutional framework   292

I   THE ESTABLISHMENT AND PURPOSE OF THE
AUTHORITY   293

II   THE ORGANS OF THE AUTHORITY   293
1. The principal organs   295
   1.1   The Assembly   295
     1.1.1   Composition   295
     1.1.2   Decision-making   295
     1.1.3   Powers and functions   296
   1.2   The Council   297
     1.2.1 Composition   297
       1.2.1.1   Equitable geographical representation
           – the 'floating seat' system

                                              300
       1.2.1.2   Council membership – Groups A - E   301
     1.2.2   Powers, functions and decision-making   307
     1.2.3   Subsidiary organs of the Council   311
       1.2.3.1 The two Commissions   312
       1.2.3.2 The Finance Committee   313
   1.3   The Secretariat   317
2. The Enterprise   317
   2.1   Rôle of the Enterprise and relationship to Authority   317
     2.1.1   The work of Special Commission 2(SCN.2)   319
     2.1.2   The UN Secretary-General's Informal
           Consultations   321
     2.1.3   The Implementation Agreement of 28 July
           1994   321
   2.2   Legal personality   322
   2.3   Structure   323
   2.4   Operations   324
     2.4.1   Capacity to carry out activities   324
     2.4.2   Plans of work   325
     2.4.3   Reserved areas   326
     2.4.4   Enterprise operations outside reserved areas   327
     2.4.5   Transfer of technology to the Enterprise   327
     2.4.6   Financial aspects   327
     2.4.7   Title to minerals and processed substances   328

		2.4.8	Non-discrimination and commercial basis of Enterprise operations	328
	2.5		Financial arrangements	328
		2.5.1	Basic principle	329
		2.5.2	Sources of funding	329
		2.5.3	Enterprise liability to make payments to Authority and the question of immunity from national taxation	331
		2.5.4	Allocation of net income	332
		2.5.5	Accounting, audit and annual report	332
	2.6		Immunities and privileges	332
	2.7		Liability of Enterprise	333
3.			Financial arrangements of Authority	335
	3.1		Budget and audit	335
	3.2		Funds established	336
	3.3		Sources of Authority funds	337
	3.4		Disbursement of funds	338
4.			Legal status, privileges and immunities of the Authority	339
5.			Suspension of rights of members of the Authority	340
6.			Relationship Agreement between the Authority and the United Nations	340
7.			Headquarters Agreement between the Authority and Jamaica	342

III			THE PREPARATORY COMMISSION	343
1.			The provisions of Resolution I	343
	1.1		Membership	343
	1.2		Duration	344
	1.3		Funding	344
	1.4		Functions	344
	1.5		Subsidiary bodies	345
	1.6		Decision-making	345
2.			The development by the Preparatory Commission of its institutional features	345
	2.1		The Preparatory Commission's organs and functions	346
		2.1.1	The Plenary	346
		2.1.2	The Special Commissions	347
		2.1.3	The General Committee	347
		2.1.4	Group of Technical Experts	347
		2.1.5	Training Panel	348
	2.2		Decision-making in the Preparatory Commission	348
3.			The Preparatory Commission's Final Report	348

xx

CHAPTER 9

The UN Convention regime of sea-bed mining:
VII. Settlement of disputes — 350

I	GENERAL OUTLINE OF THE SYSTEM	350
	1. The UN Convention in historical perspective	350
	2. The UN Convention model in outline	353

II THE INSTITUTIONS CONCERNED — 354
1. International Tribunal for the Law of the Sea — 354
   1.1 Composition of Tribunal — 354
   1.2 Special Chambers — 355
      1.2.1 Summary Procedure Chamber — 355
      1.2.2 Particular Category Chambers — 355
      1.2.3 *Ad hoc* Chambers — 356
2. Sea-Bed Disputes Chamber — 356
   2.1 Composition — 356
   2.2 *Ad hoc* Chambers — 356
3. Commercial Arbitral Tribunal — 357

III THE RANGE OF DISPUTES — 357

IV DISPUTES BETWEEN STATES PARTIES CONCERNING (1) THE INTERPRETATION OR APPLICATION OF PART XI AND RELATED ANNEXES, AS MODIFIED BY THE IMPLEMENTATION AGREEMENT AND (2) THE MINING CODE — 361
1. Part XI and related Annexes, as modified by the Implementation Agreement — 361
2. The Mining Code — 363

V DISPUTES BETWEEN A STATE PARTY AND THE AUTHORITY CONCERNING ACTS OR OMISSIONS OF A STATE PARTY ALLEGED TO BE IN VIOLATION OF PART XI OR RELATED ANNEXES, AS MODIFIED BY THE IMPLEMENTATION AGREEMENT, OR RULES, REGULATIONS AND PROCEDURES OF THE AUTHORITY; AND DISPUTES OVER ALLEGATIONS THAT A STATE PARTY HAS GROSSLY AND PERSISTENTLY VIOLATED PART XI, AS MODIFIED — 363
1. The exclusive jurisdiction of the Sea-Bed Disputes Chamber — 363
2. Disputes over transfer of technology — 364

VI	DISPUTES CONCERNING THE PRODUCTION POLICY OF THE AUTHORITY	365

VII	DISPUTES BETWEEN A STATE PARTY AND THE AUTHORITY CONCERNING : (1) ACTS OR OMISSIONS OF THE AUTHORITY ALLEGED TO BE IN VIOLATION OF PART XI OR RELATED ANNEXES, AS MODIFIED BY THE IMPLEMENTATION AGREEMENT, OR RULES, REGULATIONS AND PROCEDURES OF THE AUTHORITY; (2) ACTS OF THE AUTHORITY ALLEGED TO BE IN EXCESS OF JURISDICTION; OR (3) ACTS OF THE AUTHORITY ALLEGED TO BE A MISUSE OF POWER	366
	1. Exclusive jurisdiction of Sea-Bed Disputes Chamber	366
	2. Acts or omissions of the Authority alleged to be in violation of Part XI, as modified by the Implementation Agreement, or Rules, Regulations and Procedures of the Authority	366
	3. Acts of the Authority alleged to be in excess of jurisdiction	367
	4. Acts of the Authority alleged to be a misuse of power	367
	5. Limitations on jurisdiction of Chamber	368

VIII	DISPUTES CONCERNING CONFORMITY WITH THE CONVENTION OF PROPOSAL BEFORE ASSEMBLY	369

IX	CONTRACTUAL DISPUTES	369
	1. Disputes between parties to a contract concerning the interpretation or application of a relevant contract or plan of work.	369
	2. Disputes over the interpretation or application of the rules and regulations for financial terms of contracts; and disputes between the Authority and a contractor over the interpretation or application of the financial terms of a contract.	371
	3. Disputes between parties to a contract concerning acts or omissions of a party to the contract relating to activities in the Area and directed to the other party or directly affecting its legitimate interests.	372
	4. Disputes between the Authority and a prospective contractor concerning the refusal of a contract or a legal issue arising in the negotiation of the contract.	372

xxii

5.	Disputes between the Authority and a State Party, State enterprise or natural or juridical person, where alleged that Authority is liable for damage arising out of wrongful acts, including disclosure of industrial secrets etc.	372

X	ADMINISTRATIVE DISPUTES	373
1.	Disputes concerning alleged violations of responsibilities by Secretary-General of Authority or of a staff member	373
2.	Disputes concerning alleged disclosure by Secretary-General of the Authority or a staff member of industrial secrets etc.	373

XI	DISPUTES CONCERNING THE LIMITS OF THE AREA	373
1.	Disputes between States Parties	373
2.	Disputes between a State Party and the Authority	374

XII	DISPUTES CONCERNING OVERLAPPING PIONEER AREA CLAIMS	375

XIII	DISPUTES CONCERNING THE ENTERPRISE	375

XIV	CONCLUSION	375

Part 3

SEA-BED MINING AND THE MARINE ENVIRONMENT

CHAPTER 10

	Protection and preservation of the marine environment	379
I	INTRODUCTION	379
II	ASSESSMENT OF ENVIRONMENTAL IMPLICATIONS OF SEA-BED MINING	380
1.	United States research	380
1.1	Principal phases of sea-bed mining	382
1.2	*Modus operandi* of sea-bed mining	383
1.3	Conclusions drawn from NOAA research	383
2.	Japanese research	387
3.	Research by Interoceanmetal (IOM)	387

	4.	Indian research		387
	5.	Korean research		388
	6.	Chinese research		388
	7.	German research		388
	8.	Russian research		389

III	THE UN CONVENTION REGIME		389
	1.	Principles and policies	389
		1.1 Common heritage of mankind	389
		1.2 International responsibility and liability for damage	389
		1.3 Rights and legitimate interests of coastal States	389
		1.4 Protection of the marine environment	390
		1.5 Accommodation of activities in the Area and in the marine environment	390
		1.6 Policies relating to activities in the Area	390
		1.7 Principles entrenched against review	390
	2.	Part XII: environmental rules	391
		2.1 General obligation	391
		2.2 Best practicable means	391
		2.3 Duty not to transfer pollution	391
		2.4 Use of technologies	391
		2.5 Alien or new species	391
		2.6 Notification of imminent or actual damage and contingency plans	392
		2.7 Monitoring and environmental assessment	392
	3.	The setting and enforcement of environmental standards	393
		3.1 Setting environmental standards	393
		3.2 Enforcing environmental standards	394
		3.3 Rôle of Authority organs and Preparatory Commission	394
		3.3.1 Rôle of Assembly	394
		3.3.2 Rôle of Council	394
		3.3.3 Rôle of Legal and Technical Commission	395
		3.3.4 Rôle of Preparatory Commission	396
	4.	The Implementation Agreement	396

IV	THE MINING CODE: REGULATIONS ON PROSPECTING AND EXPLORATION FOR POLYMETALLIC NODULES IN THE AREA		398
	1.	Introduction: drafting history	398
	2.	Scope and structure of the Regulations	401

3.		Key environmental terms defined	402
	3.1	'Marine environment' defined	402
	3.2	'Serious harm to the marine environment' defined	402
4.		Prospecting and the marine environment	411
5.		Applications for approval of plans of work	413
	5.1	Data and information required before designation of a reserved area	413
	5.2	Data and information required after designation of a reserved area	414
	5.3	The position of registered pioneer investors	414
	5.4	Consideration of applications by the Legal and Technical Commission	416
6.		The contract for exploration: environmental aspects	416
	6.1	The precautionary principle and best available technology	416
	6.2	The contract	419
	6.3	'Exploration' defined	419
	6.4	Standard clauses	419

6.4.1	Environmental monitoring	420
6.4.2	Contingency plans and emergencies	423
	6.4.2.1 'Emergency orders' and 'immediate measures of a temporary nature' – Regulation 32	423
	6.4.2.2 Rights of coastal States – Regulation 33	427
6.4.3	Contractor's Annual Report	428
6.4.4	Data and information to be submitted on expiration of the contract	429
6.4.5	Confidentiality of data versus environmental protection	429
6.4.6	Due regard undertaking	429
6.4.7	Inspection	429
6.4.8	Responsibility and liability	429
6.4.9	Suspension and termination of contract and penalties	430

V		**THE PROVISIONS OF NATIONAL LEGISLATION**	430
1.		Overview	430
	1.1	United States	431
	1.2	Germany	431
	1.3	United Kingdom	432
	1.4	France	434
	1.5	Russia (formerly the Soviet Union)	435
	1.6	Japan	436
	1.7	Italy	437

		xxv

2. Analysis of United States Law — 437
 2.1 Purpose and strategy of legislation — 438
 2.2 Environmental safeguards in the exploration phase — 439
  2.2.1 Safeguards prior to the issue of licence — 439
  2.2.2 Safeguards incorporated in the licence — 441
  2.2.3 Safeguards provided by NOAA — 443
 2.3 Environmental safeguards in the commercial recovery phase — 445
  2.3.1 Safeguards prior to the issue of the commercial recovery permit
  2.3.2 Safeguards incorporated in commercial recovery permit — 449
  2.3.3 Safeguards provided by NOAA — 451
 2.4 Environmental safeguards for pre-enactment exploration — 453
 2.5 Polymetallic sulphide ores — 453
3. The co-ordination of national legislation — 453

VI CONCLUSIONS — 454

INDEX OF PERSONS — 455

SUBJECT INDEX — 457

Preface

This book is Volume 2 of a three-volume work on *Sea-Bed Energy and Minerals: The International Legal Regime.* Volume 1, published in 1992, was concerned with *The Continental Shelf.* Volume 3 embodies a selection of key documents referred to in Volumes 1 and 2.

In the Preface to Volume 1, written in 1992, it was noted that the exploitation of the polymetallic nodules of the deep sea-bed was unlikely to take place before the early years of the next century. It was suggested that, in one sense, this was fortunate, in that it gave the international community much-needed time to reach agreement on the highly complex legal regime needed to govern it. Although the new Millennium has now arrived, exploitation is still some years away. However, much progress has been made and, following the adoption in July 2000 of a first instalment of the Mining Code, the time now seems opportune to present an account of the current state of the law. I have tried to take account of developments down to 1 October 2000.

In preparing this volume, I have incurred debts to a number of friends and colleagues. For advice on the national legislation of their countries and on the current status of sea-bed mining licences, I am grateful to Prof. Jean-Pierre Beurier of the University of Nantes; Prof. Rainer Lagoni of the University of Hamburg, Dr. Renate Platzöder of the Institute for International Affairs, Ebenhausen, and Herr Joachim Koch, President of the Council of the International Seabed Authority for 1998; Judge Tullio Treves of the International Tribunal for the Law of the Sea and University of Milan; Prof. Moritaka Hayashi of the Unversity of Waseda; and Mr. James Lawless and Mr. Joseph Flanagan, both of the US National Oceanic and Atmospheric Administration (NOAA). Mr. Michael Lodge, Chief of the Office of Legal Affairs and Mrs. Michelle Bond, Librarian, both of the International Seabed Authority, have responded generously to my frequent requests for documentation and information on current developments.

Two of my colleagues in Cardiff have greatly eased my task. Louise Deeley has cheerfully and expertly produced camera-ready copy from a difficult manuscript and Mr. Alun Rogers of the Cartographic Unit of the Department of Maritime Studies of Cardiff University has generously given of his time and

xxviii *Preface*

expertise to redraw the sketch-map which appears in Chapter 7 and to process the Table in Chapter 10.

Finally, a special word of thanks is due to Mrs. Annebeth Rosenboom, Publisher, of Kluwer Law International for her advice and support over the years and especially for her patience in agreeing to delay delivery of the manuscript until the Mining Code had at long last been adopted by the Authority.

October 2000   E.D.B.

Table of Cases

Aegean Sea Continental Shelf (Greece *v*. Turkey), Judgment (ICJ – 1978) … 352

Anglo-Iranian Oil Co. Ltd. *v*. Jaffrate and Others (*The Rose Mary*) (Aden Supreme Court, 1951) … 254

Fisheries Jurisdiction Case (Spain *v*. Canada), Jurisdiction of the Court (ICJ – 1998) … 352

Fisheries Jurisdiction (United Kingdom *v*. Iceland), Jurisdiction of the Court (ICJ – 1973) … 352

Military and Paramilitary Activities in and against Nicaragua (Nicaragua *v*. United States of America), Jurisdiction and Admissibility, Judgment (ICJ – 1984) … 255

Nuclear Tests cases (Australia *v*. France; New Zealand *v*. France), Judgments (ICJ – 1974) … 352

Rose Mary, The case (Aden Supreme Court, 1951) … 254

South West Africa, Second Phase, Judgment (ICJ – 1966) … 255

South West Africa – Voting Procedure, Advisory Opinion (ICJ – 1955) …24-27

Table of UN and UNCLOS Resolutions

1. UN General Assembly Resolutions

1960   Declaration on the Granting of Independence to Colonial Countries and Peoples (Resolution 1514 (XV) of 14 December 1960) ... 60, 62, 65, 66, 67, 68, 69, 75

1965   The Question of the Cook Islands (Resolution 2064 (XX) of 16 December 1965) ... 59-60

1969   Moratorium Resolution (Resolution 2574 (XXIV) of 15 December 1969) ... 23, 27-28, 45

1970   Declaration of Principles Governing the Sea-Bed and the Ocean Floor, and the Subsoil thereof, beyond the Limits of National Jurisdiction (Resolution 2749 (XXV) of 17 December 1970) ... 15, 16, 17, 28-32, 34,35, 36, 37, 39, 40, 41, 43, 44, 45,50, 51, 52, 57, 69, 248, 277
Declaration on Principles of International Law Concerning Friendly Relations and Co-operation among States in Accordance with the Charter of the United Nations (Resolution 2625 XXV) of 24 October 1970) ... 35

1974   Charter of Economic Rights and Duties of States (Resolution 3281 (XXIX) of 12 December 1974) ... 23, 31, 32-33
The Question of Niue (Resolution 3285 (XXIX) of 13 December 1974) ... 59-60

1982   Third United Nations Conference on the Law of the Sea (Resolution 37/66 of 3 December 1982) ...344

1983   Third United Nations Conference on the Law of the Sea (Resolution 38/59 of 14 December 1983) ... 344

1994   Resolution on the Agreement Implementing Part XI of the United Nations Convention on the Law of the Sea of 10 December 1982 (Resolution 48/263 of 28 July 1994) ... 4, 8, 10, 16, 50, 97, 99, 298, 349

1996   Resolution Inviting the International Seabed Authority to Participate in the General Assembly's Deliberations as an Observer (Resolution 51/6 of 24 October 1996) ... 341

1997   Resolution Approving the Agreement Concerning the Relationship between the United Nations and the International Seabed Authority (1996) (Resolution 52/27 of 26 November 1997) ... 341

xxxii *Table of UN and UNCLOS resolutions*

2. UN Security Council Resolutions
1990   Resolution Terminating the Trusteeship Agreement for the Federated
        States of Micronesia, the Marshall Islands and the Northern Mariana
        Islands (Resolution 683/1990) ... 60
1994   Resolution 963/1994 concerning Palau ... 60

3. UNCLOS Resolutions
1982   Resolution I on the Establishment of the Preparatory Commission for the
        International Sea-Bed Authority and for the International Tribunal for
        the Law of the Sea ... 96, 189, 260, 292, 317, 318, 343, 345
                        Preamble ... 344
                        Paragraph 1 ... 344, 348
                        Paragraph 2 ... 63, 343
                        Paragraph 4 ... 195, 345
                        Paragraph 5 ... 343
                            5(a)-(g) ... 344
                            (g) ... 96, 343, 346, 347, 366, 396
                            (h) ... 195, 344, 346
                        (i) ... 128, 260, 345, 347
                        Paragraph 7 ... 195, 345, 348
                        Paragraph 8 ... 317, 319, 345, 347
                        Paragraph 9 ... 260, 345, 347
                        Paragraph 10 ... 97, 345
                        Paragraph 11 ... 97, 345, 346, 348
                        Paragraph 12 ... 347
                        Paragraph 13 ... 97, 344, 348
                        Paragraph 14 ... 344
        Resolution II Governing Preparatory Investment in Pioneer Activities
        Relating to Polymetallic Nodules ... 5, 17, 19, 39, 170, 187, 189, 190,
        195, 196, 199, 200, 201, 202, 203, 204, 206, 208, 212, 215, 216, 219,
        220, 221, 223, 225, 226, 240, 256, 258, 260, 266, 276, 283, 288, 289,
        292, 317, 318, 343, 347
                        Paragraph 1(a) ... 7, 193, 207
                            1(a)(i) ... 191, 213, 219
                        1(a)(ii) ... 191, 219, 283, 286
                        1(a)(iii) ... 192, 231, 232
                        1(b) ... 193
                        1(c) ... 191
                        1(d) ... 149
                        1(e) ... 168, 193, 222, 241
                        Paragraph 2 ... 193, 202, 283, 344
                        2(a) ... 191
                        Paragraph 3 ... 193, 214, 220, 221, 256, 257, 322
                            3(a) ... 202, 224, 238
                            3(b) ... 193, 196, 202, 222, 238
                        Paragraph 4 ... 192, 193, 283
                        Paragraph 5 ... 193, 203, 213

5(a) ... 196, 197, 201, 202
5(c) ... 197, 198, 199, 202, 206, 214, 216
5(d) ... 198, 214
Paragraph 7(a) ... 159, 160, 193, 235
Paragraph 7(b) ... 194, 229, 231, 261
Paragraph 7(c) ... 194, 229
Paragraph 8 ... 193, 194, 233, 241
8(a) ... 190
8(c) ... 194, 240
Paragraph 11 ... 230, 234, 241
11(a) ... 159, 164, 236, 237, 238, 344
Paragraph 12 ... 319, 347
12(a)(i) ... 222, 243
12(a)(i)-(iii) ... 319
12(a)(ii) ... 174, 194, 229, 348
12(a)(iii) ... 229
12(b) ... 194
12(b)(i)-(ii) ... 319
Paragraph 13 ... 233, 287
Paragraph 14 ... 287
Resolution III relating to territories whose people have not obtained
either full independence or some other self-governing status recognised
by the United Nations or territories under colonial domination ... 65
Resolution IV relating to national liberation movements ... 63

4. UNCTAD Resolutions
1972   Resolution 52(III) of 19 May 1972 ... 34
1978   Resolution of Trade and Development Board of 17 September 1978 on
        'The Exploitation of the Seabed beyond the Limits of National
        Jurisdiction' ... 23, 31, 33

5. UNCED Resolutions
1992   Rio Declaration on Environment and Development ... 417, 418, 419

Table of Statutes and Other Municipal Instruments

1945   United States: Presidential Proclamation No. 2667 of 28 September 1945 ('Truman Proclamation') ... 3

1970   Canada: Arctic Waters Pollution Prevention Act ... 352

1972   United States: Coastal Zone Management Act ... 449
       United States: Marine Mammal Protection Act ... 442, 449

1973   United States: Endangered Species Act ... 442, 449

1976   United States: Magnuson Fishery Conservation and Management Act ... 449

1980   Germany: Act of Interim Regulation of Deep Seabed Mining ... 188, 246, 249, 431-432
       United States: Deep Seabed Hard Mineral Resources Act ... 187, 211, 244-245, 246, 247, 249-268, 381, 382, 431, 437-453
       United States: Deep Seabed Mining Regulations Affecting Pre-Enactment Explorers ... 437, 453

1981   France: Law on the Exploration and Exploitation of Mineral Resources on the Deep Sea-Bed ... 188, 245, 246, 249-268, 434-435
       United Kingdom: Deep Sea Mining (Temporary Provisions) Act ... 188, 245, 246, 249-268, 432-434

1981/82 United States: Deep Seabed Mining Regulations for Exploration Licences ... 188, 244, 258, 437-453

1982   Federal Republic of Germany: Act of 12 February 1982 amending Act of Interim Regulation of Deep Seabed Mining (1980) ... 431-432
       France: Arrête du 29 janvier 1982 fixant le contenu des demandes de permis d'exploration et d'exploitation des grand fonds marins ... 188, 245, 435
       France: Décret du 29 janvier 1982 pris pour l'application de la loi du 23 décembre 1981 ... 188, 245, 435
       Japan: Law on Interim Measures for Deep Seabed Mining ... 188, 245, 246, 247, 249-268, 436-437
       Japan: Enforcement Regulations for the Law on Interim Measures for Deep Seabed Mining ... 188, 245, 436
       Soviet Union: Edict on Provisional Measures to Regulate the Activity of Soviet Enterprises Relating to the Exploration and Exploitation of

xxxvi   *Table of statutes*

Mineral Resources of Seabed Areas beyond the Limits of the
Continental Shelf ... 188, 244, 435-436
United Kingdom: Deep Sea Mining (Exploration Licences)
(Applications) Regulations ... 188, 245, 433
United Kingdom: The Deep Sea Mining (Reciprocating Countries)
(Federal Republic of Germany) Order 1982 ... 269
United Kingdom: The Deep Sea Mining (Reciprocating Countries)
(French Republic) Order 1982 ... 269
United Kingdom: The Deep Sea Mining (Reciprocating Countries)
(United States of America) Order 1982 ... 269

1984   United Kingdom: Deep Sea Mining (Exploration Licences) Regulations
        ... 188, 245, 252, 259, 267, 433
        United Kingdom: Deep Sea Mining (Reciprocating Countries) Order
        1984 ... 269

1985   Italy: Law No. 41 of 20 February 1985: Regulations on the Exploration
        and Exploitation of the Mineral Resources of the Deep Seabed ... 188,
        245, 246-247, 249-268, 269, 437
        United Kingdom: Deep Sea Mining (Reciprocating Countries) Order
        1985 ... 188, 245

1988   Italy: Presidential Decree No. 200 of 11 March 1988 ... 437

1989   United States: Deep Seabed Mining Regulations for Commercial
        Recovery Permits ... 188, 244, 258, 437-453

1992   Papua New Guinea: Mining Act ... 150

1994   Canada: An Act to Amend the Coastal Fisheries Protection Act ... 352
        Italy: Law No. 689 of 2 December 1994 Authorising Ratification and
        Implementation of the United Nations Convention on the Law of the Sea
        of 10 December 1982 and the Agreement of 29 July 1994 on the
        Implementation of Part XI of the United Nations Convention ... 188,
        245, 437
        Russia: Decree by the President of the Russian Federation on the
        Activities of Russian Natural and Juridical Persons in the Exploration
        and Exploitation of the Mineral Resources of the Seabed beyond the
        Limits of the Continental Shelf ... 188, 244, 436

1995   Germany: Law for the Implementation of the United Nations
        Convention on the Law of the Sea 1982 and the Implementation
        Agreement of 29 July 1994 ... 244-245, 431
        Russia: Order No. 410 of 25 April 1995 on Activities for Exploration
        and Exploitation of the Mineral Resources of the Seabed beyond the
        Limits of the Continental Shelf ... 188, 244, 436

1997   United Kingdom: Deep Sea Mining (Temporary Provisions) Act 1981
        (Guernsey) Order 1987 ... 432
        United Kingdom: Deep Sea Mining (Temporary Provisions) Act 1981
        (Jersey) Order 1987 ... 432

1998   United Kingdom: Petroleum Act 1998 ... 87

1999   United Kingdom: Petroleum (Current Model Clauses) Order 1999 ... 87

2000   United Kingdom: Deep Sea Mining (Temporary Provisions) Act 1981
        (Isle of Man) Order 2000 ... 432

Table of Treaties and International Regulations

1945   United Nations Charter
        Article 2(2) ... 28
                2(3) ... 353
                2(4) ... 73
        Article 10 ... 28
        Article 13 ... 28
        Article 33(1) ... 353
        Statute of International Court of Justice ... 354
            Article 36(2) ... 255, 351
1946   Convention on the Privileges and Immunities of the United Nations ... 340
1957   Treaty Establishing the European Community ... 367
1958   Geneva Convention on the High Seas
        Article 2 ... 18-19, 20, 21
        Optional Protocol of Signature concerning the Compulsory Settlement of Disputes ... 351
1959   Agreement on the Privileges and Immunities of the International Atomic Energy Agency ... 340
1961   Optional Protocol to the Vienna Convention on Diplomatic Relations concerning Compulsory Settlement of Disputes ... 351
1963   Optional Protocol to the Vienna Convention on Consular Relations ... 351
1969   European Convention on the Protection of the Archaeological Heritage ... 93-94
        Vienna Convention on the Law of Treaties ... 8
            Article 18 ... 208
            Article 26 ... 74
            Article 31 ... 50
            Article 34 ... 59
            Article 34-38 ... 57, 59
            Article 38 ... 59
            Article 53 ... 57
            Article 64 ... 57

xxxviii *Table of treaties*

1972   Convention on the International Regulations for Preventing Collisions at Sea ... 86, 87
1974   International Convention for the Safety of Life at Sea ... 86
1978   Convention on Future Multilateral Co-operation in the Northwest Atlantic Fisheries ... 352
       Protocol Relating to the International Convention for the Safety of Life at Sea ... 86
1982   Agreement Concerning Interim Arrangements Relating to Polymetallic Nodules of the Deep Sea Bed ... 42, 200, 245-246, 268-270, 453
1982   United Nations Convention on the Law of the Sea
       Preamble ... 16
       Article 1(1) ... 52, 341
            1(1)(1) ... 373
            1(1)(3) ... 94, 108, 152, 325, 401
            1(2) ... 337
            1(2)(2) ... 66, 78
            1(3) ... 53, 79 401
       Article 33 ... 94, 95
       Article 57 ... 53
       Article 60 ... 87
            60(2) ... 87
            60(7) ... 87
       Article 76 ... 53, 373
            76(8) ... 374
       Article 80 ... 87
       Article 82 ... 70, 71, 310, 367
            82(4) ... 70
       Article 84(2) ... 373, 374
       Article 87(1)(d) ... 21
            87(2) ... 86
       Article 111(1) ... 95
       Article 133 ... 53, 93
            133(a) ... 53, 79, 94, 100, 149, 401
       Part XI (Articles 133-191) ... 5, 6, 8, 9, 16, 17, 46, 50, 52, 53, 59, 61, 99
       Section 2 ... 75, 80
       Article 134(1) ... 52
            134(2) ... 53
            134(3) ... 53, 374
            134(3)-(4) ... 373
       Article 135 ... 53
       Article 136 ... 16,49, 52, 58, 100, 149, 208, 389
       Article 137 ... 72, 207-208
            137(1) ... 248, 374
            137(2) ... 65, 72
            137(3) ... 73, 210, 248
       Article 138 ... 73

Table of treaties   xxxix

Article 139 ... 75, 76, 77, 78, 112, 116, 333, 363, 389, 425
     139(2) ... 76
     139(3) ... 77
Article 140 ... 66, 67, 68, 69 70, 75, 81, 88, 94, 103, 338
     140(1) ... 65, 66, 67, 68, 338
     140(2) ... 69, 70, 71
Article 141 ... 53, 73, 74, 88
Article 142 ... 78, 389, 428
     142(3) ... 428
Article 143 ... 53, 79, 88, 91, 105, 106
     143(3) ... 267
Article 144 ... 75, 81, 82, 83, 88, 89, 91, 105, 106, 364
     144(2) ... 92, 173
Article 145 ... 53, 84, 390, 416, 418
Article 146 ... 53, 85, 86
Article 147 ... 87, 88, 108, 162, 390
     147(1) ... 86
     147(2) ... 86, 87
     147(3) ... 86
Article 148 ... 74, 82, 88, 89
Article 149 ... 53, 54, 92, 94, 95, 109
Part XI, Section 3 (Articles 150-155) ... 96, 102
Article 150 ... 54, 81, 89, 100, 101, 102, 124, 390
     150(a) ... 101, 102,103
     150(a)(b)(e)(f) and (i) ... 101
     150(a)-(j) ... 101
     150(b) ... 102
     150(c) ... 82, 101
     150(d) ... 82, 101
     150(e) ... 102
     150(f) ... 103
     150(g) ... 101
     150(h) ... 101, 124
     150(i) ... 103, 124
     150(j) ... 103
Article 151 ... 54, 89, 123, 124, 125, 168, 260, 365
     151(1) ... 124
     151(1)-(7) ... 125
     151(2) ... 102
     151(2)-(7) ... 324
     151(3) ...122
     151(8) ... 125, 126
     151(9) ... 124, 125
     151(10) ... 89, 90, 127-128, 130, 131, 142, 336
Article 152 ... 75, 88, 104
     152(1) ... 74, 104
Article 152(1)-(2) ... 104

xl   *Table of treaties*

152(2) ... 74
Article 153 ... 109, 111, 112
153(1) ... 112
153(2) ... 75, 112, 113, 147 153, 324
153(2)(b) ... 76, 77, 114,117, 136, 146,172, 326 329, 334, 372
153(3) ... 117, 118, 119, 147, 174, 325, 326
153(4) ... 76, 112, 117
153(5) ... 88, 112
153(6) ... 123, 147, 174, 175
Article 154 ... 56
Article 155 ... 16, 54, 55, 390
155(1) ... 54
155(1)(f) ... 89
155(2) ... 16, 55, 58, 398
155(4) ... 54, 55
Part XI, section 4 (Articles 156-185) ... 113
Article 156(1) ... 293, 337
156(2) ... 293, 295
156(3) ... 63, 293
156(4) ... 293, 342
Article 157 ... 93, 307
157(1) ... 293
157(2) ... 293
157(3) ... 296, 307
Article 158(1) ... 295, 317
158(2) ... 317
158(3) ... 311
Article 159(1) ... 295
159(6) ... 295
159(7) ... 296
159(8) ... 295, 364
159(9) ... 296
159(10) ... 296, 359, 369
Article 160 ... 69, 70
160(1) ... 296, 311
160(2)(1) ... 90, 131
160(2)(a)-(c) ... 296
160(2)(d) ... 296
160(2)(e) ... 296, 316, 337
160(2)(f) ... 296
160(2)(f)(i) ... 70, 71, 264 367
160(2)(f)(ii) ... 85, 367, 394
160(2)(g) ... 70, 296, 338
160(2)(k) ... 90
Article 160(2)(m) ... 364
Article 161 ... 90

Table of treaties xli

161(1) ... 297, 299
161(2) ... 298, 299
161(2)(a)-(b) ... 298
161(3) ... 299, 301
161(4) ... 299
161(8) ... 124
161(8)(a) ... 308
161(8)(b)-(e) ... 308
161(8)(c) ... 364
161(8)(d) ... 309, 310, 367
161(8)(e) ... 295, 308
Article 162 ... 69, 70, 307
162(2)(j) ... 119, 120, 307, 310, 372
162(2)(k) ... 310, 311
162(2)(m) ... 309
162(2)(n) ... 90, 307
162(2)(o) ... 307, 395
162(2)(o)(i) ... 71, 88, 310
162(2)(o)(ii) ... 85, 100, 124, 149-150, 166, 310, 367, 394,
             395, 401
162(2)(q) ... 125, 307
162(2)(r) ... 335
162(2)(t) ... 364
162(2)(u) ... 363, 395
162(2)(v) ... 363, 395
162(2)(w) ... 143, 395, 403, 423
162(2)(x) ... 106, 120,121, 163,395, 403
162(2)(y) ... 307, 311, 313
162(2)(z) ... 395
Article 163 ... 311
163(1) ... 313
163(2) ... 312, 313
163(3) ... 312
163(4) ... 312
163(6) ... 312
163(8) ... 224
163(9) ... 312
163(11) ...312
Article 164 ...312
164(1) ... 312
164(2)(d) ... 90, 131,142
Article 165 ... 312, 421
165(1) ... 312, 395
165(2) ... 408, 420
165(2)(b) ... 119
Article 165(2)(d) ... 395
165(2)(e) ... 395, 412

xlii   *Table of treaties*

165(2)(f) ... 85, 366, 395
165(2)(g) ... 395
165(2)(h) ... 396
165(2)(i) ... 396
165(2)(j) ... 396
165(2)(k) ... 396, 403, 423
165(2)(l) ... 396, 403
165(2)(m) ... 396
165(2)(n) ... 125,131
Articles 166-169 ... 317
Article 167(2) ... 317
Article 168 ... 160, 373
168(1) ... 147, 360, 373
168(2) ... 144, 146,147, 182, 185, 360, 372
168(2)-(3) ... 224
168(3) ... 146, 147, 360, 373
168(4) ... 146
Article 169 ... 317
Article 170 ... 317, 318
170(1) ... 113, 322, 324
170(2) ... 322, 334
170(4) ... 329, 338, 339
Article 171 ... 9, 264
171(a) ... 313, 337
171(b) ... 337
171(c) ... 313
171(d) ... 337
171(e) 337
171(f) 90, 131, 313,336, 337
Articles 171-175 ... 313, 335
Article 172 ... 313, 316 335
Article 173 ... 264,313,338
173(1) ... 337
173(2) ... 70, 337, 338
173(2)(a) ... 338
173(2)(b) ... 329, 338
173(2)(c) ... 90, 131,313
Article 174 ... 337
174(1) ... 313
Article 175 ... 336
Article 176 ... 339
Articles 177-183 ... 339
Article 178 ... 145, 334
Article 184 ... 340
Article 185 ... 85, 86, 340, 394
Article 185(1) ... 364
185(2) ... 359, 364

Table of treaties xliii

Section 5 ... 143, 167, 184, 186, 353, 356,358, 361, 362, 363, 375
Article 187 ... 148, 293, 368, 369
    187(a) ... 77, 358, 361, 362
    187(b) ... 77, 334,358, 359, 363, 366
    187(b)(i) ... 364, 374
    187(c) ... 143, 144, 145,334,360, 369
    187(c)(i) ... 359, 369, 370, 371
    187(c)(ii) ... 360, 372
    187(d) ... 360, 372
    187(e) ... 145, 147, 334,360
Article 188 ...148
    188(1) ... 362
    188(1)(a) ... 356, 358,361, 362
    188(1)(b) ... 357, 358, 361
    188(2) ... 140, 145, 359, 369, 370, 371
    188(2)(a) ... 370, 371
    188(2)(b) ... 371
    188(2)(c) ... 357, 370
Article 189 ... 293, 359, 368
Article 190 ... 369
    190(2) ... 145
Article 191 ... 368, 369
Part XII (Articles 192-237)... 84, 389, 391-392
Article 192 ... 391
Article 194 ... 391
Article 195 ... 391
Article 196 ... 391
    196(1) ... 391
Article 198 ... 392
Article 199 ... 392
Article 204 ... 392, 418, 420
Article 205 ... 322, 418, 420
Article 206 ... 392, 418, 420
Article 209 ... 84, 393
    209(1) ... 430
    209(2) ... 430
Article 215 ... 84, 85, 394
Article 235 ... 389, 425
Part XIII (Articles 238-265) ... 79
Article 256 ... 79
Part XV (Articles 279-299) ... 353, 374
Section 1 (Articles 279-285) ... 353, 361, 362
Section 2 (Articles 286-296) ... 353
Section 3 (Articles 297-299) ... 353
Article 279 ... 353
Article 280 ... 353, 361, 362
Article 285 ... 361, 362

xliv   *Table of treaties*

Article 286 ...353
Article 287(1) ... 353, 362
        287(1)(a) ... 354
        287(2) ... 362
Article 293 ... 361
        293(1) ... 357
Article 296 ... 361
        296(1) ... 363, 368, 369
Article 298(1)(a)(i) ... 374
Article 300 ... 74
Article 301 ... 73
Article 303 ... 94
        303(1) ... 94
        303(2) ... 94, 95
Articles 303-319 ... 309
Article 304 ... 75, 77
Article 305 ... 337, 343
        305(1)(c)-(e) ... 60, 63
        305(1)(f) ... 61, 63, 78
Article 306 ... 62
Article 307 ... 62
Article 308 ... 7
        308(1) ... 58
        308(4) ... 366, 396
        308(5) ... 233
Article 311(3) ... 58
        311(6) ... 16, 58, 59, 208
Articles 312-316 ... 309
Article 314 ... 56, 309
        314(1) ... 55, 56
        314(2) ... 54
Articles 314-316 ... 56
Article 315 ... 56
Article 316 ... 56
Article 319(3)(a) ... 64
        319(3)(b) ... 64
Annex III ... 75, 83, 91, 96, 97, 98, 111, 112, 324
Article 1 ... 104, 328
Article 2 ... 104-105
        2(1)(b) ... 91, 412
        2(2) ... 106
Article 3 ... 117-118
Article 3(2) ... 326
        3(4)(c) ... 118, 167
        3(5) ... 118, 141, 326
Articles 3-6 ... 109
Article 4 ... 113, 114, 115, 118

Table of treaties xlv

```
          4(1) ... 113, 114, 191
          4(2) ...114, 191
          4(3) ... 115-116, 122
          4(4) ... 76, 115-116
          4(6) ... 114,116, 372
Article 5 ... 81, 83, 114, 116, 117, 324, 364
          5(2) ...324
          5(4) ... 364
          5(6) ... 83, 84
Article 6 ... 115, 117, 118
          6(1) ... 118-119
          6(2) ... 118-119
          6(3) ... 119, 120
          6(3)(a) ... 120, 162
          6(3)(b) ... 106
          6(3)(c) ... 120, 121, 122, 148, 258
          6(3)(c)(i) ... 121, 122,163
          6(3)(c)(ii) ... 121-122, 163
          6(4) ... 121-122, 258
          6(5) ... 122
Article 7 ... 115, 123,125
Article 8 ... 121, 131, 132, 134, 168, 327
          8(a) ... 230
          8(b) ... 234
          8(c) ... 234
Article  9 ... 91, 117, 131, 157, 326
          9(1) ... 134, 326
          9(1)-(2) ... 327
          9(2) ... 91, 134, 326
          9(3) ... 134
          9(4) ... 91, 134
Article 10 ... 118, 167
Article 11 ... 91, 117, 131, 134,136, 326,327
          11(1) ... 327
          11(2) ... 327
          11(3) ... 327
Article 12(2) ... 326
Article 13 ... 53, 134, 135, 137, 261, 313, 327, 329, 331, 337, 371
          13(1) ... 135, 136
          13(1)(d)  ... 91
          13(1)(e) ... 329
Article 13(2) ... 135, 138, 159, 313, 372
          13(3) ... 229, 231
Articles 13(3)-(10) ... 135, 137, 313
Article 13(5) ... 139, 331
          13(6) ... 139
          13(10) ... 140
```

xlvi   *Table of treaties*

13(11) ... 140
Articles 13(11)-(15) ... 135
Article 13(12) ... 140
13(13) ... 140
13(14) ... 92
13(15) ... 140, 359, 370, 371
Article 14 ... 136, 140, 146, 224, 225
14(1) ... 140-141
14(2) ... 141
Article 15 ... 92, 142, 173
Article 16 ... 123, 142, 147, 175
Article 17 ... 85, 96, 132, 142, 167
17(1) ... 142
17(1)(b)(viii) ... 88
17(1)(b)(ix) ... 87
17(1)(b)(xii) ... 85, 393
17(1)(c) ... 313
17(1)(c)(iii) ... 92
17(2) ... 142, 167, 234, 258
17(2)(a) ... 167
17(2)(b) ... 99, 143, 233, 258
17(2)(b)(i) ... 105
17(2)(b)(ii) ... 234
17(2)(b)(iii) ... 234
17(2)(c) ... 99, 143, 233, 258
17(2)(e) ... 168
17(2)(f) ... 148-149, 180, 393
Article18 ... 85, 86, 123, 143, 174, 176, 334, 394
18(1) ... 143
18(2) ... 143
18(3) ... 143
Article 19 ... 123, 147, 174, 175
19(1) ... 147, 148
19(2) ... 148
Article 20 ... 148
Article 21 ... 148
21(1) ... 148
21(2) ... 148
21(3) ... 180
Article 22 ... 76, 77, 85, 144, 145, 146, 160, 179, 181, 334, 360,
372
Annex IV ... 317, 329, 339
Article 1 ... 318
1(1) ...318
1(2) ... 318
1(3) ... 318
Article 2 ... 318, 334

Table of treaties xlvii

2(1) ... 318, 334
2(2) ... 318
2(3) ... 318, 333, 334
Article 3 ... 334
Article 5 ... 323
5(1) ... 323
5(4) ... 323
5(5) ... 323
5(8) ... 323
5(9) ... 324
Article 6 ... 323, 324
6(c) ... 324
6(d) ... 324
6(e) ... 324
6(f) ... 324
6(g) ... 324
6(i) ... 324
6(n) ... 322
6(o) ... 323
Article 7(1) ... 323
7(2) ... 322, 323
7(5) ... 147, 224
Article 9(1) ... 332
Article 10 ... 337
10(1) ... 331
10(2) ... 332
10(3) ... 325, 331, 332
Article 11 ... 330
11(1) ... 329
11(2) ... 330
11(3) ... 330, 334
11(3)(a) ... 330
11(3)(b) ... 330
11(3)(c) ... 330
11(4) ... 332
11(5) ... 332
Article 12 ... 326
12(3)(a) ... 328
Article 12(3)(b) ... 328
12(3)(c) ...328
12(4) ... 328
12(5) ... 328
12(7) ... 328
Article 13 ... 147, 322
13(1) ... 322, 332
13(2) ... 322
13(3) ... 322, 334

xlviii *Table of treaties*

13(4)(a) ... 332, 333
13(4)(b) ... 332, 333
13(4)(d) ... 333
13(4)(e) ... 333
13(6) ... 322
Annex VI ...354, 362
Section 4 ... 356
Article 1(2) ...354
Article 2(1) ... 354
2(2) ... 354
Article 3(1) ... 354
3(2) ... 354
Article 4(1) ... 354
4(3) ... 345, 354
4(4) ... 354
Article 5(1) ... 355
Article 14 ... 356
Article 15(1) ... 355
15(2) ... 356
15(3) ... 355
15(5) ... 356
Article 17 ... 356
17(1) ... 355
Articles 17(2)-(6) ... 355
Article 17(4) ... 355
Article 32(3) ... 361
Article 33 ... 361
33(3) ... 361
Article 35(1) ... 356
35(2) ... 356
35(3) ... 356
Article 36(3) ... 357
Article 38(a) ... 358, 361
38(b) ... 358
Article 39 ... 358
Article 40 ... 361
Annex VII ...353
Annex VIII ... 353
Annex IX ... 61, 62, 78
Article 5 ... 78
Article 6 ... 78

1984 Provisional Understanding Regarding Deep Seabed Matters of 3 August
1984 ... 42, 199, 204, 207, 208, 209, 245-246, 268, 270, 271-275,
453- 454
Understanding on the Resolution of Conflicts among Applicants for
Registration as Pioneer Investors of 31 August 1984 ... 204, 213-220

1986	New York Understanding on the Implementation of Resolution II of 5 September 1986 ... 7, 19, 39-40, 168, 170, 192, 221-226, 227, 231, 238, 239, 241, 246, 256, 283, 285, 288, 322
1986	Arusha Understanding of 7 February 1986 ... 39-40, 221-226
1987	Agreement on the Resolution of Practical Problems with Respect to Deep Sea-bed Mining Areas and Related Exchanges of Notes (the 'Midnight Agreement') ... 40, 221, 226-228, 232, 246, 283-284, 285, 288, 289
	Exchange of Notes between the United Kingdom and the Soviet Union concerning Deep Sea-bed Mining Areas ... 288
1988	Convention on the Regulation of Antarctic Mineral Resource Activities (CRAMRA) ... 398, 399
	Protocol Relating to the International Convention for the Safety of Life at Sea ... 86
1990	Understanding on the Fulfilment of Obligations by the Registered Pioneer Investors of 30 August 1990 ... 229-230, 231, 232, 241, 242
1991	Memorandum of Understanding between Belgium, Canada, Germany, Italy, the Netherlands, the United Kingdom and the United States, on the one hand, and China on the other hand ('China MOU') ... 228, 230, 284, 285, 289
	Protocol on Environmental Protection to the Antarctic Treaty ... 399
1992	Understanding on the Fulfilment of Obligations by the Registered Pioneer Investor COMRA and its Certifying State China ... 231, 241, 242
	Understanding on the Fulfilment of Obligations by the Registered Pioneer Investor the Interoceanmetal Joint Organisation (IOM) ... 232, 241, 242
1994	Agreement Relating to the Implementation of Part XI of the United Nations Convention on the Law of the Sea (Implementation Agreement) ... 4, 5, 6, 14, 16,31, 40, 46, 50, 81, 96, 99, 100, 114,115, 232- 243, 260, 261, 288, 289, 292, 295, 315,321-322, 350, 356, 379, 390, 396

        Preamble ... 397
        Article 2 ... 99
            2(1) ... 6, 8, 59, 309, 358
            2(2) ... 309
        Article 3 ... 7
            3(a) ... 7
        Article 3(c) ... 8
            3(d) ... 8
        Articles 3-8 ... 59
        Article 4(1) ... 7, 8
            4(2) .. 7, 8, 235, 290
            4(3)(a) ... 8
            4(3)(b) ... 8
            4(3)(c) ... 240
        Article 5 ... 8, 240
            5(1) ... 9

l *Table of treaties*

Article 6 ... 235
    6(1) ... 7, 9
    6(2) ... 7
Article 7 ... 9, 10, 115, 235, 290
    7(1) ... 11
    7(3) ... 10, 235, 290, 291
Annex
 Section 1(1) ... 112, 113, 293
    1(2) ... 292
    1(3) ... 293, 321
    1(4) ... 293, 313
    1(5) ... 233
    1(5)(a) ... 233
    1(5)(e) ... 131
    1(5)(f) ... 99, 143, 170, 233, 234, 258
    1(5)(g) ... 397
    1(5)(h) ... 397
    1(5)(k) ... 397
    1(6)(a) ... 117
    1(6)(a)(i) ... 115, 290
    1(6)(a) (ii) ... 153, 156, 159, 160, 164, 165, 190, 236, 237,
                238, 239, 290, 415
    1(6)(a)(iii) ... 167, 236, 237, 242
    1(6)(a)(iv) ... 11
    1(6)(a)(v) ... 240
 Section 1(6)(b) ... 117
    1(7) ... 120, 397
    1(9) ... 122, 170, 171, 234
    1(10) ... 131, 132
    1(11) ... 123, 170, 171, 235, 291
    1(12) ... 10, 115, 290
    1(12)(a) ... 10, 11, 235, 290
    1(12)(c) ... 10, 301
    1(12)(c)(ii) ... 235, 290
    1(12)(d) ... 10, 123, 170, 172, 235, 291
    1(13) ... 118
 Section 1(14) ... 11, 313, 335, 337, 338
    1(15) ... 85, 307, 310, 367, 394, 395, 401
    1(16) ... 86, 99, 310, 395, 401
    1(17) ... 113, 394, 395
 Section 2 ... 134, 310, 311, 329, 338
    2(1) ... 321, 325
    2(1)(a) ... 322
    2(1)(b) ... 398
    2(1)(d) ... 398
    2(1)(e) ... 322
    2(2) ... 321, 322, 324, 325, 326, 327, 332, 338

Table of treaties li

2(3) ... 330, 331, 339
2(4) ... 118, 324, 326, 331, 332, 334, 339
2(5) ... 326, 327
2(6) ... 331, 332, 338
Section 3 ... 90, 297
3(2) ... 91, 295, 308, 313, 364
3(2)-(3) ... 364
3(3) ... 295, 296
3(4) ... 296
3(5) ... 91, 309, 364
3(6) ... 91, 308
3(7) ... 296, 309, 310, 315
3(8) ... 364
3(9) ... 91
3(9)(a) ... 91, 307
3(9)(b) ... 298
3(10) ... 298
3(11) ... 307, 311, 372
3(11)(a) ... 120, 122
3(11)(b) ... 120
3(11)-(12) ... 164
3(12) ... 360, 372
3(13) ... 310, 312
3(15) ... 297, 301
3(15)(a) ... 297, 302, 307
3(15)(a)-(d) ... 314
3(15)(b) ... 297
3(15)(c) ... 298
3(15)(d) ... 91, 298
3(15)(e) ... 91, 298, 300
3(16) ... 297, 299
Section 4 ... 16, 54, 55, 58, 89, 398
Section 5 ... 310, 324
5(1) ... 83, 364
5(1)(b) ... 364
Section 5(1)(c) ... 92, 173, 398
5(2) ... 83, 117, 364
Section 6 ... 123, 125, 126, 127, 310, 365
6(1) ... 127
6(1)(a) ... 126
6(1)(b) ... 126
6(1)(b)-(d) ... 365
6(1)(c) ... 126
6(1)(d) ... 127
6(1)(e) ... 127
6(1)(f) ... 127
6(1)(f)(i) ... 365

lii   *Table of treaties*

6(10(f)(ii) ... 365
6(1)(g) ... 126, 365, 366
6(2) ... 127
6(3) ... 126, 366
6(4) ... 127, 365, 366
6(5) ... 127, 365
6(6) ... 125
6(7) ... 102, 122, 124, 125, 195, 307, 324
Section 7 ... 89, 130, 310
7(1) ... 336
7(1)(a) ... 90
7(1)-(2) ... 90, 130
7(2) ... 90, 307, 313, 336
Section 8 ... 134, 137, 310, 327
8(1) ... 137, 371
8(1)(a) ... 137
8(1)(b) ... 137
8(1)(c) ... 139, 140
8(1)(d) ... 138, 139
8(1)(e) ... 138, 371
8(1)(f) ... 138
8(2) ... 313, 371
8(3) ... 313
Section 9(1) ... 311, 313, 314
9(2) ... 314
9(3)-(4) ... 314
9(7) ... 315, 316, 317
9(7)(c) ... 313, 335
9(7)(f) ... 310, 338
9(8) ... 309, 310, 315
9(9) ... 307, 311

1994   Understanding on the Fulfilment of Obligations by the Registered
Pioneer Investor the Government of the Republic of Korea ... 232, 241,
242
1996   Agreement Concerning the Relationship between the United Nations
and the International Seabed Authority ... 341
1998   Protocol on the Privileges and Immunities of the International Seabed
Authority ... 340, 342
1999   Agreement between the International Seabed Authority and the
Government of Jamaica regarding the Headquarters of the International
Seabed Authority ... 332, 333, 342
2000   Regulations on Prospecting and Exploration for Polymetallic Nodules in
the Area (The Mining Code). See separate Table on 'The Mining Code'.

Table of the Mining Code

2000   Regulations on Prospecting and Exploration for Polymetallic Nodules in the Area – 'The Mining Code'... 5, 84, 86, 99, 100, 124, 135, 143, 146, 152-186, 363, 379, 393, 398-430

Preamble ... 149, 152, 153

Part I ... 402

Reg. 1 ... 402, 408, 419

1(3)(b) ... 419

1(3)(d) ... 149, 166

1(3)(e) ... 104, 411

1(3)(f) ... 407, 409

1(5) ... 409

Part II ... 104, 401, 402, 411

Reg. 2 ... 105

2(1) ... 105, 411

2(2) ... 411

2(3) ... 105, 411

2(4) ... 106

2(5) ... 105

2(6) ... 105, 107

Reg. 3 ... 106, 107

3(1)-(2) ... 106

3(2) ... 412

3(3)(c) ... 324

3(4) ... 106

3(4)(d) ... 107

3(4)(d)(i)(a) ... 91

3(4)(d)(i)(b) ... 412

Reg. 4 ... 106, 411

4(2) ... 105, 107, 411

4(3) ... 107, 411

4(5) ... 107

Reg. 5 ... 107, 108

5(1) ... 107

5(1)(b) ... 412

liii

liv   *Table of mining code*

5(2) ... 108
Reg. 6 ... 107, 108, 429
6(1) ... 108
6(2) ... 109
Reg. 7 ... 109, 412
Reg. 8 ... 93, 109
Part III ... 401, 402, 413
Reg. 9 ... 153, 234
Reg. 10 ... 158, 159, 236, 415
Reg. 10(1) ... 154, 413
10(2) ... 155
10(3) ... 155
10(4) ... 155
Reg. 11 ... 155, 235, 240
11(4) ... 155
Reg. 12 ... 155, 156, 237, 414
12(1) ... 414
12(3) ... 326
12(7)(c) ... 156, 414
Reg. 13 ... 156
Reg. 14 ... 156, 161, 164, 235, 236, 237
Reg. 15 ... 156
Reg. 16 ... 156
Reg. 17 ... 154, 157, 163, 326
17(1)-(2) ... 326
17(1)-(4) ... 158
17(3) ... 327
17(4) ... 326
Reg. 18 ... 158, 236, 414
18(a)-(e) ... 414, 415
Reg. 19. ...138, 159, 160, 237
Reg. 20 ... 160
Reg. 21 ... 159, 160, 164, 237
21(1)-(2) ... 160
21(3)(a)-(d) ... 161
21(4)(a) ... 86, 161
21(4)(b) ... 162, 416
21(4)(c) ... 87, 162
21(5) ... 163
21(6) ... 416
21(6)(a) ... 162
21(6)(b) ... 163
21(6)(c) ... 106, 163, 416
21(6)(d)(i)-(ii) ... 163
21(6)-(7) ... 163
21(7) ... 163
21(8) ... 164

Table of mining code lv

21(9) ... 161
21(10) ... 160
21(11) ... 161
Reg. 22 ... 164, 165
Part IV ... 165, 401, 402, 419
Reg. 23 ... 237, 238
23(1) ... 165, 239, 419
23(2) ... 166
Reg. 23(3) ... 167
Reg. 24(1) ... 149, 166
24(2) ... 167
24(3) ... 167
Reg. 25 ... 169, 170
25(1) ... 169
25(2)-(3) ... 170
Reg. 26 ... 170, 171
26(1)-(2) ... 171
Reg. 27 ... 92
27(1) ... 173
27(2) ... 174
Reg. 28 ... 175-176
Reg. 30 ... 179, 181
Part V ... 182, 402, 420
Reg. 31 ... 165, 180, 419, 422
31(2) ... 418, 419
31(3) ... 418
31(4) ... 409, 420
31(5) ... 409, 421
31(6) ... 421
31(7) ... 421, 422
Reg. 32 ... 109, 165, 412, 423
32(1) ... 424, 428
32(2) ... 424, 428
32(3) ... 424
32(4) ... 425
32(5) ... 425
32(6) ... 425
32(7) ... 425, 426
Reg. 33 ... 423, 427, 428
33(1) ... 428
33(2) ... 428
33(3) ... 428
Reg. 34 ... 93
Part VI ... 182
Reg. 35 ... 108, 182, 183
35(1) ... 183

lvi   *Table of mining code*

35(2) ... 183-184
35(3) ... 109, 184
35(4) ... 184
35(5) ... 184
Reg. 36 ... 108, 182, 184
36(1)-(4) ... 185
Part VII ... 402
Reg. 38 ... 402, 408, 409, 419, 420, 421
38(1) ... 408
38(2) ... 408
Reg. 39 ... 186, 363
39(2) ... 186
Reg. 40 ... 149, 166
Annex 1 ... 106, 412
Annex 2 ... 154, 402, 413
Sec. I ... 154, 155
Sec. II ... 154, 155
Para. 19(b) ... 413
Para. 24(a)-(d) ... 413
Sec. III ... 154, 156, 161
Para. 21(a) ... 326
Sec. IV ... 155, 158
Sec. V ... 155, 156
Sec. VI ... 155, 156, 161
Sec. VII ... 155
Annex 3 ... 165, 239, 402, 419
Paras. A-D ... 165, 166
Annex 4 ... 165, 239, 402, 419, 420
Sec. 1.1(c) ... 408
Sec. 2 ... 174
2.1 ... 175
2.2 ... 175
2.4 ... 149, 166
Sec. 3.1 ... 170, 171, 419
3.2 ...171
3.3 ... 173
Sec. 4.3 ... 178-179
4.4 ... 176
Sec. 5 ... 419
5.2-5.4 ... 422
5.5 ... 422, 423
Secs. 5-6 ... 165
Sec. 6 ... 419
6.1 ... 426
6.2 ... 423, 427
6.3 ... 427
6.4 ... 427

Table of mining code lvii

Sec. 8 ... 173-174
   8.1-8.3 ... 173
   Sec. 10 ... 179
   Sec. 10.2(a) ... 428
      10.2(d) ... 179
      10.3 ... 428
   Sec. 11.2(a) ... 429
   Sec. 12 ... 182, 186
   Sec. 13.2 ... 408
        13.2(e) ... 408, 419, 421
  13.3(b) ... 429
    13.3(c) ... 87
   Sec. 14 ... 88
     14.1(b) ... 429
   Sec. 15 ... 86, 161, 162
   Sec. 16 ... 179, 181, 427
     16.1 ... 179, 429
     16.2 ... 180
     16.3 ... 182
     16.4 ... 182
     16.5 ... 180
   Sec. 17.1 ... 180
     17.2-17.4 ... 181
   Sec. 19 ... 171, 172
   Sec. 20 ... 175
     20.1 ... 172
   Sec. 21 ... 172, 175, 177
     21.1 ... 176-177
     21.1(a) ... 430
     21.1(a)-(b) ... 177
     21.1(a)-(c) ... 172
     21.1(c) ... 177
     21.2-21.4 ... 177
     21.5 ... 427
     21.6 ... 427
     21.7 ... 178, 430
   Sec. 24 ... 175, 178
     24.1-24.3 ... 178
   Sec. 25 ... 186, 359, 369

Tables and Figures

Table 7.1	Duration of Licences in Five States	250
Table 7.2	Sea-Bed Mining Sites	279
	1. Pioneer Areas	279
	2. Areas Reserved for the Authority	280
	3. Sites Licensed under National Legislation	281
	Sketch-Map	282
Midnight Agreement Network		284
Figure 8.1	Institutional Framework of Sea-bed Mining	294
Membership of Council of Authority		
	The Floating Seat System	300
	Group A Council Membership 1999-2004	302
	Group B Council Membership 1999-2004	304
	Group C Council Membership 1999-2004	305
	Group D Council Membership 1999-2004	305
	Group E Council Membership 1999-2004	306
Table 9.1	The Legal Regime of Activities in the Area: Classification of Disputes	359
Table 10.1	Deep seabed mining perturbations and environmental impact concerns	384

lix

Abbreviations

AFERNOD ...Association française pour l'étude et la recherche des nodules
AMR ... Arbeitsgemeinschaft meerestechnisch gewinnbare Rohstoffe
Area, The ... The Area beyond the limits of national jurisdiction
A/RES ... Resolution of UN General Assembly
ATESWPP ... Impacts of potential technical interventions on the deep-sea
    ecosystems of the south-east Pacific off Peru
BAT ... Best available technology
BIE ... Benthic Impact Experiment
CFR ... Code of Federal Regulations (US)
China MOU ... Memorandum of Understanding on the Avoidance of Overlaps
    and Conflicts Relating to Deep Sea-bed Areas between China and Potential
    Applicant States, 1991
Cm ... Command Papers (United Kingdom)
Cmnd ... Command Papers (United Kingdom)
COLREG ... Convention on the International Regulations for Preventing
    Collisions at Sea, 1972, as amended
COMRA ... China Ocean Mineral Resources Research and Development
    Association
CRAMRA ... Convention on the Regulation of Antarctic Mineral Resource
    Activities, 1988
Declaration of Principles Resolution ... Declaration of Principles Governing the
    Sea-bed and the Ocean Floor and the Subsoil thereof beyond the Limits of
    National Jurisdiction, adopted by UN General Assembly on 17 December
    1970
DISCOL ... DISturbance and reCOLonisation project
DOMES ... Deep Ocean Mining Environmental Study
DORD ... Deep Ocean Resources Development Co. Ltd. (Japan)
Draft Convention ... Draft Convention on the Law of the Sea, A/CONF.62/L.78,
    28 August 1981
Draft Convention (Informal Text) ... Draft Convention on the Law of the Sea
    (Informal Text), A/CONF.62/WP.10/Rev.3, 22 September 1980
DSSRS ... Deep Sea Sediment Resuspension System
EA ... Environmental Assessment

lxii *Abbreviations*

ECOBENT ... Benthic investigations in the Abyssal ecosystem in the south-east
   Pacific
EEC ... European Economic Community
EEZ ... Exclusive Economic Zone
EIA ... Environmental Impact Assessment
EIS ... Environmental Impact Statement
EPA ... Environmental Protection Agency
FAO ... Food and Agriculture Organisation
*Final PrepCom Report ... Report of the Preparatory Commission, under
   Paragraph 11 of Resolution I of the Third United Nations Conference on the
   Law of the Sea, on All Matters within its Mandate Except as Provided in
   Paragraph 10, for Presentation to the Assembly of the International Seabed
   Authority at its First Session,* LOS/PCN/153(Vols. I-XIII) June-July 1995.
FRG ... Federal Republic of Germany
G-77 ... Group of 77
GAOR ... [UN] General Assembly Official Records
GATT ... General Agreement on Tariffs and Trade
Hague *Recueil ... Recueil des Cours, Académie de Droit International de la Haye*
HMSO ... Her Majesty's Stationery Office (United Kingdom)
IAEA ... International Atomic Energy Agency
ICJ ... International Court of Justice
ICJ Reports ... International Court of Justice Reports
I.C.L.Q. ... *International and Comparative Law Quarterly*
ICNT ... Informal Composite Negotiating Text
ICNT/Rev.1 ... Informal Composite Negotiating Text/Revision 1
ICNT/Rev.2 ... Informal Composite Negotiating Text/Revision 2
IFREMER ... Institut français de recherche pour l'exploitation de la mer
IHB ... International Hydrographic Bureau
IJECL ... *International Journal of Estuarine and Coastal Law*
ILA ... International Law Association
ILC ... International Law Commission
ILM ... *International Legal Materials*
Int. L. Rep. ... *International Law Reports*
IMCO ... Intergovernmental Maritime Consultative Organisation
IMO ... International Maritime Organisation
Implementation Agreement ... Agreement Relating to the Implementation of Part
   XI of the United Nations Convention on the Law of the Sea, 1994
INDEX ... Indian Deepsea Experiment
IOM ... Interoceanmetal Joint Organisation
IRA ... Impact Reference Area
ISBA ... International Seabed Authority
ISNT ... Informal Single Negotiating Text
Italian YBIL ... Italian Yearbook of International Law
ITLOS ... International Tribunal for the Law of the Sea
JET ... Japan Deep Sea Impact Experiment
KCON ... Kennecott Consortium
KODOS ... Korean Deep Ocean Study

Abbreviations lxiii

LOS Bull. ... *Law of the Sea Bulletin* (United Nations, Division for Ocean Affairs and the Law of the Sea, Office of Legal Affairs)

L. Sea.Inst. Proc. ... Law of the Sea Institute (US), Proceedings

Midnight Agreement ... Agreement on the Resolution of Practical Problems with respect to Deep Sea-Bed Mining Areas, 1989

Mining Code ... Regulations on Prospecting and Exploration for Polymetallic Nodules in the Area, ISBA/6/A/18, 13 July 2000

MIT ... Massachusetts Institute of Technology

MMAJ Symposium Proceedings 1997 ... Metal Mining Agency of Japan, *International Symposium on Environmental Studies for Deep-Sea Proceedings*, Tokyo, 1997

MOU ... Memorandum of Understanding

NaVaBa ... Natural Variability Baseline study

NEPA ... National Environmental Policy Act

NIEO ... New International Economic Order

NILOS ...Netherlands Institute for the Law of the Sea

NOAA ... National Oceanic and Atmospheric Administration (US)

Nordquist/Park ... M.H. Nordquist and Choon Ho Park, *North America and Asia-Pacific and the Development of the Law of the Sea*, New York, Oceana Publications, Inc., 1981-

NPDES ... National Pollutant Discharge Elimination System

NRC ... National Research Council (US)

OAU ... Organisation of African Unity

ODIL ... *Ocean Development and International Law*

OJ ... *Official Journal of the European Communities*

OMA ... Ocean Mining Association

OMCO ... Ocean Minerals Company

OMI ... Ocean Mining Inc.

PCA ... Permanent Court of Arbitration

PCIJ ... Permanent Court of International Justice

PEE ... Pre-Enactment Explorer

PEIS ... Programmatic Environmental Impact Statement

PIP ... Preparatory Investment Protection

PIPRA ... Provisional Interim Preservational Reference Area

PIRA ... Provisional Impact Reference Area

Platzöder, *Documents* ... R. Platzöder (ed.), *Third United Nations Conference on the Law of the Sea: Documents*, Vols. I – XVIII, Oceana, 1982-1989

Platzöder PrepCom ... R. Platzöder (ed.), *The Law of the Sea: Documents 1983-1989*, Vols. I – XIII, Oceana, 1989 – 1992

PLO ... Palestinian Liberation Organisation

Preparatory Commission ... Preparatory Commission for the International Sea-Bed Authority and for the International Tribunal for the Law of the Sea

PrepCom ... Preparatory Commission for the International Sea-Bed Authority and for the International Tribunal for the Law of the Sea

RECIEL ... *Review of European Community and International Environmental Law*

lxiv *Abbreviations*

Recueil des Cours ... *Recueil des Cours, Académie de Droit International de la Haye*
Resolution I ... See under UNCLOS Resolution I
Resolution II ... See under UNCLOS Resolution II
RGDIP ... *Revue générale de droit international public*
RPA ... Rules of Procedure of the Assembly
RPC ... Rules of Procedure of the Council
RSNT ... Revised Single Negotiating Text
San Diego L.R. ... *San Diego Law Review*
Sanya Workshop Proceedings 1999 ... Deep-Seabed Polymetallic Nodule Exploration: Development of Environmental Guidelines. Proceedings of the International Seabed Authority's Workshop held in Sanya, Hainan Island, People's Republic of China, 1-5 June 1999
SBDC ... Sea-Bed Disputes Chamber
SCN.1, SCN.2. SCN.3 ... Special Commissions of the Preparatory Commission
SD & D ... International Seabed Authority, *Selected Decisions and Documents*
S.I. ... Statutory Instrument
SOLAS ... International Convention for the Safety of Life at Sea, 1974, as amended
SRA ... Stable reference area
ST/LEG/SER.B/1, ... United Nations, *Laws and Regulations on the Regime of the High Seas*, Vol.1 *(United Nations Legislative Series*, ST/LEG/SER.B/1, 11 January 1951)
ST/LEG/SER.B/8, 1959 ... United Nations, *Supplement to Laws and Regulations on the Regime of the High Seas*, Vols. I and II *(United Nations Legislative Series*, ST/LEG/SER.B/8, 1959)
ST/LEG/SER.B.15, 1970 ... United Nations, *National Legislation and Treaties relating to the Territorial Sea, the Contiguous Zone, the Continental Shelf etc. (United Nations Legislative Series*, ST/LEG/SER.B/15, 1970
ST/LEG/SER.B.16, 1974 ... United Nations, *National Legislation and Treaties relating to the Law of the Sea, (United Nations Legislative Series*, ST/LEG/SER.B/16, 1974)
ST/LEG/SER.B.18, 1976 ... United Nations, *National Legislation and Treaties relating to the Law of the Sea (United Nations Legislative Series*, ST/LEG/SER.B/18, 1976)
ST/LEG/SER.B.19, 1980 ... United Nations, *National Legislation and Treaties relating to the Law of the Sea (United Nations Legislative Series*, ST/LEG/SER.B/19, 1980)
TCR ... Terms, conditions and restrictions
UK Treaty Series ... *United Kingdom Treaty Series*
UN ... United Nations
UNCLOS I ... First United Nations Conference on the Law of the Sea (Geneva, 1958)
UNCLOS II ... Second United Nations Conference on the Law of the Sea (Geneva, 1960)
UNCLOS III ... Third United Nations Conference on the Law of the Sea (1973-1982)

Abbreviations lxv

UNCLOS I Off.Rec. ... United Nations Conference on the Law of the Sea
(Geneva, 1958). *Official Records*
*UNCLOS II Off.Rec. ... Second United Nations Conference on the Law of the
Sea* (Geneva, 1960). *Official Records*
*UNCLOS III Off.Rec. ... Third United Nations Conference on the Law of the Sea.
Official Records*
UNCLOS Resolution I ... Resolution of UNCLOS III on Establishment of the
Preparatory Commission for the International Seabed Authority and for the
International Tribunal for the Law of the Sea
UNCLOS Resolution II ... Resolution II of UNCLOS III on Governing
Preparatory Investment in Pioneer Activities Relating to Polymetallic Nodules
UN Convention ... United Nations Convention on the Law of the Sea, 1982
UNCTAD ... United Nations Conference on Trade and Development
UNEP ... United Nations Environment Programme
UNESCO ... United Nations Educational Scientific and Cultural Organisation
UN, *Multilateral Treaties 1999* ... United Nations, *Multilateral Treaties
Deposited with the Secretary-General. Status as at 31 December 1999,* 2000
UNRIAA ... United Nations Reports of International Arbitral Awards
UNTS ... *United Nations Treaty Series*
USC ... United States Code
Virginia JIL ... Virginia Journal of International Law
Vol. 3 ... Volume 3 of this work
WHO ... World Health Organisation
WMO ... World Meteorological Organisation
WTO ... World Trade Organisation
YBILC ... *Yearbook of the International Law Commission,* 1949 -

PART 1

INTRODUCTION

CHAPTER 1

Introduction

I. THE SCOPE OF VOLUME 2

The purpose of this study is to present an analysis of the legal regime governing the exploration and exploitation of the mineral resources of the 'Area' beyond the limits of national jurisdiction, that is, the area lying seaward of the outer limit of the continental shelf.

The international community was first made aware of the need to develop a regulatory framework for the exploitation of the mineral resources of the bed of the oceans in 1967, when Ambassador Pardo, in his historic speech in the UN General Assembly's First Committee, called for the recognition of the Area and its resources as the common heritage of mankind.[1] In a sense, the position at that time was somewhat similar to that which had existed with respect to the continental shelf when, in 1945, President Truman had proclaimed that the United States had exclusive jurisdiction and control over the natural resources of the continental shelf.[2] In both situations there was an awareness that the exploitation of a submarine mineral resource was imminent; that the rules of international customary law which might apply to such exploitation lacked clarity and precision; and that the very considerable investment needed to finance such exploitation would become available only if a legal regime could be created under which potential exploiters could acquire secure legal titles. The solution to which the Truman initiative led was of course the recognition in international law of the coastal State's sovereign rights to explore the continental shelf and exploit its natural resources, thereby extinguishing any conflicting rights which might have been based on the principle of the freedom of the seas.

Ambassador Pardo too wished to ensure that the principle governing the exploitation of the minerals of the Area should not be the freedom of the high seas but his preferred solution was to create a radically new international regime, under which exploitation of the Area and its resources would be for the benefit of mankind as a whole, taking into particular consideration the interests and needs of the developing countries.[3]

---

[1] See Further Chap.2, section III.1 on 'The Maltese Initiative'.

[2] Presidential Proclamation No. 2667 of 28 September 1945 (United Nations, *Laws and Regulations on the Regime of the High Seas*, ST/LEG/SER.B/1, 11 January 1951, pp. 38-40; reproduced in Vol. 3 as Doc. No. 1); See further E.D. Brown, *Sea-Bed Energy and Minerals: The International Legal Regime, Vol.1: The Continental Shelf*, 1992, at p.9.

[3] See excerpt from Maltese Memorandum quoted in Chap. 2, text, at note 30.

4   *Chapter 1*

The history of the international community's attempt since 1967 to create a stable international regime for sea-bed mining is essentially a record of the conflict between those States, particularly the Group of 77, which supported the view that the fundamental principle on which the regime of sea-bed mining should be based was the principle of the common heritage of mankind, and those other States, particularly among the industrially advanced States, which maintained that sea-bed mining was a freedom of the high seas and would continue to be undertaken on the basis of the principle of the freedom of the seas until such time as they consented to its replacement by an alternative regime. As will be seen in the chapters which follow, the conflict between the two sides was not resolved until 1994. Indeed, prior to 1994, it was impossible to say that a single regime of sea-bed mining existed. There were in fact two alternative regimes, the United Nations regime, based upon the common heritage principle as embodied in the United Nations Convention on the Law of the Sea, 1982, and the Reciprocating States regime, based upon the principle of the freedom of the high seas and the national legislation of leading industrialised States.

Following the entry into force of the United Nations Convention on the Law of the Sea, 1982 (the 'UN Convention') on 16 November 1994, it is now possible to say that the conflict has been resolved in favour of the principle of the common heritage of mankind, the fundamental principle embodied in Part XI of the UN Convention.   However, unless heavily qualified, any such conclusion would be somewhat simplistic and misleading.   In reality, the United Nations regime which emerged victorious in 1994 was far from being the original UN Convention model.   Rather, it was the UN Convention model as substantially modified by an agreement adopted by the UN General Assembly on 28 July 1994, giving effect to the results of Informal Consultations sponsored by the UN Secretary-General between 1990 and 1994.[4]   It was this instrument – the Agreement Relating to the Implementation of Part XI of the United Nations Convention on the Law of the Sea[5] (hereafter the 'Implementation Agreement') – which opened the way for the industrialised States to support the UN Convention regime of sea-bed mining.

If the current United Nations regime and its expected development over the next few years are to be thoroughly understood, it will not suffice to consider the final product in isolation.   It is the need to understand also the antecedents of the UN Convention regime, including its relationship to the competing Reciprocating States regime, which has determined the shape of this study.

---

[4] For a brief account of the Informal Consultations, see E.D. Brown, ' "Neither necessary nor prudent at this stage " : the regime of seabed mining and its impact on the universality of the UN Convention on the Law of the Sea', 17 *Marine Policy* (1993), pp.81-107 and 'The 1994 Agreement on the Implementation of Part XI of the UN Convention on the Law of the Sea: breakthrough to universality', 19 *ibid.* (1995), pp.5-20;   or E.D. Brown, *The International Law of the Sea*, Vol .I, 1994, Chap.17, section IV.

[5] For the texts of (1) General Assembly Resolution 48/263 of 28 July 1994 on the 'Agreement Implementing Part XI of the United Nations Convention on the Law of the Sea of 10 December 1982' (the 'Implementation Agreement') and (2) the Implementation Agreement, see Vol. 3, Docs. Nos. 22 and 23; also reproduced in *LOS Bull., Special Issue IV*, 16 November 1994, pp.8-25 and Misc.No.44 (1994), Cm 2705.

The volume falls into three parts. Following this introduction, the remainder of Part 1 is concerned with *The Common Heritage of Mankind as a Fundamental Principle: Ideology or Reality?* It places the United Nations regime in historical perspective by examining the forces which have shaped the compromise embodied in the UN Convention, as modified by the Implementation Agreement.

Part 2 is a comprehensive study of *The United Nations Regime of Sea-Bed Mining,* based upon Part XI of the UN Convention; the related Resolution II, 'Governing Preparatory Investment in Pioneer Activities Relating to Polymetallic Nodules', adopted at the same time as the Convention in April 1982; [6] the Implementation Agreement of 28 July 1994; and the Mining Code, approved on 13 July 2000.[7] Part 2 opens with an examination in Chapter 3 of *The Principles of the Regime* governing the Area and Chapter 4 deals with *The Basic Regime for the Development of the Resources of the Area* laid down in the UN Convention, as modified by the Implementation Agreement. Detailed though the provisions of Part XI of the Convention and of the Implementation Agreement are, they require for their practical implementation a set of even more detailed rules, regulations and procedures. It is the purpose of Chapter 5 to present an analysis of the Mining Code which embodies such rules, regulations and procedures for the prospecting and exploration phases of the sea-bed mining of polymetallic nodules.

If the Third United Nations Conference on the Law of the Sea (UNCLOS III) had been more of a legal conference and less of a political forum, it might have been reasonable to expect that the section of the UN Convention on the 'Development of Resources of the Area' would have incorporated whatever provision was deemed necessary for the protection of the interests of pioneer mining consortia, which had invested heavily in preparations for sea-bed mining prior to the adoption of the Convention. Regrettably, the reality was quite different. Despite warnings from the industrialised States that their attitude to the conventional regime would depend in part on the adequacy of its provision for the protection of pioneer investors, the Conference paid very little attention to this aspect of the matter until its closing session. As a result, the Convention itself dealt mainly with the 'normal' situation, in which the development of the resources of the Area would proceed without any need to cater for the special interests of the pioneer investor, and it was left to Conference Resolution II to make provision for a preferential status to be accorded to pioneer investors. This need have occasioned no great concern, had Resolution II been drafted with care after adequate consideration of the problem. In fact, however, it bore all the marks of hasty preparation and proved to be a quite inadequate foundation for the inauguration of the new regime. One of the results of this state of affairs was that a heavy burden fell upon the Preparatory Commission of the International Sea-Bed Authority; it had to salvage the pioneer investor scheme through a series of questionable 'adjustments' and 'understandings', while at the same time being constrained by the terms of the UN Convention and Resolution II. The Mining Code too had to reflect the special position of the registered pioneer investors and

---

[6] Reproduced in Vol. 3 as Doc. No. 14.2.

[7] Regulations on Prospecting and Exploration for Polymetallic Nodules in the Area (Mining Code), 13 July 2000 (ISBA/6/A/18); reproduced in Vol. 3 as Doc. No. 25.

6   Chapter 1

does so in a series of footnotes which indicate how the status of the pioneer investor differs from that of other contractors. Given the complexity of these developments, it has been thought wise to deal with *The Pioneer Investor Scheme* in a separate Chapter 6, though it should of course be understood that it is an integral part of the overall UN Convention regime.

Prior to the adoption in 1994 of the Implementation Agreement, it was by no means certain that the UN regime of sea-bed mining would achieve near-universality. There was a distinct possibility that a significant proportion of sea-bed mining would take place under the alternative Reciprocating States regime, based upon the principle of the freedom of the high seas and embodied in the unilateral legislation of some of the industrially advanced States, reciprocally co-ordinated by international agreement. Chapter 7, on *The UN Regime versus the Reciprocating States Regime: A Compromise Solution,* provides an account of the conflict between the two regimes and shows how a compromise solution was facilitated by the adoption of the Implementation Agreement.

Given the complexity of this conventional regime, new institutions were clearly required for its development and administration. An account of the new International Sea-Bed Authority (the 'Authority'), its several organs and related institutions will be found in Chapter 8 on *The Institutional Framework.*

One of the most remarkable features of the United Nations regime is the elaborate – some would say over-elaborate – provision which it makes for the settlement of disputes. Part 2 closes with an examination of this system in Chapter 9 on *Settlement of Disputes.*

Whatever regime was to govern sea-bed mining, there was obviously a need to ensure that it would not involve an undue risk of damage to the marine environment. Fortunately, the evidence suggests that both UNCLOS III and national administrations have been fully aware of the risks and made serious and responsible efforts to safeguard the marine environment. These efforts are reviewed in the final Part 3 of this volume on *Sea-Bed Mining and the Marine Environment..*

II. THE STATUS OF THE UN CONVENTION

As has been noted above, it was the compromise embodied in the Implementation Agreement, adopted in 1994, which persuaded the industrialised States to support the UN Convention regime of sea-bed mining. The Implementation Agreement substantially amended the regime of sea-bed mining in Part XI of the UN Convention and these changes will be fully considered in later chapters. It also introduced complex additional provisions on the entry into force of the two instruments and, by way of introduction, these are considered below.

1. Entry into Force and Transitional Arrangements
1.1 Entry into Force
Since Part XI of the UN Convention and the Implementation Agreement are to be interpreted and applied as a single instrument,[8] and the provisions of the two instruments governing their entry into force are accordingly intertwined, it is now

---

[8] Implementation Agreement, Art.2(1).

necessary, in considering the current status of the United Nations regime, to refer to both the straightforward provisions of the UN Convention itself and the considerably more complex rules embodied in the Implementation Agreement.

Article 308 of the UN Convention provides for its entry into force twelve months after the date of deposit of the sixtieth instrument of ratification or accession. This target was reached on 16 November 1993 and the Convention entered into force on 16 November 1994.[9]

As has been seen, the Implementation Agreement was *adopted* on 28 July 1994 and, under its Article 3, remained open for *signature* for twelve months thereafter. Under Article 6, the Agreement was to *enter into force* thirty days after forty States had established their *consent to be bound*, provided that they included at least seven of the States referred to in Paragraph 1a of Resolution II of the Third United Nations Conference on the Law of the Sea. This paragraph identifies the States entitled to apply for registration as pioneer investors and its scope was further extended by a New York Understanding of 5 September 1986.[10] The group included the following States: Belgium, Canada, China, France, Germany, India, Italy, Japan, the Netherlands, the Republic of Korea, Russia, the United Kingdom and the United States. In addition, five of this group of at least seven States had to be 'developed States'. This provision offered some reassurance to the developing States that the compromise package produced by the Secretary-General's Informal Consultations would receive the real support of the industrialised States, including those with an interest in the pioneer investor scheme. It was also provided that, if these conditions were satisfied before the entry into force of the UN Convention on 16 November 1994, the Agreement would also enter into force on that date.[11]

For any State establishing its consent to be bound after the above requirements were fulfilled, the Agreement enters into force on the thirtieth day following establishment of its consent to be bound.[12]

Central to these rules on entry into force is the concept of consent to be bound. States may establish their consent to be bound by the Agreement in a variety of ways:

(i) *under Article 4(1)*: by deposit of an instrument of ratification or formal confirmation of, or accession to, the UN Convention after the adoption of the Agreement on 28 July 1994;

(ii) *under Article 4(2) and (3)(a)*: by 'Signature not subject to ratification, formal confirmation or the [simplified] procedure set out in article 5'. Under Article 4(2), this route is open only to entities which have previously established or establish at the same time their consent to be bound by the UN Convention. Of course, those establishing their consent to be bound by the UN Convention at the same time would automatically be consenting to be bound by the Agreement as well under (i) above.

---

[9] On the status of the UN Convention as at 1 October 2000, see Vol.3, Table 1.
[10] See further below, Chap. 6, sections II.1.1 and III.6.
[11] Art. 6(1).
[12] Art. 6(2).

8   Chapter 1

Article 4(3)(a) does not expressly require the signatory to declare that its signature is definitive and, at first sight, it might appear that any unqualified signature would be deemed to be definitive.   After all, States wishing to subject their signatures to ratification etc. may do so under Article 4(3)(b). However, according to UN Secretariat practice, a formal, written indication of the intention of a State to be bound by a treaty is required before it will be so recorded.[13]

(iii)   *under Article 4(2) and (3)(b)*: by signature subject to ratification or formal confirmation, followed by ratification or formal confirmation.   Here too, under Article 4(2), this mode may be adopted only by States which have previously established or establish at the same time their consent to be bound by the UN Convention;

(iv)   *under Article 4(2) and (3)(c)*:   by signature subject to the simplified procedure set out in Article 5.   Once again, such signatories must already have established or establish at the same time their consent to be bound by the UN Convention;

(v)   *under Article 4(2) and(3)(d)*: by accession to the Agreement, subject to the same proviso under Article 4(2).

Given the fact that the Implementation Agreement and Part XI of the UN Convention are to be interpreted and applied together as a single instrument,[14] it is not surprising that provision should be made for an expression of consent to be bound by one of them to constitute also consent to be bound by the other.   What is surprising at first sight is that any ratification of or accession to the UN Convention after simply the *adoption* of the Implementation Agreement should also constitute consent to be bound by the Agreement.[15]   However, given the desirability of creating a single regime of sea-bed mining as speedily as possible – an end also served by the provision made for the provisional application of the Agreement[16] – this novel effect of mere adoption of a treaty is understandable.   It will be noted that the rule is reciprocal.   States establishing their consent to be bound by the Agreement must have previously established, or establish at the same time, their consent to be bound by the UN Convention.[17]

The simplified procedure for consenting to be bound which is embodied in Article 5 of the Agreement was inserted to accommodate the constitutional problems of those States which had already ratified or acceded to the UN Convention.   The intention was to obviate the need for such States to secure further legislative authority by providing them with the option of a form of tacit or implied consent.   The rule is that such a State, by signing the Agreement subject to the simplified procedure set out in Article 5, will be considered to have

---

[13] The writer is indebted to Prof. M. Hayashi, formerly Director of the UN Division for Ocean Affairs and the Law of the Sea, for confirming this practice.

[14] Art. 2(1).

[15] Art. 4(1).   See also para.6 of General Assembly Resolution A/48/263 (*loc.cit.* in note 5) which calls upon States which consent to the *adoption* of the Agreement to refrain from any act which would defeat its object and purpose.   *Cf.* Art.18 of the Vienna Convention on the Law of Treaties, 1969, which ties this obligation to signature or an expression of consent to be bound.

[16] See next section below.

[17] Art. 4(2).

established its consent to be bound by the Agreement twelve months after the date of the adoption of the Agreement, that is, on 28 July 1995, unless, before that date, it notifies the depositary to the contrary.[18] Consideration of the constitutional effect of such a device is beyond the scope of this study but it will be noted that signature subject to the Article 5 procedure would perhaps be more accurately described as accession with delayed effect, subject to a right to opt out. Moreover, the delayed effect could have been purely notional if, as was possible under Article 7, the Agreement had been applied provisionally by the State concerned between 16 November 1994 and 28 July 1995.[19]

1.2 Provisional Application of Implementation Agreement and Interim Budgetary Arrangements

Since the UN Convention was due to enter into force on 16 November 1994 quite independently of the existence or fate of the Implementation Agreement, there was obviously a possibility that the UN Convention would enter into force in its original form before the conditions for entry into force of the Agreement could be fulfilled. In that event, the parties to the UN Convention, predominantly developing States, would have been burdened with the budgetary implications of entry into force[20] and, on the other hand, the principal industrialised States, though relieved of this burden, would have been debarred from membership of the organs of the International Sea-bed Authority and deprived of any opportunity to influence the development of the regime in its early formative stage. Added to these problems, which would have existed in any event, was the need to ensure that there should be only one UN regime of sea-bed mining – that provided by Part XI of the UN Convention, as amended by the Implementation Agreement. It was in order to avoid these problems that special provision was made for the provisional application of the Agreement and for interim budgetary arrangements.

So far as provisional application is concerned, Article 7 provided that if, on 16 November 1994, the Agreement had not entered into force, it would be applied provisionally by four categories of States:

(a) States which had consented to the *adoption* of the Agreement (by voting in favour of the General Assembly resolution adopting it), unless notifying the depositary to the contrary before 16 November 1994;

(b) signatories of the Agreement, unless notifying the depositary to the contrary upon signature;

(c) States consenting to provisional application by so notifying the depositary. States which had neither voted for the General Assembly resolution nor signed the Agreement might fall into this category;

(d) States acceding to the Agreement.

Such provisional application was to continue until the date of entry into force of the Agreement or, if earlier, 16 November 1998, if at that date expressions of consent to be bound had not been made by the seven States whose support was required for entry into force under Article 6(1). In fact, the Agreement entered

---

[18] Art. 5(1).

[19] On provisional application, see next section below.

[20] See UN Convention, Art. 171.

10   Chapter 1

into force on 28 July 1996 and, therefore, the provisional application of the Agreement was terminated on that date.[21]

If a State applied the Agreement provisionally under Article 7, it automatically became a member of the Authority on a provisional basis.[22] Since, however, the provisional application of the Agreement had to terminate at the latest upon the entry into force of the Agreement,[23] the possibility existed (and indeed became a reality) that this event might occur before particular States, which were applying the Agreement provisionally, had been able to fulfil the conditions for entry into force of the Agreement for them, thus depriving them of the advantages they had enjoyed as members of the Authority on a provisional basis.   The Agreement dealt with this problem by providing that such States might continue to be members of the Authority on a provisional basis for a limited period, provided they complied with specified conditions.[24]

Two situations were envisaged.   First, if the Agreement entered into force before 16 November 1996, States might continue their provisional membership of the Authority simply by notifying such intention to the depositary.   Normally, such membership would have terminated on 16 November 1996 or upon the entry into force of the Agreement for the State concerned, whichever was earlier. However, the Council of the Authority was empowered to extend it for a further period or periods not extending beyond 16 November 1998, if satisfied that the State concerned had been making efforts in good faith to become a party to the Agreement and the UN Convention.[25]

Secondly, provision was made for the contingency that the Agreement would enter into force after 15 November 1996.   However, with the entry into force of the Agreement on 28 July 1996, this provision became redundant.

Members of the Authority on a provisional basis had the same rights and obligations as other members, including: (1) the obligation to contribute to the administrative budget of the Authority;   and (2) the right to sponsor an application for approval of a plan of work for exploration.[26]   Plans of work so approved would terminate, however, if provisional membership ceased and the State had not become a party to the Agreement.[27]

Complementary to these provisions on the provisional application of the Agreement and provisional membership of the Authority were the interim budgetary arrangements incorporated in the Agreement.   Developing the decision of the General Assembly to this effect,[28] the Agreement provided that, during an interim period extending to the end of the year following the year in which the Agreement entered into force, that is, in fact, until the end of 1997, the

---

[21] *LOS Bull.*, No.32, 1996, p.14.

[22] This is not stated in Art. 7 but is clearly implied in the opening paragraph of Section 1, para.12 of the Annex to the Agreement.

[23] Art. 7(3).

[24] Agreement, Annex, Section 1, para.12.

[25] Para.12(a).

[26] Para.12(c).

[27] Para.12(d).

[28] A/48/263, 28 July 1994 (*loc.cit.* in note 5), para.7.

administrative expenses of the Authority would be met through the regular budget of the United Nations.[29]

Taken together, these provisions provided solutions for all three of the aforementioned problems. First, States which had already ratified the UN Convention would not be disproportionately burdened with the expenses of the Authority during any period between the entry into force of the UN Convention on 16 November 1994 and the time when the industrialised States might have been expected to assume their share of the burden following the later entry into force of the Convention for them. Secondly, these arrangements ensured that the industrialised States would enjoy a number of advantages: the right to attend meetings of the Assembly of the Authority; eligibility for election to the Council of the Authority; and the right to sponsor an application for the approval of a plan of work for exploration. Thirdly, provisional application of the Agreement ensured the immediate establishment and future development of a unitary UN regime for the Area.

2. Breakthrough to Universality? Current Status

The first statistic to note is that the UN Convention entered into force on 16 November 1994 for the 68 States which had already ratified or acceded to the Convention or were otherwise bound as successor States. As at 1 October 2000, that figure had increased to 134 (133 States and the European Community).[30]

So far as the Implementation Agreement is concerned, it is useful to consider first the data relevant to the entry into force of the Agreement and then the data relevant to provisional membership of the Authority.

Data on entry into force. As has been seen, the Agreement entered into force on 28 July 1996 and, as at 1 October 2000, was binding upon 98 States and the European Community.[31]

Data on provisional membership of Authority. As has been seen, following termination of the provisional application of the Implementation Agreement on 28 July 1996, those States (and the European Community) which had enjoyed provisional membership of the Authority until then, under Article 7(1) of the Agreement, were entitled to continue their provisional membership by simply notifying the depositary of the Agreement in writing under Section 1, paragraph 12(a) of the Annex to the Agreement. Eighteen States (and the European Community) exercised this option.[32] Although such extensions terminated on 16 November 1996 [33], further extensions could be granted by the Council for a further period or periods not exceeding in total two years. It was up to the State or entity concerned to submit a request to the Council and to satisfy it that it had been making efforts in good faith to become a party to the Agreement and the UN Convention.[34] At the second (resumed), third and fourth sessions of the Authority

---

[29] Agreement, Annex, Section 1, para.14; *cf.* UN Convention, Art.171.

[30] For details, see Vol. 3, Table 1, which may be updated by referring to the UN website http://www.un.org/Depts/los/los94st.htm.

[31] *Loc. cit.* in note 30.

[32] Listed in *LOS Bull.*, No.32, 1996, p.14.

[33] Implementation Agreement, Annex, Section 1, para.12 (a).

[34] *Ibid.*

12   *Chapter 1*

in August 1996, March 1997 and March 1998, the Council approved requests for extension of provisional membership as shown in the following table. [35]

Most of the extensions were to 16 November 1998, when, under the Implementation Agreement, provisional membership came to an end.

Provisional Member	Expiry Date	Became State Party on (correct at 1.10.00)
Bangladesh	16.11.98	-
Belarus	16.11.98	-
Belgium	16.11.98	13.12.98
Canada	16.11.97	-
Chile	16.11.98	24.09.98
European Community	16.11.98	01.05.98
Gabon	16.11.98	10.04.98
Lao People's Democratic Republic	16.11.98	05.07.98
Mozambique	16.11.98	12.04.97
Nepal	16.11.98	02.12.98
Poland	16.11.98	13.12.98
Qatar	16.11.98	-
Russian Federation	16.11.97	12.04.97
Solomon Islands	16.11.98	23.07.97
South Africa	16.11.98	22.01.98
Switzerland	16.11.98	-
Ukraine	16.11.97	26.07.99
United Arab Emirates	16.11.98	-
United Kingdom	16.11.97	24.08.97
United States	16.11.98	-

As the table shows, some provisional members became full States Parties either before or after the date set for the expiry of their particular provisional membership but, as at 16 November 1998, eight of the former provisional members were still not States Parties. [36] As was noted at the Authority's fourth session in August 1998, this situation had serious budgetary implications since the Authority had previously assessed contributions for both regular and provisional members. [37] The scale of the problem is indicated in the figures for the contributions assessed against three of the eight States in the 1998 budget. Out of a total budget of $4,703,900, $1,175,975 was assessed against the United States, $149,532 against Canada and $58,178 against Switzerland. [38]

Conclusion. Given the very strong level of support indicated by the fact that the Convention and Agreement are now binding upon 134 States and entities and

---

[35] ISBA/C/9; ISBA/3/C/3; ISBA/3/C/11; and Press Release SEA/1574.
[36] Bangladesh, Belarus, Canada, Qatar, Switzerland, Ukraine, United Arab Emirates and United States.
[37] Press Release SB/4/30, 28 August 1998.
[38] *Ibid.*

The scope of volume 2   13

99 States and entities respectively, and that a number of other States, including the United States, collaborated as members of the Authority on a provisional basis until provisional membership ended on 16 November 1998, there would seem to be good reason for cautious optimism that, before long, the United Nations regime will be of near-universal scope. Nonetheless, it has also to be noted that, as at 1 October 2000, no less than 35 members of the Authority which became States Parties to the UN Convention prior to the adoption of the Implementation Agreement had still not taken the steps required to become parties to the Agreement;[39] nor, of course, is the United States a party even to the UN Convention.

As will be seen in later chapters, the UN regime of sea-bed mining is far from complete. The first instalment of the Mining Code, approved in July 2000, covers only prospecting and exploration activities and only one type of sea-bed resource, polymetallic nodules. It will need to be supplemented in due course by additional regulations governing the commercial exploitation phase of sea-bed mining and other types of sea-bed resources such as polymetallic sulphides and cobalt-bearing crusts. [40] Accordingly, this volume can present only an interim report on the progress so far made in constructing a workable regime for sea-bed mining. It is the writer's hope, however, that it may assist the reader in understanding the Byzantine complexities of the present position and in following and assessing the importance of subsequent developments.

---

[39] Angola, Antigua and Barbuda, Bahrain, Bosnia and Herzegovina, Botswana, Brazil, Cameroon, Cape Verde, Comoros, Costa Rica, Cuba, Democratic Republic of the Congo, Djibouti, Dominica, Egypt, the Gambia, Ghana, Guinea-Bissau, Guyana, Honduras, Iraq, Kuwait, Mali, Marshall Islands, Mexico, Saint Kitts and Nevis, Saint Lucia, Saint Vincent and the Grenadines, Sao Tome and Principe, Somalia, the Sudan, Tunisia, Uruguay, Viet Nam and Yemen. (source: *loc. cit.* in note 30).
[40] See further below Chap. 4, section XVIII.

CHAPTER 2

The Common Heritage of Mankind as a Fundamental Principle: Ideology or Reality?

I. INTRODUCTION: FUNDAMENTAL PRINCIPLES IN CONFLICT

If there is one 'fact' which is generally known about the regime of sea-bed mining embodied in the UN Convention on the Law of the Sea, it is that it is based upon the fundamental principle that the deep-sea area and its mineral resources are the common heritage of mankind. Implicit in this proposition is the corollary that sea-bed mining may no longer be conducted as a high seas freedom. Both of these propositions are true; however, in so far as they imply that the advocates of a common heritage regime have won an unqualified victory over the defenders of a regime based upon the freedom of the high seas, they are misleading.

It is true that the principle of the common heritage of mankind has survived as the fundamental principle of the regime of sea-bed mining incorporated in the UN Convention, as amended by the 1994 Implementation Agreement.[1] However, in reality, the model which has survived is a pale shadow of its former self and represents the compromise which resolved the long-running conflict between the advocates of the two principles. It is the object of this chapter to bring out this point and to provide a sense of historical perspective by reviewing the course of that conflict over the past three decades.

1. Freedom of the Seas versus Sovereignty: The Classical Conflict

For centuries past, many of the principal features of the international law of the sea have been formed by the interplay between two opposing fundamental principles of international law: the principle of sovereignty and the principle of the freedom of the high seas. The ascendancy of one over the other during any particular historical period has tended to reflect the interests of the predominant powers of the day. Thus, the monopolist ambitions of the Iberian powers in the fifteenth and sixteenth centuries were mirrored in their attempts to establish a *mare clausum* over large parts of the seas, just as the United Provinces of the seventeenth century and Elizabeth's England recognised that their best interests

---

[1] See further above, Chap.1, text, at note 4 and Chap.3, section I.

lay in promoting the opposite doctrine of *mare liberum*.[2]   That these dynamic forces are by no means exhausted is witnessed by the still continuing changes brought about in maritime boundaries in recent years.   The days are not so far distant when the outer limit of the territorial sea could be taken to mark the boundary landward of which sovereignty held sway and enjoyed legal presumptions in its favour, while seawards, the presumptions favoured the predominant principle of the freedom of the high seas.   With the recent introduction of legal continental shelves and exclusive fishing zones, sovereignty made considerable inroads on the scope of the freedom of the seas *ratione materiae*.   The exploration and exploitation of the natural resources of the continental shelf were to be henceforth the object of the sovereign rights of the coastal State.   Similarly, the fishery resources of the exclusive fishery zone were to be the exclusive preserve of the coastal State.   On the other hand, this seaward push of sovereignty did not affect the scope of the freedom of the seas *ratione loci* or alter the legal presumptions in its favour.   With the even more recent acceptance of the concept of the exclusive economic zone (EEZ), the balance has swung more heavily in favour of the principle of sovereignty.   Admittedly, the EEZ is a zone *sui generis* but the safeguards for the freedom of the high seas written into the UN Convention on the Law of the Sea appear less than impressive when measured against the exclusive rights accorded to the coastal State.[3]

2. Freedom of the Seas versus Common Heritage of Mankind: A Modern Conflict
From about the late 1960s, while the principle of the freedom of the seas continued the traditional battle with its ancient adversary in these offshore zones, it found that it was now also coming under attack right in the heart of its empire by a new pretender whose objective was to establish the fundamental principle that the sea-bed beyond the limits of national jurisdiction and the resources thereof were the common heritage of mankind.   The international community was thus faced with the paradoxical position that, on one front, the principle of the freedom of the seas was under attack by a principle of sovereignty motivated by the desire of coastal States to acquire exclusive rights in the fishery and mineral resources of the offshore zones, while, on another front, the principle of the freedom of the seas was being advanced in defence of exclusive rights to exploit sea-bed resources and against the attempt to establish these resources as a new species of *res communis*, a common heritage of mankind.

At first sight, the several references to the common heritage of mankind made in relevant General Assembly resolutions and treaties would seem to leave no room for doubt as to the outcome of the conflict between these two fundamental principles.   According to the Declaration of Principles, adopted by the General Assembly in 1970, the sea-bed and ocean floor beyond the limits of national jurisdiction and the resources of this 'Area' 'are the common heritage of mankind' and the exploration of the Area and the exploitation of its resources are

---

[2] See further E.D. Brown, *The International Law of the Sea*, Vol.1, 1994, Chap.2.
[3] See further *ibid.*, Chap.12.

16 *Common heritage of mankind*

to be carried out for the benefit of mankind as a whole.[4] The Preamble of the UN Convention on the Law of the Sea expressed the desire of States Parties to develop these principles and went on to confirm in Article 136 that, 'The Area and its resources are the common heritage of mankind'. Moreover, the principle was attended by strong safeguards against its subsequent erosion. The Review Conference envisaged in Article 155 was required to ensure the maintenance of the principle of the common heritage of mankind and States Parties agreed, in Article 311(6), that:

> ... there shall be no amendments to the basic principle relating to the common heritage of mankind set forth in article 136 and that they shall not be a party to any agreement in derogation thereof.

Similarly, on the surface at least, neither the General Assembly Resolution of 28 July 1994[5] nor the Implementation Agreement which it adopted[6] was any less stalwart in reaffirming the continuing validity of the principle of the common heritage of mankind. The Resolution reaffirmed that the Area and its resources are the common heritage of mankind[7] and the Agreement, in revising the UN Convention's provisions on the Review Conference, reiterated that 'the principles [including the common heritage of mankind], regime and other terms referred to in article 155, paragraph 2, of the Convention shall be maintained.'[8] It may be noted too that the Implementation Agreement purports to be an 'Agreement relating to the Implementation of Part XI ...' of the UN Convention rather than an amending instrument.

In keeping with this terminology, the industrialised States, in entering into the informal consultations which led to the Implementation Agreement, acknowledged that, in so doing, they were implicitly accepting the principle of the common heritage of mankind.[9]

It will be observed, however, that all of these indicators are expressed in very general terms. When one looks behind the facade, it becomes clear that, although the superficial ideology has been preserved, there has been a marked erosion of the substance of the common heritage regime as originally embodied in the UN Convention. To those who have closely followed the evolution of the common heritage doctrine, this will come as no surprise. The principal landmarks in that evolution were the Declaration of Principles on the Sea-Bed

---

[4] Declaration of Principles Governing the Sea-Bed and the Ocean Floor, and the Subsoil Thereof, Beyond the Limits of National Jurisdiction, A/RES/2749 (XXV), 17 December 1970; text reproduced in Vol. 3 as Doc. No.11.

[5] General Assembly Resolution A/48/263 of 28 July 1994 on the Agreement Implementing Part XI of the United Nations Convention on the Law of the Sea. For text, see Vol.3, Doc.No. 22.

[6] Agreement Relating to the Implementation of Part XI of the United Nations Convention on the Law of the Sea of 10 December 1982 (the 'Implementation Agreement'). For text, see Vol.3, Doc.No. 23.

[7] *Loc.cit.* in note 5, second preambular para.

[8] Implementation Agreement, Annex, Section 4.

[9] See, *e.g.*, D. H. Anderson (leader of UK delegation), 'Further Efforts to Ensure Universal Participation in the United Nations Convention on the Law of the Sea', 43 ICLQ (1994), pp.886-893, at p.893.

Chapter 2 17

and the Ocean Floor adopted in 1970[10] and Part XI of the UN Convention itself. The Declaration was not accepted by the industrialised States as prescribing binding principles or as creating even an interim regime for sea-bed mining; it was more a moral declaration of intent.[11] Similarly, the UN Convention regime, in its original form, was never accepted by the industrialised States, even though a last-minute attempt was made to accommodate their concerns by grafting onto the Convention, by way of Conference Resolution II, a scheme to protect the interests of pioneer investors.[12] The history of the period since 1982 has been one of attempts to reconcile the two competing regimes. Through a series of understandings and agreements, the two sides gradually edged towards a *modus vivendi* which, though difficult to square with the terms of the UN Convention, would have permitted exploration and exploitation to proceed under the two competing regimes.[13] Seen in this perspective, the Implementation Agreement simply extends the compromise further. The principle of the common heritage survives but it has been shorn of many of its most significant features.

In later chapters, the scope and meaning of the common heritage principle and the common heritage regime, as they have been remoulded by the Implementation Agreement, will be considered in some depth. In the remainder of this chapter, an attempt will be made to place these recent developments in historical perspective by reviewing the course of the conflict between the advocates of the common heritage of mankind and those who continued to rely upon the principle of the freedom of the high seas.

II. THE FREEDOM OF THE HIGH SEAS VERSUS THE COMMON HERITAGE OF MANKIND: THE CONFLICT IN HISTORICAL PERSPECTIVE

Strictly speaking, the history of the conflict between these two principles dates back only to the period between 1967 and 1970, when the proposition was first advanced that the Area and its resources should be the common heritage of mankind[14] and that principle was incorporated in the Declaration of Principles adopted by the UN General Assembly.[15] However, if the post-1970 debate and the more recent attitude of the industrialised States to the legal regime of sea-bed mining are to be properly understood, it is necessary also to refer briefly to the period prior to 1967 and to the arguments which were then being developed to provide a legal basis for exclusive rights to exploit deep sea-bed minerals.

1. The Pre-1967 Debate
Prior to 1967, two lines of argument were open to any Government which wished to support the right of one of its nationals to exploit deep sea-bed minerals.

---

[10] *Loc.cit.* in note 4 above.
[11] See further below, section III.2.3.
[12] See further below, Chap. 6.
[13] See further below, Chap. 6, sections III and IV and Chap.7.
[14] See further below, section III.1.
[15] *Loc.cit.* in note 4 above.

18 Common heritage of mankind

The first argument drew upon the analogy provided by the practice of States, over many centuries, of claiming and securing recognition of exclusive rights in the sedentary fisheries of the sea-bed beyond territorial sea limits. The argument was fully considered in the first edition of this work.[16] It was concluded that such rights had later been subsumed under the concept of the legal continental shelf and the argument that they furnished a fruitful source of analogy for the acquisition of exclusive rights to the mineral resources of the deep sea-bed was not persuasive.

The second argument, which proved to be much more enduring, was that deep-sea mining was a high seas freedom. It was this argument which was to be used in the 1980s as the basis of the unilateral sea-bed mining legislation adopted by the principal industrialised States.[17] The Reciprocating States regime developed by these States was in essence a mechanism for co-ordinating claims based upon that legislation.[18] Given the fact that the State practice and attitudes of the industrialised States continued to be based upon the freedom of the high seas argument until very recently and that the modifications of the United Nations regime effected in 1994 by the Implementation Agreement represented a compromise between the two regimes, it is clearly necessary to examine the nature of the principle of the freedom of the seas rather more closely.

2. The Freedom of the High Seas
2.1 Essential Character of the Principle

Despite recent inroads upon it, the freedom of the high seas may still be described as one of the fundamental principles of international law. The powerful presumption in favour of freedom of user of the high seas, which is one of the most important rules underlying the principle, was described thus by Schwarzenberger in 1955:

> Under international customary law, the right of user of the high seas, the air space above them and the seabed may be exercised for any purpose not expressly prohibited by international law as, for instance, for sea and air navigation, fishing, laying of cables and pipelines, naval exercises and wartime operations.[19]

The doubt which existed at that time as to whether the right of user was of an absolute character has since been clearly resolved and it is now recognised that only a right of *reasonable* user exists. This was confirmed by, *inter alia*, Article 2 of the Geneva Convention on the High Seas, 1958, the provisions of which were 'generally declaratory of established principles of international law'. Article 2 provided that:

---

[16] E.D. Brown, *Sea-Bed Energy and Mineral Resources and the Law of the Sea, Vol.2: The Area Beyond the Limits of National Jurisdiction*, 1986, Chap.2, section II.

[17] See further below, Chap.7, especially section II.1.

[18] On the Reciprocating States regime, see further below, Chap.7.

[19] G. Schwarzenberger, 'The Fundamental Principles of International Law', Hague Academy, 87 *Recueil des Cours* (1955), p. 195, at p. 360.

Chapter 2 19

Article 2

The high seas being open to all nations, no State may validly purport to subject any part of them to its sovereignty. Freedom of the high seas is exercised under the conditions laid down by these articles and by the other rules of international law. It comprises, *inter alia*, both for coastal and non-coastal States:

(1) Freedom of navigation;
(2) Freedom of fishing;
(3) Freedom to lay submarine cables and pipelines;
(4) Freedom to fly over the high seas.

These freedoms, and others which are recognised by the general principles of international law, shall be exercised by all States with reasonable regard to the interests of other States in their exercise of the freedom of the high seas.

It follows from these characteristics of the freedom of the high seas that the principal questions to be considered here are whether there was, prior to 1970, any rule of international law prohibiting deep sea mining as a freedom of the high seas and, if there was no such general prohibitory rule, what was the effect on the freedom of deep sea mining of the rule that this freedom had to be exercised by all States with reasonable regard to the interests of other States in their exercise of the freedom of the high seas?

2.2 Was there a Prohibitory Rule?

The most obvious candidate for this rôle was the rule prohibiting the appropriation of areas of the high seas. As will be seen below, this was by no means an absolute rule and the more precise question which has to be answered is whether it extended to the type of 'appropriation' involved in claims to exclusive rights of exploitation in specific deep sea-bed mining sites.

The first point to clarify, therefore, is the nature of the appropriation typically involved in such a claim. The area of a sea-bed mine site will depend upon various physical variables but in this context it will suffice to provide a rough indication of the size of area involved by referring to the dimensions specified in UNCLOS Resolution II Governing Preparatory Investment in Pioneer Activities Relating to Polymetallic Nodules.[20] In terms of this Resolution, 'pioneer investors' may have single 'pioneer areas' allocated to them. Such pioneer areas are not to exceed 150,000 square kilometres but 50 per cent of this area (and possibly more) has to be relinquished to the international Area over an 8-year period.[21] The ultimate exploitation area in each site will thus not exceed 75,000 square kilometres. According to one authoritative source, the pre-production stages of a pioneer venture would take about 23 years to complete.

---

[20] Annex I to the Final Act of UNCLOS III (United Nations, *The Law of the Sea, Official Text of the United Nations Convention on the Law of the Sea*, 1983), at pp. 177-182; reproduced in Vol.3, as Doc.No.

[21] However, under para.9 of the 'New York Understanding' of 5 September 1986 (*LOS Bull., Special Issue III,* September 1991, p.231; or Vol.3, Doc.No.), voluntary earlier relinquishment is permitted in certain circumstances. See further below, Chap.5, section III.6.1 (iii).

20   *Common heritage of mankind*

Full production would then run for about 20-24 years.[22] The physical presence of the miner on the mine site would not present much of a threat to the freedom of the high seas, assuming, of course, that the area was chosen and such operations were conducted with reasonable regard for the interests of other users.   The 'fleet' of one or two mining ships, support vessels, bulk ore carriers and possibly spoil-dumping vessels would be of modest proportions.   There would unquestionably be some environmental impact but, assuming again that the site was selected with reasonable regard for the interests of other users, it would probably not be disproportionate or long-lasting.[23]   It seems fair to say too that the degree of control over the movements of third parties in the waters superjacent to the site would be of a very limited nature.   Apart from protecting their exclusive rights in the site, miners would be chiefly concerned with the physical protection of their mining operations and safety at sea.

Thus, to sum up, the question is whether an operation conducted in such an area, for such a time, with such a fleet and involving such an environmental impact and surface control would be tantamount to the kind of appropriation of an area of the high seas which would fall within the scope of the prohibition. *Prima facie*, the answer would seem to be that it would not.   The claim would be to a usufruct rather than to the sea-bed itself and would be for a limited period of time.   Subject to its being kept within the bounds of reasonableness, both in terms of locus and conduct of operation, it would seem to be a legitimate user.

Nor is this tentative conclusion invalidated by a consideration of the proposition that an *exclusive* claim would necessarily be contrary to the freedom of the high seas.   It has been suggested by Nyhart that since exclusivity is a *sine qua non* of deep-sea mining in economic terms, an exclusive user is a reasonable user.[24]   This is a persuasive argument.   In determining whether a particular freedom is being exercised 'with reasonable regard to the interests of other States in their exercise of the freedom of the high seas',[25] one is concerned with questions of balance, proportionality, equity.   In this case, the elements to be weighed in the balance would be, on the one hand, the commercial necessity of the security of tenure which only an exclusive user could give and, on the other hand, the damage suffered by other States as a result.   In the context of the pre-1970 regime of the sea-bed, it is difficult to see that any significant damage would have been suffered by other States, provided, of course, that the areas worked were well away from established shipping routes and fishing areas, that appropriate measures were adopted for the protection of the environment, and surface operations were conducted in such a manner as not to create shipping hazards.

As was mentioned above, the prohibition of the exclusive appropriation of areas of the high seas is not in any event an absolute rule unless it is much more

---

[22] J.D. Nyhart *et al.*, *Toward Deep Ocean Mining in the Nineties* (Massachusetts Institute of Technology, Report No. MITSG 82-1), 1982, at p. 30.

[23] See further below, Chap. 10 on Protection and Preservation of the Marine Environment.

[24] J.D. Nyhart, 'The Interplay of Law and Technology in Deep Seabed Mining Issues', 15 *Virginia JIL* (1974-75), p. 827, at p. 865.

[25] As required by Art. 2 of the Geneva Convention on the High Seas, 1958.

Chapter 2 21

precisely defined. It is all a question of degree and, once again, of reasonableness and proportionality. It is, of course, true that the exercise of any user by State A involves an element of exclusivity in the sense that State B is thereby prevented from exercising that user at the same time and place. In most cases, however, such as navigation and fishing, the exclusion is virtually momentary and not of the essence of the exercise of the freedom. If navigation and fishing are at one end of the spectrum and sea-bed mining is at the other, intermediate cases are presented by the freedom to lay cables and pipelines, the freedom to construct artificial islands and other installations on the sea-bed and the freedom to close off areas of the high seas for military manoeuvres and weapons testing.

So far as cables and pipelines are concerned, the exclusivity is still minimal. They involve a very limited part of the sea-bed and they exclude neither other cables and pipelines in the same part of the sea-bed nor other users exercised with reasonable regard to the interests of the owners of the cables and pipelines.

Similarly, artificial islands and other installations, to the extent to which they are permitted in the high seas under international customary law,[26] do not involve a disproportionate 'appropriation' of the high seas, though undeniably they do exclude other users in their immediate vicinity and create a potential hazard for shipping.

Perhaps the users which approximate most closely to that of sea-bed mining are military manoeuvres, weapons testing and dumping of toxic materials. None of these needs to be a permanent appropriation but some are certainly semi-permanent and constitute more of an interference with other users than would sea-bed mining.

In short, if one descends from the level of generalised rules, abstractly formulated, to examine the particular rules actually operating in State practice, one finds an absence of any rule prohibiting sea-bed mining as a freedom of the seas. The only prohibition is of sea-bed mining unreasonably conducted.

It was stressed at the beginning of this section that the right of user of the high seas may be exercised for any purpose not expressly prohibited by international law. Thus, the onus of proof lies on those seeking to assert the existence of a prohibitory rule. There is no need to establish positively the existence of a right of user. This is not to say, of course, that it would not have been useful to buttress the presumption in favour of freedom of user by adducing positive evidence that deep sea-bed mining was a recognised user. In fact, however, the evidence is thin.

The *travaux préparatoires* of Article 2 of the 1958 Geneva Convention on the High Seas are frequently cited in support of the existence of such a user. While it is true that passages in the International Law Commission's Reports do support this view, it has to be said that the passages in question are unreasoned and very much *obiter*. All that the Commission said in its 1955 Report was that: 'It is aware that there are other freedoms, such as freedom to explore or exploit

---

[26] See N. Papadakis, *The International Legal Regime of Artificial Islands*, 1977, Chap. 1. See too Art. 87(1)(d) of the UN Convention on the Law of the Sea.

22   Common heritage of mankind

the subsoil of the high seas ...'[27]   Moreover, in its 1956 Report it added simply that:

> The Commission has not made specific mention of the freedom to explore or exploit the subsoil of the high seas. It considered that apart from the case of the exploitation or exploration of the soil or subsoil of a continental shelf –a case dealt with separately in Section III below – such exploitation has not yet assumed sufficient practical importance to justify special regulation.[28]

2.3 Tentative Conclusion

In the light of the above review, the most reasonable, if still somewhat tentative, conclusion would seem to be that, prior to 1967, sea-bed mining conducted with reasonable regard to the interests of other States in exercising the freedoms of the high seas was a legitimate user of the high seas.   The next question is whether that position changed as a result of developments in the United Nations and elsewhere following the Maltese initiative in 1967.

III.   THE EFFECT OF DEVELOPMENTS AFTER 1967

1. The Maltese Initiative

On 17 August 1967 Malta addressed a *Note Verbale* to the Secretary-General of the United Nations requesting the inclusion in the General Assembly's agenda of the following item:

> Declaration and Treaty concerning the reservation exclusively for peaceful purposes of the sea-bed and of the ocean floor, underlying the seas beyond the limits of present national jurisdiction, and the use of their resources in the interests of mankind.[29]

In the supporting Memorandum, the following passages occur:

> It is, therefore, considered that the time has come to declare the sea-bed and the ocean floor a common heritage of mankind and that immediate steps should be taken to draft a treaty embodying, *inter alia*, the following principles:
>
> (a) The sea-bed and ocean floor, underlying the seas beyond the limits of present national jurisdiction, are not subject to national appropriation in any manner whatsoever; ...
>
> (c) The use of the sea-bed and of the ocean floor, underlying the seas beyond the limits of present national jurisdiction, and their economic exploitation shall be undertaken with the aim of safeguarding the interests of mankind.   The net financial benefits derived from the use

---

[27] 2 YBILC (1955), p. 21.
[28] 2 YBILC (1956), p. 278.
[29] UN DOC. A/6695, 19 August 1967, 22 GAOR, Annex 1 (Agenda item 92), at p. 1.

Chapter 2   23

and exploitation of the sea-bed and of the ocean floor shall be used primarily to promote the development of poor countries.[30]

The question which has to be considered in this section is the extent to which this initiative and the State practice within and outside the United Nations to which it ultimately gave rise, have affected international customary law as it was prior to 17 August 1967.   The State practice in question takes a variety of forms.   The first significant fruits of Ambassador Pardo's initiative were the series of General Assembly resolutions on the subject.   They are examined below in order to determine, first, whether the resolutions themselves have had a law-creating effect and, if not, whether they have formed part of a wider law-creating process which has changed the law.   This requires the examination of related State practice.   Part of that State practice reflects the attitudes and interests of developing States and includes the Charter of Economic Rights and Duties of States of 12 December 1974, a Resolution adopted by the Trade and Development Board of UNCTAD on 17 September 1978 and a number of instruments and statements expressing the views of the Group of 77.   There is, of course, another side to State practice on sea-bed mining, reflecting the attitudes and interests of the principal industrialised States with an interest in sea-bed mining.   It thus becomes necessary to refer to the municipal sea-bed mining legislation of these States and to the treaties whereby it is co-ordinated.   Finally, attention will have to be focussed upon the UN Convention on the Law of the Sea and the associated Resolutions adopted by UNCLOS III on 30 April 1982.   Is the Convention simply a treaty creating rules for the parties to it or may it be regarded as having a wider, third-party effect, as being the culmination, the point of crystallisation, of a body of gradually developing State practice?

2. General Assembly Resolutions
While it is true that the germinal ideas reflected in the Maltese *Note Verbale* were incorporated in General Assembly resolutions regularly over the years,[31] it must be said that, with two exceptions, these ideas were not appreciably developed in those resolutions.   The notion of the 'common heritage of mankind', the prohibition of national appropriation and the commitment to benefit poor countries remained on their original high level of abstraction and generality except in the so-called Moratorium Resolution and the Declaration of Principles Resolution.   It will suffice therefore to consider the effect of these two resolutions alone.   Before doing so, however, it is necessary to clarify the law relating to the legal effect of General Assembly resolutions.

---

[30] *Ibid.*
[31] See, *e.g.,* A/RES/2340(XXII), 18 December 1967; A/RES/2467 (XXIII), 21 December 1968; A/RES/2754 (XXIV), 15 December 1969; A/RES/2749 (XXV), 17 December 1970; A/RES/2750 (XXV), 17 December 1970; A/RES/2881 (XXVI), 21 December 1971; A/RES/3029 (XXVII), 18 December 1972; A/RES/3067 (XXVIII), 16 November 1973; A/RES/3334 (XXIX), 17 December 1974; A/RES/3483 (XXX), 12 December 1975; A/RES/31/63 (XXXI), 10 December 1976.

24 *Common heritage of mankind*

2.1 The Legal Effect of General Assembly Resolutions

Given the existence of a very full literature on this subject,[32] it will suffice to state the writer's position briefly.

The general rule is quite clear and has been stated as follows by Judge Lauterpacht in his Separate Opinion in the *South West Africa – Voting Procedure* case:

> Although decisions of the General Assembly are endowed with full legal effect in some spheres of the activity of the United Nations and with limited legal effect in other spheres, it may be said, by way of a broad generalisation, that they are not legally binding upon the Members of the United Nations. In some matters - such as the election of the Secretary-General, election of members of the Economic and Social Council and of some members of the Trusteeship Council, the adoption of rules of procedure, admission to, suspension from and termination of membership, and approval of the budget and the apportionment of expenses – the full legal effects of the Resolutions of the General Assembly are undeniable. But, in general, they are in the nature of recommendations and it is in the nature of recommendations that, although on proper occasions they provide a legal authorisation for Members determined to act upon them individually or collectively, they do not create a legal obligation to comply with them.[33]

Nor does it make any difference if the resolution is called a 'Declaration' or a 'Charter'. Those seeking to bestow greater law-creating powers on the General Assembly frequently resort to selective quotation from the Memorandum of the United Nations Office of Legal Affairs on the 'Use of the Terms "Declaration and Recommendation" '.[34] Read out of context, paragraph 3 of the Memorandum does indeed appear to assist their cause in stating that:

> 3. In United Nations practice, a 'declaration' is a formal and solemn instrument, suitable for rare occasions when principles of great and lasting importance are being enunciated, such as the Declaration of Human Rights. A recommendation is less formal.

However, paragraph 4 puts rather a different gloss on the matter:

> 4. Apart from the distinction just indicated, there is probably no difference between a 'recommendation' or a 'declaration' in United Nations practice as far as strict legal principle is concerned. A 'declaration' or 'recommendation' is adopted by resolution of a United Nations organ.

---

[32] See bibliography in G. Arangio-Ruiz, 'The Normative Role of the General Assembly of the United Nations and the Declaration of Principles of Friendly Relations', Hague Academy, 137 *Receuil des Cours* (1972) p.419, at pp.732-742. See also contributions by Cheng, Higgins and MacGibbon to B. Cheng (ed.), *International Law: Teaching and Practice*, 1982.

[33] *South-West Africa – Voting Procedure, Advisory Opinion of June 7th, 1955, I.C.J. Reports 1955*, p. 67, at p. 115.

[34] UN Doc. E/CN.4/L.610, 2 April 1962, pp. 1-2.

> As such it cannot be made binding upon Member States, in the sense that a treaty or convention is binding upon the parties to it, purely by the device of terming it 'a declaration' rather than a 'recommendation'. However, in view of the greater solemnity and significance of a 'declaration', it may be considered to impart, on behalf of the organ adopting it, a strong expectation that Members of the international community will abide by it. Consequently, in so far as the expectation is gradually justified by State practice, a declaration may by custom become recognised as laying down rules binding upon States ...

There are two main points to note from this quotation. Negatively, General Assembly resolutions, irrespective of nomenclature, do not create binding legal rules except in the limited category of cases referred to in the above passage from Judge Lauterpacht's Opinion. Positively, however, the adoption of the resolution may constitute part of a wider process through which binding rules are created. The Memorandum speaks of the declaration gradually maturing into rules of customary law binding upon States and of course it may well be that a particular declaration will reflect and give precise formulation to an *opinio juris* which has been maturing in the international community; or it may act as a catalyst and, by 'impart[ing] ... a strong expectation that Members of the international community will abide by it',[35] encourage the development of rules of customary law. Again, the wider process of law creation, of which the adoption of the declaration is part, may take an alternative form. A number of States might enter into a treaty or other consensual engagement committing them to recognise the binding effect of the terms of the declaration; or individual States might bind themselves to observance of its terms through unilateral acts.

In all such cases, however, the text of the declaration and the act of its adoption provide little more than the inert material. It is the additional catalyst provided by (i) State practice before, during and following the adoption of the resolution, or (ii) a related consensual engagement, or (iii) a unilateral act, which creates the binding legal rule. This is not to deny, of course, that the form, the degree of precision and the vote by which the declaration is adopted are without influence. Clearly, if the resolution is called a 'declaration' rather than a 'recommendation' or 'resolution'; if it purports to be a declaration of 'legal principles'; if it is formulated in precise, treaty-like form; if it is adopted unanimously or by a very substantial majority, all of these factors will lend weight to 'the strong expectation that Members of the international community will abide by it'. They will doubtless influence State practice in the matter. They are strong formative factors. But the operation of the law-creating process is still necessary to complete the act of creating a binding rule.

Does regular repetition of similar resolutions or frequent recitation of a resolution affect its capacity to create binding legal rules? If one is considering the legal effect of the resolution as such, it is difficult to differ from Professor MacGibbon's conclusion that: 'However many times a recommendation is multiplied it is still at the end of the day a recommendation and not a binding

---

[35] *Ibid.*, para. 4.

26   Common heritage of mankind

legal obligation.'[36] As he said, '... however many times nothing was multiplied by [,] the result was still nothing.'[37] On the other hand, it is obvious – and, of course, Professor MacGibbon was not denying this – that a series of resolutions adopted by large majorities may well have a greater impact on State behaviour than one such resolution.   Even here, however, it would be advisable to ponder Professor MacGibbon's perceptive comment that:

> It is by no means obvious whether the twentieth or thirtieth resolution in any series should be viewed as adding to the strength (quite apart from the legal weight) of the call for action or rather as drawing attention to the ineffectuality of the predecessor in the series.[38]

Judge Lauterpacht's above-mentioned Separate Opinion is frequently cited on this subject and, as will be seen, it has apparently influenced the attitude of the United States Government.[39]   It must be said, however, that in seeking guidance from this Opinion, one has to proceed with great caution.   Practically everything which was said about the legal effect of General Assembly recommendations referred to those addressed to South Africa by the General Assembly, acting in a supervisory capacity in relation to the South West Africa Mandate.   In one passage, for example, Judge Lauterpacht expressed the view that:

> Although there is no automatic obligation to accept fully a particular recommendation or series of recommendations, there is a legal obligation to act in good faith in accordance with the principles of the Charter and of the System of Trusteeship.   An Administering State may not be acting illegally by declining to act upon a recommendation or series of recommendations on the same subject.   But in doing so it acts at its peril when a point is reached when the cumulative effect of the persistent disregard of the articulate opinion of the Organisation is such as to foster the conviction that the State in question has become guilty of disloyalty to the Principles and Purposes of the Charter.   Thus an Administering State which consistently sets itself above the solemnly and repeatedly expressed judgment of the Organisation, in particular in proportion as the judgment approximates to unanimity, may find that it has overstepped the imperceptible line between impropriety and illegality, between discretion and arbitrariness, between the exercise of the legal right to disregard the recommendation and the abuse of that right, and that it has exposed itself to consequences legitimately following as a legal sanction.[40]

---

[36] I. MacGibbon, 'Means for the Identification of International Law. General Assembly Resolutions: Custom, Practice and Mistaken Identity', in B. Cheng (ed.), *International Law: Teaching and Practice*, 1982, p.10, at p. 17.

[37] *Ibid.*

[38] *Ibid.*, at p. 16, note 24.

[39] See passage quoted in text below, at note 44.

[40] *I.C.J. Reports 1955*, p. 67, at p. 120.

Chapter 2 27

This may well be true in relation to recommendations on South Africa's responsibilities as an Administering State but it is almost certainly not true in relation to recommendations generally. Indeed, it is difficult to find any dictum in the Opinion which is clearly of general application. It is no doubt true generally that a recommendation 'is ... a legal act of the principal organ of the United Nations which Members of the United Nations are under a duty to treat with a degree of respect appropriate to a Resolution of the General Assembly'[41] and that it would be wrong to treat General Assembly resolutions 'as nominal, insignificant and having no claim to influence the conduct of the Members'.[42] That, however, does not take us very far.

Summing up, then, it is the writer's view that General Assembly resolutions on the legal regime of sea-bed mining, singly or in series and irrespective of nomenclature or voting figures, do not in themselves as a matter of law, create binding rules. On the other hand, they may well constitute an important part of a broader law-creating process in the several ways described above and in this context their various characteristics may be significant. Accordingly, the objective of the following analysis of the key General Assembly resolutions is to examine them in the broader context in order to determine whether, taken with evidence of related State practice, they have created binding legal rules.

2.2 The Moratorium Resolution
The first of the two key resolutions, the Moratorium Resolution, was adopted on 15 December 1969 by a vote of 62 in favour to 28 against, with 28 abstentions.[43] The votes against included Australia, Canada, France, Japan, the Netherlands, Norway, the Soviet Union, the United Kingdom and the United States. Given the number and importance of the States opposing the Resolution (not to mention the 28 abstentions), the adoption of this Resolution simply underlines the fact that something like half of the States in the United Nations were not prepared to give their support to the following declaration embodied in the Resolution:

> *Declares* that, pending the establishment of the aforementioned international regime:
> (a) States and persons, physical or juridical, are bound to refrain from all activities of exploitation of the resources of the area of the sea-bed and ocean floor, and the subsoil thereof, beyond the limits of national jurisdiction;
> (b) No claim to any part of that area or its resources shall be recognised.

The attitude of Governments opposed to the Resolution is well reflected in the following statement by Mr. Stevenson, the Legal Adviser of the United States Department of State:

---

[41] *Ibid.*, at p.120.
[42] *Ibid.*, at p.122.
[43] A/RES/2574 (XXIV), 15 December 1969, 24 GAOR Supp. (No. 30), at p. 11, UN Doc. A/7834 (1969).

28 *Common heritage of mankind*

The Resolution is recommendatory and not obligatory. The United States is, therefore, not legally bound by it. The United States is, however, required to give good faith consideration to the Resolution in determining its policies.

Article 2, paragraph 2 of the Charter states that 'All Members, in order to ensure to all of them the rights and benefits resulting from membership, shall fulfil in good faith the obligations assumed by them in accordance with the present Charter'. With the exception of certain expressly delineated areas such as membership and the budget, however, the General Assembly is not empowered to make decisions which impose obligations upon Members. The Moratorium Resolution does not fall within one of the special areas in which the General Assembly is empowered to make binding decisions, but rather within the mandate of Articles 10 and 13 that permits the General Assembly to discuss a matter within the scope of the Charter and make recommendations. There is an extensive authority that such a resolution cannot impose upon a Member a legal obligation to implement it.

The United States considers the recommendations contained in the Moratorium Resolution an important statement to be given weight in the determination of United States policy. The United States is not, however, obligated to implement the recommendations and has made clear its opposition to the concept.[44]

It must be concluded that, particularly for the 28 States voting against it, the Moratorium Resolution neither created binding rules immediately nor provided a significant basis for the future development of such rules. At the very most, it could be said, with Mr. Stevenson, that States were simply required to give weight in the determination of their national policies to the 'important statement' contained in this recommendation of the majority in the General Assembly.

2.3 *The Declaration of Principles Resolution*

The Declaration of Principles Resolution was adopted on 17 December 1970 by a vote of 108 in favour to none against, with 14 abstentions.[45] Moreover, the draft adopted by the First Committee of the General Assembly was itself the result of a majority vote (90 to none, with 11 abstentions) rather than of a consensus.[46] It was hardly surprising, therefore, that the Bulgarian delegation in the First Committee should have considered that:

> the presentation by this Committee of a document on which many delegations have serious reservations and objections, and which does not result from a consensus, will neither facilitate our work nor contribute to the solution of the problem.[47]

The Soviet delegation, in announcing that it too would abstain from the vote in the First Committee, also stressed that: 'Naturally approval by the General

---

[44] J.R. Stevenson's letter of 16 January 1970 to Senator Metcalf, in Hearings before the Senate Special Subcommittee on the Outer Continental Shelf, 91st Cong., lst and 2nd Sess. 210 (1970).
[45] *Loc.cit.* in note 4 above.
[46] UN Doc. A/C.1/PV.1798, 15 December 1970, p.37.
[47] UN Doc. A/C.1/PV.1799, pp.23-25.

Chapter 2 29

Assembly of this draft cannot impose legal consequences on States, since such decisions are merely of a recommendatory character.'[48]

The majority, even of those States voting in favour of the Declaration, were equally careful to limit the significance of the Declaration. Thus, the United Kingdom delegation expressed two general reservations:

> First, like any other resolution of the General Assembly, the draft declaration has in itself no binding force. Secondly and arising from this, the draft declaration of principles must be regarded as a whole and interpreted as a whole; and as a whole it has no dispositive effect until we have agreement on an international regime and, as part of that agreement, we have a clear, precise and internationally accepted definition of the area to which the regime is to apply. My delegation entirely endorses the view expressed by other delegations that it is not the purpose of the draft declaration of principles to establish an interim regime for the sea-bed.[49]

Galindo Pohl (El Salvador), who played an important part in the preparatory work which preceded the adoption of the Declaration, confirmed that it was clearly understood in the informal negotiations which paved the way for the adoption of the final compromise text, that it was not intended that the Declaration should provide a provisional regime pending the conclusion of a definitive conventional regime.[50]

Perhaps the most accurate description was given by Sir Laurence McIntyre (Australia), when he expressed his country's understanding of the principles as 'general guidelines for the establishment of a regime for the sea-bed and as an earnest of the desire of the great majority of members to have a regime; but we would not see them as having any binding or mandatory effect upon States in the meantime'.[51]

Sir Laurence went on to make it clear that the Declaration:

> should not prejudice or restrict the scope of matters that in fact can be determined effectively only through the negotiation of an international agreement or agreements at a conference on questions of the law of the sea and the sea-bed. A declaration of principles cannot be used as a substitute for the decisions that will ultimately emerge from such a conference.[52]

Similar statements were made by, *inter alia, Canada* – 'balanced and comprehensive enough to serve as the foundation and framework for an international regime'[53]; *Norway* – the principles 'are indications ... of the rules and enforceable ... we shall later have to hammer out detailed provisions'[54]; and

---

[48] UN Doc. A/C.1/PV.1798, p.32.
[49] UN Doc. A/C.1/PV.1799, p.6.
[50] UN Doc. A/C.1/PV.1781, pp.11-12.
[51] UN Doc. A/C.1/PV.17, p.27.
[52] *Ibid.*
[53] UN Doc. A/C.1/PV.1779, p.8.
[54] UN Doc. A/C.1/PV.1774, pp.18-20.

30 *Common heritage of mankind*

Peru – 'only a basis for the preparation of a regime and must not be interpreted as an interim regime'.[55]

Comments on the status of the concept of the common heritage of mankind also indicated the limited effect of the Declaration of Principles. Thus, the Byelorussian delegate rejected it as a legal principle:

> Speaking of legal principles, we should like to stress that, as in the past, the Byelorussian delegation cannot support the concept that the sea-bed and ocean floor beyond the limits of national jurisdiction and the resources thereof are the common heritage of mankind – in other words, a kind of collective property of all countries. That concept does not take into account the objective realities of the contemporary world, in which there are States having different social systems and different property regimes. Such a concept, as was evident in the work of the Sea-bed Committee, makes more difficult the working out and adoption of legal principles consonant with the interests of all States.[56]

Even the Canadian delegation did not regard the concept as a legal principle at this stage:

> We agree also that the resources of the area should be considered to be the common heritage of mankind, although we view this not so much as a legal principle at this stage, but rather as a concept to which the international community can give specific legal meaning and as a concept upon which we can together construct the machinery and the rules of international law which will together comprise the legal regime for the area beyond national jurisdiction.[57]

Speaking in the General Assembly on 18 December 1970, the late Mr. Amerasinghe, the President of UNCLOS III, said that:

> The Declaration cannot claim the binding force of a treaty internationally negotiated and accepted, but it is a definite step in that direction and ... it has – if I may adapt the words of Walt Whitman – that fervent element of model authority that is more binding than treaties.[58]

Echoing this assessment, the most reasonable conclusion would seem to be that, *at the time of the adoption of the Declaration of Principles*, the concept of the common heritage of mankind could not properly be regarded as a legal principle but embodied, rather, agreed moral and political guidelines which the community of States had undertaken a moral commitment to follow in good faith in the

---

[55] UN Doc. A/C.1/PV.17, p.1.8
[56] UN Doc. A/C.1/PV.1780, pp.47-50.
[57] UN Doc. A/C.1/PV.1779, p.4.
[58] UN Doc. A/C.1/PV.1933, p.100.

Chapter 2 31

elaboration of a legal regime for the area beyond the limits of national jurisdiction.

On the other hand, the Declaration of Principles was a much more important instrument than the Moratorium Resolution, in the sense that it clearly had a number of features which gave it the potential to constitute a significant part of a wider law-creating process. It had the 'formality' and 'solemnity' of a Declaration, arguably enunciating 'principles of great and lasting importance'[59]; it purported to be a declaration of principles and the principles 'solemnly declared' in its operative paragraphs were formulated in relatively precise, treaty-like language. Although incapable of creating binding legal rules in itself, as a General Assembly resolution, it did therefore nonetheless provide an eminently suitable basis for the generation of legally binding rules through a broader process. Before a final judgment can be made on its longer-term impact, therefore, it is necessary to examine related evidence in subsequent State practice in order to determine whether a rule of international customary law has grown out of it, and the extent to which States have become bound by consensual engagements or unilateral acts formulated by reference to it.

There have, of course, been innumerable statements made between 1970 and 1994 (when the Implementation Agreement was adopted and the UN Convention entered into force) on the status of the Declaration of Principles and more particularly on that of the common heritage principle. It will suffice, however, to examine a number of the more important instruments and statements which reflect the attitudes of the two main schools of thought, that of the Group of 77 that the common heritage principle was now part of international law, and that of some of the leading industrialised States that it would not attain that status until it was incorporated in an acceptable convention.

It would be fair to say that, although many leading members of the Group of 77 acknowledged in 1970 that the Declaration of Principles was not legally binding and did not create an interim regime for sea-bed mining, they later argued that the Declaration, taken with other General Assembly resolutions, statements made in the course of UNCLOS III and the work of other international institutions and conferences, provided clear evidence that the common heritage principle was now binding upon all States as a matter of international customary law. Four instruments may be taken as illustrating this point of view: the Charter of Economic Rights and Duties of States (1974); a Resolution adopted by the UNCTAD Trade and Development Board on 17 September 1978 on 'The Exploitation of the Seabed beyond the Limits of National Jurisdiction'; a Statement Declaring the Position of the Group of 77 on Unilateral Legislation Affecting the Resources of the Deep Seabed, made in the Plenary of UNCLOS III on 15 September 1978 by a representative of Fiji on behalf of the Group of 77; and a Letter dated 23 April 1979 to the Chairman of the Group of 77 from the Group of Legal Experts on the Question of Unilateral Legislation. In addition, brief reference will be made to more recent statements and to Declarations

---

[59] Memorandum cited in note 34 above.

32   *Common heritage of mankind*

adopted by the Preparatory Commission in 1985 and 1986, which condemned the Provisional Understanding concluded among eight States in 1984.

3. The Charter of Economic Rights and Duties of States, 1974
The Charter was adopted by the General Assembly on 12 December 1974[60] and had as its fundamental purpose the promotion of 'the establishment of the new international economic order, based on equity, sovereign equality, interdependence, common interest and co-operation among all States, irrespective of their economic and social systems'.[61]   There is no doubt that the intention of the General Assembly was 'to establish or improve norms of universal application'[62] and that the elaboration of the Charter was seen as 'the first step in the codification and development of the matter'.[63]   Neither this intention, however, nor the 'adoption and solemn proclamation' of a 'Charter' alters the fact that the Charter was adopted as a part of a General Assembly resolution.   It is in this context that Article 29 of the Charter has to be appreciated.   Article 29, part of Chapter III on 'Common responsibilities towards the international community', provided that:

> The sea-bed and ocean floor and the subsoil thereof, beyond the limits of national jurisdiction, as well as the resources of the area, are the common heritage of mankind.   On the basis of the principles adopted by the General Assembly in resolution 2749 (XXV) of 17 December 1970, all States shall ensure that the exploration of the area and exploitation of its resources are carried our exclusively for peaceful purposes and that the benefits derived therefrom are shared equitably by all States, taking into account the particular interests and needs of developing countries;   an international regime applying to the area and its resources and including appropriate international machinery to give effect to its provisions shall be established by an international treaty of a universal character, generally agreed upon.[64]

Article 29 contains the only reference to this question in the Charter and although UNCTAD continued to take an interest in sea-bed mining, it cannot be said that this aspect of the new international economic order was significantly developed by UNCLOS III.   An examination of the voting figures simply serves to underline that the Charter has little evidentiary value in relation to the legal regime of sea-bed mining.   The following six States voted against the adoption of the Resolution: Belgium, Denmark, the Federal Republic of Germany, Luxembourg, the United Kingdom and the United States.[65]   The ten countries abstaining were Austria, Canada, France, Ireland, Israel, Italy, Japan, the

---

[60] A/RES/3281 (XXIX), 12 December 1974, 29 GAOR (2315th mtg.) at p. 100, UN Doc. A/3281 (1974), reproduced in XIV ILM (1975), p. 251.
[61] Preamble of Charter (*ibid.*, at p. 252).
[62] Preamble of Resolution (*ibid.*, at pp. 251-252).
[63] *Ibid.*, at p.252.
[64] *Ibid.*, at p.260.
[65] *Ibid.*, at p.265, where voting figures are given.

Chapter 2 33

Netherlands, Norway and Spain.[66]   In the Second Committee of the General Assembly, Article 29 was adopted by 113 votes to none and with 17 abstentions.[67]

4. The UNCTAD Resolution of 17 September 1978

The Resolution on 'The Exploitation of the Seabed beyond the Limits of National Jurisdiction', adopted by the Trade and Development Board of UNCTAD on 17 September 1978[68], originated in a draft submitted by Colombia on behalf of the Group of 77.[69]   The Preamble to the resolution made reference to the Moratorium Resolution and the Declaration of Principles and to the 'consideration' 'that any unilateral actions designed to carry on the exploitation of the area before a Convention on the Law of the Sea is adopted, would violate the aforementioned resolutions of the General Assembly ...'[70]   The operative paragraphs went on, *inter alia*, to call upon all States to refrain from adopting unilateral legislation pending the conclusion of the UNCLOS negotiations;[71] to reiterate 'that any unilateral actions in contravention of the pertinent resolutions of the General Assembly would not be recognised by the international community and would be invalid according to international law';[72] and to stress 'that States which might undertake such unilateral actions would have to assume the responsibility for their consequences both on the outcome of [UNCLOS III] and on negotiations on commodities related to the exploitation of mineral resources from the sea-bed'.[73]

Although adopted by a large majority (65 to 8, with 12 abstentions), the evidentiary value of this Resolution is again blighted by the fact that a significant number of powerful industrialised States voted against its adoption.   The dissenters included the Federal Republic of Germany, France, Japan, the United Kingdom and the United States.   The United States representative, speaking on behalf of the dissenters, reaffirmed their view that deep sea-bed mining legislation was lawful.   The final passage of his statement is typical of innumerable official statements made since that time, in placing emphasis on (i) the interim nature of the legislation and (ii) the need to ensure continuity of investment pending ratification and entry into force of a generally acceptable convention.

5. Group of 77 Statements

Two of the clearest statements of the position of the Group of 77 are to be found in, first, a speech made by the Chairman of the Group of 77 in the UNCLOS Plenary on 15 September 1978 and, secondly, a Letter addressed to the said Chairman by a Group of Legal Experts.   Since the latter is more detailed and comprehensive, attention will be concentrated on its arguments first, before turning to comment briefly on the earlier statement.

---

[66] *Ibid.*
[67] *Ibid.*
[68] UNCTAD Doc. TD/B (XVI)/SC.1/L.2, 5 September 1978.
[69] *Ibid.*, at p.1.
[70] *Ibid.*, at p.2.
[71] Para.1 (*ibid.*, at p. 2).
[72] Para.2 (*ibid.*, at p. 2).
[73] Para.3 (*ibid.*, at p. 2).

34   Common heritage of mankind

5.1 Letter Dated 23 April 1979 from the Group of Legal Experts on the Question of Unilateral Legislation to the Chairman of the Group of 77 [74]
The Group of Legal Experts was established to express in the most precise form possible the Group of 77's repeatedly declared 'clear legal conviction concerning the binding nature of the principles set out in' the 1970 Declaration of Principles and its position on interim unilateral legislation.[75]   The 12-member Group included no fewer than 5 members of the International Law Commission[76] and the Letter, which was circulated in UNCLOS III at the request of the Chairman of the Group of 77, can be taken as a precise statement of the considered legal opinion of some of the leading international lawyers drawn from all regions of the developing world.   It is therefore deserving of careful analysis.

The Group's 'basic points' are presented under six heads:

(i)   *'Development of the international law of the sea'.*   In this section, the Group opens by stating that:

> Neither the Convention on the High Seas, signed in 1958,[77] nor general international law includes among the freedoms of the high seas the exploration and exploitation of the mineral resources of the sea-bed and the ocean floor beyond the limits of national jurisdiction.

Without a supporting analysis of the principle of the freedom of the seas, such a bald statement is virtually worthless. *Inter alia*, it makes no attempt to refute, and indeed betrays no awareness of the existence of the argument that any activity which is not expressly prohibited by international law is a permitted freedom of the high seas.

The Group then goes on to review the history of the United Nations' concern with this subject but, it must be said, in a highly biased fashion.   For example, in referring to the Moratorium Resolution and UNCTAD Resolution 52 (III) of 19 May 1972, no indication at all is given of the clear statements of opposition or reservation of positions made by the principal Western industrialised States. Similarly, it hardly suffices to refer, without supporting argument, to the 'mandatory principles' incorporated in the 1970 Declaration of Principles.

(ii)   *'The binding nature of the fundamental principles governing the area'.* This section of the letter deserves quotation in full:

> The principles set out in the Declaration contained in resolution 2749 (XXV) are legally binding principles which were proclaimed in this Declaration and upheld by the affirmative vote of 108 States.   It should be added that a number of the few States (14) which abstained on that occasion, although

---

[74] *Third United Nations Conference on the Law of the Sea. Official Records* (hereafter *UNCLOS III Off. Rec.*), Vol. XI, pp. 80-82.
[75] *Ibid.*, at p.81.
[76] Listed, *ibid.*, at p.81.
[77] Note omitted.

Chapter 2 35

without formulating any objection, subsequently expressed, either explicitly or implicitly, their support for those principles, as did other States members of the international community, thus recognising by their attitude the force of international custom as expressed in resolution 2749 (XXV).

This custom has given rise to new general principles of public international law which are the basis or legal foundation of any substantive norms regulating the exploration of the area of the sea-bed and the ocean floor and the subsoil thereof and the exploitation of their resources.

It is, to put it mildly, more than a little misleading to describe the States abstaining from voting on the Declaration of Principles as having done so 'without formulating any objection' and as having subsequently expressed their support for those principles. As has been seen above, the leading industrialised States were consistently careful, in 1970 and thereafter, to place on record their view that the Declaration had not led to the establishment of new rules of international law.

The law-creating capacity of General Assembly resolutions in general and the potential law-generating capacity of the Declaration of Principles have already been considered above. It is, therefore, unnecessary to comment further on the claim that the Declaration and the subsequent expressions of support for its principles have generated new 'international custom' and that this custom 'has given rise to new general principles of public international law'.

(iii) *'Normative relationship of the principles applicable to the area'*. The Group here asserts that all of the principles contained in the Declaration of Principles

> ... form a normative unity that is indivisible and applicable to the area. This normative unity consolidates the applicable principles laid down in the Charter of the United Nations and the Declaration on Principles of International Law concerning Friendly Relations and Co-operation among States in accordance with the Charter of the United Nations.[78]

Comment on this passage is difficult in the absence of further elaboration. No one, probably, would deny that the principles of the Declaration form part of an indivisible unity. This is another way of saying that the principle of the common heritage of mankind is the sum total of all the more particular principles incorporated in the Declaration. Such a proposition does not, however, have any bearing on the legal force of these principles.

(iv) *'Legal status of the area'*. This section opens with the statement that:

---

[78] Note omitted.

36   *Common heritage of mankind*

> The customary principle of the freedom of the high seas is not an absolute principle; it does not apply to the exploitation of the sea-bed and ocean floors beyond national jurisdiction, because the exploitation thereof was beyond the capacity of States at the time when that principle came into being.

Once again, this argument reflects an inadequate understanding of the nature of the principle of the freedom of the high seas. It suggests that a closed list of freedoms existed at some time in the past and that positive evidence is required to prove that a new user has subsequently been added to that list. In reality, as has been seen, the onus lies on those seeking to establish that a particular user is a prohibited user. The scope of the freedom of the high seas is not static or frozen at any point of time.

The Group then goes on to argue as follows:

> But even on the assumption that this customary principle would be applicable to this exploitation, it would certainly have ceased to be applicable in consequence of the Declaration of Principles of 1970, not only because the Declaration is a resolution adopted by the General Assembly but also because it is an event reflecting a conviction incompatible with *opinio juris sive necessitatis* indispensable to the operation of the principle as an international custom in the exploitation of the sea-bed or ocean floor beyond national jurisdiction.

Here, too, we encounter a novel view of the law-creating processes of international law. The Group's case can be restated as follows:

(i) Assume that sea-bed mining was a high seas freedom under international customary law.

(ii) Its status as a high seas freedom has now been terminated as a consequence of the adoption of the Declaration of Principles.

There are two reasons for this consequence:

(a) the Declaration is a Resolution adopted by the General Assembly;

(b) the adoption of the Declaration extinguishes one of the essential constituent elements (*opinio juris*) of the rule of customary law that sea-bed mining is a high sea freedom.

In other words, the contention is that the rights of a number of powerful industrialised States established in international customary law may be extinguished without their consent – indeed over their protests – by a General Assembly resolution. Once again the onus has been misplaced. It lies upon those seeking to deprive States of rights enjoyed under international customary law to prove that, as a result of the operation of the recognised law-creating processes, a new rule of international law, binding upon such States, has been created, extinguishing their rights. This onus has certainly not been discharged in this Letter.

Chapter 2 37

Finally, under this head, the Group argues that:

There is an obvious difference in legal status as regards the superjacent waters of the area and as regards the sea-bed, subsoil and resources of the area.
    Whereas the legal status of the superjacent waters is that of *res communis*, the legal nature of the sea-bed, subsoil and resources thereof is that of an indivisible and inalienable common heritage of mankind ...

It will suffice to say that this proposition assumes what has to be proved and the remainder of the paragraph offers no convincing proof.

(v) *'The legal principles applicable to the area and unilateral acts or limited agreements for its exploration and exploitation'*. This section of the Letter too deserves quotation *in extenso*, representing as it does the firmly held opinion of the Group of 77 developing States:

The principles of law laid down in resolution 2749 (XXV) form the basis of any international regime applicable to the area and its resources.
    All activities connected with the exploration and exploitation of the area and other related activities will be governed by the international regime to be established by the conclusion of an international treaty that is generally acceptable and includes appropriate international machinery for implementing the principles of law referred to.
    Consequently, any unilateral act or mini-treaty is unlawful in that it violates these principles, for the legal regime, whether provisional or definitive, can only be established with the consent of the international community.
    The adoption of unilateral measures, draft legislation and limited agreements would merely be an event without international legal effect and hence incapable of being invoked vis-à-vis the international community.
    The great majority of States would not admit the validity of such legislation, nor could such legislation constitute valid grounds for any juridical claim to explore or exploit the area. Furthermore, if such unilateral legislation or mini-treaty should be put into operation, the international responsibility of the States concerned would be engaged in respect of damage caused by such activities incompatible with the principles applicable in the area.
    It should be stressed that no investor would have any legal guarantee for his investments in such activities, for he would likewise be subject to individual or collective action by the other States in defence of the common heritage of mankind, and no purported diplomatic protection would carry any legal weight whatsoever.

In the light of the above comments on earlier sections of the Letter, it is not necessary to comment further on the legal arguments implicit in these several propositions beyond saying that none of them is soundly based in law. These

38 *Common heritage of mankind*

assertions stand or fall with the principal arguments on the legal regime of sea-bed mining.

(vi) *Rule of law.* In the final sections of the Letter, the Group alleges *inter alia* that the conclusion of a mini-treaty or the adoption of unilateral legislation and any attempt to carry them into effect would be inconsistent with the principles of good faith in the conduct of negotiations at international plenipotentiary conferences such as UNCLOS III. Given the protracted duration of the Conference, the declared interim nature of the unilateral legislation and the reservation of position made by the States concerned, this is clearly not a tenable proposition.

5.2 Speech of Chairman of Group of 77, 15 September 1978[79]

Mr. Nandan's speech covers much the same ground as the later Letter from the Group of Legal Experts and is open to much the same criticism. It is interesting to see what response it evoked from spokesmen for the principal industrialised States.

Perhaps the clearest and most concise statement of a position shared by the principal industrialised States was contained in the French representative's contribution, when he said that:

> ... legally speaking, the argument put forward by the spokesman for the Group of 77 to the effect that unilateral exploitation of the sea-bed was unlawful was not valid. It should be clearly understood that no Government could be bound under international law unless it agreed to be so bound in a treaty, and that in no case could a Government be bound by a legal rule which others sought to impose on it. France had never agreed to any limitation on the freedoms of the sea in so far as they related to the exploitation of the sea-bed apart from those limitations which it might have accepted by treaty or within the framework of the development of international customary law. There were no provisions in existing international positive law which prohibited the reasonable exploitation of the sea-bed on an individual basis.[80]

Similar statements were made by representatives of Belgium,[81] the Federal Republic of Germany,[82] Italy,[83] the United Kingdom[84] and the United States.[85] Japan, too, though stating that it had 'no plan at present for national legislation regarding the exploitation of the sea-bed', nevertheless went on record as believing that 'the unilateral legislation which some countries intended to adopt in no way contradicted the concept of the common heritage of man embodied in

---

[79] *UNCLOS III Off. Rec.*, Vol. IX, pp. 103-104.
[80] *Ibid.*, at p. 106, para.43.
[81] *Ibid.*, at p. 107, para.53.
[82] *Ibid.*, at p. 106, paras. 45-46.
[83] *Ibid.*, at p. 107, paras. 51-52.
[84] *Ibid.*, at pp. 107-108, paras. 60-61.
[85] *Ibid.*, at pp. 104-105, paras. 27-29.

Chapter 2 39

General Assembly resolution 2749 (XXV), and that the question of the legality of such measures could not be raised as long as no convention had been concluded'.[86]

5.3 Condemnation of Provisional Understanding

As will be seen below in Chapters 6 and 7, the industrialised States which adopted interim legislation on sea-bed mining also entered into 'mini-treaties' to co-ordinate that legislation.[87] One of the more important of these treaties was the Provisional Understanding Regarding Deep Seabed Matters concluded in 1984[88] by Belgium, the Federal Republic of Germany, France, Italy, Japan, the Netherlands, the United Kingdom and the United States. Five of the eight parties to the Provisional Understanding were at the time of signature, or later became, signatories of the UN Convention.[89] Moreover, two of them, France and Japan, subsequently submitted applications to the Preparatory Commission for registration as pioneer investors under the scheme established under UNCLOS Resolution II.[90]

The parties to the Provisional Understanding claimed that it was 'without prejudice to, nor does it affect, the positions of the Parties, or any obligations assumed by any of the Parties in respect of the United Nations Convention on the Law of the Sea'.[91] However, as will be seen when this agreement is analysed in detail, there are grounds for challenging the validity of this assertion.[92] In the present context, it will suffice to draw attention to the prompt denunciation of the Provisional Understanding by the Group of 77 and the Group of East European Socialist Countries and to the Declarations in similar terms 'adopted' by the Preparatory Commission on 30 August 1985 and 11 April 1986. A full account of these responses is given in Chapter 6.[93] As might be expected, the arguments deployed by the two groups and in the Declaration to condemn the agreement as being illegal and contrary to the letter and spirit of the UN Convention were similar to those reviewed above.

5.4 Towards a modus vivendi

After about 1985, the attitude of the Group of 77 began to change. While remaining committed to the principle of the common heritage of mankind and still determined to prevent its erosion, there were signs that they now accepted the need for an 'adjustment' of the UN Convention regime of sea-bed mining. The new attitude was evident, for example, in the negotiations which led to the series of Understandings and Agreements concluded in 1986 and 1987 in order to overcome practical difficulties in the implementation of the pioneer investor scheme provided for in Resolution II. These instruments – the Arusha and New

---

[86] *Ibid.*, at p. 107, para.54.
[87] See Chap. 7, section III and Chap.6, section III.4.
[88] For text see Vol.3, Doc. No.33.3; also reproduced in XXIII ILM (1984), p. 1354.
[89] The non-signatories being Germany, the United Kingdom and the United States.
[90] See further, Chap. 6, section III.4.4, text following note 118.
[91] Provisional Understanding, *loc. cit.* note 88, para. 15.
[92] See Chap. 6, section III.4.4, text following note 101.
[93] See Chap. 6, section III.4.4, text following note 104.

40   Common heritage of mankind

York Understandings of 1986 and the 'Midnight Agreement' of 1987 – are considered in detail in Chapter 6 but, in essence, gave effect to departures from the UN Convention and Resolution II in order to render their poorly drafted and outdated provisions practicable.   As will be seen, the two Understandings achieved a break-through in the negotiations by taking account of a range of interests, including those of the Group of 77.

Further evidence of greater flexibility was provided in 1989 when the Zambian representative in the Preparatory Commission, speaking for the Group of 77, made it clear that the Group was ready to have discussions on any issues relating to the UN Convention and work of the Preparatory Commission.[94] In July 1990, the Chairman of the Preparatory Commission confirmed the readiness of the Group of 77 to undertake a fundamental re-think of the sea-bed regime and specified the issues which called for reconsideration.[95]   At about the same time, in July 1990, the UN Secretary-General sponsored the first of a series of Informal Consultations which continued until 1994[96] and eventually bore fruit in the form of the Implementation Agreement of 28 July 1994.   As will be seen in more detail in later chapters, this Agreement introduced radical amendments of the original UN Convention regime of sea-bed mining.

5.5   The Significance of the 'Practice' of the Group of 77

The purpose of the above review of the 'practice' of the Group of 77 was to provide a basis for assessing the extent to which that practice had contributed to the development into binding rules of law of the principles enunciated in the Declaration of Principles.

As has been seen, down until about 1985, that practice was uniform.   It clearly signified that some 119 States recognised the principles enunciated in the Declaration as having become part of international law and regarded the adoption and application of unilateral interim legislation as being in breach of binding rules of international law.   However, it is doubtful if this amounted to anything more than an indication that a large number of developing States shared the same view of the law.   Given the resolute opposition of a group of large, highly industrialised States which alone had the capacity, financially and technologically, to engage in sea-bed mining, it is difficult to see how the practice of the developing States could be regarded as having transformed the non-binding principle of the Declaration of Principles into rules of international law.   As has been seen, the Declaration itself has no law-creating status; nor, taken with the related practice, does it enable us to say that it provides evidence of the *opinio*

---

[94] The Zambian statement of 1 September 1989 is reproduced in *LOS Bull.*, No.15, May 1990, at pp. 54-57.

[95] See José Luis Jesus, 'Statement on the Issue of the Universality of the Convention', in R. Wolfrum (ed.), *Law of the Sea at the Crossroads: The Continuing Search for a Universally Accepted Regime* (Proceedings of Symposium of Kiel Institute of International Law, July 1990), 1991, pp. 21-30; and 'Further Comments by José Luis Jesus, Chairman of the Preparatory Commission', in *Ocean Policy News*, September 1990, pp.7-8. See further E.D. Brown, *The International Law of the Sea*, Vol.1, 1994, at pp.461-462; or Brown, 'Neither necessary nor prudent at this stage', 17 *Marine Policy* (No.2, 1993), p.81, at pp.97-98.

[96] See further Brown, *op. cit.*, in note 95 (1994), at pp. 462-470.

juris generalis which constitutes a vital ingredient of a new rule of international customary law.

As was noted above, the attitude of the Group of 77 to the UN Convention regime has become more flexible since 1985. Its commitment to the principle of the common heritage of mankind has not lessened but it has been prepared to accept a marked change in the substance of the legal rules underlying the principle. The principle is now that which is stated and developed in the UN Convention regime as modified by the Implementation Agreement. Its substance will be considered further in the chapters which follow.

6. Practice of the Industrialised States

Much of this practice has already been considered above. Recapitulating, the industrialised States voted in favour of the Declaration of Principles but made it clear both in statements at the time, and consistently during the subsequent UNCLOS III debate, that they did not regard the Declaration as constituting an interim legal regime and would continue to regard sea-bed mining as a high seas freedom until the principles were transformed into an acceptable convention.

There are, however, various other aspects of the industrialised States' practice which remain to be considered. The first is that there is a consistent theme running through Conference statements made by the principal industrialised States to the effect that they remained committed to the conclusion and entry into force of a Convention on the Law of the Sea which would give legal precision to the principle that the mineral resources of the deep sea-bed are the common heritage of mankind. For example, responding to the statement of the Group of 77's position made in Plenary on 15 September 1978,[97] the British representative said that:

> As far as the Conference was concerned, interim legislation pending a successful convention would simply aim, as a piece of domestic housekeeping, to regulate entry into the new field in order to ensure orderly progress and the essential continuity of investment needed to develop the new technology. Progress must not be held up, for it was in the interests of the world's consumers of minerals, which included not only the United Kingdom but most developing countries. Interim legislation would be no more than a temporary umbrella which would in no way jeopardize the results of the Conference if it continued to do its work. The Government of the United Kingdom remained fully committed to the successful conclusion of a comprehensive and generally acceptable convention as soon as it could be achieved.[98]

Paradoxically, the same commitment to the achievement of a comprehensive conventional regime based on the principle of the common heritage of mankind was reflected in the unilateral legislation adopted by seven States and in a number of official statements made about the relationship of the legislation to the

---

[97] See text above, at note 79.
[98] *UNCLOS III Off. Rec.*, Vol. IX, pp. 108-109.

42 *Common heritage of mankind*

Declaration of Principles and the UN Convention on the Law of the Sea. Moreover, as has been seen,[99] the Provisional Understanding reached in 1984 to co-ordinate this legislation was declared by the parties to it to be without prejudice to their positions on the UN Convention. A full analysis of the legislation of the six 'Western' States[100] will be found in Chapter 7,[101] together with an examination of the two related agreements concluded in 1982 and 1984.[102] Here, it will suffice to comment briefly on three aspects of it – its alleged interim character, its alleged compatibility with the emerging UNCLOS regime and its embodiment of certain common heritage elements.

The principal justification offered for the adoption of most of these statutes so late in the UNCLOS proceedings was that the work of the mining consortia had reached a critical stage, at which it was necessary to make a crucial decision whether or not to proceed to the next stage, which would involve very large investments. The legislation was therefore needed to ensure continuity of investment at a high level and the retention by the consortia of the specialised teams working on their pilot projects. It was, however, reiterated time and again that the legislation was only interim and designed to provide a secure legal basis for investment only until a Convention entered into force. The passage quoted above from the British statement of 15 September 1978[103] is typical of many such assurances.

As further proof of their positive attitude to the achievement of a conventional regime based on the common heritage doctrine, the industrialised States stressed from the beginning that their unilateral legislation was designed to be 'consistent' or 'compatible' with the emerging UNCLOS regime. For example, it was claimed during the passage of the British Act through Parliament that:

> The Bill is consistent with the proposals developed at the Conference. It has been specifically designed to be compatible with an internationally agreed regime, as envisaged in the draft convention.[104]

Similarly, Mr. Richardson informed the UNCLOS Plenary that:

> The United States Government had ... worked with the Congress in framing legislation compatible with the primary goal of the Conference, namely, the negotiation of a comprehensive law of the sea convention. As he had already said ... that legislation was fundamentally consonant with the aims of the Conference, which it could be hoped would adopt an international sea-bed

---

[99] See text above, at note 91.
[100] Legislation was adopted by the following six Western States: United States (1980), Federal Republic of Germany (1980), United Kingdom (1981), France (1981), Japan (1982) and Italy (1985).
[101] See Chap. 7, sections I and II.
[102] The Agreement Concerning Interim Arrangements Relating to Polymetallic Nodules of the Deep Sea Bed, 1982 and the Provisional Understanding Regarding Deep Seabed Matters 1984. See further Chap. 7, section III. For texts, see Vol.3, Docs. Nos. 33.1 and 33.3.
[103] At note 98.
[104] Parliamentary Debates. House of Commons Official Report. Special Standing Committee on Deep Sea Mining (Temporary Provisions) Bill [Lords], Second Sitting, 2 June 1982, col.58 (Memorandum submitted by the Foreign and Commonwealth Office).

Chapter 2 43

regime well before exploitation could begin under the terms of national legislation.[105]

A full analysis will be found in Chapter 7 of the extent to which the national legislation fell short of the provisions of the UN Convention on the Law of the Sea in such matters as site-banking, anti-monopoly provisions, production controls and transfer of technology.[106] The fact remains, however, that it did include some common heritage elements. The legislation was intended to be interim; it made provision for the imposition of levies on mining licensees and the establishment of revenue-sharing funds; and it was compatible with the Convention regime at least in the sense that provision could be made by delegated legislation under it for such matters as site-banking[107] and transfer of technology.

What, then, is the significance of this practice of the industrialised States? Did they, by their support for the Declaration of Principles; their reiterated expressions of commitment to the objective of creating a conventional regime based upon the common heritage principle; their assurance of the interim nature of their unilateral legislation and of its compatibility with the emerging Conventional regime, contribute to the transformation of the common heritage principle into binding rules of international law? The obstacle in the way of any such finding is that all such Governmental actions and statements were invariably accompanied by clear reservations to the effect that, pending the acceptance by them of a Conventional regime giving precision to the common heritage principle, they regarded deep sea mining as being a freedom of the high seas.

On the other hand, there are perhaps grounds for questioning if this practice left the freedom of deep-sea mining in its pristine, pre-1970 position. There may be room for a more modest conclusion: that the industrialised States which adopted unilateral legislation were bound to exercise the freedom of deep-sea mining not only with reasonable regard to the interests of other States in their exercise of the freedom of the high seas, but also in accordance with the *fundamental principle* of the common heritage of mankind. The argument starts from the premise that, although the 1970 Declaration of Principles incorporated and developed the fundamental principle of the common heritage of mankind, it was only one of many possible models whereby the fundamental principle could be developed into more detailed norms and, as has been seen, this particular model was not binding in law. If the truth of this premise is not self-evident, it will become readily apparent when the history of the UNCLOS negotiations is recalled. Over the years, the Conference considered a number of quite different models to give detailed effect in the Convention to the principle of the common heritage of mankind and any one of them, had it eventually emerged as the preferred model for incorporation in Part XI of the UN Convention, would have been regarded as the legitimate concretisation of the fundamental principle.

---

[105] *UNCLOS III Off. Rec.*, Vol. IX, pp. 104-105.
[106] Chap. 7, section II.
[107] For British Ministerial statement to this effect, see Chap.7, at notes 49 and 50.

44 *Common heritage of mankind*

Having established the distinction between the fundamental principle itself and any particular development of it, the next step in the argument is that the above review of the State practice of the industrialised States suggests that they did accept the fundamental principle, but not its detailed development in either the Declaration of Principles or the UN Convention on the Law of the Sea. It is then necessary to consider what limitations on the freedom of deep-sea mining were imposed by this acceptance of the fundamental principle. Arguably, the answer is that the industrialised States became bound by the most basic of the principles enunciated in the Declaration of Principles and accepted by them in practice. Thus, for example, they were bound by paragraph 2 of the Declaration, forbidding appropriation of *the Area* or claims to sovereignty or the exercise of sovereign rights over it. Again, they were bound by paragraph 7, which provides that the exploration of the Area and the exploitation of its resources must be carried out for the benefit of mankind as a whole and taking into particular consideration the interests and needs of developing countries. However, these obligations were stated at a very high level of abstraction and left a considerable scope for interpretation by the States concerned. It is thus possible to contend that the unilateral legislation of the industrialised States was not inconsistent with these principles: they did not involve any appropriation of, or assertion of sovereign rights over, the Area, and their provisions for revenue-sharing did take account of the interests and needs of developing countries. On the other hand, pending their acceptance of a precise conventional regime, paragraphs 4 and 9 of the Declaration of Principles (envisaging the establishment of an international regime and appropriate international machinery) did not affect the interim right of the industrialised States to continue to exercise the high seas freedom of sea-bed mining, subject only to observance of the basic rules referred to above.

Thus, to sum up, the argument is that the practice of the industrialised States reviewed above indicated that what they had accepted was a fundamental principle which was open to elaboration in countless different ways (in relation, for example, to production controls, transfer of technology, financial arrangements and representation in institutions); that they had not yet accepted a moratorium on sea-bed mining pending the acceptance of such a detailed regime; and that their unilateral legislation was designed to reflect their acceptance that the exercise of the high seas freedom of sea-bed mining was now limited by the basic norms stated above.

Clearly, this whole argument rests on shaky foundations since, to survive, it has to surmount the obstacle presented by the insistence over the years by the industrialised powers that sea-bed mining would remain a high seas freedom until they accepted an alternative conventional regime. Moreover, even if valid, the argument is of dubious worth. What it would prove would simply be that the industrialised States were bound, negatively, not to appropriate or make sovereign claims to the Area – which they had no wish to do – and, positively, to take into particular consideration the interests and needs of developing countries. As has been seen, the statutory provisions on revenue-sharing can be considered as having given some effect to this obligation. Closer inspection of these provisions shows, however, that the funds were clearly intended to have a short life and it is by no means clear if, or how, on winding up, they would be distributed for the benefit of the developing States.[108]

7. The UN Convention on the Law of the Sea, 1982

It is not unusual for rules embodied in a treaty to generate or form the basis of similar rules of international customary law and it has been argued that the adoption of the UN Convention marked the culmination, the point of crystallisation, of a gradually maturing body of State practice and must therefore be regarded as the expression of rules of general international law binding on all States, whether parties to the Convention or not. The argument is considered in more detail in Chapter 3[109] and here it will suffice to state the conclusions there reached. First, there is no case for saying that rules of customary law emerged between 1967 and 1982 to oblige third parties to comply with the principles of the common heritage regime embodied in the UN Convention. Secondly, despite attempts to have the principle of the common heritage of mankind, as developed in the UN Convention, recognised as *jus cogens*, there is no reason to depart from the normal rule that *pacta tertiis nec nocent nec prosunt*. Thirdly, although it was of course theoretically possible that the conventional rules might be transformed into generally binding rules of international customary law as a result of developments in State practice, in reality it was never likely, given the clearly stated opposition of the industrialised States. Indeed, as has been seen, events have taken quite a different turn. The UN Convention itself has had to be amended to accommodate the opposition of the industrialised States to the original model of the common heritage regime incorporated in the Convention.

IV. CONCLUSIONS

It has been the object of this chapter to clarify the scope and meaning of the principle of the common heritage of mankind by examining its evolution over the past three decades. In the light of this historical survey, the following conclusions may be presented:

(i) Prior to the adoption of the Declaration of Principles in 1970, sea-bed mining conducted with reasonable regard to the interests of other States in exercising the freedoms of the high seas was a legitimate user of the high seas.[110]

(ii) General Assembly resolutions on the legal regime of sea-bed mining, singly or in series and irrespective of nomenclature or voting figures, do not in themselves, as a matter of law, create binding legal rules. They may, however, constitute part of a broader law-creating process.[111] Nonetheless, the Moratorium Resolution (1969) neither created binding rules immediately nor provided a significant basis for the future development of such rules. The Declaration of Principles Resolution (1970) did not create binding rules in itself but did provide a significant basis for the potential

---

[108] See further Chap. 7, section II.1.7.2.
[109] Chap. 3, section I.5.1.
[110] See further above, section II.
[111] See further above, section III.2.

46 *Common heritage of mankind*

generation of legally binding rules through a broader law-creating process.[112]

(iii) The practice of the Group of 77 indicates that a large number of developing States recognise the principles enunciated in the Declaration of Principles as part of international law. Nonetheless, the Declaration and the related practice of the Group of 77 do not provide evidence of the creation of generally applicable rules of international law opposable to the industrialised States. Moreover, after about 1985 the attitude of the Group of 77 became more flexible and they have now in effect accepted that the substance of the principle of the common heritage of mankind is laid down in the UN Convention, as substantially modified by the Implementation Agreement of 1994.[113]

(iv) The practice of the industrialised States did not contribute significantly to the transformation of the common heritage principle into binding rules of international law. At most, it modified the conditions subject to which States might exercise the freedom of deep sea mining. It had now to be exercised in accordance with the basic rules underlying the fundamental principle of the common heritage of mankind. In practice, however, any such obligations would have been of very limited scope.[114]

(v) The principle of the common heritage of mankind, as incorporated in its original form in the UN Convention, was never transformed into rules of general international law binding upon non-parties to the Convention.[115]

(vi) In effect, the conflict between the principle of the freedom of the high seas and the principle of the common heritage of mankind ended with the adoption of the Implementation Agreement in July 1994. It was thereby accepted by developing and industrialised States alike that the regime of sea-bed mining was based upon the principle of the common heritage of mankind. However, the substance of that principle is now to be found in Part XI of the UN Convention as substantially modified by the Implementation Agreement and reflects a compromise between the proponents of the two schools of thought.[116]

---

[112] See further above, sections III.2.2 and III.2.3.
[113] See further above, sections III.3, III.4 and III.5.
[114] See further above, section III.6.
[115] See further above, section III.7.
[116] See further, Chap.3.

PART 2

THE UNITED NATIONS REGIME
OF SEA-BED MINING

CHAPTER 3

The UN Convention Regime of Sea-Bed Mining:
I. The Principles of the Regime

UNCLOS III appears to have experienced some difficulty in deciding which of the various basic provisions of the regime of the Area should be elevated to the status of 'principles' and the pattern varied from one negotiating text to another. In the Draft Convention on the Law of the Sea (Informal Text) of September 1980[1], only Section 2 of Part XI purported to deal with 'Principles governing the Area', whereas Section 3 was concerned with 'Conduct of activities in the Area'. In fact, however, there was no discernible difference between those sections as regards the level of abstraction or importance of their provisions and both had been incorporated in a single 'Part II : Principles' in the original Informal Single Negotiating Text (ISNT) of 1975[2]. The Draft Convention on the Law of the Sea of August 1981[3] (hereafter 'Draft Convention, 1981') reverted to the earlier format and all of the 'Principles governing the Area' were grouped together in Section 2 of Part XI. This pattern survived in the UN Convention itself.

I. THE FUNDAMENTAL PRINCIPLE : THE COMMON HERITAGE OF MANKIND

The first principle – and it is clearly the fundamental principle of the regime – is stated as follows:

Article 136
Common heritage of mankind

The Area and its resources are the common heritage of mankind.

---

[1] A/CONF.62/WP.10/Rev.3, 22 September 1980 and Corr. 1 and 3.
[2] *Third United Nations Conference on the Law of the Sea. Official Records* (hereafter *UNCLOS III Off.Rec.*), Vol.IV, p.137.
[3] *UNCLOS III Off.Rec.*, Vol.XV, p.172.

50   The Principles of the Regime

The origins of the concept of the common heritage of mankind and the meaning and legal status of the principle as incorporated in the Declaration of Principles adopted by the General Assembly in 1970 have already been considered above.[4] In the context of the UN Convention, however, further analysis is required by reference to the other articles which throw light on the meaning of the concept as incorporated in Part XI. This is no simple task for, in a very real sense, the whole of Part XI and related articles and appendices may be regarded as the detailed development of the fundamental principle and account has now to be taken also of the amendments of these provisions made by the Implementation Agreement of 28 July 1994.[5]

1. Ideological Milieu – the Significance of the Preamble

According to Article 31 of the Vienna Convention on the Law of Treaties,[6] a treaty has to be interpreted in accordance with the ordinary meaning to be given to the terms of the treaty 'in their context' and the 'context' is defined to include 'the text, including its preamble.' The drafting of the preamble is thus not unimportant since it may have a bearing upon the interpretation of disputed parts of the body of the treaty.

No preamble had been drafted for the earlier Negotiating Texts,[7] and, in drafting the Informal Composite Negotiating Text (ICNT) version in advance of any discussion in the Conference, the President made '[E]very effort ... to avoid any provisions ... that could lead to needless controversy at this stage ...'[8] A number of States made it clear, however, in the preliminary discussion which took place in Plenary,[9] that they would wish to see specific references in the Preamble to 'the common heritage of mankind'[10] and the link between the Convention and the objectives of the new international economic order.[11]

A second, more elaborate text, proposed in 1978 by Fiji on behalf of the Group of 77,[12] failed to attract general support, partly because of its controversial reference to :

---

[4] See above, Chap. 2.

[5] For the texts of (1) General Assembly Resolution 48/263 of 28 July 1994 on the 'Agreement Implementing Part XI of the United Nations Convention on the Law of the Sea of 10 December 1982' (the 'Implementation Agreement') and (2) the Implementation Agreement, see Vol.3, Docs. Nos. 22 and 23; also reproduced in *LOS Bull.*, *Special Issue IV*, 16 November 1994, pp.8-25; and Misc.No.44 (1994), Cm 2705.

[6] Vienna Convention on the Law of Treaties, 23 May 1969, UK Treaty Series No. 58 (1980), Cmnd. 7964.

[7] Informal Single Negotiating Text (ISNT) (1975), *UNCLOS III Off. Rec.*, Vol. IV, p. 137 and Revised Single Negotiating Text (RSNT) (1976), *UNCLOS III Off. Rec.*, Vol. V, p.125.

[8] *Memorandum by the President of the Conference on Document A/CONF. 62/WP.10*, A/CONF.62/WP.10/Add.1, 22 July 1977 (*UNCLOS III Off. Rec.*, Vol. VIII, p.65), at p.66.

[9] Summary Records of the 94th to 97th Plenary Meetings, 3-11 May 1978, *UNCLOS III Off. Rec.*, Vol. IX, pp. 22-40.

[10] See, *e.g., ibid.*, at p.29, para.11; p.34, para.5; p.39, para.47; and p.40, para.57.

[11] See, *e.g., ibid.*, at p.29, para.11; p.34, para.5; p.35, para.22; p.39, para.47; and p.40, para. 57.

[12] A/CONF.62/L.33 (*UNCLOS III Off. Rec.*, Vol. IX, p.188).

Chapter 3 51

The need to lay down just and equitable conditions for the exploitation of the resources of the sea with a view to establishing a new international economic order in accordance with the relevant United Nations resolutions and safeguarding the special interests and needs of the developing countries.

Despite the rejection of this proposal, it was clear that the view was gaining ground that the Preamble should make reference to what had been described as the 'essential objectives' of the Convention or its 'guiding principles'. The views expressed in debate were summarised by the President as follows:

It seemed clear that the preamble should be brief, non-controversial and non-polemical. It should not be excessively brief or devoid of political content but should be sufficiently substantive as to cover the essential objectives and at the same time avoid controversial issues. The preamble would have to refer to the genesis of the Conference and its principal objectives, without dealing with the operative part of it.[13]

The President's words notwithstanding, the Preamble incorporated in ICNT/Rev.2 and maintained with only minor drafting changes in the UN Convention, is not altogether free from controversy. Its sixth paragraph, in particular, deserves close scrutiny. It reads as follows:

Desiring by this Convention to develop the principles embodied in resolution 2749 (XXV) of 17 December 1970 in which the General Assembly [of the United Nations] solemnly declared *inter alia* that the area of the sea-bed and ocean floor and the subsoil thereof, beyond the limits of national jurisdiction, as well as its resources, are the common heritage of mankind, the exploration and exploitation of which shall be carried out for the benefit of mankind as a whole, irrespective of the geographical location of States.[14]

The word 'develop' replaced the words 'give effect to' in an earlier version of this paragraph[15] and the President, 'To avoid any doubts as to the interpretation of the word "develop" ' [16], found it necessary to place on record the reasons for the change:

Many delegations were of the opinion that the Declaration of Principles contained in resolution 2749 (XXV) had from the moment of the adoption of that resolution acquired a definite juridical status, and that the present

[13] *Report of the President to the Plenary on the Work of the Informal Plenary on Preamble*, A/CONF.62/L.49/Add.2, 29 March 1980 (*UNCLOS III Off. Rec., Vol. XIII, p.79*).
[14] The text given is that of the UN Convention, with square brackets added to indicate where minor drafting changes were made as compared with the ICNT/Rev. 2 version in A/CONF.62/WP.10/Rev.2, 11 April 1980, and Corr.1-3.
[15] The earlier version is in document Preamble/1/Rev.1 of 24 March 1980.
[16] 'Note by the President on paragraph 6 of the Preamble', in *Addendum to Report of the President of the Plenary on the Work of the Informal Plenary on Preamble*, A/CONF.62/L.49/Add.1, 29 March 1980 (*UNCLOS III Off. Rec.*, Vol. XIII, p.79).

52   *The Principles of the Regime*

Convention was not required in order to invest them with such juridical status as they already possessed. It must be made clear that an expression had to be used which, while not affecting the question of the juridical status of those Principles, would express the desire and intent of the Conference to provide for the application of the concept of the common heritage of mankind by establishing through the present Convention the institutional and legal framework and machinery to give the concept practical shape and form'.[17]

This Presidential explanatory note was presented to Plenary together with, and as an addendum to, the agreed text of the Preamble.[18]

It would appear that this note was intended to bear the implication that the principle of the common heritage of mankind became a legally binding principle as soon as the Declaration of Principles was adopted. Two consequences would flow from this : first, the principle would be binding upon States (or, at the very least, States which voted in favour of the Declaration), even though they did not subsequently become parties to the Convention or the Convention failed to enter into force; secondly, in reflecting the organic link between Declaration and Convention in the language of its sixth paragraph, the Preamble would have the effect of constituting the Declaration a part of the 'context' of the Convention for purposes of interpretation. In the light of the examination of the status of the Declaration presented above in Chapter 2, and bearing in mind the reservations made by many States at the time of the adoption of the Declaration of Principles,[19] it hardly needs to be said that these are highly questionable propositions. In view of this, it should perhaps be noted that the sixth paragraph of the Preamble and the Presidential note are open to an alternative interpretation. Thus, it can be argued that this paragraph cannot have the effect of retrospectively investing the Declaration of Principles with a legal status which it lacked at the time of its adoption and failed to acquire subsequently.[20] In this view, the reference in this paragraph to 'principles' should be read as nothing more than a reference to the expressed intent of members of the General Assembly to participate in good faith in an attempt to transform the non-binding principles of the Declaration into binding norms of treaty law.

2. Scope of the Common Heritage of Mankind ratione loci

According to Article 136 of the UN Convention, it is 'the Area and its resources' which are 'the common heritage of mankind'. Similarly, under Article 134 (1), Part XI of the Convention applies to the 'Area'. The geographical scope of the common heritage of mankind is thus the same as that of the 'Area', which is defined in Article 1(1) as the 'sea-bed and ocean floor and subsoil thereof, beyond the limits of national jurisdiction'. Since, under the Convention, the continental shelf is always as broad as the 200-mile exclusive economic zone

[17] *Ibid.*
[18] A/CONF.62/L.49/Add.2, 29 March 1980, para. 12 (*ibid.*, at p.80).
[19] See above, Chap.2, section III.2.3.
[20] See further Chap.2, section III.6.

Chapter 3 53

(EEZ) and sometimes more extensive,[21] it follows that the 'limits' in question are in fact those of the legal continental shelf. This is confirmed by Article 134(3) which makes a cross-reference to the obligation in Part VI to deposit and give publicity to charts or lists of geographical co-ordinates indicating the outer limit of the continental shelf.[22]

The vertical scope of the common heritage may be determined by reference to Articles 133 and 135. Thus, the 'resources' which are the common heritage of mankind comprise 'all solid, liquid or gaseous mineral resources *in situ* in the Area *at or beneath the sea-bed*, including polymetallic nodules'[23]. It would appear that what an earlier draft described as 'metal-bearing brine'[24] (metaliferous muds) would fall within this definition only if they were 'at or beneath the seabed'. Article 135 reinforces the point by declaring that Part XI shall not affect the legal status of the waters superjacent to the Area.

3. Scope of the Common Heritage of Mankind ratione materiae

The regime of the Area extends beyond deep-sea mining to concern itself also with the use of the Area exclusively for peaceful purposes (Article 141), marine scientific research (Article 143), the protection of the marine environment (Article 145) and of human life (Article 146) and the preservation or disposal of archaeological and historical objects for the benefit of mankind as a whole (Article 149). In the present context, however, attention will be concentrated upon what are referred to in the Convention as 'Activities in the Area'.

Article 134(2) provides that 'Activities in the Area shall be governed by the provisions of this Part'. Article 1(3) defines 'activities in the Area' as 'all activities of exploration for, and exploitation of, the resources of the Area'; and Article 133(a) defines 'resources' as 'all solid, liquid or gaseous mineral resources *in situ* in the Area at or beneath the sea-bed, including polymetallic nodules'.

The principal resource and that for which Part XI is predominantly designed is, of course, manganese nodules. As will be seen below, however, the cobalt-rich manganese crusts and the sulphides found in the Area also form part of the common heritage, though their exploitation may be subject to different rules.[25]

The next question which arises is how to determine the value of the common heritage in these resources. A full examination of the system whereby the Authority obtains a share of the proceeds of exploitation of these resources will be found in Chapter 4.[26] As will be seen, provision was originally made in Article 13 of Annex III to the UN Convention for the payment by contractors of three types of charge. However, under the Implementation Agreement of 28 July 1994, these very detailed rules have been abandoned in favour of a set of six

---

[21] UN Convention, Arts. 57 and 76.
[22] See further Part VI, Art. 84.
[23] Art.133(a), emphasis added.
[24] Draft Convention, 1980 (cited in note 1 above), Art.133(b)(iv).
[25] See further below, Chap.4, section XVIII.
[26] In Chap.4, section VIII.

54 *The Principles of the Regime*

general principles which will provide the basis for the later establishment of detailed rules, regulations and procedures.[27]

Brief reference should also be made here to Article 149, dealing with the preservation or disposal for the benefit of mankind of objects or an archaeological and historical nature found in the Area. [28]

4. Scope of the Common Heritage of Mankind ratione temporis: Limited Scope for Amendment

Although the regime governing the system of exploration and exploitation of the resources of the Area is established for an unlimited time, provision was originally made in Article 155 of the UN Convention for a review of the regime by a Review Conference, to be convened fifteen years after the commencement of commercial production. The procedure for amendment was unacceptable to the major industrialised States because it would have been possible, under Article 155(4), for amendments to be adopted in the face of their opposition. To accommodate their concern, Article 155 was radically amended by the Implementation Agreement[29] and the new arrangements are now to be found in Section 4 of the Annex to the Implementation Agreement.

Under the new scheme, the Assembly of the Authority, on the recommendation of the Council, may undertake at any time a review of the matters referred to in Article 155(1) of the UN Convention. It may, therefore, consider at any time:

(a) whether the provisions of ... [the regime] which govern the system of exploration and exploitation of the resources of the Area have achieved their aims in all respects, including whether they have benefited mankind as a whole;

(b) whether ... reserved areas have been exploited in an effective and balanced manner in comparison with non-reserved areas;

(c) whether the development and use of the Area and its resources have been undertaken in such a manner as to foster healthy development of the world economy and balanced growth of international trade;

(d) whether monopolization of activities in the Area has been prevented;

(e) whether the policies set forth in articles 150 and 151 have been fulfilled; and

(f) whether the system has resulted in the equitable sharing of benefits derived from activities in the Area, taking into particular consideration the interests and needs of the developing States.[30]

Such a review may be undertaken '[n]otwithstanding the provisions of' Article 314(2) of the Convention[31] – which ensured that the limited amendments of the

---

[27] See further Chap.4, section VIII.2.
[28] This provision is considered further below in section XIII.
[29] *Loc.cit.* in note 5 above.
[30] UN Convention, Art.155(1), with text adjusted in the light of Section 4 of the Annex to the Implementation Agreement.

Chapter 3 55

regime permitted under Article 314(1), in advance of the Review Conference, would not prejudice the system of exploration for and exploitation of the resources of the Area, pending the Review Conference. It would appear, therefore, that there will be in future the same degree of freedom to amend the system as would have been enjoyed by the Review Conference under the original version of Article 155. Under the original Article 155(4), it was open to the Conference to either 'change' or 'modify' the system 'as it determines necessary and appropriate.' In adding the words 'changing or modifying' to an earlier draft of Article 155(4), the Chairman of the negotiating group concerned explained that the addition was made to make it clear that the amendments might entail not only partial modification but also a complete change of the system.[32]

However, it has to be added that, under Paragraph 2 of Article 155, the powers of the Review Conference were in fact severely limited and it was not open to it to change specified fundamentals of the system. Thus:

> The Review Conference shall ensure the maintenance of the principle of the common heritage of mankind, the international regime designed to ensure equitable exploitation of the resources of the Area for the benefit of all countries, especially the developing States, and an Authority to organise conduct and control activities in the Area. It shall also ensure the maintenance of the principles laid down in this Part with regard to the exclusion of claims or exercise of sovereignty over any part of the Area, the rights of States and their general conduct in relation to the Area, and their participation in activities in the Area in conformity with this Convention, the prevention of monopolization of activities in the Area, the use of the Area exclusively for peaceful purposes, economic aspects of activities in the Area, marine scientific research, transfer of technology, protection of the marine environment, protection of human life, rights of coastal States, the legal status of the waters superjacent to the Area and that of the air space above those waters and accommodation between activities in the Area and other activities in the marine environment.[33]

These same constraints are maintained by the Implementation Agreement, which permits amendments subject to the proviso that 'the principles, regime and other terms referred to in article 155, paragraph 2, of the Convention shall be maintained ...'[34]; nor must amendments affect rights acquired under existing contracts.[35]

Having dispensed with the Review Conference as the mechanism for amending the regime of sea-bed mining, the Implementation Agreement

---

[31] Implementation Agreement, Annex, Section 4.
[32] *Report of the Co-ordinators of the Working Group of 21 to the First Committee*, A/CONF.62/C.1/L.28 and Add.1*, 23 August 1980 (*UNCLOS III Off.Rec.*, Vol. XIV, p.161) at p.162.
[33] UN Convention, Art. 155(2).
[34] Implementation Agreement, Annex, Section 4.
[35] *Ibid.*

56   *The Principles of the Regime*

substituted for it the procedures contained in Articles 314-316 of the UN Convention[36].   Under Article 314, written proposals for amendment are to be submitted to the Secretary-General of the Authority and will be circulated by him to all States Parties.   Proposed amendments approved, first, by the Council and, then, by the Assembly will be considered adopted.[37]   They have then to be signed and ratified, or acceded to[38] and will enter into force one year after ratification or accession by three fourths of the States Parties.[39]

Finally, mention should be made of Article 154 of the UN Convention, under which a more limited review of the operation of the regime may be undertaken every five years. [40]

5. Scope of the Common Heritage of Mankind ratione personae
A number of questions arise under this head:

(1)   Does the Convention create obligations for States and other entities not parties to it?

(2)   What entities have the capacity to become parties to the Convention?

(3)   Who are the intended beneficiaries of the common heritage of mankind?

5.1 Does the Convention Create Obligations for States and Other Entities Not Parties to it?
Or, to put it another way, are States and other entities[41] which are not parties to the Convention bound, when exploring and exploiting the resources declared by the Convention to be the common heritage of mankind, to observe the principles of the regime established by the Convention?

A very clear majority of States represented at UNCLOS III would certainly say that, irrespective of the effect of the Convention on such third parties, they are bound to treat these resources as the common heritage of mankind because they are now recognised as such by principles of general international law. What is usually implied in this argument is that rules of customary law have emerged since 1967, when Ambassador Pardo first proposed that sea-bed resources should be the common heritage of mankind. The argument has been examined in detail in Chapter 2, but it will be recalled that the main contention is that the principles of the regime have crystallised out of a series of General Assembly resolutions and the general consensus reflected in the UNCLOS III proceedings that the principles of the common heritage regime, particularly as stated in the

---

[36] *Ibid.*

[37] UN Convention, Art.314(1).

[38] *Ibid.*, Art.315.

[39] *Ibid.*, Art.316.

[40] At the Sixth Resumed Session of the Authority in July 2000, the Assembly, agreeing with the Secretary-General's view that it was too early to consider any adjustments to the UNCLOS regime, decided that its discussion of the Secretary-General's Report met the requirements of Art. 154 (Press Release SB/6/22, 6 July 2000).

[41] On such other entities, see below, section 5.2.

Chapter 3 57

Declaration of Principles of 17 December 1970,[42] are now legally binding. The conclusion must remain as it was stated above that, given the reservations made at the time of the adoption of the Declaration of Principles in 1970 and reiterated by many of the industrialised States since that time, the principles embodied in the Declaration will not be binding upon any State as a matter of law unless it has either become a party to the UN Convention on the Law of the Sea, which has transformed the principles into precise conventional rules, or has clearly accepted the principles as legally binding upon it in some other way.[43]

Assuming, then, that general international law cannot provide a basis for obliging third parties to comply with the principles of the common heritage regime, the next question to consider is whether the Convention itself is capable of imposing any such obligation. As Mr. Perisíc (Yugoslavia) said during the Seventh Session of the Conference:

> The question [is] to what extent the principle *pacta tertiis nec nocent nec prosunt* could be applied in the matter of the common heritage of mankind.[44] The convention would merely define more precisely the method of exploitation of area and resources which, according to the 1970 declaration,[45] belonged to all States. Account must also be taken of the possibility that States not parties to the convention might also participate, on the basis of equitable criteria, in the exploitation of the resources of the sea-bed beyond the limits of national jurisdiction. The participation of third States was provided for in several international treaties or conventions'.[46]

Though Mr. Perisíc's thoughts were not developed any further, he seemed to be suggesting that the right of exploitation to which third parties are entitled – as being part of the 'all States' to which the Area and its resources belong – must be exercised in accordance with the equitable criteria of the conventional regime. Some other delegations wished to be very much more explicit and to make specific provision in the Convention for the recognition of the principle of the common heritage of mankind as *jus cogens*.[47] Chile, for example, proposed that the following article should be incorporated in the Negotiating Text:

---

[42] *Declaration of Principles Governing the Sea-Bed and the Ocean Floor, and the Subsoil thereof, beyond the Limits of National Jurisdiction*, A/RES/2749(XXV), 17 December 1970; reproduced in Vol.3 as Doc No. 11.

[43] For full argument, see Chap. 2.

[44] On the effect of treaties on third parties, see Vienna Convention on Law of Treaties, 1969 (*loc.cit.* in note 6 above), Arts.34-38. Art.34 provides that 'A treaty does not create either obligations or rights for a third State without its consent'. Art. 35 provides that, 'An obligation arises for a third State from a provision of a treaty if the parties to the treaty intend the provision to be the means of establishing the obligation and the third State expressly accepts that obligation in writing'.

[45] Note omitted.

[46] Plenary Meeting, 5 May 1978, *UNCLOS III Off. Rec.*, Vol. IX, p.31.

[47] On *jus cogens*, see Arts.53 and 64 of the Vienna Convention (*loc.cit.* in note 6 above) and the following: G. Schwarzenberger, *International Law and Order*, 1971, pp. 27-56; I.M. Sinclair, *The Vienna Convention on the Law of Treaties*, 2nd ed., 1984, Chap.7 (and literature cited at p.236, note 8); and A. Verdross, '*Jus dispositivum* and *jus cogens* in international law', 60 AJIL (1966), pp. 55-63.

58   *The Principles of the Regime*

Jus cogens

> The States Parties to the present Convention accept and recognise on behalf of the international community as a whole that the provision relating to the common heritage of mankind set out in article 136 is a peremptory norm of general international law from which no derogation is permitted and which, consequently, can be modified only by a subsequent norm of general international law having the same character.[48]

Following inconclusive discussions at the first part of the Ninth Session,[49] a much watered-down compromise formulation was adopted by consensus at the resumed Ninth Session for incorporation in the Draft Convention (Informal Text), 1980 as Article 311(6).[50] Apart from minor drafting changes, this text survived to become Article 311(6) of the UN Convention:

> States Parties agree that there shall be no amendments to the basic principle relating to the common heritage of mankind set forth in article 136 and that they shall not be a party to any agreement in derogation thereof.[51]

Thus, in effect, the attempt was abandoned to have the principle of the common heritage recognised as *jus cogens* – a 'peremptory norm of general international law' indissolubly binding on all States, parties to the Convention or not. The Chilean proposal was, in any event, somewhat overambitious. It assumed that sixty States (the number required to bring the Convention into force)[52] could, by a treaty provision, create rules of *jus cogens* for the international community generally.

What is the effect of the butchered remains? It is a little difficult to see what purpose is served by Article 311(6). The basic principle of the common heritage of mankind is already safeguarded by Articles 155(2) and 311(3) of the Convention. As has been seen, Article 155(2), read with Section 4 of the Annex to the Implementation Agreement, requires the maintenance of the principle of the common heritage of mankind,[53] and Article 311(3), in permitting parties to the Convention to conclude agreements modifying or suspending the operation of its

---

[48] Eighth Session, Part II. *Informal Proposal by Chile,* FC/14, 20 August 1979.

[49] *Preliminary Report of the President on the Work of the Informal Plenary Meeting of the Conference on Proposals for General Provisions,* A/CONF.62/L.53, 29 March 1980, (*UNCLOS III Off. Rec.,* Vol XIII, p.87).

[50] *Report of the President on the Work of the Informal Plenary Meeting of the Conference on General Provisions,* A/CONF.62/L.58, 22 August 1980 (*UNCLOS III Off. Rec.,* Vol. XIV, p.128), at p.129(5)-(8). The reference in this document is to Art. 305(6), later re-numbered Art. 311(6).

[51] UN Convention, Art. 311(6). The 1980 text was as follows:
'The States Parties to this Convention agree that there can be no amendments to the basic principle relating to the common heritage of mankind set forth in article 136 and that they shall not be party to any agreement in derogation thereof.'

[52] UN Convention, Art.308(1).

[53] See above, section I.4.

provisions *inter se*, adds the proviso that 'such agreements shall not affect the application of the basic principles embodied herein.' Certainly, it is clear that Article 311(6) can have no effect on the rights of third parties in relation to sea-bed resources.

The conclusion must be that there would seem to be no reason to depart from the normal rule that *pacta tertiis nec nocent nec prosunt*. This does not of course exclude the possibility that the norms laid down in the Convention may in the course of time be transformed into rules of universal international customary law[54] – but that will depend upon developing State practice.

5.2 What Entities Have the Capacity to Become Parties to the Convention?

The question of participation in the UN Convention gave rise to a surprising amount of controversy and was settled only during the final Eleventh Session of UNCLOS III. The final package of provisions covers the status of :

   (i) States;

   (ii) Namibia (which has since become an independent State);

   (iii) Self-governing associated States and territories enjoying full internal self-government;

   (iv) international organisations;

   (v) national liberation movements; and

   (vi) peoples of non-self-governing territories, territories under colonial domination and territories sovereignty over which is disputed.

The Implementation Agreement, which is to be interpreted and applied together with Part XI of the UN Convention as a single instrument,[55] is of course open to the same range of parties.[56]

5.2.1 States

The provisions of the UN Convention and the Implementation Agreement governing entry into force for States have already been considered in Chapter 1.[57]

5.2.2 Self-governing Associated States and Territories Enjoying Full Internal Self-government

A proposal to provide for participation in the Convention by territories invited to attend the Conference as observers was made by New Zealand and others at the Seventh Session of the Conference.[58] Australia and other States made a similar proposal at the Eighth Session in relation to 'fully self-governing associated States'[59] The sponsors had in mind the Cook Islands and Niue, the self-governing status of which had been recognised in UN General Assembly Resolutions

---

[54] As envisaged in Art.38 of the Vienna Convention on the Law of Treaties, 1969 (*loc.cit.* in note 6 above) which provided that: 'Nothing in articles 34 to 37 precludes a rule set forth in a treaty from becoming binding upon a third State as a customary rule of international law, recognised as such'.

[55] Implementation Agreement, Art.2(1).

[56] See *ibid.*, Arts.3-8.

[57] See Chap.1, section II.

[58] A/CONF.62/L.26, 8 May 1978 (*UNCLOS III Off. Rec*, Vol. IX, p.184).

[59] Document FC/10, 15 August 1979, discussed in Document FC/13, 20 August 1979, para. 6.

60 *The Principles of the Regime*

2064(XX) and 3285(XIX). It was emphasised that both entities had constitutional, legislative and executive power over the subject matter of the Convention.[60]

At the first (New York) part of the Tenth Session, two criteria were identified by which to determine whether a non-State was entitled to participate in the Convention: whether the entity had competence over matters falling within the scope of the Convention and whether it had the capacity to enter into treaties with regard to such matters.[61] The text finally agreed at the Eleventh Session distinguished among three groups satisfying these criteria and placed them in the same position as States in relation to signature, ratification and accession:

(c) all self-governing associated States which have chosen that status in an act of self-determination supervised and approved by the United Nations in accordance with General Assembly resolution 1514(XV) and which have competence over the matters governed by this Convention, including the competence to enter into treaties in respect of those matters;

(d) all self-governing associated States which, in accordance with their respective instruments of association, have competence over the matters governed by this Convention, including the competence to enter into treaties in respect of those matters;

(e) all territories which enjoy full internal self-government, recognized as such by the United Nations, but have not attained full independence in accordance with General Assembly resolution 1514 (XV) and which have competence over the matters governed by this Convention, including the competence to enter into treaties in respect of those matters.[62]

These provisions covered the Cook Islands, the Netherlands Antilles, Niue, the Trust Territory of the Pacific Islands[63] and St. Kitts-Nevis.

5.2.3 International Organisations
A proposal to allow participation in the Convention by international organisations was first made at the Seventh Session of the Conference on behalf of the

---

[60] Document FC/13, 20 August 1979, para.6.

[61] UN Information Centre, London: *Resumed Tenth Session of Law of the Sea Conference, Geneva, 3-28 August*, BR/81/20, 31 August 1981, p.15. See also M.H. Nordquist and Choon-ho Park, *Reports of the United States Delegation to the Third United Nations Conference on the Law of the Sea* (The Law of the Sea Institute, Occasional Paper No.33, 1983), at pp.466-472.

[62] UN Convention, Art. 305(1)(c)(d) and (e).

[63] In 1990, the Security Council, by Resolution 683 (1990), terminated the Trusteeship Agreement for three of the Trust Territories of the Pacific Islands: the Federated States of Micronesia, the Marshall Islands and the Northern Mariana Islands. They became members of the United Nations in 1991. The remaining Trust Territory became a member of the United Nations as the Republic of Palau in 1994, as recommended by Security Council Resolution 963 (1994).

Chapter 3 61

European Economic Community[64] and eventually provision was made for such organisations in Article 305(1)(f)and Annex IX of the Convention.

Article 305(1)(f) provides that the Convention is open for signature by 'international organisations, in accordance with Annex IX' and Article 1 of Annex IX defines 'international organisation' to mean 'an intergovernmental organisation constituted by States to which its member States have transferred competence over matters governed by this Convention, including the competence to enter into treaties in respect of those matters'. Such organisations were permitted to sign the Convention if a majority of its member States were signatories and, at the time of signature, the organisation had to make a declaration specifying the matters governed by the Convention in respect of which competence had been transferred to the organisation and the nature and extent of that competence.[65]

Pursuant to these provisions, the EEC signed the Convention on 7 December 1984 and declared that the member States had transferred competence to it in a number of fields. These included competences with regard to rules and regulations for the protection and preservation of the marine environment, as formulated in provisions adopted by the Community and as reflected by its participation in certain international agreements; and, with regard to the provisions of Part XI, competence in matters of commercial policy, including the control of unfair economic practices.[66] In a second Declaration made at the same time, it was added, however that :

> The Community, however, considers that significant provisions of Part XI of the Convention are not conducive to the development of the activities to which that Part refers in view of the fact that several Member States of the Community have already expressed their position that this Part contains considerable deficiencies and flaws which require rectification. The Community recognises the importance of the work which remains to be done and hopes that conditions for the implementation of a sea bed mining regime, which are generally acceptable and which are therefore likely to promote activities in the international sea bed area can be agreed. The Community, within the limits of its competence, will play a full part in contributing to the task of finding satisfactory solutions.[67]

---

[64] *Letter dated 10 September 1976 from the representative of the Netherlands to the President of the Conference* (on behalf of the EEC Council), A/CONF.62/48, *UNCLOS III Off. Rec.,* Vol. VI, pp. 119-120. The member States of the EEC argued that since powers in relation to matters covered by the Convention had been transferred from them to the EEC, it was necessary that both the Community and its member States should be eligible to become Contracting Parties. See also, Document FC/5, 3 August 1979, which offers a draft article permitting participation in the Convention by 'customs unions, communities or regional economic integration groupings, constituted by sovereign States, which exercise powers in areas covered by the present Convention'. For comment on this proposal, see Documents FC/13, 20 August 1979, paras. 7 and 9, and FC/17, 23 August 1979, para. 2(d). See too Letter dated 29 March 1980, A/CONF.62/98, 31 March 1980 (*UNCLOS III Off.Rec.,* Vol.XIII, p.74).

[65] UN Convention, Annex IX, Art.2.

[66] *Competence of the European Communities with regard to Matters Governed by the Convention on the Law of the Sea (Declaration made pursuant to Article 2 of Annex IX to the Convention),* 7 December 1984 (*Law of the Sea Bulletin,* No.4, February 1985, pp.16-19).

[67] *Declaration Made by the European Economic Community,* 7 December 1984 (*ibid.,* p.16).

62   *The Principles of the Regime*

The Convention is subject to 'formal confirmation' by international organisations which have signed the Convention or to accession where there has been no such signature.[68]

5.2.4 National Liberation Movements

At the Seventh Session of the Conference, members of the Arab Group sponsored a proposal to permit accession by liberation movements recognised by the United Nations and invited to take part in the Conference as observers.[69] This was followed up at the Eighth Session by a more far-reaching proposal sponsored by Algeria and others, whereby the Convention would be open to accession by:

> any territory which has not attained full independence in accordance with resolution 1514(XV) of the General Assembly, or any National Liberation Movement recognised by the United Nations and the Regional Intergovernmental Organisations concerned.[70]

This proposal provoked strong reactions. Some delegates argued that the Convention was an inappropriate vehicle through which to further the political process of self-determination or resolve political issues such as those pertaining to national liberation movements.[71] Others, pointing to examples of non-State participation in other instruments and institutions, contended that 'the interest of the entities which have not yet attained statehood due to reasons beyond their control' should be 'fully safeguarded by allowing them participation in the Convention'.[72]

As has been seen, the Tenth Session identified two criteria to be complied with by non-State signatories – competence over matters falling within the scope of the Convention and capacity to enter into treaties with respect to such matters. At the close of the Tenth Session, it was generally conceded that national liberation movements could not satisfy these criteria and it was not until the Eleventh Session that the President of the Conference, following consultations with 'some delegations immediately concerned', was able to pave the way to a compromise solution by putting forward a five-point proposal:[73]

---

[68] UN Convention, Arts. 306 and 307 and Annex IX, Art.3.

[69] A/CONF.62/L.26, 8 May 1978 (*UNCLOS III Off.Rec.*, Vol. IX, p.182).

[70] Document FC/12, 16 August 1979, discussed in Document FC/17, 23 August 1979. For examples of opposing but predictable responses to the proposal to allow the participation of the PLO in the Convention, see Mr. Rosenne (Israel) and Mr. Kovalev (USSR) in *UNCLOS III Off.Rec.*, Vol. IX, at pp. 39 and 40.

[71] FC/17, 23 August 1979, p.1.

[72] *Ibid.*, p.2.

[73] *Report of the President on the Question of Participation in the Convention*, A/CONF.62/L.86, 26 March 1982 (*UNCLOS III Off.Rec.*, Vol.XVI, p.197, at p.199).

Chapter 3 63

> (i) *National liberation movements which have been participating in the Third United Nations Conference on the Law of the Sea shall be entitled to sign the final act of the Conference, in their capacity as observers.*[74]

Effect was given to this proposal, in a form proposed by Iraq,[75] in Resolution IV of the Conference.[76]

> (ii) *National liberation movements which have been participating in the Third United Nations Conference on the Law of the Sea and which sign the final act of the Conference shall have the status of observers before the Preparatory Commission.*[77]

The language of Resolution I of the Conference, establishing the Preparatory Commission, permitted effect to be given to this proposal since it covered the 'representatives of signatories of the Final Act'.[78]

> (iii) *National liberation movements which have been participating in the Third United Nations Conference on the Law of the Sea and which sign the final act of the Conference shall have the status of observers before the Assembly of the International Sea-Bed Authority.*[79]

Effect was given to this proposal, in a form proposed by Iraq,[80] in Article 156(3) of the Convention:

> Observers at the Third United Nations Conference on the Law of the Sea who have signed the Final Act and who are not referred to in article 305, paragraph 1(c),(d),(e) or (f), shall have the right to participate in the Authority as observers, in accordance with its rules, regulations and procedures.

> (iv) *National liberation movements which have been participating in the Third United Nations Conference on the Law of the Sea and which sign the final act of the Conference may attend any meeting of the Parties to the Convention, in the capacity of observers.*
> (v) *Any communication sent to Parties to the Convention by the Depositary shall also be sent to national liberation movements which have been participating in the Third United Nations Conference on the Law of the Sea and which sign the final act of the Conference.*[81]

---

[74] *Ibid.*
[75] A/CONF.62/L.101, 13 April 1982 (*UNCLOS III Off.Rec.*, Vol.XVI, p.218).
[76] *The Law of the Sea. Official Text of the United Nations Convention on the Law of the Sea*, 1983, (UN Sales No. E.83.V.5), at p.183.
[77] *Loc.cit.* in note 73, at p.199.
[78] *Loc.cit.* in note 76, at p.175, para.2.
[79] *Loc.cit.* in note 73, at p.199.
[80] *Loc.cit.* in note 75.
[81] *Loc.cit.* in note 73, at p.199.

64   The Principles of the Regime

Effect was given to the latter two proposals in Article 319(3)(a) and (b) of the Convention.

The President summed up the effect of these proposals as being to allow the national liberation movements which had participated in the Conference and signed the Final Act:

> to participate in the Preparatory Commission and the International Sea-Bed Authority as observers. This will enable them to present the views of the peoples they represent and request the adoption of appropriate measures for the protection of the interests of those peoples until they attain their autonomy or independence.[82]

The following national liberation movements participated in the Conference and signed the Final Act: African National Congress of South Africa; Palestine Liberation Organisation (PLO); Pan Africanist Congress of Azania; and South West Africa People's Organisation (SWAPO).[83] Two of these organisations represented peoples in South Africa and a third (SWAPO) represented peoples in Namibia. Following the ending of apartheid in South Africa and the independence of Namibia, and given the fact that the above rights were accorded only to these four organisations, it is clear that the impact of these provisions will now be insignificant.

5.2.5 Peoples of Non-self-governing Territories, Territories under Colonial Domination and Territories Sovereignty over which is Disputed

In the Draft Convention on the Law of the Sea (1981), an un-numbered 'Transitional provision' appeared between the final Article 320 and Annex I.[84] Its purpose was to ensure that the peoples of the various categories of non-self-governing territories should be the beneficiaries of the resources of these territories. Their entitlement to the 'rights recognised or established by' the Convention was to be safeguarded by vesting these rights in the inhabitants of the territory, 'to be exercised by them for their own benefit and in accordance with their own needs and requirements.'[85] Paragraph 3 practically imposed a moratorium on exploitation of such resources by providing that :

> A metropolitan or foreign power administering, occupying or purporting to administer or occupy a territory may not in any case exercise, profit or benefit from or in any way infringe the rights [to such resources].

This 'transitional provision' referred to the 'resources of a territory' and not to the right of the peoples of these territories to share in the benefits of the common heritage of mankind. During the Eleventh Session of the Conference, however, the language of this provision was substantially altered and it was agreed, by way

---

[82] *Ibid.*
[83] *Loc.cit.* in note 76, at p.190, where there is a list of signatories of the Final Act.
[84] *UNCLOS III Off.Rec.*, Vol. XV, p.172, at p.224.
[85] Para.1.

Chapter 3 65

of a compromise, that it should become a resolution of the Conference rather than a provision of the Convention.[86] Resolution III now declares, *inter alia*, that:

> In the case of a territory whose people have not attained full independence or other self-governing status recognised by the United Nations, or a territory under colonial domination, provisions concerning rights and interests under the Convention shall be implemented for the benefit of the people of the territory with a view to promoting their well-being and development.[87]

It is clear, both from its origins and from its language, that this Resolution is concerned, at least principally, with the resources of the territory concerned in its offshore maritime zones. Given the generality of its formulation, however, it is at least arguable that Resolution III might also be employed to ensure that the peoples of such territories should enjoy a share in the common heritage of mankind.

5.3 Who are the Intended Beneficiaries of the Common Heritage of Mankind?
Article 137(2) of the Convention provides that 'All rights in the resources of the Area are vested in mankind as a whole, on whose behalf the Authority shall act'. It is followed by Article 140(1) which provides:

> *Benefit of mankind*

> Activities in the Area shall, as specifically provided for in this Part, be carried out for the benefit of mankind as a whole, irrespective of the geographical location of States, whether coastal or land-locked, and taking into particular consideration the interests and needs of developing States and of peoples who have not attained full independence or other self-governing status recognised by the United Nations in accordance with General Assembly resolution 1514 (XV) and other relevant General Assembly resolutions.

These provisions make it clear that the intention is to benefit 'mankind as a whole' and not simply those parts of mankind which are neatly distributed among the sovereign States Parties to this Convention. To find that a particular 'people' is eligible for benefit does not of course mean that such people necessarily has the capacity to become a party to the Convention or take part in the proceedings of the organs of the Authority which will decide upon the sharing out of the proceeds of the common heritage.[88] It does mean, however, that these peoples'

---

[86] See further *Report of the President on the Question of Participation in the Convention*, A/CONF. 62/L.86, 26 March 1982 (*UNCLOS III, Off.Rec.*, Vol.XVI, p.197 at p.199(19)) and *Memorandum issued by the Collegium on Changes Incorporated in the Draft Convention*, A/CONF.62/L.93, 2 April 1982 (*ibid.*, p.210).
[87] Resolution III, *loc. cit.* in note 76, at p.183, para.1(a).
[88] See further below, section 5.3.7.

66 The Principles of the Regime

interests have to be taken into account in exercising the power to share out these proceeds.

Which entities are to be regarded as eligible for benefit is less than clear from the language of Article 140 and it is necessary to consider the position of the following entities:

- States Parties to the Convention, whether coastal or land-locked;
- States not parties to the Convention, whether coastal or land-locked;
- Self-governing associated States and territories enjoying full internal self-government;
- National liberation movements;
- Peoples of non-self-governing territories, territories under colonial domination and territories sovereignty over which is disputed.

5.3.1 States Parties to the Convention

It is, of course, very obvious that States Parties to the Convention are the representatives of the greater part of mankind and it is clear from Article 140(1) that it makes no difference whether a State is coastal or land-locked.

It is relevant to note here that, under Article 1(2)(2) of the Convention, the term 'States Parties' refers not only to sovereign States which have become parties to the Convention but also to the various other entities which, as was seen above, may become parties to the Convention. However, these other entities are referred to below.

5.3.2 States not Parties to the Convention

Efforts by some delegations to restrict the benefit of the Convention to States Parties were unsuccessful and Article 140 includes no such qualification.[89]

5.3.3 Self-governing Associated States and Territories Enjoying Full Internal Self-government

Article 140(1) does not actually refer to such entities. It refers rather to independent States, developing States and 'peoples who have not attained full independence or other self-governing status recognised by the United Nations in accordance with General Assembly resolution 1514(XV) and other relevant General Assembly resolutions'. In a sense, self-governing associated States and territories enjoying full internal self-government lie between the two categories referred to in Article 140(1), that is, fully independent States and non-self-governing territories. If the peoples of non-self-governing territories are identified as intended beneficiaries of the common heritage of mankind, it surely follows, *a fortiori*, that the peoples of self-governing associated States and territories enjoying full internal self-government are also covered. The fact that such States and territories are eligible to become State Parties to the Convention simply underlines the point.

---

[89] See passage from Mr. Njenga's report quoted below in text at note 106.

Chapter 3 67

5.3.4 National Liberation Movements

As was seen above, the four national liberation movements which participated in the Conference and signed the Final Act were accorded the right to participate in the Preparatory Commission and the International Sea-Bed Authority as observers.[90] As the President of the Conference noted, they thus had the opportunity 'to present the views of the peoples they represent and request the adoption of appropriate measures for the protection of the interests of these peoples until they attain their autonomy or independence'.[91] This being so, there is clearly an argument for saying that the peoples represented by these movements fall within the terms of Article 140(1) as being among the 'peoples who have not attained full independence or other self-governing status recognised by the United Nations in accordance with General Assembly resolution 1514 (XV) and other relevant General Assembly resolutions'.

The policy of the United Nations and of UNCLOS III towards national liberation movements is, of course, highly selective. Thus, under Rule 62 of the Rules of Procedure of the Conference, the only national liberation movements entitled to participate in the Conference as observers were those 'in their respective region recognised by the Organisation of African Unity (OAU) or by the League of Arab States'.[92] This policy is also reflected in the various provisions of the Convention, reviewed above,[93] which accord observer rights in the Preparatory Commission and the organs of the International Sea-Bed Authority. These rights were to be enjoyed only by the four movements which actually participated in the Conference and signed the Final Act. It would seem to follow that such rights will not be extended either to other existing liberation movements or to others which may be formed in future, irrespective of their recognition by the OAU or the Arab League. It would further appear that the peoples of any liberation movement other than these four would not be eligible for benefit under Article 140 (1).[94] Moreover, given the end of apartheid in South Africa and the independence of Namibia, only one of the original four remains a potential beneficiary – the PLO.

As will be seen below, some delegations were strongly opposed to a ·formulation of Article 140 which would have the effect of benefitting national liberation movements but their views did not prevail.[95]

5.3.5 Peoples of Non-self-governing Territories, Territories under Colonial Domination and Territories Sovereignty over which is Disputed

As was seen above, such entities are not eligible to become parties to the Convention but their interests are protected to some extent by the provisions of

[90] Section 5.2.4.
[91] See text at note 82 above.
[92] *Third United Nations Conference on the Law of the Sea, Rules of Procedure*, A/CONF.62/30/Rev.3 (including amendments to 6 March 1980) (1981).
[93] Section 5.2.4.
[94] This argument is preferred to the weaker argument that such peoples might qualify as being 'peoples of non-self-governing territories, territories under colonial domination and territories sovereignty over which is disputed' — the category considered in section 5.3.5 below.
[95] Below, following note 106.

68   The Principles of the Regime

Resolution III of the Conference.[96] It was argued above that this resolution might be wide enough to allow it to be used to ensure that the peoples of such territories should enjoy a share in the common heritage of mankind.[97] Article 140(1) confirms their entitlement, certainly at least insofar as they fall within the category of 'peoples who have not attained full independence or other self-governing status recognised by the United Nations in accordance with General Assembly resolution 1514 (XV) and other relevant General Assembly resolutions'.

5.3.6 The travaux préparatoires
Interesting insights into the meaning of Article 140 are provided by a review of its drafting history.

The original ICNT version simply provided that :

> Activities in the Area shall be carried out for the benefit of mankind as a whole, irrespective of the geographical location of States, whether coastal or land-locked, and taking into particular consideration the interests and needs of the developing countries as specifically provided for in this Part of the present Convention.[98]

Even in this early version, it already appeared to be intention of the draftsman that the benefit should be extended beyond States Parties to the Convention. However, a revised version of Article 140, introduced at the Seventh Session[99] and subsequently incorporated in ICNT/Rev.1[100], widened the formula considerably. Under Paragraph 1, the interests and needs deserving of special consideration now included not only the developing countries but also 'peoples who have not attained full independence or other self-governing status'. A further development of this formula, based on a proposal made by the Arab Group and endorsed by the Group of 77, was introduced at the Eighth Session,[101] though it had to wait until after the first part of the Ninth Session before being formally incorporated in ICNT/Rev.2.[102] Under this revised version, the interests and needs to be taken into particular consideration were, as before, those of 'the developing countries and peoples who have not attained full independence or other self-governing status', but these words were now followed by this clause: '....recognised by the United Nations in accordance with General Assembly

---

[96] Above, section 5.2.5.
[97] Ibid.
[98] UNCLOS III Off.Rec., Vol. VIII, at p. 23.
[99] UNCLOS III Off.Rec., Vol. X, at p. 21.
[100] ICNT/Rev.1, A/CONF.62/WP.10/Rev.1, 28 April 1979 (Platzöder, Documents, Vol.I, p.375).
[101] A/CONF.62/L.43, Appendix A (UNCLOS III Off.Rec., Vol. XII, p. 84), as one of the 'Suggestions resulting from Consultations held by the Chairman and the Co-ordinators of the Working Group of 21'.
[102] ICNT/Rev.2, A/CONF.62/WP.10/Rev.2, 11 April 1980 (Platzöder, Documents, Vol. II, p. 3), at p. 66.

Chapter 3 69

resolution 1514(XV) and other relevant General Assembly resolutions ...'[103]. The intention was 'to ensure that States claiming to be self-governing but in fact dominated by colonialists or foreign countries, as well as secessionist movements, would not enjoy the benefits of the area.'[104]

Speaking at the Eighth Session, Mr. Njenga, Chairman of Negotiating Group 1, expressed the belief that 'this addition to article 140 reflects the wishes of the overwhelming majority of the Group of 21'. He was obliged to add, however, that 'in the opinion of some delegates the question of implementation of this provision [Article 140 as a whole, it would seem] is a problematic one and will require careful scrutiny at the next stage of the negotiations'.[105] Nevertheless, when he reported on the deliberations of the Working Group of 21 towards the end of Part 1 of the Ninth Session, Mr. Njenga found no grounds for any change, though he recognised the continuing difference of view among delegates:

> Some delegations had, and I believe still have, strong objections regarding the way in which this principle has been worded in this provision. They think that there is no valid reason to extend the sharing of the benefits derived from the exploitation of the area beyond the group of States which will become parties to the convention. It was suggested in this respect that the words 'amongst States Parties' should be added to paragraph 2 of article 140. This proposal did not get broad support among many of the delegations. Moreover, it is my impression that any restriction such as the one proposed would contradict other provisions of the convention, as well as the wording and the spirit of resolution 2749 (XXV) of the General Assembly, which refer to the benefit of mankind as a whole. Therefore I abstained from introducing any substantive change to this provision.[106]

The new formula was therefore incorporated in ICNT/Rev.2.

During the second part of the Ninth Session, the difference between the two points of view persisted, with some developed States – especially the United States – objecting in particular to the possibility that, under Article 140, liberation movements would be entitled to receive benefits from the Authority.[107]

Eventually, a compromise package was agreed, based on amendments to Articles 140,160 and 162.[108] First, Article 140(2) was amended by the addition of a non-discrimination clause.[109] The Authority was to provide for the equitable sharing of financial and other benefits derived from activities in the Area 'on a

---

[103] Resolution 1514(XV) is the *Declaration on the Granting of Independence to Colonial Countries and Peoples.*

[104] Mr. Hamad (United Arab Emirates), speaking in the First Committee on 25 April 1979 (*UNCLOS III Off.Rec.*, Vol. XI, pp.55-56, at p. 56).

[105] *UNCLOS III Off.Rec.*, Vol. XII, p. 83.

[106] *Report of the Co-ordinators of the Working Group of 21 to the First Committee,* A/CONF.62/C.1/L.27(Part II), 27 March 1980 (*UNCLOS III Off.Rec.*, Vol. XIII, p.113).

[107] *Report of the Co-ordinators of the Working Group of 21 to the First Committee,* A/CONF. 62/C.1/L.28, 23 August 1980 (*UNCLOS III Off.Rec.*, Vol.XIV, p.161), at p.172.

[108] See further, *ibid.*

[109] See further, text, at note 111 below.

70 The Principles of the Regime

non-discriminatory basis.' What this means is obscure. At first sight, it appears to be ensuring that the Authority should not discriminate in favour of any particular beneficiaries, though not apparently excluding any particular category such as liberation movements from being beneficiaries. However, Article 140(2) goes on to say that the equitable sharing is to be effected 'in accordance with Article 160(2)(f)(i)', which quite clearly prescribes that the equitable sharing is to be effected 'taking into particular consideration the interests and needs of developing States and peoples who have not attained full independence or other self-governing status.'

The second amendment, to Article 160(2)(f)(i), added 'the payments and contributions made pursuant to article 82', that is, those made in respect of exploitation of the continental shelf beyond 200 miles, to the financial and other economic benefits derived from activities in the Area; both were now to be equitably shared out by the Authority. It may be noted in passing that, as a result of this amendment, this provision is no longer consistent with Article 82(4) which restricts distribution of payments to 'States Parties to this Convention'. Even bearing in mind the extensive definition of 'States Parties' in Article 1(2)(2) of the Convention, there remains a conflict between these two provisions. However, the intention behind the amendment to Article 160(2)(f)(i) is clear. It is to ensure that 'peoples who have not attained full independence or other self-governing status' will be placed in the same position as other potential beneficiaries so far as benefits derived from Article 82 are concerned.

The third part of the compromise package consisted of amendments to Articles 160 and 162, designed to create a system of checks and balances between the Council and the Assembly of the Authority. These amendments are considered in the following section.

5.3.7 Distribution of the Benefit of Mankind

Once the peoples entitled to benefit from the common heritage of mankind have been identified, there remains the practical problem of determining how these various peoples' shares of the benefits from the Area are to be assessed and distributed.

Under Article 173(2) of the Convention, the balance of Authority funds remaining after payment of the administrative expenses of the Authority may, *inter alia*, '(a) be shared in accordance with article 140 and article 160, paragraph 2(g)'. As was noted above,[110] compromise amendments were made to Article 140(2) and to Articles 160 and 162 at the Ninth Session. As amended, Article 140(2) provides that :

> 2. The Authority shall provide for the equitable sharing of financial and other economic benefits derived from activities in the Area through any appropriate mechanism, on a non-discriminatory basis, in accordance with article 160, paragraph 2(f)(i).[111]

---

[110] Text, at note 108 and following.

[111] Para. 2 of Art. 140 was previously para. 9 of Art. 151 of ICNT. In transferring it to Article 140 of ICNT/Rev.1 at the Seventh Session, Mr. Njenga said that the reformulated version would 'give the Authority more flexibility in selecting ways in which the equitable sharing of benefits will be

Chapter 3 71

Under the earlier version of what is now Article 160(2)(f)(i) of the Convention (namely Article 160(2)(j) of ICNT/Rev.2), 'the powers and functions of the Assembly' included the :

> Adoption of rules, regulations and procedures for the equitable sharing of financial and other economic benefits derived from activities in the Area, taking into particular consideration the interests and needs of the developing countries and peoples who have not attained full independence or other self-governing status;[112]

Acting by two-thirds majority (Article 159(6)), the Assembly would thus have had a very wide discretion.[113] However, quite a different pattern was incorporated in Article 160(2)(f)(i) of the Convention, which has to be read with Article 162(2)(o)(i). Under these provisions, the Council of the Sea-Bed Authority is empowered to :

> recommend to the Assembly rules, regulations and procedures on the equitable sharing of financial and other economic benefits derived from activities in the Area and the payments and contributions made pursuant to article 82, taking into particular consideration the interests and needs of the developing States and peoples who have not attained full independence or other self-governing status;[114]

The Assembly's much-reduced role is now to consider and approve the Council's recommendations and, if it fails to approve them, its only option is to return them to the Council for reconsideration in the light of the views expressed by the Assembly.[115] As the Chairman of the First Committee of the Conference remarked, 'In this way a system of checks and balances has been constructed between the Assembly and the Council'.[116]

---

accomplished'. (UN Information Centre, London: *Round Up of Session. Seventh Session (First Part) of Third United Nations Conference on the Law of the Sea, Geneva, 28 March - 19 May*, BR/78/21, 6 June 1978, p.7). Commenting on the revised Art. 140(2), the United States Delegation reported that: 'The U.S. Delegation sought to remove the Authority from responsibility for distribution of benefits by requiring the use of some already existing international mechanism rather than a new one created by the Authority. No objections were voiced to this proposal, but by the end of the session the desired changes had not appeared. The text is slightly improved by the change in wording from shall "establish a system for equitable sharing of benefits" to "shall provide for equitable sharing of benefits"' (Nordquist and Park, *loc.cit.* in note 61 above, at p.197).

[112] ICNT/Rev.2, A/CONF.62/WP.10/Rev.2, 11 April 1980 and Corr. 1-3; Platzöder, *Documents*, Vol. II, p. 3, at p. 77.
[113] *Ibid.*
[114] UN Convention, Art. 162(2)(o)(i).
[115] UN Convention, Art. 160(2)(f)(i).
[116] *Loc. cit.* in note 107, at p. 172.

72 *The Principles of the Regime*

II. LEGAL STATUS OF THE AREA AND ITS RESOURCES[117]

The proposition that part of the globe and its resources are the common heritage of mankind looks at first sight more like the language of an electioneering politician than that of an international statesman or lawyer. It is exceedingly vague, seeming to promise bounty for all while at the same time avoiding definition or precise commitment. That the concept is of doubtful utility as a 'principle governing the Area' is suggested by the fact that, in earlier phases of the UNCLOS III negotiations, it lent itself to such diverse interpretations as that of the Soviet Union, that it entitled every State, as part of mankind, to exploit the resources of the area,[118] and that of the Group of 77, that it required that all exploitation should be the preserve of the Authority.[119]

Article 137, dealing with the legal status of the Area and its resources, introduces a little more precision – though not in relation to the provision in Paragraph 2 that 'All rights in the resources of the Area are vested in mankind as a whole, on whose behalf the Authority shall act'. The difficulties of interpretation which this paragraph presents have already been noted.[120]

Paragraph 2 goes on to provide that the *resources* of the Area are not subject to alienation and that the *minerals* recovered from the Area may only be alienated in accordance with Part XI of the Convention and the rules, regulations and procedures of the Authority.

As a corollary to the vesting in mankind, Paragraph 1 provides that:

No State shall claim or exercise sovereignty or sovereign rights over any part of the Area or its resources, nor shall any State or natural or juridical person appropriate any part thereof. No such claim or exercise of sovereignty or sovereign rights nor such appropriation shall be recognised.

---

[117] Only a brief comment is offered here on this principle. For further consideration of the legal status of the Area and its resources, see Chap. 2 above and Chaps. 4 - 7 below.

[118] See, for example, the summary of the Soviet Union's *Workshop Paper No.2* (which did not become a formal document of the Conference) provided in the *Final Report by the Co-Chairmen on the Activities of the Workshop* (established by the First Committee at the Fifth Session of the Conference), A/CONF. 62/C.1/WR.5 (*UNCLOS III Off.Rec.*, Vol. VI, pp. 165-168, at p.167, para. 14). In an earlier report on the activities of the workshop (A/CONF. 62/C.1/WR.3, *UNCLOS III Off.Rec.*, Vol. VI, pp. 164-165), it had been stated that ' ... several delegations stressed the fundamental character of the international area as the common heritage of mankind, and the commitment of all States to seek a practical realisation of that concept, which in the first place requires that the international community, through the Authority, exercise joint sovereignty over the area, and not alienate any part of it to States Parties or other entities' (para.2). Commenting on this passage, the Soviet delegate 'said that his delegation had always felt that the Authority should be concerned only with promoting and regulating the exploitation of the common heritage. The fact that the resources of the area were the common heritage of mankind did not mean that the international community should exercise sovereignty over it' (*UNCLOS III Off.Rec.*, Vol. VI, p. 64, para. 4). The Soviet Union's proposals on the basic provisions of the regime were given in A/CONF. 62/C.1/L.12, 21 March 1975 (*UNCLOS III Off.Rec.*, Vol. IV, p. 182).

[119] For the extreme view proposed at an early stage of the negotiations, see A/CONF.62/C.1/L.7, 16 August 1974 (*UNCLOS III Off.Rec.*, Vol. III, at pp. 172-173).

[120] See above, section I.5.3.

Chapter 3   73

Such a provision would effectively ensure that no part of the Area or its resources would be subjected to sovereign claims or to appropriation by States Parties to the Convention. However, it could hardly in itself debar such claims or appropriations by non-parties and, in fact, during the period between 1982 and 1994, the sanction of non-recognition did not deter such free enterprise by third parties claiming to exercise a freedom of the high seas.[121] The same can be said of Paragraph 3 of Article 137 which provides that:

> No State or natural or juridical person shall claim, acquire or exercise rights with respect to the *minerals* recovered from the Area except in accordance with this Part. Otherwise, no such claim, acquisition or exercise of such rights shall be recognised.[122]

III. GENERAL CONDUCT OF STATES; USE FOR PEACEFUL PURPOSES; NON-DISCRIMINATION

Article 138 ('General conduct of States in relation to the Area') provides that :

> The general conduct of States in relation to the Area shall be in accordance with the provisions of this Part, the principles embodied in the Charter of the United Nations and other rules of international law in the interests of maintaining peace and security and promoting international cooperation and mutual understanding.

It is difficult to see that this adds anything to what would have been understood in any event. In what is already an extremely long Convention, it might have been thought that the Conference would have seen some virtue in pruning out clauses such as this which simply reiterate duties incumbent on States under the United Nations Charter. However, not content with one such reminder, the Conference saw fit to include among the 'General Provisions' of Part XVI of the Convention Article 301 on 'Peaceful uses of the seas' which amounts to no more than the self-evident application to the seas of the prohibition against the use or threat of force in Article 2(4) of the United Nations Charter.

'Peace' features yet again in Article 141, on 'Use of the Area exclusively for peaceful purposes', which provides that :

> The Area shall be open to use exclusively for peaceful purposes by all States, whether coastal or land-locked, without discrimination and without prejudice to the other provisions of this Part.

The futility of incorporating such vague provisions on peaceful purposes in such conventions has been stressed elsewhere.[123]

---

[121] See further above, Chap. 2 and below, Chaps. 6 and 7.
[122] Emphasis added.
[123] See, *e.g.*, E. D. Brown, *Arms Control in Hydrospace: Legal Aspects*, 1971 (Woodrow Wilson International Center for Scholars, Ocean Series 301), especially at p. 46 *et seq.*

74 *The Principles of the Regime*

The non-discrimination clause in Article 141 is complemented by Article 152(1), requiring the Authority to avoid discrimination in the exercise of its powers and functions, including the granting of opportunities for activities in the Area. However, this non-discrimination clause is heavily qualified by the later provisions of the Convention, starting with Paragraph 2 of Article 152, which provides that :

> Nevertheless, special consideration for developing States, including particular consideration for the land-locked and geographically disadvantaged among them, specifically provided for in this Part shall be permitted.[124]

The phrase 'shall be permitted' replaced an earlier formulation that such special consideration 'shall not be deemed to be discrimination', which, according to the Chairman of Negotiating Group 1, 'some delegates rightly considered quite misleading'.[125] The fact remains that it is positive discrimination.

Mention may also be made here of two further 'principles', though they are not referred to in Part XI but in Part XVI – 'General Provisions'. Article 300 provides that:

Good faith and abuse of rights

> States Parties shall fulfil in good faith the obligations assumed under this Convention and shall exercise the rights, jurisdiction and freedoms recognised in this Convention in a manner which would not constitute an abuse of right.

Here, too, it must be wondered what purpose is served by this provision. The rule that 'States Parties shall fulfil in good faith the obligations assumed under this Convention' is a well established rule of international customary law which is, moreover, codified in Article 26 of the Vienna Convention on the Law of Treaties, 1969[126]. The same cannot be said of the concept of the abuse of rights[127] and, given the reservations expressed by some delegates during the Ninth Session,[128] it might have been wiser to have omitted any reference to this contentious doctrine.

---

[124] See also, Art. 148 on 'Participation of developing States in activities in the Area', considered in section XII below.

[125] *Explanatory memorandum by the Chairman of Negotiating Group 1 concerning document NG1/16,* Document NG1/17, 17 April 1979, p. 2.

[126] *Loc.cit.* in note 6.

[127] See further G. Schwarzenberger and E.D. Brown, *A Manual of International Law*, 6th ed., Revised Second Impression, 1978, at pp. 84-85 and 444.

[128] The Conference President reported that the proposed inclusion of a provision on abuse of rights 'met with some criticism as it was not in accord with some legal systems, certain concepts were not sufficiently founded [sic], and there was a problem of interpretation in some languages'. (A/CONF.62/L.53, 29 March 1980, *UNCLOS III Off. Rec.*, Vol. XIII, p.87).

Chapter 3 75

IV. BENEFIT OF MANKIND

Some of the implications of this 'principle governing the Area'[129] – that activities in the Area are to be carried out for the benefit of mankind as a whole – have been considered in section I.5.3 above, where the intended beneficiaries were identified and the system for the sharing of benefits was commented upon. Further aspects are dealt with below in relation to Article 144 on transfer of technology[130] and in Chapter 4 on the development of the resources of the Area.[131] Here it will suffice to note that the bias in favour of developing countries, noted above in relation to Article 152,[132] is again evident in Article 140. Although exploration and exploitation of the resources of the Area are to be carried out 'for the benefit of mankind as a whole', 'particular consideration' is to be given to the 'interests and needs of developing States and of peoples who have not attained full independence or other self-governing status recognised by the United Nations in accordance with General Assembly resolution 1514(XV) and other relevant General Assembly resolutions.'[133]

V. RESPONSIBILITY TO ENSURE COMPLIANCE AND LIABILITY FOR DAMAGE

If activities in the Area are not carried out in conformity with the provisions of the Convention, damage may be caused. It was necessary therefore to include in the Convention clear provision for the establishment of liability for such damage. The Convention deals with the question in two ways. First, under Article 139, it imposes a responsibility on States Parties to ensure that activities are carried out in conformity with the Convention and holds them liable for damage caused by their failure to discharge this responsibility; and a similar responsibility applies to international organisations for activities undertaken by them. It is with this 'principle governing the Area' that this section is concerned.[134]

Secondly, in Annex III ('Basic conditions of prospecting, exploration and exploitation'), the Convention provides for liability for damage on a contractual level. This aspect is dealt with below in Chapter 4.[135]

1. State Responsibility

Under Article 153(2) of the Convention, activities in the Area may be carried out by:

(i) the Enterprise (an organ of the International Sea-Bed Authority);
(ii) States Parties or State enterprises;

---

[129] Title of Part XI, Section 2 of UN Convention.
[130] See below section VIII.
[131] Chap. 4, sections I and VII.
[132] Above, section III.
[133] See further below section XII.
[134] See also Art. 304 of the Convention, under which, 'The provisions of this Convention regarding responsibility and liability for damage are without prejudice to the application of existing rules and the development of further rules regarding responsibility and liability under international law.'
[135] Chap. 4, sections XIII and XIV.

76 The Principles of the Regime

> (iii) natural or juridical persons which posses the nationality of States Parties or are effectively controlled by them or their nationals, when sponsored by States Parties; or
>
> (iv) any group of the entities referred to in (ii) and (iii) above.

Leaving the Enterprise for separate consideration later,[136] the question is to what extent is a State Party responsible for damage caused by the failure of any of the entities in (ii)-(iv) above to comply with the provisions of Part XI of the Convention when undertaking activities in the Area? The answer is supplied by Article 139 which provides that :

> 1. States Parties shall have the responsibility to ensure that activities in the Area, whether carried out by States Parties, or state enterprises or natural or juridical persons which possess the nationality of States Parties or are effectively controlled by them or their nationals, shall be carried out in conformity with this Part ...
> 2. Without prejudice to the rules of international law and Annex III, article 22, damage caused by the failure of a State Party ... to carry out its responsibilities under this Part shall entail liability; States Parties ... acting together shall bear joint and several liability. A State Party shall not however be liable for damage caused by any failure to comply with this Part by a person whom it has sponsored under article 153, paragraph 2(b), if the State Party has taken all necessary and appropriate measures to secure effective compliance under article 153, paragraph 4, and Annex III, article 4, paragraph 4.

Article 139 envisages two types of State responsibility. First, so far as concerns damage caused by one of the natural or juridical persons referred to in (iii) above, or by any group referred to in (iv) above, Paragraph 2 imposes a responsibility upon the sponsoring State akin to the *indirect responsibility* of States under general international law, in that responsibility arises not from the fault of the operator but from the supervisory fault of the State.[137] The State Party will not be liable, however, if it has taken all necessary and appropriate measures to secure effective compliance under Article 153(4) and Annex III, Article 4(4). Under the latter provision, the sponsoring State would avoid liability if it had 'adopted laws and regulations and taken administrative measures which are, within the framework of its legal system, reasonably appropriate for securing compliance by persons under its jurisdiction'. Secondly, Paragraph 2 envisages the *direct*

---

[136] See below, Chap. 8, sections II.2.2, II.2.6 and II.2.7.

[137] In international law, States are directly responsible for the tortious acts of organs of Government and indirectly responsible for a secondary failure to carry out a duty to exercise due diligence in the prevention, suppression and repression of illegal acts directed against foreigners within their jurisdiction. Thus, *e.g.*, denial of a right of innocent passage of a foreign merchant vessel through the territorial sea would render the coastal State directly responsible, whereas failure to exercise due diligence in preventing a mob from endangering the lives of foreign fishermen would incur indirect responsibility.

responsibility of the State for damage caused by the activities of the State itself or a State enterprise. It would seem that, in the majority of cases, such direct responsibility would be indistinguishable from the contractual liability for damage for which provision is made in Article 22 of Annex III. Such contractual liability is considered in detail in Chapter 4, together with the question of the forum in which proceedings may be instituted for the recovery of damages.[138]

So far as the failure of the State to carry out its indirect responsibility is concerned, damage may as a result be caused to the Authority, the Enterprise, other States or State enterprises and any of the natural or juridical persons referred to in (iii) above. In what forum may an action to recover damages be brought?[139]

The Authority may bring an action in the Sea-Bed Disputes Chamber under Article 187(b) of the Convention.

States may bring an action in the Chamber under Article 187(a).

As regards State enterprises and the natural or juridical persons referred to in (iii) above, it would appear that, in the first instance at least, the Chamber would not have jurisdiction and proceedings would have to be instituted in a municipal forum. If such domestic remedies were exhausted without satisfaction, it might be open to the home State Party of the aggrieved entity to institute proceedings before the Chamber under Article 187(a). Should the Chamber find that it lacked jurisdiction, recourse would have to be had to the normal channels of general international law, relying on Article 304 of the Convention.

2. Responsibility of International Organisations

Article 139 also provides for the responsibility of international organisations. Paragraph 1 lays down that 'The same responsibility [as lies on States Parties] applies to international organisations for activities in the Area carried out by such organisations'. Given its drafting history, it would appear that the reference is principally, though not perhaps exclusively, to international institutions, other than the Authority or the Enterprise, which might undertake activities in the Area as juridical persons controlled by States Parties and sponsored by them under Article 153(2)(b). Paragraph 3 of Article 139 correspondingly requires States Parties which are members of such institutions to 'take appropriate measures to ensure the implementation of this article with respect to such organisations.'

The meaning of this provision can best be explored by taking an example. Suppose that States A,B and C, parties to the Convention, establish an international institution – Inter-Metal – to engage in activities in the Area. This institution (unless itself a party to the Convention[140]) will be entitled to carry out such activities only if it is qualified to do so under Article 153(2)(b). In short, it must be a juridical person effectively controlled by States Parties to the Convention and sponsored by them. Suppose, next, that damage has been caused by failure of Inter-Metal to carry out activities in the Area in conformity with Part

---

[138] See Chap. 4, sections XIII and XIV.

[139] For a detailed consideration of the Convention's provisions for the settlement of sea-bed disputes, including a study of the composition and jurisdiction of the Sea-Bed Disputes Chamber, see Chap.9.

[140] See further below, text, at note 141.

78 *The Principles of the Regime*

XI. Who would be liable for such damage under Article 139? The sponsoring States, States A, B and C, would be liable for any supervisory failure on their part to take 'all necessary and appropriate measures to secure effective compliance' by Inter-Metal. Inter-Metal would not share this *indirect responsibility* but would of course be directly liable under its contract.

A second situation has to be considered, however, in view of the recognition of the rights of international organisations to participate in the Convention as 'States Parties'.[141] Suppose, for example, that competence was transferred to the European Community to conduct activities in the Area under the Convention,[142] and that the European Community established a commercial entity, Euro-Metal, to undertake such activities. In this case, the European Community would be in the same position as a State Party to the UN Convention as regards indirect responsibility and Euro-Metal would be in the same position as any similar commercial entity sponsored by such a State Party. This conclusion is confirmed by Articles 5 and 6 of Annex IX of the Convention. Under Article 5, the instrument of formal confirmation or of accession of an international organisation has to contain a declaration specifying the matters in respect of which competence has been transferred to the organisation by its members which are parties to the Convention. Article 6 imposes upon parties having competence under Article 5 responsibility for failure to comply with obligations or for any other violation of the Convention.

VI. RIGHTS AND LEGITIMATE INTERESTS OF COASTAL STATES

Article 142 regulates the exploration and exploitation of resources which lie partly within the Area and partly within the limits of national jurisdiction. In such cases, activities in the Area must be conducted with due regard to the rights and legitimate interests of the coastal State concerned. Consultations, including a system of prior notification, have to be maintained with the State and its consent obtained to any activities which 'may result' in the exploitation of resources within national limits.

Article 142 also preserves the rights of coastal States to take measures, consistent with Part XII of the Convention,

> as may be necessary to prevent, mitigate or eliminate grave and imminent danger to their coastline, or related interests from pollution or threat thereof or from other hazardous occurrences resulting from or caused by any activities in the Area.[143]

---

[141] UN Convention, Art. 1(2)(2), read with Art. 305(1)(f). See further section I.5.2.3. above.

[142] For the position of the European Community as regards Part XI of the Convention, see above, section I.5.2.3, text, following note 65.

[143] See further below, Chap. 10, section IV.6.4.2.2, on the development of this provision in the Mining Code.

Chapter 3 79

VII. MARINE SCIENTIFIC RESEARCH

Article 143 of the Convention provides that:

1. Marine scientific research in the Area shall be carried out exclusively for peaceful purposes and for the benefit of mankind as a whole, in accordance with Part XIII.
2. The Authority may carry out marine scientific research concerning the Area and its resources, and may enter into contracts for that purpose. The Authority shall promote and encourage the conduct of marine scientific research in the Area, and shall co-ordinate and disseminate the results of such research and analysis when available.
3. States Parties may carry out marine scientific research in the Area. States Parties shall promote international co-operation in marine scientific research in the Area by :
   (a) participating in international programmes and encouraging co-operation in marine scientific research by personnel of different countries and of the Authority;
   (b) ensuring that programmes are developed through the Authority or other international organisations as appropriate for the benefit of developing States and technologically less developed States with a view to :
       (i) strengthening their research capabilities;
       (ii) training their personnel and the personnel of the Authority in the techniques and applications of research;
       (iii) fostering the employment of their qualified personnel in research in the Area.
   (c) effectively disseminating the results of research and analysis when available, through the Authority or other international channels when appropriate.

The only provision of Part XIII which refers specifically to marine scientific research in the Area is Article 256:

Article 256
Marine scientific research in the Area

All States, irrespective of their geographical location, and competent international organizations have the right, in conformity with the provisions of Part XI, to conduct marine scientific research in the Area.

The scope *ratione materiae* of Article 143 is not beyond doubt. The question arises whether this provision extends to all marine scientific research in the Area or only to that which relates to 'activities in the Area', that is, 'all activities of exploration for, and exploitation of', mineral resources.[144] Article 143 itself

---

[144] UN Convention, Arts. 1(3) and 133(a).

80   *The Principles of the Regime*

suggests that it embraces all marine scientific research carried out in the Area for peaceful purposes, irrespective of any connection with mineral resources. Such an interpretation is quite consistent with the fundamental principle of Article 136 that 'The Area ... [is] the common heritage of mankind'.

The ambiguity arose because of changes which took place in the text after the Informal Single Negotiating Text (ISNT) was produced in 1975. In the original ISNT, what is now Section 2 of Part XI of the Convention ('Principles governing the Area') was embodied in a single 'Part II: Principles', and 'Activities in the Area' were more broadly defined as follows:

> 'Activities in the Area' means all activities of exploration of the Area and of the exploitation of its resources, *as well as other associated activities in the Area including scientific research.* [145]

The Revised Single Negotiating Text (RSNT), issued in 1976, simply included all the articles on the regime in an undivided Part I[146] and introduced the more restricted definition of 'Activities in the Area' now embodied in the Convention. Commenting on the change, the Chairman of the First Committee said that:

> This does not mean that other activities would not be covered or governed by this Part of the Convention. On the contrary, they are regulated under specific articles. For example, article 10 deals with scientific research, article 11 with transfer of technology and articles 12 and 13 with protection of the marine environment and of human life.[147]

This commentary still left open the question whether Article 10 of RSNT related only to that scientific research which was associated with the exploration or exploitation of the mineral resources of the Area. The question was further complicated when the 1980 Draft Convention (Informal Text) rearranged the provisions of Part XI into a number of 'Sections'.[148] Section 2 covered the 'Principles governing the Area' but Article 143 appeared in a separate Section 3 on 'Conduct of Activities in the Area'. Given the fact that 'Activities in the Area' were defined to mean 'activities of exploration for and exploitation of' mineral resources,[149] this rearrangement could be read as bearing the implication that Article 143 was confined to scientific research associated with such activities in the Area.

However, the 1981 Draft Convention[150] reincorporated Article 143 in the single 'Section 2: Principles Governing the Area'. Given this fact and having regard particularly to the language of Article 143, the better view, on balance,

---

[145] *UNCLOS III Off. Rec.*, Vol. IV, p. 137 (Art.1(ii)), emphasis added.
[146] *UNCLOS III Off. Rec.*, Vol. V, p. 125.
[147] *Ibid.*, at p. 126, para. 10.
[148] A/CONF.62/WP.10/Rev.3, 22 September 1980 and Corr. 1 and 3; Platzoder, *Documents*, Vol. II, p. 179.
[149] Arts. 1(3) and 133(a).
[150] *UNCLOS III Off. Rec.*, Vol. XV, p.172, at pp. 194-195.

Chapter 3 81

would seem to favour the more extensive interpretation, under which the provisions of this Article would extend to all marine research carried out in the Area for peaceful purposes.

VIII. TRANSFER OF TECHNOLOGY

During the negotiations in UNCLOS III, it was accepted by developing and developed States alike that if the mineral resources of the Area were to be effectively exploited as the common heritage of mankind and the developing States given a real opportunity to benefit from the preferential position they enjoy under Article 140, for example,[151] then provision would have to be made to ensure that the Enterprise (the operating arm of the Sea-Bed Authority) and the developing States should receive from the industrialised States the substantial transfer of technology without which the right to participate in sea-bed mining would be meaningless. Accordingly, an obligation to assist the Enterprise and developing countries by transfer of technology relating to 'activities in the Area' was laid down as a principle in Article 144 of the Convention and was further developed in Article 150 and Annex III, Article 5. However, as will be seen below, these provisions were radically amended by the Implementation Agreement of 28 July 1994 in order to accommodate the concerns of the industrialised States.

1. The Principle Stated
The obligation to transfer technology is stated as follows:

Article 144
Transfer of technology

1. The Authority shall take measures in accordance with this Convention:
   (a) to acquire technology and scientific knowledge relating to activities in the Area; and
   (b) to promote and encourage the transfer to developing States of such technology and scientific knowledge so that all States Parties benefit therefrom.
2. To this end the Authority and States Parties shall cooperate in promoting the transfer of technology and scientific knowledge relating to activities in the Area so that the Enterprise and all States Parties may benefit therefrom. In particular they shall initiate and promote:
   (a) programmes for the transfer of technology to the Enterprise and to developing States with regard to activities in the Area, including, *inter alia*, facilitating the access of the Enterprise and of developing States to the relevant technology, under fair and reasonable terms and conditions;

---

[151] See further above, section IV.

82   *The Principles of the Regime*

> (b)   measures directed towards the advancement of the technology of the Enterprise and the domestic technology of developing States, particularly by providing opportunities to personnel from the Enterprise and from developing States for training in marine science and technology and for their full participation in activities in the Area.

Article 144 is supplemented by Article 150, dealing with 'Policies relating to activities in the Area'. Under Paragraphs (c) and (d), activities in the Area are to be carried out so as

> to promote international co-operation for the over-all development of all countries, especially developing States, and with a view to ensuring:
> (c)   the expansion of opportunities for participation in such activities consistent in particular with articles 144 and 148;
> (d)   participation in revenues by the Authority and the transfer of technology to the Enterprise and developing States as provided for in this Convention;

The developing States are understandably anxious to participate in activities in the Area and not to be simply the passive recipients of the fruits of its exploitation. This concern is reflected in the above-mentioned Article 148, which provides that :

> The *effective participation* of developing States in activities in the Area shall be promoted as specifically provided for in this Part, having due regard to their special interests and needs, and in particular to the special need of the land-locked and geographically disadvantaged among them to overcome obstacles arising from their disadvantaged location, including remoteness from the Area and difficulty of access to and from it.[152]

2. Mechanisms for Transfer of Technology

Although the need to transfer technology was fairly readily accepted as one of the principles of the regime of the Area in every Negotiating Text since the original ISNT was published in 1975,[153] the task of transforming the general principle into detailed, specific rules and regulations proved to be less easy.

Throughout the UNCLOS III negotiations, the objective was to formulate a set of obligations which would be sufficiently demanding to ensure that the Enterprise and developing States would have access to the best available technology on reasonable terms, but not so onerous as to be unacceptable to the industrialised States and their investors. The Conference's final attempt to achieve this golden mean was embodied in the complex provisions of Article 5 of

---

[152] Emphasis added.
[153] *UNCLOS III Off.Rec.*, Vol.IV, p.137, at p.139, Art.11.

Chapter 3 83

Annex III's 'Basic conditions of prospecting, exploration and exploitation'.[154] Unfortunately, the labours of the Conference have proved to be in vain, for, under Section 5, Paragraph 2 of the Annex to the Implementation Agreement,[155] 'The provisions of Annex III, article 5 of the Convention shall not apply'. The scope of the obligation to transfer technology is now determined by Section 5, Paragraph 1 of the Annex to the Implementation Agreement, which lays down 'the following principles', described as being in 'addition to the provisions of article 144 of the Convention'[156]:

(a) The Enterprise, and developing States wishing to obtain deep seabed mining technology, shall seek to obtain such technology on fair and reasonable commercial terms and conditions on the open market, or through joint-venture arrangements;

(b) If the Enterprise or developing States are unable to obtain deep seabed mining technology, the Authority may request all or any of the contractors and their respective sponsoring State or States to cooperate with it in facilitating the acquisition of deep seabed mining technology by the Enterprise or its joint venture, or by a developing State or States seeking to acquire such technology on fair and reasonable commercial terms and conditions, consistent with the effective protection of intellectual property rights. States Parties undertake to cooperate fully and effectively with the Authority for this purpose and to ensure that contractors sponsored by them also cooperate fully with the Authority;

(c) As a general rule, States Parties shall promote international technical and scientific cooperation with regard to activities in the Area either between the parties concerned or by developing training, technical assistance and scientific cooperation programmes in marine science and technology and the protection and preservation of the marine environment.

The key which opened the way to this compromise is reflected in the reference made in sub-paragraph (a) to joint venture arrangements as being one of the means whereby the Enterprise and developing States may obtain deep sea-bed mining technology. The now-redundant provisions of Annex III of the UN Convention had also recognised joint ventures as one of the ways in which the Enterprise might acquire the necessary technology.[157] However, under the Implementation Agreement, it has been given much greater emphasis. As will be seen in Chapter 8, the Implementation Agreement provides for the initial

---

[154] For text, see *loc.cit.* in note 76 above, at pp.115-117. For analysis, see the first edition of this work: E.D. Brown, *Sea-Bed Energy and Mineral Resources and the Law of the Sea, Vol.2: The Area Beyond the Limits of National Jurisdiction*, 1986, Chap.3, at pp.II.3 43-52.

[155] *Loc. cit.* in note 5 above.

[156] Implementation Agreement, Annex, Section 5, para.1.

[157] UN Convention, Annex III, Art.5(6).

84 *The Principles of the Regime*

operations of the Enterprise to be conducted by way of joint ventures.[158] For the foreseeable future, therefore, it may be expected that, as envisaged in the discarded Article 5(6) of Annex III, 'In the case of joint ventures with the Enterprise, technology transfer will be in accordance with the terms of the joint venture agreement.'

IX. Protection of the Marine Environment

Chapter 10 of this work presents a detailed study of the legal regime governing pollution from sea-bed mining. Here, only brief reference will be made to the 'protection of the marine environment' as one of the 'principles governing the Area'.

Article 145 of the Convention embodies this principle and provides that :

> Necessary measures shall be taken in accordance with this Convention with respect to activities in the Area to ensure effective protection for the marine environment from harmful effects which may arise from such activities. To this end the Authority shall adopt appropriate rules, regulations and procedures for *inter alia*:
>
> (a) the prevention, reduction and control of pollution and other hazards to the marine environment, including the coastline, and of interference with the ecological balance of the marine environment, particular attention being paid to the need for protection from harmful effects of such activities as drilling, dredging, excavation, disposal of waste, construction and operation or maintenance of installations, pipelines and other devices related to such activities;
>
> (b) the protection and conservation of the natural resources of the Area and the prevention of damage to the flora and fauna of the marine environment.

In an earlier draft of this provision[159], such 'necessary measures' were to be taken 'in accordance with Part XII' of the Convention and although the reference to Part XII later disappeared, the principal relevant provisions are still to be found there in Article 209 (Pollution from activities in the Area) and 215 (Enforcement with respect to pollution from activities in the Area). Article 209 provides for the establishment of international rules, regulations and procedures in accordance with Part XI of the Convention, that is, by the Authority pursuant to Article 145.[160] States Parties have the complementary duty to adopt national laws and regulations to prevent, reduce and control pollution from activities in the Area

---

[158] Chapter 8, section II, especially section II.2.1.3, referring to Implementation Agreement, Annex, Section 2, para.2.

[159] Draft Convention on the Law of the Sea (Informal Text), A/CONF.62/WP.10/Rev.3, 22 September 1980 and Corr. 1 and 3.

[160] For an analysis of the relevant regulations included in the Mining Code, see below, Chap. 10, section IV.

Chapter 3 85

undertaken by 'vessels, installations, structures and other devices flying their flag, or of their registry or operating under their authority, as the case may be'.

As regards enforcement, Article 215 simply provides that enforcement of international rules etc. shall be governed by Part XI. The relevant provisions are in Article 185 and Annex III, Article 18. Article 185 provides that if a State Party has grossly and persistently violated the provisions of Part XI, it may be suspended from the exercise of the rights and privileges of membership of the Authority by the Assembly upon the recommendation of the Council. However, no such action may be taken until the Sea-Bed Disputes Chamber has found that there has indeed been such a gross and persistent violation. Article 18 of Annex III makes provision for the imposition of penalties on contractors for violation of the terms of contracts. They range from suspension or termination of rights under the contract to monetary penalties.

The provisions on responsibility will also help to make the rules on protection of the environment more effective. As has been seen[161], Article 139 places a qualified liability on States Parties for damage caused by their failure to ensure compliance with Part XI. In addition, Article 22 of Annex III imposes liability on the contractor for any damage arising out of wrongful acts in the conduct of its operations.[162]

X. PROTECTION OF HUMAN LIFE

Article 146 provides that :

> With respect to activities in the Area, necessary measures shall be taken to ensure effective protection of human life. To this end the Authority shall adopt appropriate rules, regulations and procedures to supplement existing international law as embodied in relevant treaties.

The power of the Authority to 'adopt and uniformly apply rules, regulations and procedures' for the implementation of Part XI of the Convention is further spelled out in Annex III, Article 17. Though no specific reference is made to the protection of human life, Article 17(1)(b)(xii) does refer to 'mining standards and practices, including those relating to operational safety'. Three of the organs of the Authority have a part to play in adopting these rules, regulations and procedures. First, under Article 165 (2)(f), the Legal and Technical Commission has to formulate and submit rules, regulations and procedures to the Council. It also has the duty to keep them under review and recommend necessary or desirable amendments (Article 165(2)(g)). Secondly, under Article 162(2)(o)(ii), the Council adopts the rules, regulations and procedures and applies them provisionally, pending final adoption by the Assembly under Article 160(2)(f)(ii).[163] Under the Implementation Agreement, in adopting rules,

---

[161] Section V above.
[162] See further below, Chapter 4, section XIV.
[163] See also Implementation Agreement, Annex, Section 1, para.15, which further develops the role of the Council in the adoption of rules, regulations and procedures under Art.162(2)(o)(ii).

86 The Principles of the Regime

regulations and procedures, the Authority has to take into account the draft rules, regulations and procedures and any recommendations relating to the provisions of Part XI contained in the reports and recommendations of the Preparatory Commission.[164]

Enforcement would again be effected under Article 185 and Annex III, Paragraph 18.[165]

The reference in Article 146 to 'existing international law as embodied in relevant treaties' is a masterpiece of vagueness. However, it is clear from the Mining Code that the 'relevant treaties' include the International Convention for the Safety of Life at Sea (SOLAS), 1974,[166] the Convention on the International Regulations for Preventing Collisions at Sea (COLREG), 1972[167], and the conventions and recommendations of the International Labour Organisation. [168]

XI. ACCOMMODATION OF ACTIVITIES IN THE AREA AND IN THE MARINE ENVIRONMENT

Article 147(1) of the UN Convention provides that 'Activities in the Area shall be carried out with reasonable regard for other activities in the marine environment'. It is thus reciprocal to Article 87(2) which provides that the freedoms of the high seas 'shall be exercised by all States ... with due regard for the rights under this Convention with respect to activities in the Area.' More comprehensively, Article 147(3) requires that 'Other activities in the marine environment shall be conducted with reasonable regard for activities in the Area.'

Paragraph 2 of Article 147 embodies rules concerning the erection, emplacement and removal of installations used for carrying out activities in the Area:

Installations used for carrying out activities in the Area shall be subject to the following conditions:

---

[164]Implementation Agreement, Annex, Section 1, para.16. Part XI of the draft Sea-Bed Mining Code prepared by the Preparatory Commission's Special Commission 3 deals with 'Labour, Health and Safety Standards'. See further, Draft Regulations on Prospecting, Exploration and Exploitation of Polymetallic Nodules in the Area, Part XI, LOS/PCN/SCN.3/WP.6/Add.8/Rev. 1, 15 January 1993, in *XIII Final PrepCom Report*, pp. 245-251.

[165] See under IX above.

[166] See *SOLAS. Consolidated Edition, 1992*, IMO-110E, 1992, which contains the text of SOLAS 1974 (entered into force 25 May 1980), SOLAS PROT 1978 (entered into force 1 May 1981) and a consolidated text of these two instruments embodying also all amendments up to and including the 1990 amendments (the 1991 amendments, which entered into force on 1 January 1994 are in Appendix 2). Further amendments have since been made and entered into force. A further Protocol to the Convention (SOLAS PROT 1988) was adopted on 11 November 1988 (*Protocol of 1988 relating to the International Convention for the Safety of Life at Sea, 1974 (1989 edition)*, IMO Doc. IMO-150E) and entered into force on 3 February 2000.

[167] For COLREG 1972, as amended in 1981, 1987 and 1989, see *International Conference on Revision of the International Regulations for Preventing Collisions at Sea, 1972* (1990 edition), IMO Doc. IMO-904E. Further amendments made in 1993 entered into force on 4 November 1995.

[168] On the provisions of the Mining Code, particularly Reg.21(4)(a) and Annex 4, Section 15, see below, Chap. 5, section I.4.2.2.2.

Chapter 3 87

(a) such installations shall be erected, emplaced and removed solely in accordance with this Part and subject to the rules, regulations and procedures of the Authority. Due notice must be given of the erection, emplacement and removal of such installations, and permanent means for giving warning of their presence must be maintained;
(b) such installations may not be established where interference may be caused to the use of recognised sea lanes essential to international navigation or in areas of intense fishing activity;
(c) safety zones shall be established around such installations with appropriate markings to ensure the safety of both navigation and the installations. The configuration and locations of such safety zones shall not be such as to form a belt impeding the lawful access of shipping to particular maritime zones or navigation along international sea lanes;
(d) such installations shall be used exclusively for peaceful purposes;
(e) such installations do not possess the status of islands. They have no territorial sea of their own, and their presence does not affect the delimitation of the territorial sea, the exclusive economic zone or the continental shelf.

Difficulties might arise over whether a sea lane is 'essential to international navigation' or an area is one of 'intense fishing activity' under Sub-paragraph (b). No doubt they can be overcome, however, by the adoption by the Authority of rules, regulations and procedures designed for the 'prevention of interference with other activities in the marine environment' under Annex III, Article 17(l)(b)(ix) and/or by contractual clauses regarding the location of such installations.[169] So far as exploration is concerned, provision has already been made requiring the Legal and Technical Commission to determine, when considering an application for approval of a plan of work, whether the proposed plan of work will 'ensure that installations are not established where interference may be caused to the use of recognised sea lanes essential to international navigation or in areas of intense fishing activity'. [170]

Article 147 is of course concerned with installations in the Area only in so far as they may cause a conflict with other activities in the marine environment. It is therefore understandable that Article 147(2) does not contain rules on jurisdiction over such installations similar to those found in Articles 60(2) and 80

---

[169] *Cf.* Arts.60 and 80 of the UN Convention concerning the EEZ and the continental shelf. Art.60(7) provides that 'Artificial islands, installations and structures and the safety zones around them may not be established where interference may be caused to the use of recognised sea lanes essential to international navigation'. Compliance is secured by way of licence conditions which may be framed by reference to the routing schemes adopted by IMO and made mandatory under the 1972 Collision Regulations. For model licence clauses, see the United Kingdom's Petroleum Act 1998, s. 5 and sch. 1 and the Petroleum (Current Model Clauses) Order 1999 (S.I. 1999/160).
[170] Mining Code, Reg. 21(4)(c). Contractors must give an undertaking to carry out the programme of activities 'with reasonable regard for other activities in the marine environment' (Mining Code, Annex 4, Section 13.3(c)).

88 *The Principles of the Regime*

for installations in the EEZ and on the continental shelf.[171] At first sight, it may be thought to be surprising that Article 147 does not follow these Articles in specifying a maximum breadth for safety zones around installations. However, this may well be due to the fact that the provision applies to both stationary and mobile installations[172] and it would, of course, be difficult to prescribe for the latter anything like the 500-metre zones applicable to EEZ/continental shelf installations.

XII. PARTICIPATION OF DEVELOPING STATES IN ACTIVITIES IN THE AREA

Article 148 provides that:

> The effective participation of developing States in activities in the Area shall be promoted as specifically provided for in this Part, having due regard to their special interests and needs, and in particular to the special need of the land-locked and geographically disadvantaged among them to overcome obstacles arising from their disadvantaged location, including remoteness from the Area and difficulty of access to and from it.

Although Article 148 is concerned only with the 'participation' of developing States, its provisions can be best understood if viewed in the wider context of the principle of preferential treatment accorded to developing States throughout Part XI. Some of the rules underlying this principle have already been referred to above. Thus, under Article 140 ('Benefit of mankind') and Article 162(2)(o)(i), particular consideration was to be given, in sharing the benefits derived from activities in the Area, to the interests and needs of the developing States and peoples who had not attained full independence or other self-governing status.[173] Again, it was seen that, under Article 141, read with Article 152, special consideration for developing countries in granting opportunities for activities in the Area was permitted.[174] Under Article 143, marine scientific research programmes were to be developed for the benefit of developing States[175] and provision was made for the transfer of technology to them under Article 144.[176] Finally, reference was made above to the provision made for review of the regime of sea-bed mining.[177] One of the matters which might be considered at any time is whether the Convention system has 'resulted in the equitable sharing

---

[171] See, however, Art.153(5) of the Convention, under which the Authority has the right to inspect all installations in the Area used in connection with activities in the Area and Annex III, Art.17(1)(b)(viii), which provides for the adoption by the Authority of rules, regulations and procedures on 'inspection and supervision of operations'. Provision for inspection is made in Section 14 of the 'Standard Clauses for Exploration Contract' (Mining Code, Annex 4).

[172] Art.147(2) of the Draft Convention on the Law of the Sea, 1981 (*UNCLOS III Off.Rec.*, Vol.XV, p.172) specifically referred to 'stationary and mobile installations.'

[173] See further above, sections I.5 and IV.

[174] See further above, section III.

[175] See further above, section VII.

[176] See further above, section VIII.

[177] See above, section I.4.

Chapter 3 89

of benefits derived from activities in the Area, taking into particular consideration the interests and needs of the developing States'.[178]

Article 150 lays down 'Policies relating to activities in the Area'. They include the promotion of 'international co-operation for the over-all development of all countries, especially developing States', with a view to ensuring, *inter alia*:

> ...
> (c) the expansion of opportunities for participation in such activities consistent in particular with articles 144 [transfer of technology] and 148 [participation of developing countries];
> (d) participation in revenues by the Authority and the transfer of technology to the Enterprise and developing States as provided for in this Convention;
> ...
> (h) the protection of developing countries from adverse effects on their economies or on their export earnings resulting from a reduction in the price of an affected mineral, or in the volume of exports of that mineral, to the extent that such reduction is caused by activities in the Area, as provided in article 151.

The said Article 151 embodied a set of 'Production policies', and made complex provision for limitations to be placed on production of minerals from the Area during an interim period. However, the Implementation Agreement abandoned this policy of production limitation and provided that most of the paragraphs of Article 151 'shall not apply' any longer. Nonetheless, Paragraph 10 survives and provides that:

> Upon the recommendation of the Council on the basis of advice from the Economic Planning Commission, the Assembly shall establish a system of compensation or take other measures of economic adjustment assistance including co-operation with specialised agencies and other international organisations to assist developing countries which suffer serious adverse effects on their export earnings or economies resulting from a reduction in the price of an affected mineral or in the volume of exports of that mineral, to the extent that such reduction is caused by activities in the Area. The Authority on request shall initiate studies on the problems of those States which are likely to be most seriously affected with a view to minimising their difficulties and assisting them in their economic adjustment.

Although the principle of helping developing countries through some form of economic assistance thus survived, its implementation is now governed by the Implementation Agreement. Under Section 7 of the Annex to the Agreement, the policy of the Authority on economic assistance is to be based on four principles and Article 151(10) of the Convention is to be implemented by means

---

[178] Implementation Agreement, Annex, Section 4 and UN Convention, Art.155(1)(f).

90 *The Principles of the Regime*

of the measures of economic assistance referred to in these principles.[179] Assistance is to be provided from an economic assistance fund to be established by the Authority and based on a portion of the funds of the Authority which exceeds those necessary to cover its administrative expenses. The size of the fund will be determined from time to time by the Council, acting on the recommendations of the Finance Committee.[180] Given the composition of the Finance Committee, the industrialised States should be in a position to ensure that excessive amounts are not set aside for this purpose.[181] In any event, only funds from payments received from contractors, including the Enterprise, and voluntary contributions are to be used for the establishment of the economic assistance fund.[182] The economic assistance fund was set up by Regulation 5.8 of the Authority's Financial Regulations, which became effective on 23 March 2000. [183]

Several of the organs of the International Sea-Bed Authority have parts to play in giving effect to the preferential position of the developing States. The roles of the Council and the Assembly in the equitable sharing of benefits derived from the Area have already been referred to above[184] and it has been noted too that the Council, Assembly and Economic Planning Commission were all to be involved in establishing the system of economic assistance for developing State mineral exporters.[185] The 'Powers and functions' of the Assembly also include the consideration of :

> problems of a general nature in connection with activities in the Area arising in particular for developing States, as well as those problems for States in connection with activities in the Area that are due to their geographical location, particularly for land-locked and geographically disadvantaged States;[186]

The interests of the developing countries were again catered for in the provision made in Article 161 of the UN Convention for the representation of developing States Parties in the 36-member Council. However, these provisions have now been replaced by the new rules embodied in the Implementation Agreement, which introduced a system of 'chambered' voting.[187] As a general rule, decision

---

[179] Implementation Agreement, Annex, Section 7, paras.1 and 2.

[180] *Ibid.*, para.1(a). The UN Convention allocated roles in the implementation of Art.151(10) to the Assembly (Art.160(2)(l)), the Council (Art.162(2)(n)) and the Economic Planning Commission (Art.164(2)(d)) and authorised the use of the Authority's funds for this purpose (Arts.171(f) and 173(2)(c)). These provisions have now to be interpreted in the light of the new scheme for the implementation of Article 151(10) laid down in the Implementation Agreement (Implementation Agreement, Annex, Section 7, para.2).

[181] On the Finance Committee, see further Chap.8, section II.1.2.3.2.

[182] Implementation Agreement, Annex, Section 7, para.1(a).

[183] ISBA/6/A/3, 28 March 2000, Annex. On the 'Financial Arrangements of the Authority', see further, Chap. 8, section II.3. On the new arrangements for economic assistance, see further , Chap. 4. Section VI.2.

[184] See above, section I.5.3.7.

[185] See note 180 above.

[186] Art.160(2)(k).

[187] Implementation Agreement, Annex, Section 3.

Chapter 3 91

making in the Council is to be by consensus[188] and decisions may be deferred to facilitate the achievement of consensus.[189] If, however, all efforts to reach a decision by consensus have been exhausted, decisions on most questions of substance are to be taken by a two-thirds majority vote, provided that such decisions are not opposed by a majority in any one of four chambers or groups of States, representing respectively sea-bed mineral consumers, investors in sea-bed mining, major net exporters of minerals derived from the Area, and developing States elected to the Council.[190] The most contentious element of this compromise formula concerned representation of developing States. Eventually, it was agreed that the developing States elected to the Council under Section 3, paragraph 15(d) of the Annex to the Agreement (6 developing States representing a range of 'special interests') and paragraph 15(e) (18 States, developing or developed, elected to ensure equitable geographical representation in the Council as a whole) should be treated as a single chamber.[191]

Annex III of the Convention on 'Basic conditions of prospecting, exploration and exploitation' contains a number of provisions embodying preferences favourable to developing States:-

Prospecting. Under Article 2(b), prospecting may be conducted only after the Authority has received a written undertaking that the proposed prospector will comply with the Convention and the rules, regulations and procedures of the Authority concerning *inter alia* 'co-operation in the training programmes referred to in articles 143 [on marine scientific research] and 144 [on transfer of technology]'.[192]

Reservation of sites. As will be seen in Chapter 4,[193] the Authority has to designate one of the two parts of the area specified in an application for a contract as a reserved site in which activities may be conducted only by the Authority through the Enterprise or in association with developing States. Article 9 of Annex III regulates activities in reserved sites and provides that, when the Enterprise is considering entering into a joint venture, it 'shall offer to State Parties which are developing States and their nationals the opportunity of effective participation'.[194] Paragraph 4 of the same Article allows developing States or their nationals to submit plans of work for such reserved sites which 'shall be considered' if the Enterprise decides not to carry out activities in that site itself.

Joint Arrangements and 'incentives'. Under Article 11 of Annex III, contractors entering into 'joint arrangements' (including joint ventures or production sharing) with the Enterprise may receive financial incentives and it is provided in Article 13(1)(d) that the Authority, in adopting rules, regulations, and

---

[188] *Ibid.*, Section 3, para.2.
[189] *Ibid.*, para.6.
[190] *Ibid.*, paras.5 and 9.
[191] *Ibid.*, para.9(a).
[192] Reg. 3(4)(d)(i)(a) of the Mining Code is to the same effect. On marine scientific research, see further above, section VII and on transfer of technology, section VIII.
[193] Chap.4, section VII.
[194] UN Convention, Annex III, Art.9(2).

92 *The Principles of the Regime*

procedures concerning the financial terms of a contract and in negotiating these terms, is to be guided by a number of objectives, including that of providing incentives on a uniform and non-discriminatory basis for contractors to undertake joint arrangements with the Enterprise and developing States or their nationals, to stimulate the transfer of technology thereto, and to train the personnel of the Authority and of developing States.

Article 13(14) complements this provision:

The Authority may, taking into account any recommendations of the Economic Planning Commission and the Legal and Technical Commission, adopt rules, regulations and procedures that provide for incentives, on a uniform and non-discriminatory basis, to contractors to further the objectives set out in paragraph 1.

Article 17(1)(c)(iii) provides for the adoption of rules, regulations and procedures for these incentives.

Training programmes. The obligation to provide training programmes for personnel of developing countries has been referred to above[195] and it is further specified in Article 15 of Annex III:

Training programmes

The contractor shall draw up practical programmes for the training of personnel of the Authority and developing States, including the participation of such personnel in all activities in the Area which are covered by the contract, in accordance with article 144, paragraph 2.[196]

Regulation 27 of the Mining Code is in similar terms.

XIII. ARCHAEOLOGICAL AND HISTORICAL OBJECTS

Provision is made for the preservation or disposal of objects of an archaeological and historical nature found in the Area by Article 149 of the UN Convention, as follows:

Article 149
Archaeological and historical objects

All objects of an archaeological and historical nature found in the Area shall be preserved or disposed of for the benefit of mankind as a whole, particular regard being paid to the preferential rights of the State or country of origin,

---

[195] In sections VII and VIII.

[196] Art.144(2) has now to be read with Section 5, para.1(c) of the Annex to the Implementation Agreement. See further section VIII above. See also below, Chap. 6, section III.8-11 and section IV.3 for obligations of registered pioneer investors as regards training.

Chapter 3 93

or the State of cultural origin, or the State of historical and archaeological origin.

It seems most unlikely that this Article will be of any practical significance unless it is subsequently used as a basis for further developments elsewhere. This is so for a number of reasons. First, it is irrelevant in important areas, such as the Mediterranean, where there is no 'Area' beyond the limits of national jurisdiction. Secondly, since archaeological and historical objects are not 'resources' of the Area, as defined in Article 133, and the Authority is not empowered, under Article 157, to organise and control activities in relation to them or to administer them, it is difficult to see how effect is to be given to this principle. Thirdly, the meaning of the phrase 'shall be preserved or disposed of for the benefit of mankind as a whole' is quite obscure. Presumably, the benefit envisaged is one of cultural enrichment rather than material gain, but what would constitute an acceptable arrangement and how effect would be given to the preferential rights identified in this provision are questions to which no clear answers can be given.[197]

The limited rôle of the Authority is also reflected in the Mining Code. Regulation 8 requires a prospector to immediately notify the Secretary-General in writing of any finding of an object of an archaeological or historical nature and its location. The Secretary-General must then transmit this information to the Director-General of UNESCO. Regulation 34 imposes a similar obligation upon a contractor engaged in seabed mining exploration and also requires that, following a finding in the exploration area, the contractor must take all reasonable measures to avoid disturbing such object.

The position of the underwater cultural heritage of the Area has also been considered in UNESCO in the course of the still-continuing efforts to draft a

---

[197] However, it is arguable that the reference to disposal suggests that the objects may be sold. If so, by whom, to whom and how would the proceeds be employed 'for the benefit of mankind as a whole'? An early Turkish proposal submitted to the UN Sea-Bed Committee in 1973, prior to UNCLOS III, envisaged that if the 'State of the country of origin' did not exercise its preferential right, the object might be sold to 'authorised third parties' (Draft article under Point 23. Archaeological and Historical Treasures on the Sea-Bed and the Ocean Floor beyond the Limits of National Jurisdiction, A/AC.138/SC.I/L.21, 28 March 1973).

On the status of submarine antiquities, see further A.C. Arend, 'Archaelogical and Historical Objects: the International Legal Implications of UNCLOS III', 22 *Virginia* JIL (1982), pp. 777-803; F.M. Auburn, 'Deep Sea Archaeology and the Law', 2 *International Journal of Nautical Archaeology and Underwater Exploration* (1973), pp.159-162; L. Caflisch, 'Submarine Antiquities and the International Law of the Sea', *Netherlands YBIL* (1982), pp.3-32; L.V. Prott and P.J. O'Keefe, *Law and the Cultural Heritage*, Vol.I, 1984; and L.V. Prott and P.J. O'Keefe, 'International Legal Protection of the Underwater Cultural Heritage', 14 *Revue belge de droit international* (1978-1979), pp.85-103; A. Strati, *The Protection of the Underwater Cultural Heritage*, 1995; L.H. van Meurs, *Legal Aspects of Marine Archaeological Research*, 1985; and *The Protection of the Underwater Cultural Heritage* (Special Issue of *Marine Policy* in Vol.20, No.4, 1996, Guest Editor A. Couper).

On the related question of freedom of archaeological research in the continental shelf and the European Convention on the Protection of the Archaeological Heritage of 6 May 1969, see E.D. Brown 'Freedom of Scientific Research and the Legal Regime of Hydrospace', 9 *Indian Journal of International Law* (No. 3, 1969), p. 327, at pp.353 and 357-358. See also H. Crane Miller, *International Law and Marine Archaeology* (Monograph of U.S. Academy of Applied Science), 1973.

94   *The Principles of the Regime*

Convention on the Protection of the Underwater Cultural Heritage. [198] The latest version of the Draft Convention [199] makes provision for the underwater cultural heritage in the Area in Article 7 bis. It provides that any discovery of underwater cultural heritage in the Area must be reported by the finder to the Secretary-General of the International Seabed Authority, which must then transmit the information to the UNESCO Director-General. This version would, of course, be consistent with the provisions of the Mining Code. There is, however, an alternative version in draft Article 7, under which the reporting obligations would fall upon the State Party whose nationals or vessels flying its flag made the discovery. The report would be made to the Director-General of UNESCO who would then transmit it to the Secretary-General of the Authority. Given the Authority's very limited rôle in relation to the underwater cultural heritage, [200] it is not clear what action is expected to follow the transmission of such information. It is true that Article 7(2) of the Draft Convention provides that UNESCO shall inform of the discovery all States that enjoy preferential rights under Article 149 of the UN Convention. However, how such rights are to be asserted vis-à-vis seabed activities in the Area is not clear.

Although it is not concerned with the regime of the Area or the common heritage of mankind, it may be appropriate to refer here to the only other provision of the Convention on archaeological and historical objects. Article 303, on 'Archaeological and historical objects found at sea', is included among Part XVI's 'General Provisions'. Paragraph 1 is straightforward enough, providing that:

> States have the duty to protect objects of an archaeological and historical nature found at sea and shall co-operate for this purpose.

Paragraph 2, on the other hand, calls for a word of explanation. It provides that:

> In order to control traffic in such objects, the coastal State may, in applying Article 33, presume that their removal from the sea-bed in the zone referred to in that article without its approval would result in an infringement within its territory or territorial sea of the laws and regulations referred to in that article.

---

[198] See further, E D Brown, 'The Draft Convention on the Protection of the Underwater Cultural Heritage' (presented at Congreso Iberoamericano de Derecho Marítimo, Huatulco, Mexico, November 1999), especially section 2.7.

[199] *Draft Convention on the Protection of the Underwater Cultural Heritage*, CLT-96/CONF.202/5 Rev. 2; CLT-98/CONF.202/CLD.5, July 1999.

[200] Although Art. 149 of the UN Convention makes provision for the preservation or disposal of underwater cultural heritage found in the Area for the benefit of mankind as a whole, the 'activities in the Area' over which the Authority has authority do not include underwater cultural heritage (see UN Convention, Arts. 1(1)(3) and 133(a)). Art. 140 (*Benefit of mankind*) enables the Authority to provide for equitable sharing, but this relates to 'financial and other economic benefits derived from activities in the Area', that is, in relation to mineral resources.

Chapter 3 95

As was seen above, the legal status of such objects situated in the Area is governed, however vaguely, by Article 149; and, at the other end of the spectrum, such objects on the bed of the territorial sea would fall within the sovereignty of the coastal State. This leaves for further consideration the intervening (and overlapping) maritime zones, the 24-mile contiguous zone and the 200-mile exclusive economic zone. No specific provision for the protection of objects of an archaeological or historical nature in the EEZ is to be found in the Convention but Article 303(2) does refer to the position in the contiguous zone, presumably on the supposition that this is where additional powers are most needed.

Normally, the preventive and punitive powers enjoyed by the coastal State in the contiguous zone under Article 33 have to be exercised in relation to the infringement of regulations *within its territory or territorial sea*. In other words, the coastal State would have, in the contiguous zone, the control necessary to prevent and punish infringement of regulations designed to prevent the removal of such objects *from its territory or territorial sea*. The effect of Article 303(2) is to empower the coastal State to treat the removal of such objects from the bed of the contiguous zone as if they were removed from its territory or territorial sea. It would thus be able to exercise preventive or punitive control over the perpetrators in the contiguous zone and, it would seem, enjoy a right of hot pursuit from the zone under Article 111(1).

Nor need there be any doubt about the import of the words 'the coastal State may ... presume that their removal ... *would result in* an infringement ... ' (emphasis added); for, reporting on the negotiations which led to this formulation, the Conference President said that ' ... the reference in the second paragraph to "result in an infringement" was understood to mean that it would constitute or constituted an infringement within its territory or territorial sea'.[201]

The remaining Paragraphs of Article 303 are less complicated, providing that:

3. Nothing in this article affects the rights of identifiable owners, the law of salvage or other rules of admiralty, or laws and practices with respect to cultural exchanges.
4. This article is without prejudice to other international agreements and rules of international law regarding the protection of objects of an archaeological and historical nature.

---

[201] A/CONF.62/L/58, 22 August 1980 (*UNCLOS III Off.Rec.*, Vol.XIV, p.128), at p.129, para.14.

CHAPTER 4

The UN Convention Regime of Sea-Bed Mining:
II. The Basic Regime for the Development of the Resources of the Area

Having considered the principles of the regime governing activities in the Area, the next task is to examine the detailed rules regulating the 'development of resources of the Area'.[1] In this chapter an account is given of the basic regime embodied in the UN Convention itself, as modified by the Implementation Agreement of 28 July 1994. As has been seen in Chapter 1, a scheme for the protection of Pioneer Investors was grafted on to the basic regime during the final session of UNCLOS III and Chapter 6 presents an examination of that scheme as it has developed from its origins in Conference Resolution II.

Unfortunately, at the present time, the presentation of an account of even the basic Convention regime is no easy task. Originally, the rules were laid down in the six articles of Section 3 of Part XI of the UN Convention, supplemented by Annex III on 'Basic conditions of prospecting, exploration and exploitation'. However, under Annex III, Article 17, it was left to the Authority to adopt rules, regulations and procedures for the exercise of its functions on a wide range of matters, and, under UNCLOS III's Resolution I, the Preparatory Commission was mandated to 'prepare draft rules, regulations and procedures, as necessary, to enable the Authority to commence its functions ...'.[2] At its first session, the Preparatory Commission established four Special Commissions and one of them, Special Commission 3 (SCN.3), was charged with the preparation of rules, regulations and procedures for the exploration and exploitation of polymetallic nodules in the Area, that is, the 'sea-bed mining code'.[3]

---

[1] Title of Section 3 of Part XI of the UN Convention on the Law of the Sea, 1982.
[2] Resolution I of UNCLOS III on the Establishment of the Preparatory Commission for the International Sea-Bed Authority and for the International Tribunal for the Law of the Sea (United Nations, *The Law of the Sea. United Nations Convention on the Law of the Sea*, 1983, UN Sales Publication No.E.83.V.5, at pp. 175-176; also reproduced in Vol.3 as Doc. No. 14.1) , para 5 (g).
[3] The Preparatory Commission had to prepare a final report on all matters within its mandate (except practical arrangements for the establishment of the International Tribunal for the Law of the Sea) for

The Basic Regime 97

From the beginning of SCN.3's work, there was 'general support for the idea of making the mining code comprehensive, that is to say a document which can be read independently of the Convention and Annex III'.[4] This meant 'that users of the code [would] ... have only one piece of reference material, i.e. the code, and [would] ... therefore have no need to refer to the Convention or to its annexes'.[5] Nonetheless, it was envisaged that certain articles of the Convention and Annex III would appear in Annex III of the code for reference purposes.[6]

The objective of SCN.3 was well summed up in the following passage from an early background paper prepared by the Secretariat:

> In the formulation of these rules, regulations and procedures, the primary objective should be to enable the Authority to better carry into effect the provisions of the Convention relating to the conduct of activities in the Area. The rules, regulations and procedures are subsidiary and supplementary to the Convention and are required to be drafted in greater detail and structured in such a way that they become in fact the day-to-day working instruments of the Authority.[7]

---

presentation to the Assembly at its first session, at the end of which, on 18 August 1995, it ceased to exist (Resolution I of UNCLOS III, paras.10, 11 and 13). When PrepCom met in August 1994, it had already adopted its provisional final report (*Consolidated Provisional Final Report*, Vol.I, LOS/PCN/130, 17 November 1993, containing reports of Plenary and Special Commissions 1-4). Vols.II-VI contain the Documents of Plenary and the four Special Commissions, as listed in LOS/PCN/130/ Add.1, 19 January 1994. It 'decided to consider as its final report the provisional final report on all matters within its mandate, except as provided in paragraph 10 of resolution I, supplemented by any further reports and recommendations which the Preparatory Commission has adopted' (LOS/PCN/L.115/Rev.1, 8 September 1994, at p.11). Referring to para.13 of General Assembly Resolution 48/263 which, in adopting the Implementation Agreement, called upon PrepCom to take into account the terms of that Agreement when drawing up its final report, PrepCom decided, 'in the light of the fact that it had had insufficient time to revise the contents of its provisional final report', to recommend to the Authority that it should take into account the terms of the Agreement in its consideration of the recommendations and the report of PrepCom 'in order to ensure consistency as necessary' (*ibid.*, at p.12). The definitive version of the Preparatory Commission's Report, as submitted to the first session of the Authority's Assembly, was re-packaged in 13 vols: *Report of the Preparatory Commission, under Paragraph 11 of Resolution I of the Third United Nations Conference on the Law of the Sea, on All Matters within its Mandate, Except as Provided in Paragraph 10, for Presentation to the Assembly of the International Seabed Authority at its First Session*, LOS/PCN/153 (Vols. I - XIII), June-July 1995 (referred to hereafter as *Final Prepcom Report*). For the reports and documentation of SCN.3, see vols. XII - XIII. For an overview of its work and a brief account of the regulations it drafted, see Vol.XIII, pp.311-323 ('Draft Provisional Report of Special Commission 3').

[4] *Statement to the Plenary by the Chairman of Special Commission 3 on the Progress of the Work in that Commission*, LOS/PCN/L.11, 4 September 1984, XII *Final Prepcom Report*, p.7, at para 3; *I Platzöder (PrepCom)*, p.462, at para.3.

[5] *Draft Regulations on Prospecting, Exploration and Exploitation of Polymetallic Nodules in the Area (Parts I-IV)*, LOS/PCN/SCN.3/WP.6/Rev.1, 6 June 1988, XIII *Final PrepCom Report*, p.66, at p.67, para. 2; VI *Platzoder (PrepCom)*, p.425, at p.426, para.2.

[6] *Ibid.*, para.3.

[7] *Special Commission for the Preparation of Rules, Regulations and Procedures for the Exploration and Exploitation of the Area (Sea-Bed Mining Code). Background paper by the Secretariat*, LOS/PCN/SCN.3/WP.1, 8 March 1984, VI *Platzöder (PrepCom)*, p.263, at para.2.

98 Chapter 4

It was of course essential, if the code was to be used as a day-to-day working instrument, that the rules, regulations and procedures contained in it should be consistent with the principal instrument, the Convention and its Annex III, and there were many occasions during the negotiation of the code when delegates had to be reminded of this fact.[8]   The relationship between the code and the Convention was accurately stated in a progress report made by the Chairman of SCN.3 in April 1985:

> It was stressed that the regulations needed to be clear and unambiguous and to leave no doubt as to what an applicant had to do and what the Authority had to do.   It was also stressed that the language of the code should correspond as closely as possible with that found in the Convention.   It was also pointed out that the code was a regulatory, not a constitutional document.   Although the code may be comprehensive and could be read independently from the Convention, it was not legally independent from the Convention.   The point was made that in drafting the regulations the right procedural order should be retained.[9]

Over a period of 10 years, SCN.3 succeeded in producing Draft Regulations on Prospecting, Exploration and Exploitation of Polymetallic Nodules in the Area[10] and completed a first revision of its various constituent parts, with the exception of the documents dealing with production authorisations and accounting principles and procedures.[11]   However, when, in March 1993, SCN.3 completed its labours, much remained to be done.   It is observed in the conclusion to its Draft Provisional Report that, 'Although some issues remain to be resolved, a number of the provisions of the draft mining code have in effect met with the approval of delegations'.[12]   Some might feel that the position was more accurately stated in the earlier draft of the conclusion, where it was acknowledged that, 'While progress has been made in identifying and resolving some issues, the Special Commission has not yet reached final agreement on any of the working papers'.[13]   This was hardly surprising.   As was pointed out by a number of delegations, '... it was impossible to reach a final agreement on any of the drafts contained in documents LOS/PCN/SCN.3/WP.6, its addenda 1-8 and

---

[8] See, *e.g.*, *Statement to the Plenary by the Chairman of Special Commission 3 of the Progress of Work in that Commission*, LOS/PCN/L.64, 1 September 1988, XII *Final Prepcom Report*, p.69, at p.71, para. 12; *II Platzöder (PrepCom)*, p.238, at p.240, para.12.

[9] *Statement to the Plenary by the Chairman of Special Commission 3 on the Progress of Work in that Commission*, LOS/PCN/L.16, 2 April 1985, XII *Final Prepcom Report*, p.14, at pp.14-15, para.3; I *Platzöder (PrepCom)*, p.479, at pp.479-480, para.3.

[10] LOS/PCN/SCN.3/WP.6 and Adds. 1-8 (XIII *Final PrepCom Report*, pp.17-238).   For Add.8/Rev.1, see LOS/PCN/SCN.3/1993/CRP.17/Add.1, 15 January 1993 (XIII *Final PrepCom Report*, pp.240-251).

[11] LOS/PCN/L.106, 19 August 1992 (XII *Final PrepCom Report*, p.146, at p.150, para. 23).

[12] *Draft Provisional Report of Special Commission 3* (XIII *Final PrepCom Report*, p.311, at p.323, para.316).

[13] LOS/PCN/SCN.3/1992/CRP.17, 22 July 1992 (XIII *Final PrepCom Report*, p.3, at p.16, para.67).

the first revisions as long as there was no agreement on the areas of concern in Part XI'.[14]

It was indeed the purpose of the Informal Consultations sponsored by the UN Secretary-General, which were conducted separately from the Preparatory Commission's proceedings between 1990 and 1994, to enable States to reach agreement on these 'areas of concern in Part XI'.[15]   The outcome of the consultations was the adoption by the UN General Assembly of the Agreement Relating to the Implementation of Part XI of the 1982 United Nations Convention on the Law of the Sea, 1994 (the Implementation Agreement).[16]   In accordance with Article 2 of this Agreement, Part XI of the UN Convention and the Agreement – which in effect amends Part XI – are to be interpreted and applied as a single instrument.

In adopting the Implementation Agreement, the General Assembly called upon the Preparatory Commission to *take into account* the terms of the Agreement when drawing up its final report.[17]   However, as has been seen, this proved to be impracticable and the Preparatory Commission left it to the Authority to take into account the terms of the Agreement when considering the Commission's recommendations and report.[18]   Accordingly, the Authority had to give full effect to the Implementation Agreement when drafting its rules, regulations and procedures.   In so doing, it is required, under the Agreement, to take into account the draft rules, regulations and procedures and any recommendations relating to the provisions of Part XI, as contained in the reports and recommendations of the Preparatory Commission.[19]   The Implementation Agreement also requires that such rules, regulations and procedures should *take into account* 'the prolonged delay in commercial deep sea-bed mining and the likely pace of activities in the Area', [20] thus granting the Authority significant scope for liberalising the Convention's criteria in relation particularly to the duration of sea-bed mining operations and performance requirements during the exploration and commercial production stages of contracts.[21]

Given the fact that the Authority, in drafting the Mining Code, was not required to break any new ground, it might have been thought that the Code would have been completed without any significant delay.   In reality, progress was painfully slow.   A draft was placed before the Authority's Legal and

---

[14] LOS/PCN/L.106, 19 August 1992 (XII *Final PrepCom Report*, p.146 at p.151, para. 25).

[15] For a brief account of the Informal Consultations, see E.D. Brown, '"Neither necessary nor prudent at this stage": the regime of seabed mining and its impact on the universality of the UN Convention on the Law of the Sea', 17 *Marine Policy* (1993), pp.81-107; or E.D. Brown, *The International Law of the Sea*, Vol.I, 1994, Chap.17, section IV.

[16] For the texts of (1) General Assembly Resolution A/48/263 of 28 July 1994 adopting the Implementation Agreement and (2) the Implementation Agreement, see Vol.3, Docs. 22 and 23; also in XXXIII ILM (1994), pp. 1311-1327.

[17] A/48/263, 28 July 1994 (*loc.cit.* in note 16), para.13.

[18] See further note 3 above.

[19] Implementation Agreement (*loc.cit.* in note 16 above), Annex, Sec.1, para.16.

[20] Implementation Agreement, Annex, Sec.1, para.5 (f).

[21] Para. 5 (f) is formulated, 'Notwithstanding the provisions of Annex III, article 17, paragraph 2(b) and (c) of the Convention', which refer to duration of operations and performance requirements.

100 *Chapter 4*

Technical Commission in March 1997 [22] but it was not until July 2000 that the Council was able to adopt Regulations on Prospecting and Exploration for Polymetallic Nodules in the Area. [23] It will be noted that this represents only part of the Mining Code and it will be necessary to complete it by adopting further regulations governing the exploitation phase. In due course, additional 'regulations' will be required on sea-bed resources other than polymetallic nodules. [24]

It follows, of course, that full reference can be made in this work only to the provisions of the Mining Code governing prospecting and exploration. The Regulations on prospecting are relatively straightforward and self-contained and are dealt with in this Chapter. The Regulations dealing with exploration, on the other hand, are much more complex and, given the fact that many of the corresponding parts of the UN Convention and the Implementation Agreement refer to both exploration and exploitation, it would be difficult and possibly confusing to attempt to integrate an account of these Regulations into this Chapter. In the interests of clarity, they are considered below in a separate Chapter 5.

As regards exploitation, all that exist are the draft regulations prepared by the Preparatory Commission [25] and, since they were prepared prior to the adoption of the Implementation Agreement in July 1994, there would be little point in referring to them except in the most general terms.

A full understanding of this complex regime also requires some reference to be made to the provisions of the Convention and related documents dealing with the composition and voting rules of the organs of the Authority. These institutional aspects are dealt with below in Chapter 8.

I. 'POLICIES RELATING TO ACTIVITIES IN THE AREA': UN CONVENTION, ARTICLE 150

This Article might be described as the explanatory development of the common heritage theme. Though still on a very general level, it provides a relatively more specific statement of the objectives, general and particular, of the common heritage regime.

---

[22] Draft Regulations on Prospecting and Exploration for Polymetallic Nodules in the Area. Provisional text prepared by the Legal and Technical Commission, ISBA/3/LTC/WP.1/Rev. 1, 27 March 1997.

[23] Regulations on Prospecting and Exploration for Polymetallic Nodules in the Area, adopted by the Council and approved by the Assembly on 13 July 2000, ISBA/6/A/18, 13 July 2000; reproduced in Vol. 3 as Doc. No. 25; hereafter referred to as 'Mining Code'.

[24] Under Art. 136 of the UN Convention, the Area and its *resources* are the common heritage of mankind and 'resources' are defined in Art.133(a) to mean 'all solid, liquid or gaseous mineral resources *in situ* in the Area at or beneath the sea-bed, including polymetallic nodules'. Art. 162(2)(o)(ii) gives priority to the adoption of regulations for polymetallic nodules but envisages that additional regulations will be adopted for other resources. See further below, section XVIII.

[25] See text above at note 10 and documentation referred to in note 10.

The Basic Regime 101

The Article opens with a statement in the most general terms of the objectives of activities in the Area. They are to be carried out in such a manner as to:

foster healthy development of the world economy and balanced growth of international trade, and to promote international co-operation for the over-all development of all countries, especially the developing States ...

The original version of Article 150 in the Informal Composite Negotiating Text (ICNT) went on to say that activities in the Area would be carried out 'specifically so as to ensure' a number of specified objectives.[26] The ICNT/Rev.1 version, however, substituted the phrase 'with a view to ensuring'.[27] This change, as the report of the United States delegation noted, 'reflects the reality that the policies in (a)-(g) are objectives rather than mandates and helps avoid the implication that the Article confers any power on the Authority other than those contained in other treaty articles'.[28] This 'reality' was further underlined by the modification introduced in ICNT/Rev.2, whereby 'Activities in the Area shall, *as specifically provided in this Part*, be carried out ...'[29]

The objectives enumerated in Paragraphs (a) - (j) reflect the various facets of the common heritage concept as it was shaped in the course of the negotiations. Reference has already been made above[30] to the heavy emphasis in some of these Paragraphs on creating a preferential position for the developing countries in relation to participation,[31] transfer of technology[32] and protection against adverse effects on their economies or earnings.[33] This obligation represents one side of the common heritage doctrine as developed by those States which were principally concerned to advocate that the system of exploitation of the Area should not create a monopolistic situation.[34]

Other States were anxious to emphasise that it was a fundamental objective of the regime to develop the resources of the Area and they were at pains too to stress the implied obligation on those administering the common heritage to ensure efficiency and avoid waste. Those objectives too were embodied in the final text of Article 150 but the provisions concerned, Paragraphs (a), (b), (e), (f) and (i), are somewhat ill-co-ordinated and confusing, reflecting their piecemeal addition through a series of amendments at successive sessions of the Conference.

---

[26] A/CONF. 62/WP.10, 15 July 1977 (*UNCLOS III Off. Rec.*, Vol. VIII, p.1, at p. 25).

[27] A/CONF. 62/WP. 10/Rev.1, 28 April 1979.

[28] M.H. Nordquist and Choon-ho Park (eds.), *Reports of the United States Delegation to the Third United Nations Conference on the Law of the Sea* (The Law of the Sea Institute, Occasional Paper No.33), *Seventh Session, Geneva, March 28 - May 19, 1978*, p. 185, at p. 199.

[29] A/CONF.62/WP.10/Rev.2, 11 April 1980 and Corr. 1-3, emphasis added.

[30] In Chap.3, section XII.

[31] Paras.(c) and (g).

[32] Para.(d).

[33] Para.(h).

[34] See also, on anti-monopoly clauses, below, section V.4.2, following note 126.

102   *Chapter 4*

Paragraph (a), reflecting the concern of the principal industrialised States that one of the fundamental objectives of the regime had received less than adequate emphasis in earlier drafts of Article 150, was added at the Seventh Session of the Conference and states the first policy objective of the regime as being 'the development of the resources of the Area.'[35] This addition was proposed by a group of eleven States in April 1982 as part of a last-minute package of compromise proposals designed to bridge the still wide gap separating the positions of various delegations but in particular those of the United States and the Group of 77.[36] It went some way towards accommodating the proposal of the group of seven industrialised States for the addition to Article 150 of a provision that:

> In the interpretation and exercise of its powers and functions the Authority shall at all times be guided by the objective of facilitating the development of the resources of the Area, without prejudice to the provisions of Article 151, paragraph 2.[37]

The sponsors of this amendment apparently considered that 'the question of production policies, as dealt with in the draft Convention, tended to give an anti-development orientation to Part XI.' They accordingly sought 'to ensure that the powers and functions of the Authority would serve to foster the development of the resources of the Area.'[38]

The desire to ensure efficiency and avoid waste is embodied in Paragraph (b), under which activities in the Area are to be conducted with a view to ensuring:

> orderly, safe and rational management of the resources of the Area, including the efficient conduct of activities in the Area and, in accordance with sound principles of conservation, the avoidance of unnecessary waste;

Paragraph (e), developing the theme of Paragraph (a), refers to the need to ensure:

> increased availability of the minerals derived from the Area as needed in conjunction with minerals derived from other sources, to ensure supplies to consumers of such minerals;

---

[35] A/CONF.62/L.132 and Add.1, 22 April 1982 (*UNCLOS III Off. Rec.*, Vol.XVI, pp.236-240, at p.237(24)-(25) and p.240(Annex V).

[36] See *Statement by the delegation of Canada dated 16 April 1982*, A/CONF. 62/WS/23, 22 April 1982 (*ibid.*, pp.262-264) and text of amendments proposed in A/CONF.62/L.104, 13 April 1982 (*ibid.*, p.219).

[37] *Belgium, France, Federal Republic of Germany, Italy, Japan, United Kingdom and United States* : *amendments*, A/CONF.62/L.121, 13 April 1982 (*ibid.*, pp.226-231, at p.226). As will be seen below in Section VI, Article 151(2) ceases to apply under the Implementation Agreement (*loc.cit.* in note 16 above), Annex, Sec.6, para.7.

[38] Mr. Ratiner (USA), at 168th Plenary Meeting, 15 April 1982 (*ibid.*, at p.87(7)).

Similarly, Paragraph (f) seeks to ensure:

> the promotion of just and stable prices remunerative to producers and fair to consumers for minerals derived both from the Area and from other sources, and the promotion of long-term equilibrium between supply and demand;

The group of seven industrialised States sought an amendment of this Paragraph, whereby the stated objective of promoting just and stable prices remunerative to producers and fair to consumers would be confined to minerals produced from the Area and not extended to minerals from other sources.[39] However, this proved to be one of many proposals which failed to attract general support.

As has been seen, the addition to Article 150 of the new Paragraph (a) was designed to ensure that the development of the resources of the Area should receive adequate emphasis as a fundamental objective of the regime. In the light of this addition, it is a little difficult to understand the purpose of Paragraph (i), which provides that activities in the Area will be carried out with a view to ensuring: 'the development of the common heritage for the benefit of mankind as a whole.' When this Paragraph was added to the Draft Convention (Informal Text) in 1980, its meaning was less than self-evident but, according to the 'co-ordinator' who drafted it, this Paragraph 'specifically reflects' the concern of a number of delegations which felt that insufficient emphasis had been placed on a role for the Authority to promote sea-bed mining.[40] He also referred to 'the over-all tenor of the complaints of the industrialised countries that the lack of reference to development of deep sea-bed mining in this article or elsewhere in the Convention did give some measure of imbalance'.[41] It thus seemed clear that the emphasis should lie on the words 'the development', the intention being to state a policy of active development of the deep sea-bed mining industry. Given the fact that this intention is now more specifically expressed in Paragraph (a), it is no longer clear what purpose is served by Paragraph (i), since it simply repeats what is already laid down as a 'principle governing the Area' in Article 140.

Finally, reference must be made to Paragraph (j) which was also added to Article 150 in 1980. It provides that activities are to be carried out with a view to ensuring that:

> conditions of access to markets for the imports of minerals produced from the resources of the Area and for imports of commodities produced from such minerals shall not be more favourable than the most favourable applied to imports from other sources.

This Paragraph was intended to alleviate the fears of some land-based producers that they might be deprived of traditional markets if the present pattern of

---

[39] *Loc.cit.* in note 37 above, at p.226.

[40] Report submitted by Mr. Nandan (Fiji) on negotiations co-ordinated by him relating to Production Policy, A/CONF. 62/C.1/L. 28, 23 August 1980 (*UNCLOS III Off. Rec.*, Vol. XIV, p. 163, at p. 166). The reference in this Report is to para.'(h)', later re-lettered '(i)'.

[41] *Ibid.*

104   *Chapter 4*

producer-consumer relationship were to be upset when some of their present customers became sea-bed producers and suppliers of their own domestic markets.[42]   It was included despite 'reservations expressed by certain industrialised countries' because of their fear that such a provision would impinge on their domestic trade policy.[43]

II. NON-DISCRIMINATION BY THE AUTHORITY: UN CONVENTION, ARTICLE 152

Reference has already been made to the policy of non-discrimination laid down in Paragraph 1 and to the preferential exception to it in favour of developing States in Paragraph 2.[44]

III. TITLE TO MINERALS: UN CONVENTION, ANNEX III, ARTICLE 1

Earlier drafts of this Article contained a number of ambiguities concerning the scope of minerals covered, the position of prospectors and of the Enterprise and participants in joint ventures.[45]   The final formulation, first introduced in ICNT/Rev.2, is shorter, clearer and more certain than the earlier versions.   It provides that, 'Title to minerals shall pass upon recovery in accordance with this Convention.'   It is now clear, therefore, that title passes automatically upon recovery in accordance with the other provisions of the Convention, including its Annexes, which are analysed below, and that this rule applies to contractors, the Enterprise, participants in joint ventures and prospectors (in relation to samples).[46]

IV. PROSPECTING: UN CONVENTION, ANNEX III, ARTICLE 2 AND MINING CODE, PART II

1. Prospecting Defined
Prospecting is defined as meaning:

> the search for deposits of polymetallic nodules in the Area, including estimation of the composition, sizes and distributions of polymetallic nodule deposits and their economic values, without any exclusive rights. [47]

2. UN Convention, Annex III, Article 2
Prospecting is regulated by the UN Convention, Annex III, Article 2 and, more extensively, by Part II of the of the Mining Code on 'Prospecting'.

---

[42] *Ibid.*, at p.164.
[43] *Ibid.*
[44] Above, Chap. 3, sections III and XII.
[45] See ICNT, Annex II, para. 1 and ICNT/Rev.1, Annex II, Art. 1.
[46] For comments of Conference officers on the changes made at the two parts of the Eighth Session, see *UNCLOS III Off.Rec.*,Vol. XI, p. 89 and Vol. XII, pp. 83-84.
[47] Mining Code Reg. 1(3)(e).

The Basic Regime 105

Article 2, which benefited from pruning carried out at the Eighth Session of UNCLOS III[48], provides that:

1. (a) The Authority shall encourage prospecting in the Area.
    (b) Prospecting shall be conducted only after the Authority has received a satisfactory written undertaking that the proposed prospector will comply with this Convention and the relevant rules, regulations and procedures of the Authority concerning co-operation in the training programmes referred to in articles 143 and 144 and the protection of the marine environment, and will accept verification by the Authority of compliance therewith. The proposed prospector shall, at the same time, notify the Authority of the approximate area or areas in which prospecting is to be conducted.
    (c) Prospecting may be conducted simultaneously by more than one prospector in the same area or areas.
2. Prospecting shall not confer on the prospector any rights with respect to resources. A prospector may, however, recover a reasonable quantity of minerals to be used for testing.

It is added in Annex III, Article 17(2)(b)(i) that prospecting shall be without time-limit.

3. The Mining Code , Part II
Regulation 2: Prospecting
When may prospecting begin? Prospecting may commence only after the prospector has been informed by the Secretary-General of the Authority that its notification of prospecting has been recorded pursuant to Regulation 4, paragraph 2. [49]
Duration of prospecting: As noted above, it is provided in the UN Convention that prospecting shall be without time limit. The Mining Code repeats this rule but goes on to add an exception to it: prospecting must cease upon written notification by the Secretary-General that a plan of work for exploration has been approved for the area concerned. [50]
Prospecting is not exclusive: Prospecting may be conducted simultaneously by more than one prospector in the same area or areas. [51]
Where may prospecting be undertaken?: Under Regulation 2(3), prospecting may be carried out in any part of the Area unless it falls into any of three categories:- (i) an area covered by an approved plan of work for exploration for polymetallic nodules; [52] (ii) a reserved area; [53] or (iii) an area which the Council

---

[48] See *UNCLOS III Off. Rec.*, Vol. XI, p. 89 and Vol. XII, pp. 83 - 84.
[49] Mining Code, Reg. 2(1).
[50] Reg. 2(5). On plans of work for exploration, see below, section V, Chap. 5 and, in relation to registered pioneer investors, Chap. 6, section IV.
[51] Reg. 2(6).
[52] On plans of work, see below, section V.4.

106   *Chapter 4*

has disapproved for *exploitation* because of the risk of serious harm to the marine environment. [54]

Prospecting gives no right to resources: Regulation 2(4) broadly follows the above-quoted provisions of Article 2(2) of Annex III of the UN Convention but specifies that the reasonable quantity of minerals which the prospector is permitted to recover is 'the quantity necessary for testing, and not for commercial use'.

Regulation 3: Notification of prospecting

A proposed prospector must notify the Authority of its intention to engage in prospecting in the form prescribed in Annex 1 of the Regulations. [55] In addition to various formal details, [56] the notification must include three attachments containing:

- The co-ordinates of the area or areas in which prospecting is to be conducted;
- A general description of the prospecting programme, including the proposed date of commencement and the approximate duration of the programme; and
- A written undertaking that the prospector will:
  - (a) comply with the Convention and the relevant rules, regulations and procedures of the Authority concerning:
    - (i) co-operation in the training programmes in connection with marine scientific research and transfer of technology referred to in articles 143 and 144 of the Convention; and
    - (ii) protection and preservation of the marine environment; and
  - (b) accept verification by the Authority of compliance therewith. [57]

Regulation 4: Consideration of notifications

Regulation 4 ensures that notifications of intention to prospect will be dealt with promptly and imposes a duty upon the Secretary-General to review and act on the notification within 45 days of its receipt.

Provided the notification conforms with the requirements of the UN Convention and the Mining Code Regulations, the Secretary-General will record

---

[53] On reserved areas, see further below, Chap. 4, section VII, Chap. 5, section 1.2.8 and, in relation to registered pioneer investors, Chap. 6, section IV.1.6.

[54] Art. 162(2)(x) and Annex III 6(3)(b) empower the Council to disapprove areas for exploitation where substantial evidence indicates the risk of serious harm to the marine environment. Reg. 21(6)(c) of the Mining Code similarly requires the Legal and Technical Commission not to recommend approval of a plan of work in such cases. See further on environmental aspects, Chap. 10 below.

[55] Reg. 3(1)-(2).

[56] See Reg. 3(4) and Annex 1(1)-(14).

[57] Reg. 3(4)(b)-(d) and Annex 1 (15)-(17). On marine scientific research and transfer of technology, see further above, Chap. 3, sections VII and VIII. On protection of the marine environment, see further below, Chap. 10.

its particulars in a register and inform the prospector in writing that this has been done. [58]

The Secretary-General will not be able to record a notification within the 45-day period if the notification includes:

- any part of an area included in an approved plan of work for exploration or exploitation of any category of resources; or
- any part of a reserved area; or
- any part of an area disapproved by the Council for exploitation because of the risk of serious harm to the marine environment.

Nor will a notification be recorded if the written undertaking required under Regulation 3(4)(d) [59] is not satisfactory.[60] In all such cases, the Secretary-General must provide the proposed prospector with a written statement of reasons and allow it to submit an amended notification within 90 days. The amended notification must be reviewed and acted upon within 45 days of its receipt by the Secretary-General. [61]

Earlier drafts also required that the proposed prospector should be informed if the notification included any part of an area included in a previous notification.[62] As noted above, however, prospectors are entitled to conduct prospecting simultaneously in the same area, [63] and the final text of the Mining Code omits this requirement.

Confidentiality of notifications. Unless he has the written consent of the prospector, the Secretary-General must not release any particulars contained in the notification, though he shall, from time to time, inform all members of the Authority of the identity of prospectors and the general areas in which prospecting is being conducted. [64] As will be seen below, provision is also made in Regulation 6 to ensure confidentiality of data contained in the prospector's annual reports to the Authority.

Regulation 5: Prospectors' annual reports
Within 90 days of the end of each calendar year, a prospector must submit to the Authority an annual report, which is then submitted by the Secretary-General to the Legal and Technical Commission. [65] Each annual report must contain:

(a) a general description of the status of prospecting and of the results obtained; and
(b) information on compliance with the undertakings referred to in Regulation 3, paragraph 4(d). [66]

---

[58] Reg. 4(2).
[59] See above under *Regulation 3: Notification of prospecting.*
[60] Reg. 4(3). See also above under *Where may prospecting be undertaken?*
[61] Reg. 4(3).
[62] *E.g.,* ISBA/6/C/2, 3 April 2000, Reg. 4(4).
[63] Reg. 2(6).
[64] Reg. 4(5).
[65] Reg. 5(1).
[66] *Ibid.*

108   *Chapter 4*

An earlier draft of Regulation 5 required the prospector to include also in his annual report 'observations on any incident involving safety at sea or accommodation with other marine activities and any location or finding in the Area of objects of an archaeological or historical nature.'[67]   As will be seen below, objects of an archaeological or historical nature are now dealt with in a separate regulation. In deleting the above-quoted passage from Regulation 5, the view appears to have been taken that the Authority's competence does not extend to safety at sea or marine activities other than activities in the Area. Although it is true that the International Maritime Organisation is the United Nations specialised agency for safety at sea, it has to be noted that Article 147 of the UN Convention makes provision to ensure that activities in the Area will be carried out with reasonable regard for other activities in the marine environment. [68] Strictly speaking, prospecting is not included in the definition of 'activities in the Area'. [69]   However, a simple obligation upon the prospector to include 'observations' on such matters in its annual report might have been considered to be in accordance with the spirit of Article 147 and a helpful contribution to realising its objective.

Prospecting expenditure as development costs. If the prospector wishes to claim expenditures for prospecting as part of the development costs incurred prior to the commencement of commercial production, it must submit an annual statement of the actual and direct expenditures incurred in carrying out prospecting. [70]

Regulation 6: Confidentiality of data and information   from prospecting in annual report
The Secretary-General must ensure the confidentiality of *all* data and information contained in the annual reports required under Regulation 5.[71] In an earlier draft of this Regulation, data and information of commercial value were protected for a period of ten years, with the possibility of an extension for a further period of up to ten years. [72] In the final version, however, no term is specified and the Secretary-General is simply required to ensure confidentiality in accordance with the provisions of Regulations 35 and 36. [73] Those Regulations, considered in detail in Chapter 5, [74] make no direct reference to prospecting and are clearly designed to apply principally to data and information submitted in connection with contracts for exploration. If applied, *mutatis mutandis,* to prospecting, it would appear that confidentiality would be preserved for an initial period of ten years. At that point, and every five years thereafter, the Secretary-General and the prospector would review the data and information and determine if they should remain confidential. The onus would be on the prospector to establish that

---

[67] ISBA/4/C/4, 2 April 1998.
[68] See further above, Chap. 3, section XI.
[69] UN Convention, Art. 1(1)(3).
[70] Reg. 5(2).
[71] Reg. 6(1).
[72] ISBA/5/C/4/Rev.1, 14 October 1999, Reg. 6(1).
[73] Reg. 6(1).
[74] Chap. 5, section IV.

there would be a substantial risk of serious and unfair economic prejudice if the data and information were to be released. [75]

The Secretary-General may, however, at any time, release data and information relating to prospecting if he has the consent of the prospector concerned. [76]

Regulation 7: Notification of incidents causing serious harm to the marine environment
The prospector is required to notify the Secretary-General immediately of any incident arising from prospecting which causes serious harm to the marine environment. The Secretary-General must then 'act in a manner consistent with regulation 32', which permits him to take immediate measures of a temporary nature pending any action by the Council which may, in appropriate cases, issue emergency orders. [77]

Regulation 8: Objects of an archaeological or historical nature
The prospector is required to 'immediately notify the Secretary-General in writing of any finding in the Area of an object of an archaeological or historical nature and its location'.

The Authority is not empowered to organise and control activities in relation to such objects or to administer them. However, given the principle established in Article 149 of the UN Convention, it is not unreasonable to take the view that an obligation to notify findings would not place a significant burden upon either the prospector or the Authority and would enable the latter to collaborate with more specialised agencies such as UNESCO in seeking to give effect to the objectives embodied in Article 149. [78]

V. THE SYSTEM OF EXPLORATION AND EXPLOITATION: WHO MAY EXPLORE AND EXPLOIT THE RESOURCES OF THE AREA; PLANS OF WORK: UN CONVENTION, ARTICLE 153 AND ANNEX III, ARTICLES 3-6, AS MODIFIED BY THE IMPLEMENTATION AGREEMENT

1. Article 153 : The Background
Given the fundamental principle that the resources of the Area were to be the common heritage of mankind, it was inevitable that one of the most central and difficult questions for the Conference would be: who may exploit the resources of the Area? In the beginning, in 1974, the main protagonists were poles apart, the Group of 77 insisting that the Authority alone should exploit the sea-bed, whereas the developed States insisted that States and enterprises should be entitled to undertake operations. The negotiations on this aspect of the regime between that time and the publication of the 1980 version of the Draft Convention, following

---

[75] Reg. 35(3), *mutatis mutandis*.
[76] Reg. 6(2).
[77] On Reg. 32, see further below, Chap. 10, section IV.6.4.2.
[78] On Article 149, see further above, Chap. 3, sections I.3 and XIII, which also refers to the draft Convention on the Protection of the Underwater Cultural Heritage under consideration in UNESCO.

110   Chapter 4

the close of the Ninth Session, can be best described as a series of attempts to find a compromise solution acceptable to the two sides, though satisfying neither of them completely. Gradually, the two sides moved closer, each accepting elements in the other's proposals. Thus, by the time the Fourth Session was held in March-May 1976, the developed States had accepted that an enterprise run by an international Authority would exploit the Area alongside States and enterprises, and the Group of 77 had agreed that States and enterprises could participate in sea-bed mining in association with the Authority. The Chairman of the First Committee incorporated such a 'dual' or 'parallel' system in his Revised Single Negotiating Text (RSNT) at the close of the Fourth Session.[79] Under it, mining would have been conducted either directly by the Authority, or by the States or their nationals acting 'in association with the Authority and under its control'.[80] Unfortunately, it became clear at the Fifth Session that the 'mix' incorporated in the RSNT was unacceptable to the Group of 77 in particular. As a result, the question was again discussed extensively at the Fifth Session, largely on the basis of three working papers.[81] The Group of 77 paper[82] favoured a 'unitary system', giving pre-eminence to the Authority and enabling it to exercise full and effective control over exploitation. It was opposed by some developed countries on the ground that it gave no assurance of access to sea-bed resources to States and enterprises. The United States, in a paper[83] supported by other industrialised countries, advocated a 'parallel system' which would permit direct operations by the Authority but would, in addition, guarantee access for States and enterprises qualifying for the award of a contract by virtue of financial standing and technological capability. A third paper, from the Soviet Union,[84] provided for exploitation by States and by the Authority but stressed particularly the equal opportunity of all States to mine the sea-bed.

By the end of the Fifth Session, the First Committee had reached what its Chairman described as an impasse on this question. He formulated 'the central and most difficult problem of all' as follows:

> should the new system of exploitation provide for a guaranteed permanent role in sea-bed mineral exploitation for States Parties and private firms? Or should such a role for States Parties and private firms be considered only at the option of and subject to conditions negotiated by the Authority? Or again,

---

[79] A/CONF.62/WP. 8/Rev. 1, 6 May 1976 (*UNCLOS III Off. Rec.*, Vol. V, p. 125).

[80] Art.22.

[81] The three working papers - Workshop Papers Nos. 1, 2 and 3 - did not become formal documents of the Conference. They are, however, summarised in the *Final report by the Co-Chairmen on the activities of the workshop* (established by the First Committee), A/CONF.62/C.1/WR.5, 9 September 1976 (*UNCLOS III Off. Rec.*, Vol. VI, p.165, at pp. 166-167) and are reproduced in Platzöder, *Documents*, Vol. VI, at pp. 174-180.

[82] *Workshop Paper No.1, ibid.*, pp. 174-176.

[83] *Workshop Paper No.3, ibid.*, pp. 177-180.

[84] *Workshop Paper No.2, ibid.*, pp. 176-177.

The Basic Regime 111

should their role be conceived of as essentially temporary, to be phased out over a defined period agreed to beforehand?[85]

Inter-sessional talks chaired by Mr. Evensen of Norway, continued during the Sixth Session (23 May - 15 July 1977), were widely considered to have produced the basis for a way out of the impasse acceptable to both sides. Unfortunately, however, it was at this point that the First Committee Chairman saw fit to produce a draft of Part XI of the ICNT in a form which did not reflect the tenor of the negotiations and was completely unacceptable to the industrialised States.[86] As will be seen in more detail below, the United States administration became thoroughly disenchanted with the Conference as a result and, after years of stalling, put its support fully behind efforts in Congress to place a Seabed Mineral Resources Act on the statute book.[87]

However, the ship was brought more or less back on course as a result of the work at the first part of the Seventh Session of Mr. Njenga's Negotiating Group 1. In Mr. Njenga's words, 'It is precisely with the object of finding the point of equilibrium between the partisans of guaranteed access by States and other entities to the Area and the partisans of absolute discretion of the Authority that changes have been made in the text of article 151 [now Article 153 of the UN Convention] which, while ensuring the participation of the States Parties and other entities in the activities to be carried out in the Area, also give the Authority a predominant role in the organisation, conduct and control of those activities. This was the intention behind the amendments made to article 151, which constitutes the heart of the system of exploration'.[88]

Article 153 is the heart of the sea-bed mining system, but a judgment on how successful it has been in finding the point of balance between the interests of the developed and developing States can be made only in a wider context which allows reference to be made too to the related provisions of the Convention on the financial terms of contracts, the composition and voting rules of the organs of the Authority and settlement of disputes, as well as to the amendments introduced in 1994 by the Implementation Agreement. First, however, it is necessary to present an analysis of Article 153 and of the related rules of Annex III.

As was noted above, Article 151 of the original ICNT was radically revised at the Seventh Session and the version which emerged as Article 153 of ICNT/Rev. 1 has survived virtually unchanged as Article 153 of the Convention. It is still useful, however, in order to bring out some of the features of the final Convention version, to compare it with the ICNT version.

Article 153 provides little more than the framework of the system of exploration and exploitation, the details being contained in other articles of Part XI and in the Annexes of the Convention, as modified by the Implementation

---

[85] *Report by Mr. P. B. Engo, Chairman of the First Committee on the work of the Committee*, 6 September 1976 (*UNCLOS III Off. Rec.*, Vol. VI, p. 130, at p. 132).
[86] A/CONF/62/WP.10, 15 July 1977 (*UNCLOS III Off.Rec.*, Vol.VIII, p.1, at p.22).
[87] See further Chap. 7, especially section II.
[88] *Explanatory memorandum by the Chairman concerning document NG1/10/Rev. 1* (Doc. NG1/12, *UNCLOS III Off. Rec.*, Vol. X, p. 19).

112 *Chapter 4*

Agreement, and in the rules, regulations and procedures provided for under Article 153. It is concerned with four main aspects of the system: the role of the Authority; the question of who may carry out activities in the Area; the requirement that activities must be carried out in accordance with plans of work; and security of tenure for contractors.

2. *Rôle of Authority*

The first noticeable change in the revised version of the old Article 151[89] is in its title. The original title of 'Functions of the Authority' reflected the almost omnipotent role accorded to the Authority in the body of the Article. The revised title is much more neutral, referring simply to the 'System of exploration and exploitation'.

This changed emphasis is found again in Paragraphs 1 and 2. Under the original Paragraph 1, 'Activities in the Area' were to be 'carried out by the Authority on behalf of mankind as a whole'. Under the revised version, however, they are to be 'organised, carried out and controlled by the Authority on behalf of mankind as a whole' – a formula which reduces the role of the Authority, while increasing that of States and their nationals. Similarly, in Paragraph 2, whereas, under the original ICNT, the activities of the Enterprise and of States and their nationals were described as being 'carried out on the Authority's behalf', in the revised version they are simply 'carried out'.

The control and supervisory functions of the Authority are further specified in Paragraphs 4 and 5:

4. The Authority shall exercise such control over activities in the Area as is necessary for the purpose of securing compliance with the relevant provisions of this Part and the Annexes relating thereto, and the rules, regulations and procedures of the Authority, and the plans of work approved in accordance with paragraph 3. States Parties shall assist the Authority by taking all measures necessary to ensure such compliance in accordance with article 139.
5. The Authority shall have the right to take at any time any measures provided for under this Part to ensure compliance with its provisions and the exercise of the functions of control and regulation assigned to it thereunder or under any contract. The Authority shall have the right to inspect all installations in the Area used in connection with activities in the Area.

The Implementation Agreement refers to the rôle of the Authority as being to 'organise and control' activities in the Area, thus omitting the reference in Article 153(1) to also carrying out such activities.[90]   There would not appear to be any significance in this different formulation, since the Enterprise, 'the organ of the

---

[89] *UNCLOS III Off. Rec.*, Vol. VIII, at p. 26.
[90] Implementation Agreement (*loc.cit.* in note 16 above), Annex, Sec.1, para.1.

The Basic Regime 113

Authority which shall carry out activities in the area directly,'[91] continues to play that rôle. In any event, the Agreement confirms that the powers and functions of the Authority are those expressly conferred on it by the UN Convention, and goes on to provide that it 'shall have such incidental powers, consistent with the Convention, as are implicit in, and necessary for, the exercise of those powers and functions with respect to activities in the Area.'[92]

3. Who May Carry Out Activities?
Paragraph 2 of Article 153 provides that activities in the Area shall be carried out (i) by the Enterprise and (ii) *in association with the Authority*: [93]

> by States Parties or state enterprises or natural or juridical persons which possess the nationality of States Parties or are effectively controlled by them or their nationals, when sponsored by such States, or any group of the foregoing ...

Those in the second category must, however, meet 'the requirements provided in this Part and in Annex III'. In this context, the most important of Annex III's requirements are those of Article 4 on the qualifications of applicants for contracts.

3.1 Article 4 of Annex III - Qualifications of Applicants for Contracts
The developing States would have preferred that the Authority should have enjoyed a wide discretion to negotiate the requirements to be met by applicants for contracts as terms of the contract. Throughout the negotiations, however, the developed States attached great importance to the need to specify in the Convention precisely what requirements had to be met by applicants in order to qualify for the award of a contract. The objective of the industrialised States, and particularly of the United States, was to ensure guaranteed access to sea-bed mining for their nationals, subject only to satisfaction of agreed conditions incorporated in the Convention (including its Annexes). Looked at from this point of view, the original ICNT version of what is now Article 4 of Annex III left much to be desired. In empowering the Authority to prescribe the required qualifications for an application, Paragraph 4 of Annex II of ICNT provided simply that, 'Such qualifications shall *include* financial standing, technological capability and satisfactory performance under any previous contracts with the Authority'.[94] There was thus nothing to prevent the Authority from adding qualifications relating to other considerations.

Article 4 of Annex III of the Convention is much more tightly drawn. Paragraph 1 provides that:

---

[91] UN Convention, Art.170(1).
[92] Implementation Agreement (*loc.cit.* in note 16 above), Annex, Sec.1, para.1. Para.17 adds that the 'relevant provisions of Part XI, section 4 shall be interpreted and applied in accordance with Part XI and this Agreement'.
[93] Emphasis added.
[94] *UNCLOS III Off.Rec., Vol.*VIII, at p.50, emphasis added.

Applicants, other than the Enterprise, *shall be qualified* if they have the nationality or control and sponsorship required by article 153, paragraph 2(b), and *if they* follow the procedures and *meet the qualification standards set forth in the rules, regulations and procedures of the Authority.* [Emphasis added]

The scope of such 'qualification standards' is exclusively determined by Paragraph 2:

Except as provided in paragraph 6, such qualification standards shall relate to the financial and technical capabilities of the applicant and his performance under any previous contracts with the Authority.

In order to stress the exclusive nature of these standards as a basis for the award of a contract, the word 'qualification' was added before 'standards' in both Paragraphs 1 and 2 'for the sake of clarification'.[95]

Paragraph 6 complements Paragraphs 1 and 2 by providing that:

The qualification standards shall require that every applicant, without exception, shall as part of his application undertake:
(a) to accept as enforceable and comply with the applicable obligations created by the provisions of Part XI, rules, regulations and procedures of the Authority, the decisions of the organs of the Authority and terms of his contracts with the Authority;
(b) to accept control by the Authority of activities in the Area, as authorised by this Convention;
(c) to provide the Authority with a written assurance that his obligations under the contract will be fulfilled in good faith;
(d) to comply with the provisions on the transfer of technology set forth in article 5 of this Annex.[96]

The establishment in the revised Article 4 of objective criteria for the qualifications of applicants went some way towards satisfying the demands of the industrialised States for guaranteed access for their nationals to sea-bed mining, subject only to satisfaction of specified conditions inserted in the Convention.

---

[95] *UNCLOS III Off.Rec.*, Vol.XII, p.84 (the reference is to Art.4, paras.1 and 4 of Annex II, the forerunners of Art.4, paras.1 and 2 of Annex III).
[96] This undertaking on transfer of technology was rendered inapplicable by the Implementation Agreement. See section 3.2 below.

The Basic Regime 115

The further progress towards this goal reflected in Articles 6 and 7 of Annex III[97] rendered the package acceptable to the industrialised States.[98]

Under the Implementation Agreement, special provision is made for applications for approval of plans of work for exploration submitted by applicants (other than the Enterprise and registered pioneer investors[99]) which had already undertaken substantial activities in the Area prior to the entry into force of the Convention. They are to be considered to have met the financial and technical qualifications necessary for approval of a plan of work, if the sponsoring State or States certify that the applicant has expended an amount equivalent to at least US$ 30 million in research and exploration activities and has expended not less than ten per cent of that amount in the location, survey and evaluation of the area referred to in the plan of work.[100] Moreover, such applications could be sponsored by a State which was applying the Implementation Agreement provisionally (during the interim period between the entry into force of the UN Convention on 16 November 1994 and the entry into force of the Implementation Agreement on 28 July 1996 [101]) or by a State which was allowed to remain a provisional member of the Authority (between the entry into force of the Agreement and its entry into force – at latest by 16 November 1998 – for that State[102]).[103] These provisions would have applied in cases such as applications sponsored by the United States which had not previously sought pioneer investor registration for United States companies, though they had satisfied the expenditure criterion.

Paragraphs 3 and 4 of Article 4, which were added to the text of Article 4 of Annex III at the Eighth Session of UNCLOS III, gave rise to some controversy, some delegations feeling that they were not needed at all.[104] Their intended purpose was to fill a lacuna in the existing text by setting forth general rules on sponsorship of national and multinational entities and on responsibility of sponsors.[105] They provide that:

---

[97] On Annex III, Art.6, see section 4.2 below. As noted in section VI below, Art.7 of Annex III was rendered inapplicable by the Implementation Agreement.

[98] Nordquist and Park, *op. cit.* in note 28 above. *Eighth Session, Geneva, March 19 - April 27, 1979*, p. 251, at p. 264. A group of seven of the industrialised States attempted to press their demands further at the Eleventh Session of the Conference. They sought to introduce a more specific text than that laid down in Art.4, based upon the applicant's ability to raise funds. Compliance with the test would have been certified by the sponsoring State. However, in the end this amendment was not incorporated in the Convention. See further A/CONF.62/L.121, 13 April 1982 (*UNCLOS III Off.Rec.*, Vol.XVI, p.226, at pp.228-229).

[99] On pioneer investors, see below Chap 6.

[100] Implementation Agreement (*loc.cit.* in note 16 above), Annex, Sec.1, para.6(a)(i).

[101] Implementation Agreement (*loc.cit.* in note 16 above), Art.7.

[102] *Ibid.*, Annex, Sec.1, para.12.

[103] *Ibid.*, Sec.1, para.6(a)(iv). On provisional application of the Implementation Agreement and provisional membership of the Authority, see further Chap.1, sections II.1.2 and II.2.

[104] *Loc.cit.* in note 95 above, where reference is made to the earlier numbering of these provisions as Art.4, paras.2 and 3 of Annex II.

[105] *Ibid.*

116   *Chapter 4*

3. Each applicant shall be sponsored by the State Party of which it is a national unless the applicant has more than one nationality, as in the case of a partnership or consortium of entities from several States, in which event all States Parties involved shall sponsor the application, or *unless the applicant is effectively controlled by another State Party or its nationals*, in which event both States Parties shall sponsor the application. The criteria and procedures for implementation of the sponsorship requirements shall be set forth in the rules, regulations and procedures of the Authority.

4. The sponsoring State or States shall, pursuant to article 139, have the responsibility to ensure, within their legal systems, that a contractor so sponsored shall carry out activities in the Area in conformity with the terms of its contract and its obligations under this Convention. A sponsoring State shall not, however, be liable for damage caused by any failure of a contractor sponsored by it to comply with its obligations if that State Party has adopted laws and regulations and taken administrative measures which are, within the framework of its legal system, reasonably appropriate for securing compliance by persons under its jurisdiction. [Emphasis added]

It was recognised that the clause italicised in Paragraph 3, governing sponsorship in cases where a company's nationality and control are separate, raised problems of implementation for some developed countries.[106] The final sentence, added at the Ninth Session, was intended to provide a solution,[107] though some States would have been happier to see the requirement of sponsorship by more than one State in such cases deleted altogether.[108]

Finally, it may be noted that Paragraph 4 assists in the clarification of Article 139 of the Convention[109] by stating more specifically what a sponsoring State is required to do in order to avoid indirect responsibility for damage done by the person sponsored. The obligation upon the sponsoring State to ensure compliance with the Convention will be met by the adoption of laws and regulations and the taking of administrative measures which are, within the framework of its legal system, reasonably appropriate for securing compliance by persons under its jurisdiction.

3.2 Article 5 of Annex III - Transfer of Technology

As was seen above,[110] Article 4(6) of Annex III includes among the qualification standards of applicants for contracts an undertaking 'to comply with the provisions on the transfer of technology set forth in article 5 of this Annex'. As

---

[106] A/CONF.62/C.1/L.28, 23 August 1980 (*UNCLOS III Off. Rec.*, Vol..XIV, p. 161, at p. 162, referring to the earlier numbering as Art.4 (2)).
[107] *Ibid.*
[108] Nordquist and Park, *op. cit.* in note 28 above (*Resumed Ninth Session, Geneva, July 28 - August 29, 1980*, p. 409, at p. 424).
[109] On State responsibility for damage and Art. 139, see above, Chap. 3, section V.1.
[110] Above, text following note 95.

noted above in Chapter 3, section VIII, where the question of transfer of technology is fully considered, the rules governing this subject have been amended by the Implementation Agreement and the provisions of Annex III, Article 5 of the UN Convention no longer apply. [111]

4. Plans of Work

Under Article 153(3) of the UN Convention, all activities in the Area have to be carried out in accordance with a formal written plan of work drawn up in accordance with Annex III and approved by the Council after review by the Legal and Technical Commission. Under the Implementation Agreement, the application for approval of a plan of work for exploration 'shall be considered by the Council following the receipt of a recommendation on the application from the Legal and Technical Commission', [112] and it is confirmed that the approval of such a plan shall be in accordance with Article 153(3) of the UN Convention.[113]

The plan of work must be in the form of a contract and such contracts may provide for joint arrangements in accordance with Article 11 of Annex III. The principal provisions of Annex III governing applications for and approval of plans of work are contained in Articles 3 and 6, as revised by the provisions of the Implementation Agreement.

4.1 Article 3 of Annex III – Applications for Plans of Work

Article 3 provides that:

1. The Enterprise, States Parties, and the other entities referred to in article 153, paragraph 2(b), may apply to the Authority for approval of plans of work for activities in the Area.
2. The Enterprise may apply with respect to any part of the Area, but applications by others with respect to reserved areas are subject to the additional requirements of article 9 of this Annex.
3. Exploration and exploitation shall be carried out only in areas specified in plans of work referred to in article 153, paragraph 3, and approved by the Authority in accordance with this Convention and the relevant rules, regulations and procedures of the Authority.
4. Every approved plan of work shall:
   (a) be in conformity with this Convention and the rules, regulations and procedures of the Authority;
   (b) provide for control by the Authority of activities in the Area in accordance with Article 153, paragraph 4;
   (c) confer on the operator, in accordance with the rules, regulations and procedures of the Authority, the exclusive right to explore for and exploit the specified categories of resources in the area covered by the plan of work. If, however, the applicant presents for approval a

---

[111] Implementation Agreement (*loc. cit.* in note 16 above), Annex, Sec. 5, para. 2.

[112] *Ibid.*, Annex, Sec.1, para.6(a).

[113] *Ibid.*, Annex, Sec.1, para.6(b). On plans of work for registered pioneer investors, see below Chap.6, section IV.1.

118 *Chapter 4*

> plan of work covering only the stage of exploration or the stage of exploitation, the approved plan of work shall confer such exclusive right with respect to that stage only.
>
> 5. Upon its approval by the Authority, every plan of work, except those presented by the Enterprise, shall be in the form of a contract concluded between the Authority and the applicant or applicants.

Only a few brief comments are called for at this stage. First, it will be recalled that, in some cases, applications could be sponsored by States non-parties to the UN Convention if they were applying the Implementation Agreement provisionally or were provisional members of the Authority.[114]

Secondly, it will be noted that where an applicant applies for only one of the two stages of exploration and exploitation, the plan of work may confer exclusive rights on him only in relation to that stage (Paragraph 4(c)); and, under Article 10 of Annex III, where the approved plan of work is for exploration only, it confers on the operator a preference and a priority among applicants for a plan of work for exploitation of the same area and resources – unless his performance has not been satisfactory. Under the Implementation Agreement, this reference to a performance which has not been satisfactory is to be interpreted to mean that the contractor has failed to comply with the requirements of an approved plan of work despite written warning or warnings from the Authority to the contractor to comply therewith.[115]

Finally, it should be noted that Article 3, Paragraph 5 of Annex III (and Article 153(3) of the UN Convention) has been revised by the Implementation Agreement. The obligations applicable to contractors now apply also to the Enterprise and a plan of work for the Enterprise, upon its approval, will also be in the form of a contract.[116]

4.2 Article 6 of Annex III – Approval of Plans of Work Submitted by Applicants
As was seen above, Article 4 establishes objective criteria for the qualification of applicants[117] and Article 3 prescribes the procedure to be followed by applicants.[118] Article 6 goes on to specify the procedures to be followed for the processing of applications from such qualified applicants.

Paragraphs 1 and 2 are quite straightforward recitals of the time limits and administrative formalities to be observed by the Authority in considering proposed plans of work:

> 1. Six months after the entry into force of this Convention, and thereafter each fourth month, the Authority shall take up for consideration proposed plans of work.

---

[114] See text above, following note 100.
[115] Implementation Agreement (*loc.cit.* in note 16 above), Annex, Sec.1, para.13.
[116] *Ibid.*, Annex, Sec.2, para.4.
[117] Section 3.1 above.
[118] Section 4.1 above.

2. When considering an application for approval of a plan of work in the form of a contract, the Authority shall first ascertain whether:
   (a) the applicant has complied with the procedures established for applications in accordance with article 4 of this Annex and has given the Authority the undertakings and assurances required by that article. In cases of non-compliance with these procedures or in the absence of any of these undertakings and assurances, the applicant shall be given 45 days to remedy these defects;
   (b) the applicant possesses the requisite qualifications provided for in article 4 of this Annex.

The central provision of Article 6 is in Paragraph 3. This is one of the very few provisions of the Convention which were amended at the final Eleventh Session of the Conference in an effort to render it acceptable to the United States and other industrialised States.[119] The change relates to the rôle to be played by the Authority in determining whether the proposed plans of work conform with the requirements laid down. Under the penultimate Conference text, the Draft Convention on the Law of the Sea (1981), the Authority, when considering proposed plans of work, was authorised to conduct an inquiry into their compliance with the terms of the Convention and the rules, regulations and procedures of the Authority, including the operational requirements, the financial contributions and the undertakings concerning the transfer of technology.[120] The Draft Convention text went on to provide that 'the Authority shall approve such plans of work' as soon as the Authority has 'settled' the issues under investigation (which had to be conducted 'as expeditiously as possible'), provided the plans 'conform to the uniform and non-discriminatory requirements established by the rules, regulations and procedures of the Authority'.[121] The revised chapeau of Paragraph 3 makes no reference to any inquiry by the Authority and, accordingly, the Authority's powers are confined to those specified much more precisely in Articles 153(3), 165(2)(b) and, until revised by the Implementation Agreement, 162(2)(j) of the Convention.

As has been seen, Article 153(3) requires the plan of work to be approved by the Council after review by the Legal and Technical Commission, which, under Article 165 (2)(b), is instructed to:

> review formal written plans of work for activities in the Area in accordance with article 153, paragraph 3, and submit appropriate recommendations to the Council. The Commission shall base its recommendations solely on the grounds stated in Annex III and shall report fully thereon to the Council;

---

[119] See *Report of the President to the Conference*, A/CONF.62/L.141 and Add.1, 29 April 1982 (*UNCLOS III Off. Rec.* Vol.XVI, pp.247-248, at p.248, para.10 *et seq.* and Annex).

[120] Draft Convention on the Law of the Sea (1981), *UNCLOS III Off. Rec.*, Vol. XV, p.172, Annex III, Art. 6(3).

[121] *Ibid.*

120   *Chapter 4*

The Council's rôle was originally specified in Article 162 (2)(j).   Under the Implementation Agreement, however, Article 162(2)(j) has been replaced by the following provisions:

> The Council shall approve a recommendation by the Legal and Technical Commission for approval of a plan of work unless by a two-thirds majority of its members present and voting, including a majority of members present and voting in each of the chambers of the Council, the Council decides to disapprove a plan of work.   If the Council does not take a decision on a recommendation for approval of a plan of work within a prescribed period, the recommendation shall be deemed to have been approved by the Council at the end of that period.   The prescribed period shall normally be 60 days unless the Council decides to provide for a longer period.   If the Commission recommends the disapproval of a plan of work or does not make a recommendation, the Council may nevertheless approve the plan of work in accordance with its rules of procedure for decision-making on matters of substance.[122]

The result of the revision of Article 6, Paragraph 3 is thus clear; it is to remove any suspicion that the Authority possesses any powers of inquiry into proposed plans of work other than those specified in the above provisions, which clearly indicate the responsible organs and time limits.

Even if a proposed plan of work complies with the above requirements, it may fail to secure approval by the Authority because of other provisions of Article 6, Paragraph 3, which recognise certain qualifications to the obligation of the Authority to approve plans of work.   Thus, where there is more than one application for the same site, the rule is 'first come, first served'[123] and, similarly, the Authority will not approve a plan where part or all of the proposed area is included in a previously approved plan or a proposed plan not yet finally acted on by the Authority.[124]   Again, no approval can be given in respect of areas 'disapproved' by the Council for exploitation because 'substantial evidence indicated the risk of serious harm to the marine environment'.[125]   It may be noted that, under the Implementation Agreement, an application for approval of a plan of work has now to be accompanied by an assessment of the potential environmental impacts of the proposed activities and by a description of a programme for oceanographic and baseline environmental studies in accordance with the rules, regulations and procedures adopted by the Authority.[126]

However, the most important qualifications to the Council's obligation to approve plans of work are contained in the two anti-monopoly clauses of Paragraph 3(c), designed to ensure that no one State, including entities sponsored

---

[122] Implementation Agreement (*loc.cit.* in note 16 above), Annex, Sec.3, para.11(a).   Under para.11(b), the provisions of Art.162(2)(j) 'shall not apply'.
[123] UN Convention, Annex III, Art.6(3), first sentence.
[124] Art.6(3)(a).
[125] Under Art.162(2)(x).
[126] Implementation Agreement (*loc.cit.* in note 16 above), Annex, Sec.1, para.7.

The Basic Regime 121

by it, should hold plans of work covering excessive areas of the sea-bed. Under the first clause, the Authority may not approve a proposed plan of work when the proposed plan has been submitted or sponsored by a State Party already holding:

> plans of work for exploration and exploitation of polymetallic nodules in non-reserved areas that, together with either part of the area covered by the application for a plan of work, exceed in size 30 per cent of a circular area of 400,000 square kilometres surrounding the centre of either part of the area covered by the proposed plan of work.[127]

It will be noted that the limitations refer only to plans already held for polymetallic nodule mining (that is, manganese nodules) and not to other mineral resources. Nor does it refer to any participation which the applicant may have in a reserved site.[128] The reference to 'either part of the area covered by the application for a plan of work' is to the two parts of equal estimated commercial value into which applicants have to divide areas under Article 8 of Annex III. Finally, *ex abundanti cautela*, it should be noted that the words 'already holds' were included in Subparagraph (c) with the specific intention of making it clear that sites to be counted for anti-monopoly purposes are limited to those which the applicant State (or entities sponsored by it) already *holds* and do not include sites *once held* but now exhausted or abandoned – a construction which might have been possible under an earlier draft of this provision.[129]

The effect of this first of the two anti-monopoly clauses will be to limit the proportion of prime mining sites which may be exploited by any one State (including entities sponsored by it).

Under the second anti-monopoly clause, the Authority may not approve a plan of work submitted or sponsored by a State Party which already holds:

> plans of work for the exploration and exploitation of polymetallic nodules in non-reserved areas which, taken together, constitute 2 per cent of the total sea-bed area which is not reserved or disapproved for exploitation pursuant to article 162, paragraph 2(x).[130]

In an earlier draft the limit had been set at 3 per cent but this was reduced following complaints from India and other developing States.[131]

Under paragraph 4 of Article 6, for the purpose of the calculations required under the anti-monopoly clauses of Paragraph 3(c),

---

[127] UN Convention, Annex III, Art. 6(3)(c)(i).

[128] On reserved areas, see below, section VII. France unsuccessfully urged that such participation should be taken into account in the calculation. See *Proposal Suggesting a New Wording for Articles 6 and 7 of Annex II (Anti-dominant position clause)*, WG. 21/Informal Paper 3, 10 August 1979, and US Delegation Report on the *Ninth Session, New York, March 3 - April 4 1980*, in Nordquist and Park, *op.cit.* in note 28 above, p. 351, at pp. 367-368.

[129] *Ibid.*, at p. 368. The earlier draft was ICNT/Rev.1, which referred in Annex II, Art.6(3)(d) to '... a State party which has already had approved ...'

[130] Annex III, Art. 6(3)(c)(ii).

[131] US Delegation Report cited in note 28 above, at p.368.

122   *Chapter 4*

> a plan of work submitted by a partnership or consortium shall be counted on a *pro rata* basis among the sponsoring States Parties involved in accordance with article 4, paragraph, 3 of this Annex.

If the language is somewhat complex, the meaning of this provision is quite clear. Unfortunately, the same cannot be said of the remaining, second sentence of Paragraph 4, which provides that:

> The Authority may approve plans of work covered by paragraph 3(c) if it determines that such approval would not permit a State Party or entities sponsored by it to monopolise the conduct of activities in the Area or to preclude other States Parties from activities in the Area.

Though the natural expectation might be that this second sentence related only to the plans of work referred to in the first sentence, that is those proposed by partnerships or consortia, there seems to be no other reason for such a supposition and the language suggests that it applies to all proposed plans of work 'covered by paragraph 3(c)'. Assuming this to be so, what is meant by the clause 'to monopolise the conduct of activities in the Area or to preclude other States Parties from activities in the Area'? *Prima facie*, it would seem that a State would reach a position of monopoly when either of the situations described in Paragraph 3(c)(i) and (ii) came into existence. If this is so, then this sentence can only mean that the Authority has the discretion, notwithstanding the result of a calculation under Paragraph 3(c), to determine that approval of the plan of work in question would not permit a State Party or person sponsored by it to monopolise the conduct of activities in the Area (or to preclude other States from activities in the Area). Such a determination would be made by the Council under Section 3, paragraph 11(a) of the Annex to the Implementation Agreement, following receipt of a recommendation from the Legal and Technical Commission under Article 165(2)(b).

Finally, it should be noted that Paragraph 5 of Article 6, which referred to rules governing selection among applicants following the expiry of a 25-year interim period specified in Article 151(3) of the UN Convention, has been rendered inapplicable by the Implementation Agreement – as has been Article 151(3) itself.[132]

Under the Implementation Agreement,[133] plans of work for exploration are approved for a period of fifteen years in the first instance. The contractor must then apply for a plan of work for exploitation unless it has already done so or has obtained an extension for the plan of work for exploration. Such extensions, for periods of not more than five years, may be approved if the contractor has made efforts in good faith to comply with the requirements of the plan of work but, for reasons beyond its control, has been unable to complete the necessary preparatory

---

[132] Implementation Agreement (*loc.cit.* in note 16 above), Annex, Sec.6, para.7.
[133] *Loc.cit.* in note 16 above, Annex, Sec.1, para.9.

work for proceeding to the exploitation stage, or the prevailing economic circumstances do not justify proceeding to the exploitation stage. However, notwithstanding these provisions, where the approved plan of work was sponsored by at least one State which was provisionally applying the Implementation Agreement, it was to terminate if the State ceased to apply the Agreement provisionally and had not become either a member of the Authority on a provisional basis or a State Party to the Implementation Agreement.[134] Similarly, where the application was sponsored by a State which was a member of the Authority on a provisional basis, the approved plan of work was to terminate if such membership ceased and the State had not become a State Party.[135]

5. Security of Tenure for Contractors
Paragraph 6 of Article 153 provides that:

> A contract under paragraph 3 shall provide for security of tenure. Accordingly, the contract shall not be revised, suspended or terminated except in accordance with Annex III, articles 18 and 19.

Further protection is provided by Article 16 of Annex III:

Article 16
Exclusive right to explore and exploit

> The Authority shall, pursuant to Part XI and its rules, regulations and procedures, accord the operator the exclusive right to explore and exploit the area covered by the plan of work in respect of a specified category of resources and shall ensure that no other entity operates in the same area for a different category of resources in a manner which might interfere with the operations of the operator. The operator shall have security of tenure in accordance with article 153, paragraph 6.

VI. PRODUCTION POLICIES: UN CONVENTION, ARTICLE 151 AND IMPLEMENTATION AGREEMENT, ANNEX, SECTION 6

Under the original UN Convention, the question of production policies was dealt with in Article 151 and Annex III, Article 7. Pursuant to these provisions, approval of a plan of work did not in itself authorise the contractor to proceed with production. This required a separate production authorisation which would be issued only if the production in question, when added to the production authorised for other operators, would be within the limits set by the Authority in accordance with the 'production policies' laid down in Article 151.

---

[134] *Ibid.*, para.11. See too text above, following note 100.
[135] *Ibid.*, para.12(d). See too text above, following note 100.

124   *Chapter 4*

As has been seen,[136] under Article 150(h) of the UN Convention, activities in the Area are to be carried out with a view to ensuring, *inter alia:*

> the protection of developing countries from adverse effects on their economies or on their export earnings resulting from a reduction in the price of an affected mineral, or in the volume of exports of that mineral, to the extent that such reduction is caused by activities in the Area, as provided in article 151.

The production policies laid down in Article 151 sought to ensure such protection in three ways – through commodity arrangements, production controls and compensatory economic assistance. Special provision was also made for non-nodule minerals.[137] In designing these mechanisms, it had of course to be borne in mind that a balance had to be maintained between this need to protect developing States and the need to facilitate the development of sea-bed mining, one of the policy objectives recognised in Article 150(i).[138] To put it crudely,

---

[136] In Chap.3, section XII.

[137] Art.151(9) provided that:

> The Authority shall have the power to limit the level of production of minerals from the Area, other than minerals from polymetallic nodules, under such conditions and applying such methods as may be appropriate by adopting regulations in accordance with article 161, paragraph 8.

In addition, Art.162(2)(o)(ii), after according priority to the provisional adoption by the Council of rules, regulations and procedures for the exploration for and exploitation of manganese nodules, provided that:

> Rules, regulations and procedures for the exploration for and exploitation of any resource other than polymetyallic nodules shall be adopted within three years from the date of a request to the Authority by any of its members to adopt such rules, regulations and procedures in respect of such resource.

Being part of the 1982 regime designed to place limits on the level of production, Art.151(9) was rendered inapplicable by the Implementation Agreement (Annex, Section 6, para.7). Art.162(2)(o)(ii), however, survives. See further below, section XVIII.

PrepCom's Special Commisison 1 (SCN.1) decided early in its proceedings to concentrate its attention on polymetallic nodules (LOS/PCN/L.2, 11 April 1984, VI *Final PrepCom Report*, p.34, at p.35(5); I *Platözder (PrepCom)*, p.428, at p.429(5)). This policy was later reflected in its Draft Provisional Recommendations, in which it recommended that: 'The Authority should concentrate its work on polymetallic nodules, including the projected timing of commercial production from the Area.' (Provisional Report of Special Commission 1, in PrepCom, *Consolidated Provisional Final Report* Vol.I, LOS/PCN/130, 17 November 1993, p.39, at p.51; VI *Final PrepCom Report*, p.5, at p.17, 'Draft provisional recommendation 1'). However, it was added that: 'It should also keep in view the trends and developments regarding seabed minerals other than polymetallic nodules, for example, polymetallic sulphides, cobalt-rich crusts, etc.' (*ibid.*).

Similarly, SCN.3, in drafting the 'Mining Code', decided to restrict it in the first instance to polymetallic nodules, recognising that it could be extended to cover other sea-bed resources later (*Statement to the Plenary by the Chairman of Special Commission 3 on the Progress of Work in that Commission*, LOS/PCN/L.16, 2 April 1985, XII *Final PrepCom Report*, p.14, at p.15(4) and Draft Regulations on Prospecting, Exploration and Exploitation of Polymetallic Nodules in the Area, LOS/PCN/SCN.3/WP.6, 15 March 1985, in PrepCom, *Draft final report of Special Commission 3*, LOS/PCN/SCN.3/1992/CRP.17, 22 July 1992 (XIII *PrepCom Final Report*, p.19, at p.24, Art.1). On the position under the Mining Code adopted in July 2000, see Chap. 5, introductory paras., at notes 6-7 and section II.1.3.

[138] Para.1 of Art.151 was 'Without prejudice to the objectives set forth in article 150 . . .'

production from the sea-bed must be high enough to make sea-bed mining economically viable but low enough to protect the interests of land-based producers.

Over the years following the adoption of the UN Convention, it became clear that these production policies were not acceptable to the developed States and were indeed regarded as one of the features of Part XI which constituted an obstacle to ratification of the Convention. Fortunately, following intensive consultations within the framework of the Secretary-General's Informal Consultations, the highly detailed and complex provisions of Article 151 and Annex III, Article 7[139] have been replaced by a new 'Production Policy' embodied in Section 6 of the Annex to the Implementation Agreement. As will be seen below, Section 6 confines itself to setting out the principles on which the production policy of the Authority is to be based and a few complementary rules expressed in general terms. It is left to the Authority to ensure the implementation of these provisions by developing rules, regulations and procedures, including those required to govern the approval of plans of work.[140]

Under Section 6(7) of the Annex to the Implementation Agreement, it is provided that the following provisions of the UN Convention 'shall not apply': Article 151(1)-(7) and Annex III, Article 7. The effect of this is to eliminate a very large part of the provision made for 'production policies' in the Convention. Articles 162(2)(q) and 165(2)(n) – which refer to the powers of the Council and the Legal and Technical Commission in the implementation of these policies – are also rendered inapplicable.

As a result of this radical surgery, production policy is now governed by the remains of Article 151 of the UN Convention, that is, Paragraphs 8 and 10, and Section 6 of the Annex to the Implementation Agreement.

1. Unfair Economic Practices – UN Convention, Article 151(8) and Section 6 of Annex to the Implementation Agreement
Article 151(8) of the UN Convention provides that:

> Rights and obligations relating to unfair economic practices under relevant multilateral trade agreements shall apply to the exploration for and exploitation of minerals from the Area. In the settlement of disputes arising under this provision, States Parties which are Parties to such multilateral trade agreements shall have recourse to the dispute settlement procedures of such agreements.

This provision was added at the Eleventh Session of UNCLOS III[141] in an effort to accommodate the anxiety of some land-based mineral producers, including in

---

[139] For details, see the first edition of this work: *Sea-Bed Energy and Mineral Resources and the Law of the Sea, Vol.2: The Area Beyond the Limits of National Jurisdiction*, Graham & Trotman, 1986, Chap.4, section VI.

[140] Implementation Agreement, (*loc.cit.* in note 16 above), Annex, Sec.6, para.6.

[141] *Report of the President to the Conference*, A/CONF.62/L.141 and Add.1, 28 April 1982 (*UNCLOS III Off.Rec.*, Vol.XVI, p.247, at p.248, Annex); the reference is to 'Article 151(2) bis'.

126   *Chapter 4*

particular Australia.[142]   Their fear was that a State Party, desiring to develop a sea-bed mining industry for reasons other than purely commercial, might give the project some aid, financial or otherwise, which was not available to commercially operated land-based projects, thus giving the sea-bed producer an advantage in the market and enabling him to undercut prices.[143]   The Australian delegation made a proposal to the effect that States Parties, in the production, processing, transport and marketing of minerals and commodities, derived from the resources of the Area, should avoid economic practices which caused or threatened to cause, material injury to the interest of another State Party.[144]   However, some difficulty was experienced in finding a generally acceptable formula[145], some delegations feeling that any constraints on trade practices should apply equally to the mineral industry as a whole, both to the land-based and to the sea-bed mining sectors[146].   As can be seen, Article 151(8) reflects this thinking.

Section 6 of the Annex to the Implementation Agreement, in essence, develops these provisions of Article 151(8) of the UN Convention.   It does so by elaborating a set of seven 'principles' on which the production policy of the Authority is to be based.   These principles and related provisions may be summarised as follows:

(i) Sound commercial principles.   Development of the resources of the Area is to take place in accordance with sound commercial principles.[147]

(ii) GATT made applicable.   The provisions of the General Agreement on Tariffs and Trade and its relevant codes and successor or superseding agreements (hereafter 'GATT etc.') are made applicable to activities in the Area.[148]

(iii)   No subsidies.   The subsidisation of activities in the Area is prohibited, except as may be permitted under GATT etc.[149]   The acceptance of forbidden subsidies by a contractor will constitute a violation of the fundamental terms of the contract forming a plan of work.[150]   Where, under GATT etc. arrangements, a State Party is determined to have engaged in 'subsidisation which is prohibited or has resulted in adverse effects to the interests of another' State Party, and 'appropriate steps' have not been taken by the relevant State Party or Parties, a State Party may request the Council (of the Authority) 'to take appropriate measures.'[151]

(iv) No discrimination or preferences.   There must be no discrimination between minerals from the Area and from other sources.   Nor must there be any preferential access to markets for such minerals, or commodities produced from

---

[142] Australia raised the question at the Ninth Session. See further A/CONF.62/C.1/L.27, 27 March 1980 (*UNCLOS III Off. Rec.*, Vol. XIII, p. 113), at p. 123(22)-(25).

[143] See A/CONF.62/C.1/L.28 and Add.1, 23 August 1980 (*UNCLOS III Off. Rec.*, Vol. XIV, p. 161), at p. 163.

[144] See A/CONF.62/L.81, 29 September 1981 (*UNCLOS III Off. Rec.*, Vol. XV, p. 241), at p. 242(6).

[145] See, *e.g.*, Mr. Nandan's remarks in *loc. cit.* in note 143 above, at p. 163.

[146] *Ibid.*

[147] Implementation Agreement (*loc.cit.* in note 16 above), Annex, Sec.6, para.1(a).

[148] *Ibid.*, Sec.6, para.1(b).

[149] *Ibid.*, Sec.6, para.1(c).

[150] *Ibid.*, Sec.6, para.3.

[151] *Ibid.*, Sec.6, para.1(g).

them. Particular reference is made to preferences effected by use of tariff or non-tariff barriers and to preferences given by States to their State enterprises or their nationals.[152]

(v) Plans of work to estimate maximum production. The plan of work for exploitation will have to indicate an anticipated production schedule, including an estimate of the maximum amounts of minerals to be produced per year.[153]

(vi) Dispute settlement. As noted in (ii) above, the provisions of GATT etc. are made applicable to States Parties to the Implementation Agreement with respect to activities in the Area. Where, however, a dispute arises concerning those provisions, the dispute settlement procedure to be adopted depends upon whether or not the disputing States are parties to GATT etc. If all of them are parties to GATT etc., they will have recourse to the dispute settlement procedures of GATT etc. Where, on the other hand, one or more of the disputing States are not parties to GATT etc., they will have recourse to the dispute settlement procedures provided in the UN Convention.[154] In either case, the dispute settlement procedure may be initiated by any State Party to the Implementation Agreement which has reason to believe that there has been a breach of the above-mentioned provisions of GATT etc., or the principles banning subsidisation and discrimination.[155] A State Party may also at any time bring to the attention of the Council activities which in its view are inconsistent with these provisions or principles.[156]

(vii) Priority to GATT etc. and free trade and customs union agreements. It is provided that the principles of the production policy of the Authority laid down in paragraph 1 of Section 6 shall not affect rights and obligations under GATT etc., as well as relevant free trade and customs union agreements, in relations between States Parties which are parties to such agreements.[157]

2. Economic Assistance to Developing Countries – UN Convention, Article 151(10) and Section 6 of Annex to the Implementation Agreement

As has been noted above, one of the three ways in which the UN Convention sought to ensure protection for developing countries was through compensatory economic assistance. The original production control system was based on a nickel production ceiling linked to the annual increase in nickel consumption, and this nickel ceiling also sets the limits for production of other metals from nodules. Unfortunately, however, because of the ratio of metals contained in nodules, this system would have allowed production of, for example, cobalt and manganese, far in excess of any increase in consumption of these minerals and thus would have posed a real threat to land-based producers of these minerals.[158] Article 151(10) sought to deal with this problem by providing that:

---

[152] *Ibid.*, Sec.6, para.1(d).
[153] *Ibid.*, Sec.6, para.1(e).
[154] *Ibid.*, Sec.6, para.1(f). On the dispute settlement provisions of the UN Convention, see Chap.9.
[155] *Ibid.*, Sec.6, para.4.
[156] *Ibid.*, Sec.6, para.5.
[157] *Ibid.*, Sec.6, para.2.
[158] For further details, see *op.cit.* in note 139 above, Chap.4, section VI.3.

128   *Chapter 4*

> Upon the recommendation of the Council on the basis of advice from the Economic Planning Commission, the Assembly shall establish a system of compensation or take other measures of economic adjustment assistance including co-operation with specialized agencies and other international organizations to assist developing countries which suffer serious adverse effects on their export earnings or economies resulting from a reduction in the price of an affected mineral or in the volume of exports of that mineral, to the extent that such reduction is caused by activities in the Area. The Authority on request shall initiate studies on the problems of those States which are likely to be most seriously affected with a view to minimizing their difficulties and assisting them in their economic adjustment.

It was recognised in the Conference that the problem was a very complex one, the solution of which would depend upon a detailed study of the mining industry which was beyond the scope of the Conference but should have a high priority in the work of the Economic Planning Commission. In fact, this difficult task was assigned to the Preparatory Commission's Special Commission 1 (SCN.1),[159] with a mandate to:

> undertake studies on the problems which would be encountered by developing land-based producer States likely to be most seriously affected by the production of minerals derived from the Area with a view to minimising their difficulties and helping them to make the necessary economic adjustment, including studies on the establishment of a compensation fund ...[160]

SCN.1 made considerable progress in its highly technical work [161] and went a long way towards the production of a set of recommendations for submission to the Authority.[162] However, at the close of the eleventh session, there were still significant areas of disagreement, especially over the formulation of measures to minimise the problems of affected developing land-based producer States. In particular, the European Community States and the Group of 77 took up fundamentally opposing positions on the nature and extent of assistance to be

---

[159] See further below, Chap.8, section III.2.

[160] Resolution I of UNCLOS III, para.5(i).

[161] See further (1) *Statement to the Plenary by the Chairman of Special Commission 1 on the Progress of Work in that Commission*, LOS/PCN/L.104, 20 August 1992 (VI *Final PrepCom Report*, p.173); (2) *Statement to the Plenary by the Chairman of Special Commission 1 on the Progress of Work in that Commission*, LOS/PCN/L.109, 1 April 1993 (VI *Final PrepCom Report*, p.179); (3) *Draft Provisional Report of Special Commission 1*, LOS/PCN/SCN.1/ 1992/CRP.22, 20 August 1992 and Adds. 1-4, 30 November 1992,and revised version entitled *Provisional Report of Special Commission 1* (PrepCom, *Consolidated Provisional Final Report*, Vol.I, LOS/PCN/130, 17 November 1993, pp.39-67; VI *Final PrepCom Report*, pp.5-33); and (4) Press Releases SEA/1353, 24 March 1993, SEA/1357, 26 March 1993, SEA/1363, 30 March 1993, SEA/1365, 31 March 1993 and SEA/1370, 2 April 1993.

[162] For 'Draft Provisional Recommendations', see PrepCom, *Consolidated Provisional Final Report*, Vol.I, LOS/PCN/130, 17 November 1993, at pp.51-67; VI *Final PrepCom Report*, pp.17-33.

The Basic Regime   129

provided by the Authority itself and the role that the Authority would have in deciding upon and implementing the assistance measures. Briefly, the European Community favoured a cost-effective use of resources, with the Authority acting as a catalyst to stimulate assistance from other international organisations already providing assistance to developing States. The Group of 77, on the other hand, insisted that the primary responsibility for deciding upon and implementing the requisite measures lay with the Authority.[163]   Some progress was made in bridging the gap at the tenth session of SCN.1, with agreement on the creation of a fund for the purpose of assistance to developing land-based producer States.[164] However, it was recognised in the Chairman's report that disagreements persisted, the three most significant ones being:

(a) whether the assistance to be provided by the Authority to developing land-based producer States, and the fund to be created for this purpose, could be termed economic adjustment assistance or compensation;

(b) what would be the role of the Authority *vis-à-vis* existing organisations in deciding upon and implementing assistance measures; and

(c) whether the Authority would be in a position to contribute to the financing of assistance measures, when such assistance was provided prior to the commencement of commercial production from the Area.[165]

The atmosphere of continuing divergence of views which permeated the final meeting of SCN.1 is accurately reflected in the following report which refers to a last-ditch effort by the European Community and its Member States to amend the Draft Provisional Report:

The amendments proposed by the European Community underline the provisional nature of the conclusions and recommendations of the Special Commission and the fact that divergent views existed on many critical issues and on the provisional recommendations.   Several representatives of developing countries stated that the European Community amendments painted a gloomy picture of the negotiations in the Special Commission and gave the entire report a negative slant by emphasizing what had not been accomplished.   In response, the representative of the European Community, supported by some speakers, said that the draft report must represent accurately the status of the Special Commission's deliberations even if that meant saying that critical issues had not been resolved.[166]

---

[163] See further *Progress Report of the Chairman of the Preparatory Commission*, LOS/PCN/L.103, 7 July 1992 (LOS/PCN/152 (Vol. IV), 1 May 1995, p.122), at pp.142-143, paras.77-81.
[164] LOS/PCN/L.104, 20 August 1992 (VI *Final PrepCom Report*, p.173, at pp.174-175, para.8).
[165] Ibid., at p.175., para.11.
[166] Press Release SEA/1365, 31 March 1993, p.1.   For the European Community's suggested amendment to the Draft Provisional Report, see LOS/PCN/SCN.1/1993/CRP.23 (IX *Final PrepCom Report*, p.181).

130   *Chapter 4*

It is true that the Special Commission was able to annex to its *Draft Provisional Report* a set of thirteen Draft Provisional Recommendations to be submitted to the Authority.[167]   However, agreement on some of the recommendations was secured only at a cost.   In some cases, the need to compromise resulted in vague recommendations[168]; and '... some issues, including some critical ones, remained unresolved ...'[169]

More recently, the provisions of Article 151(10) of the UN Convention have been supplemented by the Implementation Agreement.   Section 7 of the Annex to the Agreement – on 'Economic Assistance' – provides that Article 151(10) is to be 'implemented by means of measures of economic assistance referred to in paragraph 1.' [170]   Paragraph 1 states that the policy of the Authority is to be based on the following four principles:

(a)   The Authority shall establish an economic assistance fund from a portion of the funds of the Authority which exceeds those necessary to cover the administrative expenses of the Authority.   The amount set aside for this purpose shall be determined by the Council from time to time, upon the recommendation of the Finance Committee.   Only funds from payments received from contractors, including the Enterprise, and voluntary contributions shall be used for the establishment of the economic assistance fund;

(b)   Developing land-based producer States whose economies have been determined to be seriously affected by the production of minerals from the deep seabed shall be assisted from the economic assistance fund of the Authority;

(c)   The Authority shall provide assistance from the fund to developing land-based producer States, where appropriate, in cooperation with existing global or regional development institutions which have the infrastructure and expertise to carry out such assistance programmes;

(d)   The extent and period of such assistance shall be determined on a case-by-case basis.   In doing so, due consideration shall be given to the nature and magnitude of the problems encountered by affected developing land-based producer States.

The economic assistance fund was established by Regulation 5.8 of the Authority's Financial Regulations, which became effective on 23 March 2000. [171]

---

[167] *Loc. cit.* in note 162 above.

[168] See, *e.g.,* draft provisional recommendations 6, 7 and 12.

[169] *Provisional Report of Special Commission 1*, in PrepCom, *Consolidated Provisional Final Report*, Vol.I, LOS/PCN/130, 17 November 1993, p.39, at p.44(176); VI *Final PrepCom Report*, p.5, at p.10 (176).   Such issues are square-bracketed in the text.   However, the identification of passages to be square-bracketed had not been completed at the time of writing the *Provisional Report (ibid.)*.

[170] Implementation Agreement *(loc.cit.* in note 16 above), Annex, Sec.7, para.2.

[171] ISBA/6/A/3, 28 March 2000, Annex.   See further on the 'Financial Arrangements of the Authority', Chap. 8, section II.3.   On the 'Participation of Developing States in Activities in the Area', see Chap. 3, section XII.

Several other provisions of the UN Convention which are related to Article 151(10) are to be 'interpreted accordingly'[172]: Article 160(2)(1), referring to the powers and functions of the Assembly as including the establishment, upon the recommendation of the Council, on the basis of advice from the Economic Planning Commission, of a system of compensation or other measures of economic adjustment assistance as provided in Article 151(10); Articles 162(2)(n) and 164(2)(d), referring to the roles of the Council and the Economic Planning Commission; Article 171(f), referring to the funds of the Authority as including payments to a compensation fund, in accordance with Article 151(10), the sources of which are to be recommended by the Economic Planning Commission; and, finally, Article 173(2)(c), which authorised the use of Authority funds, after payment of administrative expenses, for compensation under Article 151(10).

The task of assessing the impact of mineral production from the Area on the economies of developing land-based producers remains a formidable one. As was noted above, the Preparatory Commission's Special Commission 1 was mandated to study this question. Under the Implementation Agreement, the burden has now been passed on. One of the tasks on which the Authority is to concentrate between the entry into force of the UN Convention and the approval of the first plan of work for exploitation is:

> Study of the potential impact of mineral production from the Area on the economies of developing land-based producers of those minerals which are likely to be most seriously affected, with a view to minimising their difficulties and assisting them in their economic adjustment, taking into account the work done in this regard by the Preparatory Commission;[173]

VII. RESERVATION OF SITES (THE 'BANKING' SYSTEM): RIGHTS, OBLIGATIONS AND OPPORTUNITIES OF OPERATORS OTHER THAN THE ENTERPRISE IN RELATION TO RESERVED SITES: ANNEX III, ARTICLES 8, 9 AND 11 AND IMPLEMENTATION AGREEMENT, ANNEX, SECTION 1(10)

Mention has already been made above[174] of what is sometimes referred to as the 'banking' system, first introduced in the Revised Single Negotiating Text in 1976[175] and now embodied in Article 8 of Annex III of the Convention. The obligations imposed on the applicant for a contract under this provision are perhaps best regarded as part of the price paid by the contractor for his concession. In its essentials, the system requires that the applicant should give the Authority the opportunity to reserve one half of the proposed contract area for exploitation 'through the Enterprise or in association with developing States'. The 'half' refers not to area but to estimated commercial value. The reserved half may thus be 'banked' by the Authority.

---

[172] *Loc. cit.* in note 170 above..

[173] Implementation Agreement (*loc.cit.* in note 16 above), Annex, Sec.1, para.5(e).

[174] Above, Chap.3, section XII, following note 192.

[175] *UNCLOS III Off.Rec.*, Vol.V, p.125, Part One, Annex I, Para.8(d).

132   *Chapter 4*

The purpose of this section is to provide an analysis of the rights, obligations and opportunities of operators other than the Enterprise in relation to such reserved sites. Clearly, this is only half of the story, the other half being concerned with the rights and obligations of the Enterprise. Since, however, the position of the Enterprise can be understood only in the context of a more comprehensive study of its institutional features and financial structure, consideration of this side of the system will be excluded from this section and is dealt with in Chapter 8. Article 8 of Annex III provides that:

> Each application, other than those submitted by the Enterprise or by any other entities for reserved areas, shall cover a total area, which need not be a single continuous area, sufficiently large and of sufficient estimated commercial value to allow two mining operations. The applicant shall indicate the co-ordinates dividing the area into two parts of equal estimated commercial value and submit all the data obtained by him with respect to both parts. Without prejudice to the powers of the Authority pursuant to article 17 of this Annex, the data to be submitted concerning polymetallic nodules shall relate to mapping, sampling, the abundance of nodules, and their metal content. Within 45 days of receiving such data, the Authority shall designate which part is to be reserved solely for the conduct of activities by the Authority through the Enterprise or in association with developing States. This designation may be deferred for a further period of 45 days if the Authority requests an independent expert to assess whether all data required by this article has been submitted. The area designated shall become a reserved area as soon as the plan of work for the non-reserved area is approved and the contract is signed.

In a supplementary provision, Section 1, Paragraph 10 of the Annex to the Implementation Agreement now adds that designation of a reserved area in accordance with Annex III, Article 8 is to take place 'in connection with approval of an application for a plan of work for exploration or approval of an application for a plan of work for exploration and exploitation'.

There are a number of points to note about the above provisions:

(i) The proposed contract area must be sufficiently large and of sufficient estimated commercial value to allow the Authority to determine that one half of it should be so reserved. The point of this provision is, of course, that, given the costs involved in the development of any site, irrespective of size or value, there is a certain minimum below which sites will not be economically viable.

(ii) During the UNCLOS III consideration of this Article, the industrialised States were anxious to place clear restrictions on the scope of the obligation to supply data to the Authority. Fears were expressed that earlier drafts of this provision were so vaguely formulated as to enable the Authority to interpret 'relevant data' as extending to data not only from the 'prospecting' stage but also

The Basic Regime 133

from the very much more expensive 'exploration' stage.[176] Even as recently as in its ICNT/Rev. 1 version, Article 8 would clearly have allowed the Authority to call for additional data from the applicant, since it was required to designate a reserved site only 'within 45 days of receiving *the data necessary to make the assessment of the value of the sites from the applicant'*.[177] The United States delegation described this clause as 'an undesirable provision permitting the Authority to require the prospector to do additional prospecting before it chooses the reserved site'[178] and succeeded in having an acceptably amended version incorporated in ICNT/Rev.2.[179] Commenting on this version, which, apart from minor drafting revisions, remains unchanged in the UN Convention, the United States delegation reported that:

> The revised text makes clear that the obligation of the applicant to submit data to the Authority concerning the area covered by his application is limited to that data which already has been obtained by him. This clarification is accompanied by a new provision which permits the Authority to defer action on the application for an additional forty-five day period if the Authority requests an independent expert to assess whether all data required has been submitted to the Authority. This provision would presumably permit the Authority to verify that the applicant has not withheld data already obtained by him but, unlike the earlier text, does not authorise the Authority to require the applicant to obtain additional data for submission to the Authority.[180]

With respect, this seems to be a remarkably optimistic interpretation of this provision. Given the underlying purpose for which data is to be supplied (to enable the Authority to check that the two parts of the proposed area are of equal estimated commercial value and to choose one of them for designation as a reserved site) and the description of the role of the independent expert as being 'to assess whether all data required by this article has been submitted', it is a little difficult to think that the expert's only function would be to determine whether the applicant had withheld data already obtained by him. A similar claim was made by the United States delegation at the Ninth Session of the Conference, when it was asserted that Article 8 preserved 'for the applicant the necessary

---

[176] *Report of the Committee on the Law of the Sea of the American Branch of the International Law Association*, March 1978, pp. 29-30 and note 4. The complaint referred to the ICNT version (1977 - Annex II, para. 5(j)(i)), under which the designation was to be made by the Authority 'as soon as the Authority had been able to examine the relevant data as may be necessary to decide that both parts are equal in estimated commercial value.'

[177] A/CONF.62/WP.10/Rev.1, 28 April 1979, Annex II; Platzöder, *Documents*, Vol. I, p. 375, at p. 505.

[178] *Loc.cit.* in note 28, at p. 266.

[179] A/CONF.62/WP.10/Rev.2, 11 April 1980 and Corr. 1-3, p. 157; Platzöder, *Documents*, Vol. II, p. 3, at p. 135.

[180] US Delegation Report on *Eighth Session (Resumed), New York, July 19 - August 24, 1979*, in Nordquist and Park, *op.cit.* in note 28 above, p.301, at pp. 313-314.

134   *Chapter 4*

decision as to when he has sufficient data to submit his application and obtain assurance of receiving his site'.[181]

(iii) Assuming that the Authority is satisfied that it has received the necessary data from the applicant, it is bound to designate the part of the proposed area which is to be a reserved site within 45 days; or within a further 45 days if it wishes to have an independent expert assessment as to whether all data required by Article 8 has been submitted. In the absence of a negative report from the expert, the Authority would not therefore be able to delay such designation beyond this 90-day period. It follows, of course, that there should be no delay from this quarter in the approval under Article 6 of the plan of work for the non-reserved part of the proposed area.

As will be seen below in Chapter 8, the expectation is that the Enterprise, alone or in association with other entities, will carry out activities in reserved sites. Should it decide not to do so, however, it is open to *developing* States (or entities sponsored by them) to apply for a contract.   The procedure is laid down in Article 9 of Annex III. First, under Paragraph 4:

> Any State Party which is a developing State or any   natural or juridical person sponsored by it and effectively controlled by it or by other developing State which is a qualified applicant, or any group of the foregoing, may notify the Authority that it wishes to submit a plan of work pursuant to article 6 of this Annex with respect to a reserved area. The plan of work shall be considered if the Enterprise decides, pursuant to paragraph 1, that it does not intend to carry out activities in that area.

Under Paragraph 1, the Enterprise must decide 'within a reasonable time'. [182]

The opportunities which States and other entities may have for participation in activities in the Area through contracts or joint ventures with the Enterprise[183] are considered below in Chapter 8.[184]

VIII. FINANCIAL TERMS OF CONTRACTS: UN CONVENTION, ANNEX III, ARTICLE 13 AND IMPLEMENTATION AGREEMENT, ANNEX, SECTION 8

The rules governing the financial terms of contracts were originally laid down in the exceedingly complex provisions of the UN Convention, Annex III, Article 13.[185]   That Article was radically revised by the Implementation Agreement. However, since the relevant provisions of the Implementation Agreement – Section 8 of the Annex on 'Financial Terms of Contract' – largely take the form of a set of six principles designed to provide a basis for the later establishment of

---

[181] US Delegation Report cited in note 128 above, at p.369.
[182] See further on the operations of the Enterprise in reserved areas, below, Chap. 8, section II.2.4.3.
[183] Under Annex III, Art. 9(2) and (3) and Art. 11 and the Implementation Agreement, Annex, Sec.2.
[184] See Chap.8, section II. 2.4.4.
[185] For a detailed account, see the first edition of this work, *op.cit.* in note 139 above, Chap.4, section VIII.

The Basic Regime 135

rules, regulations and procedures for financial terms of contract, it is difficult to gauge how far-reaching this revision will eventually prove to be.

The original Article 13 of Annex III consisted of fifteen paragraphs. Pursuant to the Implementation Agreement, Paragraphs 1, 2 and 11-15 will continue to apply but Paragraphs 3-10 'shall not apply'.[186] Moreover, as will be seen below, Paragraph 2 has been revised, 'with regard to [its] ... implementation'.[187] Following a brief note on the negotiation of the original 1982 regime, an account will be given in this section of the surviving paragraphs of Article 13 and of the framework of principles established by the Implementation Agreement as a basis for the elaboration of a revised regime.

As so often in the negotiation of the regime for the exploitation of the Area, the process of negotiating the provisions of the Convention governing the financial terms of contracts was one of gradually moving towards a compromise between the wishes of the Group of 77 and those of the developed States. As might be expected, the former have tended to base their proposals on highly optimistic assumptions about the profitability of sea-bed mining, whereas the latter stressed in their proposals the high degree of risk for participants in this infant industry.

Two other strands of thinking may be noted before the details of Article 13 of Annex III are considered. First, the developing countries were concerned to ensure not only that the overall share of the Authority in the proceeds of deep-sea mining should be substantial but also that a significant part of the Authority's share should take the form of 'front-end' payments, that is, payments made at the beginning or in the early years of the contract before commercial production has started to generate income for the contractor. The reason for this preference was the need, as then perceived, to provide funds to enable the Enterprise to commence operations without too much delay.

Secondly, it should be noted that the system in Article 13 does not apply to operations undertaken by the Enterprise, although several industrialised countries suggested that it should[188].

Obviously, the Implementation Agreement reflects a change in the balance of influence as between the developing and developed States but it will not be possible to evaluate fully the significance of this change until the general principles which are to govern the financial terms of contracts have been developed in detail in a further instalment of the Mining Code devoted to the exploitation of polymetallic nodules.

---

[186] Implementation Agreement (*loc.cit.* in note 16 above), Annex, Sec.8, para.2.

[187] *Ibid.*, Sec.8, para.3.

[188] See further *The Chairman's Explanatory Memorandum on document NG2/7, UNCLOS III Off. Rec.*, Vol. X, p. 63, at para. 1. There was, however, a close relationship between the financing of the Enterprise and the financial terms of contracts under the original UN Convention regime. See further Chap. 8, section II.2.5 and *UNCLOS III Off. Rec.*, Vol. XIII, p. 124. Moreover, as will be seen in Chap. 8, section II.2, the Implementation Agreement has removed many of the differences between the Enterprise and other contractors.

136   Chapter 4

1. The Objectives of the Financial Terms of Contracts: UN Convention, Annex III, Article 13(1)

As has been seen, Article 13(1) has survived the revision effected by the Implementation Agreement. Under this paragraph, the Authority, in adopting rules, regulations and procedures concerning the financial terms of contracts, and in negotiating these terms, is to be guided by the following six objectives:

(a) to ensure optimum revenues for the Authority from the proceeds of commercial production;

(b) to attract investments and technology to the exploration and exploitation of the Area;

(c) to ensure equality of financial treatment and comparable financial obligations for contractors;

(d) to provide incentives on a uniform and non-discriminatory basis for contractors to undertake joint arrangements with the Enterprise and developing States or their nationals, to stimulate the transfer of technology thereto, and to train the personnel of the Authority and of developing States;

(e) to enable the Enterprise to engage in sea-bed mining effectively at the same time as the entities referred to in article 153, paragraph 2(b); and

(f) to ensure that, as a result of the financial incentives provided to contractors under paragraph 14, under the terms of contracts reviewed in accordance with article 19 of this Annex or under the provisions of article 11 of this Annex with respect to joint ventures, contractors are not subsidised so as to be given an artificial competitive advantage with respect to land-based miners.

Clearly, some of these objectives conflict with others and Mr. Koh, who presided over the negotiations which led to this formulation, saw his task as being to produce compromise proposals which would embody a balance among these objectives, 'in particular the objective of ensuring optimum revenues for the Authority, the objective of attracting investment to sea-bed mining and the objective of enabling the Enterprise to engage in sea-bed mining as early as possible.'[189]

Some of the developed countries asked for the deletion of objectives four and five (sub-paragraphs (d) and (e) above). Mr. Koh justified his decision to retain them on the ground that he considered them 'part of the package offered by the developed countries to the developing countries for the acceptance of the parallel system of exploration and exploitation.'[190]

The sixth objective (sub-paragraph (f)) appeared for the first time in ICNT/REV.2 (1980) and was based on a proposal made by the Group of 77. As it was put by the Chairman of the Working Group of 21:

---

[189] *Report by the Chairman of Negotiating Group 2 to the First Committee*, NG2/10/Rev.1, 14 September 1978, *UNCLOS III Off. Rec.*, Vol. X, p. 144.

[190] *UNCLOS III Off. Rec.*, Vol. X, p. 63(2).

The evil which the Group of 77 wishes to avoid is that investment would be artificially diverted from land-based mining to sea-bed mining if the financial terms of sea-bed mining were unduly favourable compared to those of land-based mining.[191]

2. Types of Payment Envisaged: UN Convention, Annex III, Article 13(2)-(10) and the Implementation Agreement, Annex, Section 8(1) and (3)

Article 13, in its original 1982 form, made provision for three types of payment: (i) an application fee; (ii) an annual fixed fee; and (iii) *either* a production charge (royalty) only *or* a mixed system of production charge (royalty) and share of net proceeds.

The Implementation Agreement also refers to these three types of payment. However, whereas the original 1982 version went on to define the various types of payment in very great and complex detail, the Implementation Agreement remains on the level of general principle.

Given the fact that the 1982 provisions are not now to apply, it will suffice to refer to the detailed analysis of these provisions provided in the first edition of this work[192] and to concentrate here on the provisions of the Implementation Agreement. Whether or to what extent the Authority will draw upon the earlier formulae in elaborating the 1994 principles remains to be seen.

2.1 The System of Payments under the Implementation Agreement: the Implementation Agreement, Annex, Section 8

Section 8 includes both principles of a more general nature and principles specifically referring to the various types of payments which may be incorporated in the system to be adopted by the Authority.

The more general principles are as follows:

(i) 'The system of payments to the Authority shall be fair both to the contractor and to the Authority and shall provide adequate means of determining compliance by the contractor with such system.'[193]

(ii) 'The rates of payments under the system shall be within the range of those prevailing in respect of land-based mining of the same or similar minerals in order to avoid giving deep seabed miners an artificial competitive advantage or imposing on them a competitive disadvantage.'[194]

(iii) 'The system of payments may be revised periodically in the light of changing circumstances. Any changes shall be applied in a non-discriminatory manner. Such changes may apply to existing contracts only at the election of the contractor. Any subsequent change in choice

---

[191] *UNCLOS III Off. Rec.*, Vol. XII, p. 78.
[192] *Loc.cit.* in note 185 above.
[193] Implementation Agreement, Annex, Sec.8, para.1(a).
[194] *Ibid.*, para.1(b).

138 *Chapter 4*

between alternative systems shall be made by agreement between the Authority and the contractor.'[195]

(iv) Disputes concerning the interpretation or application of the rules and regulations based on these principles shall be subject to the dispute settlement procedures set out in the Convention.'[196]

In relatively more specific terms, reference is made to the various types of payment which may be adopted under the system to be developed by the Authority, as follows:

2.1.1 An Application Fee: UN Convention, Annex III, Article 13(2) and the Implementation Agreement, Annex, Section 8(3)

There appears to have been general agreement in UNCLOS III that applicants should pay an application fee to cover the cost of processing the applications and that the amount should be regularly reviewed. There were wide divergences, however, in the amounts proposed by various delegations. The European Community countries favoured a fee of $US 100,000, while the developing countries and the United States proposed $US 500,000.[197] In the event, the higher figure was adopted but subject to the proviso that, if the cost of processing an application was less than $US 500,000, the balance would be refunded. The amount of the fee is to be reviewed 'from time to time' by the Council in order to ensure that it covers the administrative cost of processing an application.[198]

The Implementation Agreement now provides, however, that:

With regard to the implementation of Annex III, article 13, paragraph 2, of the Convention, the fee for processing applications for approval of a plan of work limited to one phase, either the exploration phase or the exploitation phase, shall be US$ 250,000.[199]

Since this provision purports to be in 'implementation' of Article 13(2) of Annex III of the UN Convention and makes no reference to either the Council's power to review the fee or the Authority's obligation to refund any surplus over the actual administrative cost, it may be presumed that no change in these arrangements was intended and, indeed, this is confirmed by the Mining Code.[200]

2.1.2 An Annual Fixed Fee: Implementation Agreement, Annex, Section 8(1)(d)

Provision for an annual fixed fee was originally made in Article 13(3) of Annex III of the UN Convention. As noted above, however, that provision was

---

[195] *Ibid.*, para.1(e).
[196] *Ibid.*, para.1(f).
[197] Nordquist and Park, *op. cit.* in note 28 above. *Seventh Session, Geneva, March 28-May 19, 1978,* p. 185, at p. 203.
[198] *Ibid.*
[199] Implementation Agreement, Annex, Sec.8, para.3.
[200] Mining Code, Reg. 19. See further below, Chap. 5, section I.3.

The Basic Regime 139

rendered inapplicable by the Implementation Agreement.[201], which now provides instead that:

> An annual fixed fee shall be payable from the date of commencement of commercial production. This fee may be credited against other payments due under the system adopted in accordance with subparagraph (c). The amount of the fee shall be established by the Council.[202]

Perhaps the most important difference between the two formulae is that, whereas the 1982 version required a 'front-end' payment of an annual fixed fee of US$ 1 million from the date of entry into force of the contract, the 1994 type of payment (of a still to be specified amount) is payable only from the date of commencement of commercial production and may in any case be credited against the further payments to be made in the form of royalties or profit sharing.

2.1.3 Royalty System or Combined Royalty/Profit-Sharing System: *Implementation Agreement, Annex, Section 8(1)(c)*

On the assumption that sea-bed mining will prove to be highly profitable, the bulk of the payments to be made by the contractor will take the form of a payment related to production – whether as a royalty only, or as a royalty plus a share of the profits. When this element of the system of payments was being negotiated in UNCLOS III, the different views expressed on how best to design it were a reflection of the socio-economic philosophies of the States concerned. Thus, it came as no surprise that the European Community, Japan and the United States favoured a mixed system of nominal royalty plus profit-sharing which avoids heavy front-end payments and allows both profits and risks to be shared. The Authority benefits in good times; the contractor survives in bad times. The Soviet Union, on the other hand, considered that the royalty-only system was more consistent with its economic ideology and it was joined by Canada and Australia, both of which considered that royalties were relatively easy to administer and uniform in application.

Eventually, a compromise was arrived at which allowed either system to be used, at the option of the contractor. The provisions of the UN Convention which embody this compromise, Annex III, Article 13(5)-(6), are almost certainly the most complex in the Convention and were the product of long and arduous negotiations.[203] Fortunately, they have been rendered inapplicable by the Implementation Agreement. Unfortunately, it is by no means clear what will be put in their place. In referring to this element of the system, the Implementation Agreement simply provides that:

---

[201] *Ibid.*, para.2. For details of the original, UN Convention version, see *op.cit.* in note 139 above, Chap.4, section VIII 2.2.

[202] Implementation Agreement, Annex, Sec.8, para.1(d).

[203] For a detailed account, see the first edition of this work, *op.cit.* in note 139 above, Chap.4, section VIII 2.3.

140   *Chapter 4*

> The system should not be complicated and should not impose major administrative costs on the Authority or on a contractor. Consideration should be given to the adoption of a royalty system or a combination of a royalty and profit sharing system. If alternative systems are decided upon, the contractor has the right to choose the system applicable to its contract. Any subsequent change in choice between alternative systems, however, shall be made by agreement between the Authority and the contractor;[204]

While the expressed wish to avoid a complicated and costly system is admirable, it remains to be seen how the negotiators can improve on the system embodied in the original provisions of Annex III.

3. Accounting and Audit

Rules are laid down in Annex III of the UN Convention (Article 13, Paragraphs 10, 11 and 13) concerning the financial data to be made available by the contractor to the Authority and on the applicable accounting principles and financial rules, regulations and procedures. The Implementation Agreement provides that Paragraph 10, which obliges the contractor to supply such financial data as are required to determine compliance with the financial system, shall no longer apply, but leaves the other Paragraphs in place.[205]

4. Currency of Payments or Payments in Kind

Under Article 13, Paragraph 12 of Annex III, the contractor may make his payments to the Authority in freely usable currencies or currencies which are freely available and effectively usable on the major foreign exchange markets or, at the contractor's option, in the equivalents of processed metals at market values. The latter method is of course designed to accommodate States whose currencies are not freely convertible. This provision is unaffected by the Implementation Agreement.

5. Disputes over Financial Terms of Contracts

Under Article 13, Paragraph 15 of Annex III and Article 188, Paragraph 2 of the UN Convention, disputes between the contractor and the Authority over the interpretation or the application of the financial terms of a contract may be submitted by either party to binding commercial arbitration, unless both parties agree to settle the dispute by other means.[206] The Implementation Agreement leaves this provision undisturbed.

IX. Transfer of Data: UN Convention, Annex III, Article 14

Article 14, Paragraph 1 provides that:

---

[204] Implementation Agreement, Annex, Sec.8, para.1(c).
[205] *Ibid.*, para.2. On the accounts of the Authority and their audit, see also Financial Regulations of the Authority, ISA/00/01, June 2000, Regs. 11 and 12 and Annex.
[206] On dispute settlement more generally, see Chap. 9.

The operator shall transfer to the Authority, in accordance with its rules, regulations and procedures and the terms and conditions of the plan of work, at time intervals determined by the Authority all data which are both necessary for and relevant to the effective exercise of the powers and functions of the principal organs of the Authority in respect of the area covered by the plan of work.

The original ICNT version of this provision[207] referred to 'organs of the Authority' rather than 'principal organs of the Authority'. Since the paragraph in question referred specifically to 'the contract area', it was unlikely that it could have been interpreted to require the transfer of data needed to make the operation of the Enterprise in 'the Area' possible.[208] Mr. Njenga proposed the removal of any possible ambiguity, however, by substituting 'principal organs' for 'organs'.[209] The Enterprise is not of course one of the principal organs of the Authority. The point was in any event further emphasised by the subsequent addition of a third paragraph whereby:

Data transferred to the Authority by prospectors, applicants for contracts or contractors, deemed proprietary, shall not be disclosed by the Authority to the Enterprise or to anyone external to the Authority, but data on the reserved areas may be disclosed to the Enterprise. Such data transferred by such persons to the Enterprise shall not be disclosed by the Enterprise to the Authority or to anyone external to the Authority.

The need for the reservation concerning data on the reserved areas is of course self-evident.[210]

Finally, Paragraph 2 of Article 14 adds that:

Transferred data in respect of the area covered by the plan of work, deemed proprietary, may only be used for the purposes set forth in this article. Data necessary for the formulation by the Authority of rules, regulations and procedures concerning protection of the marine environment and safety, other than equipment design data, shall not be deemed proprietary. [211]

The specific protection granted to equipment design data should be noted.[212]

---

[207] ICNT (1977), *UNCLOS III Off. Rec.*, Vol. VIII, p. 1, at p. 53 (Annex II, para. 8).

[208] Under Annex III, Art.3(5), plans of work for the Enterprise were not to take the form of a contract. As noted above (text, at note 116), this position has been changed by the Implementation Agreement.

[209] *UNCLOS III Off. Rec.*, Vol.X, p.133, at pp.135-136.

[210] See *UNCLOS III Off. Rec.*, Vol.XIII, p.116 (30).

[211] See further on confidentiality of data and information, Chap. 5, section IV and Chap. 10, section IV.6.4.5.

[212] See further *ibid.*

142   *Chapter 4*

X. TRAINING PROGRAMMES: UN CONVENTION, ANNEX III, ARTICLE 15

The obligation placed upon the contractor to draw up programmes for the training of personnel of the Authority and developing countries has been referred to above.[213]

XI. EXCLUSIVE RIGHT TO EXPLORE AND EXPLOIT: UN CONVENTION, ANNEX III, ARTICLE 16

This provision has been referred to above in section V.5.

XII. RULES, REGULATIONS AND PROCEDURES OF THE AUTHORITY: UN CONVENTION, ANNEX III, ARTICLE 17

Article 17 consists of two paragraphs, the first of which enjoins the Authority to adopt and uniformly apply rules, regulations and procedures for the exercise of its functions as set forth in Part XI on, *inter alia*, the following matters:
(a) administrative procedures relating to prospecting, exploration and exploitation in the Area;
(b) operations;
(c) financial matters; and
(d) the implementation of decisions taken pursuant to Article 151(10) and Article164(2)(d).[214]

Paragraph 2 requires that rules, regulations and procedures on seven specified items must fully reflect the objective criteria laid down. The seven items for which such detailed criteria are provided are as follows:
(a) size of areas for exploration;
(b) duration of prospecting, exploration and exploitation operations;
(c) performance requirements;
(d) categories of resources;
(e) renunciation of areas;
(f) protection of the marine environment;
(g) commercial production.

The Preparatory Commission was made responsible for the preparation of the draft rules, regulations and procedures required to enable the Authority to commence its functions.   However, as has been seen, the Preparatory Commission's Special Commission 3 had not completed this task by the time it wound up its work in 1993.[215] It was accordingly provided in the Implementation Agreement that one of the tasks on which the Authority would concentrate during the interval between the entry into force of the Convention and the approval of the first plan of work for exploitation would be:

---

[213] See above, Chap. 3, sections VII, VIII and XII (text, at note 195). On the training obligations of registered pioneer investors, see below, Chap.6, sections III.8-11 and IV.3.

[214] On Art.151(10), see further above, section VI.2.

[215] See the opening section of this chapter, including note 3.

adoption of rules, regulations and procedures necessary for the conduct of activities in the Area as they progress ...[216]

The first part of this Mining Code, adopted in July 2000 and fully considered below in Chapter 5, is limited to prospecting and exploration for polymetallic nodules in the Area.

It is further provided that, notwithstanding the provisions of Annex III, Article 17(2)(b) and (c) (on the duration of operations and performance requirements), such rules, regulations and procedures are to take into account the terms of the Implementation Agreement, the prolonged delay in commercial deep sea-bed mining and the likely pace of activities in the Area.[217]

XIII. PENALTIES: UN CONVENTION, ANNEX III, ARTICLE 18

Article 18 of Annex III provides the Authority with a range of graduated penalties which may be imposed on a contractor.

The most serious sanctions, suspension or termination of the contract, may be imposed only in two cases:

(a) if, in spite of warnings by the Authority, the contractor has conducted his activities in such a way as to result in serious, persistent and wilful violations of the fundamental terms of the contract, Part XI and the rules, regulations and procedures of the Authority; or

(b) if the contractor has failed to comply with a final binding decision of the dispute settlement body applicable to him.[218]

The Authority does, however, have the option of imposing monetary penalties in lieu of suspension or termination.[219]

For less serious violations, monetary penalties proportionate to the seriousness of the violation may be imposed.[220]

Normally, the Authority may not execute a decision involving monetary penalties, suspension or termination until the contractor 'has been accorded a reasonable opportunity to exhaust the judicial remedies available to him pursuant to Part XI, section 5', that is, by recourse to the Sea-Bed Disputes Chamber of the International Tribunal for the Law of the Sea under Article 187(c) of the UN Convention.[221] Immediate execution may be ordered by the Authority, however, in cases where emergency orders are required under Article 162(2)(w) to prevent serious harm to the marine environment.[222]

---

[216] Implementation Agreement (*loc.cit.* in note 16 above), Annex, Sec.1, para.5(f).
[217] *Ibid.*
[218] Annex III, Art. 18(1).
[219] Annex III, Art.18(2).
[220] *Ibid.*
[221] Annex III, Art.18(3).
[222] *Ibid.*

144　*Chapter 4*

XIV. 'RESPONSIBILITY OR LIABILITY': UN CONVENTION, ANNEX III, ARTICLE 22

In section V of Chapter 3 it was seen that States Parties might be indirectly responsible for damage caused by the failure of a contractor sponsored by them to carry out sea-bed activities in conformity with the Convention. It was noted that, in addition, the Convention made provision for liability for damage on a contractual level and it is this liability, provided for in Annex III, Article 22, which is dealt with here. It was also noted above that, in certain circumstances, the Authority may impose penalties on contractors.[223]

Article 22 of Annex III provides as follows:

Responsibility

The contractor shall have responsibility or liability for any damage arising out of wrongful acts in the conduct of its operations, account being taken of contributory acts or omissions by the Authority. Similarly, the Authority shall have responsibility or liability for any damage arising out of wrongful acts in the exercise of its powers and   functions, including violations under article 168, paragraph 2, account being taken of contributory acts or omissions by the contractor. Liability in every case shall be for the actual amount of damage.

1. The Liability of the Contractor

Article 22 of Annex III places liability upon the contractor for 'any damage arising out of wrongful acts in the conduct of its operations'. There would seem to be no reason to restrict such liability to damage suffered by the other party or parties to the contract and the plain meaning would appear to extend such liability to damage suffered by:

other parties to the contract	*third parties*
the Authority	States
States	State entities
State entities	natural or juridical persons
natural or juridical persons sponsored by States Parties	

On looking for the forum or fora in which claims might be lodged, however, difficulties arise.

Dealing first with claims against the contractor by other parties to the contract, there is no difficulty in finding a competent forum. Thus, under Article 187(c), disputes concerning (i) 'the interpretation or application of a relevant contract or a plan of work', or (ii) 'acts or omissions of a party to the contract relating to activities in the Area and directed to the other party or directly affecting its legitimate interests' may be submitted to the Sea-Bed Disputes

---

[223] Above, section XIII.

Chamber. Moreover, under Article 188(2), disputes concerning category (i) may also be submitted, at the request of any party to the dispute, to binding commercial arbitration, unless the parties otherwise agree. It is to be noted, however, that the arbitration tribunal has no jurisdiction to determine any question of interpretation of the Convention.

For example, it follows from Articles 187(c) and 188(2), and is confirmed by Article 190(2), that actions may be brought by a natural or juridical person of State A nationality against State B in the Sea-Bed Disputes Chamber or, in relation to category (i) disputes, before a commercial arbitral tribunal. Of course, in both cases, such opportunities would be available only on the assumption that both of the disputing parties are contracting parties to the same contract. Thus, if a contract is concluded between the Authority on the one hand and State A and a company registered in State B (Company B) on the other hand, it would be possible for Company B to sue State A before the Sea-Bed Disputes Chamber.

Turning to the position of third-party claimants, however, there are gaps in these jurisdictional provisions. They may be illustrated by two examples. First, where the Authority has concluded one contract with State A and Company B, as above, and a second contract with Company C (registered in State C), it would not seem to be possible for Company C to sue State A or Company B in respect of the wrongful activities of State A and Company B.[224] A second situation which appears to escape the net is that where damage is caused by a contractor to an entity having no contractual relationship at all with the Authority. For example, State D (a party to the Convention) or a Company registered in State D (Company D), neither being a contractor with the Authority, might suffer damage as a result of the wrongful activities of a contractor. Neither the Sea-Bed Disputes Chamber nor a commercial arbitral tribunal would have jurisdiction in relation to a resulting claim. It might be possible in these two cases to institute proceedings in a municipal forum but this is hardly a satisfactory situation.

2. The Liability of the Authority

As was seen above, Article 22 of Annex III imposes liability on the Authority for any damage arising out of wrongful acts in the exercise of its powers and functions and, under Article 187(e) of the Convention (and possibly Article 187(c) also), the Sea-Bed Disputes Chamber would have jurisdiction over claims made by aggrieved contracting parties. As noted above, however, third parties are not catered for in Article 187(c) and it is at least questionable whether the Chamber has jurisdiction over such third-party claims under Article 187(e) or any other provision. Article 187(e) gives the Chamber jurisdiction over disputes between the Authority and other entities 'where it is alleged that the Authority has incurred liability as provided in Annex III, article 22', but, unfortunately, the formulation of both this paragraph and of Article 22 strongly suggests that only claims by contracting parties are covered. Nor would it be possible to sue the

---

[224] This gap is referred to in the *Report by the Chairman of the Group of Legal Experts on the Settlement of Disputes relating to Part XI* (A/CONF.62/L.43, 29 August 1979, *UNCLOS III Off. Rec.*, Vol. XII, p. 74, at p. 92).

146   Chapter 4

Authority in the municipal courts of a State Party unless it waived the immunity from legal process which it enjoys under Article 178.

2.1 Liability for Disclosure of Industrial Secrets

The liability of the Authority and of the Secretary-General of the Authority and his staff for disclosure of industrial secrets is provided for in Article 168 of the Convention and Article 22 of Annex III.

Article 168(2) places an obligation upon the Secretary-General and his staff not to disclose, even after the termination of their functions, any industrial secret, proprietary data which are transferred to the Authority in accordance with Annex III, Article 14, or any other confidential information coming to their knowledge by reason of their employment with the Authority.

Paragraph 3 then goes on to provide that:

> Violations of the obligations of a staff member of the Authority set forth in paragraph 2 shall, on the request of a State Party affected by such violation, or a natural or juridical person, sponsored by a State Party as provided in article 153, paragraph 2(b), and affected by such violation, be submitted by the Authority against the staff member concerned to a tribunal designated by the rules, regulations and procedures of the Authority. The Party affected shall have the right to take part in the proceedings. If the tribunal so recommends, the Secretary-General shall dismiss the staff member concerned.

It will be noted that no specific tribunal is identified, this being left, under Paragraph 4, for elaboration in the rules, regulations and procedures of the Authority. In fact, as will be seen in Chapter 5, provision is made in the Mining Code and in Staff Regulations for the establishment of *ad hoc* tribunals, from which there is a right of appeal. [225]

It is not clear whether the delinquent member of staff is personally liable for damages or simply liable to disciplinary penalties, including dismissal. When the matter was considered in April 1979, it was reported merely that:

> The question of monetary penalties and damages arising out of improper disclosure ... would have to be considered together with the question as to whether the Authority as such may be made liable.[226]

Progress was made at the subsequent sessions of the Conference[227] but the position remains obscure. As a result of the specific addition made to Article 22 of Annex III at the Resumed Eighth Session, the Authority itself is now clearly

---

[225] See further, Chap. 5, section IV.4.

[226] A/CONF.62/C.1/L.25 and Add. 1, 26 April and 23 May 1979 (*UNCLOS III Off. Rec.*, Vol. XI, p. 109), at p.111.

[227] At the Resumed Eighth Session (*UNCLOS III Off. Rec.*, Vol. XII, p. 91) and at the Ninth Session (*UNCLOS III Off. Rec.*, Vol. XIII, p. 135).

liable for such wrongful damage.[228] Moreover, the Sea-Bed Disputes Chamber clearly has jurisdiction over such claims against the Authority under Article 187(e). What is still not clear, however, is whether any liability for damages lies upon the staff member concerned. The commentary in the Report of the Chairman of the Group of Legal Experts responsible for these articles is less than helpful in this respect in reporting simply that 'this liability [of the Authority] would be in addition to the liability of the staff member concerned, which article 168, paragraph 2, already provided for'.[229]

Attention has been drawn to the fact that, whereas Article 168(1) speaks of an 'administrative tribunal', Article 168(3) refers simply to 'a tribunal' and it has been suggested that the intention in the latter case may have been to leave the way open for the inclusion of national courts which, unlike international tribunals, would have the capacity to deal with the criminal law aspects of unlawful disclosures.[230]

It is to be hoped too that the position of the staff of the Enterprise will be clarified in further regulations. As a result of the late addition of a fifth paragraph to Article 7 of Annex IV,[231] the responsibilities set forth in Article 168(2) are made 'equally applicable to the staff of the Enterprise'. There is no specific provision, however, identifying the forum in which disputes over violations would be heard. Any such forum would have to be in conformity with the provisions of Article 13 of Annex IV on the legal status, privileges and immunities of the Enterprise.

XV. REVISION OF CONTRACT: UN CONVENTION, ANNEX III, ARTICLE 19

Article 19, Paragraph 1 provides that:

> When circumstances have arisen or are likely to arise which, in the opinion of either party, would render the contract inequitable or make it impracticable or impossible to achieve the objectives set out in the contract or in Part XI, the parties shall enter into negotiations to revise it accordingly.

At first sight, this provision seems to pose a serious threat to the sanctity of the contractual relationship and the contractor's security of tenure under Article 153(6) and Annex III, Article 16. However, a different complexion is put on the matter by Paragraph 2, under which any contract entered into in accordance with Article 153, Paragraph 3 may be revised only with the consent of the parties. Reading the two paragraphs together, it would seem that a party to the contract which alleges that such circumstances have arisen or are likely to arise has a right

---

[228] A specific reference to violations under Article 168(2) was added. See further *UNCLOS III Off. Rec.*, Vol. XII, at p. 91.

[229] *Ibid.*

[230] L.C. Caflisch, 'The Settlement of Disputes Relating to the Seabed', in C.L. Rozakis and C.A. Stephanou (eds.), *The New Law of the Sea* (1983), pp. 303-344, at p. 308.

[231] This paragraph was added by the Conference, on the recommendation of the Drafting Committee, on 24 September 1982 (*UNCLOS III Off. Rec.*, Vol. XVII, pp. 4(4) and 5(9)).

148 *Chapter 4*

to require the other party to the contract to enter into negotiations, the initial purpose of which will be to examine the evidence adduced in order to determine whether such circumstances have indeed arisen or are likely to arise. There would seem to be no question at this stage of treating **Paragraph 1** as a *pactum de contrahendo*, that is, an obligation to negotiate in good faith with a view to agreeing upon a revision of the contract. Such an obligation would arise only if the parties agreed on the existence or likely future occurrence of 'such circumstances'. Even then, under Paragraph 2, the consent of the parties would be required to the revision. If the parties failed to agree on the existence of such circumstances, the matter might be referred to the Sea-Bed Disputes Chamber under Article 187 or to a commercial arbitral tribunal under Article 188.

XVI. TRANSFER OF RIGHTS AND OBLIGATIONS: UN CONVENTION, ANNEX III, ARTICLE 20

Article 20 is straightforward, providing that:

> The rights and obligations arising under a contract may be transferred only with the consent of the Authority, and in accordance with its rules, regulations and procedures. The Authority shall not unreasonably withhold consent to the transfer if the proposed transferee is in all respects a qualified applicant and assumes all of the obligations of the transferor and if the transfer does not confer to the transferee a plan of work, the approval of which would be forbidden by article 6, paragraph 3(c) of this Annex.

The rules governing approval of plans of work are dealt with above in section V.4.2.

XVII. APPLICABLE LAW: UN CONVENTION, ANNEX III, ARTICLE 21

Paragraphs 1 and 2 are unremarkable in providing that:

> 1. The contract shall be governed by the terms of the contract, the rules, regulations and procedures of the Authority, Part XI and other rules of international law not incompatible with this Convention.
> 2. Any final decision rendered by a court or tribunal having jurisdiction under this Convention relating to the rights and obligations of the Authority and of the contractor shall be enforceable in the territory of each State Party.

The remainder of Article 21 protects the contractor from having conditions imposed on it by a State Party that are inconsistent with Part XI of the Convention. There is, however, one exception for the benefit of the environment. Thus, the application by a State Party of environmental or other laws and regulations to contractors sponsored by it or to ships flying its flag, more stringent than those imposed by the Authority pursuant to Article 17, Paragraph

2(f) of Annex III, is not to be deemed to be inconsistent with Part XI. While this power introduces a degree of unpredictability as to the costs which a contractor might have to bear, it is at least restricted to the sponsor/flag State.

XVIII. RESOURCES OF THE AREA OTHER THAN
POLYMETALLIC NODULES

This book is primarily concerned with the legal regime governing prospecting and exploration for, and exploitation of, polymetallic nodules (or manganese nodules). There is good reason for this. Whereas the potential of polymetallic nodules as a rich source of minerals has been well known for many years and a good deal of research has been conducted on them, recognition of the potential of other types of submarine mineral resources has been much more recent. [232] Accordingly, the UN Convention, in declaring the 'Area and its *resources*' to be the common heritage of mankind, [233] defined 'resources' to mean 'all solid, liquid or gaseous mineral resources *in situ* in the Area at or beneath the seabed, *including polymetallic nodules*'. [234] It made no specific reference to other types of mineral resources. The same emphasis on polymetallic nodules is to be found in Article 162(2)(o)(ii) of the Convention which gives priority to the development of rules, regulations and procedures for the exploration for and exploitation of polymetallic nodules. As a consequence, the 'first set of Regulations' [235] – the Mining Code adopted in July 2000 – is principally concerned with polymetallic nodules. [236]

However, the UN Convention does prescribe a procedure for the adoption of rules, regulations and procedures for other resources. Article 162(2)(o)(ii) provides that:

---

[232] On submarine mineral resources, see generally W.J. Broad, *The Universe Below*, Simon & Schuster, New York, 1997. Recently, a great deal of interest has been shown in the genetic resources of the deep seabed, including, in particular, hyperthermophilic (heat-loving) bacteria associated with hydrothermal vents. However, not being within the definition of 'resources' in Art. 133(a) of the UN Convention, such creatures are not covered by the Convention's regime for the Area. See further, L. Glowka, 'The Deepest of Ironies: Genetic Resources, Marine Scientific Research, and the Area', 12 *Ocean Yearbook* (1996), pp. 154-178; and L. Glowka, 'Genetic Resources, Marine Scientific Research and the International Seabed Area', RECIEL (vol. 8(I), 1999). See also P.W. Birnie, 'Legal Problems Concerning Bioprospecting for Genetic Resources Located in Marine Hydorthermal Vents Beyond National Jurisdiction' (paper presented to the Conseil Européen du Droit de l'Environnement, May 1997); W.T. Burke, 'State Practice, New Ocean Uses, and Ocean Governance under UNCLOS', *Proceedings of the Law of the Sea Institute's 28ᵗʰ Annual Conference* (1994), pp. 219-234, at pp. 229-234; and G. Verhoosel, 'Prospecting for Marine and Coastal Biodiversity: International Law in Deep Water ?', 13 *International Journal of Marine and Coastal Law* (No. 1, 1998), pp. 91-104.
[233] UN Convention, Art. 136, emphasis added.
[234] UN Convention, Art. 133(a), emphasis added. Polymetallic nodules are defined in UNCLOS III's Conference Resolution II, para. 1(d) and Reg. 1(3)(d) of the Mining Code as meaning, 'one of the resources of the Area consisting of any deposit or accretion of nodules, on or just below the surface of the deep seabed, which contain manganese, nickel, cobalt and copper.'
[235] Mining Code, Preamble.
[236] As will be seen in Chap. 5, section II.1.3, brief reference to other resources is made in Regs. 24(1) and 40 and Annex 4, section 2.4.

150   *Chapter 4*

Rules, regulations and procedures for the exploration for and exploitation of any resource other than polymetallic nodules shall be adopted within three years from the date of a request to the Authority by any of its members to adopt such rules, regulations and procedures in respect of such resource.

On 17 August 1998, the Russian delegation to the Authority, referring to discoveries of large, rich deposits of hydrothermal polymetallic sulphides and cobalt-bearing crusts by United States and Russian scientists, made 'an official request to the Authority', invoking the procedure set out in Article 162(2)(o)(ii). [237]

Polymetallic sulphides, also known as seafloor massive sulphides, are reported to have 'economically attractive metal contents of gold, silver, copper and zinc'. [238] The Secretary-General of the Authority described them in a recent Report as follows:

Polymetallic sulphide mineral deposits are formed by precipitation from hydrothermal solutions that convect through seafloor spreading centres driven by volcanogenic heat sources. The geographical distribution of deposits of polymetallic sulphides is less well known than that for polymetallic nodules, although it is understood that, compared to polymetallic nodules, deposits of sulphides are highly concentrated. Recent discoveries in areas under national jurisdiction have led to the suggestion that mining of such deposits may become technically and economically feasible in the relatively near future. [239]

The first licences for the exploration for polymetallic sulphides were issued by Papua New Guinea in 1997 for deposits within its exclusive economic zone. [240]

Following the Russian initiative, the Secretariat of the Authority began work in 1999 on a review of the status of knowledge and research on resources other than polymetallic nodules and, to further its work, convened a workshop in Kingston, Jamaica, in June 2000. [241] Although the focus was mainly on 'deep sea polymetallic massive sulphide deposits and cobalt bearing ferromanganese encrustations', it was reported that:

The workshop [was] also [to] review the current status of activities in relation to the conversion of the valuable components of methane hydrates,

---

[237] ISBA/4/A/CRP.2, 24 August 1998.
[238] *Oceans and the law of the sea, Report of the Secretary-General*, A/53/456, 5 October 1998, para. 34.
[239] *Report of the Secretary-General of the International Seabed Authority under article 166, paragraph 4 of the United Nations Convention on the Law of the Sea*, ISBA/6/A/9, 6 June 2000, para. 53.
[240] Under Papua New Guinea's 1992 Mining Act. See further, *Oceans and the law of the sea, Report of the Secretary-General*, A/54/429, 30 September 1999, paras. 339-340.
[241] *Loc. cit.* in note 239, at para. 54. At the time of writing, publication of the proceedings of the workshop is awaited.

oil and gas, marine phosphorites and deposits of precious metals into reserves of the commodities which they contain. [242]

The proceedings of the workshop were distributed to the members of the Legal and Technical Commission during the resumed sixth session of the Authority in July 2000 and it was reported that:

> Members briefly considered the type of legal framework which will be appropriate for minerals other than polymetallic nodules, taking into account the natural variability in the types of deposits and the sharing of the resources as the common heritage of mankind as outlined in the Convention. [243]

---

[242] *Ibid.* Cobalt-bearing crusts have a metal composition similar to polymetallic nodules but with a much higher cobalt content (*loc. cit.* in note 238, para. 34). They 'can be found at depths of 2,500 to 8,000 feet, distributed in various forms and sizes on the ocean floor above the substrates as well as buried beneath the sediment' (*Law of the Sea,Report of the Secretary-General*, A/51/645, 1 November 1996, para. 283).

[243] Report of the Chairman of the Legal and Technical Commission on the Work of the Commission during the Resumed Sixth Session, ISBA/6/C/11, 11 July 2000, para. 13.

CHAPTER 5

The UN Convention Regime of Sea-Bed Mining:
III. The Mining Code: Exploration

This chapter is concerned with those parts of the Regulations on Prospecting and Exploration for Polymetallic Nodules in the Area[1] (the 'Mining Code') which deal with the exploration phase of 'activities in the Area'.[2]

As the Preamble to the Mining Code makes clear, these Regulations are subject to the provisions of the UN Convention, the Implementation Agreement and other rules of international law not incompatible with the UN Convention. As was explained in Chapter 4,[3] the presentation of a single, comprehensive account of all of the rules on exploration in the UN Convention, the Implementation Agreement and the Mining Code gives rise to certain practical problems and, in the interests of clarity, the Mining Code Regulations governing exploration are dealt with separately here. There is an additional reason for such separate treatment. It is intended that the Mining Code should be used as the day-to-day working instrument of the Authority and of the sea-bed mining industry and it may be helpful to have it considered separately. However, this chapter is fully cross-referenced to Chapter 4, which contains an analysis of the corresponding provisions of the UN Convention, as amended by the Implementation Agreement.

Chapter 4 also deals with the provision of the Mining Code which regulate prospecting.[4] As has been seen, however, Regulations on the exploitation phase of 'activities in the Area' have still to be finalised [5] and the existing draft regulations are not considered here.

---

[1] Regulations on Prospecting and Exploration for Polymetallic Nodules in the Area, ISBA/6/A/18, as approved by the Assembly on 13 July 2000; reproduced in Vol. 3 as Doc. No. 25.
[2] The UN Convention, Art. 1(1)(3) defines 'activities in the Area' to mean 'all activities of exploration for, and exploitation of, the resources of the Area'.
[3] See introductory paragraphs of Chap. 4.
[4] Chap. 4, section IV.
[5] See Chap. 4 above, text, at note 10, and documentation referred to in that note.

It has also to be noted that this chapter, like the Regulations dealing with exploration, covers only the exploration of the Area for polymetallic nodules.[6] Other resources of the Area will be covered by separate regulations yet to be drafted.[7]

I. THE APPLICATION FOR A PLAN OF WORK FOR EXPLORATION

1. Who May Make an Application for a Plan of Work for Exploration
1.1 The General Position
Regulation 9 contains a general statement of the position, as follows:

Regulation 9
General

Subject to the provisions of the Convention, the following may apply to the Authority for approval of plans of work for exploration:
(a) the Enterprise, on its own behalf or in a joint arrangement;
(b) States Parties, state enterprises or natural or juridical persons which possess the nationality of States Parties or are effectively controlled by them or their nationals, when sponsored by such States, or any group of the foregoing which meets the requirements of these Regulations. [footnote omitted].

Regulation 9 is based upon Article 153(2) of the UN Convention. An analysis of that provision and of related provisions is given above in Chapter 4.[8]

As the final clause of Regulation 9 indicates, applicants covered by paragraph (b) have to meet the requirements of these Regulations. In particular, they must have the qualifications required of applicants by other Regulations considered below in such matters as financial standing,[9] technological capability[10] and satisfactory performance under any previous contracts with the Authority.[11]

1.2 Applications by Registered Pioneer Investors
A footnote to Regulation 9 adds that:

A request by a registered pioneer investor for approval of a plan of work for exploration under paragraph 6(a)(ii) of section 1 of the annex to the

---

[6] See further Chap. 4 above, text, at note 24. See also below, section II.1.3 on the 'Scope of the contract *ratione materiae*'.
[7] The Preamble to the Regulations describes them as 'this first set of Regulations', the objective of which 'is to provide for prospecting and exploration for polymetallic nodules'. Russia has requested the Authority to start work on further regulations to cover other resources of the Area. See above, Chap. 4, section XVIII and below, section II.1.3.
[8] Chap. 4, section V.3.
[9] See below, section I.2.1, under 'Financial and technical information'; section I.2.4 on 'The financial and technical capabilities of the applicant'; and section I.4.2.2.1 on 'Criteria relating to the applicant'.
[10] See sections referred to in note 9 above.
[11] See below, section I.2.1, under 'Previous contracts' and section I.2.5 on 'Previous contracts with the Authority'.

154　*Chapter 5*

Agreement shall be submitted within 36 months of the entry into force of the Convention.

The position of the registered pioneer investor is considered more fully below in Chapter 6.[12]

2. The Content of the Application
2.1 The Form of the Application

The application has to be submitted in the form prescribed in Annex 2 of the Regulations [13] and falls into seven sections dealing with:

- *Information on the applicant.* The required information includes not only formal data on the identity and location of the applicant but also the identity of the sponsoring State and a statement of its status in relation to the UN Convention and the Implementation Agreement. Certificates of sponsorship have also to be attached.[14]
- *Information on the area under application.* This information includes the definition of the boundaries of the area and its division into two parts of equal estimated commercial value. Detailed data enabling the Council to designate a reserved area has also to be given. Such data will relate to both the location, survey and evaluation of the polymetallic nodules in the areas, and environmental parameters. If the application refers to any part of a reserved area, its co-ordinates must be given and an indication of the applicant's qualifications to apply under Regulation 17.[15]
- *Financial and technical information.* This section specifies the detailed information which is required to enable the Council to determine (i) if the applicant is financially capable of carrying out the proposed plan of work and of fulfilling its financial obligations to the Authority; and (ii) if the applicant is technically capable of carrying out the proposed plan of work.[16]

As was seen in Chapter 4, the Implementation Agreement made special provision for applicants (other than the Enterprise and registered pioneer investors) which had already undertaken substantial activities in the Area prior to the entry into force of the Convention.[17] This provision is reflected in a footnote to the Regulations whereby such entities or their successors in interest will 'be considered to have met the financial and technical qualifications necessary for approval of a plan of work if the sponsoring State or States certify that the applicant has expended an amount equivalent to at least US$30 million in research and exploration activities and has expended no less than 10 per cent of that amount in the location, survey and evaluation of the area referred to in the plan of work.' [18]

---

[12] On applications by registered pioneer investors for plans of work, see Chap. 6, section IV.1.
[13] Mining Code, Reg. 10(1). On the position of registered pioneer investors, see below, section I.2.9.
[14] Mining Code, Annex 2, section I.
[15] Mining Code, Annex 2, section II.
[16] Mining Code, Annex 2, section III.
[17] See further above, Chap. 4, section V.3.1.
[18] Mining Code, Annex 2, section III, footnote a.

- *The plan of work for exploration.* The information required under this section includes a general description and schedule of the proposed exploration programme, as well as a schedule of anticipated expenditure for the immediate 5-year period. There is also heavy emphasis on the supply of environmental information, including information which would enable an environmental impact assessment to be conducted.[19]
- *Undertakings.* Under this section, applicants are required to submit a written undertaking to accept as enforceable the obligations applicable to them and control by the Authority of activities in the Area 'as authorised by the Convention'. A written assurance has also to be provided that obligations under the contract will be fulfilled in good faith.[20]
- *Previous contracts.* Specified information on the dates of previous contracts and on reports submitted in connection with such contracts has to be submitted.[21]
- *Attachments.* Finally, this section requires a list to be supplied of all attachments and annexes and specifies the format in which data and information must be submitted.[22]

2.2 Who Submits the Application

Regulation 10(2) specifies who shall submit applications on behalf of States, entities, and the Enterprise. Regulations 10(3) and (4) require further information on such matters as the nationality of the applicant which would have been better included in Annex 2, Section 1 on *Information concerning the applicant.* Indeed, there is a degree of repetition as between these two parts of the Code.

2.3 Requirement of Certificate of Sponsorship

Regulation 11 gives details of the requirement that every applicant other than the Enterprise must submit a certificate of sponsorship by its sponsoring State or States. States or entities in a joint arrangement with the Enterprise are also bound by this requirement.[23] Special provision for registered pioneer investors is again made in a footnote to the Regulations. It indicates that:

> the certifying State or States at the time of registration or their successors shall be deemed to be the sponsoring State or States provided such State or States are States Parties to the Convention or are provisional members of the Authority at the time of the request.[24]

2.4 The Financial and Technical Capabilities of the Applicant

The provision made in Regulation 12 for the submission by the applicant of detailed information on its financial and technical capabilities by and large covers

---

[19] Mining Code, Annex 2, section IV.
[20] Mining Code, Annex 2, section V.
[21] Mining Code, Annex 2, section VI.
[22] Mining Code, Annex 2, section VII.
[23] Mining Code, Reg. 11(4).
[24] Mining Code, Reg. 11, footnote 3. Provisional membership of the Authority terminated for all States on 16 November 1998. See further Chap. 1, section II.

156   Chapter 5

the same ground as Annex 2, Section III of these Regulations, referred to above in section 2.1. However, reflecting the increasingly heavy emphasis in the Mining Code on environmental protection, the information to be submitted was extended in a new paragraph added to Regulation 12 at the Resumed Fourth Session of the Authority in August 1998. As a result, applicants must include 'a general description of the applicant's financial and technical capacity to respond to any incident or activity which causes serious harm to the marine environment'. [25]

Regulation 12 also refers to the special position of registered pioneer investors:

> A registered pioneer investor requesting approval of a plan of work for exploration under paragraph 6(a)(ii) of section 1 of the annex to the Agreement shall be considered to have satisfied the financial and technical qualifications necessary for approval of a plan of work.[26]

2.5 Previous Contracts with the Authority
Here too, Regulation 13 is to the same effect as Annex 2, Section VI of these Regulations, referred to above in section 2.1

2.6 Undertakings
Once again, there is a considerable degree of repetition in Regulation 14 of the provision made for written undertakings to be given by the applicant in Annex 2, Section V of the Regulations, referred to above in section 2.1. A footnote to Regulation 14 indicates that such undertakings have also to be provided by registered pioneer investors.

2.7 'Total area covered by the application' and 'Data and information to be submitted before the designation of a reserved area'
The requirements of Regulations 15 and 16 are similar to those specified in Annex II, Section II of the Regulations ('Information relating to the area under application'), referred to above in section 2.1.

2.8 Applications for Approval of Plans of Work with Respect to a Reserved Area
The provision made for the designation of reserved areas in the UN Convention and the Implementation Agreement is analysed above in Chapter 4 [27] and the position of the Enterprise in relation to such reserved areas is considered in Chapter 8. [28]

As was seen in Chapter 4, developing States (or entities sponsored by them) may apply for approval of a plan of work for a reserved area provided the Enterprise has indicated, 'within a reasonable time', that it does not intend to carry out activities in the area concerned. [29]

---

[25] Mining Code, Reg. 12(7)(c).
[26] Mining Code, Reg. 12, footnote 4.
[27] See further above, Chap. 4, section VII.
[28] See further below, Chap. 8, section II.2.4.3.
[29] See further above, Chap. 4, section VII.

As will be seen in Chapter 8, it would also be open to the contractor which contributed a particular area to the Authority as a reserved area to apply for a plan of work for that area if the Enterprise did not submit an application within a specified 15-year period. [30] In such a case, the contractor would be bound to offer in good faith to include the Enterprise as a joint-venture partner.[31]

Regulation 17 of the Mining Code develops these provisions further. Building upon Annex III, Article 9 of the UN Convention, Regulation 17 provides that:

Applications for approval of plans of work with respect to a reserved area

1. Any State which is a developing State or any natural or juridical person sponsored by it and effectively controlled by it or by any other developing State, or any group of the foregoing, may notify the Authority that it wishes to submit a plan of work for exploration with respect to a reserved area. The Secretary-General shall forward such notification to the Enterprise, which shall inform the Secretary-General in writing within six months whether or not it intends to carry out activities in that area. If the Enterprise intends to carry out activities in that area, it shall, pursuant to paragraph 4, also inform in writing the contractor whose application for approval of a plan of work for exploration originally included that area.

2. An application for approval of a plan of work for exploration in respect of a reserved area may be submitted at any time after such an area becomes available following a decision by the Enterprise that it does not intend to carry out activities in that area or where the Enterprise has not, within six months of the notification by the Secretary-General, either taken a decision on whether it intends to carry out activities in that area or notified the Secretary-General in writing that it is engaged in discussions regarding a potential joint venture. In the latter instance, the Enterprise shall have one year from the date of such notification in which to decide whether to conduct activities in that area.

3. If the Enterprise or a developing State or one of the entities referred to in paragraph 1 does not submit an application for approval of a plan of work for exploration for activities in a reserved area within 15 years of the commencement by the Enterprise of its functions independent of the Secretariat of the Authority or within 15 years of the date on which that area is reserved for the Authority, whichever is the later, the contractor whose application for approval of a plan of work for exploration originally included that area shall be entitled to apply for a plan of work for exploration for that area provided it offers in good faith to include the Enterprise as a joint-venture partner.

4. A contractor has the right of first refusal to enter into a joint venture arrangement with the Enterprise for exploration of the area which was included in its application for approval of a plan of work for exploration and which was designated by the Council as a reserved area.

---

[30] See further below, Chap. 8, section II.2.4.3.
[31] See further *ibid.*

158   *Chapter 5*

More simply put, the various options as to who may apply, and when applications may be made, are as follows:

- *A developing State, or an entity sponsored by it,* may notify the Authority that it wishes to submit a plan of work and the Authority has to forward such notification to the Enterprise.[32] Within 6 months, the Enterprise must either decide whether or not to carry out activities in the area, or notify the Secretary-General that it is engaged in discussions regarding a potential joint venture. In the latter case, the Enterprise has one year from the date of 'such notification' (presumably its notification to the Authority rather than the Authority's earlier notification to the Enterprise) in which to decide whether to conduct activities in the area. [33]

  If, within the 6-month period or the extended 12-month period, the Enterprise decides not to conduct activities in the area, the developing State will immediately be entitled to submit an application. [34] If, on the other hand, the Enterprise fails, within the initial 6-month period, to either take a decision or notify the Authority of ongoing joint venture discussions, the developing State may submit its application at the end of the initial 6-month period. [35]

- *The position of the original contractor.* If, within the initial 6-month period, the Enterprise notifies its intention to carry out activities in the reserved area, it must also inform the contractor whose application for approval of a plan of work originally included that area. [36] That contractor will then have a right of first refusal to enter into a joint-venture arrangement with the Enterprise. [37]

  An alternative opportunity will arise for the contractor if neither the Enterprise nor a developing State (or entity sponsored by it) applies for approval of a plan of work within a specified 15-year period. In that event, the contractor will be entitled to apply for a plan of work provided it offers in good faith to include the Enterprise as a joint-venture partner.[38]

2.9 Data and Information to be Submitted for Approval of the Plan of Work for Exploration

Regulation 18 covers the same ground as Annex 2, Section IV of the Regulations, considered above in section 2.1. It requires the applicant to submit specific information on its programme of work. It is added in a footnote that this Regulation is to be implemented by registered pioneer investors in the light of Regulation 10.[39] A footnote to Regulation 10 details the different form in which applications are to be submitted by registered pioneer investors as follows:

---

[32] Mining Code, Reg. 17(1).
[33] Mining Code, Reg. 17(2).
[34] *Ibid.*
[35] *Ibid.*
[36] Mining Code, Reg. 17(1).
[37] Mining Code, Reg. 17(4).
[38] Mining Code, Reg. 17(3).
[39] Mining Code, Reg. 18, footnote 6.

The Mining Code: Exploration 159

A request by a registered pioneer investor for approval of a plan of work for exploration under paragraph 6(a)(ii) of section 1 of the annex to the Agreement shall consist of documents, reports and other data submitted to the Preparatory Commission both before and after registration and shall be accompanied by a certificate of compliance, consisting of a factual report describing the status of fulfilment of obligations under the registered pioneer investor regime, issued by the Preparatory Commission in accordance with resolution II, paragraph 11(a). The registered pioneer investor shall, where such information has not already been provided, update the information, using, as far as possible, the provisions of regulation 18 as a guide, and submit its programme of work for the immediate future, including a general assessment of the potential environmental impacts of the proposed activities.[40]

It may be noted that this procedure was followed when, in August 1997, the Legal and Technical Commission recommended to the Council that it consider as approved the plans of work submitted by the seven registered pioneer investors, and the Council, accepting this recommendation, requested the Secretary-General to take the necessary steps to issue the plans of work in the form of contracts 'in accordance with the regulations on prospecting and exploration for polymetallic nodules in the Area and a standard form of contract to be approved by the Council.'[41]

3. Fee for Applications
Provision is made for this fee in the UN Convention, Annex III, Article 13(2), as 'implemented' by the Implementation Agreement, Annex, Section 8(3). As was seen in Chapter 4, there was some doubt about the impact of the latter provisions on the original terms of the Convention.[42] Regulation 19 clarifies the situation. The fee is set at US$ 250,000. This amount is to be reviewed from time to time by the Council to ensure that it covers the costs of processing the application. However, if the costs of processing are less than the fixed amount, the Authority has to refund the difference to the applicant.

Special provision is again made by footnote for the fee payable by registered pioneer investors. Under UNCLOS Resolution II, Paragraph 7(a), it was originally provided that the pioneer investor would pay a fee of US$ 250,000 when applying for a plan of work for exploration *and exploitation*. [43] However, the Implementation Agreement (Annex, Section 1, Paragraph 6(a)(ii)) provided that this fee was to 'be deemed to be the fee relating to the exploration phase, [44] and the footnote to Regulation 19 now reflects this amendment in providing that:

---

[40] Mining Code, Reg. 10, footnote 2.
[41] See *Report and recommendation of the Legal and Technical Commission*, ISBA/3/C/7, 22 August 1997 (International Seabed Authority, *Selected Decisions & Documents of the First, Second and Third Sessions*, ISA/98/01.E, pp 69-70) and *Requests for approval of plans of work for exploration*, ISBA/3/C/9, 28 August 1997 *(ibid. ,*pp. 71-72). See also below, section I.4.2.3, for the procedure to be followed by the Commission when acting on applications from registered pioneer investors under Regulation 21, note 8.
[42] See further above, Chap. 4, section VIII.2.1.1.
[43] See further below, Chap. 6 section II.1.4.
[44] See further below, Chap. 6, section IV.1.4.

160   *Chapter 5*

In the case of a registered pioneer investor requesting approval for a plan of work for exploration under paragraph 6(a)(ii) of section 1 of the annex to the Agreement, the fee of US$ 250,000 paid pursuant to resolution II, paragraph 7(a), shall be deemed to be the fee referred to under paragraph 1 relating to the exploration phase. [45]

4. Processing of Applications
4.1 Receipt, Acknowledgment and Safe Custody of Applications
Regulation 20 is quite straightforward in providing that:

1. The Secretary-General shall:

   (a) acknowledge in writing receipt of every application for approval of a plan of work for exploration submitted under this Part, specifying the date of receipt;
   (b) place the application together with the attachments and annexes thereto in safe custody and ensure the confidentiality of all confidential data and information contained in the application; and
   (c) notify the members of the Authority of the receipt of such application and circulate to them information of a general nature which is not confidential regarding the application.

As was seen in Chapter 4, provision is made in Article 168 of the UN Convention and Annex III, Article 22 for the protection of the confidentiality of data and information submitted by applicants. [46]

4.2 Consideration of Applications by the Legal and Technical Commission
The procedure for consideration by the Commission of applications for approval of a plan of work is laid down in Regulation 21. The normal procedure, considered below in sections 4.2.1 and 4.2.2, is dealt with in the body of the Regulation. The different procedure to be followed in the case of applications submitted by registered pioneer investors is set out in a footnote to the Regulation and is considered below in section 4.2.3.

4.2.1 When is an Application Considered?
The Secretary-General , upon receipt of an application, places it on the agenda for the next meeting of the Commission and the Commission examines applications in the order in which they are received. [47] The Commission is required to consider applications 'expeditiously' and has to submit its report and recommendations to the Council on the designation of the areas and on the plan of work for exploration at the first possible opportunity, taking into account the schedule of meetings of the Authority. [48]

---

[45] Mining Code, Reg. 19, footnote 7.
[46] See above, Chap. 4, section XIV.2.1. On confidentiality, see further below, section IV.
[47] Mining Code, Reg. 21(1) and (2).
[48] Mining Code Reg. 21(10).

The Mining Code: Exploration 161

4.2.2 Criteria to be Considered by the Commission
In considering applications, the Commission has to make determinations relating both to the applicant and to the proposed plan of work. In doing so, it must apply the Mining Code Regulations and the rules, regulations and procedures issued by the Authority in a uniform and non-discriminatory manner. [49]It has also to have regard to the principles, policies and objectives relating to activities in the Area as provided for in Part XI and Annex III of the UN Convention, and the Implementation Agreement. [50]

4.2.2.1 Criteria Relating to the Applicant
The Commission has to determine whether the applicant:
- has complied with the provisions of these regulations,[51] as considered above; [52]
- has given the undertakings and assurances specified in Regulation 14,[53] also considered above; [54]
- possesses the financial and technical capability to carry out the proposed plan of work.[55] As was seen above, the prescribed form for applications specified in Annex 2 of the Regulations includes a Section III on 'Financial and technical information' which will ensure that the Commission has the necessary information on which to base its determination; [56]
- has satisfactorily discharged its obligations under any previous contract with the Authority, details of which will again have been submitted by the applicant under Section VI of Annex 2 of the Regulations. [57]

4.2.2.2 Criteria Relating to the Proposed Plan of Work
The Commission has also to determine, in accordance with the requirements set forth in the Regulations and its procedures whether the proposed plan of work for exploration:
- will provide for effective protection of human health and safety. [58] The implications of this provision are made more apparent in one of the standard clauses for exploration contracts specified in Annex 4 of the Regulations. Section 15 is in the following terms:

---

[49] Mining Code, Reg. 21(11).
[50] Mining Code, Reg. 21(9).
[51] Mining Code, Reg. 21(3)(a).
[52] See above, sections I.1 and 2.
[53] Mining Code, Reg. 21(3)(b).
[54] See above, sections I.2.1 ('Undertakings') and I.2.6.
[55] Mining Code, Reg. 21(3)(c). See above, sections I.2.1 ('Financial and technical information') and I.2.4.
[56] See above, section I.2.1 ('Financial and technical information').
[57] Mining Code, Reg. 21(3)(d). See further above, sections I.2.1 ('Previous contracts') and I.2.5.
[58] Mining Code, Reg. 21(4)(a).

162   *Chapter 5*

Safety, labour and health standards

15.1 The Contractor shall comply with the generally accepted international rules and standards established by competent international organisations or general diplomatic conferences concerning the safety of life at sea, and the prevention of collisions and such rules, regulations and procedures as may be adopted by the Authority relating to safety at sea. Each vessel used for carrying out activities in the Area shall possess current valid certificates required by and issued pursuant to such international rules and standards.

15.2 The contractor shall, in carrying out exploration under this contract, observe and comply with such rules, regulations and procedures as may be adopted by the Authority relating to protection against discrimination in employment, occupational safety and health, labour relations, social security, employment security and living conditions at the work site. Such rules, regulations and procedures shall take into account conventions and recommendations of the International Labour Organisation and other competent international organisations.

The Draft Regulations on Prospecting, Exploration and Exploitation of Polymetallic Nodules in the Area prepared by the Preparatory Commission included a Part XI on Labour, Health and Safety Standards [59] which will no doubt be drawn upon by the Authority in adopting further rules, regulations and procedures, as envisaged in the above-quoted Section 15.2.

- will provide for effective protection and preservation of the marine environment. [60] This environmental aspect is considered more fully below in Chapter 10.
- will ensure that installations are not established where interference may be caused to the use of recognised sea lanes essential for international navigation or in areas of intense fishing activity.[61]

This criterion reflects the principle laid down in Article 147 of the UN Convention, considered above in Chapter 3. [62]

4.2.2.3 Grounds for Not Recommending Approval

The Commission will not recommend approval of the plan of work in the following circumstances:

- if part or all of the area covered by the proposed plan of work for exploration is included in a plan of work for exploration approved by the Council for polymetallic nodules; [63]

---

[59] See further LOS/PCN/SCN.3/WP.6/Add.8, 11 February 1992; and Corr. 1, 25 February 1992; and Rev. 1, 15 January 1993 (*Report of the Preparatory Commission*, LOS/PCN/153, Vol. XIII, 30 June 1995, at pp. 231-236, 237-238 and 245-251).

[60] Mining Code, Reg. 21(4)(b).

[61] Mining Code, Reg. 21(4)(c).

[62] See further above, Chap. 3, section XI.

[63] Mining Code, Reg. 21(6)(a). This first-come, first-served rule is based on the UN Convention, Annex III, Art. 6(3)(a), considered above in Chap. 4, section V.4.2. Art. 6(3)(a) also gives priority to 'a previously submitted proposed plan of work which has not been finally acted upon by the Authority'.

- if part or all of the area covered by the proposed plan of work for exploration is included in a plan of work approved by the Council for exploration for or exploitation of other resources if such proposed plan of work for exploration for polymetallic nodules might cause undue interference with activities under such an approved plan of work for such other resources; [64]
- if part or all of the area covered by the proposed plan of work for exploration is included in an area disapproved for exploitation by the Council in cases where substantial evidence indicates the risk of serious harm to the marine environment; [65]
- if the proposed plan of work for exploration has been submitted or sponsored by a State that already holds:
  (i) plans of work for exploration and exploitation or exploitation only in non-reserved areas that, together with either part of the area covered by the application, exceed in size 30 per cent of a circular area of 400,000 square kilometres surrounding the centre of either part of the area covered by the proposed plan of work;
  (ii) plans of work for exploration and exploitation or exploitation only in non-reserved areas which, taken together, constitute 2 per cent of that part of the Area which is not reserved or disapproved for exploitation pursuant to article 162, paragraph (2)(x), of the Convention. [66]
  These criteria are a restatement of the two anti-monopoly clauses embodied in the UN Convention, Annex III, Article 6(3)(c)(i)-(ii), considered above in Chap.4. [67]
- if part or all of the area covered by the proposed plan of work for exploration is included in a reserved area or an area designated by the Council to be a reserved area. [68] However, this obstacle does not of course exist in the case of applications by the Enterprise, on its own behalf or in a joint venture, or in applications made by developing States (and entities sponsored by them) or by contractors under Regulation 17. [69]

4.2.2.4 Commission Recommendation to Council

Provided the above criteria relating to the applicant and the criteria relating to the proposed plan of work are met, and none of the grounds for not recommending approval applies, the Commission will recommend approval of the plan or work to the Council. [70] If, however, the Commission finds that an applicant has not complied with the Regulations , it has to notify the applicant in writing, through the Secretary-General, indicating the reasons. The applicant may then, within 45 days of such notification, amend its application. If, after further consideration,

---

[64] Mining Code, Reg. 21(6)(b). On activities concerning resources other than polymetallic nodules, see further below, section II.1.3 and above, Chap. 4, section XVIII.
[65] Mining Code, Reg. 21(6)(c). See further below Chap. 10, section IV.5.4 and above, Chap. 4, section V.4.2.
[66] Mining Code, Reg. 21(6)(d)(i)-(ii) .
[67] See further above, Chap.4, section V.4.2.
[68] Mining Code, Reg. 21(7).
[69] *Ibid.* See further above, section I.1.2.
[70] Mining Code, Reg. 21(5), read with Reg. 21(6)-(7).

164   *Chapter 5*

the Commission is of the view that it should not recommend approval of the plan of work, it must so inform the applicant and provide it with a further opportunity to make representations within thirty days of such 'information'. It is then left to the Commission to 'consider any such representations made by the applicant in preparing its report and recommendation to the Council'. [71]

4.2.3 Procedure for Pioneer Investor Applications

Where the request for approval of a plan of work is one made by a registered pioneer investor, the following much simpler procedure, as laid down in footnote 8 to Regulation 21, has to be followed:

In the case of a request by a registered pioneer investor for approval of a plan of work for exploration under paragraph 6(a)(ii) of section 1 of the annex to the Agreement, the Secretary-General shall ascertain whether:

(a) the documents, reports and other data submitted to the Preparatory Commission both before and after registration are available;

(b) the certificate of compliance, consisting of a factual report describing the status of fulfilment of obligations under the registered pioneer investor regime, issued by the Preparatory Commission in accordance with resolution II, paragraph 11(a), has been produced;

(c) the registered pioneer investor has updated the information provided in the documents, reports and other data submitted to the Preparatory Commission both before and after registration and has submitted its programme of activities for the immediate future, including a general assessment of the potential environmental impacts of the proposed activities; and

(d) the registered pioneer investor has given the undertakings and assurances specified in regulation 14.

If the Secretary-General informs the Commission that the provisions of (a), (b) (c) and (d) have been satisfied by a registered pioneer investor, the Commission shall recommend approval of the plan of work.

In short, the procedure consists of a straightforward administrative process carried out by the Secretariat, followed by an automatic recommendation to Council by the Commission. This procedure was followed by the Commission when, on 22 August 1997, it recommended to the Council 'that the Council consider as approved the plans of work for exploration submitted by' the seven registered pioneer investors. [72]

4.3 Consideration and Approval by the Council of Plans of Work

Regulation 22 provides simply that the Council shall consider the reports and recommendations of the Commission relating to approval of plans of work for exploration in accordance with the Implementation Agreement, Annex, Section 3, paragraphs 11 and 12. The Council's role is considered above in Chapter 4. [73]

---

[71] Mining Code, Reg. 21(8).
[72] ISBA/3/C/7, *loc. cit.*. in note 41 above, at pp. 69-70.
[73] See above Chap. 4, section V.4.2.

The Mining Code: Exploration 165

A footnote to Regulation 22 dealing with plans of work of registered pioneer investors provides simply that, once the Commission submits a recommendation to approve a plan of work, it shall be considered approved by the Council in accordance with paragraph 6(a)(ii) of Section 1 of the Annex to the Implementation Agreement.

II. THE CONTRACT FOR EXPLORATION

1. The Contract
Once a plan of work has been approved by the Council, it has to be prepared in the form of a contract between the Authority and the applicant. The rules governing the contract are to be found in:
- Part IV of the Regulations on 'Contracts for Exploration';
- Annex 3 of the Regulations on 'Contract for Exploration', which prescribes the form of the contract; and
- Annex 4 of the Regulations on 'Standard Clauses for Exploration Contract'.

1.1 The Form of the Contract
Under Regulation 23(1), the contract must be prepared in the form prescribed in Annex 3. The text of Annex 3 is reproduced in Volume 3 [74] and here it will suffice to note a few of its principal features:
- *Incorporation of standard clauses.* The standard clauses set out in Annex 4, also reproduced in Volume 3, [75] are incorporated by reference into the contract. [76]
- *Exploration area.* The exploration area allocated to the Contractor is to be defined by co-ordinates to be listed in a schedule to the contract, as reduced from time to time in accordance with the standard clauses and the Regulations. [77]
- *Grant of exclusive right to explore.* The contractor is granted the exclusive right to explore for polymetallic nodules in the exploration area in accordance with the terms and conditions of the contract.[78]
- *Contract term.* The contract is for a period of 15 years unless the Contractor obtains a contract of exploitation prior to the expiry of that period or the contract is sooner terminated. [79]

Although the final text of Regulation 23(1) does not refer specifically to environmental clauses, the standard clauses on environmental monitoring and contingency plans and emergencies would of course be incorporated in contracts. [80]

---

[74] Vol. 3, Doc. No. 25.
[75] Vol. 3, Doc. No. 25.
[76] Mining Code, Annex 3, para. A.
[77] Mining Code, Annex 3, para. B.
[78] Mining Code, Annex 3, para. C.
[79] Mining Code, Annex 3, para. D.
[80] See Mining Code, Regs. 31 and 32 and Annex 4, Sections 5 and 6. *Cf.* The earlier draft of Reg. 23(1) in ISBA/5/C/4/Rev. 1, 14 October 1999.

166   *Chapter 5*

1.2 Parties to the Contract
The contract is executed by the Secretary-General on behalf of the Authority and
by the applicant [81] and enters into force on signature. [82]

1.3 Scope of Contract ratione materiae
As has been seen, regulations have yet to be adopted to govern the exploration
and exploitation of resources of the Area other than polymetallic nodules. [83]
Regulation 24(1) accordingly provides that:

> The contractor shall have the exclusive right to explore an area covered by a
> plan of work for exploration in respect of polymetallic nodules.   The
> Authority shall ensure that no other entity operates in the same area for
> resources other than polymetallic nodules in a manner that might interfere
> with the operations of the contractor.

Moreover, under Section 2(4) of the Standard Clauses for Exploration Contract,
the Authority reserves the right to enter into contracts with respect to resources
other than polymetallic nodules with third parties in the area covered by the
contract.
   However, under Regulation 40, on 'Resources other than polymetallic
nodules', it is provided that:

> If a prospector or contractor finds resources in the Area other than
> polymetallic nodules, the prospecting and exploration for and exploitation of
> such resources shall be subject to the rules, regulations and procedures of the
> Authority relating to such resources in accordance with the Convention and
> the Agreement.

As was seen in Chapter 4, on 17 August 1998, the Russian delegation made 'an
official request to the Authority,' invoking the procedure set out in Article
162(2)(o)(ii) of the UN Convention for initiating the adoption of rules for
exploration for such resources.[84] The Authority is thus bound to adopt such rules,
regulations and procedures not later than 17 August 2001.

1.4 Non-discrimination as Compared with Registered Pioneer Investors
Provision is made to ensure equality of treatment as between registered pioneer
investors and other contractors (other than the Enterprise). Thus, a contract with
such other contractor must include arrangements similar to and no less favourable
than those agreed with any registered pioneer investor. Similarly, if such other
contractors are granted more favourable arrangements, the Council must make
similar arrangements with regard to the obligations assumed by the registered

---

[81] Mining Code, Reg. 23(2).
[82] Mining Code, Annex 3, para. D.
[83] See further above, Chap. 4, section XVIII. 'Polymetallic nodules' are defined in Reg. 1(3)(d) of the
Mining Code as 'one of the resources of the Area consisting of any deposit or accretion of nodules, on
or just below the surface of the deep seabed, which contains manganese, nickel, cobalt and copper.'
[84] ISBA/4/A/CRP.2, 24 August 1998.

pioneer investors, provided that they do not affect or prejudice the interests of the Authority. [85]

1.5 Contractor's Priority for Exploitation

It is made clear in the UN Convention that an approved plan of work for exploration confers upon the operator exclusive rights with respect only to the exploration stage of activities. [86] However, Article 10 of Annex III of the Convention adds that such an operator will enjoy a preference and priority among applicants for a plan of work for exploitation of the same area and resources, unless its performance has not been satisfactory. Reflecting these provisions, Regulation 24(2) of the Mining Code provides that:

> A contractor who has an approved plan of work for exploration only shall have a preference and a priority among applicants submitting plans of work for exploitation of the same area and resources. Such preference or priority may be withdrawn by the Council if the contractor has failed to comply with the requirements of its approved plan of work for exploration within the time period specified in a written notice or notices from the Council to the contractor indicating which requirements have not been complied with by the contractor. The time period specified in any such notice shall not be unreasonable. The contractor shall be accorded a reasonable opportunity to be heard before the withdrawal of such preference or priority becomes final. The Council shall provide the reasons for its proposed withdrawal of preference or priority and shall consider any contractor's response. The decision of the Council shall take account of that response and shall be based on substantial evidence.

Regulation 24(3) adds a further judicial safeguard:

> A withdrawal of preference or priority shall not become effective until the contractor has been accorded a reasonable opportunity to exhaust the judicial remedies available to it pursuant to Part XI, section 5, of the Convention.

1.6 Size of Area, Renunciation and Relinquishment

The UN Convention does not specify the size of areas for exploration or require relinquishment of portions of such areas during the period of exploration. It does, however, in Annex III, Article 17, make provision for the adoption of rules, regulations and procedures on, *inter alia*, 'size of areas' and 'renunciation of areas'. [87] Such rules, regulations and procedures must 'fully reflect the objective criteria' set forth in Article 17(2).

As regards size of areas, Article 17(2)(a) provides that:

---

[85] Mining Code, Reg. 23(3). This provision reflects the provisions of the Implementation Agreement, Annex, Section 1(6)(a)(iii). See further below, Chap. 6, section IV.1.5.

[86] UN Convention, Annex III, Art. 3(4)(c). See further Chap. 4, section V.4.1.

[87] See above, Chap. 4, section XII.

168   *Chapter 5*

The Authority shall determine the appropriate size of areas for exploration which may be up to twice as large as those for exploitation in order to permit intensive exploration operations. The size of area shall be calculated to satisfy the requirements of article 8 of this Annex on reservation of areas as well as stated production requirements consistent with article 151 in accordance with the terms of the contract taking into account the state of the art of technology then available for sea-bed mining and the relevant physical characteristics of the areas. Areas shall be neither smaller nor larger than are necessary to satisfy this objective.

On renunciation of areas, Article 17(2)(e) simply provides that:

The operator shall have the right at any time to renounce without penalty the whole or part of his rights in the area covered by a plan of work.

Although the Convention did not specify the size of areas or impose relinquishment obligations for exploration contracts, UNCLOS III's Resolution II did make such provision in relation to the 'pioneer activities' to be carried out by registered pioneer investors. [88] Resolution II , Paragraph (1)(e) provided that:

...A pioneer area shall not exceed 150,000 square kilometres. The pioneer investor shall relinquish portions of the pioneer area to revert to the Area, in accordance with the following schedule:
(i)   20 per cent of the area allocated [by the Preparatory Commission to the pioneer investor] by the end of the third year from the date of the allocation;
(ii)   an additional 10 per cent of the area allocated by the end of the fifth year from the date of allocation;
(iii) an additional 20 per cent of the area allocated or such larger amount as would exceed the exploitation area decided upon by the Authority in its rules, regulations and procedures, after eight years from the date of the allocation of the area or the date of the award of a production authorisation, whichever is earlier.

Sub-paragraph (iii) is hardly a model of clear drafting. However, it would appear that if, for example, the Authority decides in future to include in the Mining Code a regulation limiting exploitation areas to, say, 70,000 square kilometres, the final 20 per cent relinquishment would be raised to 23.33% in order to reduce the pioneer area to 70,000 square kilometres.

As will be seen in Chapter 6, the New York Understanding of 5 September 1986, in order to overcome certain practical problems, introduced a departure from these provisions by permitting pioneer investors to voluntarily relinquish portions of the application areas simultaneously with their registration as pioneer investors. [89]

---

[88] See also below Chap. 6, sections III.6.1(ii)-(iii) and IV.2.
[89] See further Chap. 6, section III.6.1(iii).

The Mining Code: Exploration 169

Although 'pioneer activities' are different from exploration and, indeed, pioneer investors have to apply for approval of a plan of work for exploration, the Authority, in drafting Regulation 25 of the Mining Code on 'Size of area and relinquishment', adopted a very similar formula. Regulation 25(1) first provides that:

> The total area allocated to the contractor under the contract shall not exceed 150,000 square kilometres. The contractor shall relinquish portions of the area allocated to it to revert to the Area, in accordance with the following schedule:
> (a) 20 per cent of the area allocated by the end of the third year from the date of the contract;
> (b) an additional 10 per cent of the area allocated by the end of the fifth year from the date of the contract; and
> (c) an additional 20 per cent of the area allocated or such larger amount as would exceed the exploitation area decided upon by the Authority, after eight years from the date of the contract.

However, Regulations 25(1) goes on to make this schedule of relinquishment subject to the proviso that:

> a contractor shall not be required to relinquish any portion of such area when the total area allocated to it does not exceed 75,000 square kilometres.

The penultimate version of this provision, still current at the close of the first part of the Authority's Sixth Session in March 2000, was significantly different, providing that:

> a contractor shall not be required to relinquish any portion of such area when the total *remaining* area allocated to it does not exceed 75,000 square kilometres [emphasis added].

Under the earlier formulation, if the original, total area allocated to the contractor was, say, 100,000 square kilometres, it would have fallen by 20% to 80,000 at the end of the third year. At the end of the fifth year, since 'the total remaining area' would still have exceeded 75,000, a further relinquishment would have been required, though it is not entirely clear whether a full 10% would have been relinquished (bringing the remainder to 70,000) or only a 5% reduction, to bring the remainder to 75,000.

Under the final version of this clause, the position is quite different and, on the face of it, it would appear that the three-step reductions of 20%, 10% and 20% would be required in all cases except where the original total area allocated did not exceed 75,000 square kilometres. Using the same model as above, this would mean that the original total area of 100,000 would be reduced below the 75,000 level – in fact to 50,000 – after eight years. Thus, a contractor with an original allocation of 100,000 square kilometres would end up with an area of 50,000, whereas a contractor allocated 75,000 square kilometres would end up with

170   *Chapter 5*

75,000. Since this would clearly be an absurdity, it seems likely that the intention was simply to ensure that the reductions would be of such a size as would be required to bring the remaining area down to 75,000 square kilometres. If so, a clearer formulation could surely have been found.

Special provision had to be made in Regulation 25 for pioneer investors since, as noted above, they were already subject to the relinquishment provisions of Resolution II and the 1986 New York Understanding. Paragraph 2 accordingly provides that:

> In the case of a registered pioneer investor, the contract shall take into account the schedule of relinquishment, where applicable, in accordance with the terms of its registration as a registered pioneer investor. [90]

Accordingly, the French, Japanese and Russian contracts will take into account the 'voluntary advance relinquishments' provided for in the New York Understanding and specified in detail in the registration documentation. [91]

The Council is empowered by Regulation 25(3) to defer the schedule of relinquishment in exceptional circumstances:

> The Council may, at the request of the contractor, and on the recommendation of the Commission, in exceptional circumstances, defer the schedule of relinquishment. Such exceptional circumstances shall be determined by the Council and shall include, *inter alia*, consideration of prevailing economic circumstances or other unforeseen exceptional circumstances arising in connection with the operational activities of the Contractor.

The legal basis of this provision in the UN Convention or Implementation Agreement is not stated but may be Paragraph 5(f) of Section 1 of the Annex to the Implementation Agreement which permits the Authority, when adopting regulations, to take into account, *inter alia*, 'the prolonged delay in commencing deep seabed mining and the likely pace of activities in the Area'.

1.7 Duration of Contracts

The duration of the contract for exploration is governed by:
- The Implementation Agreement, Annex, Section 1, Paragraphs 9,11 and 12(d);
- Regulation 26 of the Mining Code; and
- Standard Clauses for Exploration Contract (Mining Code, Annex 4) Section 3.

---

[90] The provision for early relinquishment made in the New York Understanding was designed to accommodate the difficulties of those pioneer investors which, because of overlapping claims, had difficulty in complying with the requirements of Resolution II. France, Japan and the Soviet Union fell into this category whereas India, *e.g.*, did not; hence the need to refer in Reg.25(2) to the schedule of relinquishment 'where applicable'.

[91] For details, see 'Statement on the Implementation of Resolution II' (New York Understanding), 5 September 1986 (*LOS Bull.*, Special Issue III, September 1991, pp. 231-235), paras. 9-13; and the registration documentation for France (*ibid.*, pp. 41-74), Japan (*ibid.*, pp. 75-109) and Russia (*ibid.*, pp. 110-146).

The Implementation Agreement[92] and Regulation 26 [93] specify that the plan of work shall be approved for a period of 15 years and Section 3.1 of the Standard Clauses indicates that the period runs from the entry into force of the contract upon signature by both parties. [94]

Upon expiration of the plan of work for exploration, the contractor must apply for a plan of work for exploitation subject to four exceptions:

- The contractor has already made such an application. [95]
- The contractor has obtained an extension of the plan of work for exploration. Such extensions, for periods of not more than five years, may be approved by the Council, on the recommendation of the Commission, if the contractor has made efforts in good faith to comply with the requirements of the plan of work but, for reasons beyond its control, has been unable to complete the necessary preparatory work for proceeding to the exploitation stage, or the prevailing economic circumstances do not justify proceeding to the exploitation stage. [96] Applications for such extensions have to be submitted not later than six months before the expiration of the contract. [97] Extensions may also be granted if the contractor's performance of its obligations has been delayed by *force majeure*.[98]
- The contractor decides to renounce its rights in the area covered by the plan of work for exploration.[99]
- The contract is sooner terminated. [100] Such earlier termination may arise in a number of ways:
  (i) Under the Implementation Agreement, it was provided that, where the approved plan of work was sponsored by at least one State which was provisionally applying the Implementation Agreement, it would terminate if the State ceased to apply the Agreement provisionally and had not become either a member of the Authority on a provisional basis or a State Party to the Implementation Agreement. [101] However, this provision is now redundant, provisional application of the Implementation Agreement having terminated on 28 July 1996, although States in this position were permitted to continue their membership of the Authority on a provisional basis for a limited period terminating at the latest on 16 November 1998. [102]

---

[92] Implementation Agreement, Annex, Section 1, para. 9.
[93] Mining Code, Reg. 26(1).
[94] Standard Clauses, Mining Code, Annex 4, Section 3.1.
[95] Implementation Agreement, Annex, Section 1, para. 9; Mining Code, Reg. 26(1).
[96] Implementation Agreement, Annex, Section 1, para. 9; Mining Code, Reg. 26(1)-(2).
[97] Mining Code, Reg. 26(2); Standard Clauses, Mining Code, Annex 4, Section 3.2.
[98] See further below, section 1.10, under *Force majeure*.
[99] Mining Code, Reg. 26(1); Standard Clauses, Mining Code, Annex 4, Section 19. See also above, section 1.6.
[100] Standard Clauses, Mining Code, Annex 4, Section 3(1)(b).
[101] Implementation Agreement, Annex, Section 1, para. 11.
[102] See further above, Chap. 1, section II.1.2 and Chap.6, section IV.1.2.

172   *Chapter 5*

(ii)   Under the Implementation Agreement, it was further provided that, where the application had been sponsored by a State which was a member of the Authority on a provisional basis, the approved plan of work would terminate if such membership ceased and the State had not become a State Party to the Agreement. [103] As noted above, the status of provisional membership of the Authority terminated on 16 November 1998 and this provision too is therefore now redundant.

(iii)   Under Article 153(2)(b) of the UN Convention, the contractor must possess the nationality of a State Party or be effectively controlled by it or its nationals. It is accordingly provided in Section 19 of the Standard Clauses that:

> If the nationality or control of the Contractor changes or the Contractor's sponsoring State, as defined in the Regulations, terminates its sponsorship, the Contractor shall promptly notify the Authority forthwith. [104]

In either such event, the contract would terminate forthwith unless the Contractor obtained another sponsor, meeting the requirements prescribed in the Regulations, which submitted to the Authority a certificate of sponsorship for the Contractor in the prescribed form within the time specified in the Regulations.[105]

(iv)   The contract may be terminated by the Council in the circumstances provided for in Section 21 of the Standard Clauses:

(a)   if, in spite of written warnings by the Authority, the Contractor has conducted its activities in such a way as to result in serious persistent and wilful violations of the fundamental terms of this contract, Part XI of the Convention, the Agreement and the rules regulations and procedures of the Authority; or

(b)   if the Contractor has failed to comply with a final binding decision of the dispute settlement body applicable to it; or

(c)   if the Contractor becomes insolvent or commits an act of bankruptcy or enters into any agreement for composition with its creditors or goes into liquidation or receivership, whether compulsory or voluntary, or petitions or applies to any tribunal for the appointment of a receiver or a trustee or receiver for itself or commences any proceedings relating to itself under any bankruptcy, insolvency or readjustment of debt law, whether now or hereafter in effect, other than for the purpose of reconstruction. [106]

---

[103] Implementation Agreement, Annex, Section 1, para. 12(d).
[104] Standard Clauses, Mining Code, Annex 4, Section 20.1.
[105] *Ibid.,* Section, 20.2.
[106] *Ibid.,* Section 21.1(a)-(c). See further below, section 1.9.4 on *Suspension and Termination of Contracts.*

Finally, it may be noted that the Contractor's rights and obligations may continue for a time after the expiration of the contract. One of the Standard Clauses provides that:

> Notwithstanding the expiration of this contract in accordance with section 3.1 hereof, if the Contractor has, at least ninety days prior to the date of expiration, applied for a contract for exploitation, the Contractor's rights and obligations under this contract shall continue until such time as the application has been considered and a contract for exploitation has been issued or refused. [107]

1.8 Training

Contractors are required to provide training for personnel of the Authority and developing States under the UN Convention, Article 144(2) and Annex III, Article 15. Article 144(2) has to be read with the Implementation Agreement, Annex, Section 5, Paragraph 1(c). [108] These provisions are further developed in the Mining Code and its Standard Clauses for Exploration Contracts.

Regulation 27(1) of the Mining Code is in the following terms:

> *Regulation 27*
> *Training*
>
> 1. Pursuant to article 15 of Annex III to the Convention, each contract shall include as a schedule a practical programme for the training of personnel of the Authority and developing States and drawn up by the contractor in co-operation with the Authority and the sponsoring State or States. Training programmes shall focus on training in the conduct of exploration, and shall provide for full participation by such personnel in all activities covered by the contract. Such training programmes may be revised and developed from time to time as necessary by mutual agreement.

This provision appears to suggest that the training programme would be drawn up in pre-contract negotiations and included as a schedule to the contract prior to signature. However, the corresponding Standard Clause seems to be at variance with this interpretation. Section 8.2 provides that, 'The scope and financing of the training programme shall be subject to negotiation between the contractor, the Authority and the sponsoring State or States.' [109] Section 8.1 specifies, however, that the contractor will submit proposed training programmes to the Authority for approval 'prior to the commencement of exploration under this contract', which seems to indicate that the contract will be signed first and the terms of the training programme will be, or at least may be, approved afterwards for incorporation in the contract as schedule 3.[110] The full text of Section 8 reads as follows:

---

[107] *Ibid.*, Section 3.3.
[108] See further Chap. 3, sections VII, VIII and XII (text at note 195); Chap. 6, sections III.8-11 and IV.3; and Chap. 4, section X.
[109] Standard Clauses, Mining Code, Annex 4, Section 8.2.
[110] In accordance with Section 8.3.

174   *Chapter 5*

Section 8
Training

8.1 In accordance with the Regulations, the Contractor shall, prior to the commencement of exploration under this contract, submit to the Authority for approval proposed training programmes for the training of personnel of the Authority and developing States, including the participation of such personnel in all of the Contractor's activities under this contract.
8.2 The scope and financing of the training programme shall be subject to negotiation between the Contractor, the Authority and the sponsoring State or States.
8.3 The Contractor shall conduct training programmes in accordance with the specific programme for the training of personnel referred to in section 8.1 hereof approved by the Authority in accordance with the Regulations, which programme, as revised and developed from time to time, shall become a part of this contract as schedule 3.[111]

Separate provision is made in UNCLOS Resolution II, Paragraph 12(a)(ii) for the training programmes to be provided by Pioneer Investors and their special position is also reflected in Regulation 27(2) of the Mining Code, which provides that the contract, 'shall take into account the training provided in accordance with the terms of its registration as a registered pioneer investor'. Developments pursuant to these provisions are considered in Chapter 6 below. [112]

1.9 Security of Tenure and Contractor's Exclusive Right to Explore
A very important part of any mining contract is the provision made for the contractor's security of tenure. In the Mining Code, direct provision is made for security of tenure in Standard Clause 2 but, for a fuller understanding of the position, reference has also to be made to a number of related provisions dealing with the contractor's exclusive right to explore, suspension and termination of contracts, revision of contracts, and proposals made for adjustments in the contractor's annual reports.

1.9.1 Security of Tenure
Starting with the basic provisions of the UN Convention on security of tenure, Article 153(6) provides that:

A contract under paragraph 3 shall provide for security of tenure. Accordingly, the contract shall not be revised, suspended or terminated except in accordance with Annex III, articles 18 and 19. [113]

Annex III, Article 18 deals with 'penalties' and specifies the circumstances in which, as a penalty, a contractor's rights may be suspended or terminated for

---

[111] Standard Clauses, Mining Code, Annex 4, Section 8.
[112] See Chap. 6, sections III.8 and IV.3.
[113] See further Chap. 4, section V.5.

The Mining Code: Exploration   175

breaches of contract. [114] Annex III, Article 19 lays down the rules for revision of contracts. [115]

The Mining Code deals with security of tenure in Section 2 of the Standard Clauses. Section 2.1, reflecting Article 153(6) of the UN Convention, provides simply that:

> The Contractor shall have security of tenure and this contract shall not be suspended, terminated or revised except in accordance with sections 20 , 21 and 24 hereof.

Sections 20, 21 and 24 embody the Standard Clauses on 'termination of sponsorship' (and possible termination of contract as a consequence);[116] 'suspension and termination of contract and penalties'; [117] and revision of contracts. [118]

1.9.2 Contractor's Exclusive Right to Explore

Under Annex III, Article 16 of the UN Convention, the contractor enjoys the exclusive right to explore the area covered by the plan of work and the Authority has to ensure that no other entity operates in the same area for a different category of resources in a manner which might interfere with the contractor's operations.[119]

Reflecting these provisions, Section 2.2 of the Standard Clauses provides that:

> The Contractor shall have the exclusive right to explore for polymetallic nodules in the exploration area in accordance with the terms and conditions of this contract. The Authority shall ensure that no other entity operates in the exploration area for a different category of resources in a manner that might unreasonably interfere with the operations of the Contractor. [120]

1.9.3 Periodic Review of the Programme of Work

Regulation 28 of the Mining Code provides that:

> *Periodic review of the implementation of the plan of work for exploration*
>
> 1. The contractor and the Secretary-General shall jointly undertake a periodic review of the implementation of the plan of work for exploration at intervals of five years. The Secretary-General may request the contractor to submit such additional data and information as may be necessary for the purposes of the review.

---

[114] See further Chap.4, section XIII.
[115] See further Chap.4, section XV.
[116] See further above, section II.1.7, text following note 100.
[117] See further below, section 1.9.4.
[118] See further below, section 1.9.5.
[119] See further Chap. 4, section V.5.
[120] Standard Clauses, Mining Code, Annex 4, Section 2.2.

176   *Chapter 5*

2. In the light of the review, the contractor shall indicate its programme of activities for the following five-year period, making such adjustments to its previous programme of activities as are necessary.
3. The Secretary-General shall report on the review to the Commission and to the Council. The Secretary-General shall indicate in the report whether any observations transmitted to him by States Parties to the Convention concerning the manner in which the contractor has discharged its obligations under these Regulations relating to the protection and preservation of the marine environment were taken into account in the review. [121]

Further detail is provided by Section 4.4 of the Standard Clauses:

Not later than 90 days prior to the expiration of each five-year period from the date on which this contract enters into force in accordance with section 3 hereof, the Contractor and the Secretary-General shall jointly undertake a review of the implementation of the plan of work for exploration under this contract. The Secretary-General may require the Contractor to submit such additional data and information as may be necessary for the purposes of the review. In the light of the review, the Contractor shall indicate its programme of activities for the following five-year period, including a revised schedule of anticipated yearly expenditures, making such adjustments to its previous programme of activities as are necessary. Schedule 2 hereto shall be adjusted accordingly. [122]

In the penultimate draft of those provisions (ISBA/6/C/2, 3 April 2000), any necessary adjustments to the plan of work would have had to be agreed between the contractor and the Secretary-General and approved by the Council, thus ensuring that no adjustment would be forced upon the contractor without its consent. Although there is no such provision in the final text of the Mining Code, it is true that it is left to the contractor to indicate any adjustments believed to be necessary in the light of the jointly conducted review.

1.9.4 Suspension and Termination of Contracts
As has been seen in Chapter 4, the suspension or termination of the contract is among the range of penalties which the Authority may impose upon the Contractor under Annex III, Article 18 of the UN Convention. [123] That article identifies two cases in which the sanction of suspension or termination may be imposed. The same two cases are identified in the corresponding part of the Mining Code, Section 21.1 of the Standard Clauses, as follows:

The Council may suspend or terminate this contract, without prejudice to any other rights that the Authority may have, if any of the following events should occur:

---

[121] Mining Code, Reg. 28.
[122] Standard Clauses, Mining Code, Annex 4, Section 4.4.
[123] See Chap. 4, section XIII.

(a) if, in spite of written warnings by the Authority, the Contractor has conducted its activities in such a way as to result in serious persistent and wilful violations of the fundamental terms of this contract, Part XI of the Convention, the Agreement and the rules, regulations and procedures of the Authority; or

(b) if the Contractor has failed to comply with a final binding decision of the dispute settlement body applicable to it; [124]

However, Section 21.1 adds a third case:

(c) if Contractor becomes insolvent or commits an act of bankruptcy or enters into any agreement for composition with its creditors or goes into liquidation or receivership, whether compulsory or voluntary, or petitions or applies to any tribunal for the appointment of a receiver or a trustee or receiver for itself or commences any proceedings relating to itself under any bankruptcy, insolvency or readjustment of debt law, whether now or hereafter in effect, other than for the purpose of reconstruction. [125]

As has been seen in section I.2.1 and I.2.4 above, an applicant for an exploration contract has to supply the detailed information required to enable the Council to determine that it is financially capable of carrying out the proposed plan of work and of fulfilling its financial obligations to the Authority. If a contractor is financially embarrassed to the extent indicated in Section 21.1(c), it is evident that it is no longer financially capable in this sense. The detailed procedure for effecting a suspension or termination is set forth in the remaining paragraphs of Section 21 of the Standard Clauses. The suspension or termination will be effected 60 days after notice through the Secretary-General unless, within that time, the Contractor disputes the Authority's right to suspend or terminate the contract in accordance with the dispute settlement provisions of Part XI of the Convention. [126] In the latter case, the contract may be suspended or terminated only in accordance with a binding decision of the dispute settlement body concerned.[127]

All is not lost if the contract has simply been suspended. Section 21.4 of the Standard Clauses provides that:

If the Council has suspended this contract, the Council may by notice require the Contractor to resume its operations and comply with the terms and conditions of this contract, not later than 60 days after such notice. [128]

---

[124] Standard Clauses, Mining Code, Annex 4, Section 21.1(a)-(b).
[125] *Ibid.*, Section 21.1(c).
[126] *Ibid.*, Section 21.2. On the dispute settlement provisions of Part XI of the Convention, see further below, Chap. 9, especially section IX on *Contractual Disputes*.
[127] *Ibid.*, Section 21.3.
[128] *Ibid.*, Section 21.4.

178   *Chapter 5*

Termination is, of course, much more drastic in its effect and, under Section 21.7 of the Standard Clauses:

> In the event of termination or expiration of this contract, the Contractor shall comply with the Regulations and shall remove all installations, plant, equipment and materials in the exploration area and shall make the area safe so as not to constitute a danger to persons, shipping or to the marine environment. [129]

1.9.5 Revision of Contracts

The provision made for revision of contracts in Section 24 of the Standard Clauses poses no threat to the contractor's security of tenure and, indeed, may be to its advantage, in that it facilitates revision when changed circumstances render the contract inequitable or make it impracticable or impossible to achieve its objectives.

Section 24 envisages two sets of circumstances which may justify a revision:

> 24.1   When circumstances have arisen or are likely to arise which, in the opinion of the Authority or the Contractor, would render this contract inequitable or make it impracticable or impossible to achieve the objectives set out in this contract or in Part XI of the Convention or the Agreement, the parties shall enter into negotiations to revise it accordingly.
>
> 24.2   This contract may also be revised by agreement between the Contractor and the Authority to facilitate the application of any rules, regulations and procedures adopted by the Authority subsequent to the entry into force of this contract. [130]

Paragraph 24.1 commits the contractor only to negotiations and Paragraph 24.2 makes any revision subject to agreement between the contractor and the Authority. The element of consent is further emphasised in the final paragraph of Section 24:

> 24.3   This contract may be revised, amended or otherwise modified only with the consent of the Contractor and the Authority by an appropriate instrument signed by the authorised representatives of the parties. [131]

Section 4.3 of the Standard Clauses similarly envisages changes in the programme of activities and the expenditures specified therein, but again, on the basis of consent:

> 4.3   The Contractor, with the consent of the Authority, which consent shall not be unreasonably withheld, may from time to time make such changes in the programme of activities and the expenditures specified therein as may be necessary and prudent in accordance with good mining industry practice, and

---

[129] *Ibid.*, Section 21.7.
[130] *Ibid.*, Sections 24.1 and 24.2.
[131] *Ibid.*, Section 24.3.

taking into account the market conditions for the metals contained in polymetallic nodules and other relevant global economic conditions. [132]

One way in which the Contractor may initiate adjustments to the programme of activities is indicated in Section 10 of the Standard Clauses. Section 10 includes in a list of matters to be incorporated in the contractor's annual report, 'details of any proposed adjustments to the programme of activities and the reasons for such adjustments'.[133]

1.10 Responsibility and Liability

Although more elaborate provision was made in earlier drafts of the Mining Code for the responsibility and liability of the contractor and of States and international organisations, [134] the final version of the Mining Code deals with the 'responsibility and liability' of the contractor and the Authority much more concisely.

1.10.1 Liability of the Contractor for Damage

Regulation 30 of the Mining Code provides that the liability of the contractor 'shall be in accordance with the Convention'. As was seen in Chapter 4, the UN Convention made provision for liability for damage on a contractual level under Annex III, Article 22. [135]

Regulation 30 goes on to add that:

> The contractor shall continue to have responsibility for any damage arising out of wrongful acts in the conduct of its operations, in particular damage to the marine environment, after the completion of the exploration phase. [136]

The Standard Clauses develop these provisions further by providing that:

> The Contractor shall be liable for the actual amount of any damage, including damage to the marine environment, arising out of its wrongful acts or omissions, and those of its employees, subcontractors, agents and all persons engaged in working or acting for them in the conduct of its operations under this contract, including the costs of reasonable measures to prevent or limit damage to the marine environment, account being taken of any contributory acts or omissions by the Authority. [137]

The contractual implications of this liability are further drawn out in the following paragraph:

---

[132] *Ibid.*, Section 4.3.
[133] *Ibid.*, Section 10.2(d).
[134] See ISBA/5/C/4/Rev.1, 14 October 1999, Reg. 30 and Standard Clauses, Section 16.
[135] See further above, Chap. 4, section XIV.1.
[136] Mining Code, Reg. 30.
[137] Standard Clauses, Mining Code, Annex 4, Section 16.1.

180   *Chapter 5*

> The Contractor shall indemnify the Authority, its employees, subcontractors and agents against all claims and liabilities of any third party arising out of any wrongful acts or omissions of the Contractor and its employees, agents and subcontractors, and all persons engaged in working or acting for them in the conduct of its operations under this contract.[138]

Moreover, the Standard Clauses require the Contractor to have insurance cover, as follows:

> The Contractor shall maintain appropriate insurance policies with internationally recognised carriers, in accordance with generally accepted international maritime practice.[139]

An earlier draft of the Mining Code made provision permitting States to apply to contractors sponsored by them, or to ships flying their flag, national environmental rules more stringent than those in the UN Convention regime. This draft regulation did not survive in the final version of the Mining Code. [140] However, this is of course without prejudice to the provisions of Annex III, Article 21(3) of the UN Convention under which:

> No State Party may impose conditions on a contractor that are inconsistent with Part XI. However, the application by a State Party to contractors sponsored by it, or to ships flying its flag, of environmental or other laws and regulations more stringent than those in the rules, regulations and procedures of the Authority adopted pursuant to article 17, paragraph 2(f), of this Annex shall not be deemed inconsistent with Part XI.[141]

It will be noted that reference is made to rules etc. adopted by the Authority under Article 17(2)(f) of Annex III, that is, rules drawn up in order to secure effective protection of the marine environment. In other words, the exception allowed under Annex III, Article 21(3) applies only to 'environmental or other laws and regulations' designed to secure effective protection of the marine environment. Presumably, the reference to 'other' laws and regulations was intended to cover laws relating to fishing or navigation, for example, which are not strictly speaking 'environmental' but which may nonetheless help to secure effective protection of the marine environment.

Force majeure. Where delay or failure to perform contractual obligations has been caused by *force majeure*, the contractor is relieved of liability. [142] *Force majeure* is defined as meaning 'an event or condition that the Contractor could not reasonably be expected to prevent or control; provided that the condition was

---

[138] *Ibid.*, Section 16.2.
[139] *Ibid.*, Section 16.5.
[140] See ISBA/5/C/4/Rev.1, 14 October 1999, Reg. 31.
[141] UN Convention, Annex III, Art. 21(3).
[142] Standard Clauses, Mining Code, Annex 4, Section 17.1.

The Mining Code: Exploration   181

not caused by negligence or by a failure to observe good mining industry practice'.[143]

In such cases the Contractor is, upon request, granted a time extension equal to the period of the delay and the term of the contract is extended accordingly.[144] However, the Contractor has to take reasonable measures to contain the situation in accordance with the Standard Clauses, Section 17.3:

> In the event of *force majeure*, the Contractor shall take all reasonable measures to remove its inability to perform and comply with the terms and conditions of this contract with a minimum of delay; provided that the Contractor shall not be obligated to resolve or terminate any labour dispute or any other disagreement with a third party except on terms satisfactory to it or pursuant to a final decision of any agency having jurisdiction to resolve the dispute.[145]

In addition, the Contractor must keep the Authority informed under Section 17.4:

> The Contractor shall give notice to the Authority of the occurrence of an event of *force majeure* as soon as reasonably possible, and similarly give notice to the Authority of the restoration of normal conditions.[146]

1.10.2 Liability of the Authority for Damage

Regulation 30 provides that the 'Responsibility and liability ... of the Authority shall be in accordance with the Convention',[147] that is, in effect, in accordance with the UN Convention, Annex III, Article 22, which is considered in detail in Chapter 4.[148]

Regulation 30 is supplemented by Section 16 of the Standard Clauses, under which:

> 16.3 The Authority shall be liable for the actual amount of any damage to the Contractor arising out of its wrongful acts in the exercise of its powers and functions, including violations under article 168, paragraph 2, of the Convention, account being taken of contributory acts or omissions by the Contractor, its employees, agents and subcontractors, and all persons engaged in working or acting for them in the conduct of its operations under this contract.
>
> 16.4 The Authority shall indemnify the Contractor, its employees, subcontractors, agents and all persons engaged in working or acting for them in the conducts of its operations under this contract, against all claims and liabilities of any third party arising out of any wrongful acts of omissions in

---

[143] *Ibid.*
[144] *Ibid.*, Section 17.2.
[145] *Ibid.*, Section 17.3.
[146] *Ibid.*, Section 17.4.
[147] Mining Code, Reg. 30.
[148] See above, Chap. 4, section XIV.2.

182   *Chapter 5*

the exercise of its powers and functions hereunder, including violations under article 168, paragraph 2, of the Convention. [149]

Article 168(2) of the UN Convention is concerned with the duty of the Secretary-General and the Secretariat staff not to disclose confidential material. [150]

III. PROTECTION AND PRESERVATION OF THE MARINE ENVIRONMENT

The provision made in Part V of the Mining Code and the Standard Clauses for Exploration Contracts for the protection and preservation of the marine environment is considered below in Chapter 10 on *Protection and Preservation of the Marine Environment.* [151]

IV. CONFIDENTIALITY OF DATA AND INFORMATION

As has been seen in Chapter 4, the UN Convention places an obligation upon the Secretary-General and his staff, and members of the Legal and Technical Commission, to maintain the confidentiality of proprietary data and industrial secrets supplied to them by applicants for contracts, and makes provision for the liability of the Authority and the Secretary-General of the Authority for improper disclosures. [152] These provisions are developed further in Regulations 35 and 36 of the Mining Code, Regulations 10 and 11 of the Staff Regulations and Section 12 of the Standard Clauses.

The drafting of those parts of the Mining Code which deal with the question of confidentiality proved to be very difficult and the final version was completed only at the sixth session of the Authority in July 2000. Earlier drafts attempted to tie the concept of confidentiality to notions of 'data and information of a proprietary or commercially sensitive nature' [153] or 'data and information of commercial value'. [154] It may be noted that the term 'proprietary' is not defined either in the UN Convention or any of the drafts of the Mining Code.

In the final version of the Mining Code, Part VI, on 'Confidentiality', is now split into two Regulations and embodies a new approach, divorced from any notions of commercial value or commercial sensitivity. This new formulation is considered below in relation to:

- What constitutes confidential data and information;
- Limitations on use by Authority of confidential data and information;
- Period of confidentiality;
- Procedures to ensure confidentiality;
- Standard Clause on confidentiality.

---

[149] Standard Clauses, Mining Code, Annex 4, Sections 16.3 and 16.4.

[150] On confidentiality of data and information, see further below, section IV.

[151] See especially Chap. 10, section IV.

[152] See above, Chap. 4, section XIV.2.1.

[153] ISBA/4/C/4, 2 April 1998, Reg. 31(1).

[154] ISBA/5/C/4/Rev.1, 14 October 1999, Reg. 36(1).

The Mining Code: Exploration   183

1. What Constitutes Confidential Data and Information

Although Regulation 35 is titled 'Proprietary data and information and confidentiality', the definition in paragraph 1 of what constitutes confidential data and information makes no mention of 'proprietary' data and, as noted above, 'proprietary' is nowhere defined.

Paragraph 1 provides that:

> Data and information submitted or transferred to the Authority or to any person participating in any activity or programme of the Authority pursuant to these Regulations or a contract issued under these Regulations, and designated by the contractor, in consultation with the Secretary-General, as being of a confidential nature, shall be considered confidential unless it is data and information which:
> (a) is generally known or publicly available from other sources;
> (b) has been previously made available by the owner to others without an obligation concerning its confidentiality; or
> (c) is already in the possession of the Authority with no obligation concerning its confidentiality.

Two aspects of this definition deserve to be noted. First, it relates to data and information submitted or transferred not only to the Authority (as in earlier drafts) but also to 'any person participating in any activity or programme of the Authority' etc.

Secondly, a more verifiable test is introduced for the identification of such confidential material. It will no longer suffice for the contractor to identify it as such, as in previous drafts. It has now to be 'designated by the contractor, in consultation with the Secretary-General, as being of a confidential nature'.

In the penultimate draft of the Mining Code, it was provided that:

> Data and information which is necessary for the formulation by the Authority of rules, regulations and procedures concerning protection of the marine environment and safety, other than equipment design data, shall not be deemed proprietary. [155]

In the final version, no such provision appears and data and information falling into this category will now be subject to the normal rules on confidentiality.

2. Limitations on Use by Authority of Confidential Data and Information

The fact that data and information are confidential does not of course necessarily mean that they cannot be used by Authority organs or personnel. Paragraph 2 of Regulation 35 specifies the limits within which they may be used:

> Confidential data and information may only be used by the Secretary-General and staff of the Secretariat, as authorised by the Secretary-General, and by the members of the Legal and Technical Commission as necessary

---

[155] ISBA/6/C/2, 3 April 2000, Reg. 35(2).

184   *Chapter 5*

for and relevant to the effective exercise of their powers and functions. The Secretary-General shall authorise access to such data and information only for limited use in connection with the functions and duties of the staff of the Secretariat and the functions and duties of the Legal and Technical Commission.

3. Period of Confidentiality

During the drafting of Regulation 35 there was much debate over the length of time during which confidentiality was to be enjoyed. Some favoured protection indefinitely; others argued for confidentiality while the contract remained in force, unless it were followed by a contract for exploitation; yet others wished to see the obligations of Authority staff made more specific. [156] In the end, a balanced formula was found whereby confidentiality will be preserved for ten years after the date of submission of the material or until the expiry of the contract, whichever is later; thereafter, the onus is upon the contractor to establish, at periodical reviews conducted with the Secretary-General, that the release of the material would present a substantial risk of serious and unfair economic prejudice. Paragraph 3 of Regulation 35 is as follows:

> Ten years after the date of submission of confidential data and information to the Authority or the expiration of the contract for exploration, whichever is the later, and every five years thereafter, the Secretary-General and the contractor shall review such data and information to determine whether they should remain confidential. Such data and information shall remain confidential if the contractor establishes that there would be a substantial risk of serious and unfair economic prejudice if the data and information were to be released. No such data and information shall be released until the contractor has been accorded a reasonable opportunity to exhaust the judicial remedies available to it pursuant to Part XI, section 5, of the Convention.

If, however, at any time after the expiry of the contract, the contractor enters into a contract for exploitation in respect of any part of the exploration area, confidential data and information relating to that part of the area will remain confidential in accordance with the new contract for exploitation. [157]

It is recognised, however, that the contractor may, at any time, waive confidentiality of data and information. [158]

4. Procedures to Ensure Confidentiality

The final version of Regulation 36, on 'Procedures to ensure confidentiality', for the most part follows the same lines as the penultimate draft in placing duties of confidentiality upon the Secretary-General and the staff of the Authority and

---

[156] *Outstanding Issues with Respect to the Draft Regulations on Prospecting and Exploration for Polymetallic Nodules in the Area. Note by the Secretariat,* ISBA/6/C/INF.1, March 2000, para. 22.

[157] Reg. 35(4).

[158] Reg. 35(5).

members of the Legal and Technical Commission, and in imposing responsibility upon the Secretary-General to establish the necessary administrative procedures. [159] However, in a clear effort to give added assurances to prospective contractors, it goes further than the earlier draft in two respects. First, Paragraph 2 introduces stringent security safeguards applicable to personnel having access to confidential material:

> A person who is authorised pursuant to these Regulations to have access to confidential data and information shall not disclose such data and information except as permitted under the Convention and these Regulations. The Secretary-General shall require any person who is authorised to have access to confidential data and information to make a written declaration witnessed by the Secretary-General or his or her authorised representative to the effect that the person so authorised:
> (a) acknowledges his or her legal obligation under the Convention and these Regulations with respect to the non-disclosure of confidential data and information;
> (b) agrees to comply with the applicable regulations and procedures established to ensure the confidentiality of such data and information.

Secondly, further disincentives are provided by Paragraph 5, envisaging action by the Authority against any person acting in breach of the obligations relating to confidentiality:

> Taking into account the responsibility and liability of the Authority pursuant to Annex III, article 22, of the Convention, the Authority may take such action as may be appropriate against any person who, by reason his or her duties for the Authority, has access to any confidential data and information and who is in breach of the obligations relating to confidentiality contained in the Convention and these Regulations.

Regulations 10 and 11 of the Staff Regulations [160] offer some guidance on the types of action which the Authority may take. First, the Secretary-General may impose disciplinary measures on staff members whose conduct is unsatisfactory and may summarily dismiss a member of staff for serious misconduct. [161] Secondly, if staff members act in violation of their obligation under Article 168(2) of the UN Convention not to disclose industrial secrets, etc., complaints by affected States Parties or persons sponsored by them must be submitted to a three-person *ad hoc* tribunal appointed by the UN Secretary-General. If the tribunal so recommends, the Secretary-General of the Authority must dismiss the staff member concerned. [162] If the staff members allege 'non-observance of their terms of appointment, including all pertinent regulations and rules', there will be

---

[159] See Reg. 36(1), (3) and (4).
[160] Staff Regulations of the International Seabed Authority, ISBA/6/C/10, 13 July 2000, Annex.
[161] *Ibid.*, Reg. 10.2.
[162] *Ibid.*, Reg. 10.3.

186　*Chapter 5*

a right of appeal to 'administrative machinery with staff participation', established by the Secretary-General, and to the United Nations Administrative Tribunal. [163]

5. Standard Contractual Clause on Confidentiality

Section 12 of Annex 4 of the Mining Code simply incorporates by reference into contracts the confidentiality provisions of the Regulations reviewed above:

Confidentiality

Data and information transferred to the Authority in accordance with this contract shall be treated as confidential in accordance with the provisions of the Regulations.

V. SETTLEMENT OF DISPUTES

Part VIII of the Mining Code, on 'Settlement of Disputes' consists of the single Regulation 39, under which disputes concerning the interpretation or application of the Regulations are to be settled in accordance with Part XI, section 5 of the UN Convention. Similarly, Section 25 of the Standard Clauses requires any dispute between the parties concerning the interpretation or application of the contract to be settled in the same way. [164] Part XI, section 5 of the UN Convention is fully considered below in Chapter 9 on 'Settlement of Disputes'. [165]

It is further provided in Regulation 39(2) and Standard Clause 25.2 that:

Any final decision rendered by a court or tribunal having jurisdiction under the Convention relating to the rights and obligations of the Authority and of the Contractor shall be enforceable in the territory of each State Party to the Convention.

---

[163] *Ibid.*, Regs. 11.1 and 11.2.
[164] Standard Clause 25.1.
[165] See further Chap. 9, section IV.

CHAPTER 6

The UN Convention Regime of Sea-Bed Mining:
IV. The Pioneer Investor Scheme

An account was given in Chapter 3 of the principles underlying the UN Convention regime of sea-bed mining and in Chapter 4 an examination was made of the basic regime for the development of the resources of the Area laid down in Part XI of the UN Convention, as modified by the Implementation Agreement. This chapter is concerned with the third main component of the regime, the Pioneer Investor Scheme, for which provision was originally made in Resolution II of UNCLOS III.

I. Origins and Raison d'Etre

It was clear, prior to the Eleventh Session of UNCLOS III, and confirmed during it, that the establishment of a Preparatory Investment Protection scheme (PIP) which would offer adequate protection to pioneer investors in sea-bed mining was a *sine qua non* of a conventional regime for sea-bed mining acceptable to the principal industrialised States. Accordingly, the Eleventh Session of UNCLOS III was essentially concerned with the attempt to devise a PIP scheme which would, on the one hand, provide acceptable safeguards for the very heavy investments already made by a number of pioneer enterprises and, on the other hand, satisfy the Group of 77 (G-77) by preserving the main principles of the UN Convention regime as already drafted. Both sides were under considerable pressure to reach a compromise. The G-77 were aware that five of the principal industrialised States had already adopted unilateral legislation, following the lead given by the United States in 1980,[1] and that there was talk of a Reciprocating

---

[1] Legislation was adopted by the following States: United States (1980), Federal Republic of Germany (1980), United Kingdom (1981), France (1981) and the Soviet Union (1982). The following citations refer to this legislation as subsequently amended or replaced and to the legislation later adopted by Japan (1982) and Italy (1985):
United States : Deep Seabed Hard Mineral Resources Act 1980, Public Law 96-283, 28 June 1980, 94 Stat.553; 30 USC 1401 *et seq*.; reproduced (as amended to 1 July 2000) in Vol. 3 as Doc. No. 26.1. See too related Deep Seabed Mining Regulations for Exploration Licenses, *Federal Register*, Vol.

188   *Chapter 6*

States Regime being established by these States on the basis of a co-ordinating mini-treaty. They acknowledged too that failure to meet the minimum demands of the United States Government and its consequent refusal to become a party to the Convention would, at the very least, seriously weaken the conventional system and possibly render it impracticable. There were, however, strong pressures on the other side too. Not only would failure to ratify the UN

46, No. 178, 15 September 1981, pp. 45890-45920; 15 CFR Part 970; XX ILM (1981), pp. 1228-1258 (as amended); Subpart C issued separately in *Federal Register*, Vol. 47, No. 110, 8 June 1982, pp. 24948-24951; 15 CFR Part 970 (as amended); and Deep Seabed Mining Regulations for Commercial Recovery Permits, *Federal Register*, Vol. 54, No.525, 6 January 1989; 15 CFR Part 971.

Germany: The FRG originally adopted the Act of Interim Regulation of Deep Seabed Mining 1980, *Bundesgesetzblatt*, Part I, 9080, No. 50, 22 August 1980, p.1457 (English translation in XX ILM (1981), p.393), as amended by the Act of 12 February 1982, *Bundesgesetzblatt*, Part I, No. 5, 17 February 1982, p.136 (English translation in XXI ILM (1982), p.832). Following accession to the UN Convention in 1994, Germany replaced this legislation with the more comprehensive Law for the Implementation of the UN Convention and the Implementation Agreement of 29 July 1994 (*Ausführungsgesetz Seerechtsübereinkommen* 1982/1994) of 6 June 1995, BGBl. I 778 9510-23; part of this Law is reproduced in English translation in Vol.3 as Doc. No. 27.1 ('Act Governing Deep Seabed Mining').

United Kingdom: Deep Sea Mining (Temporary Provisions) Act 1981 as amended, reproduced in Vol.3 as Doc. 28.1. See too Deep Sea Mining (Exploration Licences) (Applications) Regulations 1982, S.I. 1982/58; the Deep Sea Mining (Exploration Licences) Regulations 1984, S.I.1984/1230; and the Deep Sea Mining (Reciprocating Countries) Order 1985, S.I.1985/2000; reproduced in Vol.3 as Docs. Nos. 28.2 to 28.4.

France: Law on the Exploration and Exploitation of Mineral Resources on the Deep Sea-Bed 1981, Law No. 81-1135 of 23 December 1981, *Journal officiel*, 24 December 1981, pp. 3499-3500; English translation in Vol.3 as Doc. No. 29.1. See too Decree No. 82-111 of 29 January 1982 passed in application of the law of 23 December 1981 in respect of the exploration and exploitation of mineral resources of the deep seabed, *Journal officiel*, 31 January 1982, p. 431 and Arrêté of 29 January 1982 determining the contents of applications for permits for the exploration and exploitation of the deep seabed, *Journal officiel*, 31 January 1982 ; English translations in Vol. 3 as Docs. Nos. 29.2 and 29.3.

Russia: The former Soviet Union originally adopted the Edict on Provisional Measures to Regulate the Activity of Soviet Enterprises Relating to the Exploration and Exploitation of Mineral Resources of Seabed Areas beyond the Limits of the Continental Shelf, 17 April 1982, *Izvestiia*, 18 April 1982, pp. 1-2; English translation in XXI ILM (1982), p.551. More recently the Russian Federation issued a Decree by the President of the Russian Federation on the activities of Russian natural and juridical persons in the exploration and exploitation of the mineral resources of the seabed beyond the limits of the continental shelf, Decree No. 2099 of 22 November 1994 (*Collected Laws of Russian Federation*, 1994, No.31, p.3252); English translation in *LOS Bull.*, No. 28, 1995, pp. 28-30; reproduced in Vol.3 as Doc. No. 30.1. See also the related Order No. 410, 25 April 1995 concerning the way in which activities are to be carried out by Russian natural and juridical persons for exploration and exploitation of the mineral resources of the seabed beyond the limits of the continental shelf (*Collected Laws of the Russian Federation*, 1995, No. 18, p. 1675); English translation reproduced in Vol.3 as Doc. No. 30.2.

Japan: Law on Interim Measures for Deep Seabed Mining 1982; English translation reproduced in Vol. 3 as Doc. No. 31.1. See too Enforcement Regulations for the Law on Interim Measures for Deep Seabed Mining, *Official Register of the Ministry of International Trade and Industry*, No. 9770, 26 July 1982.

Italy: Italy originally adopted Law No.41 of 20 February 1985: Regulations on the Exploration and Exploitation of the Mineral Resources of the Deep Seabed, *Gazzetta Ufficiale*, No.52, 3 March 1985, pp.1593-1596; English translation in XXIV ILM (1985), pp.983-996. These Regulations were repealed by Law No. 689 of 2 December 1994 authorising ratification and implementation of the United Nations Convention on the Law of the Sea of 10 December 1982 and the Agreement of 29 July 1994 on the Implementation of Part XI of the United Nations Convention, *Gazzetta Ufficiale*, No. 295 of 19 December 1994, Supplement No. 164; English translation reproduced in Vol.3 as Doc. No. 32.1.

Convention put in peril many of the valued features of the package-deal Convention on matters other than sea-bed mining but it would also heighten the commercial risks for the consortia of operating under national legislation by denying them the internationally recognised security of tenure which the conventional regime would provide. Nor were the industrialised States unaware of the political costs likely to be incurred by rejection of a conventional scheme which had been designed to give substance to the common heritage concept.

In the end, these pressures proved to be insufficient to create enough common ground between a G-77 which felt that it had reached the limit of the concessions it was prepared to make and a United States Administration which may well have been moved as much by fundamental ideological objections to the common heritage system as by dissatisfaction with particular features of it. The Conference did, however, succeed in reaching a compromise which, on the one hand, allowed the negotiations on some elements of the regime to continue in the Preparatory Commission and, on the other, held out some hope that the other principal industrialised States participating in the pioneer multinational consortia would find the ultimate Convention-PIP package sufficiently attractive to enable them to become parties to the Convention. The compromise finally arrived at was embodied in Conference Resolutions I and II,[2] which respectively established the Preparatory Commission and a scheme designed to provide protection for investments already made in pioneer deep-sea mining activities.

The original rationale of the PIP scheme was explained thus by the two UNCLOS officers, Messrs. Koh and Engo, who introduced the first draft of it in March 1982:

It is a demonstrable reality that six consortia and one State have been investing funds in the development of sea-bed mining technology, equipment and expertise. The programme of their research and development has arrived at a point when they must invest substantial amounts of funds in site-specific activities. The industrialised countries representing these consortia have been demanding that the Conference and the Convention on the Law of the Sea should recognise these preparatory investments. We feel that this is a legitimate request provided that the preparatory investments of these pioneers will be brought within the framework of the Convention and provided that the interim arrangement is transitory in character.[3]

As will be seen below, the protection provided by the scheme was in later drafts extended well beyond the originally intended beneficiaries.

Not the least of the peculiarities of the original PIP scheme was the fact that it permitted the first stage of sea-bed operations (the 'pioneer activities' stage) to proceed under the UN Convention regime, as modified by Resolution II, quite

---

[2] Resolution I: Establishment of the Preparatory Commission for the International Sea-Bed Authority and for the International Tribunal for the Law of the Sea; and Resolution II: Governing Preparatory Investment in Pioneer Activities relating to Polymetallic Nodules. The two Resolutions, together with the UN Convention on the Law of the Sea, were adopted on 30 April 1982 and can be found in Annex I to the Final Act of UNCLOS III (United Nations, *The Law of the Sea. Official Text of the United Nations Convention on the Law of the Sea* (1983) (UN Sales No. E.83.V.5), at pp. 175-182); also reproduced in Vol.3 as Docs. Nos. 14.1 and 14.2..
[3] *Report of the Co-ordinators of the Working Group of 21*, A/CONF. 62/C.1/L.30, 29 March 1982 (*UNCLOS III Off.Rec.*, Vol.XVI, p.271, at p.272(15); VII Platzöder, *Documents*, p.60, at p.62).

190   *Chapter 6*

independently of the entry into force of the UN Convention.   Moreover, it allowed pioneers to obtain, through registration as pioneer investors, what amounted to a secure, international recognition of their mine-sites which, even if the UN Convention had failed to enter into force, would have given them a strong, preferential position.   On the other hand, one must beware of giving the impression that the Convention regime was practically superseded by the PIP scheme.   As will be seen, enterprises operating under the integrated Convention-PIP regime were in fact bound by the essential features of Part XI of the Convention.   Under Resolution II, they were required to apply for a plan of work for exploration and exploitation, in accordance with the Convention, within six months of the entry into force of the Convention[4] – though the 1994 Implementation Agreement later revised the timetable and required requests for approval of plans of work for exploration to be submitted within thirty-six months of the entry into force of the Convention.[5]

II. THE ORIGINAL PIONEER INVESTOR SCHEME

Resolution II was drafted in haste and based on what proved to be highly optimistic assumptions concerning the time scale within which exploitation of sea-bed resources would commence.   As a result, the original regime had to be extensively developed and adapted by the Preparatory Commission.   Given the complexity of the negotiations and of the revised regime to which they led, it is advisable, in the interests of clarity, to describe in this section the original regime as laid down in Resolution II;   its further development and adaptation are then dealt with in the following sections.

Under the original Convention-PIP regime, there were three main steps in the process whereby an enterprise might finally achieve the right to engage in commercial exploitation of sea-bed resources.   The first was registration as a 'pioneer investor', the second approval of a plan of work by the Authority and the third allocation of a production authorisation.   These procedures are examined below in turn.

1. Registration as a Pioneer Investor
1.1 Three Categories of Pioneer Investor
As a result of the radical changes made to the original draft of Resolution II,[6] the notion of a pioneer investor became much broader than originally intended. Originally, as was seen above, [7] the protection was intended to benefit 'six consortia and one State' which had 'been investing funds in the development of sea-bed mining technology, equipment and expertise'.   The six consortia consisted of a French consortium, a Japanese consortium and four consortia made up of firms from the following eight States: Belgium, Canada, Germany, Italy, Japan, the Netherlands, the United Kingdom and the United States.   The final

---

[4] Resolution II, para.8(a).
[5] Agreement Relating to the Implementation of Part XI of the 1982 United Nations Convention on the Law of the Sea, 1994 (*LOS Bull., Special Issue* IV, 1994, pp.10-25; reproduced in Vol..3 as Doc. No. 23), Annex, Sec.1, para.6(a)(ii). See further below, Section IV.1.1.
[6] The original version is in A/CONF.62/C.1/L.30, 29 March 1982, Annex II (*loc.cit.* in note 3 above, at p.273; VII Platzöder, *Documents*, p.67).
[7] Above, at note 3.

version of Resolution II extended the scope of prospective pioneer investors beyond these consortia to include Russian and Indian entities and developing State entities. The provision in question, Paragraph 1(a) of Resolution II, calls for close analysis. It identified three categories of pioneer investor, as follows:

Category 1 [8] consisted of :
- France, Japan, India and the former Soviet Union; or
- a State enterprise of each State; or
- *one* natural or juridical person possessing the nationality of, or effectively controlled by, each State or its nationals.

Three conditions had to be satisfied before entities in this category might qualify for registration as pioneer investors:
(i) The State concerned had to sign the Convention before it or its State enterprise or natural or juridical person would qualify.
(ii) Prior to 1 January 1983, at least $US 30 million had to be spent on pioneer activities, including not less than 10 per cent of that amount on the location, survey and evaluation of the area specified in the application for registration.
(iii) Evidence of the level of investment specified in (ii) had to be produced. Where the prospective pioneer investor was a State, the evidence was to take the form of a statement by that State certifying the level of expenditure. In other cases, a certificate was required from the State concerned.[9]

Category 2 consisted of 'four entities, whose components being natural or juridical persons [1] possess the nationality of one or more of the following States, or are effectively controlled by one or more of them or their nationals: Belgium, Canada, the Federal Republic of Germany, Italy, Japan, the Netherlands, the United Kingdom of Great Britain and Northern Ireland, and the United States of America ...'[10] The original footnote reference specified the four entities as being the Kennecott Consortium; Ocean Mining Associates; Ocean Management Incorporated; and the Ocean Minerals Company.[11]

The qualifying conditions for prospective pioneer investors in this category were identical to those in Category 1 so far as expenditure requirements were concerned. There was a significant difference, however, as regards signature of the Convention and certification. It must be said that this difference is not readily apparent on the face of the document but it seems to have been generally understood in the Conference that if, for example, a consortium consisted of, say, four companies from four States, it would not be necessary for all four States to sign the Convention. It would suffice to have signature of the Convention and certification of expenditure by one such State.[12]

---

[8] Resolution II, para.1(a)(i).
[9] Resolution II, para. 2(a).
[10] Resolution II, para.1(a)ii).
[11] The footnote refers to another document: 'Sea-bed mineral resource development: recent activities of the international consortia' and addendum, published by the Department of International Economic and Social Affairs of the United Nations (ST/ESA/107 and Add.1.); Add.1 is reproduced in III *Platzöder*, pp.190-196.
[12] The relevant provisions are Resolution II, paras. 1(a)(ii), 1(c) and 2(a); and Convention, Annex III, Article 4(1) and (2). Reading these provisions together, it would appear that certification and, therefore, by definition, signature, were required by all four States. However, this is not the

192 *Chapter 6*

The Soviet Union protested vigorously against the alleged discriminatory nature of this distinction but without avail.[13]   Indeed, responding to their complaint, Mr. Koh, the Conference President, suggested that the Resolution even discriminated in favour of the Soviet Union.   Despite the fact that it was a relative newcomer in the development of sea-bed mining technology, equipment and expertise, it had nevertheless been guaranteed one pioneer area as against the four to be shared by seven Category 2 States (excluding Japan).[14] He pointed out too that no plan of work would be approved for a Category 2 consortium unless all the States whose companies made up the consortium had become parties to the Convention.[15]   If the Soviet Union had had its way, it would have meant, in the light of the United States decision not to sign the Convention, that none of the four Category 2 consortia would have qualified   for registration as pioneer investors since there was United States participation in all of them.[16] The later decisions of the Governments of Germany and the United Kingdom not to sign the Convention would of course have complicated matters even further.

Category 3 [17] consisted of:
- any developing State; or
- any State enterprise of such State; or
- any natural or juridical person possessing the nationality of, or effectively controlled by, such State or its nationals; or
- any group of the foregoing.

Two conditions had to be satisfied before entities in this category might qualify for registration as pioneer investors:
(i) the developing State concerned had to be a signatory of the Convention;
(ii) evidence had to be produced by the State concerned of the same level of expenditure as required for Category 1 entities. However, the deadline for such expenditure was not 1 January 1983 - as it was for Categories 1 and 2 - but 1 January 1985.[18]

It was made impossible for a component part of a multinational pioneer investor to register under Category 3.[19]

---

interpretation generally accepted in the Conference. See, *e.g.*, statements of Soviet delegation in A/CONF.62/L.133, 23 April 1982 and A/CONF.62/L.144, 29 April 1982 (*UNCLOS III Off.Rec.*, Vol.XVI, pp.240 and 250; XVI Platzöder, *Documents*, pp.72 and 100); Opinion of UN Legal Counsel in A/CONF.62/L.139, 28 April 1982 (*UNCLOS III Off.Rec.*, Vol.XVI, p.245, at p.246(12); XVI Platzöder, *Documents*, p.84, at p.87); and Report of President Koh in A/CONF.62/L.141, 29 April 1982 (*UNCLOS III Off.Rec.*, Vol.XVI, pp.247-248, at p.247(7); XVI Platzöder, *Documents*, p.89, at p.91).

[13] See Soviet statements cited in note 12.
[14] A/CONF.62/L.141, 29 April 1982 (*UNCLOS III Off.Rec.*, Vol.XVI, at p.247(9); XVI Platzöder, *Documents*, p.89, at p.91).
[15] *Ibid.*, at para.8.
[16] For a tabular analysis of the four Category 2 consortia, as composed in 1986, see the first edition of this work (*Sea-Bed Energy and Mineral Resources and the Law of the Sea, Vol. II. The Area Beyond the Limits of National Jurisdiction*, Graham & Trotman, London, 1986), at pp.II.7 12-13.
[17] Resolution II, para. 1(a)(iii).
[18] Under the New York Understanding of 5 September 1986, this cut-off date was extended to the entry into force of the UN Convention. See further below, section III.6.1, at note 195.
[19] Resolution II, para.4.

Finally, it should be noted that it was possible for the rights of the pioneer investor to devolve upon its successor in interest if, for example, one of the original consortia decided to withdraw from sea-bed mining, disposing of its interest to another consortium.[20]

1.2 Applications for Registration of Pioneer Investors

Under Paragraph 2 of Resolution II, it was provided that '*as soon as the Commission begins to function*', any State which had signed the Convention could apply to the Commission on its own behalf or on behalf of any of the potential pioneer investors in categories 1-3 above for registration as a pioneer investor. Provided that the application was accompanied by a certification of expenditure, as referred to above, and 'was in conformity with the other provisions of this resolution, including paragraph 5', the Commission was required to register the applicant. The problems resulting from the alleged ambiguity of the clause italicised above and from the requirement in Paragraph 5 that a State must ensure, before making an application, that areas for which applications were made did not overlap one another, will be considered in detail below.[21] It will suffice for the moment to note that in this respect Resolution II bears the scars of its hasty preparation and proved to be quite impracticable.

1.3 Allocation of Pioneer Areas

Paragraph 3 of Resolution II incorporated a 'site-banking' system similar to that of the Convention and it was left to the Preparatory Commission to designate the part of the total area submitted which was to be reserved for the Authority. The remaining part would be allocated to the pioneer investor as a 'pioneer area' in which it had the exclusive right to conduct 'pioneer activities'.[22] It will be noted that each pioneer investor was entitled to only *one* pioneer area,[23] which 'shall not exceed 150,000 square kilometres'.[24] Moreover, portions of this area, amounting in total to 50%, had to be gradually relinquished to the Area over a period of eight years.[25]

'Pioneer activities' were defined in Paragraph 1(b) and included the elements of what is normally known as exploration, despite the fact that the pioneer investor had later to apply for approval of a plan of work for both exploration and exploitation (Paragraph 8). Pioneer activities included, for example, 'the recovery from the Area of polymetallic nodules with a view to the designing, fabricating and testing of equipment which is intended to be used in the exploitation of polymetallic nodules'.

1.4 Financial Arrangements

Each pioneer investor had to pay a $US 250,000 registration fee plus a further $US 250,000 when it applied to the Authority for a plan of work.[26] An additional fee of $US 1 million per year was payable from the time the pioneer area was

---

[20] Resolution II, para. 1(a), last sentence.
[21] See below, section III.3 and 4.3.
[22] Resolution II, para.3(b).
[23] Resolution II, para.4.
[24] Resolution II, para.1(e).
[25] *Ibid.*
[26] Resolution II, para.7(a).

194   *Chapter 6*

allocated, payable once the Authority approved the plan of work.[27]   Pioneer investors would furthermore have to spend a minimum amount on their sites, the amount to be determined by the Preparatory Commission.[28]

1.5 Assistance to the Enterprise

Pioneer investors had three obligations imposed upon them '[i]n order to ensure that the Enterprise is able to carry out activities in the Area in such a manner as to keep pace with States and other entities'.   They related to carrying out exploratory work at the request of the Preparatory Commission on a cost-reimbursable basis plus interest at ten per cent; the provision of training at all levels for personnel designated by the Commission; and an undertaking, before the entry into force of the Convention, to perform the obligations prescribed in the Convention relating to transfer of technology.[29]

In addition, every certifying State was required to ensure that the necessary funds were made available to the Enterprise in a timely manner in accordance with the Convention upon its entry into force; and to report periodically to the Preparatory Commission on its activities and those of its sea-bed entities.[30]

2. Approval of Plans of Work

Pioneer investors could not proceed beyond the pioneer activities stage until they had received a contract approving their plans of work. Under Paragraph 8 of Resolution II, application had to be made to the Authority within six months of the entry into force of the Convention and certification by the Commission that the pioneer investor had complied with the provisions of Resolution II. The application had to be made in accordance with the Convention and the plan of work had to comply with, and be governed by, the relevant provisions of the Convention and the rules, regulations and procedures of the Authority, including those on the operational requirements, the financial requirements and the undertaking concerning the transfer of technology. The pioneer investor was, however, secure in the knowledge that, if the provisions of the Convention and the Resolution were complied with, '[a]ccordingly,the Authority shall approve such application.'

One of the provisions of the Resolution which had to be complied with is to be found in Paragraph 8(c). It was noted above that the failure of Germany, the United Kingdom and the United States to sign or become a party to the Convention would not prevent the registration as pioneer investors of the four Category 2 multinational consortia which included components of the nationality of one or more of these three States. Registration could be effected provided that the consortium included at least one component which possessed the nationality of a signatory State or was effectively controlled by one or more such States or their nationals. The position was quite different, however, when the time came to apply for approval of a plan of work. Under Paragraph 8(c) of Resolution II, a plan of work would not be approved for a Category 2 consortium unless all the States whose natural or juridical persons participated in it were parties to the Convention. Given the changes effected by the 1994 Implementation Agreement,

---

[27] Resolution II, para.7(b).
[28] Resolution II, para.7(c).
[29] Resolution II, para.12(a).
[30] Resolution II, para.12(b).

it is no longer necessary to explore the implications of this requirement in relation to the national make-up of the multinational consortia concerned.[31]

3. Production Authorisations

Under the original 1982 regime, one further permit was required before commercial production could commence – a production authorisation. Although Resolution II secured priority status for the pioneer investor here too, the rights of the pioneer investor were limited, first, by reference to the preferential position of the Enterprise and, secondly, by reference to the production limitation provisions of the Convention. Since, however, these production controls and, therefore, the need for production authorisations have been abolished by the 1994 Implementation Agreement, it is no longer useful to consider them further.[32]

III. THE DEVELOPMENT AND ADAPTATION OF THE PIONEER INVESTOR SCHEME

1. The Preparatory Commission: Responsibilities, Organs, Rules and Procedures

Resolution I, establishing the Preparatory Commission, included among its responsibilities that of exercising the powers and functions assigned to it by Resolution II, relating to preparatory investment.[33] It was left to the Commission to adopt its own rules of procedure (applying for this purpose the UNCLOS III Rules of Procedure) and to establish such subsidiary bodies as were necessary for the exercise of its functions.[34]

During the Spring 1983 part of its first session, the Commission adopted a Consensus Statement of Understanding concerning the general features of the structure of the Commission, its agenda and decision making.[35] This was followed, during the resumed part of the first session in Autumn 1983, by the adoption by consensus of a package of three papers on (i) the Commission's structure, functions of its organs and bodies, officers and venue; (ii) procedures and guidelines for registration of pioneer investors; and (iii) rules of procedure on decision-making.[36] Finally, at this session, the Commission adopted its rules of procedure on 8 September 1983.[37]

In the Consensus Statement of Understanding, it was emphasised that the Preparatory Commission would adopt by consensus the rules and procedures for the implementation of Resolution II and the establishment of adequate machinery to administer the regime for the protection of pioneer investors. The subsequently adopted package of three papers made provision for the establishment of a number of organs and, in particular assigned preparatory-

---

[31] See further below, section IV.1.2. On the earlier position, see the first edition of this work (cited in note 16 above), at pp.II.7 10-14.

[32] See Implementation Agreement, Annex, Sec. 6, para. 7. On the earlier position, see the first edition of this work (cited in note 16 above), at pp.II.7 14-15.

[33] Resolution I (*loc.cit.* in note 2), para 5(h).

[34] Resolution I, paras.4 and 7.

[35] LOS/PCN/3, 8 April 1983 (I *Final PrepCom Report*, p.38; I *Platzöder (PrepCom)*, p.188).

[36] Suggestions by the Chairman adopted at the 5th Plenary meeting of the Committee on 8 September 1983, LOS/PCN/27, 8 September 1983 (I *Final PrepCom Report*, p. 41; I *Platzöder (PrepCom)*, p.224).

[37] LOS/PCN/28, 23 November 1983, and Corr. 1, 31 January 1984, and Corr. 2, 17 May 1984 (I *Final PrepCom Report*, pp. 57, 74 and 75; I *Platzöder (PrepCom)*, p.238).

196 *Chapter 6*

investment functions to a Plenary, a General Committee and a 'technical body'.[38] Plenary's functions included the implementation of Resolution II's scheme governing preparatory investment in pioneer activities. The General Committee was to act on behalf of the Preparatory Commission as the executive organ for the administration of Resolution II's pioneer investor scheme and was to be convened by the Chairman of the Commission within 15 days of the receipt of an application for registration as a pioneer investor. The 'technical body' was to be established to assist the General Committee in examining the application and, once all necessary data had been received, the pioneer area was to be allocated within 45 days and a certificate of registration issued as required by Paragraph 3(b) of Resolution II.

As regards decision-making, it was specified that decisions in Plenary on rules and procedures for the implementation of Resolution II and for the establishment of adequate machinery to administer the regime for the protection of pioneer investors would require consensus. This requirement was subsequently embodied in the Preparatory Commission's Rules of Procedure.[39]

Under Rule 46 of the Rules of Procedure of the Preparatory Commission, the UN Secretary-General was required, in agreement with the Commission, to promulgate procedures for the handling of confidential data referred to in Resolution II.[40]

2. The Preparation of the Rules for the Implementation of the Pioneer Investor Scheme: The Preparatory Commission's 1984 Session
At the 1984 session of the Preparatory Commission, priority was given to the adoption of rules for the registration of pioneer investors and, in particular, to the three most difficult issues: a procedure and timetable for the elimination of overlapping claims among the pioneer investors; the rules designed to ensure strict confidentiality of data; and the rules on the composition and decision-making role of the 'technical body' which was to assist the General Committee in examining applications for registration as pioneer investors. The Plenary completed the first reading of the draft rules for the registration of pioneer investors and on confidentiality of data and provisionally adopted over two-thirds of them.[41] The question of confidentiality and the technical body will be reverted to below.[42] First, however, the particularly difficult problem of overlapping areas must be considered.

3. The Obligation to Avoid Overlapping Areas: Original Provisions of Resolution II
Paragraph 5(a) of Resolution II provided that :

> Any State which has signed the Convention and which is a prospective certifying State shall ensure, before making applications to the Commission under paragraph 2, that areas in respect of which applications are made do not

---

[38] On the later establishment of a Group of Technical Experts, see further below, section III. 6.2.
[39] *Loc.cit.* in note 37, Rule 35(1)(b).
[40] *Ibid.* See further below, section III 6.3.
[41] *Law of the Sea. Report of the Secretary-General*, A/39/647, 16 November 1984, at p.22, paras.81-82. The draft rules are in LOS/PCN/WP.16/Rev.1 (III *Platzöder (PrepCom)*, p.56).
[42] See below, section III. 6.2 and 6.3.

overlap one another or areas previously allocated as pioneer areas. The States concerned shall keep the Commission currently and fully informed of any efforts to resolve conflicts with respect to overlapping claims and of the results thereof.

It is clear that, under this provision, the onus rested upon the 'prospective certifying States' to ensure, before making applications for registration of pioneer investors, that application areas did not overlap with one another or with areas previously allocated as pioneer areas. Although they had to 'keep the Commission currently and fully informed of any efforts to resolve conflicts ... and of the results thereof', there was nonetheless no doubt that conflict resolution was the responsibility of the States concerned and was not a function of the Commission. Unfortunately, however, the original Resolution II scheme embodied an obligation to complete the process of conflict resolution in accordance with a prescribed timetable and the failure to comply with this timetable seriously undermined the scheme and delayed its implementation. Paragraph 5(c) provided that:

The prospective certifying States, including all potential claimants, shall resolve their conflicts as required under sub-paragraph (a) by negotiations within a reasonable period. If such conflicts have not been resolved by 1 March 1983, the prospective certifying States shall arrange for the submission of all such claims to binding arbitration in accordance with UNCITRAL Arbitration Rules to commence not later than 1 May 1983 and to be completed by 1 December 1984. If one of the States concerned does not wish to participate in the arbitration, it shall arrange for a juridical person of its nationality to represent it in the arbitration. The arbitral tribunal may, for good cause, extend the deadline for the making of the award for one or more 30-day periods.

Comparing sub-paragraphs 5(a) and 5(c), it is a little difficult to determine which States were supposed to be included in the consultations, negotiations and conflict-resolving procedures which might be required under sub-paragraph 5(a). Sub-paragraph 5(a) was concerned only to ensure that 'areas in respect of which applications are made do not overlap with one another or areas previously allocated as pioneer areas'. In referring to 'areas in respect of which applications are made', this formulation seemed to confine the exercise to areas in respect of which applications were about to be made and to exclude areas in respect of which it might still be possible to submit applications at a later date. The reference to 'areas previously allocated' also suggested that it was envisaged that applications would be made at different times and that the conflict-resolving exercise was one which would have to take place every time an application was made.

If this interpretation had been correct, it would have had significant implications. Suppose, for example, that the Category 1 pioneer investors had decided to submit applications for registration as pioneer investors in 1985 and that the Category 2 pioneer investors had announced that (i) they would not submit applications in 1985 and (ii) they had not yet reached a decision on whether to submit applications later. It would then have been open to the

198   *Chapter 6*

Category 1 pioneer investors to conduct the overlap-avoidance exercise among themselves and in disregard of any interest which Category 2 pioneer investors might have been able to claim over the areas in question. This would hardly have been consistent with the underlying purpose of Resolution II, which was to protect the pioneer investments already made. This purpose could not have been achieved without safeguarding the interests which pioneer investors had established in particular areas. That such area-specific interests were relevant was further borne out by the criteria prescribed in Paragraph 5(d) for the resolution by arbitration of conflicts with respect to overlapping claims. In any event, Paragraph 5(c) suggested the need for the overlap avoidance exercise to be conducted among a wider group of States. As has been seen, this sub-paragraph referred to the requirement for conflict resolution to be conducted by 'the prospective certifying States, *including all potential claimants'*.[43] It followed that all States which qualified as prospective certifying States for pioneer investors under Categories 1, 2 or 3 should have been given the opportunity to take part.

The identification of these States was the next problem. They clearly included the four States referred to in respect of Category 1 pioneer investors. All four - France, India, Japan and the Soviet Union - had signed the Convention and their pioneer investors met the expenditure deadline criterion.

Equally clearly, they included the following four States referred to in relation to Category 2 pioneer investors: Belgium, Canada, Italy and Japan. These States had signed the Convention and were the home States of entities participating in one or more of the four multinational consortia pioneer investors in Category 2. These pioneers had again satisfied the expenditure deadline criterion. The Netherlands was in the same position as these four States but, with the termination of Dutch participation in the consortia in 1985, it would appear to have lost its status as a potential claimant.[44]

On the other hand, Germany, the United Kingdom and the United States, the remaining three States referred to in relation to Category 2 pioneer investors, did not qualify as prospective certifying States since they failed to sign the Convention by the closing date of 9 December 1984. It should be noted, however, that the interests of companies registered in these non-signatory States could be protected in the negotiations by the certifying States associated with the same consortia. For example, Canada, acting as certifying State for the Kennecott Consortium (KCON), was entitled to seek to protect the pioneer area claimed by KCON, thus incidentally protecting the interest of the three British companies participating in KCON.

As regards Category 3 pioneer investors, there were, of course, a very large number of developing States which had signed the Convention. However, so far as is known to the writer, none of these States would in fact have qualified as a prospective certifying State under the original terms of Resolution II, since none of them was the home State of an entity which had satisfied the financial criterion by the deadline of 1 January 1985. As will be seen below, however, the deadline was later extended to the date of the entry into force of the UN Convention.[45]

---

[43] Emphasis added.
[44] *Ocean Policy News*, March 1988, p.6.
[45] See below, section III. 6.1(vii).

4. State Practice 1982-84 and the Provisional Understanding of 3 August 1984
Whether a State with an interest in sea-bed mining was a party to the UN Convention or not, it would clearly concerned to avoid or resolve conflicts concerning overlapping sea-bed claims. It is not surprising, therefore, that several attempts were made between 1982 and 1984 to design a mechanism for this purpose. The failure of the first of these attempts had a significant impact on subsequent State practice.

4.1 The Abortive MOU Negotiations
Canada initiated negotiations in July 1982, involving a number of States which had either signed the UN Convention or, like the United Kingdom, had not definitely said that they would not. The objective was to draft a Memorandum of Understanding on the Settlement of Conflicting Claims with Respect to Seabed Areas (generally known as MOU).[46] MOU was firmly tied to Resolution II, its purpose being 'to ensure that areas in respect of which applications are made to the Preparatory Commission do not overlap with one another'.[47] It was envisaged that a rudimentary organisation would be provided in the form of a neutral State designated to act as Registrar.[48]

Had the MOU negotiations proved successful, it might well have been possible to comply with the timetable prescribed in Resolution II, Paragraph 5(c), that is resolution of conflicts by 1 March 1983 and, in the absence of such resolution, submission to binding arbitration which was to commence not later than 1 May 1983 and to be completed by 1 December 1984. For a number of reasons, however, the negotiations in the end proved fruitless. The fact that some participants had reservations over the apparent amendment of Resolution II which would have been effected by MOU and the failure of the Memorandum to cater for non-signatories of the UN Convention certainly contributed to the abandonment of the negotiations. Also important was the attitude of the Soviet Union to the negotiations. The Soviet Union later 'express[ed] regret that it was not possible during the consultations to reach an understanding, in particular on such an important question as the date of the exchange of co-ordinates of sea-bed areas.'[49] It went on to criticise 'certain participants in these consultations' for having 'insistently advocated the setting of time-limits for the exchange of co-ordinates which were considerably later than the time-limits established in resolution II - an arrangement which would be to the advantage only of countries which have not signed the Convention and are not interested in its application.'[50] The Soviet Union returned to the attack again a year later in a letter addressed to the Chairman of the Preparatory Commission, asserting that:

---

[46] A copy of MOU was transmitted to the Chairman of the Preparatory Commission on 8 April 1983 (Canadian letter of 28 April 1983, LOS/PCN/15, 29 April 1983, I *Platzöder (PrepCom)*, p.207) and it was published as a conference document on 1 September 1983 (LOS/PCN/24, Annex II, I *Platzöder (PrepCom)*, p.217, at p.218).
[47] Art.2.
[48] Art.3.
[49] Letter dated 29 April 1983 to the Chairman of the Preparatory Commission, LOS/PCN/17, 2 May 1983 (I *Platzöder (PrepCom)*, p.209, at p.210).
[50] *Ibid.*

200   Chapter 6

In other words, these countries were endeavouring to ensure that the formal resolution of conflicts in line with the procedure being elaborated at the initiative of Canada could begin only after they had in practice completed among themselves the above mentioned division [of the most promising sea-bed areas] by means of a separate agreement.[51]

4.2 The Agreement Concerning Interim Arrangements Relating to Polymetallic Nodules of the Deep Sea Bed, 1982

The second attempt to establish a conflict-resolving mechanism was successful, though it involved only four States - France, the Federal Republic of Germany, the United Kingdom and the United States. The Agreement concerning Interim Arrangements relating to Polymetallic Nodules of the Deep Sea Bed entered into force on signature on 2 September 1982[52] and it was without prejudice to the decisions of the parties on signature of the UN Convention.[53] The basic object of the Agreement was to facilitate the identification and resolution of conflicts which might arise from applications for authorisations made by Pre-Enactment Explorers on or before 12 March 1983.[54] International conflicts not otherwise resolved had to be settled, 'if a Party so elects', by an arbitration procedure specified in Appendix 1, on the basis of Principles for the Resolution of Conflicts laid down in Appendix 2.[55] Although this Agreement embodied only a conflict-resolution procedure, further developments were foreshadowed in the agreement of the parties to consult together to consider an arrangement to facilitate mutual recognition of national authorisations.[56]

4.3 Soviet and Indian Applications to the Preparatory Commission and Responses Thereto 1983-84

It was against the background of the failed MOU negotiations and the conclusion of the four-Power Agreement of 2 September 1982 that the Soviet Union took action to force the pace in a letter dated 6 April 1983 addressed to the Preparatory Commission.[57] As was subsequently explained, the Soviet Union considered that it would have been helpful to achieve a 'gentleman's agreement' in the context of the MOU consultations but did 'not consider this to be essential, since all questions concerning conflict resolution are settled by resolution II.'[58] It was on the basis of this understanding that the letter of 6 April 1983 was written. In it, the Soviet Union proposed that other prospective certifying States should indicate their readiness by 1 May 1983 to exchange co-ordinates of areas and initiate negotiations on the resolution of possible conflicts concerning the boundaries of such areas. It was further declared that if these other States had not notified the

---

[51] Letter of 3 April 1984, LOS/PCN/36*, 5 April 1984 (I *Platzöder (PrepCom)*, p.266, at p.267). For refutation of these allegations, see letters to Chairman of the Preparatory Commission from Canada (LOS/PCN/40, 11 April 1984, *ibid.*, p.275), a group of seven Western States and Japan (LOS/PCN/41, 12 April 1984, *ibid.*, p.277), Japan (LOS/PCN/42, 12 April 1984, *ibid.*, p.279) and France (LOS/PCN/44, 12 April 1984, *ibid.*, p.282).
[52] UK Treaty Series No.46 (1982), Cmnd. 8685; XXI ILM (1982), pp. 950-962.
[53] Preamble.
[54] Para.1.
[55] The Schedule, Part II, para.9.
[56] Para. 4(c) of the Agreement.
[57] LOS/PCN/4, 8 April 1983 (I *Platzöder (PrepCom)*, p.191).
[58] *Loc. cit.* in note 49, at p.210.

Pioneer Investor Scheme 201

Commission of their readiness to exchange co-ordinates by that date, the Soviet Union would consider that it had fully complied with the provisions of Paragraph 5(a) of Resolution II, that no conflict had arisen and that the Soviet enterprise on behalf of which an application would be submitted on 1 May 1983 would be registered as the first pioneer investor.

In a *Note Verbale* dated 24 April 1983, the Indian Government submitted a very similar statement to the Commission.[59] It reported that it had already been engaged in consultations with other prospective certifying States; that it was ready to exchange co-ordinates; that it intended to submit an application under Resolution II; and that, if it did not receive any response about the exchange of geographical co-ordinates by 1 May 1983, it 'would feel free to take further action in this matter as may be appropriate pursuant to the provision of resolution II.'

Responding to French criticism of its letter of 6 April 1983, the Soviet Union again wrote to the Commission on 29 April 1983 and stated that, in view of the fact that it had informed the Commission of 'the Soviet position regarding the substance of the question', it now considered itself entitled to take further action in accordance with Resolution II. On this occasion it confirmed 'its readiness immediately to enter into negotiations' with France for the resolution of any conflict over sea-bed areas.[60]

In the absence of any response from other States by 1 May 1983, the Soviet Union and India wasted no time in making their next move. In a Soviet letter dated 3 May 1983[61] and an Indian *Note Verbale* dated 12 May 1983,[62] the Chairman of the Preparatory Commission was informed that representatives of the two States had met on 29 and 30 April 1983 and assured themselves that there was no conflict or controversy between them. It was revealed in the Indian communication that the Soviet Union intended to apply to the Commission for registration and allocation of a pioneer area in the Pacific Ocean, whereas India's application would relate to the central Indian Ocean.

The way was now clear for the actual applications to the Commission. The Soviet application was lodged on 20 July 1983[63] and was followed by the Indian application on 10 January 1984.[64]

By way of preface to the actual submission of the application, the Soviet letter referred to three relevant facts: first, it reported that the Soviet Union had 'done everything possible to exchange co-ordinates of areas with other prospective pioneer investors, and to initiate negotiations with them to resolve possible conflicts concerning the boundaries of areas by 1 May 1983'; secondly, it referred to the successful conclusion of the above-mentioned negotiations with India; and thirdly, it recorded the fact that, so far, no notifications had been received from other States of their readiness to exchange co-ordinates. The letter then proceeded to make formal application for the registration as a pioneer investor of the Soviet enterprise Southern Production Association for Marine Geological Operations (Yuzhmorgeologiya). The letter was accompanied by a

---

[59] LOS/PCN/7, 26 April 1983 (I *Platzöder (PrepCom)*, p.197).
[60] *Loc.cit.* in note 49.
[61] LOS/PCN/19, 4 May 1983 (I *Platzöder (PrepCom)*, p.212).
[62] LOS/PCN/21, 13 May 1983 (I *Platzöder (PrepCom)*, p.214).
[63] LOS/PCN/30, 24 October 1983 (I *Final PrepCom Report*, p. 76; I *Platzöder (PrepCom)*, p.258).
[64] LOS/PCN/32, 14 February 1984 (I *FinalPrepCom Report*, p. 79; I *Platzöder (PrepCom)*, p.260).

202   *Chapter 6*

sealed package containing the bulk of the data required by Paragraph 3(a) of Resolution II.   The co-ordinates of the area, 'because of their strict confidentiality', were, however, retained in a second sealed packet which was to be transmitted to the Commission immediately it was requested.

In acknowledging receipt of the package, the Chairman of the Commission simply stated that he would inform the Commission of the Soviet communication and would deposit the first sealed package with the Secretary-General for safe-keeping.[65]

The only notable feature of the similar application submitted by India in its letter of 10 January 1984[66] is that it was transmitted to the Commission through the UN Secretary-General who, in informing the Commission of its receipt, stated that he was doing so 'in accordance with the procedures and guidelines for registration of pioneer investors under resolution II of [UNCLOS III], as contained in annex II of document LOS/PCN/27 dated 8 September 1983.'[67] As has been seen,[68] this document was adopted in the Commission by consensus. It should be noted, however, that, in a Statement made on 8 September 1983 by the Chairman of the Group of Western European and Other States,[69] it was made clear, *inter alia*, that in the view of these States:

(1) annex II should 'not in any way prejudg[e] the rules and procedures to be drawn up by the Preparatory Commission, notably with regard to the form of the application and its content';[70]
(2) annex II could not prejudge the provisions of Resolution II concerning overlapping applications;[71] and
(3) annex II could not 'create an order of priority that might be derived from the recording of an application according to the procedure envisaged by the provisions of sections I, B, C and D.'[72]

There appears to have been no expectation on the part of either the Soviet Union or India that the Commission would proceed to apply Paragraph 3(b) of Resolution II. It is there provided that, within 45 days of receiving the data required by Paragraph 3(a), the Commission has to designate the part of the area submitted which is to be a reserved area and allocate the other part to the pioneer investor as a pioneer area.

This series of actions by the Soviet and Indian Governments was met by a flurry of notes addressed to the Commission by other interested States.

The most comprehensive responses were submitted by France and Japan. Like the Soviet Union and India, they had already signed the Convention on 10 December 1982 and 7 February 1983 respectively. The principal points made by

---

[65] LOS/PCN/31, 24 October 1983 (I *Final PrepCom* Report, p. 78; I *Platzöder (PrepCom)*, p.259).
[66] *Loc.cit.* in note 64.
[67] *Ibid.*
[68] Text above at note 36.
[69] LOS/PCN/29, (I *Platzöder (PrepCom)*, p.254, at p.255).
[70] *Ibid.*, at p.256.
[71] *Ibid.*
[72] *Ibid.*

the two Governments in letters addressed to the Chairman of the Commission[73] may be summarised as follows:

Need for agreement on procedure for identifying and resolving overlapping area conflicts. The two States took the view that the provisions of Paragraph 5 of Resolution II could not be applied until an agreement had been reached among the prospective certifying States on a procedure - preferably a multilateral one - for the identification of overlapping claims and the resolution of resulting conflicts. Both States were at the time participating in the MOU negotiations and clearly hoped that they would lead to the desired agreement.

As has been seen, the Soviet Government did not dissent from the view that such an agreement was desirable. It was of the opinion, however, that it was not essential since Resolution II itself settled all questions concerning conflict resolution.[74] While that is hardly true, it is nonetheless difficult to discern in Resolution II any requirement that prospective certifying States should agree upon a particular *modus operandi* for conflict resolution.

Rejection of Soviet/Indian deadline for start of negotiations. As has been seen, the Soviet Union and India had called upon other prospective certifying States to indicate their readiness to exchange co-ordinates and commence negotiations for the resolution of possible conflicts before 1 May 1983. Otherwise, they would consider that they had fully complied with their obligations under Paragraph 5(a) of Resolution II. The French Government pointed out that there was no justification for prescribing 1 May 1983 as the compulsory starting point for negotiations and argued that, 'even if one were to stick to a literal interpretation of the resolution, the date 1 March would mark the end of the negotiations and the date 1 May the start of arbitration. Accordingly, on the latter date it would be too late to open negotiations'.[75] But, of course, both States took the view that the timetable in Paragraph 5(c) had proved to be impracticable and that it was therefore necessary to continue negotiations to reach agreement as speedily as possible.

Applications may be made 'as soon as the Commission begins to function'. Paragraph 2 of Resolution II permits States to apply for pioneer investor registration 'as soon as the Commission begins to function' and here again there was a clear difference of view in the interpretation of the resolution. In one sense, of course, it could be said that the Commission began to function when it met for its first session on 15 March 1983. France and Japan, supported by the other prospective certifying States, argued, however, that applications could not properly be made until the Commission had begun to function *for the purpose of implementing the resolution* and that this position would not be reached until the Commission had adopted rules, regulations and procedures for the implementation of Resolution II. As has been seen, this view is certainly in line with the approach to its mandate adopted by the Preparatory Commission and it is difficult to see how the Commission could discharge its function in relation to the

---

[73] For the French response, see Letters dated 27 April 1983 (LOS/PCN/8, I *Platzöder (PrepCom)*, p.198), 28 April 1983 (LOS/PCN/12, *ibid.*, p.204) and 20 June 1983 (LOS/PCN/22, *ibid.*, p.215). For the Japanese response, see Letter dated 28 April 1983 (LOS/PCN/11, *ibid.*, p.202).

[74] Text above, at note 58.

[75] LOS/PCN/8, 27 April 1983 (I *Platzöder (PrepCom)*, p.198, at p.199).

204   *Chapter 6*

pioneer investor scheme responsibly in the absence of agreed, detailed rules and procedures.[76]

Reservation of rights. France and Japan, again joined by other prospective certifying States, made it clear that they did not recognise any legal rights or priorities alleged to have been established by the Soviet and Indian actions[77] and reserved their own rights to submit pioneer investor applications once the necessary machinery was in place.

States which, at that time, had not yet signed the Convention but still had the option to do so until 9 December 1984, were careful to reserve their rights as still being prospective certifying States.

The United Kingdom's letter of 27 April 1983[78] and Belgium's two letters of the same date[79] and in similar terms, raised interesting questions, especially given the fact that the United Kingdom later decided not to sign the Convention. They expressed the view that it was 'in the interests of all States with deep sea mining interests' (in the Belgian formulation 'all States having means to explore the sea-bed and the ocean floor') that there should not be overlapping of exploration areas. They pointed out that generally agreed arrangements for the elimination of possible overlaps did not exist. In their absence, the two States, having regard to their 'contingent interest' (United Kingdom) or 'the rights that [they] may at some future date have to invoke' (Belgium), reserved their positions with regard to the Soviet and Indian actions.

These reservations raised a number of questions. What contingent interest or right did the two Governments have in mind? What was the *locus standi* of non-signatory States in relation to the implementation of Resolution II; and, in particular, how was the situation affected by the subsequent decision of one of the States, the United Kingdom, not to sign the Convention? These questions will be considered below in relation to the 'Understanding' of 31 August 1984 negotiated by the Chairman of the Preparatory Commission to permit a first group of pioneer investors to apply for registration. First, however, it is necessary to note the further exchanges which took place prior to and during the second session of the Preparatory Commission (19 March - 13 April 1984).

In February 1984, France and Japan, acting in association with each other, invited the Soviet Union to enter into consultations with them to identify overlapping areas and decide how to resolve any conflicts found to exist.[80] In reporting their initiatives to the Preparatory Commission at the end of March

---

[76] For an indication of the matters requiring consideration, see Statement by the Chairman of the Group of Western European and Other States at Plenary of Commision on 8 September 1983, LOS/PCN/29, 29 September 1983 (I *Platzöder (PrepCom),* p.254, at pp. 256-257). See too the provisions of the Provisional Understanding Regarding Deep Seabed Matters of 3 August 1984, referred to below in section 4.4.

[77] See too the position taken by the Group of Western European and Other States, referred to in text above at notes 69-72.

[78] LOS/PCN/13, 29 April 1983 (I *Platzöder (PrepCom),* p.205).

[79] LOS/PCN/14, 29 April 1983 (I *Platzöder (PrepCom),* p.206) and LOS/PCN/16, 29 April 1983 (*ibid.,* p.208).

[80] The French Government's letter of 20 February 1984 is reproduced in LOS/PCN/35, 2 April 1984 (I *Platzöder (PrepCom),* p.263). According to this document, the Soviet Government replied on 19 March 1984. For the similar Japanese letter of 21 February 1984, see LOS/PCN/34, 29 March 1984 (I *Platzöder (PrepCom),* p.262).

1984, the two Governments indicated that it appeared from the Soviet replies that the Soviet Government was not prepared to 'answer that proposal positively'.[81]

The Soviet Government, in a long letter addressed to the Preparatory Commission on 3 April 1984,[82] placed on record their own very different account of these developments. It was noted first that Japan and France, together with the other Western countries concerned, had failed to respond to the Soviet Government's letter of 6 April 1983[83] declaring its readiness to exchange co-ordinates and open negotiations for the resolution of possible conflicts.[84] It was suggested that the fact that, almost a year later, France and Japan had now themselves made a similar proposal could be explained by the fact that '... the Western countries and Japan, together with their consortia, have only recently finished dividing up the most promising sea bed areas in the Pacific Ocean ...'[85] The Soviet letter went on to indicate how it had replied to the French and Japanese proposals. *Inter alia*, it had :

> stated that the delegation of the USSR at the second session of the Preparatory Commission [which was due to meet shortly afterwards on 19 March 1984] would be prepared to hold consultations with the delegations of Japan and France as well as India, if they so desired, with a view to ensuring the adoption as soon as possible of mutually acceptable rules for the registration of applications. Thus, these consultations would involve the representatives of all the four States which, under resolution II, are entitled, after the signing of the Convention, to become pioneer investors and which have either already submitted applications for sea-bed areas to the Preparatory Commission or intend to do so in the very near future.[86]

It will be noted that the offer was not to exchange co-ordinates and consult on the resolution of possible conflicts; it was, rather, to consult with a view to adopting rules for the registration of applications. The implication that the Soviet Government intended to rely upon its compliance with the timetable prescribed in Resolution II and the failure of the Western countries and Japan so to do was made more explicit in the passage which followed:

> ... the Soviet side also noted that subsequently the delegations of these four countries, if they so agreed, could begin an exchange of views concerning an early registration of applications of the above four countries, bearing in mind that the Soviet and Indian applications had already been made. In so doing, the Soviet side proceeded from the fact that it was precisely the USSR and India that had entirely fulfilled the provisions of resolution II, paragraph 5, and were ready to identify and resolve possible conflicts within the period specified by resolution II. Yet they were deprived of that opportunity because

---

[81] Japan : Letter dated 29 March 1984, LOS/PCN/34, 29 March 1984 (I *Platzöder (PrepCom)*, p.262); France : Letter dated 30 March 1984, LOS/PCN/35, 2 April 1984 (*ibid.*, p.263).

[82] LOS/PCN/36*, 5 April 1984 (*ibid.*, p.266).

[83] LOS/PCN/4, 8 April 1983 (*ibid.*, p.191).

[84] LOS/PCN/36*, 5 April 1984 (*ibid.*, p.266, at p.268).

[85] *Ibid.*, at p.268.

[86] *Ibid.*, at pp.268-269.

206   *Chapter 6*

other countries refused to conduct negotiations with them within the period specified by resolution II and went so far as to violate that timeframe.[87]

In essence, the Soviet Government appeared to be making two points. First, since the Soviet Union had complied with Resolution II and others had not, it was no longer obliged to enter into conflict-resolution procedures in relation to the pioneer areas applied for by the Soviet Union. Secondly, it seemed to envisage the early registration of the four Category 1 pioneer investors without any need for any further conflict-resolution consultations with other potential certifying States. This was, of course, quite consistent with the Soviet view that the time for such consultations had expired.

That the Soviet position was quite unacceptable to other prospective certifying States was immediately made clear in a series of letters addressed to the Chairman of the Preparatory Commission. The Federal Republic of Germany had already reserved its position in relation to the Soviet application on 27 April 1983,[88] pointing out that, since the Convention would remain open for signature until 9 December 1984, States specified in paragraph 1 of Resolution II, which as yet had not signed the Convention but decided to do so at a later stage, might still avail themselves of all rights conferred upon them under Resolution II. It reserved its position as such a prospective certifying State. Consistently with this position, the German Government wrote to the Chairman of the Preparatory Commission on 6 April 1984, referring to the above-mentioned letters from the French and Japanese Governments and indicating its readiness to participate with other relevant Governments in overlap consultations.[89]   The German Government's letter provoked a predictable response from the Soviet Government, critical of this and similar proposals by other members of the 'group of 7' 'contrary to resolution II, on the holding of consultations on matters related to the identification and resolution of conflicts ...'[90]

The Canadian Government's position was similar to that of the German Government. In its view:

> ... any registration of application for a mine site would be incompatible with the requirements of resolution II unless, prior to registration, the applicant could demonstrate that the area in respect of which the application is made does not overlap with any other pioneer site. It is the Canadian position that the resolution of such conflicts among prospective pioneer States, including all potential claimants, is essential in the interest of a successful implementation of the Convention ...[91]

In urging that 'renewed efforts should be made to resolve conflicts among all interested pioneer investors',[92] the Canadian delegation reminded the Preparatory

---

[87] *Ibid.*, at p.269.

[88] Note Verbale of 27 April 1983, LOS/PCN/9, 28 April 1983 (I *Platzöder (PrepCom)*, p.200).

[89] LOS/PCN/37, 6 April 1984 (*ibid.*, p.270).

[90] LOS/PCN/38, 10 April 1984 (*ibid.*, p.271, at p.272). The 'group of 7' consisted of Belgium, France, Germany, Italy, Japan, the Netherlands and the United Kingdom.

[91] Letter dated 11 April 1984, LOS/PCN/40, 11 April 1984 (*ibid.*, p.275). It is relevant to note here that para.5(c) of Resolution II refers to the 'prospective certifying States, including all potential claimants.'

[92] *Ibid.*

Pioneer Investor Scheme 207

Commission of the very limited effect which registration would have for any pioneer investor if at the end of the day all the States whose natural or juridical persons participated in the entity concerned did not become parties to the Convention. No plan of work would of course be approved for any such pioneer investor.[93]

The 'group of 7' also responded to the Soviet letter and, *inter alia*, reiterated their desire to consult on procedures to identify overlapping claims and resolve any conflicts found to exist.[94]

4.4 Provisional Understanding of 3 August 1984 and its Relation to Resolution II

It was noted above that the efforts initiated by Canada to establish an agreed Memorandum of Understanding (MOU) for the settlement of conflicts over overlapping areas had come to nothing. As was seen, one of the reasons for the failure of the negotiations to produce an agreement was that the draft Memorandum envisaged that only signatories of the UN Convention would be parties to it.[95] Reference was also made above to the view expressed by the United Kingdom and Belgium that it was in the interests of all States with deep sea mining interests that there should be generally agreed arrangements for the elimination of possible overlaps of exploration areas.[96] The next landmark in the development of the pioneer investor scheme took the form of such an arrangement and it paved the way for France and Japan to submit pioneer investor applications to the Preparatory Commission.

The Provisional Understanding Regarding Deep Seabed Matters[97] was signed on 3 August 1984 by eight States, including - as at that date - three signatories of the UN Convention (France, Japan and the Netherlands) and five non-signatories (Belgium, Federal Republic of Germany, Italy, the United Kingdom and the United States). On the same date, the three signatory States addressed letters to the Preparatory Commission[98] to inform it of 'the progress in the efforts to resolve conflicts arising out of possible overlappings in the areas claimed by pioneer investors'[99] effected by the Provisional Understanding. In essence, each of the eight parties to the Provisional Understanding had encouraged the pioneer investors in which they or their companies participated to resolve possible overlapping conflicts with the other pioneer investors referred to in Paragraph 1(a) of Resolution II. The purpose of the Provisional Understanding was 'to assure on governmental level the results'[100] of the industry agreement reached by the six pioneer investors concerned.

It was of course obvious to the parties to the Provisional Understanding that, in formulating it, they had to be very careful not to fall foul of the provisions of the UN Convention and Resolution II. It will be recalled that Article 137 of the Convention provides that:

---

[93] *Ibid.* See further above, section II.2.
[94] Letter dated 12 April 1984, LOS/PCN/41, 12 April 1984 (I *Platzöder (PrepCom)*, p.277).
[95] Text above, following note 46.
[96] Text above, following note 78.
[97] XXIII ILM (1984), p.1354; reproduced in Vol. 3 as Doc. No. 33.3.
[98] Japan, LOS/PCN/45, 16 August 1984 (I *Platzöder (PrepCom)*, p.284); Netherlands, LOS/PCN/46, 16 August 1984 (*ibid.*, p.286); France, LOS/PCN/47, 16 August 1984 (*ibid.*, p.288).
[99] In identical terms in all three communications.
[100] Japanese communication, LOS/PCN/45, 16 August 1984, at p.2 (I *Platzöder (PrepCom)*, p.284, at p.285); similarly in communications of Netherlands and France.

208   Chapter 6

Article 137
Legal status of the Area and its resources

1. No State shall claim or exercise sovereignty or sovereign rights over any part of the Area or its resources, nor shall any State or natural or juridical person appropriate any part thereof. No such claim or exercise of sovereignty or sovereign rights nor such appropriation shall be recognised.
2. All rights in the resources of the Area are vested in mankind as a whole, on whose behalf the Authority shall act. These resources are not subject to alienation. The minerals recovered from the Area, however, may only be alienated in accordance with this Part and the rules, regulations and procedures of the Authority.
3. No State or natural or juridical person shall claim, acquire or exercise rights with respect to the minerals recovered from the Area except in accordance with this Part. Otherwise, no such claim, acquisition or exercise of such rights shall be recognised.

There would thus be an obligation upon parties to the UN Convention not to recognise the appropriation by any State or natural or juridical person of any part of the Area or its resources; nor any claim, acquisition or exercise by such persons of rights with respect to the mineral resources from the Area, except in accordance with Part XI of the Convention.

There is also an obligation upon parties under Article 311(6) not to be party to any agreement in derogation of the basic principle relating to the common heritage of mankind set forth in Article 136, that is, the principle that 'The Area and its resources are the common heritage of mankind'; and, of course, the reference is to that principle as developed in Part XI of the Convention, as opposed to the looser concept embodied in earlier UN General Assembly Resolutions or in national legislation.[101]

There can be little doubt that recognition of any claim made, or licence granted, outside the framework of the UN Convention and Resolution II would constitute a breach of the obligations of a State Party under the above provisions. Moreover, it should be recalled that, under Article 18 of the Vienna Convention on the Law of Treaties,[102] both signatory States and States which have ratified or acceded to a treaty are bound, prior to its entry into force, to refrain from acts which would defeat the object and purpose of the treaty. Although non-signatories would have no such obligation, such States would of course have to be aware, in signing the Provisional Understanding, that they would have to honour the obligations of the Convention if they later decided to accede to it.

The parties to the Provisional Understanding sought in advance to refute any allegation that it might run counter to the provisions of the Convention by inserting in their letters to the Preparatory Commission a paragraph in the following terms:

The essential purport of this governmental agreement is that the contracting governments must refrain from issuing an authorisation to a pioneer investor

---

[101] See further on this distinction, Chap. 7, especially at section IV.2.
[102] Vienna Convention on the Law of Treaties, 1969, U.K. Treaty Series No. 58, Cmnd. 7964 (1980).

for an area which overlaps the mine sites allotted to the other pioneer investors in accordance with the above-mentioned agreement among the six pioneer investors. Thus the obligation of the contracting governments under the agreement is one of self-restraint in its character, and it does not involve an obligation on the part of these governments to recognise or support any particular claim of the other pioneer investors. In effect, the agreement aims to ensure the minimum need of avoiding possible future conflicts due to overlapping claims for mine sites, and, as such, fulfils in part the requirement of resolution II to resolve overlapping claims.[103]

However, since it was of the essence of the conventional regime for sea-bed mining that it excluded participation by non-parties or their natural or juridical persons, it was surely more than a little disingenuous to contend that an agreement not to make claims in areas claimed by non-parties whose known intention was to exploit their resources outside the Convention, did not amount to a breach of both the letter and the spirit of the conventional regime. In form, there may have been no grant of recognition to such claims; in substance, such recognition was clearly implied.[104]

Predictably, the Group of 77 and the Group of East European Socialist Countries were prompt in issuing their denunciations of the Provisional Understanding. *Inter alia*, the Group of 77 reiterated its 'opposition to documents based on national legislation and reciprocal agreements that purport to regulate and authorise deep sea-bed activities'.[105] They held 'strongly that such agreements are contrary to the letter and the spirit of the Law of the Sea Convention and have no legal validity.'[106] They went on to view the Provisional Understanding as:

> constituting an unacceptable attempt, by some entities, to engage in deep sea-bed activities under reciprocally recognised national legislations of the signatory States, which seem to arrogate to themselves the powers of the International Sea-bed Authority to authorise sea-bed operations. Furthermore, the Provisional Understanding goes beyond the resolution of conflicts arising from overlapping claims, by including provisions regarding exploration and exploitation of the sea-bed resources, outside the Law of the Sea Convention. The Group of 77 rejects this Provisional Understanding as a basis for creating legal rights and regards it as wholly illegal.[107]

The East European States were equally uncompromising in condemning and rejecting the agreement as illegal. *Inter alia*, they described it as being:

---

[103] LOS/PCN/45 (I *Platzöder (PrepCom)*, p.284, at p.285) and in similar terms in LOS/PCN/46 (*ibid.*, p.286) and LOS/PCN/47 (*ibid.*, p.288).

[104] No doubt, the provisions of para. 14 of the Provisional Understanding, on denunciation, would permit parties to the UN Convention to avoid breach of the Convention after its entry into force. Those provisions would not, however, affect the obligation arising from signature of the Convention.

[105] Statement by the Chairman of the Group of 77 delivered on 13 August 1984, LOS/PCN/48, 16 August 1984 (I *Platzöder (PrepCom)*, p.290, at para.4).

[106] *Ibid.*

[107] *Ibid.*, at p.291, para.5.

210   *Chapter 6*

in fact a 'mini-treaty', i.e. an attempt to establish a regime for the exploitation of the resources of the international sea-bed area that is completely contradictory to the United Nations Convention on the Law of the Sea. Indeed, it seeks, as is clear from the memorandum concerning its application, to substitute for the rules, regulations and procedures for activities in the area that have been elaborated in detail in the Convention on the Law of the Sea and are to be rendered more specific by the Preparatory Commission its own 'standards' permitting western consortia to act without control in exploring and exploiting the resources of the deep sea-bed.[108]

Specific reference was also made to the obligations incumbent upon signatories of the UN Convention under the Vienna Convention on the Law of Treaties and to Article 137 (3) of the UN Convention cited above.

This East European onslaught was followed up by the tabling in the Commission of a draft resolution sponsored by the Group of Eastern European Socialist Countries, the operative paragraphs of which read as follows:

1. *Declares* that States which refuse to observe the Convention as a whole or any parts thereof deprive themselves of the opportunity of enjoying the rights and benefits deriving therefrom, in particular with respect to access to the mineral resources of the International Sea-Bed Area;
2. *Rejects* the above-mentioned agreement of 3 August 1984, as a basis for creating legal rights and regards it as wholly illegal;
3. *Decides* that that agreement, like any other agreements concerning the International Sea-Bed Area that are not compatible with the Convention, shall not be recognised by the Preparatory Commission.[109]

The sponsors decided not to press the matter to a vote at the Autumn 1984 session[110] and, even at the Spring 1985 session, consideration of a revised version of the draft resolution was deferred.[111] However, matters came to a head at the Autumn 1985 session when a Plenary meeting of the Preparatory Commission was convened to consider both this draft resolution and a draft Declaration submitted by Pakistan on behalf of the Group of 77.[112] On 30 August 1985 the draft Declaration was adopted without change. Its operative paragraphs read as follows:

---

[108] Statement by the Chairman of the Group of East European Socialist Countries delivered on 13 August 1984, LOS/PCN/49 (I *Platzöder (PrepCom)*, p.292).

[109] Letters dated 21 August 1984, with annexed draft resolution, LOS/PCN/L.7/Rev.1, 21 August 1984 (I *Platzöder (PrepCom)*, p.444).

[110] LOS/PCN/L.14, 14 September 1984 (I *Platzöder (PrepCom)*, p.476). The charge of illegality was levelled against the Provisional Understanding not only by the Group of 77 and the Eastern European States but also by China and Mongolia. See also the somewhat half-hearted attempt to refute the charge in the statement made by the Chairman of the Netherlands delegation on behalf of the eight parties to the Provisional Understanding (LOS/PCN/52, 24 August 1984, *ibid.*, p.299). It added nothing to the earlier letters to the Preparatory Commission referred to above (text at note 98 and following).

[111] The revised draft resolution submitted on 29 March 1985 by Czechoslovakia on behalf of the Group is in LOS/PCN/L.7/Rev.2 (I *Platzöder (PrepCom)*, p.446).

[112] See *Report of the Chairman of the Preparatory Commission*, LOS/PCN/L.27, 3 September 1985 (I *Platzöder (PrepCom)*, pp.530-531). The Draft Declaration is in LOS/PCN/L.21, 12 August 1985 (*ibid.*, p.506).

Pioneer Investor Scheme 211

1. Declares that:
   a) The only régime for exploration and exploitation of the Area and its resources is that established by the United Nations Convention on the Law of the Sea and related resolutions adopted by the Third United Nations Conference on the Law of the Sea.
   b) Any claim, agreement or action regarding the Area and its resources undertaken outside the Preparatory Commission which is incompatible with the United Nations Convention on the Law of the Sea and its related resolutions shall not be recognised.
2. Rejects such claim, agreement or action as a basis for creating legal rights and regards it as wholly illegal.[113]

The ferocity of the debate on this Declaration was very largely a reflection of the feelings engendered by the grant in August 1984 of exploration licences to four consortia under the United States Deep Seabed Hard Mineral Resources Act 1980.[114] One of these consortia, Ocean Mining Associates, wrote to the Soviet enterprise, Yuzhmorgeologiya, on 2 November 1984, informing it of the issue of a United States licence numbered USA-3 for area 'Delta-Gamma', in the Clarion-Clipperton zone of the Pacific and requesting that those having an interest in the matter should be informed.[115] The Soviet Union took this opportunity to mount a strong attack on the American action, which it described as unlawful and an attempt to appropriate the powers of the Preparatory Commission and undermine the UN Convention.[116] It perceived this attempt to establish a separate regime for sea-bed mining as further evidence of the need for the Preparatory Commission to condemn the Provisional Understanding as unlawful and to make it clear that it would not be recognised by the Preparatory Commission.[117]

It has to be added that the significance of the Declaration was seriously prejudiced by the manner in which it was adopted, as reflected in the statement read out by the President of the Preparatory Commission at the Plenary meeting on 30 August 1985:

> After consultation with delegations it is my understanding that the Draft Declaration contained in document LOS/PCN/L.21 of 12 August 1985 commands a large majority in the Preparatory Commission. I, therefore, take it that consequently the Draft Declaration has been approved and has been adopted.

---

[113] LOS/PCN/72, 2 September 1985 (*ibid.*, p.333). This document is reproduced in Vol. 3 as Doc. No. 16.

[114] In August 1984 exploration licences were issued to Ocean Minerals Company (OMCO), Ocean Mining Associates (OMA) and Ocean Management, Inc. (OMI) and in October 1984 a licence was issued to Kennecott Consortium (KCON). See also Chap.7, section V for table and map showing sea-bed mining sites.

[115] The letter is described in *Letter dated 10 June 1985 from the Acting Permanent Representative of the USSR to the United Nations addressed to the Chairman of the Preparatory Commission*, LOS/PCN/64, 1 July 1985 (I *Platzöder (PrepCom)*, p.317). Annex II embodies the Soviet reply to OMA.

[116] *Ibid.*, at p. 317.

[117] *Ibid.*, at pp. 317-318.

212   *Chapter 6*

I note that a number of delegations, while appreciating the pre-occupations of that majority, could not give support to the declaration because of their concerns about some aspects of the substance and the effect of the declaration.[118]

Returning to the mainstream of developments following the adoption of the Provisional Understanding on 3 August 1984, the next step was not long in coming. On 3 and 21 August 1984 respectively, France and Japan submitted applications to the Commission for the registration as pioneer investors of the French enterprise AFERNOD[119] and the Japanese enterprise DORD.[120] In the UN Secretary-General's Notes to the Commission, informing it of the receipt of the applications,[121] reference was again made to the procedures and guidelines for registration of pioneer investors contained in annex II of document LOS/PCN/27 of 8 September 1983.[122]

It was recorded in both applications that the co-ordinates of the areas identified in the applications had been amended in the light of the settlement of a conflict between DORD and AFERNOD. It was acknowledged in both cases that the possibility of a conflict with the Soviet pioneer investor still subsisted. The French document added that 'exchanges of views between the interested delegations [were] being pursued with a view to reaching a satisfactory solution'.[123] Both Notes stressed that the submission of their applications did not imply any change in their previously stated position on the implementation of Resolution II. They still maintained the view that no applications for allocation of a pioneer area could be examined by the Commission until all possible overlappings between the areas applied for by signatory States had been settled, the organs of the Commission were ready to function and the rules for the registration of applications had been adopted. The matter was put bluntly by the French Government as follows: '... the present application and similar applications cannot for the time being be taken into consideration, since not all the conditions required have as yet been fulfilled'.[124]

---

[118] Report of the Chairman of the Preparatory Commission, LOS/PCN/L.27, 3 September 1985 (I *Platzöder (PrepCom)*, p.530, at p.531). For views critical of the legal validity and political wisdom of the declaration, see Letters from the Chairmen of the British and German Delegations to the Chairman of the Preparatory Commission (LOS/PCN/74 and LOS/PCN/73, 9 January 1986, *ibid.*, pp.337 and 335). A complementary Declaration was adopted on 11 April 1986 (LOS/PCN/78, 21 April 1986; *ibid.*, at p.344) by a vote of 59 in favour to 7 against, with 10 abstentions. It deplored the fact that Germany and the UK had issued exploration licences and reiterated its conviction that any such claim, agreement or action, including the issuing of licences, which were incompatible with the UN Convention on the Law of the Sea, were 'wholly illegal and devoid of any basis for creating legal rights.' A significant number of the delegations which voted against the Declaration or abstained took the view that the legal judgments incorporated in the Declaration were beyond the competence of the Preparatory Commission whose mandate did not permit it to pass judgment on the legality of the behaviour of any State.
[119] LOS/PCN/51, 23 August 1984, Annex (*ibid.*, p.297).
[120] LOS/PCN/50, 22 August 1984, Annex (*ibid.*, p.295).
[121] LOS/PCN/50, 22 August 1984 (*ibid.*, p.294) and LOS/PCN/51, 23 August 1984 (*ibid.*, p 297).
[122] See further text above following note 66.
[123] LOS/PCN/51, Annex (I *Platzöder (PrepCom)*, p.297, at p.298).
[124] *Ibid.*

4.5 State Practice 1982-84: Summing Up

The most striking result of the State practice analysed above was that, despite their differing views on the interpretation and implementation of Resolution II, the two pairs of States which had submitted applications to the Preparatory Commission for pioneer investor registration - the Soviet Union and India on the one hand and France and Japan on the other - found themselves in very similar situations. All four States then had applications pending before the Commission; they recognised the need to resolve possible conflicts over exploration areas in the Pacific[125]; and thus accepted in practice that registration and allocation of pioneer areas would take place only subsequent to adoption by the Commission of the Rules and Procedures for Registration of Pioneer Investors. Differences remained of course in relation to the Provisional Understanding but there seemed to be no reason why these should affect negotiations among these four States, despite the fact that such negotiations might well have implications for the other parties to the Provisional Understanding.[126]

It will be noted that the four pioneer investors on behalf of which the four States had submitted applications are the four Category 1 'State' pioneer investors referred to in Paragraph 1(a)(i) of Resolution II. As will be seen below, they were also the four pioneers whose interests were catered for in the Understanding on Resolution of Conflicts Among Applicants for Registration as Pioneer Investors presented to the Preparatory Commission by its Chairman at the end of August 1984.

5. The Understanding on Resolution of Conflicts Among Applicants for Registration as Pioneer Investors of 31 August 1984

As has been seen,[127] under Paragraph 5 of Resolution II, the onus of ensuring that application areas did not overlap rested upon the prospective certifying States and conflict resolution was the responsibility of the States concerned and not a function of the Preparatory Commission. During the April 1984 session of the Commission, Mr Warioba, the Commission Chairman, had accordingly taken the view that it must be left to the States concerned to find a solution. However, he was given a mandate to use his good offices to help the parties concerned to reach an understanding and was able to announce on 31 August 1984 that they had reached agreement on an Understanding on Resolution of Conflicts among Applicants for Registration as Pioneer Investors.[128] The Understanding was in two parts. Part I was declared to be 'an understanding on resolution of conflicts among applicants for registration as pioneer investors'[129] and Part II was 'an understanding on the *procedure* for conflict resolution among the *first group* of applicants'.[130] As will be seen below, following an account of the principal features of the Understanding, the status of this instrument was far from clear and a number of States reserved their positions in relation to it.

---

[125] This follows from the terms of the Understanding on Resolution of Conflicts reached among the four States in August 1984 and analysed below in section III. 5.
[126] See further below under section III. 5.
[127] Above, section III.3.
[128] LOS/PCN/L.8, 31 August 1984; II *Final PrepCom Report*, p. 5; Vol. 3, Doc. No. 15.
[129] *Ibid.*, title of Part I.
[130] *Ibid.*, title of Part II, emphasis added.

214   *Chapter 6*

5.1 Principal Features of Understanding
The Understanding laid down a timetable and a procedure for the resolution of conflicts among the first group of applicants and the adoption of the rules for registration of pioneer investors under which the first group of applicants was to be registered.

The first group of applicants included all those applicants which submitted their applications to the Commission not later than 9 December 1984. In practice, therefore, as was noted above,[131] the group comprised the four Category 1 pioneer investors on behalf of which applications had been submitted by, in chronological order, the Soviet Union, India, France and Japan.

As regards the timetable for conflict resolution, it was provided that the first group of applicants would meet on 17 December 1984 to exchange co-ordinates of areas applied for.[132] In case of overlaps, the applicants concerned were to resolve the conflicts among themselves.[133] The negotiations were to begin no later than 11 January 1985, to be completed by 4 March 1985 and to be reported to the Chairman of the Commission not later than 8 March 1985.[134] Unlike Paragraph 5(c) and (d) of Resolution II, the Understanding made no provision for binding arbitration to settle conflicts remaining unsettled by the due date.

At a meeting held in Geneva from 3 to 6 December 1984, representatives of the four States drew up an agreement to ensure the confidential nature of data and information and a *procés verbal* setting out the terms for the exchange of co-ordinates.[135] These instruments were signed and mine site co-ordinates were exchanged in Geneva on 17 December 1984.[136] Following a further series of meetings in January and February 1985, the three Governments which had overlap problems reported to the Chairman of the Preparatory Commission on 28 February 1985 that, although the conflict concerning the overlapping between the Japanese and Soviet application areas had been provisionally solved, the French and Soviet delegations had not been able to settle their conflict 'due to the magnitude of the overlapping ascertained.'[137] They were apparently unable to reach agreement 'on the basis of a fair sharing of the overlapping area' because:

> the implementation of this principle could not allow the Parties to fulfil the other condition set out in Resolution II, paragraph 3, which provides that 'each application shall cover a total area which need not be a single continuous area, sufficiently large and of sufficient estimated commercial value to allow two mining operations', a part of which being reserved for the International Sea-Bed Authority.[138]

---

[131] Text above, following note 126.

[132] Part II, para. 1.

[133] Part II, para. 2.

[134] Part II, paras. 3-5.

[135] Mr. Schricke (France), speaking in the General Assembly on 13 December 1984 (Provisional Verbatim Record of the Ninety-ninth Meeting, A/39/PV.99, 21 December 1984, pp. 168-170).

[136] *Ocean Policy News*, January-February 1985, p. 4.

[137] Letter dated 28 February 1985 from the Governments of France, Japan and the USSR addressed to the Chairman of the Preparatory Commission, LOS/PCN/56, 12 March 1985 (I *Final PrepCom Report*, p. 88; I *Platzöder (PrepCom)*, p.303).

[138] *Ibid.*

Pioneer Investor Scheme 215

It followed, of course, that no further progress towards adoption of rules for the registration of pioneer investors could be made at the Spring 1985 session of the Preparatory Commission.[139]

At the close of the following Autumn 1985 session of the Preparatory Commission, the Chairman reported that, despite further intensive negotiations between France and the Soviet Union, the two Governments had still not reached agreement.[140] He had accordingly come to an understanding with them that further 'very serious efforts to resolve the issues' would be made prior to the next Spring 1986 session of the Commission.[141] If, by then, an understanding had been reached, 'the Commission will revert to the examination of the rules for registration, adopt them and proceed to the next stage.'[142] Failing agreement between France and the Soviet Union, on the other hand, he would report to the Plenary by not later than the beginning of the second week of the session and 'request the Commission to take an appropriate decision on how we should continue.'[143]

In closing his report, the Chairman noted that already two years had passed since the Preparatory Commission, in adopting document LOS/PCN/27,[144] had accorded high priority to the elaboration and adoption of rules, regulations and procedures for the implementation of Resolution II.[145] The timetable for adoption of the rules for registration of pioneer investors embodied in the Understanding of 31 August 1984 had also, of course, been proved to be over-optimistic. The Understanding provided that the rules were to be adopted by the Commission 'immediately after the convening of its next session,' which was scheduled to meet from 4 March to 5 April 1985.[146] Rule 35 of the Commission's Rules of Procedure[147] required the rules to be adopted by consensus and the possibility was not envisaged that such a consensus might not be forthcoming 'immediately after the convening' of the session.

The registration of the first group of applicants was to proceed following adoption of the rules for registration.[148] However, 'No application for an area located in a geographical region [was to] be registered if there [was] a pending conflict over areas claimed in the same geographical region between pioneer investors of the first group of applicants.'[149] In practical terms, this meant that an unresolved overlap between two or more of the first group of applicants for sites in the Clarion-Clipperton region of the Pacific would block the registration of all first-group applicants for sites in that area.

The Understanding proceeded on the assumption that the registration of the first group of applicants was independent of later applications. The fact that there

---

[139] See further, Statement made by the Chairman of the Preparatory Commission at the close of the Spring 1985 session, LOS/PCN/L.19, 3 April 1985 (I *Platzöder (PrepCom)*, p.495, at pp.499-500).
[140] Report of the Chairman of the Preparatory Commission, LOS/PCN/L.27, 3 September 1985 (*ibid.*, p.530, at pp.532-533).
[141] *Ibid.,* at p.533.
[142] *Ibid.*
[143] *Ibid.*
[144] See above, text at note 36.
[145] *Loc. cit.* in note 140, at p. 533.
[146] *Loc. cit.* in note 128, Part I, para. 7.
[147] *Loc. cit.* in note 37.
[148] *Loc. cit.* in note 128, Part I, para. 8.
[149] *Ibid.*

216   *Chapter 6*

might be unresolved overlaps between a first-group applicant and another potential pioneer investor was not apparently considered a good reason to block the registration of first-group applications. As Paragraph 10 of Part I of the Understanding made clear, the registration of the first group was to be without prejudice to the right of other potential pioneer investors to submit applications for registration. However, such applications were to be submitted 'taking into account the areas already allocated or designated as reserved areas.'[150]

5.2 Status of the Understanding

The status of the Understanding, its relationship to Resolution II and its capacity to bind States other than those belonging to the first group of applicants were far from clear. As has been seen, it was found necessary during the final substantive session of UNCLOS III to adopt the pioneer investor scheme embodied in Resolution II. Conceived in haste and amounting in effect to an amendment to the sea-bed mining regime in the Convention, Resolution II had proved to be impracticable, especially as regards its timetable for the resolution of conflicts over overlapping areas. There was perhaps, therefore, a case for saying that the Preparatory Commission should be considered to enjoy the implied powers necessary to ensure the effective implementation of the pioneer investor scheme in Resolution II and that such powers would enable it to substitute a new timetable for that envisaged in Paragraph 5(c) of Resolution II. In so proceeding, however, it would be bound to limit the amendment to the minimum required to render the scheme practicable; not otherwise to prejudice the rights established by the Convention and Resolution II; and to adopt the amendment by consensus.[151] Consensus in this context would mean the absence of any formal objection by any member of the Commission.[152] States like the United Kingdom, which, as signatories of the Final Act of UNCLOS III, enjoyed the status of observers in the Commission, would have no power to prevent the formation of a consensus since they were not 'entitled to participate in the taking of decisions'.[153]

There must be grave doubts whether the Understanding fulfilled these conditions. First, in conferring a preferential position upon the first group of applicants, it would appear to have introduced a novel feature which was both unnecessary for the purpose of rendering the scheme practicable and prejudicial to the rights of other States. If other States were to be bound by its terms, it would certainly have been necessary to show that they had consented to it either as parties to the Understanding or in some other way. Unfortunately, it was not at all clear who the parties to the Understanding were.

At the time of its presentation to the Preparatory Commission by Chairman Warioba, the Understanding was described as an 'understanding ... achieved amongst the parties concerned', following consultations conducted by the Chairman.[154] It was 'later on' to 'be issued as an official document so that it can be available to all delegations.'[155] It is not clear from the document which States were numbered among 'the parties concerned'. Part I was entitled

---

[150] *Ibid.*, Part I, para. 10.
[151] Rules of Procedure of Preparatory Commission (*loc. cit.* in note 37), Rule 35(1)(b).
[152] *Ibid.*, Rule 35 (2).
[153] *Ibid.*, Rule 2.
[154] LOS/PCN/L.8, 31 August 1984 (I *Final PrepCom Report*, p.5; I *Platzöder (PrepCom)*, p.448).
[155] *Ibid.*

'Understanding on Resolution of Conflicts among Applicants for Registration as Pioneer Investors' and in a preambular paragraph indicated that the Understanding was reached '[i]n order to facilitate the registration as pioneer investors of the *first group* of applicants'.[156] Under Paragraph 2, the first group included 'all those who have submitted applications to the Preparatory Commission by 9 December 1984.'[157] Paragraph 9 declared that 'This understanding will apply to all applicants who will have submitted their applications to the Preparatory Commission by 9 December 1984'.[158] Since, in addition, the whole of Part II was concerned with the *procedure* for conflict resolution among this *first group* of applicants, it would appear that the 'parties concerned' were confined to the members of the first group, though it is known that other States took part in the Chairman's consultations.[159]

Further light was cast on the process whereby the Understanding was adopted and on the attitude to it of interested third parties during the debate on the Law of the Sea at the 39th session of the UN General Assembly in December 1984. The General Assembly had before it the Secretary-General's report on the *Law of the Sea* which included a description of the work accomplished by the Preparatory Commission during 1984. In Paragraph 83 of this report it was stated that:

> The Commission has decided that, following the adoption of the rules for the registration of pioneer investors, it will proceed to register the first group of applicants at the third session of the Preparatory Commission, to be held in Kingston from 11 March to 5 April 1985. In the meantime the Commission has requested the first group of applicants to resolve as soon as possible conflicts with respect to the overlapping of the areas claimed.[160]

Paragraph 86 went on to report that:

> At the end of the Geneva meeting the Chairman announced that an understanding had been reached on the procedure and on a timetable for conflict resolution for the first group of applicants.[161]

These paragraphs were the subject of extensive comments in almost identical terms by the Canadian and Netherlands delegations, with which the Belgian and

---

[156] *Ibid.*, emphasis added.

[157] *Ibid.*, Part I, para.2

[158] *Ibid.*, Part I, para.9.

[159] According to a statement read for Chairman Warioba at the Eighteenth Annual Conference of the Law of the Sea Institute, San Francisco, September 1984, 'Consultations were held among the four states which have submitted applications (under the Chairman's auspices). The Group of Seven Western industrial states also submitted a memo which contained their views and was submitted to the Chairman by the Netherlands' (J.L. Kateka, *The Status of the International Seabed Authority: The Work of the PrepCom*, in R.B. Krueger and S.A. Riesenfeld (eds.), *The Developing Order of the Oceans*, 18 *L.Sea Inst. Proc.* (1985), p.200, at p.203. See also United Kingdom letter to the Commission dated 4 September 1984, LOS/PCN/54, 24 September, 1984 (I *Platzöder (PrepCom)*, p.301).

[160] *Law of the Sea. Report of the Secretary-General*, A/39/647, 16 November 1984, at p. 23.

[161] *Ibid.*

218   *Chapter 6*

Italian Governments associated themselves.[162] It will suffice to refer to the views expressed by Mr. van Lanschot (Netherlands).

After pointing out that the Chairman of the Preparatory Commission had twice confined himself to reporting that 'an understanding has been reached among the parties concerned',[163] Mr. van Lanschot criticised Paragraph 86 as being ambiguous, in that it failed to specify that the understanding was not reached by the Preparatory Commission but by the parties concerned.[164] He added that:

> In order to avoid misunderstandings I may add that the words 'parties concerned' do not refer to the Members of the Group of 77 on the one hand and the Soviet Union on the other hand - that is, the States that participated in the informal consultations conducted by Chairman Warioba. No, the words 'the parties concerned' refer only to France, India, Japan and the Soviet Union.[165]

In a very significant passage and in language almost identical to that used by his Canadian counterpart, Mr. van Lanschot went on to say that:

> The very notion of a 'first group of applicants' has not been used by the Preparatory Commission nor by its Chairman, except by reference to the terms of the understanding itself.It is an expression limited only to the understanding that was reached by the four States concerned. The only decision that the Preparatory Commission itself took with respect to negotiations of pioneer investors is contained in paragraph 14 of document LOS/PCN/L.13 and it is to 'complete the consideration of the draft rules on pioneer investors and adopt them.' Both part I and part II of the understanding therefore reflect the views of the parties to that understanding only and as such have no effect on other States.[166]

The Netherlands delegation was clearly anxious to make his Government's position crystal clear on this question, for, in a passage which went beyond the scope of the otherwise similar Canadian statement, he continued:

> The rules and regulations will have to be drawn up on their own merits, that is, without reference to the understanding among the four States. The fact that those four States reached an understanding among themselves cannot prejudge the freedom of discretion nor the responsibility of each member State as regards its participation in the decision-making process - notably in the General Committee - with regard to the registration of applications. In this context I may add that in our view the issue of conflict resolution can be

---

[162] General Assembly, Provisional Verbatim Record of the Ninety-ninth Meeting, 13 December 1984, A/39/PV.99, 21 December 1984, at pp. 146-155 (Canada);   156-157 (Belgium); 157-161 (Netherlands); and 162-167 (Italy).
[163] A/39/PV.99, 21 December 1984, at p. 157, citing LOS/PCN/L.8, 31 August 1984 (I *Platzöder (PrepCom)*, p.448) and LOS/PCN/L.13, 4 September 1984 (*ibid.*, p.471).
[164] A/39/PV.99, at pp. 158-160.
[165] *Ibid.*
[166] *Ibid.*, at p. 161.

Pioneer Investor Scheme 219

satisfactorily solved only by agreements which encompass all parties that may be affected by overlapping on any particular site.[167]

Battle was rejoined in 1985 in a series of letters addressed to the Chairman of the Preparatory Commission by the delegations of Belgium,[168] Canada,[169] Italy,[170] and the Netherlands[171] on the one side and France[172] and the Soviet Union[173] on the other.

The Netherlands letter repeated the points made in its earlier statements, referred to above, but elaborated further its view that 'the issue of conflict resolution can only be satisfactorily solved by agreements which encompass all parties which may be affected by overlapping on any particular site'.[174] It was argued that:

> The fundamental objective of resolution II must therefore be preserved *with regard to all identified pioneers* as long as resolution II is valid and may not be given up because of the expiration of the date of 9 December 1984. *It is the sovereign right of a State to become party to a convention* by signature followed by ratification or *by accession.*[175]

They were anxious to ensure that a settlement of the question would be reached which would not discourage either the signatory sea-bed miners which had not yet filed a claim, or the non-signatory sea-bed miners when they were considering the possibility of acceding to the Convention.[176]

The Belgian, Canadian and Italian letters emphasised these same two points: the need to reach agreements among all parties which might be affected by overlapping on any particular site and the desirability of not discouraging potential claimants who were still considering accession to the Convention. The Canadian letter referred to 'the rights of all prospective certifying States, including all potential claimants',[177] while Italy described 'all potential claimants' as being those identified in paragraph 1(i) and (ii) of resolution II.'[178]

The Soviet Union was the first to respond and was at pains, first, to refute the contention that the Understanding of 31 August 1984 was reached outside the framework of the Preparatory Commission and, secondly, to deplore the attempt of the four Western signatory-States to demand the resolution of disputes among all potential applicants, irrespective of whether they had signed the Convention.[179] The French delegation followed the same line, arguing that the Understanding was 'merely in necessary implementation of the mandatory provisions of

---

[167] *Ibid.*
[168] LOS/PCN/61, 26 April 1985 (I *Platzöder (PrepCom)*, p.314).
[169] LOS/PCN/63, 26 April 1985 (*ibid.*, p.316).
[170] LOS/PCN/62, 26 April 1985 (*ibid.*, p.315).
[171] LOS/PCN/60, 26 April 1985 (*ibid.*, p.312).
[172] LOS/PCN/67, 68, 69 and 70, 16 August 1985 (*ibid.*, pp.326, 328, 329 and 330).
[173] LOS/PCN/65, 8 July 1985 (*ibid.*, p.322) and LOS/PCN/66, 15 July 1985 (*ibid.*, p.325).
[174] *Loc. cit.* in note 171, at p. 312.
[175] *Ibid.*, at p. 313, emphasis added.
[176] *Ibid.*
[177] *Loc. cit.* in note 169, at p. 316.
[178] *Loc. cit.* in note 170, at p. 315. The reference should in fact be to para. 1(a)(i) and (ii).
[179] *Loc. cit.* in note 173.

220   Chapter 6

resolution II'.[180] The demand for comprehensive conflict resolution among all potential claimants to any particular site was dismissed with the comment that it would be 'tantamount to asserting that, henceforth, the decisions the commission will be called upon to take will be subject to the good-will of private commercial undertakings which were unable or unwilling to benefit from the rights introduced by resolution II'.[181]

5.3 Autumn 1985: Impasse

By the end of the Autumn 1985 session of the Preparatory Commission, something of an impasse had been reached in the Chairman's efforts to produce a formula which would allow conflict resolution to take place, thus opening the way for the adoption of rules for the registration of pioneer investors and the registration of the first group of applicants. As has been seen, it had not proved possible for France and the Soviet Union to resolve the conflict over their overlapping claims in the Clarion-Clipperton zone, partly because of the magnitude of the overlap and partly because of the impossibility, as perceived by the parties, of fulfilling the conditions set out in Resolution II, paragraph 3.[182] Matters were further complicated by the fact that the Soviet claim was known to overlap with those of the multinational consortia which were both potential pioneer investors under the UN regime and licensees under the unilateral legislation of the Reciprocating States. Indeed, one of the obstacles in the way of a settlement of the Franco-Soviet conflict was the desirability of avoiding a solution which would leave either the Enterprise (in relation to the reserved part of the Soviet application area) or the Soviet Union with an area overlapping any area allocated to a Reciprocating State licensee.

The Reciprocating States were by no means powerless in the face of the failure of the Understanding to respect what the Canadian delegation described as 'the rights of all prospective certifying States, including all potential claimants.'[183] As has been seen,[184] consensus is required for the adoption of the rules for the registration of pioneer investors. It was thus possible for the four States which were full members of the Preparatory Commission (Belgium, Canada, Italy and the Netherlands) to delay the achievement of a consensus until the rules required that applicants for registration should provide proof that overlap conflicts with all prospective pioneer investors (and not only with Category 1 pioneer investors) had been resolved.

It was against this background that Chairman Warioba had to continue to employ his good offices in an effort to achieve a more satisfactory settlement. Following consultations with the first group of applicants, especially with France, Japan and the Soviet Union, Mr. Warioba invited them to a meeting in Arusha, Tanzania in February 1986, the outcome of which was the 'Arusha Understanding'.

---

[180] Loc. cit. in note 172 (LOS/PCN/67), at p.327.
[181] Ibid.
[182] See text above at notes 137-138.
[183] LOS/PCN/63, 26 April 1985 (I Platzöder (PrepCom), p.316).
[184] Above, section III.1, at note 39.

6. The Arusha Understanding of 7 February 1986 and the New York Understanding of 5 September 1986

The Arusha Understanding[185] of 7 February 1986 constituted a break-through in the continuing negotiations and paved the way for the later New York Understanding[186] of 5 September 1986 and the 'Midnight Agreement' of 14 August 1987. Since the New York Understanding was a more developed 'package of understanding'[187] built upon the Arusha Understanding, it may be helpful to present a combined account of the two documents.

The two Understandings achieved a break-through in the negotiations in the Preparatory Commission because they took account of the interests of: (i) the first group of applicants, France, India, Japan and the Soviet Union; (ii) the Group of 77 and other States which were strongly opposed to any undermining of the UN Convention regime; (iii) the potential applicants, that is, the Western multinational consortia which possessed the nationality of or were controlled by the nationals of Belgium, Canada, Germany, Italy, Japan, the Netherlands, the United Kingdom and the United States; and (iv) the Enterprise, the operating arm of the Authority.

6.1 Principal Ingredients of Understandings

The principal ingredients of the two Understandings were as follows:

(i) Procedure for registration of first group of applicants (France, India, Japan and the Soviet Union). As has been seen, a General Committee was established to act as the Preparatory Commission's executive organ for the purpose of registration of pioneer investors and it was to be assisted by a technical body.[188] Under the New York Understanding, the General Committee, in considering applications, had to take into account the reports of a 15-member Group of Technical Experts appointed by the Chairman of the Preparatory Commission in accordance with a procedure laid down in the Understanding.[189]

(ii) Resolution of overlap conflicts among first group of applicants. France and the Soviet Union, and Japan and the Soviet Union agreed to resolve their overlapping-sites problem on the basis of equal sharing of overlapping areas and early relinquishment of parts of the areas applied for.[190]

(iii) Early relinquishment of areas - departures from Resolution II. As was noted above,[191] one of the main obstacles to an earlier resolution of the Franco-Soviet conflict, in particular, was the fact that a solution based on a fair sharing of the overlapping areas would not have permitted the parties to comply with the requirements of Resolution II, paragraph 3. This paragraph provides that 'each application shall cover a total area ... sufficiently large and of sufficient estimated

---

[185] On the Arusha Understanding, see further *LOS Bull.*, No.8, November 1986, pp.35-36; *LOS Bull., Special Issue III,* pp.9-10; and *Ocean Policy News*, May 1986, pp.5-6.

[186] The text of the New York Understanding takes the form of a 'Statement on the Implementation of Resolution II' and is reproduced in XXV ILM (1986), pp.1326-1330; *LOS Bull., Special Issue III,* pp.231-235; reproduced in Vol.3 as Doc. No. 17.

[187] 'Statement made by the Acting Chairman of the Preparatory Commission' on 5 September 1986, LOS/PCN/L.41/Rev.1, *LOS Bull., Special Issue III,* p.223, at p.228, para.35.

[188] See above, section III.1, at note 38.

[189] See further below, section III.6.2.

[190] Under New York Understanding, paras.13(1) and (2) and 9.

[191] See text above, at notes 137-138.

222   Chapter 6

commercial value to allow two mining operations' and the Preparatory Commission had to designate which part was to be reserved for the Authority, acting through the Enterprise or in association with developing States.   The Understandings provided a way round this problem by permitting the applicant States to voluntarily relinquish portions of the application areas simultaneously with their registration as pioneer investors.[192]   Such advance relinquishment was, of course, a departure from Paragraph 1(e) of Resolution II, which envisaged relinquishment of half of the application areas in stages over an eight-year period.

(iv) Self-allocation of areas - a departure from Resolution II, Para.3(b). Paragraph 3(b) of Resolution II made it clear that the Preparatory Commission would allocate to applicants one of the two parts of the mine-site area which had to be identified by applicants for pioneer-investor registration.   The two Understandings permitted a departure from this provision by allowing the first group of applicants to identify an area of up to 52,300 square kilometres each for incorporation by the Preparatory Commission in the area to be allocated to each applicant.[193]

(v) The position of potential applicants.   The provision for early relinquishment of parts of pioneer areas also facilitated an improvement in the position of potential applicants since, under Paragraph 12 of the New York Understanding, the relinquished areas were to be deposited with the Preparatory Commission.   They were to be reserved to form part of the application areas of potential applicants 'until the Convention enters into force'.

It was further provided in Paragraph 15 of the New York Understanding that potential applicants would be treated in the same way as the first group of applicants, provided that they assumed similar obligations and submitted their applications before the entry into force of the Convention.   *Inter alia*, this entitled them to the right, referred to in (iv) above, to select areas of up to 52,300 square kilometres for incorporation in their pioneer areas.

(vi) Mine site for the Authority.   Under Paragraph 13(1)(c) and (d) of the New York Understanding, the three first-group applicants with overlapping claims, France, Japan and the Soviet Union, agreed to contribute portions of areas covered by their applications to constitute part of the area to be reserved for the Authority.   In total, the three contributions amounted to an area of 52,300 square kilometres, which had to be of equal estimated commercial value to the average of the three similar areas which these States had selected for inclusion in their own pioneer areas (see iv above).

Paragraph 14 of the New York Understanding also required the first group of applicants to assist the Preparatory Commission and the Authority in the exploration of a mine site for the first operation of the Enterprise and in preparing a plan of work for it.   This too marked a departure from the terms of Resolution II, Paragraph 12(a)(i) of which related only to exploration, only to the area reserved for the Authority in connection with each pioneer investor's own application, and made provision for reimbursement of the costs incurred.   Under the New York formula, the conditions of this assistance were to 'be discussed and agreed to following registration ...'[194]

---

[192] New York Understanding, paras. 9 and 19(d).
[193] See New York Understanding, paras. 13(2) and (3).
[194] Para.14.

(vii) Enhancement of position of 'developing States' and 'socialist States of Eastern Europe'. As has been seen, Resolution II recognised developing States or their enterprises as a third category of potential pioneer investor and discriminated in their favour by stipulating 1 January 1985 (rather than 1983) as the cut-off date for the qualifying $30 million expenditure on pioneer activities. The New York Understanding extended this cut-off date until the entry into force of the Convention.[195]

The 'socialist States of Eastern Europe' also benefited from the New York Understanding. In addition to the Soviet Union's entitlement under Resolution II, it was now provided that a group of all or several such States or their State enterprises could apply for one pioneer area until the Convention entered into force.[196] The group was defined in a note (later overtaken by political developments in Eastern Europe) to include Bulgaria, the Byelorussian SSR, Czechoslovakia, the German Democratic Republic, Hungary, Poland, the Ukranian SSR and the USSR.[197]

(viii) Apologia for departures from the Convention or Resolution II. The authors of the New York Understanding sought to protect themselves from charges of inconsistency with the terms of the UN Convention or Resolution II by asserting that:

(a) the procedures and mechanisms outlined in the Understanding had been devised to overcome practical difficulties in the implementation of Resolution II and to facilitate the registration of the first group of applicants as soon as possible; and

(b) 'These procedures and mechanisms shall not be construed as setting a precedent for the implementation of the regime for seabed mining under the Convention, nor do they purport to alter or amend that regime in any way ...'[198]

It was added that the 'integrated package' of procedures, mechanisms and provisions of the Understanding was to be implemented as a whole and respected by all concerned.[199]

6.2 General Committee and Group of Technical Experts

As was seen above,[200] at its Autumn 1983 session, the Preparatory Commission made provision for the establishment of a number of organs and, in particular, assigned preparatory-investment functions to a General Committee and a 'technical body'. The General Committee was to act on behalf of the Preparatory Commission as the executive organ for the administration of Resolution II. The function of the technical body was to assist the General Committee in examining applications for registration as pioneer investors.

Detailed provision was made for a Group of Technical Experts (GTE) in the New York Understanding as follows:

Composition. Under Paragraph 6, the Group was not to exceed 15 members, including 4 representing the first four applicants. Each member of the Preparatory Commission was permitted to propose up to 3 candidates for

---

[195] Para.20.
[196] Para.21.
[197] Note to para.21
[198] Paras. 16 and 18.
[199] Para.17.
[200] See above, section III.1.

224   *Chapter 6*

inclusion in a list of qualified candidates to be compiled by the UN Secretary-General.   Members of the GTE were to be appointed by the Chairman of the Preparatory Commission from this list, in consultation with the regional groups, and the composition of the Group had to reflect the principle of equitable geographical distribution.[201]   In inviting nominations, the Secretary-General asked nominating States to indicate the qualifications of candidates and their specific fields of competence.[202]

Functions.   Under Paragraph 4, the functions of the GTE were to determine whether the applications were in conformity with Resolution II, in particular with the principle of equal estimated commercial value, subject to the guidelines and procedures set forth in the New York Understanding; and to submit a report on each application to the General Committee.[203]

Confidentiality.   Under Paragraph 8, the UN Secretary-General was authorised to make available to the GTE applications and related data and information.   Members were required to 'maintain the confidentiality of the data and information submitted to them, even after the conclusion of their functions.'

Expenses.   Under Paragraph 6, the expenses of technical experts were to be borne by the States nominating them.   However, the Preparatory Commission later decided that these costs should be paid out of the special trust fund made up of registration fees paid by pioneer investor applicants.[204]

6.3 Confidentiality of Data and Information

Paragraph 3(a) of Resolution II, after specifying the data to be submitted in support of applications for registration as pioneer investors, went on to provide that:

> In dealing with such data, the Commission and its staff shall act in accordance with the relevant provisions of the Convention and its annexes concerning the confidentiality of data.

The relevant provisions of the Convention are Article 163(8); Article 168(2)-(3), as extended by Annex IV, Article 7(5); and Annex III, Article 14.[205]

Under Rule 46, Paragraph 2 of the Rules of Procedure of the Preparatory Commission, the Secretary-General was required, in agreement with the Commission, to 'promulgate procedures for the handling of confidential data

---

[201] The original membership was as follows: *Africa*: Cameroon, Kenya, Zambia; *Asia:* China, India, Indonesia, Japan; *Eastern Europe*: German Democratic Republic, Soviet Union; *Latin America*: Brazil, Colombia, Cuba; *Western Europe and Others*: Canada, France, Norway (*LOS Bull., Special Issue III*, p.31).   When the GTE considered the Chinese application in December 1990, a member from 'Germany' was still listed (*ibid.*, p.170).   By July 1991, a German member was no longer listed and the GTE was reduced to 14 members (*ibid.*, pp.206-207).

[202] Statement by Acting Chairman of the Preparatory Commission on 5 September 1986 (LOS/PCN/L.41/Rev.1, *LOS Bull., Special Issue III*, p.223, at p.229 (40)).

[203] For texts of Reports, see *LOS Bull., Special Issue III*, at pp.17, 44, 80, 112, 155 and 190; and LOS/PCN/BUR/R. 40, 25 July 1994.

[204] Decision of 21 August 1987 (LOS/PCN/96, 1 September 1987, I *Platzöder (PrepCom)*, p.377).

[205] See further LOS/PCN/WP.16/Rev.1, 12 April 1984, Annex I (III *Platzöder (PrepCom)*, p.56, at p.68).

referred to in resolution II of the Third United Nations Conference on the Law of the Sea.'[206]

As was pointed out in a Secretariat working paper,[207] separate rules were required to cover the Preparatory Commission and its various organs on the one hand - that is, intergovernmental political bodies - and, on the other hand, the staff of the Commission - that is, international civil servants.   So far as Commission staff were concerned, they would be subject to obligations arising from the oath or statement made on assuming their functions and from the Staff Regulations.[208]   The Secretariat did, however, draft additional rules on procedures for the handling of confidential data by staff members of the Secretariat servicing the Commission.   They were designed 'to reduce the likelihood that confidential information might be transmitted between or disseminated among persons outside the Commission and members of the Secretariat servicing the Commission.'[209]

As regards the Commission itself, draft Rule 16 simply provided as follows:

Confidentiality of data and information
[In the exercise of their functions, the members of the Commission shall act in accordance with the relevant provisions of the Convention, its annexes and such rules as the Commission may adopt concerning the confidentiality of data.][210]

The Secretariat working paper suggested that the Commission, pursuant to draft Rule 16, might approve a rule similar to Annex III, Article 14 of the Convention (which applies to the Authority and the Enterprise) which would prevent the confidential information received by the Commission from applicants from being disseminated or transmitted to other organs, enterprises or persons without the authorisation of the party providing the information.[211]   It was pointed out that additional rules would be required for the handling of confidential data by the technical body.[212]

In September 1984 the Plenary of the Preparatory Commission began but did not complete consideration of draft Rule 16.[213]   Plenary had before it, in addition to the Secretariat working paper, a Group of Seven working paper[214] and 'Suggestions' by the Chairman,[215] which included a fully developed Rule 16. Further consideration of these rules appears to have been deferred pending resolution of the problem of overlapping areas.   However, brief reference to confidentiality was included in the New York Understanding of 5 September 1986.

As has been seen,[216] Paragraph 8 of the New York Understanding required members of the Group of Technical Experts to maintain the confidentiality of the

---

[206] *Loc. cit.* in note 37 above, at p.251.
[207] *Loc. cit.* in note 205, at pp.68-71.
[208] *Ibid.*, at p. 69(7).
[209] *Ibid.*, at p. 70(9)-(10), with draft rules at pp. 72-73.
[210] *Ibid.*, at p. 64.
[211] *Ibid.*, at p.69(5).
[212] *Ibid.*, at p.70(11).
[213] LOS/PCN/L.13, 4 September 1984, (I *Platzöder (PrepCom)*, p.471, at pp.472-473(13)).
[214] LOS/PCN/WP.18, 21 March 1984 (III *Platzöder (PrepCom)* p.93, at p.99, section V.
[215] LOS/PCN/WP.24, 4 September 1984 (III *Platzöder (PrepCom)*, p.181).
[216] In section III. 6.2 above.

226   *Chapter 6*

data and information submitted to them, even after the conclusion of their functions.   When the Group met for the first time to consider the Indian application for pioneer investor registration, the Secretary-General's Special Representative for the Law of the Sea outlined the specific procedures that would be in effect to ensure confidentiality.[217]   More details were provided in the Special Representative's Report to the Preparatory Commission in March 1988:

> The Secretary-General has taken measures to ensure the confidentiality of data and information relating to the registration of pioneer investors and the safe-keeping of such data and information.   In this regard, it should be noted that before the examination of the applications, each member of the Group of Technical Experts gave a written undertaking to the Secretary-General to maintain confidentiality with respect to data and information made available to him.   The duty of the members of the Group of Technical Experts not to disclose confidential information constitutes both an obligation in respect of the individual's appointment for the purposes of the Preparatory Commission and a personal responsibility to the applicants.   It should be recalled that, in accordance with document LOS/PCN/L.41/Rev.1, Annex, paragraph 8, 'the members of the Group of Technical Experts will maintain the confidentiality of the data and information submitted to them even after the conclusion of their functions'.[218]

7.   The 'Midnight Agreement' of 14 August 1987
7.1 Registration of Indian Pioneer Investor
Under the New York Understanding, France, India, Japan and the Soviet Union were due to submit revised applications for pioneer investor registration by 25 March 1987.   However, acknowledging that further time   was needed, the Preparatory Commission, in a further Statement of Understanding of 10 April 1987, extended the deadline until 20 July 1987[219] and applications were in fact submitted by that date.   The Indian application was then examined by the Group of Technical Experts and, on 17 August 1987, the General Committee of the Preparatory Commission, acting on their report, decided to register India as the first pioneer investor.[220]

7.2 The 'Midnight Agreement' Network
Registration of the other three applicants was further delayed because of the need to accommodate the results of very important negotiations between the Soviet Union and the potential applicants with which it had overlapping claims.   The negotiations were complex, partly for technical reasons but more particularly because they involved both States signatories to the Convention and non-signatories; and both applicant States and potential applicants.
No less than six States had interests in the multinational consortia which qualified as potential applicants under Resolution II.   Three of them, Belgium,

---

[217] *LOS Bull., Special Issue III*, p.19(3).
[218] LOS/PCN/L.57, 16 March 1988 (II *Platzöder (PrepCom)*, p.194, at p.195(7)).
[219] *LOS Bull., Special Issue III*, p.236, at p.237, para.8
[220] *Ibid.*, p.33.   Full documentation on the Indian application is reproduced ibid., at pp.14-40.   For co-ordinates of 'pioneer area' and 'reserved area', see pp.36-39 and for illustrative map, p.40.   For Certificate of Registration, see *LOS Bull.*, No.12, December 1988, p.41.

Canada and Italy, had signed the UN Convention and were therefore full members of the Preparatory Commission. The remaining three, the Federal Republic of Germany, the United Kingdom and the United States, had not signed the UN Convention, though, as signatories of the UNCLOS III Final Act, they were entitled to observer status in the Preparatory Commission. The United States had not, however, taken advantage of this and had not participated in the Preparatory Commission's work. To complicate matters further, the overlaps between the Soviet Union's claim and those of the potential applicants related to areas allocated to the consortia under licences granted to them in 1984 and 1986 under American, British and German national legislation.

In this tangled situation, the three signatory States which had interests in the consortia (Belgium, Canada and Italy) and the Netherlands (a signatory which previously had an interest[221]) were alone in a position to oppose the Soviet claim in the Preparatory Commission until an acceptable accommodation was achieved to protect consortia interests. Accordingly, they conducted negotiations with the Soviet Union but, during the process, consulted closely with the three non-signatory States (Germany, the United Kingdom and the United States). The negotiations led to the Agreement on the Resolution of Practical Problems with respect to Deep Sea-bed Mining Areas, signed at a midnight ceremony on 14 August 1987 and therefore known subsequently as the 'Midnight Agreement'.[222]

The Midnight Agreement was in fact part of an interlinked network of agreements which resolved the conflicts between the Soviet Union and the consortia and committed all of the States concerned, whether signatories of the UN Convention or not, to respect boundaries of sea-bed mining areas specified in the Midnight Agreement. Thus, in addition to the Midnight Agreement itself, concluded between the Soviet Union and the four UNCLOS-signatories (Belgium, Canada, Italy and the Netherlands), there were also two sets of bilateral Exchanges of Notes. The first series, concluded by the Soviet Union with each of the three UNCLOS-non-signatories (Germany, the United Kingdom and the United States),[223] built upon and referred to an unpublished understanding reached by the four States in New York on 3 September 1986, that is, two days before the adoption of the New York Understanding of 5 September 1986. Each of the Western parties to these Notes agreed to be bound by the Midnight Agreement on the understanding that the Soviet Union would also be so bound. Thus, although the Soviet reluctance to be seen to be negotiating with UNCLOS-non-signatories had been respected so far as the direct negotiations for the Midnight Agreement were concerned, the reality was rather different. Not only had the non-signatories been indirectly involved in the Midnight negotiations (see above); they were also now concluding formal agreements with the Soviet

---

[221] Dutch participation in the OMCO consortium ended in December 1985. However, 'the Netherlands continued to take part in the negotiations, mainly because they fulfilled an intermediary role as a signatory of the 1982 Convention. Without such an intermediary signatory taking part, the OMCO consortium, in which now only American companies participated, could not have been involved in the negotiations. The Netherlands considered its involvement in the negotiations as an important contribution on the way to a working deep seabed mining regime.' (*NILOS Newsletter*, Vol.1, No.1, January 1988, p.6).

[222] XXVI ILM (1987), pp.1505-1508; *LOS Bull., Special Issue III*, pp.242-244; Vol. 3, Doc. No. 18.1.

[223] See, *e.g.*, the Exchange of Notes between the United States and the Soviet Union of 14 August 1987, XXVI ILM (1987), pp.1510-1512; *LOS Bull., Special Issue III*, pp.247-248; Vol. 3, Doc. No. 18.2.

228   Chapter 6

Union. The fact that the bilateral Notes were stated to be without prejudice to the position of either side with respect to the UN Convention hardly alters this basic fact.

The Midnight Agreement network was completed by a second series of bilateral Exchanges of Notes between each non-signatory (Germany, the United Kingdom and the United States) and each of the four western parties to the Midnight Agreement (Belgium, Canada, Italy and the Netherlands).[224]   The parties undertook not to take steps to terminate the Midnight Agreement or the bilateral Exchanges of Notes with the Soviet Union except by common accord.

The Midnight Agreement itself is a relatively straightforward instrument. The parties agreed on boundary lines and undertook to respect the agreed resolution of practical problems regarding deep-sea mining areas based on these boundary lines.[225]   Being subject to an earlier agreement on preservation of confidentiality of data, however, the annexes describing these boundaries and the accommodations based upon them were published only in part.[226]

The parties undertook not to prevent registration of applications to the Preparatory Commission for areas referred to in the annex to the Agreement or to create additional practical problems over such areas.   Accordingly, they would not engage in or support deep sea-bed mining in, or seek or support registration in the Preparatory Commission of, a sea-bed mining area, if incompatible with the Agreement.   They also agreed to take all measures in conformity with international law and existing legislation to ensure that there should be no physical interference with the sea-bed mining activities of one another in the said areas.[227]

7.3 Registration of French, Japanese and Soviet Pioneer Investors

The way was now clear for the registration of the remaining three of the first group of applicants and, on 17 December 1987, the General Committee of the Preparatory Commission approved the applications of France, Japan and the Soviet Union for registration as pioneer investors.[228]

---

[224] See, e.g., the Exchange of Notes between the United States and the Netherlands of 14 August 1987, XXVI ILM (1987), pp.1513-1515; LOS Bull., Special Issue III, pp.249-250; Vol. 3, Doc. No. 18.3.

[225] Midnight Agreement, Arts.1 and 2.

[226] For the agreement on the preservation of confidentiality of data, see XXVI ILM (1987), p.1045. Although the versions of the Agreement published in ILM and LOS Bull., Special Issue III (loc.cit. in note 222) omit the annexed co-ordinates, they are given in part in the version published in LOS Bull., No.11 (1988), p.34, at p.36 et seq.   However, the co-ordinates of (1) pioneer areas allocated by PrepCom; (2) reserved areas allocated by PrepCom and (3) areas in which potential applicants have an interest may now be found (except for the Korean registration, 1994, on which see section III.11 and note 258 below) in the following documents:
For (1) and (2): LOS Bull., Special Issue III, at pp.36-39 (Indian application); pp.72-73 (French application); pp.106-108 (Japanese application); pp.140-145 (Soviet Union application); pp.175-181 (Chinese application); and pp.212-214 (application of socialist States of Eastern Europe).
For (3): LOS Bull., No.7 (1986), pp.74-86; No.11 (1988), pp.28-45 and 57-63; No.12 (1988), pp.27-36; and Memorandum of Understanding between Belgium, Canada, Germany, Italy, the Netherlands, the United Kingdom and the United States, on the one hand, and China on the other hand, 22 February 1991, UK Treaty Series No.52 (1991), Cm 1628, Annex II; Vol. 3, Doc. No. 21.

[227] Midnight Agreement, Arts.3, 4 and 5.

[228] For documentation, see LOS Bull., Special Issue III, pp.41-74 (French application); 75-109 (Japanese application); and 110-146 (Soviet application).   On co-ordinates of pioneer areas allocated, see note 226 above. For chart illustrating these areas, see ibid., at p.182. For Certificates

Pioneer Investor Scheme 229

8. The Understanding on Pioneer Investors' Obligations of 30 August 1990
Consultations 'on the modalities for the implementation of the obligations of the registered pioneer investors',[229] initiated in 1988, led to the adoption on 30 August 1990 of an Understanding on the Fulfilment of Obligations by the Registered Pioneer Investors and their Certifying States.[230] The consultations were said to have 'required intense negotiations and a great deal of innovative effort as well as a spirit of compromise and understanding on the part of all participants.'[231]

The Understanding included the following elements:

(i) Training. The obligation to provide training pursuant to Resolution II, Paragraph 12(a)(ii) was further specified. The training costs were to be borne by the registered pioneer investors. The precise number of trainees, the duration and the fields of training were to be agreed between the Preparatory Commission and each registered pioneer investor according to its capabilities, but the first group of trainees was to consist of 'no less than 12 individuals'.[232]

(ii) Transfer of technology. The registered pioneer investors undertook to perform the obligations prescribed in the UN Convention (in accordance with Resolution II, Paragraph 12(a)(iii)) and agreed that training in the use of such technology would be a substantial component of the training programme (see (i) above).[233]

(iii) Expenditure on exploration. Expenditure required by Resolution II, Paragraph 7(c) was to be determined by the Preparatory Commission in consultation with each registered pioneer investor within twelve months of 30 August 1990.[234]

(iv) Development of mine site for Authority. The obligation of France, Japan and the Soviet Union to undertake preparatory work and stage I of a plan for exploration was specified and a timetable laid down.[235]

(v) Waiver of annual fee. The annual fee of $US 1 million payable by registered pioneer investors under Resolution II, Paragraph 7(b) was waived as of the date of their registration, provided they complied with their obligations relating to training and development of a mine site for the Authority ((i) and (iv) above).[236] Moreover, if, following deposit of the sixtieth instrument of ratification of, or accession to the UN Convention, it was concluded that commercial production would not take place for an extended period, the Preparatory Commission could recommend waiver of the similar $US 1 million fee payable under Annex III, Article 13(3) of the UN Convention.[237]

On the adoption of the Understanding, the Chairman of the Preparatory Commission made the following statement:

---

of Registration, see *LOS Bull.*, No.12, December 1988, at pp.39, 43 and 45 and Vol. 3, Doc. No. 19 (French Certificate).

[229] Statement by the Chairman of the Preparatory Commission, LOS/PCN/L.87, 30 August 1990 (II *Final PrepCom Report*, p. 100; XI *Platzöder (PrepCom)*), pp.110-111, para.39).

[230] *LOS Bull.*, *Special Issue III*, p.261; XI *Platzöder (PrepCom)*, p.112; Vol. 3, Doc. No. 20.

[231] *Loc.cit.* in note 229.

[232] Para.2. See further below, section IV.3, text at note 322 and following.

[233] Para.3.

[234] Para.4.

[235] Paras.7 and 8.

[236] Paras.10 and 11.

[237] Para.12.

230   *Chapter 6*

(a) Should any agreement be made which would affect in any way this Understanding, such adjustments as may be necessary shall be made to it;

(b) The required date for the submission of a plan of work by each registered pioneer investor under Resolution II, paragraph 8(a), shall be reviewed in the light of the assessment of the Group of Technical Experts in accordance with paragraph 12 of the Understanding[238] [that is, an assessment of the time when commercial production may be expected to commence].

In fact, as will be seen in section IV.1.1 below, the six-month deadline for submission of plans of work laid down in Resolution II, paragraph 8(a) was extended to thirty-six months under the Implementation Agreement of 28 July 1994.

The General Committee of the Preparatory Commission has agreed that each registered pioneer investor will be provided with a certificate of compliance indicating the extent to which it has complied with its obligations under Resolution II and related understandings and decisions of the Preparatory Commission.[239]

9. The Chinese Pioneer Investor Application, 1990-91

On 22 August 1990 China submitted to the Preparatory Commission an application for registration as a pioneer investor of the State-owned China Ocean Mineral Resources Research and Development Association (COMRA).[240]   The area applied for lies in the Clarion-Clipperton Zone of the Pacific and consists of three separate parts totalling 300,000 square kilometres.   It was certified that the area claimed did not overlap with existing pioneer areas or with areas claimed by known potential pioneer investors.   The application was approved on 5 March 1991[241] following the adoption on 22 February 1991 of a Memorandum of Understanding on the Avoidance of Overlaps and Conflict relating to Deep Sea-bed Areas[242] which was signed by China on the one hand and seven potential pioneer investor States on the other hand (that is, four signatories of the UN Convention, Belgium, Canada, Italy and the Netherlands, and the three non-signatories, Germany, the United Kingdom and the United States).   Each side undertook to refrain from any actions which could prevent the registration of an application for a mining area by the other side in the future.   China's pioneer area and the sea-bed areas of the Western consortia are defined in Annexes I and II respectively.

As the terms of the Understanding on Pioneer Investors' Obligations of 30 August 1990[243] applied to only the first four registered pioneer investors, it was necessary for the Preparatory Commission to 'enter into arrangements similar to

---

[238] XI *Platzöder (PrepCom)*, p.111, para.40.
[239] Statement by the Chairman of the Preparatory Commission, LOS/PCN/L.115/Rev.1, at p.5, paras.20-21.   Certificates of compliance are provided for in Resolution II, para.11.
[240] For full documentation on the application, see *LOS Bull., Special Issue III*, at pp.147-182.
[241] *Ibid.*, p.172.
[242] UK Treaty Series No.52 (1991), Cm 1628; Vol. 3, Doc. No. 21.
[243] See section III.8 above.

Pioneer Investor Scheme 231

those'[244] in that Understanding with COMRA. After protracted consultations (because the matter of similar treatment for future applicants was still pending[245]), the Understanding on the Fulfilment of Obligations by the Registered Pioneer Investor COMRA and its Certifying State China was adopted on 12 March 1992.[246] COMRA was to provide training to not less than four persons initially; to consult the Preparatory Commission within twelve months on exploration expenditure; and to undertake, if requested, exploration of one mine site for the Enterprise within the Authority's reserved area. China had to report annually on activities carried out in the area. As in the earlier Understanding of 30 August 1990, the annual fee of $US 1 million payable under Resolution II, Paragraph 7(b) was waived and the Preparatory Commission was empowered to recommend waiver of the similar $US 1 million fee payable under Annex III, Article 13(3) of the UN Convention.[247]

10. Application by East European States and Cuba, 1991

As was seen above, developing States and Eastern European States were entitled to submit pioneer investor applications and, on 4 March 1991, the Preparatory Commission received an application to register the multinational Interoceanmetal Joint Organisation(IOM) as a pioneer investor.[248] The application identified IOM as the applicant [249] and its status was described as a 'natural or juridical person' and as 'an enterprise efficiently [effectively?] controlled by the Governments of the certifying States'. [250] The application was submitted by Poland acting on behalf of Bulgaria, Cuba, the Czech and Slovak Federal Republic, Poland and the Soviet Union as certifying States, [251] that is, four Eastern European States and one developing State, Cuba. The General Committee, conscious that such a mixed group constituted neither 'any developing State' under Resolution II, Paragraph 1(a)(iii), nor 'a group of all or several socialist States of Eastern Europe, or a group of State enterprises of such States' under the New York Understanding of 5 September 1986,[252] 'decided to recommend to the Preparatory Commission that Cuba be deemed to be included in' the list of socialist States of Eastern Europe.[253].

The certifying States declared that they had ensured that the areas applied for did not overlap with pioneer areas already delineated or those claimed by the

---

[244] Under para.17 of the Understanding of 30 August 1990, the Preparatory Commission 'shall enter into arrangements similar to those contained in this understanding with any other registered pioneer investor or applicant.'

[245] Statement by the Chairman of the Preparatory Commission, LOS/PCN/L.97, 29 August 1991 (II *Final PrepCom Report*, p. 119), para.32.

[246] Statement of the Chairman of the Preparatory Commission, LOS/PCN/L.102, 13 March 1992 (II *Final PrepCom Report*, p. 128), para.47. The text of the Understanding is annexed at pp.137-139.

[247] See section III.8 above on the Understanding of 30 August 1990, and COMRA Understanding, paras.9 and 10.

[248] For full documentation on the application, see *LOS Bull., Special Issue III*, at pp.183-214.

[249] *Ibid.*, at p. 185, para. 1 and p. 193, para. 3.

[250] *Ibid.*, at pp. 193-194, paras. 4-5 and p. 185, para. 3.

[251] *Ibid.*, at pp. 185, para. 1 and 193, para. A.1.

[252] New York Understanding (1986), para. 21. A footnote to this paragraph identified the socialist States of Eastern Europe as Bulgaria, Byelorussian SSR, Czechoslovakia, German Democratic Republic, Hungary, Poland, Ukrainian SSR and the USSR. Obviously, Cuba is not included in this group.

[253] General Committee Decision of 21 August 1991, para.3 (*LOS Bull., Special Issue III*, pp.208-209).

232   *Chapter 6*

pioneer investors referred to in Resolution II, paragraph 1(a)(ii); and that they had taken steps to make sure that there was no overlap with areas claimed by the already known potential pioneer investors.   They undertook too to conduct pioneer activities in accordance with the provisions of Resolution II, as applied by the Preparatory Commission, in particular in the Understanding on the Fulfilment of Obligations by the Registered Pioneer Investors of 30 August 1990.[254]

On 21 August 1991, the General Committee decided to register the applicants as a pioneer investor and included in the area allocated to it an area of 52,300 sq kms identified by the applicant.[255]

At its resumed tenth session in August 1992, the General Committee adopted the Understanding on the Fulfilment of Obligations by the Registered Pioneer Investor, the Interoceanmetal Joint Organisation (IOM)[256] in terms similar to those embodied in the COMRA Understanding referred to above.[257]

11. Application by the Republic of Korea, 1994

The last application for pioneer investor status was made to the Preparatory Commission by the Government of the Republic of Korea in 1994.   On 2 August 1994, the General Committee registered it as a pioneer investor and included in the area allocated to it an area of 52,300 sq kms identified by the applicant.[258]   On 12 August 1994 the Committee adopted an Understanding on the fulfilment of obligations by the registered pioneer investor and its certifying State, the Republic of Korea.[259]

IV. THE 1994 IMPLEMENTATION AGREEMENT AND THE PIONEER INVESTOR SCHEME

As has been seen in the earlier sections of this chapter, the history of the UN regime of sea-bed mining, and of the pioneer investor regime which is part of it, has been one of gradual development and adaptation necessitated by the need to effect a reconciliation between the original regime and the demands of the non-signatory States which continued to be potential applicants under the UN regime. The Midnight Agreement of 14 August 1987 was an important landmark in this process of reconciliation but its purpose was to bring about a *modus vivendi* between two different regimes rather than to introduce alterations of the UN regime which would persuade the non-signatory States to accept it.   However, as has been seen, the Agreement Relating to the Implementation of Part XI of the 1982 United Nations Convention on the Law of the Sea (the Implementation Agreement) was much more radical and aimed to promote the universality of the UN Convention by so revising its regime of sea-bed mining as to make it

---

[254] *LOS Bull., Special Issue III*, at pp.185(4) and 187(11).

[255] *Ibid.*, at pp.208-211. For co-ordinates of the designated areas, see Annex, pp.212-214.

[256] Statement of the Chairman of the Preparatory Commission,LOS/PCN/L.108, 20 August 1992, p.3, para.10, with Understanding annexed at pp.6-7.

[257] See section III.9 above.

[258] Decision adopted on 2 August 1994 by the General Committee of the Preparatory Commission, LOS/PCN/144, 12 October 1994, with Annex giving co-ordinates of designated areas.

[259] LOS/PCN/L.115/Rev.1, 8 September 1994, p.5, para.19, with Understanding annexed at pp.13-14.

acceptable to the major industrialised powers. It is the object of this section to explain how the pioneer investor regime was affected by the new Agreement.

It is provided in the Implementation Agreement that, during an initial period between the entry into force of the UN Convention and the date of the approval of the first plan of work for *exploitation*, the Authority 'shall concentrate' on certain tasks.[260] They include:

(1) The implementation of decisions of the Preparatory Commission relating to registered pioneer investors and their certifying States, including their rights and obligations, in accordance with Article 308(5) of the UN Convention and Resolution II, Paragraph 13 – under which the Authority is required to act in accordance with Resolution II and decisions of the Preparatory Commission taken pursuant to Resolution II.[261]

(2) The processing of applications for approval of plans of work for exploration in accordance with Part XI of the UN Convention and the Implementation Agreement.[262]

(3) The adoption of rules, regulations and procedures necessary for the conduct of activities in the Area as they progress. Such rules, regulations and procedures must take into account the Implementation Agreement itself, the prolonged delay in commercial deep sea-bed mining and the likely pace of activities in the Area. They may, however, depart from the provisions of Annex III, Article 17(2)(b) and (c) of the UN Convention concerning the duration of operations and performance requirements.[263] Given the fact that registered pioneer investors had to request approval of plans of work for exploration by 16 November 1997,[264] the preparation of rules, regulations and procedures clearly required the Authority's early attention. Nevertheless, as will be seen below, this part of the Mining Code was still only in draft form at that date.

1. Plans of Work of Registered Pioneer Investors: Provisions of the Implementation Agreement and the Mining Code

Section 1 of the Annex to the Implementation Agreement introduced a number of significant changes to the rules governing applications for approval of plans of work by registered pioneer investors. They relate to (i) the timing of applications and duration of plans of work; (ii) the persons who may submit applications; (iii) the content of the application; (iv) the fee payable by pioneer investors; (v) the procedure for processing an application; and (vi) the related designation of reserved areas for the Authority. In the following account of these provisions, reference is also made to the corresponding Regulations of the Mining Code which, as noted above in Chapter 5, made provision for registered pioneer investors in a series of footnotes.

1.1 The Timing of Applications and Duration of Plans of Work

Under the original provisions of Paragraph 8 of Resolution II, registered pioneer investors had to apply for approval of a plan of work for *exploration and exploitation* within six months of the entry into force of the Convention and

---

[260] Implementation Agreement, Annex, Sec.1, para.5.
[261] *Ibid.*, para.5(b).
[262] *Ibid.*, para.5(a).
[263] *Ibid.*, para.5(f). See further above, Chap.4, text following note 18.
[264] See further below in section 1.1.

234 *Chapter 6*

certification by the Preparatory Commission under Resolution II, Paragraph 11 of compliance with Resolution II. Under the Implementation Agreement, approval of a plan of work for *exploration* may be requested within thirty-six months of the entry into force of the UN Convention, that is, by 16 November 1997.[265]

So far as the duration of exploration is concerned, the UN Convention originally envisaged that exploration should be of sufficient duration to permit a thorough survey of the specific area, the design and construction of mining equipment for the area and the design and construction of small and medium-size processing plants for the purpose of testing mining and processing systems. It was left to the Authority to adopt rules, regulations and procedures to 'fully reflect' these 'objective criteria'.[266] The Implementation Agreement is more direct: a plan of work for exploration is to be approved for a period of fifteen years.[267]

Upon the expiration of a plan of work for exploration, the contractor has to apply for a plan of work for exploitation unless (a) the contractor has already done so (which clearly indicates that applications for exploitation may be submitted during the fifteen-year period), or (b) the contractor has obtained an extension of the plan of work for exploration. Extensions for periods of not more than five years each may be approved if the contractor has made efforts in good faith to comply with the requirements of the plan of work but for reasons beyond its control has been unable to complete the necessary preparatory work for proceeding to the exploitation stage or the prevailing economic circumstances do not justify proceeding to the exploitation stage.[268]

The duration of a plan of work for exploitation is not specified in either the UN Convention or the Implementation Agreement. 'Objective criteria' governing the duration of exploitation operations, which were to be reflected in the Authority's rules, regulations and procedures, are laid down in the UN Convention.[269] The Implementation Agreement adds that, notwithstanding these provisions, such rules, regulations and procedures shall take into account the terms of the Implementation Agreement, the prolonged delay in commercial deep sea-bed mining and the likely pace of activities in the Area.[270]

1.2 Who May Submit Applications for Approval of Plans of Work?

Under the original UN Convention regime, when an application for approval of a plan of work was to be made by an entity other than a State, approval would not be given unless (a) the certifying State (the sponsoring State[271]) was a party to the Convention and (b) all the States whose national or juridical persons participated in the consortium were parties to the Convention.[272]

The Implementation Agreement varied these provisions and, during a transitional period, catered for the interests of States which were members of the Authority on a provisional basis. This status was originally enjoyed by States

---

[265] Implementation Agreement, Annex, Sec. 1, para. 5(f); Mining Code, Reg. 9, note 1. See also text above, at note 238.

[266] UN Convention, Annex III, Art.17(2) (chapeau) and (2)(b)(ii).

[267] Implementation Agreement, Annex, Sec.1, para.9.

[268] *Ibid.*

[269] UN Convention, Annex III, Art.17(2)(b)(iii).

[270] Implementation Agreement, Annex, Sec.1, para.5(f).

[271] Resolution II of UNCLOS III, para.8(b).

[272] *Ibid.*, para.8(c).

which were not States Parties to the UN Convention but had been applying the Implementation Agreement on a provisional basis under Article 7 of the Implementation Agreement. Such provisional application of the Agreement terminated on its entry into force on 28 July 1996.[273] However, it was open to States to continue their membership of the Authority on a provisional basis until 16 November 1996 and indeed to 16 November 1998 provided that the Council was satisfied that they had been making efforts in good faith to become parties to the Agreement and the Convention.[274]

The revised rules governing applications by pioneer investors for approval of plans of work for exploration where such provisional members of the Authority were involved were as follows:

(i)   States members of the Authority on a provisional basis had the right to sponsor an application.[275]

(ii)   Where the pioneer investor consisted of natural or juridical persons possessing the nationality of more than one State, a plan of work for exploration would not be approved unless all the States were States Parties to the Implementation Agreement (and therefore to the UN Convention[276]) or members of the Authority on a provisional basis.[277]

(iii)   Where the State acting as sponsor for such a multinational consortium was a member of the Authority on a provisional basis, the approved plan of work would terminate if such membership ceased and the State had not become a State Party to the Implementation Agreement and the UN Convention[278].

(iv)   Similarly, an approved plan of work for exploration sponsored by at least one State provisionally applying the Implementation Agreement would terminate if such a State ceased to apply the Agreement provisionally, which it would have done automatically on entry into force of the Agreement on 28 July 1996,[279] and had not become a member of the Authority on a provisional basis or had not become a State Party.[280]

The Mining Code deals with the identification of the sponsoring State in relation to applications by registered pioneer investors in a footnote to Regulation 11:

> In the case of a request by a registered pioneer investor for approval of a plan of work, the certifying State or States at the time of registration or their successors shall be deemed to be the sponsoring State or States provided such State or States are States Parties to the Convention or are provisional members of the Authority at the time of the request. [281]

---

[273] Under Art.6 of the Agreement.

[274] Implementation Agreement, Art.7(3) and Annex, Sec. 1, para.12(a). See further Chap.1, section II.1.2 and II.2.

[275] Implementation Agreement, Annex, Sec. 1, para.12(c)(ii).

[276] Implementation Agreement, Art.4(2).

[277] Implementation Agreement, Annex, Sec.1, para.12(c)(ii).

[278] *Ibid.*, para.12(d).

[279] See Implementation Agreement, Art.7(3).

[280] Implementation Agreement, Annex, Sec. 1, para.11.

[281] Mining Code, Reg. 11, note 3.

236   Chapter 6

1.3 The Content of the Application
The content of the pioneer investor's application for approval of a plan of work for exploration may be determined by reference to the Implementation Agreement and related Regulations in the Mining Code.

In requesting approval, the pioneer investor must submit:
- The plan of work, consisting of documents, reports and other data submitted to the Preparatory Commission before and after registration as a pioneer investor. [282]
- A certificate of compliance issued by the Preparatory Commission in accordance with Resolution II, paragraph 11(a) and consisting of a factual report describing the status of fulfilment of obligations under the registered pioneer investor regime. [283] Where such information has not already been provided, the pioneer investor must also update the information contained in the certificate of compliance, using, as far as possible, the provisions of Regulation 18 as a guide, and submit its programme of activities for the immediate future, including a general assessment of the potential environmental impacts of the proposed activities. [284] The said Regulation 18 itemises the data and information to be submitted by applicants other than pioneer investors.
- An environmental impact assessment (EIA). As just noted above, the pioneer investor has to prepare 'a general assessment of the potential environmental impacts' of its proposed activities. The formulation of Regulation 10, note 2 seems to indicate that this EIA would be part of the 'programme of work for the immediate future' rather than part of the submissions filed with the request for approval. However, as will be seen in Chapter 10, all seven registered pioneer investors submitted their requests for approval of their plans of work on 19 August 1997 and included among their submissions a general assessment of the potential environmental impacts of the proposed activities. [285]
- An undertaking that the pioneer investor will:
  a) accept as enforceable and comply with the applicable obligations created by the provisions of the Convention and the rules, regulations and procedures of the Authority, the decisions of the relevant organs of the Authority and the terms of its contracts with the Authority;
  b) accept control by the Authority of activities in the Area, as authorised by the Convention; and
  c) provide the Authority with a written assurance that its obligations under the contract will be fulfilled in good faith. [286]

1.4 Fee
Under UNCLOS Resolution II, Paragraph 7(a), the fee payable by a pioneer investor when applying for a plan of work for exploration and exploitation was set at $US 250,000. However, it was made clear in the Implementation Agreement (Annex, Section 1, Paragraph 6(a)(iii)) that this fee would be deemed

---

[282] Implementation Agreement, Annex, Sec. 1, para. 6(a)(ii); Mining Code, Reg. 10, note 2.
[283] *Ibid.*
[284] Mining Code, Reg. 10, note 2.
[285] See further below, Chap. 10, section IV.5.3.
[286] Mining Code, Reg. 14, note 5.

to be the fee for the exploration phase and this understanding is confirmed by a note to Regulation 19 of the Mining Code.

1.5 The Procedure for Processing an Application

The procedure for processing an application is laid down in the Implementation Agreement and the Mining Code.

According to the Implementation Agreement, a plan of work submitted in accordance with the requirements noted above in section 1.3, 'shall be considered to be approved' and such an approved plan of work takes the form of a contract between the Authority and the registered pioneer investor.[287] Thus, subject to verification of compliance with the above-noted requirements, the process of approval is automatic.

The Mining Code deals with the process in a note to Regulation 21, which specifies the role of the Commission, and a note to Regulation 23, on the Council's role.

The procedure in the Commission is as follows:

In the case of a request by a registered pioneer investor for approval of a plan of work for exploration under paragraph 6(a)(ii) of section 1 of the annex to the Agreement, the Secretary-General shall ascertain whether:
(a) the documents, reports and other data submitted to the Preparatory Commission both before and after registration are available;
(b) the certificate of compliance, consisting of a factual report describing the status of fulfilment of obligations under the registered pioneer investor regime, issued by the Preparatory Commission in accordance with resolution II, paragraph 11(a), has been produced;
(c) the registered pioneer investor has updated the information provided in the documents, reports and other data submitted to the Preparatory Commission both before and after registration and has submitted its programme of work for the immediate future, including a general assessment of the potential environmental impacts of the proposed activities; and
(d) the registered pioneer investor has given the undertakings and assurances specified in regulation 14.
If the Secretary-General informs the Commission that the provisions of (a), (b), (c) and (d) have been satisfied by a registered pioneer investor, the Commission shall recommend approval of the plan of work. [288]

The subsequent procedure for final approval by the Council is as follows:

In the case of a request by a registered pioneer investor for approval of a plan of work for exploration under paragraph 6(a)(iii) of section 1 of the Agreement, once the Commission recommends approval of the plan of work and submits its recommendation to the Council, the plan of work shall be

---

[287] Implementation Agreement, Annex, Sec. 1, para. 6(a)(ii).
[288] Mining Code, Reg. 21, note 8. Note 4 to Regulation 12 (on Financial and technical capabilities) similarly provides that a registered pioneer investor requesting approval of a plan of work will be considered to have satisfied the financial and technical qualifications necessary for approval of a plan of work.

238   *Chapter 6*

considered approved by the Council in accordance with paragraph 6(a)(ii) of section 1 of the annex to the Agreement. [289]

1.6 Related Designation of Reserved Areas for the Authority
As has been seen, [290] Resolution II, Paragraph 3(a) requires that applications for registration as pioneer investors cover a total area which can be divided into two parts of equal estimated commercial value. Paragraph 3(b) goes on to provide that the Preparatory Commission would be responsible for deciding which of the two areas should be allocated to the pioneer investor applicant and which reserved for the conduct of activities in the Area by the Authority. However, under the New York Understanding of 5 September 1986, the first group of applicants were permitted to depart from this provision and identify an area of up to 52,300 square kilometres each for incorporation in the area to be allocated to each applicant. [291]

In registering each of the first group of applicants, the General Committee of the Preparatory Commission allocated pioneer areas to the applicants and designated areas to be reserved for the Authority in accordance with this Understanding. [292] As was noted above, plans of work submitted by registered pioneer investors in accordance with Section 1, Paragraph 6(a)(ii) of the Annex to the Implementation Agreement are 'considered to be approved'. [293] The areas allocated to them at the time of their registration as pioneer investors are thus carried forward into their plans of work which take the form of a contract with the Authority. [294]

2. Approval of Plans of Work of Registered Pioneer Investors: Progress Report
On 19 August 1997, all seven registered pioneer investors submitted requests for approval of their plans of work. In accordance with the provisions of the Implementation Agreement, [295] the plans of work consisted of documents, reports and other data submitted to the Preparatory Commission both before and after registration and (except in the case of Korea) were accompanied by a certificate of compliance consisting of a factual report describing the status of fulfilment of obligations under the pioneer investor regime issued by the Preparatory Commission.[296]

The Legal and Technical Commission considered the requests on 21 August 1997 and ascertained that the requirements of the Implementation Agreement had been complied with. [297] On 27 August 1997, the Council, acting on the

---

[289]   Mining Code, Reg. 23, note 9.
[290]   Above, section II.1.3.
[291]   See above, section III.6.1(iv).
[292]   See above, sections III.7.3 and III.9-11.
[293]   See above, section IV.1.5.
[294]   Implementation Agreement, Annex, Sec. 1, para. 6(a)(ii). On progress made in completing the process of approving plans of work in the form of contracts, see section IV.2 below.
[295]   Implementation Agreement, Annex, Section 1, para. 6(a)(ii).
[296]   Certificates of compliance were issued by the Preparatory Commission under Resolution II, para. 11(a). As Korea was unable to obtain a certificate before the Preparatory Commission concluded its work, a statement describing the status of the implementation of the obligations of this registered pioneer investor was issued in lieu of the certificate by the Secretary-General (ISBA/3/C/6, 11 August 1997).
[297]   *Report and Recommendations of the Legal and Technical Commission Concerning the Request for Approval of Plans of Work for Exploration by* [the seven registered pioneer investors] (ISBA/3/C/7,

recommendation of the Commission, noted that, in accordance with Paragraph 6(a)(ii) of section 1 of the Annex to the Implementation Agreement, the plans of work for exploration submitted by the seven registered pioneer investors were considered to be approved. It accordingly requested the Secretary-General to take the necessary steps to issue the plans of work in the form of contracts incorporating the applicable obligations under the provisions of the UN Convention, the Implementation Agreement and Resolution II, and in accordance with the Mining Code Regulations and a standard form of contract to be approved by the Council. [298]. The Secretary-General was, of course, unable to act upon this request until the Mining Code was adopted in July 2000.[299]

Given the political changes which have taken place in Eastern Europe in recent years, it may be useful to list the names of the seven registered pioneer investors whose plans of work for exploration have now been approved, together with their sponsoring State or States:

- The Government of India (India)
- Institut français de recherche pour l'exploitation de la mer (IFREMER)/ Association française pour l'étude et la recherche des nodules (AFERNOD) (France)
- Deep Ocean Resources Development Co. Ltd. (DORD) (Japan)
- Yuzhmorgeologiya (Russian Federation)
- China Ocean Minerals Research and Development Association (COMRA) (China)
- Interoceanmmental Joint Organisation (IOM) (Bulgaria, Cuba, Czech Republic, Poland, Russian Federation and Slovakia)
- Government of the Republic of Korea (Korea).

The abnormal case of IOM. As was seen above, the composition of IOM is unusual. It was sponsored by four Eastern European States and Cuba. [300] If it was to qualify for registration as a pioneer investor, it had to be shown to be 'a group of all or several socialist States of Eastern Europe or a group of State enterprises of such States' under Paragraph 21 of the New York Understanding of 5 September 1986. Unfortunately, Cuba was not included in the list of States identified as constituting this group of States in a note to Paragraph 21, and it was for this reason that the General Committee of the Preparatory Commission had to recommend that Cuba should be deemed to be included in the list. [301]

In the application for registration as a pioneer investor, IOM was identified as the applicant with an address in Poland and a certificate was submitted

---

22 August 1997). For information of a general nature regarding the requests for approval of plans of work submitted by the registered pioneer investors, together with lists of documents and reports of the Preparatory Commission relevant to plans of work for exploration, see *Report of the Secretary-General* (ISBA/4/A/1/Rev.1, 2 April 1998, Annexes I – VII).

[298] ISBA/3/C/9, 28 August 1997.

[299] Part IV of the Mining Code ('Contracts for Exploration') prescribes the form of the contract in Reg. 23(1). The contract will be in the form prescribed in Annex 3 and each contract will incorporate, as terms and conditions of the contract, the standard clauses set out in Annex 4 in effect at the date of entry into force of the contract. The Secretary-General has informed the Council that he plans to sign contracts before its next session in July 2001 (Press Release SB/6/29, 14 July 2000).

[300] See above, section III.10.

[301] See further *ibid.*

240 *Chapter 6*

confirming its registration there as a juridical person. [302] As is evident from information given in a later document, IOM was in fact recorded as having its principal place of business and its place of registration in Szczecin, Poland. [303] IOM was duly registered as a pioneer investor on this basis in 1991.

Although IOM was registered as a juridical person in Poland, it was in fact effectively controlled by the five sponsoring States [304] and it would appear that it was therefore necessary that the sponsoring States should be parties to the Implementation Agreement at the time of the request for approval of IOM's plan of work for exploration on 19 August 1997. [305] The position was quite straightforward in relation to four of the five sponsoring States, which were clearly States Parties to both the UN Convention and the Implementation Agreement. For the fifth State, Cuba, the position is less clear. Cuba ratified the UN Convention on 15 August 1984 and, according to a Report of the Secretary-General dated 2 April 1998, Cuba is bound by the Implementation Agreement under the simplified procedure set out in Article 5 of the Agreement. [306] Under that Article, a State which has signed the Agreement in accordance with Article 4(3)(c) – that is, subject to the procedure set out in Article 5 – shall be considered to have established its consent to be bound by the Agreement 12 months after the date of its adoption. If Cuba did indeed sign on this basis, it would have become bound by the Agreement on 28 July 1995. However, no record of this signature appears even in the most recent table published by the United Nations. [307]

It may be, however, that speculation on the status of Cuba in relation to the Implementation Agreement is in any event irrelevant. As has been seen, [308] Regulation 11 of the Mining Code deals with the identification of the sponsoring State or States in the case of a request by a registered pioneer investor for approval of a plan of work. According to the footnote to that Regulation, the certifying State or States at the time of registration – a category which includes Cuba – shall be deemed to be the sponsoring State or States, provided that such State or States are States Parties to *the UN Convention* at the time of the request – as Cuba was.

3. Monitoring Fulfilment of Obligations by Registered Pioneer Investors and their Certifying States: From the Preparatory Commission to the Authority
On 18 August 1995, at the conclusion of the first session of the Assembly of the Authority, the rôle of the Preparatory Commission came to an end. [309] Until then, its General Committee, which acted on behalf of the Preparatory Commission as the executive organ for the implementation of Resolution II of UNCLOS III, was

---

[302] *LOS Bull.*, Special Issue III, September 1991, at p. 185, para. 2 and pp. 193-194, paras. 4 and 5.

[303] *Plans of Work for Exploration. Report of the Secretary-General*, ISBA/4/A/1/Rev.2, 2 September 1998 (ISBA, *Selected Decisions and Documents of the Fourth Session*, ISA/99/01.E, p.1, at p. 28).

[304] See above, section III.10, at note 250.

[305] UNCLOS Resolution II, para. 8(c), as modified by section 1, para. 6(a)(v) of the Annex to the Implementation Agreement

[306] *Loc. cit.*, in note 303 above, p. 28.

[307] Table showing the current status of the UN Convention and the Implementation Agreement, http://www.un.org/Depts/los, accessed 1 September 2000. States such as Barbados and Iceland which have become bound by the Agreement in this way are specially marked on the table. No such mark appears for Cuba. Indeed, there is no indication of any kind that Cuba is a party to the Agreement.

[308] In section IV.1.2 above.

[309] See further below, Chap.8, section III.3.

responsible for monitoring fulfilment of their obligations by registered pioneer investors and their certifying States.[310] These obligations included relinquishment of parts of pioneer areas[311] and the obligations incorporated in the Understanding on Pioneer Investors' Obligations of 30 August 1990 and the related Understandings subsequently adopted in relation to the Chinese, Eastern European and Korean pioneer investors.[312]

Under Resolution II, Paragraph 11, the Preparatory Commission was required to provide each pioneer investor with the certificate of compliance with the provisions of Resolution II, which was required under Paragraph 8 before an application could be made for a plan of work. In 1994, the General Committee of the Preparatory Commission agreed that each such certificate should read as follows:

> The Preparatory Commission for the International Seabed Authority and for the International Tribunal for the Law of the Sea hereby certifies that ... has complied with the obligations under resolution II and the related understandings and decisions of the Preparatory Commission to the extent indicated in the relevant parts of the annexed report.[313]

There was to be annexed to each certificate a report on the status of the implementation of the obligations of the registered pioneer investors.[314] This document, which was subsequently issued,[315] provides a useful summary of the fulfilment of obligations as of August 1994. It did not, however, cover the most recent of the registered pioneer investors, the Government of the Republic of Korea, which was unable to obtain a certificate of compliance before the Preparatory Commission concluded its work. In lieu of such a certificate, the Secretary-General of the Authority prepared a 'Statement describing the status of the implementation of the obligations ... of this pioneer investor'. [316]

As has been seen[317], one of the obligations accepted by the French, Japanese and Soviet pioneer investors under the Understanding of 30 August 1990 related to the development of a mine site for the Authority. They were placed under an obligation to undertake preparatory work and stage I of a plan for exploration. No such burden was placed upon the Chinese, Eastern European and Korean pioneer investors under the Understandings concluded separately with them at the time of their registration. It was accordingly felt by the French, Japanese and Soviet pioneer investors that they had been denied equality of treatment and were

---

[310] See further above, section III.1. See also *Statement by the Chairman of the Preparatory Commission*, LOS/PCN/L.115/Rev.1, 8 September 1994 (II *Final PrepCom Report*, p. 167), section II. A-C.

[311] As required by Resolution II, Para.1(e), as modified by the New York Understanding of 5 September 1986. See further above, section III. 6.1(ii)-(iii).

[312] See above, sections III.8 to III.11.

[313] Statement by the Chairman of the Preparatory Commission, LOS/PCN/L.115/Rev.1, 8 September 1994 (*loc. cit.* in note 310, at p. 171).

[314] *Ibid.*

[315] *Report on the Status of the Implementation of the Obligations of the Registered Pioneer Investors under Resolution II and the Related Understandings Prepared by the Secretariat*, LOS/PCN/145, 23 September 1994 (II *Final PrepCom Report*, p. 203).

[316] ISBA/3/C/6, 12 August 1997 (ISBA, *Selected Decisions & Documents of the First, Second and Third Sessions*, ISA/98/01.E, pp. 66-68).

[317] See section III.8 above.

242   Chapter 6

entitled to have their obligations 'adjusted' in accordance with the statement made by the Chairman of the Preparatory Commission at the time of the adoption of the Understanding on pioneer investors' obligation on 30 August 1990.[318] It will be recalled that the Chairman indicated that, 'Should any agreement be made which would affect in any way this Understanding, such adjustments as may be necessary shall be made to it'.[319]

The General Committee delayed a response until the Secretary-General's consultations led to the adoption of the Implementation Agreement in July 1994. However, it then decided that the performance of the obligation 'to carry out stage I of the exploration work referred to in document LOS/PCN/L.87, annex, paras. 7 and 8' should be deferred until the Legal and Technical Commission determined that substantial exploration work was being carried out by any contractor.[320] This was to be so, 'unless the Council [of the Authority] decided, at the request of any registered pioneer investor, to make adjustments in accordance with paragraph 40(a) of document LOS/PCN/L.87 and section I, paragraph 6(a)(iii) of the annex to the [Implementation Agreement]'.[321] The latter provision is designed to ensure, in accordance with the principle of non-discrimination, equality of treatment as between registered pioneer investors and potential applicants for plans of work for exploration.   Contracts with the latter must include arrangements similar to and no less favourable than those incorporated in the contracts of registered pioneer investors. Where discrimination occurred, the Council would be required to adjust the rights and obligations of the registered pioneer investors accordingly.

After 18 August 1995, the General Committee's monitoring rôle passed to the Authority and reports submitted by the registered pioneer investors are now considered by the Legal and Technical Commission. [322]

As has been seen, one of the obligations of registered pioneer investors was to provide training at all levels for personnel designated by the Preparatory Commission [323] and, by the time the Preparatory Commission completed its work in 1995, all of the pioneer investors except Korea had fulfilled their obligations. [324]   However, Korea's proposal for a training programme was submitted in

---

[318] See Letter dated 25 March 1993, from the Coordinator of the group of registered pioneer investors on behalf of France, Japan and the Russian Federation addressed to the Chairman of the Preparatory Commission, LOS/PCN/128, 26 March 1993 (I *Final PrepCom Report*, p. 179) and the follow-up letters dated 1 October 1993, LOS/PCN/131, 6 October 1993 (*ibid.*, p. 181) and 5 July 1994, LOS/PCN/138, 11 July 1994 (*ibid*, p. 193).

[319] LOS/PCN/L.87, 30 August 1990 (II *Final PrepCom Report*, p. 100; XI *Platzöder (PrepCom)*, p.111), Annex, para. 40. See further text above, following note 237.

[320] Report cited in note 315 above, at p.12, para.42.

[321] *Ibid.*

[322] See, *e.g., Report of the Legal and Technical Commission on the work of the Commission during the fifth session* (ISBA/5/C/6, 17 August 1999), para. 5 of which lists the reports considered by it. See also ISBA/4/A/1/Rev. 2, 2 September 1998 (*Selected Decisions & Documents of the Fourth Session,* ISA/99/01.E, pp. 1-39) which includes details of all reports submitted both to the Preparatory Commission and the Authority.

[323] See above section III(8), which refers to the general Understanding on Pioneer Investors' Obligations of 30 August 1990. Section III (9)-(11) refers to the corresponding Understandings for COMRA, IOM and Korea.

[324] *Report of the Secretary-General of the International Seabed Authority under article 166, paragraph 4 of the United Nations Convention on the Law of the Sea* (ISBA/5/A/1, 28 July 1999), para. 29.

Pioneer Investor Scheme 243

1995,[325] and approved by the Legal and Technical Commission in August 1997. The Commission went on to select trainees for the programme in August 1998 and then reported as follows:

> The Legal and Technical Commission considers that, with the selection of trainees for the training programme of the Government of the Republic of Korea, the process initiated during the Preparatory Commission to implement paragraph 12(a)(i) of resolution II has been concluded. In view of the realities regarding the activities of the Enterprise at this stage, as contained in section 2 of the Implementation Agreement, it was the view of the Commission that the purposes of future training programmes of the Authority and the selection criteria for the future have to be reconsidered. The Commission requested the Secretariat to ascertain the current activities of all previous trainees under resolution II with a view to assisting it in this matter. [326]

The Secretary-General reported in July 1999 that the Secretariat was in the process of preparing an evaluation of the training carried out pursuant to Resolution II and would present the results of its study to the Commission. [327] In his Report to the Assembly in July 2000, the Secretary-General anticipated that a comprehensive report would be submitted to the Council in 2001. [328]

---

[325] ISBA/3/LTC/2.
[326] ISBA/4/C/12 and Corr. 1, 25 August 1998, para. 7.
[327] Report cited in note 324 above, at para. 32.
[328] ISBA/6/A/9, 6 June 2000, para. 36.

CHAPTER 7

The UN Convention Regime of Sea-Bed Mining:
V. The UN Regime versus the Reciprocating States Regime: A Compromise Solution

I. INTRODUCTION

Prior to the adoption in 1994 of the Implementation Agreement, it was by no means certain that the UN regime of sea-bed mining would achieve near-universality. There was a distinct possibility that a significant proportion of sea-bed mining would take place under the alternative Reciprocating States Regime, based upon the principle of the freedom of the high seas and embodied in the unilateral legislation of some of the industrially advanced States, reciprocally co-ordinated by international agreement. The object of this chapter is to provide an account of the conflict between the two regimes and to show how a compromise solution was facilitated by the adoption of the Implementation Agreement.

If any State, or its natural or juridical persons, intends to engage in sea-bed mining, it has to adopt national legislation to govern it. This is so, irrespective of the attitude of the State in question to the UN Convention. Indeed, the Reciprocating States Regime was based on the legislation of a number of industrially advanced States whose motive in adopting it was dissatisfaction with the UN Convention regime of sea-bed mining and a wish, therefore, to provide an alternative regime. National legislation of this variety was originally adopted by the following six States[1]: United States (1980)[2], Germany (1980, amended

---

[1] On similar legislation adopted by the Soviet Union in 1982, see the first(1986) edition of this work at pp.II.8 3-4 and 32-36. This legislation was superseded by Decree No.2099 of 22 November 1994 of the Russian Federation (*Collected Laws of the Russian Federation,* 1994, No.31, p.3252) and the implementing Order No.410 of 25 April 1995 (*ibid.,* 1995, No.18, p.1675. English translations reproduced in Vol.3 as Docs. Nos. 30.1 and 30.2.

[2] Deep Seabed Hard Mineral Resources Act 1980, Public Law 96-283, 28 June 1980, 94 Stat. 553; 30 U.S.C. 1401 *et seq.*; reproduced (as amended to 1 July 2000) in Vol. 3 as Doc. No. 26.1. See also related Deep Seabed Mining Regulations for Exploration Licenses, *Federal Register,* Vol. 46, No. 178, 15 September 1981, pp. 45890-45920; 15 CFR Part 970; XX ILM(1981), pp. 1228-1258 (as amended). Subpart C issued separately in *Federal Register,* Vol. 47, No. 110, 8 June 1982, pp. 24948-24951; and Deep Seabed Mining Regulations for Commercial Recovery Permits, *Federal Register,* Vol.54, No.525, 6 January 1989; 15 CFR Part 971.

244

1982)[3], United Kingdom (1981)[4], France (1981)[5], Japan (1982)[6] and Italy (1985)[7]. Of those six States, three, Germany, the United Kingdom (hereafter 'UK') and the United States (hereafter 'US'), decided against signing the UN Convention. Moreover, of the remaining three States, two, France and Italy, in making declarations when signing the Convention, referred to deficiencies and flaws in Part XI of the Convention which would require rectification by the Preparatory Commission.[8]   A similar declaration was made by the European Economic Community.[9]   There was little doubt, therefore, that, unless these States were ultimately satisfied that the minimum required rectifications had been made to the UN regime, they would decide against ratification of or accession to the Convention.   In that event, a significant part of sea-bed mining would have proceeded under the alternative 'Reciprocating States Regime'.   Such an outcome would have had serious implications for the viability of operations under the UN regime.

The legislation itself professed to be of an interim nature. However, there was a good deal of suspicion – and not only in the Group of 77 – that these statutes, while paying lip service to the principle of the common heritage of mankind, were in reality the first strands in a network of parallel municipal legislation which would gradually consolidate into a permanent alternative regime, departing to a significant degree from the provisions of the UN Convention. These suspicions were heightened, moreover, by the conclusion in 1982 and 1984 of two agreements designed to co-ordinate this network of national legislation by

---

[3] Act of Interim Regulation of Deep Seabed Mining of 16 August 1980 (BGBl.I, p.1457) as amended by Act of 12 February 1982 (BGBl.I, p.136). English translations are in XX ILM (1981), p. 393 and XXI ILM (1982), p. 832. Following German accession to the UN Convention in 1994, new provision was made for sea-bed mining in a more comprehensive Law of 6 June 1995 (BGBl.I 778 9510-23; partially reproduced in English translation in Vol.3 as Doc No. 27.1).

[4] Deep Sea Mining (Temporary Provisions) Act 1981 as amended. See also the following related Orders: Deep Sea Mining (Exploration Licences) (Applications) Regulations 1982, S.I. 1982/58; Deep Sea Mining (Exploration Licences) Regulations 1984, S.I. 1984/1230; and Deep Sea Mining (Reciprocating Countries) Order 1985, S.I. 1985/2000. Texts reproduced in Vol.3 as Docs. Nos. 28.1 - 28.4.

[5] Law on the Exploration and Exploitation of Mineral Resources on the Deep Sea-Bed 1981 (Law No. 81-1135 of 23 December 1981, *Journal officiel*, 24 December 1981, pp. 3499-3500; Decree No. 82-111 of 29 January 1982 Passed in Application of the Law of 23 December 1981 in Respect of the Exploration and Exploitation of the Mineral Resources of the Deep Sea-Bed, *Journal officiel*, 31 January 1982, p. 431; and Arrêté of 29 January 1982 Establishing the Contents of Applications for Permits for the Exploration and Exploitation of the Deep Sea-Bed, *Journal officiel*, 31 January 1982. English translations reproduced in Vol.3 as Docs. Nos. 29.1 - 29.4.

[6] Law on Interim Measures for Deep Seabed Mining, 1982; English translation reproduced in Vol.3 as Doc No. 31.1. See also Enforcement Regulations for the Law on Interim Measures for Deep Seabed Mining, *Official Register of the Ministry of International Trade and Industry*, No. 9770, 26 July 1982.

[7] Law No. 41 of 20 February 1985: Regulations on the Exploration and Exploitation of the Mineral Resources of the Deep Seabed, *Gazzetta Ufficiale*, No. 52, 1 March 1985, pp. 1593-1596; English translation in XXIV ILM (1985), pp. 983-996 and reproduced in Vol.III of the first edition of this work at pp.III.3 212-218. This Law, together with the Regulation for its implementation (Presidential Decree No.200 of 11 March 1988 (*Gazzetta Ufficiale*, No.139, 13 June 1988), was repealed by Law No.689 of 2 December 1994 (*Gazzetta Ufficiale*, No.295, 19 December 1994, Supplement No.164) which authorised ratification of the UN Convention; English translation reproduced in Vol.3 as Doc. No. 32.1.

[8] The texts of the Declarations made by France and Italy are reproduced in *LOS Bull.*, No. 5, July 1985, at pp. 11 and 15.

[9] *Ibid.*, at p.26.

246   *Chapter 7*

providing for the identification and resolution of conflicts over overlapping sea-bed claims and an undertaking by the States Parties to refrain from issuing authorisations to engage in sea-bed operations for any area which overlapped specified areas covered by authorisations already granted or applied for.[10]

As was seen in Chapter 6, an at least temporary *modus vivendi* was arranged in 1986-87 among the various groups with an interest in sea-bed mining. Under the New York Understanding, the Midnight Agreement and a series of related agreements concluded between pioneer-investor applicants and potential applicants, the interests of the potential applicants were safeguarded and equality of treatment guaranteed until the entry into force of the UN Convention; and conflicts over overlapping sites were resolved.[11]   For the time being, therefore, there was no danger of conflicts arising as a result of competition for sites among the registered pioneer investors, the Enterprise and the consortia holding sites under Reciprocating States legislation.   However, this truce was clearly fragile and it was accepted on all sides that, both in the interests of long-term stability and the entry into force of the UN Convention on a universal basis, it was desirable to find a way of making the UN regime acceptable to the Reciprocating States.   The Implementation Agreement of 28 July 1994 embodies the results of negotiations to that end.

II. THE RECIPROCATING STATES REGIME AND THE UN CONVENTION REGIME COMPARED

1. Reasons for and Legal Basis of 'Interim' Legislation and Relationship to Principle of Common Heritage of Mankind Embodied in UN Convention

The purposes of the United States' Deep Sea-bed Hard Mineral Resources Act, 1980[12] and the thinking behind it are clearly stated in section 2, the 'Findings and Purposes' section of the Act itself.   The four Western European States – Germany, the UK, France and Italy – and Japan do not practise this style of parliamentary drafting and it is necessary, where possible, to delve into the *travaux préparatoires* to discover the reasons which led to the adoption of Germany's Act of Interim Regulation of Deep Sea-bed Mining 1980-82,[13] the UK's Deep Sea Mining (Temporary Provisions) Act 1981,[14] the French Law on the Exploration and Exploitation of the Mineral Resources of the Deep Sea-bed 1981,[15] the Japanese Law on Interim Measures for Deep Sea-bed Mining 1982[16] and the Italian Law embodying Regulations on the Exploration and Exploitation

---

[10] The two treaties referred to are the Agreement Concerning Interim Arrangements Relating to Polymetallic Nodules of the Deep Sea Bed among France, Germany, United Kingdom and United States, 2 September 1982, UK Treaty Series No. 46 (1982), Cmnd. 8685; XXI ILM (1982), pp.950-962; and the Provisional Understanding Regarding Deep Sea-bed Matters among Belgium, Germany, France, Italy, Japan, the Netherlands, the United Kingdom and the United States, 3 August 1984, XXIII ILM (1984), pp. 1354-1360.   These two instruments were considered above in Chap. 6, section III.4 and are dealt with in more detail below in section III.   Texts are reproduced in Vol.3 as Docs. Nos. 33.1 and 33.3.

[11] See further Chap.6, sections III.6, 7, 9, 10 and 11.

[12] *Loc.cit.* in note 2.

[13] *Loc.cit.* in note 3.

[14] *Loc.cit.* in note 4.

[15] *Loc.cit.* in note 5.

[16] *Loc.cit.* in note 6.

of the Mineral Resources of the Deep Sea-bed 1985.[17]   In fact, however, it is clear that all six countries were motivated principally by the desire: (1) to ensure non-discriminatory access for their nationals to sea-bed resources, thus providing secure access to supplies of minerals in the national interest; (2) to encourage continued research and development pending the entry into force for the country concerned of a Convention on the Law of the Sea; (3) to encourage potential investors to support such research and development; and (4) to ensure that their nationals should not be placed at a competitive disadvantage in relation to nationals of other countries which had adopted interim legislation.

Reference was also made to a number of other factors in one or other of the six States. Thus, all six Governments were anxious to protect life, health and property against the dangers arising from deep-sea mining and to protect the environment. Again, certainly the majority were committed to a policy of establishing a revenue-sharing fund which would ensure that the proceeds of deep-sea mining would be shared with the international community.[18] Finally, it is perhaps worth noting that one of the purposes of the US Act was said to be the encouragement of the successful conclusion of a Law of the Sea Treaty which would assure, *inter alia*, 'non-discriminatory access to such resources for all nations'.[19]

Turning next to the legal basis of these statutes, the arguments of the six States were again very similar. All six insisted that their legislation was interim in nature; that it did not involve any claim to sovereignty or sovereign rights over the deep sea-bed or its mineral resources; that they remained committed to the conclusion and entry into force of a Convention on the Law of the Sea which would give legal precision to the principle that the mineral resources of the deep sea-bed are the common heritage of mankind; that they were not legally bound by the terms of United Nations General Assembly Resolutions on the common heritage of mankind; and that deep-sea mining conducted with due regard to the interests of other States in the freedom of the high seas was, under the current law, a legitimate exercise of a high seas freedom.

In introducing their unilateral legislation, most of these Governments[20] not only made it clear that they considered themselves committed to the eventual entry into force of the UN Convention; they even claimed that their interim legislation was consistent with the regime of deep-sea mining developed in UNCLOS III. The claim was perhaps most clearly made in a Memorandum submitted by the UK Foreign and Commonwealth Office to the House of Commons Special Standing Committee which examined the Bill:

> The Bill is consistent with the proposals developed at the Conference. It has been specifically designed to be compatible with an internationally agreed regime, as envisaged in the draft convention.[21]

---

[17] *Loc.cit.* in note 7.

[18] There is no reference to any levy for this purpose in the Japanese Law but this may not be significant since Article 34 provides for all fees to be designated by Cabinet Order.

[19] S.2(b)(1).

[20] This is certainly true for the US, Germany, UK and France. It may also be the position of the Japanese and Italian Governments but the writer has no evidence to substantiate this.

[21] The Special Standing Committee held seven sittings between 19 May 1981 and 23 June 1981 and its proceedings are in *Parliamentary Debate, House of Commons, Official Report, Special Standing Committee, Deep Sea Mining (Temporary Provisions) Bill [Lords]*, cols.1-266.   The passage quoted is at col. 58.

248   *Chapter 7*

Even leaving aside the legal opinion of the Group of Legal Experts established by the Group of 77[22] that such interim legislation was contrary to international law, such a claim was very difficult to sustain. It would have been easier to argue that, *prima facie*, the introduction of a regime of the kind embodied in these statutes, based on the principle of the freedom of the high seas, would be tantamount to a denial during the interim period of the fundamental principle of the UN regime - the common heritage of mankind. This charge could be dismissed only if it could be shown that the provisions of the statutes (or related subordinate legislation) did in fact approximate to a substantial degree to the central, essential provisions of the Convention regime. To provide a basis for an evaluation of these contentions, a review is provided below of the provisions of the Convention regime and the interim statutes on these central issues.

1.1 Common Heritage Doctrine versus Unilateralism

None of the six States claimed sovereignty or sovereign rights over the sea-bed Area or its resources and indeed they emphasised that this was not their intention. The statutes did not therefore fall foul of Article 137(1) of the Convention, which forbids any such claims. Unfortunately, the provisions of these instruments which authorised exploration and exploitation of the Area's mineral resources were less easy to square with the terms of the Convention. Article 137(3) of the Convention is quite clear in providing that:

> No State or natural or juridical person shall claim, acquire or exercise rights with respect to the minerals recovered from the Area except in accordance with this Part. Otherwise, no such claim, acquisition or exercise of such rights shall be recognised.

However, the argument of the unilateralists was not that their interim legislation complied with the Convention, or, for that matter, with the common heritage doctrine as laid down in outline in the Declaration of Principles of December 1970.[23] Rather, they denied that the provisions of the Declaration of Principles were legally binding or that they would be bound to comply with the provisions of the UN Convention on the Law of the Sea until it entered into force for them. Accordingly, they could argue, the charge that their unilateral legislation violated international law would be substantiated only if it could be shown that the common heritage of mankind doctrine had already been transformed into rules of international law. What, then, did they mean by saying that their legislation was 'consistent with' the proposals developed at the Conference or that it was 'compatible with' the regime envisaged in the Convention? Apparently, what was meant was that the Governments of the six States had indicated their commitment to the realisation of a common heritage regime by formulating their legislation in such a way that it was consistent or compatible with the spirit of the Convention even if, in the interim, it departed in certain respects from its detailed terms. They could point, for example, to (1) the interim nature of the regime; (2) the establishment of a revenue-sharing fund; and (3) controls for the protection

---

[22] Letter dated 23 April 1979 from the Group of Legal Experts on the Question of Unilateral Legislation to the Chairman of the Group of 77, *UNCLOS III Off. Rec.*, Vol. XI, p. 81. See further Chapter 2, section III.5.1.

[23] Declaration of Principles Governing the Sea-Bed and the Ocean Floor, and the Subsoil thereof, Beyond the Limits of National Jurisdiction, UN General Assembly Resolution A/RES/2749(XXV), 17 December 1970; text reproduced in Vol.3 as Doc. No. 11. See further Chapter 2, section III.2.3.

UN regime v reciprocating State regime 249

of the environment and of scientific research. To state the argument is, however, to emphasise its weakness. The reality was that the Reciprocating States Regime which was based on this unilateral legislation included only a selection of features suggested by the Convention, chosen and substantially modified by the States concerned. As the following examination of the key provisions of the legislation and the Convention regime shows, there was a nod rather than a bow to the common heritage regime.

1.2 The Scope of the Interim Regime ratione temporis

The description of these acts as 'interim' reflected the intention, expressly stated in some cases and implied in others,[24] to repeal them upon the entry into force for the State concerned of a Convention on the Law of the Sea. However, neither this description nor the sections of the statutes dealing with their temporal scope enabled the observer to determine how long the interim could turn out to be in practice.

The US Act and the legislation of the four Western European States contained similar, though not identical, provisions on the commencement dates for licences to explore and licences to exploit. Under the US and UK Acts,[25] an exploration licence was not to be granted in respect of any period before 1 July 1981. No date was specified in the German,[26] French[27] or Italian instruments. Under all five statutes, no exploitation licence was to authorise commercial recovery to take place prior to 1 January 1988.[28] The Japanese Law departed from this pattern and did not specify commencement dates either for exploration or commercial recovery.

On the more important question of the possible duration of licences, the Acts were less clear. The Japanese Law again lacked specificity[29] but the position in the other five States was as tabulated in Table 7.1. No licences for exploitation were in fact issued in any of those six States. However, as the table shows, licensed exploitation might well have continued until the mine site in question was no longer commercially viable, and, of course, it is also true that licences issued at later dates could have run for similar periods. In short, there was no temporal limit prescribed in this legislation.

1.3 The Scope of the Interim Regime ratione personae

Given the possibility that mining could have continued under a Reciprocating States Regime for a good many years, the next question to ask is what was the personal scope of the licensing system so established. Or, to put the question another way, to what extent did this regime establish a privileged club of

---

[24] See US Act (*loc.cit.* in note 2), ss.2(a)(16), 2(b)(2)-(3), 201 and 202; German Act (*loc.cit.* in note 3), ss. 1 and 5; UK Act (*loc.cit.* in note 4),s. 18(3)-(4); French Law (*loc.cit.* in note 5), Art. 1; Japanese Law (*loc.cit.* in note 6), Art. 1(1); and Italian Law (*loc.cit.* in note 7), Arts. 1 and 20.

[25] US Act, s. 102(c)(1)(D); UK Act, s. 2(4).

[26] However, under s. 6(1) of the German Act, a resident of the Federal Republic who was engaged in exploration activities at the time of the effective date of the Act (which under s. 22 was 23 August 1980) could continue these activities only if he applied for a licence within three months.

[27] The French Decree No. 81-555 of 12 May 1981 (*Journal officiel*, 16 May 1981), which prescribed the procedure for applications to undertake exploration of sea-bed resources, provided that the relevant dossier might be submitted as from 1 July 1981. However, it was repealed by the Decree No. 82-111 of 29 January 1982 (*loc.cit.* in note 5), Art. 18.

[28] US Act, s.102 (c)(1)(D); German Act, s.4(3); UK Act, s.2(4); French Law, Art. 7; Italian Law, Art. 20.

[29] See Arts. 4(2), 12(2), 13(2), 14, 17 and 23 for more general references to the duration of permits.

Table 7.1: Duration of Licences in Five States

	United States (S.107)		Germany (S.10)		United Kingdom (Act s.2(3) and S.I.1984/1230, reg.4)		France (Arts. 5 and 7)		Italy (Arts. 8 and 9)	
	Exploration	*Exploitation*	*Exploration*	*Exploitation*	*Exploration*	*Exploitation*	*Exploration*	*Exploitation*	*Exploration*	*Exploitation*
Initial Term	10 years	20 years and for so long thereafter as minerals are recovered in commercial quantities	20 years	20 years	10 years	For such period as the Secretary of State thinks fit (possibly* 20 years)	Initial period needed to complete exploration programme, construct and test prototype equipment and collect and process mineral resources	Initial period compatible with the general economy of the project	Must permit implement-ation of programme submitted but not exceed 10 years	Compatible with general economy of programme but not exceeding 25 years
Extension	Periods of not more than 5 years each		Periods of up to 5 years	Periods of up to 10 years	Periods of 5 years				Subsequent 3-year periods	May be extended on justified grounds

* The possible figure given is that stated by the Government as their current view at 11 June 1981. Decisions would depend upon practice in reciprocating countries and discussion within mining companies (see *loc. cit.* in note 21 above, at col. 173).

economically and technologically advanced States whose nationals would have enjoyed opportunities to engage in deep-sea mining on advantageous terms, to the detriment of other sectors of international society, particularly the developing States?

Answers must be sought to a number of questions: Who was entitled to apply for a licence under the Reciprocating States Regime? What benefits were enjoyed by the operators under this regime? What was the position of an operator either unlicensed or licensed by a non-reciprocating State?

1.3.1 Who Could Apply for a Licence Under the Reciprocating States Regime?

The legislation of the six Reciprocating States was similar, in that all six States provided for the issue of licences to their own nationals, variously defined, and, with the exception of Japan, recognised their right to operate under licences granted by another Reciprocating State. It is, however, useful to look more closely at the detailed provisions of the six statutes.

Section 2(b)(3) of the US Act stated that it was one of the purposes of the Act to establish 'an interim program' to regulate sea-bed mining by United States citizens and section 101(a) allowed US citizens to mine under authorisations granted by either the United States or a Reciprocating State. Section 3 asserted jurisdiction over United States citizens and vessels and foreign persons and vessels otherwise subject to its jurisdiction.

For the purposes of the US Act, section 4(4) defined 'United States citizens' to mean:

(a) any individual who is a citizen of the United States;

(b) any corporation, partnership, joint venture, association, or other entity organised or existing under the laws of any of the United States; and

(c) any corporation, partnership, joint venture, association, or other entity (whether organised or existing under the laws of any of the United States or of a foreign nation) if the controlling interest in such entity is held by an individual or entity described in sub-paragraphs (A) or (B).

This last subparagraph enabled the United States to pierce the corporate veil of any entity organised or existing under the laws of any other State, reciprocating or non-reciprocating, in order to determine the existence of an American 'controlling interest', defined as:

a direct or indirect legal or beneficial interest in or influence over another person arising through ownership of capital stock, interlocking directorates or officers, contractual relations, or other similar means, which substantially affect the independent business behavior of such person.[30]

The German Act was much more simply drafted and provided in section 3 that deep-sea mining could be conducted by residents of Germany only if licensed by either Germany or a Reciprocating State. The term 'resident' included 'natural persons resident or usually domiciled in the (German) economic area as well as juridical persons with the place of incorporation or management therein'.[31] It was thus clear that 'residents' in Germany could operate under licences issued by Reciprocating States (though not under those issued by third States).

---

[30] US Act, s.4(3).

[31] The term 'resident' is taken from s. 4(1)(3) of the Foreign Trade Law (Aussenwirtschaftsgesetz).

252   Chapter 7

Under section 1 of the UK Act, deep-sea mining was prohibited without a licence issued under the Act and the prohibition extended *ratione personae* to any person who: (a) was a UK national, a Scottish firm or a body incorporated in the UK; and (b) was resident in any part of the UK. The prohibition could also be extended by Order in Council to such nationals, firms and bodies as were resident outside the UK; or as were resident in any country specified in the Order; and/or to bodies incorporated in the Channel Islands, the Isle of Man, any colony or any associated State. However, under section 3(2)(b), the prohibition was lifted if such 'persons' held a licence granted by a Reciprocating State. British persons thus enjoyed the same freedom as their American and German counterparts to join foreign consortia in Reciprocating States or to operate independently under Reciprocating State licences. On the other hand, it may be noted that the Secretary of State was empowered to revoke or vary a licence if a licensee company ceased to have its central management or to be incorporated in the United Kingdom.[32]

The French and Italian Laws followed the common pattern, providing for the issue of exploration and exploitation permits to their nationals and recognising their right to operate under permits granted by another Reciprocating State.[33]

The Japanese Law again departed from the common pattern by providing in Article 11(1) that persons who were not nationals or corporations of Japan could not obtain permission to engage in deep-sea mining.

Considering the provisions of these six Acts together, it is thus clear that, while there was no barrier to the investment of foreign capital from non-reciprocating States in deep-sea mining enterprises licensed under a Reciprocating States regime, the legislation was designed to provide a favourable legal regime for the nationals of the States concerned.

1.3.2 Benefits of Operating under a Reciprocating State's Licence

There were two principal benefits of operating under a Reciprocating State's licence. The first was that the licence ensured security of tenure in the mining site vis-à-vis all potential competitors in all of the Reciprocating States. Overlapping licences would not be granted for exploration or exploitation in any area of the deep-sea bed in respect of which a current licence to explore or exploit had already been granted by a Reciprocating State.

The second benefit was that the operator would enjoy the protection of the licensing State against interference with his mining operations by third parties. However, it has to be said that this security was rather more relative. There was no problem as regards interference by other nationals of the licensing State or of another Reciprocating State. For example, section 101(c) of the US Act prohibited interference by US citizens with the activities of miners licensed by the United States or a Reciprocating State. The position was considerably more obscure, however, in relation to interference from outside the Reciprocating States nexus.

The threat to the licensee's security might have arisen from any one of at least three sources. First, the licensee might have been confronted by a competing claim to his mining site by a miner from a non-reciprocating State, either licensed

---

[32] Deep Sea Mining (Exploration Licences) Regulations 1984, S.I. 1984/1230, Schedule, cl.22(2)(g).

[33] French Law, Arts. 3 and 4; Italian Law, Arts. 3 and 16. Under Art.5, Italian nationals applying for permits from a Reciprocating State had also to register their applications with the Italian Government.

or unlicensed. Secondly, the licensee might have suffered direct physical interference by States purporting to safeguard the common heritage of mankind from illegal mining. Thirdly, the licensee or his successor in title to minerals derived from the sea-bed might have found his title to the minerals challenged in legal proceedings in the courts of a non-reciprocating State.

As regards the first question - that of competition for a site with a miner from a non-reciprocating State - the position was relatively straightforward. It must be assumed that the claims of both parties would have been founded on a shared conviction that deep-sea mining was a permissible freedom of the high seas; for, otherwise, the competitor would have been operating under the UN regime, the situation envisaged in the next paragraph. This being so, it would have been necessary to resolve any conflict arising from competing claims to a common user of the high seas through the normal means of pacific settlement under international law. The licensed operator would have enjoyed the support of the licensing State in settling the conflict.

A more difficult problem would have been presented by the second challenge – that of the States purporting to protect the common heritage of mankind. In this case there would have been no shared conviction concerning the status of deep-sea mining. It would, of course, have been possible for the Reciprocating State to take its stand on the principle of the freedom of the high seas and to endeavour to protect its licensee in the same way as in the first case. Scrutiny of the Acts does, however, reveal a very cautious attitude to the possibility of international conflict, particularly in the US, German and Italian legislation.

Looking first at the position in the United States, a number of provisions would have been directly in point and reflected the anxiety of the United States not to create conflicts with other States. Thus, section 102(b)(4), for example, provided that,

> In the event of interference with the exploration or commercial activities of a licensee or permittee by nationals of other States, the Secretary of State shall use all peaceful means to resolve the controversy by negotiation, conciliation, arbitration, or resort to agreed tribunals.

In a similar vein, the Administrator under the Act was required by section 105(a) to find, before issuing licenses or permits, that the operations proposed would not, *inter alia*:

(i) ...unreasonably interfere with the exercise of the freedoms of the high seas by other states, as recognised under general principles of international law; [or]
(ii) ...create a situation which may reasonably be expected to lead to a breach of international peace and security involving armed conflict.

The Administrator also enjoyed powers, under section 105(c), to modify or revise licences and permits to avoid the same danger. Finally, under section 106(a)(2)(B), the Administrator was empowered to suspend or modify particular activities under a licence or permit if the President determined that it was necessary to avoid any situation which might reasonably be expected to lead to a breach of international peace and security involving armed conflict.

The provisions of the German Act seemed to reflect this same ambivalent attitude, conscious of the need to protect nationals in their exercise of a high seas freedom but aware too of the risks of incurring the wrath of the defenders of the common heritage. Section 5(1)(3) provided that licences would not be granted if

254   *Chapter 7*

there was a danger that the development proposed would either 'substantially impair the rights of others in their enjoyment of the freedom of the high seas', or 'materially impair the foreign relations of the Federal Republic of Germany'. Under section 18(1), the Minister was empowered to take the measures required in individual cases to safeguard these interests.

The Italian Law was similar. Under Article 7, exploration and exploitation permits might be denied if the Minister of Foreign Affairs held that granting them might seriously harm international relations. Again, under Article 10, permits might be modified or revoked if the Minister determined that their continuation in their original form could seriously damage international relations.

The remaining three States, France, Japan and the United Kingdom, adopted a less revealing approach and made no reference to interference with their licensees by third States or their nationals. Moreover, there was nothing in the legislation to prevent licences being granted in respect of areas in which operations were being conducted by persons other than those licensed by them or by a Reciprocating State. Looked at from the licensee's point of view, there was perhaps some merit in a legislative approach which did not follow the American, German and Italian models in advertising the fact that licences would not be granted where the operations under them might be expected to impair foreign relations. Any such provision might well have been regarded as an open invitation to the Group of 77 to step up their campaign against unilateral legislation by undertaking or threatening to undertake direct action against operations in licensed mining sites.

The third risk against which the licensee might have expected protection arose from the possibility that his title to minerals derived from the sea-bed, or that of a purchaser from him, might have been challenged in the courts of a non-reciprocating State. Analogies have been drawn with the practice of tracking 'hot' oil or other commodities confiscated in violation of international law and subsequently sold to purchasers in a third State. As it was put in a US State Department memorandum,

> The theory of a suit brought in pursuance of hot oil or another hot commodity is simple. The company whose property has been seized in violation of international law maintains that the expropriating government did not, by virtue of an act that violated international law, acquire good title to the property in question. The company places prospective purchasers on notice of this contention. If nevertheless a party proceeds to purchase a hot product, the expropriated company initiates a legal action designed to regain possession of the property unlawfully taken from it, or the proceeds.[34]

One of the best known of such cases was the action brought by the Anglo-Iranian Oil Co. in the Aden Supreme Court which, in *The Rose Mary* case in 1951, declined to recognise the title of the purchaser of oil taken by the Iranian Government in violation of international law.[35]

The analogous risk faced by the deep-sea mining licensee was that if a purchaser in a non-reciprocating State of sea-bed minerals or of goods manufactured from such minerals were to refuse to pay the purchase price, the local courts might decline to enforce the contract on the ground that, having

---

[34] United States: *Statement by the Department of State on 'Hot' Libyan Oil*, XIII ILM (1974), p. 767, at pp. 768-769.

[35] *Anglo-Iranian Oil Co. Ltd. v. Jaffrate and Others (The Rose Mary)*, Aden, Supreme Court [1953] Intl. L. Rep. 316.

obtained the minerals in violation of international law, the vendor had no title to pass to the purchaser and no right therefore to sue for the purchase price.[36]

It is doubtful if such a situation would have arisen in practice. Even if the minerals or manufactured products had been sold abroad, it is unlikely that their sea-bed origins would have been identifiable. If, however, such a contingency had arisen, the licensee would clearly have been in a difficult position. His home State would certainly have been expected to afford him diplomatic protection but, given the jurisdictional hazards of international law, there would have been no guarantee that an international court or tribunal would have had the opportunity to consider the international legality of deep-sea mining under a Reciprocating State licence or, indeed, that it would have found it to be legal, given the opportunity.

The last point suggests yet another hazard for the deep-sea miner: the possibility that proceedings might have been instituted before the International Court of Justice. There are two possibilities to consider. First, the General Assembly might have requested an Advisory Opinion on the legality of unilateral legislation of the type adopted by the Reciprocating States.[37] Such a request would have related to a matter of legitimate concern to the General Assembly and would not have required the Court to rule on an actual pending dispute. It is possible, therefore, that the Court would have acceded to the General Assembly's request.

The second possibility is that contentious proceedings might have been brought against a Reciprocating State by one or more members of the Group of 77. Given the fact that France, Germany and Italy had not made Optional Clause declarations under Article 36(2) of the Court's Statute and that the United States' declaration had been terminated,[38] Japan and the United Kingdom would appear to have been the most vulnerable targets. Since the Court had held in an earlier case that the *actio popularis* is not known to international law,[39] it would have been necessary for the applicant State or States to demonstrate a legal interest. While it seems unlikely that the Court would have regarded the interest of a State or States in preventing such a depletion of the common heritage of mankind as constituting a sufficient legal interest to found an action, the position might well have been different if an applicant for registration as a pioneer investor had been

---

[36] A possibility suggested by A.V. Lowe in the House of Commons Special Standing Committee on Deep Sea Mining (Temporary Provisions) Bill [Lords] (*loc. cit.* in note 21, at cols. 92-93).

[37] Mr. T. Koh, President of UNCLOS III, is reported to have told correspondents that any attempt to permit sea-bed mining under a mini-treaty would be met by a stern legal challenge and that 'I will take it upon myself to persuade the General Assembly to ask the International Court of Justice for an advisory opinion on whether such activities under unilateral legislation are lawful'. (*Financial Times*, London, 3 May 1982). No such challenge was ever mounted.

[38] The US Declaration of 26 August 1946 (ICJ, *Yearbook 1983-84*, p. 90), accepting the Court's 'compulsory' jurisdiction, included a subjective domestic jurisdiction reservation excluding from its scope 'disputes with regard to matters which are essentially within the domestic jurisdiction of the United States of America *as determined by the United States of America*' (emphasis added). In a statement dated 6 April 1984, the United States attempted to exclude the application of the 1946 Declaration to disputes with any Central American State for a period of two years from 6 April 1984 (*ibid.*, p.91). Following a finding by the International Court of Justice that this statement could not override the obligation of the US to submit to the Court's jurisdiction in the case concerning *Military and Paramilitary Activities in and against Nicaragua, I.C.J. Reports 1984*, p. 392, at p. 421, the US terminated its Declaration of 1946 with effect from April 1986 (*The Times*, London, 9 October 1985).

[39] *South West Africa, Second Phase, Judgment, I.C.J. Reports 1966*, p.6, at para. 88.

256   Chapter 7

involved. Suppose, for example, that an application had been submitted to the Preparatory Commission by a group of developing States[40] and that the site applied for overlapped with that covered by an existing licence granted by a Reciprocating State. In that case, the applicant States would certainly have had a justifiable legal interest. The cost to the miner of the delays caused by any such action (including, possibly, an indication by the Court of interim measures of protection) might have been very considerable.

1.4 Reservation of Sites ('site-banking')

As has been seen in Chapters 4[41] and 6 [42], one of the essential elements in the UN Convention regime is the 'site-banking' system provided for both in the UN Convention and in Conference Resolution II. Under the Convention, applicants for deep-sea mining contracts are required to submit to the International Sea-Bed Authority detailed data on two parts of the total area specified in the application, each part being of equal estimated commercial value. The Authority then designates one of these two parts as a 'reserved site' in which activities may be conducted only by the Authority through the Enterprise or in association with developing States.[43] Moreover, under Resolution II, Paragraph 3, a similar obligation is placed upon applicants for registration as pioneer investors, the Preparatory Commission being empowered to designate the part of the area to be reserved or 'banked'.[44]

None of the six Acts under scrutiny contained any comparable provision[45] and it seems unlikely that the question was ever seriously considered in the course of the discussions among the Group of Like-Minded States.[46] It was, however, thoroughly debated during the passage of the British Bill, with the Government successfully opposing an Opposition amendment which would have incorporated a site-banking requirement in the Act.[47] Though protesting sympathy with the object of the amendment, the Government regarded its inclusion in the Bill as premature, for two main reasons.[48] First, the absence of any such provision in either the American or the German legislation meant that such a requirement in the UK Act would have placed British companies at a competitive disadvantage. Secondly, it would have pre-empted UNCLOS III negotiations on a clause for the protection of interim investments. The Government was willing to consider site-banking as part of the eventual arrangements but not in isolation. The Minister

---

[40] See above, Chap.6, section III.6.1 (vii).

[41] Chap. 4, section VII.

[42] Chap. 6, section II.1.3.

[43] UN Convention, Annex III, Art.8.

[44] See, however, above, Chap.6, section III.6.1(iv) for a departure from this provision permitted under the New York Understanding.

[45] But Art. 6 of the French Law may have been foreshadowing such a provision by entitling an exploration permit-holder to obtain an exploitation permit, but only for an area of not more than half of that covered by the exploration permit.

[46] The Under-Secretary of State who steered the British Bill through the House of Commons was unable to say whether or not there had been any discussion of banking of licences with the United States or German Governments. (*House of Commons Parliamentary Debates. Weekly Hansard*, Vol. 8, col. 815, 13 July 1981).

[47] See *loc. cit.* in note 21, cols. 64, 142, 153-159 and *House of Commons Parliamentary Debates. Weekly Hansard*, Vol. 8, cols. 804-815, 13 July 1981.

[48] *Loc. cit.* in note 21, cols. 156-157.

indicated that 'the matter could be considered in regulations, and so on, in due course'.[49] He added subsequently that he was:

> ... satisfied that the Bill in its present form will enable the Secretary of State to allow for a site banking arrangement within his discretion to grant licences in pursuance of clause 2(2) to comply with any preliminary investment protection arrangement that may be agreed at UNCLOS, and that could apply whether or not a treaty is in prospect or, indeed, ... no treaty eventually comes.[50]

Further pointers are to be found in statements made by a Foreign Office legal adviser and a spokesman for Rio Tinto Zinc, appearing before the House of Commons Special Standing Committee. The former, commenting on the site-banking gap in the Bill, said that:

> ... nothing in the legislation will preclude the operation of [the convention's banking system] ... from the moment that the convention comes into effect. Under the arrangements made at the conference for the protection of interim investments, the banking system *could* become partially applicable in advance of the convention, because companies *could voluntarily* submit a site to be banked by the future authority.[51]

The second statement was made by a Rio Tinto Zinc representative in response to a question about his Company's attitude to a site-banking requirement. He informed the Committee that, 'It is certainly assumed by us that we shall be putting up two sites. One will be available for the Enterprise when it is eventually formed'.[52] It is likely that his reply envisaged that this would be in compliance with regulations giving effect to a banking system and assumed the successful negotiation in the meantime of an acceptable arrangement for the protection of preliminary investment.

These statements were of course made before Resolution II was adopted in April 1982. As has been seen, Paragraph 3 of that Resolution required applicants for registration as pioneer investors to comply with a site-banking provision. However, it was never likely that any action would be taken on the site-banking question by any of these six States unless and until ways were found of revising the UN regime to the satisfaction of the Reciprocating States. It follows, of course, that companies operating under their unilateral legislation would have been able to avoid a substantial cost which was one of the central conditions of the Conventional regime.

1.5 Anti-monopoly and Diligence Provisions

It would clearly be contrary to the common heritage of mankind concept to permit any particular State to obtain a disproportionate share of deep-sea mining sites. Similarly, it would be an abuse of the system established to give effect to the common heritage doctrine if licensees were permitted to 'hoard' mine sites without meeting reasonable 'performance' or diligence standards. As was seen

---

[49] *Ibid.*, col. 157. For powers to make regulations and orders, see s.12 of the Act and the Schedule and, for a reference to those already made, note 4 above.

[50] *Loc. cit.* in note 47 (Hansard), at col. 816.

[51] *Loc. cit.* in note 21, at col. 64, emphasis added.

[52] *Ibid.*, at col. 144.

258   Chapter 7

above in Chapter 4,[53] the Convention embodies provisions to ensure that neither of these forms of monopolisation should be permitted.

Thus, under Annex III, Article 6(3)(c), the Authority would not approve a plan of work if it had been submitted or sponsored by a State Party which already held plans of work for the exploration and exploitation of manganese nodules covering specified maximum areas. Under Paragraph 4, however, approval might be granted if the Authority determined that such approval would not permit a State Party or persons sponsored by it to monopolise the conduct of activities in the Area or to preclude other States Parties from activities in the Area.[54] Although Resolution II places registered pioneer investors in a privileged position in relation to approval of plans of work, such plans have still to comply with the Convention and the rules, regulations and procedures of the Authority.[55] Moreover, as has been seen,[56] each pioneer investor is entitled to only one pioneer area not exceeding 150,000 square kilometres, portions of which, amounting in all to 50%, have to be gradually relinquished to the international area over a period of eight years (if not relinquished in advance under the New York Understanding[57]).

Diligence requirements are referred to in Annex III, Article 17(2), which prescribed the 'objective criteria'[58] to be incorporated in the regulations to be adopted by the Authority. 'Performance requirements' were specified for both exploration and commercial production.[59]

The Reciprocating States' legislation did contain diligence requirements but none of the six Acts placed any limitation on the number of sites which might be held by a licensee.

The most detailed of the diligence provisions were those laid down in section 108 of the US Act, which required the licensee to make periodic reasonable expenditures for exploration and, once commercial recovery was achieved, to maintain commercial recovery throughout the period of the permit. Further provision to ensure diligent exploration was made in the Deep Seabed Mining Regulations for Exploration Licenses, 1981[60] and the Deep Seabed Mining Regulations for Commercial Recovery Permits, 1989.[61]

Section 10(3) of the German Act was similar in requiring the licensee to make periodic and reasonable investments for exploration, while section 5(1)2 required of an applicant for an authorisation to explore for and exploit mineral resources that, as a result of his knowledge, experience and financial resources, as well as his reliability, he could guarantee an orderly development of mineral resources. According to the *Statement of Reasons* published with the German Bill, these two provisions were to be regarded as complementary to each other and as designed to 'prevent a blocking of sea-bed areas by companies not capable or willing to

---

[53] See further, Chap. 4, section V.4.2, following note 126.

[54] See further *ibid*.

[55] Resolution II Governing Preparatory Investment in Pioneer Activities relating to Polymetallic Nodules, adopted 30 April 1982 (Annex I to Final Act of UNCLOS III, in United Nations, *The Law of the Sea, United Nations Convention on the Law of the Sea*, 1983, p. 177), para.8; reproduced in Vol. 3 as Doc. No. 14.2.

[56] Above, Chap. 6, section II.1.3.

[57] See further Chap.6, section III.6.1(iii).

[58] UN Convention, Annex III, Art. 17(2), chapeau.

[59] Art. 17(2)(c). See for a later modification of the requirements of Art.17(2)(b) and (c) the Implementation Agreement, Annex, Sec.1, para.5(f).

[60] *Loc. cit.* in note 2, ss. 970.517 and 970.602.

[61] *Loc. cit.* in note 2, ss. 971.418 and 971.503.

UN regime v reciprocating State regime 259

develop the mineral resources'.[62] Section 5 was described as intended, *inter alia*, to prevent the 'hoarding' of sites by applicants having no intention of carrying out development.[63]

Characteristically, the UK Act was somewhat more economical in its language and simply provided in section 2(3)(f) that the Secretary of State might include among the terms and conditions of a licence the requirement that exploration or exploitation would be diligently carried out. The model clauses to be incorporated in exploration licences included a clause on 'Diligence', which required that:

> The Licensee shall carry out the exploration for which he is licensed in accordance with the exploration plan. It shall be the duty of the Licensee to ensure that such exploration is carried out with all due skill and diligence.[64]

The French Law dealt with diligence in Articles 6, 7 and 14. Under Article 6, the exploration permit was to set out the permit holder's obligations, especially the minimum financial commitment required of him. Similarly, Article 7 provided for the imposition of obligations upon the holder of an exploitation permit and referred in particular to a minimum programme of production. Under Article 14, failure to comply with these diligence requirements might lead to withdrawal of permits.

Under the Japanese Law, permission to engage in deep sea-bed mining would not be granted unless the applicant satisfied, *inter alia*, the following conditions: that his financial standing and technological capabilities were sufficient for proper execution of sea-bed mining and that 'rational and smooth development of deep sea-bed mineral resources shall be able to be performed properly.'[65] Permittees were required to commence their activities within six months of the grant of the permit and not to suspend their activities for more than six continuous months.[66]

Like the Japanese Law, the Italian Law required applicants for permits to have the necessary technical and financial capacity.[67] Under Article 11, the permit might be terminated if the permit holder lost such technical and financial capacity, failed to fulfil his obligations under the statute or the provisions of the permit, or seriously failed to comply with the timetable and the conditions specified in the work programme.

As noted above, none of the Acts placed any limitation upon the number of sites which a licensee might hold and it followed of course that it was quite possible that a State which had operated for some time under such an interim regime might be unable to conform with the anti-monopoly provisions of Article 6(3)(c) of Annex III of the Convention.

In the United Kingdom, a valiant but futile attempt was made by the Opposition to persuade the Government to include such an anti-monopoly provision in the Bill. The Opposition amendment sought to ensure that a licence would not be granted if, as a result, one person or group of persons would then hold or have the benefit of licences for more than two sites granted either by the UK or another Reciprocating State. The Government's view was that such

[62] *Statement of Reasons. II. Section-by-Section Analysis*, Section 10.
[63] *Ibid.*, Section 5.
[64] Deep Sea Mining (Exploration Licences) Regulations 1984, S.I. 1984/1230, Schedule, cl.8.
[65] Japanese Law, *loc. cit.* in note 6, Art. 12(3)-(4).
[66] Art. 23; unless, in both cases, an extension has been granted.
[67] Italian Law(1985), *loc. cit.* in note 7, Art. 7.

260   *Chapter 7*

provision was not only in itself much too restrictive of the activities of the consortia of which British companies were members but would also place such companies at a serious disadvantage as compared with companies operating under the American or German Acts, neither of which contained any such restrictions.[68]

1.6 Protection of Land-based Mineral Producers

As was seen in Chapter 4,[69] the Convention originally contained elaborate provisions designed to protect the economies of the developing States from the impact which sea-bed mining might have on the export earnings of land-based, mineral-producing States.[70] The production policies laid down in Article 151 sought to ensure such protection in three ways: through commodity arrangements, production controls and compensatory economic assistance. Moreover, Conference Resolutions I and II not only retained the Conventional production control provisions but also gave the Preparatory Commission a role in developing additional safeguards for land-based producers.[71]

None of the six Acts of the Reciprocating States made provision for production control, though it must be said that it is a little difficult to see how they could. Nevertheless, for any evaluation of claims that this legislation was compatible with the Convention, it is revealing to consider the provisions of section 110 of the US Act. This section was designed to ensure that licence conditions would be so framed as to have due regard to the prevention of waste and the future opportunity for the commercial recovery of the unrecovered balance of the mineral resources in the licensed area. It ends with the following provision:

> As used in this Act, the term 'conservation of natural resources' is not intended to grant, imply, or create any inference of production controls or price regulation, in particular those which would affect the volume of production, prices, profits, markets, or the decision of which minerals or metals are to be recovered, except as such effects may be incidental to actions taken pursuant to this section.

The British, German, French, Japanese and Italian legislatures did not see fit to bare their souls in public in this way, but, in effect, by including no reference to production controls in their statutes, they adopted the same position as their American counterpart.[72] The absence of production ceilings in the British Bill was the subject of questions in the House of Commons Special Standing Committee[73] but they elicited only an official's comment that, ' ... nothing in the legislation will preclude the operation of ... [production controls] from the moment that the convention comes into effect'.[74]

---

[68] See further *loc. cit.* in note 21, at cols. 159-166.

[69] Chap.4, section VI.

[70] These provisions were radically changed by the Implementation Agreement. See further Chap.4, section VI and Chap.6, section II.3.

[71] Resolution I, paras. 5(i) and 9.

[72] See, however, Art. 7 of the Italian Law(1985), under which, in granting permits, the Ministry is to take into consideration 'that they do not exceed a reasonable area, taking the interests of the other States into account'.

[73] *Loc. cit.* in note 21, cols. 47 and 64.

[74] *Ibid.*, col.64.

1.7 Financial Provisions and the Fund

Five of the six statutes under consideration - the exception being the Japanese Law[75] - made provision for the imposition of a levy on deep-sea mining operations and for payment of the proceeds into a holding fund. Indeed, Government spokesmen frequently pointed to these provisions as evidence of their good faith and commitment to the common heritage doctrine.[76]

1.7.1 Levies

Dealing first with the levy, it will be recalled that Article 13 of Annex III of the Convention originally made provision for three types of payment: (i) an application fee; (ii) an annual fixed fee; and, (iii) *either* (a) a production charge, *or* (b) a mixed system of production charge and share of net proceeds.[77] If the contractor opted for the production charge system, the levy would be payable at the initial rate of 5 per cent of the market value of the processed metals, rising after 10 years to 12 per cent. Where the alternative, mixed system was chosen, the contractor would pay a production charge set at 2 per cent in the early stage of the mining operation, rising to 4 per cent once the operator had recovered his development costs. It would remain at 2 per cent, however, where the contractor's return on his investment was less than 15 per cent per annum. In addition, under this mixed system, the contractor would pay a share of his net proceeds to the Authority, ranging from 35 per cent during the early stage of a low-profit operation to 70 per cent during the later phase of a more profitable one.

These financial provisions had to be read with the corresponding provisions applicable under Resolution II's pioneer investor scheme, referred to above.[78] As was seen, each pioneer investor has to pay a $US 250,000 registration fee, plus a further $US 250,000 when it applies to the Authority for a plan of work. An additional fee of $US 1 million was originally imposed from the time the pioneer area was allocated, payable once the Authority approved the plan of work,[79] but, as has been seen, this fee has been conditionally waived under the Understanding of 30 August 1990.[80]

The Convention levy system was designed in a form quite different from that adopted in the unilateral statutes and it is therefore very difficult to make a direct comparison between the Convention and the Acts or to compare the financial effects of the two regimes. The five Acts adopted the same rate of levy, though expressed in different forms. It seems to be generally accepted that the proceeds of a levy under the Acts would have generated approximately half of the revenue which would be produced under the Convention regime.

---

[75] Under Art.34 of the Japanese Law, the amount of the fees payable by permittees was to be determined by Cabinet Order. No reference was made to the establishment of a fund from which aid to developing States might be drawn.

[76] *E.g.*, Mr. MacGregor during the Second Reading debate. (*House of Commons Parliamentary Debates. Weekly Hansard*, Vol. 3, col. 848 (29 April 1981). See also statement by French Ministre de la Mer reported in *Journal de la marine marchande*, 24 September 1981, p.2278.

[77] See further Chap.4, section VIII, which also indicates how these provisions were radically transformed by the Implementation Agreement.

[78] In Chap. 6, section II.1.4. For later modification by the Implementation Agreement, see also Chap.6, section IV.1.4.

[79] Under Resolution II, para. 7(b).

[80] See further above, Chap.6, section III.8(v).

262   *Chapter 7*

The US Act[81] imposed a tax of 3.75 per cent of the imputed value of the resource removed.[82] Imputed value was defined as 20 per cent of the fair market value of the commercially recoverable metals and minerals contained in such a resource as at the date of removal and assuming that the metals and minerals were separated from the resource and in the most basic form for which there was a readily ascertainable market price.[83] Under section 4498(a), the tax would not be payable on any removal after (1) an international deep sea-bed treaty[84] entered into force for the United States, or (2) 10 years after the date of enactment of 'this sub-chapter',[85] whichever was earlier.

At first sight, the German provision looks quite different. Under section 12, the contractor would pay an annual fee of 0.75 per cent of the average market price in that particular year for the metals and minerals in their simplest commercial processing forms which are recovered from the mineral resources mined. In fact, however, the levy is at approximately the same level in the two Acts, 3.75 per cent of 20 per cent being equal to 0.75 per cent. The point is clarified in the legislative record of the British Bill.[86]

Section 9 of the UK Act provided that the licensee would pay (a) 3.75 per cent of the value of the unprocessed nodules. Since, however, the ascertainment of a suitable market price would be possible only when there was free trade in nodules as such, alternative (b) provided for payment of 0.75 per cent of the value of the recovered products.

Inevitably, Parliamentary defenders of the common heritage of mankind attacked these provisions and asked why the rates specified were of the order of 50 per cent below the rates established in what was then the Draft Convention. Spokesmen for the mining companies, examined before the Special Standing Committee during the passage through Parliament of the UK Bill, acknowledged that these rates were acceptable to them.[87]   They added, however, that the financial terms to be imposed on contractors under the Convention would only be acceptable if it were understood that they would not also be subject to national taxation.[88] It was apparent that the British Government – and no doubt the American and German Governments before it – had relied heavily on advice from the industry and that the companies were happy with the Government's policy.[89] Seeking to justify these relatively low rates, the Minister argued:

(i)   that it was undesirable to impose a heavier burden on British companies than that imposed on American and German companies;

(ii)   that lower levies were appropriate in an interim period when the companies did not enjoy the more favourable operating conditions in terms of long term security which an international convention would offer them;

---

[81] See 'Title IV - Tax' of the original US Act of 1980, s. 402 of which added a new Subchapter F, consisting of ss. 4495-4498 to Chap. 36 of the Internal Revenue Code 1954.

[82] *Ibid.*, s.4495.

[83] *Ibid.*, s.4497.

[84] The term 'international deep sea-bed treaty' is defined in s. 4498(b).

[85] The subchapter referred to is that cited in note 81 above. The date of enactment was 28 June 1980.

[86] See Mr. MacGregor in *loc.cit.* in note 21, cols. 7 and 245-246.

[87] *Ibid.*, cols. 131 and 142.

[88] *Ibid.*, col.131.

[89] *Ibid.*

(iii) that the payment under the Convention had been set at a higher level to meet the enormously greater expenses of the Authority and of the Enterprise, as well as to provide a royalty for the international community as a whole.[90]

Bearing in mind that the Authority would be able to distribute to the international community only the balance of its income remaining after payment of its administrative expenses,[91] this was a persuasive argument.

Article 12 of the French Law[92] and Article 15 of the Italian Law[93] adopted the same 3.75 per cent rate of levy as the three earlier Acts.

1.7.2 International Revenue-Sharing Funds

As has been seen, the Reciprocating States claimed that their legislation was compatible with the UN regime. The principal evidence usually offered in support of such contentions was the provision made in the unilateral legislation for sharing the proceeds of deep-sea mining with the international community through the establishment of a fund made up of the levies reviewed above. Thus, when the German Bill was published, it purported to be 'a contribution to the development of the common heritage of mankind' and 'not in contradiction to the common heritage principle'. 'As a concrete result, Section 13 establishes a trust fund ... which is to be put at the disposal of the international community.'[94]

Similar sentiments were expressed by a British Minister during the passage of the UK Act. Mr. MacGregor sought to demonstrate his Government's 'good intent towards the wider international community and, in particular, to developing countries, through the raising of the levy'. He argued that, ' ... without the interim legislation and the levy proposed in clause 9, there would be no bounty to pass on to the International Sea Bed Authority when the convention comes into force'. They were, he said, 'allowing the possibility of passing on a bounty to the convention when it is set up. Therefore, we are trying to get some activity prior to the setting up of the convention and to raise some revenue ready to be transferred. In that respect it is a bonus.'![95]

Again, mention may be made of one of the purposes of the American Act, as expressed in section 2(b)(2):

> to provide for the establishment of an international revenue-sharing fund the proceeds of which shall be used for sharing with the international community pursuant to such Treaty.

The French Minister for the Sea also declared his Government's intention of setting up an overseas development fund based on deep-sea mining levies[96], and such a 'Fund for the participation of developing countries in the resources of the deep sea-bed' was in fact established in 1982.[97]

---

[90] *Ibid.*, cols, cols.7 and 249-251.

[91] See further below, section 1.7.2.

[92] *Loc. cit.* in note 5.

[93] *Loc. cit.* in note 7.

[94] *Statement of Reasons. I. General Considerations.*

[95] *Loc. cit.* in note 21, col. 251.

[96] *Loc. cit.* in note 76.

[97] Finance Law 1982, Arts.52 and 65; English translation reproduced in Vol. 3 as Doc. No. 29.4.

264   Chapter 7

The provisions of the Italian Law were similar, the 3.75% levy being imposed 'for the purposes of the Italian Aid to the Developing Countries'.[98]

These being the five Governments' good intentions, how was effect to be given to them under the operative provisions of the Acts?; and how did these provisions compare with the revenue-sharing system incorporated in the Convention? Before turning to consider these questions, a brief reminder must be given of the relevant provisions of the Convention.[99] Under Article 140, deep-sea mining is to be conducted for the benefit of mankind as a whole and taking into particular consideration the interests and needs of developing States and of peoples who have not attained full independence or other self-governing status. The Authority is responsible for providing for the equitable sharing of financial and other economic benefits derived from such activities in accordance with Article 160(2)(f)(i). The mechanisms have to be approved by the Assembly on the recommendation of the Council. Finally, reference should be made to Articles 171 and 173 which govern the collection and distribution of the Authority's funds. These funds include sums transferred from the Enterprise, receipts from contractors mining the deep sea-bed and payments to a compensation fund for land-based mineral producers. After payment of administrative expenses, the Authority's funds may be:

(i)   distributed for the benefit of mankind as indicated above;
(ii) used to provide the Enterprise with Funds; and
(iii) used to compensate developing States for damage done to their economies as a result of the impact of deep-sea mining on the mineral market.

Against this background it is now possible to review and compare the corresponding provisions of the five statutes.

The US Act established a trust fund in the Treasury to be known as the 'Deep Sea-bed Revenue Sharing Trust Fund',[100] into which were to be paid the levies described above. It will be recalled that such levies were to be payable during, at most, the 10-year period commencing from the date of enactment, that is until 28 June 1990.[101] Annual reports were to be made to Congress by the Secretary of the Treasury and provision was made for investment of available portions of the Trust Fund.

So far as the common heritage is concerned, however, it was the provision made for expenditure from the Trust Fund which was most important and it must be said that the provisions of section 403(d) and (e) were hardly likely to inspire the Group of 77 with confidence in the good intentions of the United States. This section envisaged two alternative situations. If the Convention had been in force for the United States by 28 June 1990, the Trust Fund would have been available 'for making contributions required under such treaty for purposes of the sharing among nations of the revenues from deep sea-bed mining'. Given the fact that the treaty was not in force for the United States by that date, the alternative provision applied. It provided simply that 'amounts in the Trust Fund shall be available for such purposes as Congress may hereafter provide by law'.

---

[98] Art.15.

[99] For full details of these provisions, see Chap. 3, section I, especially '5.3.7 Distribution of the benefit of mankind'.

[100] S.403.

[101] See text above at note 85.

UN regime v reciprocating State regime 265

Thus, to sum up, the US Act provided for the establishment of a Fund fed by a tax on deep-sea mining, leviable until, at the latest, 1990. If, by 1990, the Convention had not entered into force for the United States, there was no specific commitment as to how the Trust Fund would be used. Even section 2(b)(2),[102] in setting out the purposes of the Act, spoke of 'sharing with the international community *pursuant to such Treaty*' (emphasis added).

The UK Act too was short on commitment. Section 10 provided for the establishment of a Deep Sea Mining Fund in the Treasury, into which the levies described above were to be paid. As noted earlier, no such levies were to be payable before 1 January 1988, when the first exploitation licenses could have taken effect. As in the US Act, provision was made for annual Treasury reports and for investment of the Fund.[103] Again, following the American model, the UK Act provided both for the entry into force for the UK of the UN Convention and for the contingency that it would not have done so within ten years of the coming into force of section 10.

If the Convention had entered into force for the UK within the ten-year period, provision would have been made under section 10(6) 'for the payment to [the designated international] ... organisation of any sums for the time being standing to the credit of the Fund'. However, since the whole Act entered into force on 25 January 1982 and the ten-year period therefore expired on 25 January 1992 without the entry into force of the Convention, there was no question of having to make such a payment. Nor, indeed, would there have been any funds to transfer since commercial exploitation had not yet taken place. The Act went on to provide that, if the Convention had not entered into force for the UK by the date specified (25 January 1992), the Fund may be wound up and section 9 (containing the levy system) repealed. No such order, which would require the approval of the Treasury and of the House of Commons,[104] has yet been made.

The Minister was pressed by the Opposition to be more generous in drafting these contingency arrangements. It was proposed, for example, that the Secretary of State might be empowered to 'provide for the application of any sums standing to the credit of the Fund to purposes identified by Her Majesty's Government as constituting overseas development aid'.[105] The Government was not to be moved, however, taking its stand on the long-established Treasury principle that revenue funds should not be hypothecated.[106] The Minister held out the hope 'that the money might go for development aid purposes, or something of that sort',[107] but he would go no further.

Next, how well does the German Act stand up to scrutiny? Certainly, on the surface at least, it was drafted in more generous terms. Section 13 provided:

> The Federal Government shall be authorised to transfer the trust fund to the international sea-bed authority after entry into force of an international agreement on deep sea-bed mining for the Federal Republic of Germany. Up to that time the trust fund shall be invested for foreign aid purposes.

While, no doubt, this formula would still have allowed the German Government to keep its total foreign aid bill steady by cutting back on funds which might

---

[102] See text above following note 95.
[103] S.10(2) and (9).
[104] S.10(7) and (8).
[105] *Loc. cit.* in note 21, col. 253.
[106] *Ibid.*, col. 255 (Mr. MacGregor).
[107] *Ibid.*

266   *Chapter 7*

otherwise have been made available, at least it was a much clearer indication of the Government's positive attitude than was to be found in either the American or the British Acts.

So far as the French Law is concerned, it will be recalled that a 'Fund for the participation of developing countries in the resources of the deep sea-bed' was set up in 1982.[108] However, as regards expenditure from the fund, Article 65 refers simply to 'payments by France in respect of public development aid'.

Finally, although, as has been seen,[109] the Italian Law clearly provided that the 3.75% levy was for the purpose of Italian aid to developing States, the law itself did not specify how the resulting fund was to be allocated to developing States.

1.8 Transfer of Technology

An analysis of the obligations originally imposed upon parties to the UN Convention and sea-bed mining contractors to transfer sea-bed mining technology to the developing States and the Enterprise has been given above.[110] Especially in view of the breadth of the definition of the technology which there would have been an obligation upon the operator to transfer, these undertakings might well have represented a significant part of the cost to the contractor of operating under the Convention regime, both in terms of direct costs and the indirect cost of placing the licensee's competitors in a relatively advantageous position. It is hardly a matter for surprise, therefore, to find that none of the six Acts under consideration exhibited its 'compatibility' with the UN regime by including among its provisions an obligation to transfer technology.

It has to be admitted that the formulation of workable provisions on the transfer of technology for incorporation in unilateral legislation would be exceedingly difficult. Some of the difficulties were alluded to during the passage of the British Bill through Parliament. The Opposition tried to amend the Bill in two respects in order to help the developing States to acquire technological know-how and hardware. The effect of the amendments would have been to empower the Secretary of State to include among the terms and conditions of a deep-sea mining licence, first, a term 'prescribing arrangements for the transfer of sea-bed technology to developing countries which apply to the Secretary of State for it' and, secondly, a term 'specifying the need to apply all reasonable endeavours to include in the operations personnel, finance and management from the developing nations'.[111]

As so often in these proceedings, the Minister was able to resist these amendments on the safe ground that to accept them would be to place British companies at a competitive disadvantage as compared with companies operating under, for example, American or German legislation, which included no such burdens.[112] He also sought to disarm his critics, however, with a rather more subtle argument. He accepted the UNCLOS aim of providing the Enterprise with the finance, technology and expertise necessary to permit it to operate a parallel system effectively from the outset, as soon as the Convention entered into force.[113] He argued, however, that the Government could most effectively secure

---

[108] Above, text at note 97.
[109] Above, text at note 98.
[110] See Chap. 3, section VIII and, in relation to obligations placed upon pioneer investors under Resolution II, Chap.6, section II.1.5.
[111] *Loc. cit.* in note 21, col. 176.
[112] *Ibid.*, col. 182 (Mr. MacGregor).
[113] *Ibid.*, col.182.

that end by encouraging British mining companies to continue with this expensive and risky development work. He went so far as to say that:

> We are keen to get the Bill on the statute book quickly and to enable the new interim arrangement to come into force so that when the convention comes into force and the Enterprise is established the technology will be ready, developed and tested and available for transfer to the Enterprise under the convention's terms.[114]

In speaking in these terms, the Minister was able to rely on the evidence given before the Special Standing Committee by representatives of the mining companies. Apart from expressing concern about the cost of transferring technology and the feasibility of transferring technological know-how which is the product of many years of experience, the companies also expressed anxiety about being blamed for the performance of only partly tested technology operated by the relatively inexperienced hands of the Enterprise.[115]

No doubt, there is much truth in these arguments. The fact remains, however, that operations conducted under Reciprocating States legislation prior to the entry into force of the Convention for the State concerned would have been unencumbered by these costs.

1.9 Other Important Provisions of the UN Regime

A comprehensive comparison of the legislation of the Reciprocating States with the UN regime would have to cover not only those aspects, reviewed above, concerned with what might be called the business aspects of deep-sea mining, but also a number of less central issues such as the provision made for the protection of scientific research, the protection of the environment and the settlement of disputes.

So far as the protection of scientific research is concerned, an analysis of the provisions of the UN Convention has been provided in Chapter 3[116] and there is little to add as regards the legislation of the Reciprocating States. All six States made it clear that they were not asserting claims to sovereignty or sovereign rights over the deep sea-bed and that mining operations must be conducted with reasonable regard to the interests of other persons in their exercise of the freedom of the high seas.[117] It would follow that freedom of scientific research in the Area would have been respected to the extent to which it was compatible with the exclusive rights of licensees operating under national legislation. Moreover, in some cases, specific reference was made to protection of the freedom of scientific research.[118] On the other hand, none of the statutes made any provision for the promotion of international co-operation in marine scientific research in the Area, as called for in Article 143(3) of the UN Convention.

As regards protection of the environment, a full analysis of both the UN regime and of national legislation is given in Chapter 10. As will be seen, the provisions of national legislation reflected a serious attempt by the States

---

[114] *Ibid.*, col.183.
[115] *Ibid.*, cols. 139-140 and 181-183.
[116] Chap. 3, section VII.
[117] See US Act, ss. 2(a)(12), 3(a), 101(a)(2)(A) and 111; German Act, s. 1(1), 1(2), 3(2) and 5(3); UK Act, ss. 1(6) and 7 and Deep Sea Mining (Exploration Licences) Regulations 1984, S.I. 1984/1230, Schedule, cl.19(1); French Law, Art. 1; Japanese Law, Art. 1(2); and Italian Law, Art. 3.
[118] US Act, s. 101(a)(2)(A); UK 1984 Regulations, Schedule, cl.19(1); French Law, Art. 1; and Italian Law, Art. 3.

268   Chapter 7

concerned to ensure that the environmental impact of deep-sea mining should be reduced to a minimum.

Finally, there is the question of settlement of disputes. It will suffice to say that the elaborate provision made for the settlement of disputes in the UN Convention, reviewed in Chapter 9, had no counterpart in the legislation of the Reciprocating States. Disputes arising under the national legislation of a particular State can of course be settled by the courts of that State or by arbitration.[119] So far as international disputes are concerned, however, with the exception of the two treaties concluded in 1982 and 1984 referred to in section III below, no specific provision was made for dispute settlement.

III. THE CO-ORDINATION OF THE LEGISLATION OF THE RECIPROCATING STATES

As was noted in the introduction to this chapter, the Reciprocating States Regime includes not only the legislation of the Reciprocating States but also the treaty arrangements for the co-ordination of this legislation. In Chapter 6, a brief account has already been given of the essential features of the two agreements concluded in 1982 and 1984 and an examination has been made of the compatibility of the 1984 Agreement with the UN Convention regime.[120] As was seen, the suspicions of the Group of 77 that the so-called 'interim' statutes might in fact turn out to be a permanent alternative regime for sea-bed mining were only heightened by the conclusion of these agreements.[121] It is clearly necessary, therefore, before arriving at a judgment on the impact of this unilateral legislation and of the compatibility of the Reciprocating States Regime with the UN regime, to provide a more detailed analysis of these two co-ordinating agreements.

1. The Agreement Concerning Interim Arrangements Relating to Polymetallic Nodules of the Deep Sea Bed, 1982[122]

This agreement was, from the beginning, of very limited scope both *ratione personae* and *ratione materiae* and its significance was further reduced subsequently by an apparent change of policy on the desirability of mutual recognition of national mining authorisations. However, it still deserves notice as reflecting the intentions of its States Parties as they were in 1982.

1.1 Scope of Agreement ratione personae

The Agreement was concluded between four States, France, Germany, the United Kingdom and the United States. Only France subsequently signed the UN Convention. Provision was made for the issue of invitations to other States to accede to the Agreement[123] but no such invitations appear to have been issued.

---

[119] See, *e.g.*, UK Act, ss. 14 and 15 and 1984 Regulations, Schedule, cl.23 and cl.24; and Japanese Law, Art. 28.

[120] See Chap.6, sections III.4.2 and III.4.4.

[121] See Introduction to this Chapter.

[122] XXI ILM (1982), pp.950-962; UK Treaty Series No.46 (1982), Cmnd.8685; text reproduced in Vol.3 as Doc. No. 33.1.

[123] Para.12.

1.2 Scope of Agreement ratione temporis
The Agreement entered into force on signature on 2 September 1982[124] and was for an unlimited period, though subject to denunciation on thirty days notice.[125]

1.3 Scope of Agreement ratione materiae
The limited object of the Agreement, as laid down in Paragraph 1, was to facilitate the identification and resolution of conflicts which might arise from the filing and processing of applications for sea-bed mining authorisations made by Pre-Enactment Explorers (PEEs) on or before 12 March 1982, under the legislation of any of the parties. PEEs were defined as entities engaged, prior to the earliest date of enactment of domestic legislation by any party, in deep sea-bed polymetallic nodule exploration by substantial surveying activity with respect to the area applied for.[126] However, the parties also agreed to consult together 'in regard to consideration of any arrangement to facilitate mutual recognition' of authorisations[127] and, as will be seen below, Paragraph 5 also referred to the possible conclusion by parties of agreements 'for the mutual recognition of authorisations granted under their respective laws in respect of deep sea-bed operations'.

That it was indeed the intention of the parties to grant mutual recognition of authorisations was confirmed by, for example, the making of a series of orders by the British Government in 1982, whereby France, Germany and the United States were designated as reciprocating countries[128]. These orders were to come into operation upon the entry into force of agreements between the United Kingdom and these three States 'with respect to the recognition of licences' issued by each country.[129] Rather late in the day, it seems to have been realised that any such recognition was very difficult to reconcile with the protestations of the Reciprocating States that their interim legislation was fully compatible with the UN regime. As a result, no mutual recognition treaties were entered into and the British orders were revoked and replaced by a new order in 1984 which designated the United Kingdom's three treaty partners and Japan as reciprocating countries, but with no reference to recognition of authorisations.[130]

Unfortunately, as will be seen, one result of this change of policy was that the provisions in the 1982 Agreement for the resolution of international conflicts became inoperable.

1.4 Identification and Resolution of Conflicts
Paragraph 3 of the Agreement, read with Part I of the Schedule, laid down a procedure whereby, once applications had been processed domestically, a final combined list of all PEE applications would be established and the exact locations of any conflicting applications determined.

Whether the conflict was domestic or international, the parties to the Agreement undertook to afford the applicants adequate opportunity, and to encourage them, to resolve the conflict 'in a timely manner by voluntary

---

[124] Under para.11.
[125] Para.13.
[126] Schedule, Part IV, para. 11(d).
[127] Para.4(c).
[128] S.I. 1982/176, S.I. 1982/177 and S.I. 1982/178.
[129] Art. 1 of each order.
[130] Deep Sea Mining (Reciprocating Countries) Order 1984, S.I 1984/1170. It may be noted that under Art. 16 of the Italian Law of 1985 (loc.cit. in note 7), a State would have been recognised by Italy as a reciprocating State only if it recognised the permits issued in accordance with the Italian Law.

270   *Chapter 7*

procedures'.[131] Domestic conflicts were to be resolved pursuant to the 'domestic requirements' of the State concerned, though the applicants might agree to employ the international conflict resolution procedures laid down in the Agreement.[132] As regards international conflicts, Paragraph 5 prescribed that:

> In the event that any of the Parties with whom applications for authorisations have been made by PEEs on or before March 12, 1982 enter into an agreement *for the mutual recognition of authorisations* granted under their respective laws in respect of deep sea bed operations, the Parties concerned shall apply the procedures and impose the requirements set out in Part II of the Schedule hereto.[133]

Inter alia, the Schedule provided for the resolution of international conflicts through the good offices of the States Parties or, at the instance of any party and in the absence of agreement on any other binding conflict resolution procedure, by binding arbitration in accordance with a prescribed arbitration procedure and on the basis of prescribed principles for resolution of conflict.[134] However, since, for the reasons explained above, no such agreements to recognise authorisations ever materialised, these provision for the resolution of international conflict became a dead letter. Needless to say, the significance of the Agreement was considerably reduced as a result.

1.5 Compatibility of Agreement with UN Regime

The Agreement was one 'concerning interim arrangements' and in its Preamble 'recalls' the 'interim character' of the legislation of the parties. The Preamble made it clear too that the object was to avoid overlaps among pioneer areas and to ensure that, 'during the interim period, pioneer activities will be carried out in an orderly and peaceful manner.' Moreover, it was emphasised that the Agreement was without prejudice to the decisions of the parties with respect to the UN Convention.[135] Finally, the parties expressed their desire 'to ensure that adequate areas containing polymetallic nodules remain available for operations by other states and entities in conformity with international law'.[136] The fact remains, however, that the Agreement envisaged the grant of mutual recognitions of authorisations. Furthermore, the establishment of the conflict resolution procedures, together with the undertakings to consult before issuing any authorisation[137] and not to issue any authorisation before 3 January 1983,[138] clearly implied that conflicting authorisations would not be granted. For the reasons given above in Chapter 6 in relation to the 1984 Provisional Understanding, such undertakings must be regarded as tantamount to implied recognition of other States' authorisations and as being incompatible with the UN regime.[139]

---

[131] Agreement, para. 2.
[132] Schedule, Part I, para. 7.
[133] Emphasis added.
[134] Schedule, Part II, para. 9 and Appendices 1 and 2.
[135] *Ibid.*
[136] *Ibid.*
[137] Agreement, para 4(b).
[138] Schedule, Part I, para. 5.
[139] See Chap. 6, section III.4.4.

UN regime v reciprocating State regime 271

2. The Provisional Understanding Regarding Deep Sea-bed Matters, 1984 [140]

As has been seen, the 1982 Agreement was of very limited scope both *ratione personae* and *ratione materiae*. The Provisional Understanding Regarding Deep Sea-bed Matters and the related Memorandum on the Implementation of the Understanding[141], signed on the same day, 3 August 1984, was of much wider scope, extending beyond the avoidance of overlaps to the co-ordination of national legislation and the prescription of common standards to be observed by licensees in conducting deep sea-bed operations.

2.1 Scope of Provisional Understanding ratione personae

The Provisional Understanding was concluded among eight States, including, as at the date of signature, three signatories of the UN Convention (France, Japan and the Netherlands) and five non-signatories (Belgium, Germany, Italy, the United Kingdom and the United States). Belgium and Italy subsequently signed the UN Convention. Under Paragraph 13, additional States could be invited to accede to the Agreement after its entry into force.

The Memorandum on Implementation was signed by the same eight States, with one exception, the Netherlands.[142]

2.2 Scope of Provisional Understanding ratione temporis

The Provisional Understanding was signed on 3 August 1984 and entered into force for the majority of the parties thirty days later on 2 September 1984. Under Paragraph 12, signatories lacking the necessary legal provisions for the issue of sea-bed mining authorisations, could, by a declaration upon signature, limit the application of the agreement to parts other than those concerned with the issue of authorisations. Belgium, Italy and the Netherlands made such declarations but Italy's sea-bed mining legislation subsequently entered into force.

The Provisional Understanding was without limit of time but was subject to denunciation on 180 days notice.[143] What amounted to partial denunciation was also permitted by Paragraph 14(2). For 'good cause related to the implementation of this Agreement', a party could serve notice on another party that it would cease to give effect to Paragraph 1 of the agreement, that is, the rules designed to prevent overlapping of sea-bed mining claims, by prohibiting authorisations or requests for registration in specified cases. Such denunciations would not, however, affect the rights and obligations of the parties concerned towards other parties to the agreement.[144]

2.3 Scope of Provisional Understanding ratione materiae
2.3.1 Prohibition of Conflicting Authorisations or Registrations

Paragraph 1 of the agreement sought to avoid the creation of overlaps among the sea-bed sites in which deep sea-bed operations had been authorised under national legislation. Prior to the conclusion of the Provisional Understanding, six of the pioneer consortia (excluding only the public enterprises of the Soviet Union, India and the Peoples Republic of China) entered into agreements for voluntary conflict resolution on 18 May 1983 and 15 December 1983.[145] The

---

[140] XXIII ILM (1984), pp.1354-1360; text reproduced in Vol.3 as Doc.No. 33.3.
[141] *Ibid.*
[142] XXIII ILM (1984), p. 1358.
[143] Para.14(1).
[144] Para. 14(2).
[145] These agreements were referred to in para. 1(1)(a) of the Provisional Understanding.

272   *Chapter 7*

Provisional Understanding reflects the recognition by eight of the States whose nationals participated in these agreements (Canada alone being excepted) of the need to assure on the Governmental level the results of these consortia agreements.[146] Paragraph 1 accordingly provided that no party could issue an authorisation to engage in sea-bed operations in an area which overlapped, in whole or part, with another area falling into one or other of the following three categories:

(i) an area covered in another application filed under the consortia agreements referred to above and still under consideration by another party;

(ii) an area claimed in any other application filed in conformity with national law and the Provisional Understanding either prior to signature of the Provisional Understanding or earlier than the application in question, if still under consideration by another party;

(iii) an area covered by an authorisation issued by another party in conformity with the Provisional Understanding.

The prohibition covered not only the issue of 'authorisations' but also the seeking of registration, defined in Appendix I as meaning 'any registration or other act by an authority which is recognised or accepted by the party in question as conferring any right or authorisation to engage in deep sea-bed operations'.

The agreements for voluntary conflict resolution referred to above were entered into by the following six consortia: Association Française pour l'Etude et la Recherche des Nodules (AFERNOD), Deep Ocean Resources Development Co., Ltd. (DORD), the Kennecott Consortium (KCON), Ocean Mining Associates (OMA), Ocean Minerals Company (OMCO), Ocean Management, Inc. (OMI).[147] Although the German consortium, Arbeitsgemeinschaft meerestechnisch gewinnbare Rohstoffe (AMR), was not a party to these voluntary agreements, the parties to the Provisional Understanding noted in a Joint Record of the same date as the Provisional Understanding that the AMR application fell under category (ii) above.[148] They did so after receiving an assurance from the German Government that the area applied for by AMR fell outside the Clarion Clipperton Zone.[149]

Paragraph 1(2) of the Provisional Understanding closed a possible loophole by further prohibiting the States Parties themselves from engaging in deep sea-bed operations in an area for which, under Paragraph 1(1), it was not permitted to issue an authorisation or seek registration.

2.3.2 Co-ordination of National Legislation and Prescription of Operating Standards

As indicated above, the Provisional Understanding was concerned not only with the limited objective of preventing the issue of overlapping authorisations. More comprehensively, it provided a framework for the establishment of a Reciprocating States Regime which called for the co-ordination of national law and practice in a number of respects:-

Application requirements. The law and practice of the States Parties as regards applications for sea-bed mining authorisations were co-ordinated in relation to, first, processing of applications, secondly, eligibility of applicants and, thirdly, the size of areas for which authorisations might be granted.

---

[146] See above Chap. 6, section III.4.4.
[147] Provisional Understanding, Appendix I.
[148] Joint Record, XXIII ILM (1984), p. 1360.
[149] *Ibid.*

Under Paragraph 8, parties had to seek consistency in their application requirements and, under Paragraph 2, had to, as far as possible, process applications without delay. Accordingly, they had first, 'with reasonable dispatch', to make an initial examination of each application to determine its compliance with requirements for minimum content under its national law. Thereafter, they had to determine the applicant's eligibility for the issuance of an authorisation.

The criteria of eligibility were laid down in Paragraph 1 of the Memorandum on Implementation. Authorisations were to be issued (or transferred) only to applicants:

(a) which [were] financially and technologically qualified to conduct the proposed deep sea-bed operations;
(b) which [complied] with all the requirements of the Party's national law; and
(c) whose deep sea-bed operations [would] be carried out in accordance with the standards prescribed below.

Moreover, consultation had to take place prior to the issuance or transfer of a licence to an applicant who had previously been denied an authorisation or had an authorisation revoked for the same area by another State Party, or who had relinquished the same area under an authorisation of another party.

The size of the area for which an authorisation might be granted was to be limited by the need to ensure that:

the deep sea-bed operations authorised can be conducted within the initial duration of the authorisation in an efficient, economic and orderly manner with due regard for conservation and protection of the environment, taking into consideration, as appropriate, the resource data, other relevant physical and environmental characteristics and the state of technology of the applicant, as set forth in the plan of operations.[150]

Compliance with this requirement was verifiable, since a party might be called upon to provide a written statement of reasons why it had approved an application area of a particular size.[151]

Standards. As noted above, authorisations could be issued only to applicants whose deep sea-bed operations would be carried out in accordance with prescribed standards and, under Paragraph 8 of the Provisional Understanding, the parties undertook to seek consistency in operating standards. The standards themselves and the means for their enforcement were prescribed in Paragraphs 3 and 4 of the Memorandum on Implementation. Each State Party had to take all necessary measures so that deep sea-bed operations under its control would comply with the following standards:

- *Freedom of the seas.* Operations to be conducted with reasonable regard to the interests of other States in the exercise of the freedom of the high seas.[152]
- *Protection of environment.* Operations to include efforts to protect the quality of the environment, not to result in significant adverse effects on

---

[150] Memorandum on Implementation, para. 2(1).

[151] *Ibid.*, para.2(2).

[152] *Ibid.*, para.3(1)(a).

274　*Chapter 7*

- the environment[153] and to be monitored for their effects on the environment.[154]
- *Conservation.* Operations to have due regard for the prevention of waste and the future opportunity for the commercial recovery of the unrecovered balance of the hard mineral resources in the authorisation area.[155]
- *Safety at sea.* Operations not adversely to affect the safety of life and property at sea in accordance with generally accepted international standards.[156]
- *Diligence.* Operations to be conducted diligently by maintaining a reasonable level of operation based on the size of area and other relevant factors.[157]
- *Non-interference.* Parties to ensure that persons under their jurisdiction minimise interference with any activity authorised under an authorisation issued by another party.[158]

Clearly, these operating standards, which reflected those incorporated in the legislation reviewed above, were stated in very broad, general terms. However, States Parties undertook to co-operate in developing measures, consistent with their national laws, needed to implement the provisions of the Provisional Understanding and the Memorandum on Implementation. They had to do so in such a manner that the measures developed would be, in general function and effect, compatible with, comparable to, and as effective as those established by the other parties.[159]

To enforce these standards effectively, the parties agreed that they would employ:

> as appropriate, measures such as: imposing reasonable penalties for violation of requirements; placing observers on vessels to monitor compliance; suspending, revoking, or modifying authorisations; and, issuing orders in an emergency to prevent a significant adverse effect on the environment or to preserve the safety of life and property at sea.[160]

No exploitation before 1988. The understanding in Paragraph 4 not to authorise or engage in exploitation of the hard mineral resources of the deep seabed before 1 January 1988 was of course in line with the provisions of the unilateral legislation of the Reciprocating States reviewed above.

Notification and consultation. The Provisional Understanding sought to ensure close co-ordination of the practice of the parties by providing for notification and consultation on a range of issues.[161] They included consultations prior to the issuance of any authorisation and with regard to 'relevant legal provisions and any modifications thereof'.[162]

---

[153] *Ibid.*, para.3(1)(b).
[154] *Ibid.*, para.3(1)(f).
[155] *Ibid.*, para.3(1)(c).
[156] *Ibid.*, para.3(1)(d).
[157] *Ibid.*, para.3(1)(e).
[158] *Ibid.*, para.3(2).
[159] *Ibid.*, para.3(3).
[160] *Ibid.*, para.4.
[161] Provisional Understanding, paras. 3 and 5.
[162] *Ibid.*, para.5(a) and (c).

Confidentiality. Provision was made in Paragraph 6 of the Provisional Understanding for the confidentiality of the co-ordinates of application areas and other proprietary or confidential commercial information to be maintained.

Dispute settlement. It was no doubt hoped that the provision made for consultation and notification would largely prevent disputes from arising over the interpretation or application of the agreement. However, Paragraph 10 did lay down a dispute settlement procedure, though it was extremely loose. Parties were required to settle any dispute over the interpretation or application of the Agreement by 'appropriate means'. The only 'means' referred to was binding arbitration, but the obligation was simply 'to consider the possibilities of having recourse to binding arbitration and, if they agree,' to have recourse to it.

2.4 Compatibility of Provisional Understanding with UN Regime

Paragraph 15 of the Provisional Understanding declared that:

> This Agreement is without prejudice to, nor does it affect, the position of the Parties, or any obligations assumed by any of the Parties, in respect of the United Nations Convention on the Law of the Sea.

However, as was seen in Chapter 6, where the question of the compatibility of the Provisional Understanding with the UN regime was considered in detail[163], there are serious grounds for arguing that an agreement not to issue authorisations in respect of areas for which authorisations have been issued by non-parties to the UN Convention, whose known intention is to exploit their mineral resources outside the Convention regime, amounts to a breach of both the letter and spirit of the UN Convention.

IV. THE INCOMPATIBILITY OF THE TWO REGIMES

Having reviewed the substance of the legislation and the co-ordinating treaty practice of the Reciprocating States and compared it with the original provisions of the UN Convention regime, it is now possible to return to the questions raised at the beginning of this chapter: to what extent did the essential provisions of the Convention regime and the Reciprocating States Regime differ, and was it true that the operation of a Reciprocating States Regime, either during an interim period prior to the entry into force of the Convention or on a semi-permanent basis, would have been tantamount to a denial of the fundamental principle that deep-sea minerals are the common heritage of mankind?

1. The Differences between the Two Regimes

On the basis of the above analysis, the answer to the first question is quite clear. There were very substantial differences between the essential provisions of the two regimes. Summing up, the principal differences were as follows:

Unilateralism.[164] The most fundamental difference was that the Reciprocating States Regime was based on the assumption that it was lawful and compatible with the common heritage doctrine to exploit the resources of the Area under unilateral legislation. The UN regime, on the other hand, prohibited the unilateral approach.

---

[163] Chap. 5, section III.4.4.
[164] See further above, section II.1.1.

276   Chapter 7

Temporal scope.[165]   In assessing the compatibility of the two regimes, it is important to determine how long the interim regime might have been expected to last. Unfortunately, as has been seen, the temporal scope of the Reciprocating States Regime was indeterminate. Moreover, it seemed likely that, had States proceeded under their own less onerous unilateral legislation, they would have found it increasingly difficult as time went by to abandon the Reciprocating States Regime in favour of the UN regime.

Beneficiaries of the two regimes.[166] The Reciprocating States Regime provided a favourable legal regime for the exploitation of deep-sea minerals by nationals of Reciprocating States and was therefore highly discriminatory as compared with the UN regime, with its emphasis on the preferential position of the developing States. Although the security of tenure offered by these instruments was by no means absolute, it was nonetheless substantial. On the other hand, the difference between the two regimes was significantly reduced by the concessions granted to the pioneer investor under Resolution II and extended further by the Preparatory Commission.[167]

Site-banking.[168]   As has been seen, a British Minister held out the possibility that provision might be made for site-banking (reservation of sites for exploitation by the Enterprise and/or developing States) through subordinate legislation if, as a *quid pro quo*, agreement could be reached on adequate protection for preliminary investment in the closing sessions of UNCLOS III.[169] The fact remains, however, that no such provision was ever made.

Anti-monopoly provisions.[170] Although all six States had provisions to ensure that licensees would develop their holdings with due diligence, none of them paid any attention to the anti-monopoly provisions of the Convention which limited the total areas which could be held by nationals of any one State.

Production control.[171]   Nor did the six Reciprocating States see fit to impose any production controls.

Financial terms and revenue-sharing funds.[172]   Here too there were radical differences between the two regimes. The levies chargeable under the national legislation were about half of those prescribed in the Convention. It has been suggested that there may have been a reasonable case for setting levies at a lower rate during a risky and expensive interim period. However, any such argument has to be treated with great caution, not only because the duration of the interim was unknown but also because the licensee might at the same time have been avoiding the additional costs of site-banking, anti-monopoly provisions, production controls and obligations to transfer technology.

Transfer of technology.[173] As has been seen, the Reciprocating States made no provision for the transfer of technology. This was of course in line with the virtual restriction of mining opportunities under the Acts to nationals of the Reciprocating States. The difficulties of including provision for transfer of technology in unilateral legislation of this sort are not to be underestimated but

---

[165] See further above, section II.1.2.
[166] See further above, section II.1.3.
[167] See further above, Chap.6, section III.
[168] See further above, section II.1.4.
[169] *Ibid.*, text, at note 50.
[170] See further above, section II.1.5.
[171] See further above, section II.1.6.
[172] See further above, section II.1.7.
[173] See further above, section II.1.8.

UN regime v reciprocating State regime 277

this does not alter the inescapable result that mining taking place under the interim legislation would have unencumbered by this cost.

Dispute settlement.[174] As compared with the elaborate provision made for the settlement of sea-bed mining disputes in the UN regime, the references to dispute settlement in the Reciprocating States Regime were very sparse.

2. A Denial of the Common Heritage Principle?

Turning to the second question, if the question is whether the operation of the Reciprocating States Regime was tantamount to a denial (in the interim or semi-permanently) of the common heritage principle *as incorporated in the Convention regime*, the answer is self-evident. It does not necessarily follow, however, that it was a denial of the fundamental principle itself - that deep-sea minerals are the common heritage of mankind.

It was suggested above[175] that the Reciprocating States had selected for inclusion in their legislation those features of the Convention regime which suited their interests and omitted other more onerous commitments; and that they had significantly modified even those features which they did adopt. This view of the matter was suggested by the claims made by the Reciprocating States that their legislation was compatible with the UN Convention. There is, however, another way of looking at the relationship between the Reciprocating States regime and the fundamental principle, which involves revisiting the origins of the common heritage doctrine. In outline, the argument would run as follows:

1. Pending the entry into force for them of the Convention, the Reciprocating States were under no obligation to accept the version of the common heritage doctrine elaborated in the UN Convention.

2. These States did accept the fundamental principle that deep-sea minerals are the common heritage of mankind and regarded the Declaration of Principles of December 1970[176] as providing morally-binding guidelines for the elaboration of an international regime based on this principle.

3. They recognised that it was of the essence of the common heritage principle that the exploitation of sea-bed resources should be carried out for the benefit of mankind as a whole and taking into particular consideration the interests and needs of the developing countries. There was an obligation to ensure the equitable sharing by States of the benefits derived from sea-bed mining, taking into particular consideration the interests and needs of the developing States.

4. They recognised, in accordance with Paragraph 2 of the Declaration of Principles, that 'The *area* shall not be subject to appropriation by any means by States or persons, natural or juridical ...'[177] and avoided violation of this principle in their Acts.

5. They recognised too, in accordance with Paragraph 3 of the Declaration of Principles, that 'No State or person, natural or juridical, shall claim, exercise or acquire rights with respect to the area or its resources incompatible with the international regime to be established and the principles of the Declaration'. Such recognition did not, however, commit the Reciprocating States to agree to accept any international regime emerging from UNCLOS III. Pending the emergence of a conventional regime acceptable to them, they reserved the right to authorise deep-sea mining under legislation which was not incompatible with the international regime which they continued to work for and which would better

---

[174] See further above, section II.1.9 and Chap.9.
[175] See above, section II.1.1.
[176] See above, note 23.
[177] Emphasis added.

278   *Chapter 7*

embody the common heritage doctrine than did the international regime of the Convention.

At this point in the argument, the underlying conflict of ideologies and economic philosophies becomes apparent. In its most extreme and undiplomatic form, the argument would be that, given the inability of the developing States to exploit deep-sea minerals without the financial and technological assistance of the industrialised States, it would be realistic to regard acceptance of the common heritage principle by the industrialised States as a form of development aid and a contribution to a new international economic order. However, a sense of realism had to be preserved. Just as it was questionable whether it was practicable to place production controls on only that part of mineral production which was sea-bed based,[178] so it was unrealistic to isolate one aspect of development aid - that represented by the common heritage principle - and impose on it an ambitious and untried system of central planning which was alien to those whose role it would be to supply the initial capital and technology. It followed that the aim should be to design a regime which would minimise waste and inefficiency and maximise the benefits of deep-sea mining which the developing States were to share.

6. Priority should therefore be given to maximising the profits from deep-sea mining (with due concern for such matters as the environment) so that the largest possible funds would be available for spending on the real development priorities of the developing States. It would be inconsistent with this aim (1) to establish costly international bureaucracies;   (2) to encourage deep-sea mining by inexperienced public international institutions; or (3) to transfer deep-sea mining technology to such inexperienced institutions or to developing States whose real technological needs were of a very different character.

7. The legislation adopted by the Reciprocating States was interim in nature but provided a basis for the negotiation of an international regime radically different from that of the Convention but more effectively securing a maximisation of the common heritage of mankind. In the course of its negotiation, the level at which levies were to be set (especially in the longer term) would need to be reconsidered and mechanisms provided for the distribution of funds through international development agencies.

8. Failure to recognise these realities would mean that scarce funds would be needlessly squandered and possibly even that exploitation would not take place at all, as being insufficiently attractive to investors.

V. MODUS VIVENDI BETWEEN THE TWO REGIMES

Despite the incompatibility between the UN regime of sea-bed mining and the Reciprocating States Regime, in practice, a *modus vivendi* was established which allowed the Preparatory Commission to proceed with the registration of pioneer investors under Resolution II, while at the same time not prejudicing the interests of the consortia to which exploration licences had been granted under the legislation of the Reciprocating States. The purpose of this section is to consider in more detail the scope and nature of that *modus vivendi* and the consequences for the two regimes of its eventual demise.

Before turning to this task, it may be useful to illustrate, by reference to the following tables and related sketch-map, how, under this *modus vivendi*, conflicts

---

[178] See doubts expressed by Mr. A.A. Archer in House of Commons Special Standing Committee (*loc.cit.* in note 21, at cols. 47-48).

Table 7.2: Sea-Bed Mining Sites

1. Pioneer Areas

	Pioneer Investor	Certifying State	Certificate of Registration	Site Co-ordinates	Map Symbol
1.1	Government of India	India	18.12.87	*LOS Bull. Special Issue III*, pp.36-37	Not shown
1.2	Association française d'études et de recherche des nodules (AFERNOD)	France	16.5.88	*Ibid.*, p.73	Fr
1.3	Deep Ocean Resources Development Co. Ltd. (DORD)	Japan	16.5.88	*Ibid.*, p.108	Japan
1.4	Yuzhmorgeologiya	USSR	16.5.88	*Ibid.*, pp.142-143	Russia
1.5	China Ocean Mineral Resources Research and Development Association (COMRA)	China	Decision 5.3.91	*Ibid.*, pp.179-181	CH-1 CH-2
1.6	Interoceanmetal Joint Organisation (IOM)	Bulgaria Cuba Czech and Slovak Federal Republic Poland USSR	Decision 21.8.91	*Ibid.*, pp.213-214	IOM-1 IOM-2 IOM-3
1.7	Government of the Republic of Korea	Korea	Decision 2.8.94	LOS/PCN/144, 12.10.94 (in Report of PrepCom to ISBA, LOS/PCN/153 (Vol.I), 30 June 1995), pp.195-202.	ROK

2. Areas Reserved for the Authority

	Related to Pioneer Investor Application of	Site Co-ordinates
2.1	India	*LOS Bull., Special Issue III*, pp.38-39
2.2	AFERNOD	*Ibid.*, p.72
2.3	DORD	*Ibid.*, pp.106-107
2.4	Yuzhmorgeologiya	*Ibid.*, pp.140-141
2.5	COMRA	*Ibid.*, pp.175-178
2.6	IOM	*Ibid.*, pp.212-213
2.7	Korea	LOS/PCN/144 (*loc. cit. supra*), pp. 198-200.

3. Sites Licensed Under National Legislation

	Issued by	Original Date	Held by	Site Co-ordinates	Map Symbol
3.1	USA	29.8.84, revised 13.4.88	Lockheed Martin Missiles & Space (LMMS); formerly OMCO.	*China MOU*, Annex II, No.4, p.15	USA-1
3.2	USA	29.8.84 revised 22.2.88	OMI. The OMI Consortium was dissolved on 31 March 1999 and its licence has been relinquished.	*Ibid.*, No.5, p.17	USA-2
3.3	USA	29.8.84 revised 22.2.88	OMA. The OMA Consortium relinquished its licence on 29 August 1997.	*Ibid.*, No.6, p.18	USA-3
3.4	USA	29.10.84	LMMS; formerly Kennecott Consortium and OMCO.	*Ibid.*, No.3, p.15	USA-4
3.5	UK	21.12.84	Carborundum Company on behalf of Kennecott Consortium. This licence was surrendered in 1993.	*Ibid.*, No.2, p.14	UK
3.6	Germany	29.11.85	AMR. Expired 16.11.98 under German Act, s.13.	*Ibid.*, No.7, p.20	Ger-1
3.7	Germany	30.11.85	AMR as Trustee for OMI (OMI was dissolved in 1999). Expired 16.11.98 under German Act, s.13.	*Ibid.*, No.1, p.14	Ger-2

Sea-bed Mining Sites

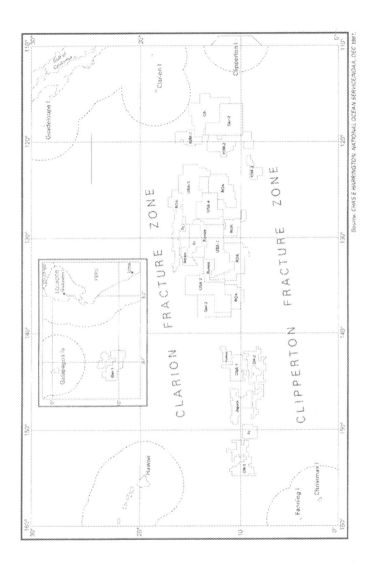

over overlapping mine sites were avoided or resolved. The tables include information on sites allocated to registered Pioneer Investors and related areas reserved for the Authority, as well as sites allocated under national legislation. The latter include sites held by consortia which qualified as Potential Applicants under Resolution II and additional licensed sites which were not eligible for registration as pioneer areas, either because the licensee was not a Potential Applicant under Resolution II, Paragraph 1(a)(ii) or because the licensee held more than one area – the limit allowed under Resolution II, Paragraph 4. The sketch-map does not cover the Indian pioneer area in the Indian Ocean; nor does it cover the areas reserved for the Authority. However, the co-ordinates of these areas may be determined by reference to the table.

1. Scope of modus vivendi ratione personae
The *modus vivendi* was based upon the provisions of the following network of understandings, agreements and declarations.

1.1 The New York Understanding of 5 September 1986
This 'understanding' took the form of a 'Statement on the Implementation of Resolution II', annexed to a 'Statement made by the Acting Chairman of the Preparatory Commission.'[179] This 'final package of understanding'[180] resulted from consultations conducted by the Chairman and Acting Chairman of the Preparatory Commission with 'all the interested groups',[181] namely:

- the group of first applicants, France, India, Japan and the Soviet Union;
- the 'potential applicants'. Strictly speaking, 'applicants' for registration of pioneer investors must be States[182] but the expression 'potential applicant' was used in the Preparatory Commission to refer to the Western multinational consortia whose components possessed the nationality of one or more of the following States or were effectively controlled by one or more of them or their nationals: Belgium, Canada, Germany, Italy, Japan, the Netherlands, the United Kingdom and the United States.[183]
- the Group of 10, representing the Group of 77.
- the Group that was popularly known as the Friends of the Convention.

1.2 The 'Midnight' Agreement of 14 August 1987 on the Resolution of Practical Problems with Respect to Deep Sea-Bed Mining Areas with Related Exchanges of Notes[184]
The Midnight network of agreements consisted of the principal Agreement and two sets of bilateral exchanges of notes referring to the principal Agreement. The parties to these interlinked agreements were as follows:

---

[179] XXV ILM (1986), pp.1326-1330; *LOS Bull., Special Issue III*, pp.231-235; reproduced in Vol.3 of this work as Doc. . On New York Understanding, see further, Chap.5, section III.6.

[180] 'Statement made by the Acting Chairman of the Preparatory Commission' on 5 September 1986, LOS/PCN/L.41/Rev.1, *LOS Bull., Special Issue III*, p.223, at p.228, para.35.

[181] *Ibid.*, at p.228, paras.32 and 34.

[182] Under Resolution II, para.2, a State applies on its own behalf or on behalf of a state enterprise or entity or natural or juridical person. However, to confuse matters, para.2 goes on to say that the Commission 'shall register the applicant as a pioneer investor'. In fact, in the case of an entity other than a State, it is that entity rather than the applicant State which is registered.

[183] Resolution II, para.1(a)(ii).

[184] On the 'Midnight' network of agreements, see further above, Chap.6, section III.7.

284   Chapter 7

Midnight Agreement Network

Western Bilaterals	State Parties to Midnight Agreement	Soviet Bilaterals
Germany UK ------------ USA	Belgium	
Germany UK ------------ USA	Canada	
	Soviet Union ------	Germany UK USA
Germany UK ------------ USA	Italy	
Germany UK ------------ USA	Netherlands	

1.3 Memorandum of Understanding on the Avoidance of Overlaps and Conflict Relating to Deep Sea-Bed Areas between China and Seven Potential Applicant States of 22 February 1991[185]
The parties to this treaty were, on the one hand, China and, on the other hand, Belgium, Canada, Germany, Italy, the Netherlands, the United Kingdom and the United States.

1.4 Declarations by Eastern European States, 1991
In their application of 4 March 1991 for pioneer investor registration of Interoceanmetal Joint Organisation[186], the certifying Eastern European States made certain declarations concerning the avoidance of overlaps with pioneer areas already delineated or those claimed by pioneer investors or known potential pioneer investors[187]. They did not, however, follow the Chinese model by entering into a memorandum of understanding on the avoidance of overlaps and conflict with the Potential Applicant States.

---

[185] See further above, Chap.6, section III.9.
[186] See further above, Chap.6, section III.10.
[187] Decision adopted on 21 August 1991 by the General Committee of the Preparatory Commission on the application submitted by Eastern European States and Cuba for registration of Interoceanmetal Joint Organisation as a pioneer investor, LOS/PCN/122, reproduced in *LOS Bull, Special Issue III*, September 1991, pp.208-214, at p.209, para.7.

UN regime v reciprocating State regime 285

1.5 Declarations by Korea, 1994
In its application of 14 January 1994 for registration of the Government of Korea as a pioneer investor,[188] Korea too made declarations on the avoidance of overlapping claims.[189] Here too, however, no memorandum of understanding was entered into on the avoidance of overlaps and conflict with the Potential Applicant States.

2. Scope of modus vivendi ratione materiae
2.1 The New York Understanding of 5 September 1986
Under the provisions of this Understanding, three of the group of first applicants, France, Japan and the Soviet Union, voluntarily relinquished portions of their application areas simultaneously with their registration as pioneer investors. The relinquished areas were deposited with the Preparatory Commission and reserved to form part of the application areas of Potential Applicants.[190] The areas are identified neither in the New York Understanding itself nor in the publicly available documents concerned with the registration of the three States as pioneer investors.[191]

2.2 The Midnight Agreement of 14 August 1987 and Related Exchanges of Notes
The parties to the principal Agreement agreed on boundary lines and undertook to respect the agreed resolution of practical problems regarding deep-sea mining areas based on these boundary lines.[192] The parties to the related network of bilateral exchanges of notes committed themselves to these same undertakings.[193] The annexes to the Midnight Agreement specify the co-ordinates of the agreed boundary lines but they have been published only in part and in a highly unintelligible form.[194]

2.3 Memorandum of Understanding between China and Seven Potential Applicant States of 22 February 1991
In return for an undertaking by the seven Potential Applicant States to respect the pioneer area to be attributed to the Chinese pioneer investor, China agreed to respect the areas referred to in Annex II to the Memorandum.[195] This Annex gives the co-ordinates of the areas in which the Potential Applicant States had an interest – co-ordinates which had been published earlier in the *Law of the Sea Bulletin*.[196] Reference must be made to the text of this Annex, reproduced in

---

[188] See further above, Chap.5, section III.11.
[189] Decision adopted on 2 August 1994 by the General Committee of the Preparatory Commission on the application submitted by the Government of the Republic of Korea for registration as a pioneer investor, LOS/PCN/144,12 October 1994, reproduced in I *Final PrepCom Report*, pp.195-202, at pp.195-196, para. 3(b).
[190] See further above, Chap.5, section III.6.1(iii) and (v).
[191] For such documentation, see *LOS Bull., Special Issue III*. See also, however, Chap.6, note 226 for references to documentation giving the co-ordinates of these areas.
[192] Midnight Agreement, Arts. 1 and 2.
[193] See further above, Chap.6, section III.7.2.
[194] See version in *LOS Bull.*, No.11, July 1988, p.34, at p.36 *et seq*. See further, however, Chap.6, note 226 for more precise information on co-ordinates.
[195] Memorandum of Understanding on the Avoidance of Overlaps and Conflicts Relating to Deep Sea-bed Areas, 22 February 1991, UK Treaty Series No.52 (1991), Cm 1628, hereafter referred to as 'China MOU'. See further on the China MOU, above, Chap.6, section III.9.
[196] For reference, see below, notes 198-204.

286   Chapter 7

Volume 3 of this work,[197] for details, but it may be noted that seven areas are identified, as tabulated below:

Interested consortium	*Holding licence granted by*
1. Arbeitsgemeinschaft meerestechnisch gewinnbare Rohstoffe (AMR) as trustee for Ocean Management Inc.	Germany [198]
2. Carborundum Co. Ltd. on behalf of the Kennecott Consortium	UK[199]
3. Kennecott Consortium	USA[200]
4. Ocean Minerals Company	USA[201]
5. Ocean Management Inc.	USA[202]
6. Ocean Mining Associates	USA[203]
7. AMR	Germany[204]

2.4 Declarations by Eastern European States, 1991

In their application dated 4 March 1991 for registration of Interoceanmetal Joint Organisation as a pioneer investor, the Eastern European States gave the following assurance:

> The certifying States ensure that the areas in respect of which the application is made do not overlap with pioneer areas and reserved areas already delineated or with those claimed by the pioneer investors referred to in paragraph 1(a)(ii) of resolution II of the Third United Nations Conference on the Law of the Sea. The certifying States have taken steps to make sure that the application area does not overlap with the areas claimed by the already known potential pioneer investors.[205]

The General Committee of the Preparatory Commission decided to register Interoceanmetal Joint Organisation as a pioneer investor on 21 August 1991 and the co-ordinates of the areas reserved for the Authority and allocated to the

---

[197] Vol.3, Doc. No. 21.

[198] See *LOS Bull.*, No. 11, July 1988, p.57; and China MOU, p.14. Expired 16 November 1998.

[199] See *LOS Bull.*, No.11, July 1988, p.58; China MOU, p.14. It is understood that this licence was surrendered in 1993.

[200] See *LOS Bull.*, No.7, April 1986, p.78; China MOU, p.15. This licence (USA-4) was surrendered by KCON on 21 May 1993 and reissued to OMCO on 22 December 1994. OMCO was later abolished and all interests consolidated in Lockheed Martin Missiles & Space (LMMS) (NOAA, *Deep Seabed Mining. A Report to Congress*, December 1995, at pp.4 and 9).

[201] See *LOS Bull.*, No.12, December 1988, p.34; China MOU, p.15. OMCO was later abolished and all interests were consolidated in LMMS – see note 200 above.

[202] See *LOS Bull.*, No.12, December 1988, p.30; China MOU, p.17. OMI was dissolved in 1999 and its licence was relinquished.

[203] See *LOS Bull.*, No.12, December 1988, p.31; China MOU, p.18. OMA relinquished its licence in 1997.

[204] See *LOS Bull.*, No.12, December 1988, p.27; China MOU, p.20. Expired 16 November 1998.

[205] *LOS Bull., Special Issue III*, p.185(4). This assurance is noted in the General Committee's Decision of 21 August 1991, granting registration (*ibid.*, p.209, para.7).

applicant as a pioneer area respectively are specified in the Annex to the Decision.[206]

2.5 Declaration by Korea, 1994

In its pioneer investor application submitted on 14 January 1994, the Government of the Republic of Korea gave an assurance of having avoided overlapping claims in terms almost identical to those incorporated in the declarations of the Eastern European States quoted above.[207] The General Committee of the Preparatory Commission decided to register the Government of the Republic of Korea as a pioneer investor on 2 August 1994 and the co-ordinates of the areas reserved for the Authority and allocated to the applicant as a pioneer area respectively are specified in the Annex to the Decision.[208]

3. Scope of modus vivendi ratione temporis

The above analysis has shown that a *modus vivendi* was achieved between the UN regime and the Reciprocating States Regime whereby it was agreed by the parties to the various understandings, agreements and declarations that (i) the Potential Applicant States would respect the pioneer areas registered by the Preparatory Commission and reserved areas allocated to the Authority; and (ii) in return, the other parties would respect the areas in which the Potential Applicant States had an interest, that is, the areas for which they had issued exploration licences under their national legislation. The next question is: what was the temporal scope of this *modus vivendi*?

In considering the question, it is essential not to confuse the temporal scope of this *modus vivendi* with the temporal scope of the rights of the Potential Applicant States under Resolution II to make applications for registration as pioneer investors.

Dealing first with the latter question, the answer must be sought first in Resolution II, which provided the legal basis of the rights of the Potential Applicants.[209] As has been seen, the pioneer investor system established by the Resolution was intended to be of a transitional character[210] and it was accordingly provided by Paragraph 14 that '... this resolution shall have effect until the entry into force of the Convention'. Being unqualified, the date intended must have been that of the entry into force of the Convention generally, that is, 16 November 1994, as opposed to its later entry into force for particular States. It would follow that the rights of the Potential Applicant States must have ceased to exist on that date unless it can be argued that they were preserved by Resolution II, Paragraphs 13 and 14. Paragraph 14, in terminating the effect of Resolution II on entry into force of the Convention, was without prejudice to Paragraph 13, which provided that:

> The Authority and its organs shall recognise and honour the rights and obligations arising from this resolution and the decisions of the Commission taken pursuant to it.

There can be little doubt that 'the rights ... arising from this resolution', whereby Potential Applicants could apply for pioneer investor registration, had to be

---

[206] *LOS Bull., Special Issue III*, p.208, at pp.212-214.
[207] The declaration in question is quoted in the General Committee's Decision of 2 August 1994 (*loc. cit.* in note 189 above, at para. 3(b)).
[208] *Ibid.*, at pp.198-202.
[209] See further above, Chap.5, section II.
[210] See further Chap.5, section I.

288   *Chapter 7*

exercised before the entry into force of the Convention, unless they had been extended beyond that date by a decision of the Preparatory Commission 'taken pursuant to' Resolution II. In considering whether any such decision was ever made, the status of the New York Understanding and the Midnight Agreement have to be considered.

Even if the New York Understanding could be considered to be a decision of the Preparatory Commission taken pursuant to the Resolution, it could not serve to extend the rights of the Potential Applicants. Under Paragraph 12, the right of Potential Applicants to include areas relinquished by France, Japan and the Soviet Union as part of their application areas lasted only 'until the Convention enters into force'. Similarly, the right to equality of treatment with the first group of applicants, guaranteed under Paragraph 19(e), was conditional upon Potential Applicants submitting their applications before the entry into force of the Convention.

The Midnight Agreement and the related exchanges of notes clearly did not constitute a decision of the Preparatory Commission and could not therefore extend rights arising from Resolution II. The same may be said of the Memorandum of Understanding concluded by the Potential Applicant States with China.

The conclusion must therefore be that the rights of the Potential Applicants to apply for registration as pioneer investors under Resolution II lapsed upon the entry into force of the UN Convention.[211]

It does not follow, however, that the *modus vivendi* between the UN Convention regime and the Reciprocating States Regime also lapsed upon the entry into force of the UN Convention. In considering this separate question, it is necessary to have regard to the effect of the Midnight Agreement network and the Memorandum concluded between the Potential Applicants and China. What is the status of these instruments? As has been seen, they do not constitute decisions taken by the Preparatory Commission. On the other hand, they are clearly treaties. Do they, however, bind the parties to them to continue to respect the areas claimed by the Potential Applicants, irrespective of the attitude of the latter to the UN Convention and, if so, for an unlimited period?

While it is true that one of the objectives of the Midnight Agreement was to remove impediments to the universal adherence to the UN Convention,[212] the obligations undertaken in the Agreement and in the related exchanges of notes are not expressed to be conditional upon the attainment of that objective. Nor do the provisions of these instruments governing their temporal scope link their termination to the fate of the UN Convention. Article 7 of the principal Agreement simply provides that it will remain in force 'until otherwise agreed by the parties' – thus requiring the consent of all of them to its termination. The related exchanges of notes with the Soviet Union similarly provide that they will remain in force for the duration of the Midnight Agreement, or until otherwise agreed by the parties, whichever is later.[213] Finally, the bilateral exchanges of

---

[211] However, as will be seen in section VI below, the Implementation Agreement of 28 July 1994 does allow Potential Applicant States to secure approval of plans of work after the entry into force of the Convention in specified circumstances.

[212] Preamble

[213] See, *e.g.*, Exchange of Notes between the UK and the Soviet Union concerning Deep Sea-bed Mining Areas, 14 August 1987, UK Treaty Series No.34 (1988), Cm 383; *LOS Bull.*, No.11, July 1988, p.29; or the US-Soviet Exchange of Notes of 14 August 1987, reproduced in Vol. 3 as Doc. No. 18.2.

UN regime v reciprocating State regime 289

notes between the non-signatory States (Germany, the United Kingdom and the United States) and the Western parties to the Midnight Agreement (Belgium, Canada, Italy and the Netherlands) contain undertakings not to take steps to terminate the Midnight Agreement or the bilateral exchanges of notes with the Soviet Union except by common accord of the respective bilateral parties.[214]

Turning next to the Memoranda of Understanding concluded between China and the Potential Applicant States, the position is similar to that in the Midnight instruments. Thus, China agrees to 'respect the areas' claimed by the seven Western parties[215] and this undertaking is separate from the additional undertaking not to act in a manner that could prevent the future registration of applications in respect of the said areas claimed by Western States.[216] The agreement remains in force, under Article 6(1), until otherwise agreed by the parties.[217]

It may be concluded, therefore, that, even after the entry into force of the UN Convention, a *modus vivendi* continues to exist whereby the parties to the Midnight network of agreements and the agreement with China are bound to respect one another's sea-bed mining areas until such time as they agree to terminate the agreement/s concerned.

VI. THE IMPACT OF THE IMPLEMENTATION AGREEMENT
THE RECIPROCATING STATES REGIME

The Implementation Agreement facilitated the transition of Potential Applicant States from the Reciprocating States Regime to the UN Convention regime by continuing to acknowledge their preferential position under Resolution II and by allowing them to secure approval of a plan of work even during an interim period prior to their being full parties to the UN Convention and the Implementation Agreement.

As has been seen, Resolution II identified three categories of entities which were to be entitled to apply for registration as pioneer investors.[218] Those in the first category – France, India, Japan and the former Soviet Union or their nationals – have since been registered as pioneer investors.[219] Of the entities falling into categories II and III (as extended by the New York Understanding of 5 September 1986 [220]), three more pioneer investors have been registered: the Chinese State-owned enterprise COMRA; the Interoceanmetal Joint Organisation (IOM), controlled by a group of Eastern European States (and Cuba); and the Government of the Republic of Korea.[221] However, when the time limit for the submission of applications expired on entry into force of the UN Convention,

---

[214] See, *e.g.*, Exchange of Notes between the UK and Italy, 14 August 1987, UK Treaty Series No. 34 (1988), Cm 383; *LOS Bull.*, No. 11, July 1988, p. 44; or the US-Netherlands Exchange of Notes of 14 August 1987, reproduced in Vol. 3 as Doc. No. 18.3.

[215] China MOU, Art.1(2).

[216] Art.2(2).

[217] On the other hand, strictly speaking, it would not appear that the Eastern European States or Korea are bound to respect the claims of the potential pioneer investors after the entry into force of the UN Convention on 16 November 1994. The declarations incorporated in their pioneer investor applications simply provided an assurance that their application areas did not overlap with areas claimed by known potential pioneer investors. They were entitled to assume that these options would have to be exercised by the potential pioneer investors by 16 November 1994; otherwise they would lapse.

[218] See Chap.6, section II.1.

[219] See Chap.6, section III.7.

[220] See Chap.6, section III.6.1 (vii).

[221] See Chap.6, section III.9,10 and 11.

290 *Chapter 7*

there remained a number of potential applicants in categories II and III, including some of the Reciprocating States, which had not submitted applications. The Implementation Agreement allowed these entities to apply for plans of work both in cases where the State concerned had become a party to the UN Convention and, subject to certain conditions, in cases where the State concerned had not yet become a full party to the Convention.

Dealing first with the more straightforward case, where the State had become a party to the UN Convention, a former potential applicant which had already undertaken substantial activities in the Area prior to the entry into force of the UN Convention, or its successor in interest, would have been entitled to submit an application for approval of a plan of work for exploration.[222] Such an application would have been considered to have met the financial and technical qualifications necessary for approval if the sponsoring State or States certified that the applicant had expended an amount equivalent to at least $30 million in research and exploration activities and had expended no less than 10 per cent of that amount in the location, survey and evaluation of the area referred to in the plan of work.[223] Provided the plan of work otherwise satisfied the requirements of the Convention, it would have been approved by the Council of the Authority in the form of a contract.[224]

Returning to the more complex case, all was not lost if the State concerned had not become a State Party to the UN Convention. It could still have proceeded with an application for approval of a plan of work for exploration if it was a member of the Authority on a provisional basis. Such status was originally enjoyed by States which were applying the Implementation Agreement on a provisional basis under Article 7 of the Implementation Agreement.[225] Although provisional application of the Implementation Agreement terminated upon its entry into force on 28 July 1996[226], it was open to States to continue their membership of the Authority on a provisional basis for a limited time, though not beyond 16 November 1998, that is, four years after the entry into force of the UN Convention.[227] The rules governing applications where such provisional members of the Authority were concerned were as follows:
(i) States members of the Authority on a provisional basis were entitled to sponsor an application[228].
(ii) Where the sponsored entity consisted of natural or juridical persons possessing the nationality of more than one State, a plan of work for exploration would not have been approved unless all the States were either States Parties to the Implementation Agreement (and therefore to the UN Convention[229]) or members of the Authority on a provisional basis.[230]

---

[222] Implementation Agreement, Annex, Sec.1, para.6(a)(i). Such applications would have had to be submitted within 36 months of the entry into force of the UN Convention, that is by 16 November 1997, the revised deadline laid down for registered pioneer investors in para.6(a)(ii).
[223] *Ibid.*
[224] *Ibid.*
[225] Implementation Agreement, Annex, Sec.1, para.12(chapeau).
[226] Implementation Agreement, Art.7(3)
[227] Implementation Agreement, Annex, Sec.1, para 12 (a). Such membership beyond 16 November 1996 was conditional upon an application to the Council, which had to be satisfied that the applicant had been making efforts in good faith to become a party to the Agreement and to the Convention. See further Chap.1, section II.1.2 and II.2.
[228] Implementation Agreement, Annex, Sec.1, para.12(c)(ii).
[229] Implementation Agreement, Art.4(2).
[230] Implementation Agreement, Annex, Sec.1, para.12(c)(ii).

UN regime v reciprocating State regime 291

(iii) Where the State acting as sponsor for such a multinational consortium was a member of the Authority on a provisional basis, the approved plan of work would have terminated if such membership ceased and the State had not become a State Party to the Implementation Agreement and the UN Convention.[231]

(iv) Similarly, an approved plan of work for exploration sponsored by at least one State provisionally applying the Implementation Agreement, was to terminate if such a State ceased to apply the Agreement provisionally (which it would have done automatically on entry into force of the Agreement on 28 July 1996 [232]) and had not become a member of the Authority on a provisional basis or a State Party.[233]

In fact, as has been seen in Chapter 6, none of the remaining potential applicants took advantage of these transitional provisions and the number of registered pioneer investors stayed at seven.

---

[231] *Ibid.*, para.12(d).
[232] See Implementation Agreement, Art.7(3).
[233] Implementation Agreement, Annex, Sec.1, para.11.

CHAPTER 8

The UN Convention Regime of Sea-Bed Mining:
VI. The Institutional Framework

Throughout the negotiation of the sea-bed mining regime in UNCLOS III, it was clear that the acceptability of much of the regime embodied in Part XI of the UN Convention depended to some extent upon the composition and voting rules of the various organs of the International Sea-Bed Authority and upon the provision made for the settlement of disputes.[1] When, towards the end of the Conference, provision was made for the establishment of the Preparatory Commission, care had again to be taken to ensure that the institutional balance achieved in the Convention should not be disturbed by the terms of Resolutions I and II.[2] However, these arrangements did not prove to be durable and were the subject of far-reaching changes made by the Implementation Agreement of 28 July 1994.[3] *Inter alia*, the Implementation Agreement introduced major changes in relation to decision-making, the role of the Enterprise and the establishment of a Finance Committee, and these and other modifications will be reviewed in later sections of this chapter. First, however, reference must be made to a number of more general changes which affected the whole approach of the international community to sea-bed mining and reflected a significantly altered balance between the interests of the industrialised powers and the developing States. The underlying rationale of these changes is the need to minimise costs and, in furtherance of that goal, the Agreement establishes three principles of management:

Cost-effectiveness: all organs and subsidiary bodies must be cost-effective and this principle will also apply to the frequency, duration and scheduling of meetings.[4]

---

[1] On settlement of disputes, see Chap. 9.
[2] The institutional features of the Preparatory Commission are dealt with in this chapter and an account of its role in administering the pioneer investor scheme is given in Chap.6.
[3] Agreement relating to the Implementation of Part XI of the United Nations Convention on the Law of the Sea of 10 December 1982, 28 July 1994 (Implementation Agreement), *LOS Bull.*, Special Issue IV, 1994, p.10; Misc.No.44 (1994), Cm 2705, reproduced in Vol. 3 as Doc. No. 23.
[4] Implementation Agreement, Annex, Section 1(2).

Evolutionary approach. The setting up and functioning of the organs and subsidiary bodies of the Authority are to be based on an evolutionary approach, taking into account their functional needs, so that they may discharge their responsibilities at various stages of the development of sea-bed mining.[5]

Streamlining. The early functions of the Authority are to be carried out by the Assembly, the Council, the Secretariat, the Legal and Technical Commission and a new body, the Finance Committee. During this early period, the functions of the Economic Planning Commission will be performed by the Legal and Technical Commission.[6]

I. THE ESTABLISHMENT AND PURPOSE OF THE AUTHORITY

The Convention establishes an International Sea-Bed Authority (the 'Authority'),[7] the purpose of which is to enable States Parties to 'organise and control activities in the [Sea-Bed] Area, particularly with a view to administering the resources of the Area'.[8] The Authority, with its seat in Jamaica,[9] consists of all States Parties[10] to the Convention and provision is made for observer status.[11] As was seen in Chapter 1,[12] provision was also made in the Implementation Agreement for membership of the Authority on a provisional basis during a transitional period which ended on 16 November 1998.

The powers expressly bestowed upon the Authority and its organs are many and complex but, lest there should be gaps, the Convention expressly confers upon the Authority the incidental implied powers which may prove necessary for the exercise of its express powers and performance of its functions.[13]

II. THE ORGANS OF THE AUTHORITY

A diagrammatic representation of the organs of the Authority and of other related institutions is given in Figure 8.1. As will be seen, the Authority consists of three 'principal organs', three subsidiary organs and the 'Enterprise'. Reference is also made to the International Tribunal for the Law of the Sea and especially its Sea-Bed Disputes Chamber. Though not organs of the Authority, they have a role to play in relation to sea-bed mining and are dealt with in detail in Chapter 9. The Preparatory Commission for the International Sea-Bed Authority and for the

---

[5] *Ibid.*, Section 1(3).
[6] *Ibid.*, Section 1 (4).
[7] Art.156(1).
[8] Art.157(1), confirmed by Implementation Agreement, Annex, Section 1(1).
[9] Art.156(4). On Headquarters Agreement with Jamaica, see below, section II.7.
[10] Art.156(2).
[11] Art.156(3).
[12] Chap.1, section II.1.2.
[13] Art.157(2), confirmed by Implementation Agreement, Annex, Section 1(1). The US Delegation commented that 'These provisions usefully limit the scope of permissible activity of the Authority and will serve to prevent the Authority from lawfully claiming powers and functions not either expressly granted or necessary for their performance'. (M.H. Nordquist and Choon-ho Park (eds.), *Reports of the United States Delegation to the Third United Nations Conference on the Law of the Sea* (The Law of the Sea Institute, Occasional Paper No.33, 1983), *Eighth Session (Resumed), New York, July 19-August 24, 1979*, p.301, at p.327). See also UN Convention, Arts. 187 and 189 on the jurisdiction of the Sea-Bed Disputes Chamber over *ultra vires* acts of the Authority.

I. THE AUTHORITY

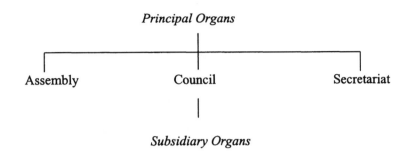

Principal Organs

Assembly — Council — Secretariat

Subsidiary Organs

Economic Planning Commission
Legal and Technical Commission
Finance Committee

The Enterprise

II. INTERNATIONAL TRIBUNAL FOR THE LAW OF THE SEA

Sea-Bed Disputes Chamber

III. PREPARATORY COMMISSION

4 Special Commissions — *Training Panel* — *General Committee*

Group of Technical Experts

IV. UN Secretary-General's Informal Consultations

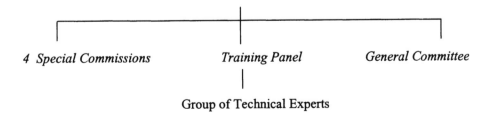

Figure 8.1. Institutional Framework of Sea-bed Mining

Institutional framework 295

International Tribunal for the Law of the Sea, though established directly by UNCLOS III and not an organ of the Authority, was of course closely related to it and played an important rôle in developing the UN Convention regime and preparing for its entry into force. Finally, brief reference must also be made here to another transient 'institution', the UN Secretary-General's Informal Consultations, a series of meetings outside the Preparatory Commission's framework, which paved the way for the Implementation Agreement of 28 July 1994.[14].

1. The Principal Organs
The Convention establishes three principal organs,[15] the Assembly, the Council and the Secretariat.

1.1 The Assembly
1.1.1 Composition
The Assembly, the Authority's plenary organ, consists of all members of the Authority.[16] It thus includes all States Parties to the UN Convention.[17] Prior to 16 November 1998, it also included those States which were members of the Authority on a provisional basis.[18]

1.1.2 Decision-making
The Implementation Agreement introduced a new general rule on decision-making which applies to all organs of the Authority: as a general rule, decision-making should be by consensus.[19] If, however, all efforts in the Assembly to reach a decision by consensus have been exhausted, the original rules laid down in the UN Convention apply.[20] Each member of the Assembly has one vote.[21] On questions of substance, decisions are taken by a two-thirds majority of members present and voting, provided they include a majority of the members participating in that session of the Assembly. In case of doubt, items are taken to be questions of substance unless otherwise decided by the Assembly by the same qualified majority.[22]

---

[14] For a detailed account of the Secretary-General's Informal Consultations, see E.D. Brown, '"Neither necessary nor prudent at this stage" : the regime of sea-bed mining and its impact on the universality of the UN Convention on the Law of the Sea', 17 *Marine Policy* (No.2, 1993), pp.81-107; and 'The 1994 Agreement on the Implementation of Part XI of the UN Convention on the Law of the Sea: breakthrough to universality?', 19 *Marine Policy* (No.1, 1995), pp.5-20; or E.D. Brown, *The International Law of the Sea*, Vol. I, 1994, Chap.17, section IV.
[15] Art.158(1).
[16] Art.159(1).
[17] Art.156(2).
[18] See further Chap.1, section II.1.2.
[19] Implementation Agreement, Annex, Section 3(2) and Rule 61(1) of Rules of Procedure of the Assembly (ISA/99/03.E, hereafter referred to as 'RPA'). 'Consensus' is not defined in the Implementation Agreement or RPA but is defined for the purpose of voting in the Council in Art.161(8)(e) of the UN Convention and Rule 59 of the Rules of Procedure of the Council (ISA/99/04.E, hereafter referred to as 'RPC') as meaning 'the absence of any formal objection'. See further below, under section 1.2.2.
[20] Implementation Agreement, Annex, Section 3(3).
[21] UN Convention, Art.159(6); Rule 60 of RPA.
[22] Art.159(8), as applied by Implementation Agreement, Annex, Section 3(3) and Rule 61(2) of RPA.

296   *Chapter 8*

The Implementation Agreement introduced a new rule clarifying the relationship between the Assembly and the Council. Decisions of the Assembly have to be based on the recommendations of the Council when they are concerned with any matter for which the Council also has competence or with administrative, budgetary or financial matters. If the Council's recommendations are unacceptable to the Assembly, it may return the matter to the Council for further consideration in the light of the views expressed by the Assembly.[23] Decisions having financial or budgetary implications have also to be based on the recommendations of the new Finance Committee.[24]

Supplementary rules allow voting on questions of substance to be deferred for a period of up to five days.[25] Voting may also be delayed when an advisory opinion of the Sea-Bed Disputes Chamber has been sought on the conformity with the Convention of a proposal before the Assembly on any matter. Voting must be stayed pending delivery of the advisory opinion.[26]

Decisions on questions of procedure are taken by a majority of the members present and voting.[27]

1.1.3 Powers and Functions

At first sight, it might be thought that the powers and functions of the Assembly are those befitting 'the supreme organ of the Authority to which the other principal organs shall be accountable as specifically provided for' in the Convention.[28] Thus, it is empowered, *inter alia*, to establish general policies (Article 160(1)); to elect the members of the Council, the Secretary-General, and the Governing Body and Director-General of the Enterprise (Article 160(2)(a)-(c)); to establish subsidiary organs (Article 160(2)(d)); to assess budgetary contributions and approve the annual budget (Article 160(2)(e) and (h)); to consider and approve rules, regulations and procedures (Article 160(2)(f)); and to decide upon the equitable sharing of financial and other economic benefits derived from activities in the Area (Article 160(2)(g)).

If the above-mentioned voting rules are recalled and it is borne in mind that well over the required two-thirds majority can always be mustered by the Group of 77 for questions of substance on which their members are like-minded, then it is not difficult to understand why the relationship between the Assembly and the Council was an issue of vital importance for the industrialised States in the Conference negotiations. If the powers and functions of the Assembly were to be constructed on the basis of the principle of the sovereign equality of States[29] and on a voting system with a built-in bias in favour of the developing States, it was essential, if agreement was to be reached, that adequate safeguards should be provided for the interests of the industrialised States which would frequently find themselves in a minority.

---

[23] Implementation Agreement, Annex, Section 3(4) and Rule 61(3) of RPA.
[24] *Ibid.*, Section 3(7) and Rule 61(4) of RPA. See further below, section II.1.2.3.2.
[25] UN Convention, Art.159(9) and Rule 64 of RPA.
[26] Art.159(10) and Rule 65 of RPA.
[27] Art.159(7), confirmed by Implementation Agreement, Annex, Section 3(3) and Rule 61(2) of RPA.
[28] Art.160(1).
[29] Under Art.157(3), 'The Authority is based on the principle of the sovereign equality of all its members'.

Institutional framework 297

After a long and bitter struggle, this objective was reached and, on closer examination, it will be found that, on many of the matters referred to above, the Assembly's powers can only be exercised on the basis of recommendations from the Council or within the confines of formulae established by the Convention. In reality, the more important powers lie with the Council, 'the executive organ of the Authority',[30] and the predominant role of the industrialised States in the Council has been further enhanced by the Implementation Agreement.   An examination of the Council's composition, its powers and functions, and the rules on decision-making in the Council reveals the fundamental nature of the Authority.

1.2 The Council
1.2.1 Composition
Article 161(1) of the UN Convention, which governed the composition of the Council in its original form, was rendered inapplicable by the Implementation Agreement[31] and the Council must now be elected in accordance with the provisions of Section 3 of the Annex to the Implementation Agreement.

As before, the Council is to consist of 36 members of the Authority elected by the Assembly[32] and, as before, five categories of States Parties are identified, from which specified numbers of members have to be elected in sequence.[33] However, the composition of the five categories has been altered and, in addition, the 36 members are divided into four 'chambers' for the purposes of the rules on decision-making in the Council.

The 36 members are to be elected in the following order:

Group A. 'Four members from among those States Parties which, during the last five years for which statistics are available, have either consumed more than 2 per cent in value terms of total world consumption or have had net imports of more than 2 per cent in value terms of total world imports of the commodities produced from the categories of minerals to be derived from the Area, provided that the four members shall include one State from the Eastern European region having the largest economy in that region in terms of gross domestic product and the State, on the date of entry into force of the Convention, having the largest economy in terms of gross domestic product, if such States wish to be represented in this group;'[34]

Group B. 'Four members from among the eight States Parties which have made the largest investments in preparation for and in the conduct of activities in the Area, either directly or through their nationals;'[35]

Group C. 'Four members from among States Parties which, on the basis of production in areas under their jurisdiction, are major net exporters of the categories of minerals to be derived from the Area, including at least two

---

[30] Art.162(1).
[31] Implementation Agreement, Annex, Section 3(16).
[32] *Ibid.*, Section 3(15), chapeau.
[33] *Ibid.*, Section 3(15).
[34] *Ibid.*, Section 3(15)(a).
[35] *Ibid.*, Section 3(15)(b).

298   *Chapter 8*

developing States whose exports of such minerals have a substantial bearing upon their economies;'[36]

Group D. 'Six members from among developing States Parties, representing special interests. The special interests to be represented shall include those of States with large populations, States which are land-locked or geographically disadvantaged, island States, States which are major importers of the categories of minerals to be derived from the Area, State which are potential producers of such minerals and least developed States;'[37] and

Group E. 'Eighteen members elected according to the principle of ensuring an equitable geographical distribution of seats in the Council as a whole, provided that each geographical region shall have at least one member elected under this subparagraph. For this purpose, the geographical regions shall be Africa, Asia, Eastern Europe, Latin America and the Caribbean and Western Europe and Others.'[38]

There is also an 'informal understanding' that:

> Once there is a widespread participation in the International Seabed Authority and the number of members of each regional group participating in the Authority is substantially similar to its membership in the United Nations, it is understood that each regional group would be represented in the Council of the Authority as a whole by at least three members.[39]

Before elections are held, the Assembly has to establish lists of the countries fulfilling the criteria of membership in Groups A to D.[40] Some may qualify for membership under more than one category but any such State may be proposed for election by only one group.[41] Each group in categories A to D will be represented in the Council by those members nominated by that group and each group is to nominate only as many candidates as the number of seats required to be filled by that group.[42] If, however, the number of potential candidates in a group (Groups A to E) exceeds the number of seats available in the group, 'as a general rule, the principle of rotation should apply.'[43] It is left to the States members of the group to determine how the principle is to apply in their group.[44]

Article 161(2) of the UN Convention obliged the Assembly, when electing members of the Council, to ensure that land-locked and geographically disadvantaged States and certain coastal States were represented to a degree which was reasonably proportionate to their representation in the Assembly.[45] However, Article 161(2) imposed this obligation upon the Assembly only when it

---

[36] *Ibid.*, Section 3(15)(c).
[37] *Ibid.*, Section 3(15)(d).
[38] *Ibid.*, Section 3(15)(e).
[39] Statement made by the President of the General Assembly at the time of the adoption of GA Resolution 48/263 of 28 July 1994 (adopting the Implementation Agreement) (Misc.No.44 (1994), Cm 2705, at p.19).
[40] Implementation Agreement, Annex, Section 3(9)(b).
[41] *Ibid.*
[42] Section 3(10).
[43] *Ibid.*
[44] *Ibid.*
[45] UN Convention, Art.161(2)(a)-(b).

was 'electing members of the Council in accordance with paragraph 1 [of Article 161]' and, of course, that paragraph has been rendered inapplicable by Section 3(16) of the Annex to the Implementation Agreement. It would appear to follow, therefore, that, even though Article 161(2) was not expressly rendered inapplicable, this particular variety of equitable geographical representation is no longer guaranteed. It may be noted, however, that the interests involved are to a substantial extent included among those covered by Group D.

Members are normally elected for a four-year term but, at the first election, half of the members of each group had to be elected to two-years terms,[46] thus, in theory at least,[47] ensuring a degree of continuity of membership within each group. Members are eligible for re-election but 'due regard has to be paid to the desirability of rotation of membership.'[48]

To avoid confusion, it has to be noted that, although the first elections took place on 21 March 1996 and it might be thought, therefore, that a 2-year term would end on 20 March 1998 and a 4-year term on 20 March 2000, in fact, the Assembly decided on 25 March 1998 to harmonise the terms of office of members of the Council with the calendar year. In order to do so, it further decided that:

- the terms of office of members elected in 1996 for a two-year term would end on 31 December 1998;
- the terms of office of members elected in 1996 for a four-year term would end on 31 December 2000; and
- the terms of office of members elected in 1998 would commence on 1 January 1999 and continue for a period of four calendar years. [49]

The negotiations required to reach agreement on the composition of the various groups proved to be difficult and protracted, in large part because of the need to reconcile the principle of equitable geographical representation with that of the representation of special interests. Eventually, an extremely complex system of rotation and duration of terms was adopted and final agreement on the composition of the Council was achieved at the 30th meeting of the Assembly in March 1996.[50] As will be seen below, the arrangements agreed upon include not only firm nominations for the first, 1996 elections, but also understandings on later elections. In attempting to present a clear account of these very complex arrangements, it may be advisable to deal first with the system adopted to ensure equitable geographical representation among the five United Nations regions. This is followed by an analysis of Council membership, by reference to the five Groups A to E defined above.

---

[46] UN Convention, Art.161(3).
[47] In practice, as will be seen below, the classic simplicity of this pattern has been obscured by the complex variations introduced during the election process in 1996.
[48] *Ibid.*, Art.161(4).
[49] Decision of the Assembly of the International Seabed Authority concerning the duration of terms of office of members of the Council, ISBA/4/A/5, 25 March 1998 (*SD & D*, vol. 2, p.40).
[50] Statement of the President of the Assembly on the work of the Assembly during the first part of the second session, ISBA/A/L.9, 2 April 1996 (*SD & D*, vol. 1, p.17), paras. 4-9.

300   *Chapter 8*

1.2.1.1 Equitable Geographical Representation - The 'Floating Seat' System
As was seen above, the eighteen members of Group E have to be elected according to the principle of ensuring an equitable geographical distribution of seats in the Council as a whole.[51] To that end, each of the five United Nations regions must have at least one member elected in this group. Moreover, there is an understanding that, once the number of members of each regional group participating in the Authority is substantially similar to its membership in the United Nations, each such regional group will be represented on the Council by at least three members.[52]

During the elections in March 1996, agreement was reached on a system of allocation among regional groups which would meet these requirements. It was agreed in principle that 10 seats should be allocated to the African Group, 9 seats to the Asian Group, 8 seats to the Western European and Others Group, 7 seats to the Latin American and Caribbean Group and 3 seats to the Eastern European Group. Given the fact that the total number of seats allocated according to that formula would have amounted to 37, a way had to be found to lose the extra 1 seat. The 'floating seat' system was devised for this purpose. Under it, for the first four years, a system of rotation was to be applied whereby, every year, one of the five regions would relinquish one seat for the year.[53] The relinquishment is only partial, however, in the sense that the regional group concerned may designate one of its members in the Assembly to participate in the deliberations of the Council without the right to vote during the one-year period.[54] The effect of this system during the first four years may be tabulated as follows. The bracketed figures indicate where a region relinquishes a seat.[55]

The Floating Seat System

UN Region	1996	1997	1998	1999
Africa	10	10	(9)	10
Asia	9	9	9	(8)
Latin America & Caribbean	(6)	7	7	7
Western Europe & Others	8	(7)	8	8
Eastern Europe	3	3	3	3
Totals	36	36	36	36

---

[51] Implementation Agreement, Annex, Section 3(15)(e).
[52] *Informal Understanding to be read by the President of the General Assembly at the time of the adoption of the resolution* [adopting the Implementation Agreement], *Law of the Sea. Report of the Secretary-General*, A/48/950, 9 June 1994, Annex II.
[53] See further, *Composition of the First Council of the International Seabed Authority*, ISBA/A/L.8, 21 March 1996 and Corr.1, 2 April 1996 (*SD & D*, vol. 1, p.15).
[54] *Ibid.*, at p.15, footnote 2.
[55] Based on data in *loc. cit.* in note 53.

Institutional framework 301

The Eastern European Group's share of 3 seats was unaffected during the first four years. Thereafter, it was envisaged that:

> the principle of burden-sharing, on an equal and equitable basis, shall continue to be respected involving the five regional groups and taking into account the situation at that time, in particular the effect of the termination of the provisional membership of the Assembly.[56]

The Eastern European Group had reservations about the application of this system, pointing out [57] that, in their case, it would reduce their share of seats below the minimum of three envisaged in the Informal Understanding which accompanied the Implementation Agreement. Their concern was accommodated in the arrangement for the period 2001-2004 agreed to in the Assembly in July 2000. It was agreed that all but the Eastern European Group would relinquish one seat in successive years: Guyana (Latin American and Caribbean Group) in 2001, Malta (Western European and Others Group) in 2002, Algeria (African Group) in 2003 and a member of the Asian Group in 2004. [58]

Having set out the system whereby equitable geographical representation is to be ensured, the next step is to show how this system has been integrated into the system of distribution of Council seats among the special interest groups.

1.2.1.2 Council Membership - Groups A-E [59]

As noted above, Article 161(3) of the UN Convention prescribes a system of staggered elections by requiring that, at the first elections (held in 1996), one half of the seats in each of the five groups be filled for a term of four years and the other half for a two-year term. It follows, of course, that, as from 1998, elections to fill one half of the thirty six seats for four-year terms have to be held every two years. As from 1 January 1999, the four-year terms run for calendar years. Thus, for example, in March 1998, the Russian Federation was elected to a Group A seat for a four-year term commencing on 1 January 1999.

Group A (consumers)

As has been seen, Group A comprises four States Parties from among the largest consumers of minerals. Since such States have also to be members of the Authority,[60] whether on a permanent or provisional basis,[61] a certain element of

---

[56] *Ibid.*, p.15, footnote 1.

[57] *Statement of the Eastern European Group*, Annex VI to *Statement of the President on the work of the Assembly during the first part of the second session*, ISBA/A/L.9, 2 April 1996 (*SD &D*, vol. 1, p.23).

[58] See further, ISBA/6/A/14, 13 July 2000, note 1.

[59] Details of the composition of the Council and the system of rotation and duration of terms are given in *Composition of the First Council of the International Seabed Authority*, ISBA/A/L.8, 21 March 1996 and Corr.1, 2 April 1996 (*SD & D*, vol. 1, p.15); and in *Election to Fill Vacancies on the Council for the Period 2001 to 2004 in Accordance with Article 161, Paragraph 3, of the Convention*, ISBA/6/A/CRP.1/Rev.1, 27 March 2000. See also 'Indicative Lists of States Members' in ISBA/6/A/CRP.2, 27 March 2000.

[60] Implementation Agreement, Annex, Section 3(15), chapeau.

[61] Members of the Authority on a provisional basis had the same rights and obligations as other members, *ibid.*, Section 1(12)(c).

302   *Chapter 8*

uncertainty necessarily arose from the fact that the States eligible for election in 1996 included the United Kingdom and the United States, whose provisional membership of the Authority was due to terminate on 16 November 1997 and 16 November 1998 respectively.[62] Although the United Kingdom subsequently became a full member following accession to the UN Convention in 1997, the United States ceased to be a member on 16 November 1998.

It will be recalled that Group A must include one State from the Eastern European region having the largest economy in that region in terms of gross domestic product, if it wishes to be represented in this group.[63] So long as the Russian Federation satisfies that criterion, it must be elected if it so wishes. Similarly, since Group A has to include the State having the largest economy in terms of gross domestic product on the date of entry into force of the Convention, if it so wishes,[64] the United States too had to be elected so long as it satisfied that criterion and so wished.

At the first elections in 1996, Japan and the United Kingdom were elected to four-year terms and the Russian Federation and the United States to two-year terms. In March 1998, the Russian Federation and the United States (which was still a provisional member of the Authority) were elected for four-year terms as from 1 January 1999.[65] However, following the termination of United States membership of the Authority on 16 November 1998, it became necessary to fill the vacancy at the next meeting of the Assembly in August 1999.Italy was elected to the vacancy for the remainder of the four-year term to the end of the year 2002, but it was stipulated that Italy would relinquish its seat in Group A in favour of the United States if the United States became a member of the Authority.[66]

Following the further elections held in July 2000, the composition of the Group A membership of the Council for the years 1999-2004 is as shown in the table below. In this table and in the corresponding tables for Groups C, D and E, States are listed in the order of the United Nations regional groups to which they belong: African Group; Asian Group; Eastern European Group; Latin American and Caribbean States Group; and Western European and Other States Group; and in alphabetical order within the regional groups.

Group A Council Membership 1999-2004 (a)

1999	2000	2001	2002	2003	2004
Japan	Japan	Japan	Japan	Japan	Japan
Russian Federation	Russian Federation	Russian Federation	Russian Federation	Note (d)	Note (d)
Italy (b)	Italy	Italy	Italy	Note (d)	Note (d)
United Kingdom	United Kingdom	United Kingdom(c)	United Kingdom	United Kingdom	United Kingdom

---

[62] See further, Chap.1, section II.2.
[63] Implementation Agreement, Annex Section 3(15)(a).
[64] *Ibid.*
[65] ISBA/4/A/6, 25 March 1998 (*SD & D*, vol. 2, p.40).
[66] ISBA/5/A/7, 17 August 1999 (*SD & D*, vol. 3, p.18).

(a)   For table showing membership for the period 1996-2002, see ISBA/6/A/CRP.1/ Rev.1, 27 March 2000, Annex I.
(b)   With possibility of relinquishment to United States. See text above at note 66.
(c)   UK re-elected on understanding that it may relinquish its seat in favour of France after two years, if so requested (ISBA/6/A/14, 13 July 2000, note 2).
(d)   Seat to be filled at elections in 2002.

Group B (investors)

As was noted above, the arrangements agreed upon in the Assembly in March 1996 covered not only the nominations for the 1996 Council elections but also what appeared to be firm understandings on the nominations to be made for subsequent elections.[67] The process was made particularly transparent in the case of the Group B nominations since it published a 'Statement by members of Group B'[68] setting out the substance of their agreement and separate statements were issued by Japan and Korea expressing their reservations.[69]

Strictly speaking, the Assembly, and, therefore, the various groups, were concerned with the 1996 elections and not with the further elections to be held subsequently at two-yearly intervals. Accordingly, Group B nominated for election in 1996 the following four States: China and France for four-year terms and India and Germany for two-year terms.

Given the fact that candidates must satisfy the Group B criterion at the time when an election is held by being among the eight States Parties which have made the largest investments in sea-bed mining, it might have been supposed that nominations for future elections would not be made until shortly before the date of the election in question. In fact, however, the statement made by the members of Group B went on to deal with the 1998 and 2000 elections. In unqualified terms, it is recorded that:

- India will not seek re-election in 1998. Therefore, India shall be renominated by the Group as a candidate for the election to the Council to be held in 2000 for a four-year term;
- Germany shall be renominated by the Group as a candidate for the election to the Council to be held in 1998 for a four-year term;
- The Netherlands, which withdrew its candidature for the first election, shall be nominated by the Group as a candidate for the election to the Council to be held in 1998 for a four-year term.[70]

Unsurprisingly, not all States were entirely happy with the outcome of Group B's deliberations and two of them, Japan and Korea, made statements of their

---

[67] See text above following note 49.

[68] The statement is in Annex I to the *Statement of the President on the work of the Assembly during the first part of the second session*, ISBA/A/L.9, 2 April 1996 (*SD & D*, vol. 1, p.17, at pp. 21-22). *Inter alia*, it indicates that, '... the principle of rotation shall be applied to all members of the Group on an equal basis' and that, 'The investors shall consult regularly on the matters which are dealt with in the Council so that the four States representing Group B in the Council can take into account the position of the other investors'.

[69] *The Statement by Japan on the composition of Group B* and the *Statement by the Republic of Korea on the composition of Group B* are Annexes III and II respectively to ISBA/A/L.9, 2 April 1996(*SD & D*, vol. 1, p.17, at p. 22).

[70] *Loc. cit.* in note 68, at pp. 21-22.

304   *Chapter 8*

position for the record. Japan pointed out that it was not possible to predetermine which countries would be the eight largest investors in the year 2000 and that provisional membership of the Authority would end at the latest on 16 November 1998. As has been seen above, Japan's membership of the Council as a nominee of Group A was not guaranteed beyond the year 2000 and this no doubt explained Japan's decision to reserve its right to stand for nomination from Group B at the Council elections in 2000.[71]

Korea took up a similar position. Noting that the eligibility of a State should be determined on the basis of its qualifications at the time of the election, it stated that:

> ...any decision or understanding by the current members belonging to a specific group beyond this mandate will not bind the future eligible members for such groups. In other words, the question of a State which is presently not a member of Group B, but would fit into the system by 1998 or 2000 or any subsequent year as one of the eight largest investors, should be dealt with where it really occurs, on the basis of the legal situation and on the principle of rotation of all members of Group B on an equal basis.[72]

Korea reserved its right 'to reopen the case as the occasion arises.'[73]

Despite these reservations, the elections have proceeded on the basis of the Group B Statement. In March 1998, Germany and the Netherlands were elected to four-year terms commencing 1 January 1999; [74] and in July 2000 India and China were elected to four-year terms commencing 1 January 2001. [75] The following table records Group B's Council membership for the year 1999 to 2004.

Group B Council Membership 1999-2004 (a)

1999	2000	2001	2002	2003	2004
China	China	China	China	China	China
France	France	India	India	India	India
Germany	Germany	Germany	Germany	Note (b)	Note (b)
Netherlands	Netherlands	Netherlands	Netherlands	Note (b)	Note (b)

(a)   For table showing membership for the period 1996-2002, see ISBA/6/A/CRP.1/ Rev.1, 27 March 2000, Annex I.

(b)   Seat to be filled at elections in 2002.

---

[71]   *Loc. cit.* in note 69. In fact, Japan was re-elected to a Group A seat in July 2000.
[72]   *Loc. cit.* in note 69.
[73]   *Ibid.*
[74]   ISBA/4/A/6, 26 March 1998.
[75]   ISBA/6/A/14, 13 July 2000.

Institutional framework 305

Group C (exporters)

The rationale behind Group C's nomination of candidates is not immediately apparent but is explained by a combination of factors: the basic rules for the election in the Implementation Agreement; the form taken by the principle of rotation in this group; and the need to maintain the agreed distribution of Council seats among the regional groups. The table which follows shows Group C's Council membership between 1999 and 2004. The accompanying notes reflect the factors referred to above and the terms of the understandings reached in 1996.

Group C's Council Membership 1999-2004 (a)

1999	2000	2001	2002	2003	2004
Gabon (b)	Gabon	South Africa	South Africa	Zambia	Gabon
Poland (c)	Poland	Indonesia	Indonesia	Note (f)	Note (f)
Chile (d)	Chile	Australia	Australia	Note (f)	Note (f)
Australia (e)	Australia	Portugal	Portugal	Portugal	Portugal

(a) For table showing membership for period 1996-2002, see ISBA/6/A/CRP.1/ Rev.1, 27 March 2000, Annex 1.

(b) In accordance with the understanding reached in 1996, Gabon assumed the seat in Group C occupied by Zambia until 31 December 1998. It was understood that South Africa would be elected to this seat for a four-year term from 2001, on the understanding that it would serve for two years and then relinquish its seat to Zambia in 2003 and to Gabon in 2004. Thereafter, the seat would be open to any State eligible to represent Group C.

(c) Poland was elected to serve in Group C for two years until the end of 2000, after which the seat would be open to any State eligible to represent Group C, on the basis that Poland would serve on the Council for two years during the period 2001 to 2006.

(d) Chile was elected on the basis that it would serve for two years (1999 and 2000) in Group C, following which it would relinquish its seat in Group C to Indonesia and occupy in 2001 and 2002 the seat in Group E occupied by Costa Rica.

(e) Canada was elected to this seat for a four-year term in 1998 but, following termination of its membership of the Authority in 1998, Australia was elected to replace Canada for the remainder of its term to the end of 2002, subject to the proviso that Group C members will consult further if Canada joins the Authority.

(f) Seat to be filled at elections in 2002.

Group D (developing States representing special interests)

The composition of the six-member Group D contingent is even more complex but may be tabulated thus:

Group D's Council Membership 1999-2004 (a)

1999	2000	2001	2002	2003	2004
Egypt (b)	Egypt	Egypt	Egypt	Note (d)	Note (d)
Sudan (c)	Sudan	Sudan	Sudan	Sudan	Sudan
Fiji	Fiji	Fiji	Fiji	Note (d)	Note (d)
Oman	Oman	Papua New Guinea	Papua New Guinea	Papua New Guinea	Papua New Guinea
Brazil	Brazil	Brazil	Brazil	Brazil	Brazil
Jamaica	Jamaica	Jamaica	Jamaica	Note (d)	Note (d)

306   Chapter 8

(a) For table showing membership for the period 1996-2002, see ISBA/6/A/CRP.1/Rev.1, 27 March 2000.

(b) Egypt was elected to a two-year term in Group E in 1996 on the understanding that it would in 1998 be elected to a four-term in Group D; it would, however, serve only two years and relinquish its seat in 2000 to the candidate to be nominated in 2000 by the African Group. However, in July 2000, it was agreed (ISBA/6/A/14, note 4) that it would keep its seat until 31 December 2002.

(c) Nigeria was elected to a four-year term in 1996 but was to relinquish the seat to Sudan in 1998.

(d) Seat to be filled at elections in 2002.

Group E (equitable geographical distribution)

The following table shows the Council membership of the 18-member Group E for the years 1999 to 2004. Given its size and its purpose – to secure an equitable geographical distribution of Council membership, as well as a balance between developed and developing States – it is not surprising that this is the most complex group of all.

Group E Council Membership 1999-2004 (a)

1999	2000	2001	2002	2003	2004
Cameroon	Cameroon	Algeria (e)	Algeria	Gabon	Algeria
Kenya	Kenya	Cameroon	Cameroon	Namibia	Namibia
Namibia	Namibia	Gabon (f)	Gabon	Senegal	Senegal
Nigeria	Nigeria	Namibia	Namibia	Czech Republic	Czech Republic
Senegal	Senegal	Nigeria	Nigeria	Poland	Poland
Tunisia	Tunisia	Senegal	Senegal	Argentina	Argentina
Indonesia (b)	Indonesia	Tunisia	Tunisia	Guyana	Guyana
Pakistan	Pakistan	Pakistan	Pakistan	Trinidad & Tobago	Trinidad & Tobago
Philippines	Philippines	Republic of Korea	Republic of Korea	Malta	Malta
Republic of Korea	Republic of Korea	Saudi Arabia	Saudi Arabia	Spain	Spain
Saudi Arabia	Saudi Arabia	Czech Republic	Czech Republic	Note (k)	Note (j)
Ukraine	Ukraine	Poland	Poland	Note (k)	Note (k)
Argentina	Argentina	Argentina	Argentina	Note (k)	Note (k)
Costa Rica	Costa Rica	Chile (g)	Chile	Note (k)	Note (k)
Paraguay	Paraguay	Paraguay	Guyana (i)	Note (k)	Note (k)
Trinidad & Tobago	Trinidad & Tobago	Trinidad & Tobago	Paraguay	Note (k)	Note (k)
Austria (c)	Italy/Malta (d)	Malta (h)	Trinidad & Tobago	Note (k)	Note (k)
Belgium	Belgium	Spain	Spain	Note (k)	Note (k)

(a) For table showing membership for the period 1996-2002, see ISBA/6/A/CRP.1/Rev.1, 27 March 2000. For details of the 'floating sea' arrangements for 2001-2004, see ISBA/6/A/14, 13 July 2000, note 1. On the 'floating seat system', see above, section 1.2.1.1

(b)   Completing remaining two years of four-year term to which Poland was elected in 1996.

(c)   Austria was re-elected in 1998 for a four-year term. It was understood that Austria would relinquish its seat at the end of 1999 in favour of Belgium. Belgium would occupy the seat for 2000. The Western European and Others Group would determine who would occupy the seat for the remaining two years of the term (2001 and 2002).

(d)   When Italy was elected to a Group A seat to replace United States, a vacancy arose in Group E for the remainder of 2000. Malta was elected to fill it (ISBA/6/A/6, 11 April 2000).

(e)   Algeria relinquishes its seat under the 'floating seat' arrangement during 2003.

(f)   Gabon will serve in Group E for the period 2001-2003; and in Group C in 2004 (ISBA/6/A/14, 13 July 2000, note 5).

(g)   In accordance with understanding in Latin American and Caribbean Group, Chile was elected to the seat previously occupied by Costa Rica for the period 2001-2002.

(h)   Malta relinquishes its seat under the 'floating seat' arrangement during 2002.

(i)   Guyana relinquishes its seat under the 'floating seat' arrangement during 2001.

(j)   In 2004 the Asian Group will occupy 8 seats. In 2002, the Asian Group will nominate the member to relinquish a seat during 2004 under the 'floating seat' arrangement.

(k)   Seat to be filled at elections in 2002.

The 'chambers' system

For the purposes of decision-making in the Council, the Implementation Agreement identifies four 'chambers'.[76] The first three chambers coincide with Groups A, B and C above but the fourth chamber consists of the developing States elected under both Group D and Group E.

Predominance of industrialised States

The considerable emphasis on the representation of special economic interest groups (as opposed to a straightforward representation based on equitable geographical distribution) has to be seen as favouring the minority of industrialised States which will always have predominant representation in chambers A and B ('consumers' and 'investors' groups) and, of course, if the United States accedes to the UN Convention, it will be guaranteed permanent membership of the Council under the formula for membership of Group A, provided only that it 'wish[es] to be represented in this group.'[77] Taken with the voting rules described below, the composition of the Council places those States in a significantly advantageous position.

1.2.2 Powers, Functions and Decision-making

A full list of the powers and functions of the Council will be found in Article 162 of the UN Convention, as amended by the Implementation Agreement.[78] Here, attention will be focused primarily on the more important powers and functions and on the related decision-making rules.

It was noted above that, under Article 157(3), the Authority is based on the principle of the *sovereign equality* of all its members and the description of this principle as a fundamental principle of the Authority[79] reflects the strong

---

[76] Implementation Agreement, Annex, Section 3(9)(a).

[77] Implementation Agreement, Section 3(15)(a).

[78] The following parts of Art.162 have been affected by the Annex to the Implementation Agreement: Art.162(2)(j) (Annex, Section 3(11)); Art.162(2)(n) (Annex, Section 7(2)); Art.162(2)(o) (Annex, Section 1(15)); Art.162(2)(q) (Annex, Section 6(7)); Art.162(2)(y) (Annex, Section 9 (9)).

[79] See title of Art.157.

308   Chapter 8

opposition of the great majority of States represented at the Conference to the introduction into the constitution of the Authority of representational or voting devices which many of them felt to be inconsistent with the fundamental principle of the regime of the Area – the principle of the common heritage of mankind.[80] At one extreme stood the representatives of the developing world who looked to this regime for the establishment of the beginnings of a new international economic order and abhorred any mention or even hint of weighted votes, blocking minorities or veto powers.   At the other extreme stood the representatives of the existing economic order, believing that the price to be paid for their agreement to the new regime must be institutional guarantees of the protection of a share in the resources of the Area to which their contributions of capital and technology entitled them.   In its essentials, the debate was not about the detailed institutional rules but about the underlying fundamental questions raised by the call for an equitable redistribution of the world's wealth.   At the end of the day the realities of power politics prevailed.   Particularly as amended by the Implementation Agreement, the rules on decision-making in the Council clearly reflect the dominant position of the industrialised powers.

Rules on decision-making.   Under the original provisions of the UN Convention, decisions of the Council on procedural questions were taken by simple majority vote.[81]   On questions of substance, the Council operated a complex, three-tier system of voting, with votes of two-thirds, three-quarters and consensus being required for different categories of decisions.[82]   These rules were radically revised by the Implementation Agreement.

As has been seen, the Implementation Agreement introduced a new rule, whereby, as a general rule, decision-making in the organs of the Authority should be by consensus.[83] The term 'consensus' is not defined in the Agreement, but Rule 59 of the Council's Rules of Procedure[84] adopts the definition provided by Article 161(8)(e) of the UN Convention, under which 'consensus' means 'the absence of any formal objection'. Article 161(8)(e) went on to say that, where it was apparent that there would be such an objection, a prescribed conciliation procedure would have to be resorted to for the purpose of reconciling the differences and producing a proposal which could be adopted by consensus. The Implementation Agreement makes no reference to the conciliation procedure but does provide that the Council may defer the taking of a decision in order to facilitate further negotiation whenever it appears that all efforts at achieving consensus on a question have not been exhausted.[85] Since Article 161(8)(e) has not been rendered inapplicable by the Implementation Agreement, it might seem that this provision for deferment of the vote is complementary to it rather than a substitution for it. On the other hand, the Council's Rules of Procedure do refer to the deferment device but make no mention of a conciliation procedure.

---

[80] See further Chap.3, section I.
[81] Art.161(8)(a).
[82] Art.161(8)(b)-(e).
[83] Implementation Agreement, Annex, Section 3(2).
[84] ISA/99/04.E.
[85] Implementation Agreement, Section 3(6).

Institutional framework 309

In any event, there is no guarantee that conciliation or further negotiations will lead to consensus and the Agreement includes rules which come into play in the absence of a consensus. So far as questions of procedure are concerned, it is provided that, if all efforts to reach a decision by consensus have been exhausted, decisions will then be taken by a majority of members present and voting.[86]

If a consensus is beyond reach on questions of substance, the new rules are much more complex and differ according as the question is or is not one for which the UN Convention specifically requires decision by consensus. If there is such a specific requirement, the decision cannot be taken until consensus is achieved.[87] If, on the other hand, no such specific requirement is included in the UN Convention, the rule is that, once all efforts to reach a consensus (under the new general rule) have been exhausted, the decision may be taken by a two-thirds majority of members present and voting, provided that such decisions are not opposed by a majority in any one of the voting chambers referred to above.[88]

The protection which these rules provide against the imposition of unacceptable decisions by a majority are further enhanced by the supplementary rule which requires that decisions having financial or budgetary implications must be based on the recommendation of the new Finance Committee.[89] Moreover, in the Finance Committee, decisions on questions of substance must be taken by consensus.[90]

Issues for which consensus required. Given the importance of the exception to the two-thirds majority rule in the case of issues for which the UN Convention specifically requires a consensus, the next question is to identify what these issues are. They are referred to in Article 161(8)(d) of the UN Convention and are as follows:

(i) the adoption of amendments to Part XI of the UN Convention. Since, under Article 2(1) of the Implementation Agreement, the provisions of the Agreement and Part XI are to be interpreted and applied together as a single instrument, it would probably follow that the adoption of amendments to the Implementation Agreement would also require consensus. That this is so is in any event confirmed by the provisions of Article 2(2) of the Agreement itself, under which Articles 309-319 of the Convention apply to the Agreement as they apply to the Convention. These articles include Articles 312-316, governing amendment of the Convention, and, in particular, Article 314, which deals with amendments to the provisions of the Convention relating exclusively to activities in the Area.

(ii) the taking of measures to provide protection of developing countries from adverse effects caused by activities in the Area.[91] Such protection is now to be given in accordance with the principles on Economic Assistance laid down in Section 7 of the Annex to the Implementation Agreement.

---

[86] *Ibid.*, Section 3(5).
[87] This follows from the terms of Section 3(5).
[88] Implementation Agreement, Annex, Section 3(5).
[89] *Ibid.*, Section 3(7).
[90] *Ibid.*, Section 9(8). See further below, section II.1.2.3.2.
[91] UN Convention, Art.161(8)(d), referring to Art.162(2)(m).

310   *Chapter 8*

(iii) the recommendation to the Assembly of rules, regulations and procedures on the equitable sharing of financial and other economic benefits derived from activities in the Area and the payments and contributions from the exploitation of the continental shelf beyond 200 miles to be made pursuant to Article 82 of the UN Convention.[92]   It is specifically provided in the Implementation Agreement that Council decisions on rules, regulations and procedures on the equitable sharing of financial and other economic benefits derived from activities in the Area (there is no mention of payments and benefits under Article 82) 'shall take into account' recommendations of the Finance Committee.[93]   It might seem, at first sight, that since such decisions clearly have 'financial or budgetary implications', they would in fact have to be 'based on the recommendations of the Finance Committee', made by consensus,[94] but this hardly seems to be a tenable conclusion.[95]

(iv) the adoption and provisional application of rules, regulations and procedures of the Authority.[96]   These rules, regulations and procedures are central to the regime of sea-bed mining since they will relate to prospecting, exploration and exploitation in the Area and the financial management and internal administration of the Authority.[97]   However, this task is now to be accomplished in accordance with the revised scheme laid down in the Implementation Agreement.[98]   Accordingly, the rules, regulations and procedures to be elaborated and adopted will now be based on the principles contained in specified sections of the Annex to the Implementation Agreement and on any additional rules, regulations and procedures necessary to facilitate the approval of plans of work for exploration and exploitation.   The specified sections of the Annex are Section 2 (on the Enterprise), Section 5 (transfer of technology), Section 6 (production policy), Section 7 (economic assistance), and Section 8 (financial terms of contracts).[99]   In adopting the rules etc., the Authority has also to take into account the draft rules etc. prepared by the Preparatory Commission.[100]

Approval of plans of work.   Under the original UN Convention regime, special provision was made in Article 162(2)(j) and (2)(k) for decision-making in relation to the approval of plans of work.   That provision was replaced by the Implementation Agreement and the new rules are as follows:

(i)   If the Legal and Technical Commission, by a majority of members present and voting,[101] recommends approval of a plan of work, the Council 'shall approve' the recommendation, unless, by a two-thirds majority of its members present and voting, including a majority of members present and

---

[92] UN Convention, Art.161(8)(d) and Art.162(2)(o)(i).
[93] Implementation Agreement, Annex, Section 9(7)(f).
[94] See Implementation Agreement, Annex, Section 3(7) and Section 9(8).
[95] The question is considered further below in section II.1.2.3.2.
[96] UN Convention, Art.161(8)(d) and Art.162(2)(o)(ii).
[97] Art.162(2)(o)(ii).
[98] See further Implementation Agreement, Annex, Section 1(15).
[99] *Ibid.*, chapeau.
[100] *Ibid.*, Section 1(16).
[101] *Ibid.*, Section 3(13).

voting in each of the chambers of the Council, the Council decides to disapprove a plan of work.[102] If the Council wishes to approve the Commission's recommendation expressly ('shall approve'), the normal rule for voting on matters of substance would apply, that is, consensus or, if unobtainable, a two-thirds majority of members present and voting, provided that the decision is not opposed by a majority in any one of the Council's four chambers. There is, however, an alternative route to Council approval. If the Council does not take a decision on a positive recommendation of the Commission within a prescribed period (normally 60 days), it will be deemed to have given its approval at the end of that period.[103]

(ii)   If the Legal and Technical Commission recommends disapproval, or does not make a recommendation, it is still open to the Council to approve the plan of work, applying its normal rule for voting on questions of substance.[104]

(iii) The procedure for approval of plans of work submitted by the Enterprise is the same, *mutatis mutandis,* as for other applicants,[105] but account would have to be taken of the radical amendments regarding the position of the Enterprise introduced by the Implementation Agreement.[106]

The predominant rôle of the Council. It is clear from this analysis that although, under Article 160 (1), the Assembly has to 'be considered the supreme organ of the Authority,'[107] the description is largely an empty formula designed to satisfy the demands of the Group of 77 in form, if not in substance, and is not matched by any residual powers whereby the Assembly may assert its authority over the Council in central areas of decision-making.

1.2.3 Subsidiary Organs of Council

The Authority is empowered to establish such subsidiary organs as may be found necessary.[108] In the UN Convention itself, provision is made for an Economic Planning Commission and a Legal and Technical Commission, described as 'organs of the Council,'[109] and, pursuant to the requirement in Article 162(2)(y) of the Convention, a Finance Committee was established by the Implementation Agreement.[110]

---

[102] *Ibid.*, Section 3(11).
[103] *Ibid.*
[104] *Ibid.*
[105] UN Convention, Art.162(2)(k).
[106] See Implementation Agreement, Annex, Section 2 and below, section 2.
[107] A formulation which replaced the form of words used in an earlier negotiating text (ICNT/Rev. 1 of 28 April 1979) to the effect that the 'Assembly is the supreme organ ...' The change, alleged to diminish the relative status of the Assembly, apparently rendered the text more acceptable to the industrialised States.
[108] Art.158(3).
[109] Art.163.
[110] Implementation Agreement, Annex, Section 9(1) and (9). See further below, section 1.2.3.2.

312   Chapter 8

1.2.3.1 The Two Commissions

Many of the Council's powers have to be exercised on the basis of advice or recommendations from its Commissions, or on the basis of, or taking account of, the recommendations of the Finance Committee. It is therefore important that the composition and decision-making processes of these organs should be such as to enable them to give well-informed advice without undue delay.

Under Article 163(2) and (6), each of the two Commissions is to be composed of fifteen members elected by the Council to serve for a term of five years but the Council may, if necessary, decide to increase the size of either Commission, having due regard to economy and efficiency. As will be seen below, this provision was employed at the first election in August 1996 to increase the size of the Legal and Technical Commission to twenty-two members. Members of the Commissions are required to have appropriate qualifications in the area of competence of the Commission concerned and States Parties must 'nominate candidates of the highest standards of competence and integrity with qualifications in relevant fields so as to ensure the effective exercise of the functions of the Commissions.'[111] In addition, due regard has to be paid to the need for equitable geographical distribution and representation of special interests.[112] The need for an appropriately qualified membership is re-emphasised in more specific form in Article 164 (which exemplifies the kind of qualifications needed for membership of the Economic Planning Commission) and Article 165 (which performs the same service for the Legal and Technical Commission). In both cases the Council is again enjoined to 'endeavour to ensure that the membership of the Commission reflects all appropriate qualifications'.[113]

The functions of the two Commissions include the proposal of measures to the Council to implement decisions relating to activities in the Area, the review of trends in the minerals market, the examination of situations likely to lead to adverse effects on the economies of developing States, the review of work plans, the supervision of activities in the Area and the assessment of the environmental impact of activities in the Area.[114] The Commissions are to exercise their functions in accordance with such guidelines and directives as the Council may adopt.[115]

As regards the decision-making process, the UN Convention simply provides that the procedures of the Commissions will be established by the rules, regulations and procedures of the Authority.[116] The Implementation Agreement, on the other hand, provides for '*Decisions by voting* in the Legal and Technical Commission' to be taken by a majority of members present and voting.[117] It is not clear from these provisions whether all decisions of the Commission are to be reached by voting or this rule applies only after all efforts to achieve a consensus have failed. As has been seen, '*As a general rule*, decision-making in the *organs*

---

[111] Art.163(3).
[112] Art.163(4).
[113] Arts.164(1) and 165(1).
[114] See further Arts.164 and 165.
[115] Art.163(9).
[116] Art.163(11).
[117] Implementation Agreement, Annex, Section 3(13), emphasis added.

of the Authority should be by consensus.[118] The question is whether the 'general rule' is departed from in the case of the Legal and Technical Commission, an organ of the Council.[119] The answer is provided by the Rules of Procedure of the Legal and Technical Commission. Rule 44(1) provides that, 'As a general rule, decision-making in the Commission should be by consensus', and Rule 44(2) prescribes that, 'If all efforts to reach a decision by consensus have been exhausted, decisions by voting shall be taken by a majority of members present and voting'. [120]

It has also to be noted in this context that the functions of the Economic Planning Commission are to be performed by the Legal and Technical Commission until such time as the Council decides otherwise, or until the approval of the first plan of work for exploitation.[121]

The first election of members of the Legal and Technical Commission took place in August 1996 and, as noted above, the Council took advantage of the provisions of Article 163(2) to raise the number of members to 22, though without prejudice to future elections.[122] The election of an additional candidate to be proposed by the Latin American and Caribbean Group was approved in August 1999, also without prejudice to future elections. [123]

1.2.3.2 The Finance Committee
Establishment. Under Article 162(2)(y) of the UN Convention, the Council is required to establish a subsidiary organ for the elaboration of draft financial rules, regulations and procedures relating to two matters. The first is the financial management of the Authority in accordance with Articles 171 to 175.[124] This covers such questions as the sources of the Authority's funds, its annual budget, the expenses of the Authority, its borrowing powers and annual audit. The second matter is the financial arrangements to be made in accordance with Annex III, Article 13 and Article 17(1)(c).[125] This requirement to establish such a subsidiary organ is deemed to have been fulfilled by the establishment of a Finance Committee under Section 9(1) of the Annex to the Implementation Agreement.

---

[118] Implementation Agreement, Annex, Section 3(2), emphasis added.

[119] UN Convention, Art.163(1).

[120] The 'Revised Draft Rules of the Legal and Technical Commission' (ISBA/5/C/L.1/Rev.2, 1 September 1999) were approved by the Council in August 1999 (ISBA/5/C/11, 2 September 1999, para. 15), with the exception of Rules 6 and 53, which were finalised at the Sixth Session in July 2000. The Rules of Procedure of the Legal and Technical Commission are now in the Annex to the Decision of the Council of 13 July 2000 (ISBA/6/C/9, 13 July 2000).

[121] Implementation Agreement, Annex, Section 1(4).

[122] ISBA/C/L.3, 11 November 1996 (*SD & D*, vol. 1, p.39(7)).

[123] ISBA/5/C/11, 2 September 1999 (*SD & D*, vol. 3, p. 47(5)).

[124] Parts of these articles have been modified by the Annex to the Implementation Agreement, as follows (with the relevant provision of the Annex in brackets): Art.171(a) (Annex, Section 1(14)); Art.171(f) (Annex, Section 7(2)); Art.172 (Annex, Section 9(7)(c)); Art.173 (Annex, Section 1(14)); Art.173(2)(c) (Annex, Section 7(2)); and Art.174(1) (Annex, Section 1 (14)).

[125] Art.13(2) and Art.13(3)-(10) of Annex III of the UN Convention have been modified by Section 8(3) and 8(2) respectively of the Annex to the Implementation Agreement.

314   *Chapter 8*

Composition. The Committee consists of 15 members,[126] no two of whom may be nationals of the same State Party,[127] elected for a five-year term by the Assembly.[128] Members must have appropriate qualifications relevant to financial matters and the highest standards of competence and integrity.[129] In their election, due account has to be taken of the need for equitable geographical distribution and the representation of special interests.[130] In particular, each of the groups (the Council chambers representing the special interests of consumers, investors, exporters and developing States) identified in Section 3(15)(a)-(d) of the Annex to the Implementation Agreement has to be represented by at least one member.[131] Until such time as the Authority has sufficient funds, other than assessed contributions, to meet its administrative expenses, the Committee must include representatives of the five largest contributors to the Authority's administrative budget. Thereafter, the election of one member from each group will be on the basis of nomination by the members of the group, without prejudice to the possibility of further members being elected from each group.[132]

Once again, the first elections were bedevilled by the need to secure agreement on the allocation of seats among the various interest groups and regional groups and the process was further complicated by the need to include representatives of the five largest contributors to the budget. Eventually, at the resumed second session of the Assembly in August 1996, the fifteen members were elected on the basis of a complex compromise formula which was declared to be without prejudice to the overall composition of the Finance Committee for future elections and, in particular, to the claims of the regional groups.[133] It was understood too that the situation would have to be reviewed in the light of the circumstances prevailing after 16 November 1998, when provisional membership of the Authority was due to terminate.[134]

As a result of these negotiations, the first Finance Committee was composed as follows: three members each were drawn from the African Group, the Asian Group and the Latin American and Caribbean Group; five members were drawn from the Western European and Other States Group; and one member came from the Eastern European Group. However, 'to accommodate some regional interests',[135] it was found necessary to agree that the Latin American and Caribbean Group would relinquish one seat after two years (1997-1998) in favour of the Asian Group for the remainder of the five-year term. Similarly the Western European and Others Group was to relinquish one of its seats after two and one half years in favour of a candidate from the Eastern European Group. The five-year term commenced on 1 January 1997.[136]

---

[126] Implementation Agreement, Annex, Section 9(1).
[127] *Ibid.*, Section 9(2).
[128] *Ibid.*, Section 9(3)-(4).
[129] *Ibid.*, Section 9(1).
[130] *Ibid.*, Section 9(3).
[131] *Ibid.*
[132] *Ibid.*
[133] See further *Statement of the President on the Work of the Assembly during the Resumed Second Session*, ISBA/A/L.13, 11 November 1996, paras.6-11.
[134] *Ibid.*, para.11.
[135] *Ibid.*, para.10
[136] *Ibid.*

Institutional framework 315

In accordance with the understanding reached in 1996, [137] in August 1999, an Indonesian candidate was elected to the Finance Committee for the remainder of the five-year term of the Mexican member and, following the resignation of the United States member, a Polish candidate was elected for the remainder of the five-year term to 31 December 2001. [138]

Decision-making. Decisions of the Finance Committee on questions of procedure are to be taken by a majority of members present and voting.[139] Decisions on questions of substance require consensus.[140] This is a very important rule because, under the Implementation Agreement, decisions taken by the Assembly and the Council on a wide range of financial and budgetary questions have to *take into account*[141] recommendations of the Finance Committee and, indeed, any decision by the Assembly or the Council having financial or budgetary implications must be *based on* the recommendations of the Finance Committee.[142]

At first sight, there might appear to be a lack of consistency in the Implementation Agreement. Section 9(7) of the Annex lists six issues on which decisions of the Assembly and the Council have merely to 'take into account' the recommendations of the Finance Committee. However, since all six are clearly financial or budgetary issues, it might seem to follow that decisions by the Assembly or the Council on such issues must have financial or budgetary implications and must therefore be based on the recommendations of the Finance Committee.[143]

However, an alternative interpretation is more persuasive. That the authors of the Implementation Agreement intended to distinguish between the financial and budgetary issues itemised in Section 9(7) and *other* issues having financial or budgetary *implications* is strongly suggested by the fact that, under an earlier draft, the Assembly and Council would have been required to take decisions *on the basis of* the Finance Committee's recommendations on the six issues now listed in Section 9(7).[144] The formula was later changed to 'take into account'. Rule 31 of the Council's Rules of Procedure, on submission of the annual budget, is consistent with this interpretation, in indicating that, 'The Council shall consider the proposed annual budget taking into account the recommendations of the Finance Committee and submit it to the Assembly, together with its own

---

[137] *Ibid.,* para. 10.
[138] ISBA/5/A/14, 2 September 1999 (*S D & D*, vol. 3, p. 39, paras. 7-9). Occasional vacancies were also filled in March 1998 (a Tunisian for another Tunisian – ISBA/4/A/9, 28 April 1998, para. 4); in August 1999 (an Indian for another Indian – ISBA/5/A/14, 2 September 1999, para. 6); and in March 2000 (a Russian for another Russian – ISBA/6/A/6, 11 April 2000, para. 5). See also Note by the Secretary-General, ISBA/6/A/1.
[139] Implementation Agreement, Annex, Section 9(8).
[140] *Ibid.*
[141] *Ibid.,* Section 9(7), chapeau.
[142] *Ibid.,* Section 3(7).
[143] *Ibid.*
[144] See the 'Boat Paper', dated 3 August 1993, prepared by several developed and developing States as a contribution to the UN Secretary-General's Informal Consultations which led to the Implementation Agreement. Annex II.I, para. 5 refers to this question.

316   Chapter 8

recommendations thereon'.[145] . The Financial Regulations of the Authority make the same distinction. Thus, under Regulation 3(7), decisions by the Assembly and the Council on the budget 'shall take into account the recommendations of the Finance Committee', whereas, under Regulation 13(1), decisions having financial or budgetary implications 'shall be based on the recommendations of the Finance Committee'. [146]

The fact remains, of course, that the recommendations of the Finance Committee have to be adopted by consensus. The consequences of failure to reach a consensus are not indicated in the Implementation Agreement, although the question was raised in the course of the Preparatory Commission's deliberations on the establishment of a Finance Committee.[147]   Draft Rules produced in 1996 provided that, 'In case the Finance Committee fails to reach consensus during a reasonable period of time, it shall prepare a report reflecting different opinions'. However, the final Rules of Procedure adopted on 20 August 1999 simply repeat that decisions on questions of substance shall be taken by consensus.[148]

Powers and functions.   The range of the Finance Committee's functions and the powers which it enjoys in relation to such functions by virtue of the above-noted decision-making rules are indicated in Section 9(7) of the Annex to the Implementation Agreement.   It has a role to play by making recommendations on the following issues:

(a) Draft financial rules, regulations and procedures of the organs of the Authority and the financial management and internal financial administration of the Authority;

(b) Assessment of contributions of members to the administrative budget of the Authority in accordance with Article 160, paragraph 2(e), of the Convention;

(c) All relevant financial matters, including the proposed annual budget prepared by the Secretary-General of the Authority in accordance with Article 172 of the Convention and the financial aspects of the implementation of the programmes of work of the Secretariat;

(d) The administrative budget;

(e) Financial obligations of States Parties arising from the implementation of the Implementation Agreement and Part XI as well as the administrative and budgetary implications of proposals and recommendations involving expenditure from the funds of the Authority;

---

[145] ISBA/C/12, 3 December 1996.

[146] The Financial Regulations of the International Seabed Authority were approved by the Assembly on 23 March 2000 and are in ISBA/6/A/3, 28 March 2000, Annex; or ISA/00/01.

[147] *Summary Report on the Secretary-General's informal consultations on outstanding issues relating to the deep sea-bed mining provisions of the UN Convention on the Law of the Sea, held on 8-12 November 1993*, 14 December 1993, p.5(12), where the question was raised, 'whether provisions should be made in case decisions could not be taken by consensus'.

[148] ISBA/F/WP.1, 24 July 1996, draft Rule 21; and Rules of Procedure of the Finance Committee, 20 August 1999 (ISA/00/01), Rule 22(2).

Institutional framework 317

(f) Rules, regulations and procedures on the equitable sharing of financial and other economic benefits derived from activities in the Area and the decisions to be made thereon.[149]

1.3 The Secretariat

The third of the 'principal organs' of the Authority is the Secretariat.[150] This is the administrative organ of the Authority, headed by the chief administrative officer of the Authority, the Secretary-General. In general, the Secretariat shares the characteristics common to the administrative organs of other international institutions.[151] It is, however, refreshing to find that although, in recruiting staff, the Secretary-General has to pay due regard to the principle of equitable geographical representation, this is subject to the 'paramount consideration' of the 'necessity of securing the highest standards of efficiency, competence and integrity.'[152] Provision is also made for consultation and co-operation with other international and non-governmental organisations recognised by the Economic and Social Council of the United Nations.[153]

Staff Regulations were adopted by the Council at the Resumed Sixth Session of the Authority in July 2000. [154]

2. The Enterprise

The Enterprise is established as an organ of the Authority in Article 158(2) of the UN Convention and its role and institutional features were originally further specified in Article 170 and in the Statute of the Enterprise which is embodied in Annex IV to the Convention. UNCLOS III also made provision for the establishment by the Preparatory Commission of a 'special commission for the Enterprise' and for the entrustment to it of functions referred to in both Conference Resolutions I and II.[155] Unfortunately, the practical value of much of the work done by this special commission - that is, Special Commission 2 of the Preparatory Commission - has been put in doubt, partly as a result of the anticipated long delay in proceeding to the exploitation of sea-bed minerals, but more especially by the substantial changes made by the Implementation Agreement to the provisions of the UN Convention dealing with the Enterprise. In analysing these various provisions below, reference will be made as appropriate to the specific changes introduced by the Implementation Agreement.

2.1 Rôle of the Enterprise and Relationship to Authority

In providing for the 'purpose' of the Enterprise and its relationship to the Authority, there is a remarkable amount of repetition between Article 170 of the

---

[149]Implementation Agreement, Annex, Section 9(7).
[150] UN Convention, Arts.158(1) and 166-169.
[151] See, *e.g.*, D.W. Bowett, *The Law of International Institutions*, 4th ed., 1982, at pp.97-104.
[152] Art.167(2).
[153] Art.169.
[154]Staff Regulations of the International Seabed Authority, (Council Decision of 13 July 2000, ISBA/6/C/10, Annex). On the duty of confidentiality of Authority staff, see above, Chap. 5, section IV.
[155] UNCLOS III, Resolution I on the Establishment of the Preparatory Commission for the International Sea-Bed Authority and for the International Tribunal for the Law of the Sea, Para.8.

318   *Chapter 8*

UN Convention and Articles 1 and 2 of the Statute of the Enterprise in Annex IV to the Convention.

The Enterprise is described (in both Article 170 of the Convention and Article 1(1) of the Statute) as '... the organ of the Authority which shall carry out activities in the Area directly ... as well as the transporting, processing and marketing of minerals recovered from the Area', the latter clause having been added at the Eighth Session of UNCLOS III to reflect the accepted view of the scope of the Enterprise's functions.[156] Despite a French attempt to have this formulation amended, it would seem to have been accepted that the Enterprise should be authorised to transport, process and market not only minerals which it recovered from the Area but also those recovered from the Area by other entities.[157]

Following an extensive debate on the Statute of the Enterprise at the Ninth Session of UNCLOS III, a consensus emerged that the Enterprise should have operational autonomy and operate on commercial principles.[158] The autonomy enjoyed by the Enterprise is, however, a limited one – limited by the rules circumscribing its freedom of action and rendering it accountable to other organs of the Authority. First, the Enterprise has to act in accordance with (i) the provisions of the Convention and the rules, regulations and procedures of the Authority, (ii) the general policies established by the Assembly and (iii) the directives of the Council.[159] Subject to all this, however, in developing the resources of the Area, the Enterprise is to 'operate in accordance with sound commercial principles'[160] and is to 'enjoy autonomy in the conduct of its operations'.[161] It must be added, however, that, as will be seen below, the 'sound commercial principles' did not exclude the possibility of the receipt by the Enterprise of considerable financial and technological assistance under the terms of the original UN Convention regime.[162] On the other hand, its autonomy was reflected in the provision that 'Nothing in this Convention shall make the Enterprise liable for the acts or obligations of the Authority, or make the Authority liable for the acts or obligations of the Enterprise'.[163]

The above description of the role of the Enterprise and its relationship to the Authority is based on the original UN Convention regime and it has now to be modified by taking account of the changes introduced by the Implementation Agreement. Before doing so, however, it may be useful to provide a brief account of the work done by the Preparatory Commission's Special Commission 2 pursuant to its mandate under Resolutions I and II of UNCLOS III and of the part played by the UN Secretary-General's Informal Consultations.

---

[156] Nordquist and Park, *op. cit.* in note 13. *Eighth Session, Geneva, March 19-April 27, 1979*, p.251, at p. 276.

[157] A/CONF.62/C.1/L.28, 23 August 1980, *UNCLOS III Off. Rec.*, Vol. XIV, p. 161, at p. 167.

[158] Nordquist and Park, *op. cit.* in note 13. *Ninth Session, New York, March 3-April 4, 1980*, p.351, at p. 377.

[159] UN Convention, Art.170 and Statute, Arts.1(2) and 2(1).

[160] Annex IV, Art.1(3).

[161] Annex IV, Art.2(2).

[162] See further below, sections 2.4.5 and 2.5

[163] Annex IV, Art.2(3).

Institutional framework   319

2.1.1 The Work of Special Commission 2 (SCN.2)

SCN.2 was mandated to take all measures necessary for the early entry into effective operation of the Enterprise and to perform the functions referred to in Resolution II, Paragraph 12,[164] the objective of which was to ensure that the Enterprise should be able to keep pace with States and other entities carrying out sea-bed mining activities in the Area. Paragraph 12 placed obligations upon both registered pioneer investors and certifying States.[165] Pioneer investors had three obligations placed upon them.[166] First, they were required to carry out exploration in reserved areas 'at the request of the Commission'. Secondly, they had to provide training at all levels for personnel 'designated by the Commission'. Finally, they were required to undertake, before the entry into force of the Convention, to perform the obligations prescribed in the Convention relating to transfer of technology. The Preparatory Commission's role in relation to these obligations was to be performed by SCN.2.[167]

Similarly, Paragraph 12 imposed two obligations upon certifying States.[168] They had to ensure that the necessary funds would be made available to the Enterprise in a timely manner in accordance with the Convention, upon its entry into force; and they had to report periodically to the Commission on the activities carried out by them, by their entities or natural or juridical persons. Here too, the Commission's role was to be performed by SCN.2.[169]

Initially, the Commission 'envisaged its work as encompassing the full range of preparatory work needed to facilitate the implementation of the Convention and to assure the ability of the Enterprise "to keep pace" with registered pioneer investors, in the event that sea-bed mining was ready to commence at the time of entry into force of the Convention'.[170] Soon, however, it was obliged to set up an Advisory Group on Assumptions to monitor economic factors pertinent to the viability of sea-bed mining and to conclude that '... virtually any concrete recommendations it could make on both operational and organisational matters would need to be revised as and when economic prospects for mining improve'.[171] From 1986, therefore, it concentrated on a more limited agenda: the development and establishment of a training programme; organisational structure of the Enterprise and consideration of a recommendation regarding a pre-operational Enterprise; operational options of the Enterprise, including project feasibility analysis, an agreed set of working assumptions and the initial operation of the Enterprise.[172]

---

[164] Resolution I, Para.8.
[165] UNCLOS III, Resolution II Governing Preparatory Investment in Pioneer Activities Relating to Polymetallic Nodules, Para.12.
[166] *Ibid.*, Para.12(a)(i)-(iii).
[167] In accordance with Resolution I, Para.8 and Resolution II, Para.12, read together.
[168] Resolution II, Para.12(b)(i)-(ii).
[169] Resolution I, Para.8, read with Resolution II, Para.12.
[170] LOS/PCN/SCN.2/1992/CRP.6, 17 August 1992, p.5(5).
[171] *Ibid.*, p.6(8).
[172] *Ibid.*, p.6(9).

320   *Chapter 8*

SCN.2 had little difficulty in dealing with the relatively uncontentious question of establishing a training scheme[173] but the same cannot be said about its work on the more essential items on its agenda.

As regards the establishment of the organisational structure of the Enterprise, it is true that it succeeded in producing 'Annotations ... on the Provisions of the Convention Relating to the Structure and Organisation of the Enterprise'.[174] However, that there had to be a very large question mark over the usefulness of this work was emphasised by the statement made by the Group of Six, explaining why they wished to reserve their position on this document.[175] It was pointed out that the prospects for commercial exploitation had receded into the next century; there was a growing acceptance that the Enterprise should operate on purely commercial terms and that its first mining operation should be carried out as a joint venture with other deep sea-bed mining companies. It was concluded that 'the provisions of the Convention relating to the Enterprise had been overtaken by events and therefore needed to be changed'.[176] It was thus premature to take any decision at that point regarding the detailed structure and organisation of the Enterprise and inappropriate to annotate provisions when it was not known whether and under which circumstances they would be applied.[177]

The same reservations, though now generally shared, are reflected in the Special Commission's 'annotations' for the initial operation and administration of the Enterprise ('transitional arrangements'). The Assembly was advised 'to proceed on the basis of an evolutionary approach where the functions of the Enterprise ... are filled (sic) and carried out according to the dictates of the prevailing circumstances'.[178] It would 'have to judge the best way in which [the functions of the Enterprise in this interim period] ... are to be carried out ...'[179]

As will be seen below, the growing caution and reservations over the role to be played by the Enterprise reflected in the later sessions of SCN.2 were even more evident in the Secretary-General's Informal Consultations and led to the radical revision of the provisions of the UN Convention dealing with the Enterprise by the Implementation Agreement. Regrettably, these changes mean that much of the considerable work done by SCN.2 and the high level of expertise reflected in the voluminous documentation which the Authority inherited from the Commission[180] will be of only limited relevance for the future.

---

[173] See further *ibid.*, at pp.7-8 and Annex 1.

[174] See further *ibid.*, at p.10(22) and its Annex 2 which embodies LOS/PCN/SCN.2/L.8/Rev.1, 17 August 1992. The original title referred to 'Recommended Annotations ...' but the word 'Recommended' was deleted after several speakers pointed out that the Special Commission had not in fact agreed on any annotations. See LOS/PCN/L.110, 31 March 1993, p.5(21) and Press Release SEA/1361, 29 March 1993, p.1.

[175] See further LOS/PCN/SCN.2/L.8/Rev.1, 17 August 1992, at p.6(6)-(7).

[176] *Ibid.*, at p.6(7).

[177] *Ibid.* See too LOS/PCN/L.110, 31 March 1993, at p.5(18).

[178] LOS/PCN/SCN.2/CRP.5/Rev.1, August 1992 (as amended by LOS/PCN/L.110, 31 March 1993), at p.9.

[179] *Ibid.*, at p.10.

[180] This documentation is published in the Preparatory Commission's 13-vol. final report (on which see further below, section III.3). For 'Provisional final report of Special Commission 2', see X *Final PrepCom Report*, pp.8-28 and for SCN.2's documentation, see X and XI *Final PrepCom Report*. See also Press Releases SEA/1352, 24 March 1993, SEA/1354, 25 March 1993, SEA/1361, 29 March 1993, and SEA/1367, 1 April 1993.

Institutional framework 321

2.1.2 The UN Secretary-General's Informal Consultations
Although the Preparatory Commission was used as a forum in which to express the need for changes in the original UN Convention regime of sea-bed mining, the task of bringing about such changes was not within its mandate. This explains why the preparatory work leading to the Implementation Agreement was left to be done through a series of Informal Consultations convened by the UN Secretary-General between July 1990 and June 1994, when the Secretary-General was able to report to the General Assembly that they had 'led to a result which ... could form the basis of a general agreement ...'[181] So far as the Enterprise is concerned, the 'findings' reported in an Information Note of 10 December 1992 included the recognition that, 'When deep sea-bed mining becomes feasible, the Enterprise should begin its operations through joint ventures.'[182] It was acknowledged too that, 'Funding obligations for the first mining operation of the Enterprise [would] ... not arise since the exploitation is to be carried out at least in the initial phase through joint ventures and funds shall be provided pursuant to the provisions of the joint venture arrangements.'[183] These 'findings' formed the basis of the amendments made in the Implementation Agreement.

2.1.3 The Implementation Agreement of 28 July 1994
First, by way of preface, it may be noted that the Implementation Agreement embodies a compromise between the position favoured by the developing States, which advocated an effective, independent organ reflecting the basic principle of the common heritage of mankind, and that of the industrialised States, which wished the Enterprise to operate via joint ventures once sea-bed mining became commercially viable. The Agreement confirms that the Enterprise will conduct its initial mining operations by way of joint ventures.[184] It also gives effect to the general principle, applicable to all of the organs of the Authority, that their setting up and functioning should be based on an evolutionary approach, taking into account their functional needs, in order that they may discharge their responsibilities effectively at various stages of the development of sea-bed mining.[185]

In the beginning, the functions of the Enterprise are to be performed by the Secretariat of the Authority, operating under an interim Director-General.[186] It will keep under review trends and developments relating to sea-bed mining and, *inter alia*, evaluate information on areas reserved for the Authority under pioneer

---

[181] *Law of the Sea. Consultations of the Secretary-General on outstanding issues relating to the deep sea-bed mining provisions of the United Nations Convention on the Law of the Sea. Report of the Secretary-General*, A/48/950, 9 June 1994, at p.7(28).
[182] *Information Note concerning the Secretary-General's Informal Consultations on outstanding issues relating to the deep sea-bed mining provisions of the UN Convention on the Law of the Sea*, 10 December 1992, at p.7.
[183] *Ibid.*
[184] Implementation Agreement, Annex, Section 2(2).
[185] *Ibid.*, Section 1(3).
[186] Implementation Agreement, Annex, Section 2(1).

322   Chapter 8

investor scheme.[187]   The question of the functioning of the Enterprise independently of the Secretariat of the Authority will be taken up by the Council of the Authority either upon the approval of a plan of work for exploitation for an entity other than the Enterprise, or upon receipt by the Council of an application for a joint venture operation with the Enterprise.   If such joint ventures 'accord with sound commercial principles', the Council must then issue a directive under Article 170(2) of the UN Convention, providing for such independent functioning of the Enterprise.[188]

2.2 Legal Personality

Though described as 'the organ of the Authority ...'[189] and subject to the general policies of the Assembly and the directives and control of the Council, the Enterprise nevertheless has separate legal capacity. Under Article 170(2), it has, 'within the framework of the international legal personality of the Authority ... such legal capacity as is provided for in the Statute set forth in Annex IV'. The scope of the Enterprise's legal capacity, as laid down in Article 13 of Annex IV, is determined on a functional basis. Under Article 13(1) and (2), the legal capacity accorded to it in the territories of States Parties is:

> such legal capacity as is necessary for the exercise of its functions and the fulfilment of its purposes and, in particular, the capacity:
> (a) to enter into contracts, joint arrangements or other arrangements, including agreements with States and international organisations;
> (b) to acquire, lease, hold and dispose of immovable and movable property;
> (c) to be a party to legal proceedings.

Each State Party is bound, under Paragraph 6 of Article 13, to take such action as is necessary 'for giving effect in terms of its own law to the principles set forth' in Annex IV. One of those 'principles' is that identified in Article 13, Paragraph 1: 'To enable the Enterprise to exercise its functions, the status, privileges and immunities set forth in this article shall be accorded to the Enterprise in the territories of States Parties'.

Under Article 13(3), actions may be brought against the Enterprise only in a court of competent jurisdiction in the territory of a State Party in which the Enterprise has an office or facility; has appointed an agent for the purpose of accepting service or notice of process; has entered into a contract for goods or services; has issued securities; or is otherwise engaged in commercial activity.

The Governing Board of the Enterprise is the organ responsible for entering into any legal proceedings, agreements and transactions and for taking any other actions in accordance with Article 13.[190] The Director-General of the Enterprise is the legal representative of the Enterprise.[191] However, as has been seen, in the

---

[187] *Ibid.*, Section 2(1)(a) and (e). Substantial areas have already been reserved for the Authority under Resolution II, Para.3 and the New York Understanding of 5 September 1986. See further Chap.6, section III.6 and 7 and section IV.1.6.

[188] Implementation Agreement, Annex, Section 2(2).

[189] UN Convention, Art.170(1).

[190] Annex IV, Art.6(n).

[191] Annex IV, Art.7(2).

Institutional framework   323

beginning, all Enterprise functions will be performed by the Secretariat of the Authority, operating under an interim Director-General.[192]

2.3 Structure

The Enterprise has a simple structure. A 15-man Governing Board, elected by the Assembly,[193] directs the business operations of the Enterprise and exercises all the powers necessary to fulfil the purposes of the Enterprise.[194] The chief executive of the Enterprise, the Director-General, is elected by the Assembly upon the recommendation of the Council and the nomination of the Governing Board.[195] The chief executive is directly responsible to the Governing Board for the conduct of the business of the Enterprise[196] and may have non-discretionary powers delegated to him by the Governing Board with the approval of the Council.[197]

The institutional features of the Governing Board are fully detailed in Article 5 and it will suffice here to draw attention to a few of the more important of them. First, in line with objectives of efficiency and avoidance of waste noted earlier,[198] States are required to bear in mind the need to nominate candidates of the highest standard of competence, with qualifications in relevant fields, so as to ensure the viability and success of the Enterprise.[199]

Secondly, in accordance with accepted standards of international administrative law, if a member of the Governing Board has a conflict of interest on a matter before the Board, he must refrain from voting.[200]

Thirdly, reflecting the principles of operational autonomy and sound commercial practice noted above,[201] the members of the Governing Board are not representatives of governments but act in their personal capacity and accept instructions from neither governments nor the Authority.[202] Their independence is buttressed by the method of their remuneration; they are paid out of Enterprise funds.[203]

Fourthly, despite a French proposal that the Board be selected for a limited time by those States which account for 70% of Enterprise financing, strong pressure from the Group of 77 ensured that members of the Board should be elected by the Assembly.[204] The Council does, however, have a role to play in the election of the Director-General, since the Assembly may elect only upon the Council's recommendation and the Governing Board's nomination.[205]

---

[192] See above, at note 186.
[193] Annex IV, Art.5(1).
[194] Annex IV, Art.6.
[195] Annex IV, Art.7(1).
[196] Annex IV, Art.7(2).
[197] Annex IV, Art.6(o).
[198] See above, Chap.4, section I, following note 34.
[199] Annex IV, Art.5(1).
[200] Annex IV, Art.5(8).
[201] Above, section 2.1.
[202] Annex IV, Art.5(4).
[203] Annex IV, Art.5(5).
[204] Annex IV, Art.5(1).   See also Nordquist and Park, *op.cit.* note 13, at p.378 and A/CONF.62/C.1/L.28, 23 August 1980, *UNCLOS III Off.Rec.*, Vol.XIV, p.161, at p.167.
[205] Annex IV, Art.7(1).

324   *Chapter 8*

Finally, attention should be drawn to Article 5(9) of the Statute, under which any State member of the Authority may ask the Board for information in respect of its operations which particularly affect that member. The Board must endeavour to provide such information.

The Board's powers and functions are listed in Annex IV, Article 6. They include powers to draw up and submit formal written plans of work to the Council[206]; to develop plans of work and programmes for carrying out activities in the Area, as well as the transporting, processing and marketing of minerals recovered from the Area[207]; to prepare and submit applications for production authorisation[208]; to authorise negotiations on the acquisition of technology[209]; to establish terms and conditions and to authorise negotiations for entering into joint ventures and other forms of joint arrangements[210]; and to approve the annual budget of the Enterprise.[211]

2.4 Operations

The earlier drafts of the UN Convention reflect the fact that, in the earlier sessions of the Conference, the regime governing activities in the Area was devised primarily to regulate the activities of entities other than the Enterprise and it was not until the Eighth and Ninth Sessions of UNCLOS III that the Conference gave serious, detailed consideration to the Statute of the Enterprise and to the question of the applicability to activities conducted by the Enterprise of Annex III's basic conditions of exploration and exploitation. It is this history which partly explains the difficulty of ascertaining the regime governing the Enterprise's operations.   Matters have been complicated yet further by the amendments introduced by the Implementation Agreement.   It may be helpful therefore to identify, and present a unified analysis of, the various provisions, scattered throughout the UN Convention, the Implementation Agreement and their annexes, bearing upon this subject.

2.4.1 Capacity to Carry Out Activities

Under Article 153(2) of the UN Convention, activities in the Area may be carried out by the Enterprise[212] and, under Article 170(1), the Enterprise is described as

---

[206] Annex IV, Art.6(c).   Under the Implementation Agreement, Annex, Section 2(4), a plan of work for the Enterprise is now, like that of other contractors, to take the form of a contract concluded between the Authority and the Enterprise. See further below, section 2.4.2.

[207] Annex IV, Art.6(d). Under the Implementation Agreement, Annex, Section 2(2), initial deep seabed mining operations are to be conducted through joint ventures. See further below, section 2.4.

[208] Annex IV, Art.6(e).   Such applications had to be submitted in accordance with Art.151(2)-(7) of the UN Convention. However, under the Implementation Agreement, Annex, Section 6(7), those provisions no longer apply. See further below, under section 2.4.3.

[209] Annex IV, Art.6(f). This paragraph referred in particular to Annex III, Art.5. However, under the Implementation Agreement, Annex, Section 5(2), Annex III, Art.5 of the UN Convention no longer applies and transfer of technology is governed by the Implementation Agreement, Annex, Section 5. See further above, Chap.3, section VIII.

[210] Annex IV, Art.6(g).   As has been seen (section 2.1.3 above), initial deep sea-bed mining operations of the Enterprise are to be conducted through joint ventures. See further below, section 2.4.

[211] Annex IV, Art.6(i).

[212] See further above, Chap. 4, section V.3. Prospecting may also be undertaken by the Enterprise. See Mining Code, Reg. 3(3)(c).

Institutional framework   325

the organ of the Authority 'which shall carry out activities in the Area directly ... as well as the transporting, processing and marketing of minerals recovered from the Area'.

2.4.2 Plans of Work

As has been seen,[213] the functions of the Enterprise are to be performed by the Secretariat of the Authority during the first phase of its existence, that is, 'until it begins to operate independently of the Secretariat'.[214]   During that phase, it will not engage in actual 'activities in the Area', that is, 'activities of exploration for, and exploitation of, the resources of the Area'.[215]   The first phase will come to an end when the Council issues a directive providing for the independent functioning of the Enterprise.[216]   According to the Implementation Agreement, the Council shall *take up this issue* of independent functioning either upon the approval of a plan of work for exploitation for an entity other than the Enterprise, or upon receipt of an application for a joint-venture operation with the Enterprise.[217]   However, the directive providing for independent functioning will be issued only after a determination by the Council that 'joint venture operations with the Enterprise accord with sound commercial principles.'[218]   The meaning of this provision is not altogether clear.   Is it open to the Council, following approval of a plan of work for exploitation for an entity other than the Enterprise, to make a general determination that 'joint-venture operations with the Enterprise accord with sound commercial principles' or may such a determination be made only after receipt of an actual application for a specific joint-venture operation with the Enterprise?

In any event, once the Enterprise is functioning independently, it must conduct its 'initial' deep sea-bed mining operations through joint ventures.[219]   It is not quite clear when such operations cease to be 'initial' operations. The original UN Convention made reference to an 'initial period required for the Enterprise to become self-supporting, which shall not exceed 10 years from the commencement of commercial production by it' and exempted the Enterprise from paying part of its net income to the Authority during this period.[220] However, as is argued below in section 2.5.3, this exemption would no longer appear to be applicable under the Implementation Agreement.

Under Article 153(3) of the Convention, all activities in the Area have to be carried out in accordance with a formal written plan of work[221]   As a result of amendments introduced by the Implementation Agreement, the obligations applicable to other contractors now apply also to the Enterprise and a plan of work for the Enterprise, upon its approval, will take the form of a contract

---

[213] Above, section 2.1.3.
[214] Implementation Agreement, Annex, Section 2(1).
[215] UN Convention, Art.1(1)(3).
[216] Implementation Agreement, Annex, Section 2(2).
[217] *Ibid.*
[218] *Ibid.*
[219] *Ibid.*
[220] UN Convention, Annex IV, Art.10(3).
[221] See further above, Chap. 4, section V.4.

326   Chapter 8

concluded between the Authority and the Enterprise.[222]   The rules affecting the Enterprise are thus for the most part the same as those for other applicants, as considered in Chapter 4, section V.4 above.   It may be noted, however, that an application by the Enterprise may refer to any part of the Area, including, of course, reserved areas,[223] whereas applications by others with respect to reserved areas are subject to additional requirements.[224]   As is the case with other contractors, applications from the Enterprise must be accompanied by evidence supporting its financial and technological capacity.[225]

2.4.3 Reserved Areas

The procedure whereby the Authority designates reserved areas has already been examined in Chapter 4.[226]   It remains to consider further the provisions of Articles 9 and 11 of Annex III and of Article 12 of Annex IV of the UN Convention, which govern the activities of the Enterprise in the Area and of entities associated with it by contract, joint venture or other joint arrangement, and the modifications introduced by the Implementation Agreement.

The Enterprise has to decide, in relation to each reserved area, whether it intends to carry out activities there.   As a general rule, this decision may be taken at any time.[227]   If, however, a developing State notifies the Authority of its wish to submit a plan of work for such a reserved area, the Enterprise must take its decision 'within a reasonable time', which is interpreted by the Mining Code as meaning within six months or, where it is engaged in discussions regarding a potential joint venture, within one year.[228]   If it decides to proceed, then, for so long as the operations may be considered to be 'initial deep sea-bed mining operations', they must be conducted through joint ventures.[229]   Under the original provisions of the UN Convention, the Enterprise was free to enter into joint ventures with any willing entities eligible to carry on activities in the Area under Article 153(2)(b) of the Convention,[230] though it was bound, when considering such joint ventures, to offer to States Parties which were developing States and their nationals 'the opportunity of effective participation.'[231]   Under the Implementation Agreement, however, priority is given to a contractor which has contributed a particular area to the Authority as a reserved area.[232]   It is granted the right of first refusal to enter into a joint-venture arrangement with the Enterprise for exploration and exploitation of that area.   Moreover, if the Enterprise does not submit an application for a plan of work within 15 years of the commencement of its functions independent of the Secretariat of the

---

[222] Implementation Agreement, Annex, Section 2(4), amending UN Convention, Art.153(3) and Annex III, Art.3(5).

[223] UN Convention, Annex III, Art.3(2). See too Mining Code, Reg. 17.

[224] See further Chap. 4, section VII.

[225] Annex III, Art.12(2) and Mining Code, Reg. 12(3) and Annex 2, III.21(a).

[226] See Chap.4, section VII.

[227] UN Convention, Annex III, Art.9(1).

[228] *Ibid.*, Art.9(1) and (4); Mining Code, Reg. 17(1)-(2).

[229] Implementation Agreement, Annex, Section 2(2).

[230] UN Convention, Annex III, Art.9(2).

[231] *Ibid.*

[232] Implementation Agreement, Annex, Section 2(5); Mining Code, Reg. 17(4).

Authority,[233] or within 15 years of the date on which the area was reserved, whichever is the later, the contractor will be entitled to apply for a plan of work for that area, provided it offers in good faith to include the Enterprise as a joint-venture partner.[234]

Once its 'initial deep sea-bed operations' are behind it, it will presumably be open to the Enterprise, whenever it decides to undertake activities in a reserved area, to either (i) engage in operations itself, or (ii) conclude a contract for the execution of part of its activities, or (iii) enter into a joint venture.[235] It would appear, however, that, even during this second phase, the contractor which contributed the reserved area would still have a right of first refusal to enter into a joint venture and, if the Enterprise itself did not submit an application, to apply for a plan of work, provided it offered to include the Enterprise as a joint-venture partner.[236]

2.4.4 Enterprise Operations Outside Reserved Areas

It was noted above[237] that the Enterprise may apply for approval of a plan of work covering activities in any part of the Area and not only in reserved areas. Needless to say, in making such applications, the Enterprise is not bound to identify two areas of equal value, a requirement which applies only to applicants other than the Enterprise.[238]

The Enterprise may also become involved in activities in the Area outside reserved areas pursuant to a contract between another applicant and the Authority providing for some form of joint arrangement under Annex III, Article 11. If such activities are 'initial deep sea-bed mining operations' of the Enterprise, the joint arrangements must take the form of a joint venture.[239] Thereafter, however, they may be either joint ventures, production sharing, or any other form of joint arrangement, and such arrangements will enjoy the same protection against revision, suspension or termination as a contract not involving the Enterprise.[240] Joint-venture partners of the Enterprise are liable for the payments required by Article 13 of Annex III but this is offset to some extent by the financial incentives offered to them in the same Article.[241]

2.4.5 Transfer of Technology to the Enterprise

This aspect of the Enterprise's operations has been dealt with above.[242]

2.4.6 Financial Aspects

The financial aspects of the Enterprise's operations are considered below.[243]

---

[233] See above, section 2.1.3.
[234] *Loc.cit.* in note 232; Mining Code, Reg. 17(3).
[235] Under UN Convention, Annex III, Art.9(1)-(2).
[236] Under Implementation Agreement, Annex, Section 2(5).
[237] Text, at note 223.
[238] Under Annex III, Art.8 of the UN Convention.
[239] Implementation Agreement, Annex, Section 2(2).
[240] UN Convention, Annex III, Art.11(1).
[241] *Ibid.*, Art.11(2) and (3). Art.13 has been heavily amended by the Implementation Agreement, Annex, Section 8. See further Chap.4, section VIII.
[242] In Chap.3, section VIII.
[243] See section 2.5 below.

328   *Chapter 8*

2.4.7 Title to Minerals and Processed Substances
The provision of Annex III, Article 1 that, 'Title to minerals shall pass upon recovery in accordance with this Convention', applies to the Enterprise as well as other entities. It is further provided in Annex IV, Article 12(4) that, 'The Enterprise shall have title to all minerals and processed substances produced by it'.

2.4.8 Non-discrimination and Commercial Basis of Enterprise Operations
Under Article 12(7) of Annex IV,

> The Enterprise shall not interfere in the political affairs of any State Party; nor shall it be influenced in its decisions by the political character of the State Party concerned. Only commercial considerations shall be relevant to its decisions, and these considerations shall be weighed impartially in order to carry out the purposes specified in article 1 of this Annex.

Accordingly, minerals and processed substances produced by the Enterprise must be sold on a non-discriminatory basis and without non-commercial discounts.[244] Again, contracts for the supply to the Enterprise of goods and services must be awarded, after inviting tenders, to bidders offering the best combination of quality, price and delivery time.[245] Once again, however, with a nice touch of Animal Farm logic, discrimination in favour of developing countries may not always be discriminatory. Thus, in deciding between two or more bids offering such a combination of quality, price and delivery time, the Enterprise is required to award the contract on the basis of two principles. The first requires non-discrimination 'on the basis of political or other considerations not relevant to the carrying out of operations with due diligence and efficiency'; but the second permits preference to be accorded to developing countries, including the land-locked or otherwise geographically disadvantaged among them, in accordance with guidelines approved by the Council.[246] It is also open to the Governing Board to adopt rules determining the special circumstances in which the requirement of invitations to bid may be dispensed with in the best interests of the Enterprise.[247]

2.5 Financial Arrangements
Given the very large cost of a sea-bed mining operation[248], and bearing in mind the need for the Governments of some of the leading industrialised States to

---

[244] Annex IV, Art.12(5).
[245] Annex IV, Art.12(3)(a).
[246] Annex IV, Art.12(3)(b).
[247] Annex IV, Art.12(3)(c).
[248] Towards the end of UNCLOS III these costs were estimated in *Potential financial implications for States Parties to the future convention on the law of the sea: Report of the Secretary-General*, A/CONF.62/L.65, 18 February 1981, *UNCLOS III Off.Rec.*, Vol. XV, p.102, at p.115. The 'low', 'medium' and 'high' 'order of magnitude' estimates of development costs of an integrated four-metal sea-bed mining operation given in this report were $700 million, $1,000 million and $1,400 million

secure the necessary support of their legislatures for the ratification of a Convention which, in its original form, would have required them to provide financial assistance to the Enterprise, it is not surprising that the problem of financing the Enterprise proved to be one of the most complex facing the Conference. Indeed, significant drafting changes were still being made during the Resumed Ninth Session of the Conference in August 1980 and the compromise formulae ultimately included in the Convention were accepted only reluctantly by some of the industrialised States. However, the compromises were in vain, for, as will be seen below, further radical changes were introduced by the Implementation Agreement. The financial arrangements of the Enterprise were not, of course, negotiated in isolation but very much as part of a package deal which also included the rules concerning the financial terms of contracts. The following analysis should therefore be read in the light of the analysis in Chapter 4 of the provisions of Article 13 of Annex III on 'Financial terms of contracts', as amended by the Implementation Agreement.[249]

2.5.1 Basic Principle
The basic principle, as laid down in Article 170(4) of the UN Convention, is that:

> The Enterprise shall, in accordance with article 173, paragraph 2, and Annex IV, article 11, be provided with such funds as it may require to carry out its functions.

However, Article 170(4) and Annex IV have now to be interpreted and applied in accordance with the provisions of the Implementation Agreement on the Enterprise, that is, Section 2 of the Annex to the Agreement.[250]

Article 170(4) of the UN Convention is complemented by Article 13(1)(e) of Annex III, under which the Authority is to be guided by a number of objectives, including that of 'enabl[ing] the Enterprise to engage in sea-bed mining effectively at the same time as the entities referred to in article 153, paragraph 2(b)' of the Convention.

2.5.2 Sources of Funding
Article 11(1) of Annex IV identifies five sources of funds for the Enterprise:
(i)   Amounts received under Article 173(2)(b). Under this provision, the balance of Authority funds left after payment of the Authority's administrative expenses may be used for a number of purposes, including the provision of the Enterprise with funds.
(ii) Voluntary contributions made by States Parties for the purpose of financing activities of the Enterprise. It may be safely assumed that this will not be a significant source of funds.
(iii) Income of the Enterprise through its operations.

1980 dollars. The costs covered were those necessary to explore and exploit one mine site, and to transport, process and market the metals recovered therefrom.
[249] Chap.4, section VIII.
[250] See further below.

330 *Chapter 8*

(iv) Other funds made available to the Enterprise to enable it to commence operations as soon as possible and to carry out its functions. Originally, this category would have included sums made available under Annex IV, Article 11(3)(c). Under that provision, if, because only a limited number of States became parties to the Convention, the sum of their financial contributions fell short of the funds necessary to enable the Enterprise to explore and exploit one mine site (which the Enterprise was assured of under Annex IV, Article 11(3)(a)), the shortfall had to be made up. However, since the Implementation Agreement has removed the obligation of States Parties to fund one mine site of the Enterprise,[251] this particular obligation no longer exists.

(v) Amounts borrowed by the Enterprise. Originally, Article 11 envisaged two types of borrowing powers, normal commercial borrowing powers under Article 11(2) and powers to borrow to fund the Enterprise's initial mining operation under Article 11(3).

Normal borrowing powers. Article 11(2) of Annex IV is concerned with the normal borrowing powers of the Enterprise, that is, powers not granted specifically to facilitate the Enterprise's initial mining operation. It simply provides that:

(a) The Enterprise shall have the power to borrow funds and to furnish such collateral or other security as it may determine. Before making a public sale of its obligations in the financial markets or currency of a State Party, the Enterprise shall obtain the approval of that State Party. The total amount of borrowings shall be approved by the Council upon the recommendation of the Governing Board.

(b) States Parties shall make every reasonable effort to support applications by the Enterprise for loans on capital markets and from international financial institutions.

Financing Enterprise's first mining operation. Article 11(3) of Annex IV originally embodied a scheme whereby funds would be provided to enable the Enterprise to conduct its first mining operation and meet its initial administrative expenses. Half of the funds required were to be made available by all States Parties in the form of long-term, interest-free loans and the other half was to be raised by the Enterprise itself, with debts so incurred being guaranteed by all States Parties.[252]

The Implementation Agreement has swept away this system by providing that:

The obligations of States Parties to fund one mine site of the Enterprise as provided for in Annex IV, article 11, paragraph 3, of the Convention shall not apply and States Parties shall be under no obligation to finance any of the

---

[251] Implementation Agreement, Annex, Section 2(3). See further below under 'Financing Enterprise's first mining operation'.
[252] UN Convention, Annex IV, Art.11(3)(b).

Institutional framework 331

operations in any mine site of the Enterprise or under its joint-venture arrangements.[253]

This new situation is, of course, consistent with the other provisions of the Implementation Agreement, noted above[254], under which the obligations applicable to contractors are made applicable to the Enterprise and a plan of work for the Enterprise is to take the form of a contract between the Authority and the Enterprise.[255]

2.5.3 Enterprise Liability to Make Payments to Authority and the Question of Immunity from National Taxation
In UNCLOS III the industrialised States and the Group of 77 had diametrically opposed views on these two questions. The industrialised States argued for the imposition on the Enterprise of financial payments to the Authority, similar to those payable by contractors, and for liability of the Enterprise to pay national taxes. Their objective was of course to maintain a competitive balance between the Enterprise and private sea-bed miners. Some of the Group of 77, on the other hand, argued that the Enterprise, as an arm of the Authority, with a 'social/political function', should be liable neither for financial payments to the Authority nor for national taxation.[256]

The formula on financial payments originally incorporated in the UN Convention leant towards the view of the industrialised States. Annex IV, Article 10(1) required the Enterprise to 'make payments to the Authority under Annex III, article 13, or their equivalent', that is, to make the same payments as private contractors or equivalent payments. However, the Enterprise was exempted from making such payments during an initial period required for the Enterprise to become self-supporting, 'which shall not exceed 10 years from the commencement of commercial production by it'.[257]

As regards national taxation, the Convention adopted a middle position. Automatic immunity was not granted but, under Annex IV, Article 13(5), the 'Enterprise shall negotiate with the host countries in which its offices and facilities are located for exemption from direct and indirect taxation'.

Once again, these provisions were changed by the Implementation Agreement, in line with the underlying policy of assimilating the position of the Enterprise to that of other contractors. The Implementation Agreement does not refer specifically to the above provisions of the UN Convention and the current position has to be inferred from the general rules that, 'The obligations applicable to contractors shall apply to the Enterprise' and that Annex IV is to be interpreted and applied in accordance with the section of the Implementation Agreement on the Enterprise.[258] It would seem to follow that, whether as a joint-venture partner

---

[253] Implementation Agreement, Annex, Section 2(3).
[254] In section 2.4.2.
[255] Implementation Agreement, Annex, Section 2(4).
[256] Nordquist and Park, *op.cit.* in note 13, *Ninth Session, New York, March 3-April 14, 1980*, p.351, at p.378. See also at p.432.
[257] UN Convention, Annex IV, Art.10(3).
[258] Implementation Agreement, Annex, Section 2(4) and (6).

332   Chapter 8

engaged in 'initial deep sea-bed mining operations'[259] or otherwise, the Enterprise will have to make the same payments to the Authority as private contractors and will no longer enjoy the 10-year moratorium provided for in the Convention. Similarly, there would no longer seem to be any basis for negotiating with host countries for exemption from national taxes. It may be noted, however, that the Headquarters Agreement between the Authority and Jamaica envisages that the Jamaican Government and the Enterprise 'shall enter into special agreements concerning the exemption of the Enterprise from direct and indirect taxation.[260]

2.5.4 Allocation of Net Income

Under Annex IV, Article 10(2), the Assembly, upon the recommendation of the Governing Board, has to determine what portion of the net income of the Enterprise is to be retained as its reserves. The remainder has to be transferred to the Authority. As has been seen,[261] under the original provisions of the UN Convention, the Assembly had to exempt the Enterprise from making financial payments to the Authority for an initial period of up to 10 years and during that time all of the net income of the Enterprise was to be left in its reserves.[262] That exemption has now apparently been withdrawn.

2.5.5 Accounting, Audit and Annual Report

Finally, attention should be drawn to the provisions of Annex IV, Article 11 (4) and (5), establishing the separate status of Enterprise funds, assets and expenses and providing for audit of the accounts of the Enterprise. An audited statement of the accounts has to be included in the Enterprise's annual report to the Council and, in addition, summary financial statements and a profit and loss account have to be transmitted to the Council 'at appropriate intervals'.[263] These provisions appear to be unaffected by the Implementation Agreement.

2.6 Immunities and Privileges

The UN Convention, in its original form, not only gave the Enterprise a privileged position in relation to fund-raising.[264] It also placed it at a considerable advantage in relation to its competitors by according to it, under Article 13 of its Statute, a number of immunities and privileges. Thus, under Paragraph 4(a), 'The property and assets of the Enterprise, wheresoever located and by whomsoever held, shall be immune from requisition, confiscation, expropriation or any other form of seizure by executive or legislative action'. Moreover, under Paragraph 4(b), such property and assets of the Enterprise were to 'be free from discriminatory restrictions, regulations, controls and moratoria of any nature'. The Implementation Agreement makes no specific reference to these provisions but, reading together the provisions of Section 2(4) and 2(6) of

---

[259] *Ibid.*, Section 2(2). See further section 2.4 above.
[260] Agreement between the International Seabed Authority and the Government of Jamaica regarding the Headquarters of the International Seabed Authority (ISBA/5/A/11, 25 August 1999, Annex), Art. 23.
[261] Text above, at note 257.
[262] Annex IV, Art.10(3).
[263] Annex IV, Art.9(1).
[264] See further above, section 2.5.2.

Institutional framework 333

the Annex, there seem to be good grounds for arguing that these privileges are incompatible with the competitive status of the Enterprise resulting from the Agreement.[265]

On the other hand, the provisions of paragraph 4(d) of Article 13 of the Statute of the Enterprise are probably unaffected by the Implementation Agreement. Under Paragraph 4(d), States Parties must ensure that the Enterprise enjoys all rights, privileges and immunities accorded by them to entities conducting commercial activities in their territories and they must be enjoyed on no less favourable a basis than accorded to entities engaged in similar commercial activities; and this equality of treatment extends to cover even special privileges provided for developing countries or their commercial entities. However, Paragraph 4(e) would again appear to be contrary to the new status of the Enterprise in providing that 'States Parties may provide special incentives, rights, privileges and immunities to the Enterprise without the obligation to provide such incentives, rights, privileges and immunities to other commercial entities'.[266]

2.7 Liability of Enterprise

Article 139 of the UN Convention imposes a responsibility on States Parties to ensure that activities are carried out in conformity with the Convention and holds them liable for damage caused by their failure to discharge this responsibility; and a similar responsibility applies to international organisations for activities undertaken by them. These provisions were considered above in Chapter 3, section V. The Convention also provides in its Annex III for liability for damage on a contractual level and this aspect was dealt with above in Chapter 4, section XIV. However, in both of these chapters, the question of the liability of the Enterprise for damage caused by its activities in the Area was left for separate treatment later and it is to this problem that attention must now be turned.

In analysing State responsibility under Article 139 of the Convention, a distinction was drawn between the indirect or supervisory responsibility of the sponsoring State and the State's direct responsibility for damage caused by the activities of the State itself.[267] The first question to be considered is whether a similar distinction has to be drawn in relation to the Enterprise.

Article 139 provides that, 'The same responsibility [as lies on States Parties] applies to international organisations for activities in the Area undertaken by such organisations'. It was suggested in Chapter 3 that the reference is principally, though not perhaps exclusively, to international institutions other than the Authority or the Enterprise, undertaking activities in the Area under Article

---

[265] However, this view is not reflected in the Headquarters Agreement (*loc. cit.* in note 260 above), Art.20 of which repeats the provisions of Art.13(4)(a)-(b) of the Statute.

[266] Here too the Headquarters Agreement (*loc. cit.* in note 260 above) repeats, in Art.22, the provisions of Art.13(4)(e) of the Statute. As the observer delegation of the United States noted in the Assembly, 'article 22 of the headquarters agreement, which encompassed provisions from annex IV, article 13, paragraph 4, of the Convention, may not fully reflect the requirements of the 1994 Implementation Agreement, which envisions the Enterprise operating in conjunction with joint ventures. In the view of the United States, in granting any special privileges to joint ventures operating in conjunction with the Enterprise, consistency must be maintained with the World Trade Organisation and various bilateral investment treaties and other relevant treaties' (ISBA/5/A/14, 27 August 1999, para. 21).

[267] See Chap.3, section V.1.

334   *Chapter 8*

153(2)(b).[268] There is, however, a case for saying that this provision is also applicable to the Authority in respect of the activities of the Enterprise. At first sight, this conclusion might seem to be ruled out by the provisions of Annex IV, Articles 2 and 3. Article 2(3) provides that, 'Nothing in this Convention shall make the Enterprise liable for the acts or obligations of the Authority, or make the Authority liable for the acts or obligations of the Enterprise'. Similarly, Article 3 provides that 'no member of the Authority shall be liable by reason only of its membership for the acts or obligations of the Enterprise.'[269] However, the Authority's liability would be for its own failure to supervise and ensure compliance by the Enterprise and not for the acts of the Enterprise itself. Consistently with this view, the Enterprise has to act in accordance with 'the rules, regulations and procedures of the Authority, as well as the general policies established by the Assembly, and shall be subject to the directives and control of the Council.'[270]

Even if this argument is accepted, jurisdictional problems might arise. States Parties might be able to institute proceedings against the Authority under Article 187(b). In other cases, it would appear to be necessary to show that the damage caused by the Authority's supervisory failure involved a breach of contract. In that case, an action might be brought under Article 187(c) or (e).[271]

As regards direct responsibility for damage caused by the operations of the Enterprise, the Authority is clearly not liable (Annex IV, Article 2(3)).   Under the original UN Convention regime (in terms of which plans of work for the Enterprise were not in the form of a contract with the Authority), the penal and tortious liability of the Enterprise for acts or omissions in the course of activities in the Area was unclear.[272]   However, under the Implementation Agreement, Enterprise plans of work will take the form of a contract and, moreover, the 'obligations applicable to contractors shall apply to the Enterprise'.[273]   It follows that Annex III, Article 18 of the UN Convention (Penalties on contractors) and Article 22 (Responsibility of contractors) will apply *mutatis mutandis* to the Enterprise.[274]

So far as jurisdiction is concerned, the original provisions of the Statute of the Enterprise are unaffected by the Implementation Agreement.   The Enterprise does not enjoy the blanket immunity from legal process in the territories of States Parties which is accorded to the Authority[275] and, under Article 13(3) of Annex IV:

> (a)   Actions may be brought against the Enterprise only in a court of competent jurisdiction in the territory of a State Party in which the Enterprise:

---

[268] Chap.3, section V.2.

[269] Without prejudice to obligations to finance the Enterprise under Annex IV, Art.11(3).

[270] UN Convention, Art.170(2) and Annex IV, Art.2(1).

[271] See further above, Chap.4, section XIV.2 and below, Chap.9.

[272] See first edition of this work, Chap.5, section II.2.7.

[273] Implementation Agreement, Annex, Section 2(4).

[274] On penalties under Annex III, Art.18 and responsibility under Annex III, Art.22, see above, Chap.4, sections XIII and XIV.

[275] See UN Convention, Art.178 and below section 4.

Institutional framework 335

(i) has an office or facility;

(ii) has appointed an agent for the purpose of accepting service or notice of process;

(iii) has entered into a contract for goods or services;

(iv) has issued securities; or

(v) is otherwise engaged in commercial activity.

(b) The property and assets of the Enterprise, wherever located and by whomsoever held, shall be immune from all forms of seizure, attachment or execution before the delivery of final judgment against the Enterprise.

3. Financial Arrangements of Authority

The financial arrangements of the Authority were originally laid down in Articles 171-175 of the UN Convention. These provisions have now to be read with Section 1(14) of the Annex to the Implementation Agreement and other related provisions of the Agreement, and the Financial Regulations of the Authority.

The Financial Regulations were approved by the Assembly and became effective on 23 March 2000 and will apply to the financial period 2001-2002 and subsequent financial periods. [276] They are based substantially on the Financial Regulations of the United Nations, adjusted to take account of the provisions of the UN Convention and the Implementation Agreement.

This brief account of the financial arrangements of the Authority will concentrate on the central provisions of these instruments dealing with:

- the budget and audit;
- funds established, including the economic assistance fund;
- sources of Authority funds; and
- disbursement of funds.

3.1 Budget and Audit

The Authority has its own budget.[277] The UN Convention and the Implementation Agreement envisage an annual budget [278] but the Financial Regulations refer to a budget for each 'financial period', defined as consisting of two consecutive calendar years.[279] A proposed budget is submitted by the Secretary-General of the Authority to the Council [280] and is also transmitted to the Finance Committee, which prepares a report, with recommendations, for the Council's consideration.[281] After consideration, Council submits it to the Assembly with any recommendations it wishes to make.[282] The Assembly has then to consider and approve the proposed budget.[283] In making decisions on the administrative budget

---

[276] Decision of the Assembly, 23 March 2000 (ISBA/6/A/3, 28 March 2000). The Financial Regulations of the International Seabed Authority are in the Annex to this document.

[277] Implementation Agreement, Annex, Section 1(14).

[278] UN Convention, Art. 172 and Implementation Agreement, Annex, Section 9(7)(c).

[279] Financial Regulations, Reg. 3.1 and Reg. 2.1. However, Reg. 3.6 requires that the budget 'be appropriated annually in accordance with the Convention'.

[280] UN Convention, Art. 172.

[281] Financial Regulations, Reg. 3.4.

[282] UN Convention, Arts. 172 and 162(2)(r) and Financial Regulations, Reg. 3.4.

[283] Financial Regulations, Reg. 3.6.

336   *Chapter 8*

of the Authority, both the Council and the Assembly must take into account the recommendations of the Finance Committee.[284]

Provision is made in Article 175 of the UN Convention for an annual audit by an auditor appointed by the Assembly but, here too, the Regulations refer to the two-year financial period. [285]

3.2 Funds Established
Provision is made for the establishments of a number of funds and accounts:
- a general administrative fund for the purpose of accounting for the administrative expenditures of the Authority; [286]
- a working capital fund made up from advances from members of the Authority, to be used for purposes to be determined from time to time by the Assembly, including to finance budgetary appropriations. Until such time as the Authority has sufficient income from other sources to meet its administrative expenses, the working capital fund will be made up from advances from States members of the Authority in accordance with an agreed scale of assessment based on the scale used for the regular budget of the United Nations or, in the case of international organisations such as the European Union, as determined by the Authority; [287]
- trust funds, reserve and special accounts, which may be established by the Secretary-General; [288] and
- an economic assistance fund.

The economic assistance fund. Originally Article 171(f) of the UN Convention made provision for payments to a compensation fund to be used to compensate developing countries whose export earnings had been reduced as a result of activities in the Area. The sources of this fund were to be recommended by the Economic Planning Commission. [289] However, this provision has now to be 'interpreted' in the light of the Implementation Agreement, Annex, Section 7(1) [290] and Regulation 5.8 of the Financial Regulations, under which an economic assistance fund is established. [291] The amount to be set aside for this purpose is to be determined by the Council from time to time, upon the recommendation of the Finance Committee. [292] Only funds from payments received from contractors, including the Enterprise, and voluntary contributions may be credited to the fund and only 'a portion' of those funds which exceeds those necessary to cover the administrative expenses of the Authority. [293]

---

[284] Financial Regulations, Reg. 3.7
[285] Financial Regulations, Reg. 12.
[286] Financial Regulations, Reg. 5.1.
[287] Financial Regulations, Reg. 5.2-5.3.
[288] Financial Regulations, Reg. 5.5-5.6.
[289] UN Convention, Arts. 171(f) and 151(10).
[290] Implementation Agreement, Annex, Section 7(2).
[291] On these new arrangements for economic assistance, see further above, Chap. 4, section VI.2 and Chap. 3, section XII.
[292] Financial Regulations, Reg. 5.8. A footnote to this paragraph adds that, 'This provision will need to be elaborated in due time'.
[293] Implementation Agreement, Annex, Section 7(2) and Reg. 5.8.

Institutional framework 337

3.3 Sources of Authority Funds

The funds of the Authority are to include:

(a) Assessed contributions made by States members of the Authority on an agreed scale of assessment based on the scale used for the regular budget of the United Nations.[294] It is envisaged that these assessed contributions will be payable only until such time as the Authority has sufficient income from other sources to meet its administrative expenses and this part of the Authority's funds is paid into a special account earmarked for the Authority's administrative expenses, the general administrative fund.[295] It would appear, nonetheless, that these administrative expenses are also a first call upon the other funds of the Authority.[296]

(b) Agreed contributions, as determined by the Authority, made by international organisations, members of the Authority, in accordance with Annex IX to the Convention. The European Union, qualified to become a member of the Authority by virtue of Article 156(1) of the UN Convention, read with Article 1(2), Article 305 and Annex IX, Article 1, would fall into this category. [297]

(c) Funds received by the Authority in connection with activities in the Area.[298]

(d) Funds transferred from the Enterprise in accordance with Annex IV, Article 10 of the UN Convention.[299]

(e) Funds borrowed pursuant to Article 174 of the UN Convention.[300] The Implementation Agreement limits the borrowing power of the Authority by prescribing that it shall not be exercised to finance its administrative budget. [301]

(f) Voluntary contributions made by members or other entities. [302]

(g) Such other funds to which the Authority may become entitled or may receive, including income from investment. [303]

As noted above, Article 171(f) of the UN Convention originally identified payments to a compensation fund as a further source of Authority funds but this no longer applies. [304]

---

[294] UN Convention, Arts.171(a) and 160(2)(e), read with Implementation Agreement, Annex, Section 1(14) and Reg. 6.1-6.2 of Financial Regulations. Note, however, that it was provided that, until the end of the year following the year in which the Implementation Agreement entered into force, that is the end of 1997, the administrative expenses of the Authority would be met through the budget of the United Nations (Implementation Agreement, Annex, Section 1(14)).

[295] UN Convention, Arts.160(2)(e) and 173(1), Implementation Agreement, Annex, Section 1(14) and Reg. 5.1 of Financial Regulations, which establishes the fund.

[296] UN Convention, Art.173(2).

[297] Financial Regulations, Reg. 6.1(b).

[298] UN Convention, Art.171(b), Annex III, Art. 13 and Financial Regulations, Reg. 6.1(c).

[299] Financial Regulations, Reg. 6.1(d).

[300] UN Convention, Art.171(d).

[301] Implementation Agreement, Annex, Section 1(14). Borrowing is not included among the sources of Authority funds listed in Financial Regulations, Reg. 6.1.

[302] UN Convention, Art. 171(e) and Financial Regulations, Reg. 6.1(e).

[303] Financial Regulations, Reg. 6.1(f).

[304] See further above, section 3.2, under *The economic assistance fund.*

338   *Chapter 8*

3.4 Disbursement of Funds

Provision for disbursement of Authority funds was made originally in Article 173 of the UN Convention. However, Article 173 has been significantly affected by the changes introduced by the Implementation Agreement in relation to the obligation of States Parties to provide the Enterprise with funds[305] and in relation to the scheme to compensate developing countries for the adverse effect on their economies resulting from sea-bed mining.[306]

As has been seen, for an initial period, the administrative expenses of the Authority were to be a charge upon the regular budget of the United Nations.[307] Thereafter, the rules governing disbursement of Authority funds were to be as follows:

(i)   Assessed contributions paid into the special account earmarked for administrative expenses, that is, the general administration fund set up under Regulation 5.1 of the Financial Regulations, will be disbursed for that purpose.[308]   Any shortfall would be a charge on other Authority funds.[309]

(ii)   Funds remaining after payment of administrative expenses, with the exception of assessed contributions by States and international organisations,[310] may be disbursed, *inter alia*, as follows:

(a)   They may be shared in accordance with Article 140 and 160(2)(g) of the UN Convention.[311] These provisions envisage the equitable sharing of benefits derived from activities in the Area, 'taking into particular consideration the interests and needs of developing States and peoples who have not attained full independence or other self-governing status.'[312] The recommendations of the Finance Committee will have to be taken into account by the Assembly and Council in drawing up the governing rules and in taking decisions in accordance with them.[313]

(b)   They may be used to provide the Enterprise with such funds as it may require to carry out its functions.[314] The Implementation Agreement provides that Article 170(4) of the UN Convention (which refers to the provision of such funds to the Enterprise) is to be interpreted and applied in accordance with Section 2 of the Agreement, on 'The Enterprise'.[315] As has been seen, that Section requires the Enterprise to conduct its initial mining operations through joint ventures;[316] removes the obligation of States Parties to fund one mine site for the Enterprise or to finance any of the operations in any mine site of the

---

[305] See above under section 2.5.2.

[306] See further above, section 3.2, under *The economic assistance fund*, and Chap.4, section VI.2.

[307] Implementation Agreement, Annex, Section 1(14). The initial period terminated at the end of 1997.

[308] See further above, section 3.2 and Financial Regulations, Reg. 5.1 and 5.7(chapeau).

[309] UN Convention, Art.173(2) and Financial Regulations, Reg. 5.7 (chapeau).

[310] Financial Regulations, Reg. 5.7(chapeau).

[311] UN Convention, Art. 173(2)(a) and Financial Regulations, Reg. 5.7(a).

[312] UN Convention, Art.140(1).

[313] Implementation Agreement, Annex, Section 9(7)(f).

[314] UN Convention, Arts.173(2)(b) and 170(4), and Financial Regulations, Reg. 5.7(b).

[315] Implementation Agreement, Annex, Section 2(6).

[316] *Ibid.*, Section 2(2).

Enterprise or under its joint-venture arrangements;[317] and imposes on the Enterprise the same contractual obligations as are applicable to other contractors.[318] It is not clear how Article 170(4) is intended to be interpreted in the light of these provisions. The trend established by the Implementation Agreement is obviously in the direction of placing the Enterprise in the same competitive position as other operators in the Area. On the other hand, Article 170(4) has not been rendered 'not applicable' by the Agreement and the Financial Regulations approved in March 2000 confirm the continuing applicability of Article 170(4).[319] The intention would appear to be to continue to allow payments to be made to the Enterprise from Authority funds, presumably to cover its administrative expenses, as distinct from the costs of operating in the Area.[320]

(c) They may be set aside for the purposes of the economic assistance fund referred to above. [321]

4. Legal Status, Privileges and Immunities of the Authority

Under Article 176 of the UN Convention, the Authority has international legal personality and such legal capacity under municipal law as may be necessary for the exercise of its functions and fulfilment of its purposes. As was seen above,[322] the Enterprise has a legal personality distinct from that of its parent body.

Under Articles 177-183 of the UN Convention, the Authority enjoys a wide range of privileges and immunities designed to enable it to fulfil its functions. Again as seen above,[323] the immunities and privileges of the Enterprise are dealt with separately in its Statute, in Annex IV.

In considering these fairly detailed provisions, the Preparatory Commission took the view that there was a need for an additional Protocol on the Privileges and Immunities of the Authority, which would both set out the Conventional provisions and, in addition, deal with aspects not covered by the Convention, such as the privileges and immunities of representatives of members of the Authority, officials and experts, and the use of the laissez-passer by Authority officials.[324] A Working Group was set up in August 1996 to consider the Preparatory Commission's draft and, following its review, the Secretariat of the Authority was instructed to undertake further work on the basis of the earlier text. The Draft Protocol which they originally submitted to the third session of the Authority in March 1997 followed the same comprehensive approach.[325] However, it was felt by many delegations that, if there was a need for a Protocol

---

[317] *Ibid.*, Section 2(3).
[318] *Ibid.*, Section 2(4).
[319] Reg. 5.7(b).
[320] See also above, section 2.5 on the 'Financial Arrangements' of the Enterprise.
[321] Financial Regulations, Reg. 5.7(c), a provision which 'will need to be elaborated in due time' (footnote to Reg. 5.7(c)). See further above, section 3.2, under *The economic assistance fund.*
[322] Above, section 2.2.
[323] Above, section 2.6.
[324] See further Draft Protocol on the Privileges and Immunities of the International Seabed Authority, LOS/PCN/WP.49/Rev.2, reproduced in V *Final PrepCom Report*, pp.126-141.
[325] ISBA/3/A/WP.1, 10 March 1997.

340   *Chapter 8*

at all (given the detailed provisions of the UN Convention), it should be confined to matters not dealt with in the Convention. Accordingly, a second draft was prepared which, following preambular cross-references to the provisions of the UN Convention, offered a much shorter text referring only to 'certain additional privileges and immunities [which] are necessary for the exercise of the functions of the' Authority.[326] It was based substantially on certain provisions of the Convention on the Privileges and Immunities of the United Nations of 13 February 1946 (the General Convention).[327] Following further work by the Working Group, a final draft was presented to the Assembly in March 1998 [328] and adopted by the Assembly on 26 March 1998.[329]

The Protocol was open for signature from 26 August 1998 to16 August 2000 [330] and will enter into force 30 days after the date of deposit of the tenth instrument of ratification, approval , acceptance or accession. [331] As will be seen below in section 7, the provisions of the Protocol are intended to be complementary to those of the Headquarters Agreement. [332]

5. Suspension of Rights of Members of the Authority

Provision is made in Article 184 of the UN Convention for the suspension of voting rights of members in arrears in the payment of their financial contributions to the Authority. Under Article 185, a member found by the Sea-Bed Disputes Chamber to have grossly and persistently violated the provisions of the sea-bed regime (Part XI of the Convention) may be suspended from the exercise of the privileges and the rights of membership.[333]

6. Relationship Agreement between the Authority and the United Nations

In August 1996, the Council of the Authority requested its Secretary-General to negotiate with the Secretary-General of the United Nations a relationship agreement,[334] taking into account the draft prepared by the Preparatory Commission.[335] The Council decided that the agreement should be provisionally

---

[326] Revised Draft Protocol on the Privileges and Immunities of the International Seabed Authority, ISBA/3/A/WP.1/Add.1, 24 March 1997, Preamble.

[327] UNTS, vol.1, p.15 and vol.90, p.327. The Secretariat note (*loc. cit.* in note 326, p.1, para.3) refers to Arts. I, II, IV, V, VI and VII of the General Convention. It may be noted that the privileges and immunities of the UN Specialised Agencies are governed by the Convention on the Privileges and Immunities of the Specialised Agencies of 21 November 1947 (UNTS, vol. 33, p. 261). The authority is not a Specialised Agency but an autonomous organisation and such entities are governed by separate instruments such as the Agreement on the Privileges and Immunities of the International Atomic Energy Agency of 1 July 1959.

[328] ISBA/4/A/L.2.

[329] ISBA/4/A/8, 26 March 1998 (*SD & D*, vol. 2, p. 42). The Protocol on the Privileges and Immunities of the International Seabed Authority is annexed to this document.

[330] ISBA/5/A/1 and Corr. 1, 5 July 1999 (*SD & D*, vol. 3, p. 1), para. 9.

[331] Under Art. 18. Provisional application is also possible under Art. 19.

[332] Art. 12 of the Protocol so provides but prescribes that, in case of conflict, the provisions of the Agreement will prevail.

[333] See further Chap.9, section V.

[334] ISBA/C/10, 14 November 1996, para.1.

[335] Draft Relationship Agreement between the International Seabed Authority and the United Nations, LOS/PCN/WP.50/Rev.3 (V *Final PrepCom Report*, pp.142-149). For a brief description of the Preparatory Commission's work, see LOS/PCN/130 (I *Final PrepCom Report*, pp.33-35).

Institutional framework 341

applied upon signature and that it would enter into force on approval by the Assembly of the Authority and the General Assembly of the United Nations.[336] The Agreement Concerning the Relationship between the United Nations and the International Seabed Authority[337] was signed by the two Secretaries-General on 14 March 1996 and was applied provisionally thereafter pending its approval by the two Assemblies. The Assembly of the Authority, acting on the Council's recommendation,[338] approved the Agreement on 27 March 1997 [339] and it entered into force on approval by the General Assembly on 26 November 1997. [340]

One aspect of the relationship had already been established, prior to the adoption of the Relationship Agreement, when the General Assembly invited the Authority to participate in its deliberations as an observer.[341] The Relationship Agreement itself 'is intended to define the terms in which the United Nations and the Authority shall be brought into relationship'.[342]

Article 2 of the Relationship Agreement lays down a number of principles. In particular, the United Nations recognises that the Authority 'shall function as an autonomous international organisation in the working relationship with the United Nations' established by the agreement[343] and as the organisation through which States Parties to the Convention and the Implementation Agreement will organise and control activities in the Area.[344]

The provision made for co-operation between the two organisations and for the co-ordination of their activities includes arrangements for reciprocal representation in relevant organs, co-operation between the two secretariats and exchange of information, data and documents.[345] *Inter alia*, the two bodies are to co-operate in obtaining from States Parties, and exchanging, copies of charts or lists of geographical co-ordinates indicating the outer limits of national jurisdiction,[346] these being also, of course, the inner limits of the Area.[347]

Careful provision is made to ensure respect for confidential material, data and information, both in general terms[348] and in relation to the obligations undertaken by the Authority to assist the Security Council and the International Court of Justice.[349]

So far as budgetary and financial matters are concerned, the Authority recognises the desirability of establishing close co-operation, 'aimed at benefiting from the experience of the United Nations in this field'.[350]

---

[336] ISBA/C/10, 14 November 1996, paras.2 and 3. Art.18 of the Relationship Agreement embodies the same provisions.
[337] ISBA/3/A/L.2 - ISBA/3/C/L.2, 24 February 1997.
[338] ISBA/3/C/4, 20 March 1997.
[339] ISBA/3/A/3, 27 March 1997.
[340] UN General Assembly Resolution 52/27 of 26 November 1997.
[341] A/RES/51/6, 24 October 1996.
[342] Relationship Agreement, Art.1.
[343] Art. 2(2).
[344] Art. 2(1).
[345] See Arts. 3-9.
[346] Art. 8(3)-(4).
[347] UN Convention, Art.1(1).
[348] Relationship Agreement, Art.8(6).
[349] Arts.4 and 5.
[350] Art.13.

342   *Chapter 8*

7. Headquarters Agreement between the Authority and Jamaica
Article 156(4) of the UN Convention makes provision for the seat of the Authority to be in Jamaica and the Preparatory Commission prepared a draft headquarters agreement between the Authority and Jamaica.[351] The Council of the Authority, at its resumed second session in August 1996, requested the Secretary-General to negotiate an agreement, taking the Preparatory Commission's draft into account.[352] The negotiations were to be under the guidance of the Council and the agreement was to be applied provisionally upon its signature and to enter into force on approval by the Assembly of the Authority and the Government of Jamaica.[353] Following negotiations in January and February 1997, a draft Agreement between the International Seabed Authority and the Government of Jamaica regarding the Headquarters of the International Seabed Authority was prepared for consideration by the Council at the first part of its third session in March 1997.[354] Following protracted negotiations, [355] the Council recommended approval of the Agreement [356] and it was approved by the Assembly on 25 August 1999.[357]

Inter alia, the Agreement deals with such matters as the legal personality and capacity of the Authority[358] and the privileges and immunities to be enjoyed by the Authority[359] and by Member State missions in Jamaica.[360] Similar provision is made for the status and rights, privileges and immunities of the Enterprise.[361]

As was noted above,[362] the provisions of the Agreement are complementary to those of the Protocol on the Privileges and Immunities of the Authority and Article 50 of the Agreement, in terms similar to those of Article 12 of the Protocol, confirms that, in case of conflict, the provisions of the Agreement will prevail.

Provision is made in Article 48 for the settlement of disputes between the Authority and competent Jamaican authorities. If they cannot be settled by other means within a period of three months, they must be referred to a panel of three arbitrators at the request of either party to the dispute.

---

[351] LOS/PCN/WP.47/Rev.2, 28 July 1992 (V *Final PrepCom Report*, pp.97-125). See also, for additional clarifications of the draft, LOS/PCN/SCN.4/WP.16/Add.2, 14 October 1993 (*Report of the Preparatory Commission*, LOS/PCN/152, Vol. I, 28 April 1995, pp.91-114).
[352] Decision of the Council, ISBA/C/11, 14 November 1996, Para.1.
[353] *Ibid.*, Paras 2-3.
[354] ISBA/3/A/L.3 - ISBA/3/C/L.3, 21 February 1997 and Corr.1, 18 March 1997.
[355] Reported in ISBA/5/A/4, 9 August 1999 and Add. 1 (*SD & D*, vol. 3, pp. 12-17) and in ISBA/5/C/11, 2 September 1999 (*SD & D*, vol. 3, p. 46 at paras. 7-9).
[356] ISBA/5/C/9, 24 August 1999 (*SD & D*, vol. 3, p. 45).
[357] ISBA/5/A/11, 25 August 199 (*SD & D*, vol. 3, p.21). The Agreement between the International Seabed Authority and the Government of Jamaica regarding the Headquarters of the International Seabed Authority is annexed to this document.
[358] Art.3.
[359] Arts.5-16, 26 and 32-43.
[360] Arts.27-31.
[361] Arts.17-25.
[362] In section II.4 above.

III. THE PREPARATORY COMMISSION

The Preparatory Commission for the International Sea-Bed Authority and for the International Tribunal for the Law of the Sea was established by Resolution I of UNCLOS III.[363] Like the preparatory commissions of other international institutions, its principal task was to prepare the draft rules, regulations and procedures, as necessary, to enable the institution - in this case the Authority - to commence its functions[364] and to deal with other preliminary matters of an institutional nature.[365] Unlike other such commissions, however, it was also required to implement the pioneer investor scheme for which provision was made in UNCLOS III's Resolution II.[366] A full account of the pioneer investor scheme and of the Preparatory Commission's role in administering it will be found in Chapter 6. The purpose of this section is simply to complete the review of the organisational framework of the sea-bed mining regime established by UNCLOS III by examining the institutional aspects of the Preparatory Commission. Only a bare outline of the Preparatory Commission's institutional features was provided by Resolution I, it being left to the Commission itself to develop them further. An account will first be given, therefore, of the provisions of Resolution I itself, before turning to outline their further elaboration by the Preparatory Commission.

1. The Provisions of Resolution I
1.1 Membership
The Preparatory Commission consisted of the representatives of the States which had signed or acceded to the UN Convention.[367] When it was wound up at the close of the first meeting of the Assembly of the Authority, the figure stood at 162.

Provision was also made for observers. Paragraph 2 of Resolution I referred only to the representatives of signatories of the Final Act and allowed them to 'participate fully in the deliberations of the Commission as observers' but not to participate in the taking of decisions.[368] Among others, Germany,[369] the United Kingdom and the United States fell into that category. However, the Preparatory Commission envisaged an additional category of observers in its Rules of Procedure, adopted in September 1983.[370] Such 'other observers' included States and other entities which were eligible to sign the Convention under Article 305

---

[363] Resolution I on the Establishment of the Preparatory Commission for the International Sea-Bed Authority and for the International Tribunal for the Law of the Sea, adopted by UNCLOS III on 30 April 1982, in *Law of the Sea* (United Nations, 1983, Sales No.E.83.V.5), at p.175; reproduced in Vol. 3 as Doc. No. 14.1.

[364] Resolution I, Para.5(g).

[365] See further Resolution I, Para.5.

[366] Resolution II Governing Preparatory Investment in Pioneer Activities Relating to Polymetallic Nodules, adopted by UNCLOS III on 30 April 1982, in *Law of the Sea, op.cit.* in note 363, at p.177; reproduced in Vol. 3 as Doc. No. 14.2.

[367] Resolution I, Para.2.

[368] Resolution I, Para.2.

[369] Prior to Germany's accession to the UN Convention on 14 October 1994.

[370] Rules of Procedure of the Preparatory Commission for the International Sea-Bed Authority and for the International Tribunal for the Law of the Sea, LOS/PCN/28, 23 November 1983, and Corr. 1 and 2 (I *Final PrepCom Report*, pp.57-75; *Platzöder (PrepCom)*, Vol.I, p.239), Rule 3.

344 Chapter 8

but in fact signed neither the Convention nor even the Final Act; the UN Specialised Agencies and the International Atomic Energy Agency; various other intergovernmental agencies; and specified national liberation movements. Such 'other observers' could participate on questions within the scope of their competence but only upon the invitation of the Chairman of the Preparatory Commission or of a Special Commission, as the case might be. Like the normal observers, they were not entitled to participate in the taking of decisions.[371] Non-governmental organisations could also be invited to sit as observers in public meetings of the Commission.[372]

1.2 Duration
The Commission began its first session on 15 March 1983 and remained in existence until the conclusion of the first meeting of the Assembly of the Authority on 18 August 1995.[373]

1.3 Funding
The Commission's expenses were paid out of the regular budget of the United Nations.[374] The United States decided to withhold its pro rata share of the cost to the United Nations budget of funding the Preparatory Commission.[375]

1.4 Functions
The broad purpose of the Preparatory Commission was to 'ensure the entry into effective operation without undue delay of the Authority and the Tribunal and to make the necessary arrangements for the commencement of their functions'.[376] More specifically, the following range of functions was specified:
(i) The exercise of the powers and functions assigned to it in relation to the preparatory investment protection scheme established by Conference Resolution II, including in particular the registration and certification of pioneer investors.[377]
(ii) The tasks traditionally performed by preparatory commissions, including the preparation of draft rules, regulations and procedures required to enable the Authority to commence its functions.[378]
(iii) The study by a special commission of the problems which would be encountered by developing land-based producer States likely to be most seriously affected by the production of sea-bed minerals and the submission

---

[371] Rule 3(2).

[372] Rule 3(4).

[373] Pursuant to Resolution I, Paras.1 and 13.

[374] Resolution I, Para.14, subject to the approval of the General Assembly given in A/RES/37/66 of 3 December 1982.

[375] The UN General Assembly recalled its approval of the financing of the Preparatory Commission from the UN regular budget in a Resolution adopted on 14 December 1983 (A/RES/38/59). In explaining his negative vote, the US representative stated his Government's view on the illegality of such funding (A/38/PV.96, 21 December 1983, pp. 25-26). See also the Singapore representative's challenge to the US to test its view by supporting a reference of the question to the ICJ for an Advisory Opinion (ibid., p. 30).

[376] Resolution I, Preamble.

[377] Resolution I, Para.5(h) and Resolution II, Paras.2 and 11.

[378] Resolution I, Para.5(a)-(g).

Institutional framework 345

to the Authority of recommendations to assist them. Such studies were also to cover the establishment of a compensation fund.[379]

(iv) The establishment of a special commission for the Enterprise, to take all measures necessary for the early entry into effective operation of the Enterprise.[380]

(v) The preparation of recommendations regarding practical arrangements for the establishment of the International Tribunal for the Law of the Sea. Such recommendations were to be embodied in a report to a meeting of States Parties to be convened within six months of the date of entry into force of the UN Convention.[381]

(vi) The preparation of a final report on all matters within its mandate (except the practical arrangements for the Tribunal) for presentation to the Assembly at its first meeting.[382]

1.5 Subsidiary Bodies
The Preparatory Commission was empowered to establish such subsidiary bodies as were necessary for the exercise of its functions,[383] in addition to the two 'special commissions' referred to above on the problems of land-based producers and on the Enterprise.

1.6 Decision-making
The Preparatory Commission's voting rules were not established in Resolution I but were left to be adopted by the Commission itself, applying for this purpose UNCLOS III's Rules of Procedure.[384]

2. The Development by the Preparatory Commission of its Institutional Features
The first session of the Preparatory Commission was held in Jamaica from 15 March to 8 April 1983 and from 15 August to 9 September 1983. By the close of the first session, the Preparatory Commission had succeeded in electing its Chairman (J.S. Warioba of Tanzania), adopting its Rules of Procedure and completing its organisational structure.

At the Spring 1983 meeting the Commission produced a 'Consensus Statement of Understanding' embodying only the general lines of its intended structure.[385] It was agreed that the Commission should consist of:

(i) The Plenary, as principal organ.

(ii) A number (still unspecified) of Special Commissions, open to all Convention signatories, enjoying equal status and reporting to Plenary. The 'bureaus' of the Plenary and of the Special Commissions were to be established with due regard to the practice of the UN General Assembly and

---

[379] Resolution I,Paras.5(i) and 9.
[380] Resolution I, Para.8.
[381] Resolution I, Para.10 and UN Convention, Annex VI, Art.4(3). See further Chap.9, section II.1.1.
[382] Resolution I, Para.11. On the final report, see further below, section 3.
[383] Resolution I, Para.7.
[384] Resolution I, Para.4.
[385] The Consensus Statement is embodied in the Statement by the Acting Chairman of the Preparatory Commission (LOS/PCN/3, 8 April 1983, I *Final PrepCom Report*, p.38; *Platzöder (PrepCom)*, Vol.I, p.188).

346   *Chapter 8*

UNCLOS III and the need for each regional group to be represented in all bureaus of the organs of the Commission by at least one member.

(iii)   In addition, a General Committee was to consist of the Chairman of the Preparatory Commission and all the members of the bureaus of the Plenary and the Special Commissions.

The Consensus Statement listed the matters to be dealt with by the various organs but was without prejudice to their allocation among these organs.   It was specified, however, that the Preparatory Commission must ensure, when adopting its rules of procedure, that decisions requiring consensus under the UN Convention also required consensus in the Commission.   It was emphasised, in particular, that the Commission would adopt by consensus the rules and procedures for the implementation of Resolution II and the establishment of adequate machinery to administer the regime for the protection of pioneer investors.[386]

At its Autumn 1983 meeting, the Preparatory Commission fleshed out its earlier Consensus Statement of Understanding by adopting, again by consensus, three papers containing the Chairman's suggestions on (i) the structure of the Commission, functions of the organs and bodies of the Commission, officers and venue; (ii) procedures and guidelines for registration of pioneer investors under Resolution II; and (iii) rules of procedure on decision-making.[387]

2.1 The Preparatory Commission's Organs and Functions
It was confirmed that a Plenary would be established and that there would be four Special Commissions.   In addition, a General Committee was established and provision was made for a 'technical body' to assist it.   The functions of these various bodies are indicated below.

2.1.1 The Plenary
The functions assigned to the Plenary as the principal organ of the Preparatory Commission[388] were as follows:

(i)   *Authority functions*: preparation of rules, regulations and procedures on the administrative, financial and budgetary matters pertaining to the various organs of the Authority.[389]

(ii)   *Pioneer investor functions*: the implementation of Resolution II's   scheme governing preparatory investment in pioneer activities.[390]

(iii)   *Final report*: the preparation and adoption of the Preparatory Commission's final report for presentation to the first session of the Assembly of the International Sea-Bed Authority.[391]

(iv)   *General business*: the general conduct of business; co-ordination of the work of the organs of the Commission and of subsidiary bodies; and, upon the

---

[386] It was subsequently so provided in Rule 35 of the Commission's Rules of Procedure (*loc.cit* in note 370 above).

[387] LOS/PCN/27, 8 September 1983 (I *Final PrepCom Report*, p.41; *Platzöder (PrepCom)*, Vol.I, p.224).

[388] Consensus Statement of Understanding (*loc.cit.* in note 385), para.1.

[389] Pursuant to Resolution I, Para.5(g).

[390] Pursuant to Resolution I, Para.5(h). See further Chap.6, section III.

[391] As required by Resolution I, Para.11.

Institutional framework 347

recommendation of the General Committee, all questions of organisation of work.

(v) *Practical arrangements for tribunal*: presentation to a meeting of States Parties, to be convened following entry into force of the UN Convention, of a report on arrangements for establishment of the International Tribunal for the Law of the Sea.[392]

(vi) *Residual matters*: all matters not specifically assigned to Special Commissions or other subsidiary bodies.

2.1.2 The Special Commissions

Special Commission 1 was to deal with the problems that could be encountered by developing land-based producers likely to be most seriously affected by the production of sea-bed minerals and was entrusted with the functions referred to in Resolution I, Paragraphs 5(i) and 9. *Inter alia*, it was mandated to undertake studies on the establishment of a compensation fund.

Special Commission 2, for the Enterprise, was made responsible for the adoption of all measures necessary for the early entry into effective operation of the Enterprise. It was entrusted with the functions referred to in Resolution I, Paragraph 8 and Resolution II, Paragraph 12.

Special Commission 3 was to be concerned with the preparation of a sea-bed mining code, that is, the rules, regulations and procedures for the exploration and exploitation of the Area, as required by Resolution I, Paragraph 5(g).

Special Commission 4, for the Tribunal, was assigned the task of preparing recommendations on practical arrangements for the establishment of the International Tribunal for the Law of the Sea.

2.1.3 The General Committee

The General Committee was assigned two functions: to act on behalf of the Preparatory Commission as the executive organ for the administration of Resolution II's pioneer investor scheme; and, secondly, to make recommendations to the Preparatory Commission on all questions of organisation of work.[393]

2.1.4 Group of Technical Experts

The 'technical body' to assist the General Committee was not established immediately. However, in 1986 it was set up as a Group of Technical Experts and made responsible for determining whether applications for registration as pioneer investors were in conformity with Resolution II.[394]

---

[392] See note 381 above.
[393] *Loc.cit.* in note 387, Annex I, section III.
[394] LOS/PCN/L.41/Rev.1, 11 September 1986 (II *Final PrepCom Report* p.24; *Platzöder (PrepCom)*, Vol.II, p.74), para.40(a) and Annex, paras. 6-8. See further Chap.6, section III.6.1 (i) and 6.2.

348   *Chapter 8*

2.1.5 Training Panel
The Training Panel was set up in 1991[395] as a subsidiary body of the Preparatory Commission.[396]   Its function was to plan and carry out a training programme in accordance with the Principles, Policies, Guidelines and Procedures for a Preparatory Commission Training Programme adopted in 1989.[397]

2.2 Decision-making in the Preparatory Commission[398]
All procedural decisions, whether in Plenary, Special Commissions or subsidiary bodies, had to be taken by a majority of the representatives present and voting.

Decisions in Plenary on matters of substance fell into two categories requiring, respectively, consensus and a two-thirds majority.   The following questions required consensus: all matters requiring consensus under the UN Convention; rules and procedures for the implementation of Resolution II and for the establishment of adequate machinery to administer the regime for the protection of pioneer investors; the rules and regulations for the exploration and exploitation of the Area; the final report of the Preparatory Commission to the Assembly and the report containing recommendations on practical arrangements for the establishment of the International Tribunal for the Law of the Sea to be submitted to the meeting of the States Parties to the Convention; and the imposition on States of financial obligations not provided for in the approved budget of the United Nations.   Other Plenary decisions on matters of substance required a two-thirds majority.

In both Special Commissions and subsidiary bodies, decisions on matters of substance had to be taken by a two-thirds majority of the representatives present and voting.

3. The Preparatory Commission's Final Report
The Preparatory Commission's first session began on 15 March 1983 and its final session ended at the conclusion of the first session of the Authority's Assembly on 18 August 1995.[399]

Resolution I, Paragraph 11 required the Commission to present to the Authority at its first session 'a final report on all matters within its mandate ... [except practical arrangements for the establishment of the International Tribunal

---

[395] See LOS/PCN/L.92, 21 March 1991   (II *Final PrepCom Report*, p.110, at pp.116 and 118; *Platzöder (PrepCom)*, Vol.XII, p.444, at pp.450-451).
[396] Under Resolution I, Para.7.
[397] Resolution II, Para.12(a)(ii) required registered pioneer investors to provide training for personnel designated by the Preparatory Commission.   'Principles, Policies, Guidelines and Procedures for a Preparatory Commission Training Programme' (LOS/PCN/SCN.2/L.6/Rev.1, X *Final PrepCom Report*, p.216; *Platzöder (PrepCom)*, Vol. V, p.320) were adopted on 31 August 1989.   See also 'Recommendations of Special Commission 2' for the 'Implementation of the Preparatory Commission Training Programme' made in 1990 (LOS/PCN/SCN.2/L.7, 23 March 1990, X *Final PrepCom Report*, p.228; *Platzöder (PrepCom)*, Vol. XI, p.307).   For report of Training Panel's sixth and final meeting in August 1994 and its final report to the General Committee, see LOS/PCN/BUR/R.47, 3 August 1994 and Corr.1 (IV *Final PrepCom Report*, pp.270-278) and LOS/PCN/BUR/R.48 (IV *Final PrepCom Report*, pp.9-280).
[398] See further LOS/PCN/27, 8 September 1983 (I *Final PrepCom Report*, p.41; *Platzöder (PrepCom)*, Vol.I, p.224), Annex III and the Rules of Procedure of the Preparatory Commission (*loc.cit.* in note 370), Sections VII and VIII.
[399] Pursuant to Resolution I, Paras.1 and 13.

Institutional framework 349

for the Law of the Sea]'. During its August 1994 session, the Plenary decided to consider as its final report the 'provisional' final report which it had earlier adopted, 'supplemented by any further reports and recommendations which the Preparatory Commission has adopted'.[400] This was despite the fact that the word 'provisional' was intended to indicate that there were still pending issues for which the Preparatory Commission or its Special Commissions had been unable to find solutions. However, a much greater weakness in the final report resulted from the fact that the substantive work of the Commission and its Special Commissions had been completed before the Implementation Agreement was adopted by the UN General Assembly on 28 July 1994. Consequently, the Preparatory Commission found itself unable to respond to the call by the General Assembly 'to take into account the terms of the Agreement when drawing up its final report'.[401] Accordingly, the Preparatory Commission simply took note of the request and decided to 'recommend to the Authority that it should take into account the terms of the Agreement ... in the consideration of the recommendations and the report of the Preparatory Commission in order to ensure consistency as necessary'.[402]

The Commission's final report consists of thirteen volumes[403] embodying the reports and related documentation of (1) the Plenary, including the General Committee and the Training Panel;[404] (2) Special Commission 1;[405] (3) Special Commission 2;[406] and (4) Special Commission 3.[407] So far as the substantive work of these organs is concerned, reference is made to the relevant chapters of this volume and the appropriate sections of the final report itself.[408]

---

[400] Statement by the Chairman of the Preparatory Commission, LOC/PCN/L.115/Rev.1, 8 September 1994 and Corr.1, 7 November 1994 (II *Final PrepCom Report*, pp.167-182, at p.177, para.4).

[401] General Assembly Resolution A/RES/48/263 of 28 July 1994 on the Implementation Agreement (*LOS Bull., Special Issue IV*, 16 November 1994, pp.8-9), para.13.

[402] *Loc.cit.* in note 400, at p.12, para.45.

[403] *Report of the Preparatory Commission under Paragraph 11 of Resolution I of the Third United Nations Conference on the Law of the Sea, on All Matters within its Mandate, Except as Provided in Paragraph 10, for Presentation to the Assembly of the International Seabed Authority at its First Session*, LOS/PCN/153, 13 vols, 1995. The reports and documentation of Special Commission 4 on arrangements for the establishment of the International Tribunal for the Law of the Sea are published in a separate document, LOS/PCN/152 (Vols. I-IV).

[404] LOS/PCN/153, Vols. I-V.

[405] LOS/PCN/153, Vols. VI-IX.

[406] LOS/PCN/153, Vols. X-XI.

[407] LOS/PCN/153, Vols. XII-XIII.

[408] See further (i) *on the Plenary*, Chap.6, section III, Chap.8, section III and *Consolidated Provisional Final Report of the Plenary* (LOS/PCN/153 (Vol. I), 30 June 1995, pp.11-37). 'Pending issues' are listed at pp.36-37; (ii) *on SCN.1* (problems of developing land-based producer States), Chap.4, section VI and *Provisional Report of Special Commission 1* (LOS/PCN/153 (Vol. VI), 26 June 1995, pp.4-33); (iii) *on SCN.2* (on the Enterprise), Chap.8, section II.2 and *Provisional Final Report of Special Commission 2* (LOS/PCN/153 (Vol. X), 5 July 1995, pp.8-28); (iv) *on SCN.3* (preparation of sea-bed mining code), Chap.4, text following note 4 and *Draft Provisional Report of Special Commission 3* (LOS/PCN/153 (Vol. XIII), 30 June 1995, pp.311-323); (v) *on SCN.4*, see further *Draft Report of the Preparatory Commission under Paragraph 10 of Resolution I*, LOS/PCN/SCN.4/WP.16, 12 October 1993 (*Report of the Preparatory Commission under Paragraph 10 of Resolution I*, LOS/PCN/152, Vol. I, 28 April 1995, p.6).

CHAPTER 9

The UN Convention Regime of Sea-Bed Mining:
VII. Settlement of Disputes

I. GENERAL OUTLINE OF THE SYSTEM

1. The UN Convention in Historical Perspective
Although the idealism which originally inspired UNCLOS III has been considerably eroded since Ambassador Pardo made his celebrated 'common heritage' speech in 1967,[1] and the Implementation Agreement of 28 July 1994 has substantially modified the regime of sea-bed mining in Part XI of the UN Convention, it remains true that this new legal regime is a revolutionary experiment in international law and relations. It may be thought fitting, therefore, that the substantive rules of the new order should be complemented by equally ambitious provisions for the settlement of disputes – provisions which, it may be noted, have not been modified in the same way but have indeed been extended by the Implementation Agreement to cover additional areas of dispute. On the other hand, given their radical novelty and complexity, it is necessary, in assessing these new dispute-settlement provisions, to preserve some sense of historical perspective and to bear in mind that these peaceful settlement procedures, produced in the hot-house atmosphere of UNCLOS III, will have to be capable of survival in a cold outside world which has not until now given much encouragement to such blooms.

It is sometimes difficult to remember that international law is still in large part a system of auto-interpretation in which the unqualified acceptance by States of an obligation to submit their disputes to a binding form of third-party settlement is still highly exceptional. Moreover, even when accepted, such obligations are frequently not honoured. These sobering facts can be illustrated

---

[1] In the First Committee of the General Assembly of the United Nations on 1 November 1967 (UN Doc.A/C. 1/PV.1515, pp.2-68 and PV.1516, pp.2-7).

Dispute settlement 351

both in relation to international law in general and to the law of the sea, prior to 1994, in particular.

On the general level, it is open to States to make a declaration under Article 36(2) (the 'optional clause') of the Statute of the International Court of Justice, accepting the Court's compulsory jurisdiction. However, the latest edition of the Court's Yearbook shows that, as at 31 July 1998, only 60 States out of a total United Nations membership of 185 States had made such declarations.[2] Moreover, many of these States had not seen fit to make a declaration in unqualified form but hedged around their declarations with objective or, much worse, subjective domestic jurisdiction reservations. An example of the objective form of such reservations is provided by the Canadian declaration of 10 May 1994, which reserves from the Court's jurisdiction 'disputes with regard to questions which by international law fall exclusively within the jurisdiction of Canada'.[3] Under this type of reservation, while it is open to a reserving State to raise a preliminary objection to proceedings brought against it on the ground that they concern matters exclusively within the jurisdiction of the State, it is left to the Court to decide objectively in accordance with international law whether or not such a claim can be sustained. On the other hand, where a subjective domestic jurisdiction reservation has been made, the Court is deprived of this power. For example, Liberia's declaration does not apply 'to any dispute *which the Republic of Liberia considers* essentially within its domestic jurisdiction'.[4]

Given the influential part played by the United States delegation in the design and formulation of the dispute settlement provisions of the UN Convention on the Law of the Sea, it is also of interest to note that the United States is one of twelve States whose optional clause declarations have expired, been withdrawn or been terminated without being replaced since 1951.[5] The other eleven are Bolivia, Brazil, China, E1 Salvador, France, Guatemala, Iran, Israel, South Africa, Thailand and Turkey.

It is true, of course, that obligations of compulsory dispute settlement have been accepted in a large number of other instruments but on a highly selective basis.[6]

The background in the law of the sea area is similarly uninspiring. As at 31 December 1999, only 37 States were bound by the Optional Protocol of Signature concerning the Compulsory Settlement of Disputes associated with the four 1958

---

[2] International Court of Justice, *Yearbook 1997-1998* (No.52, 1998), pp. 63 and 83. The texts of the declarations are reproduced at pp.84-124.

[3] *Ibid.*, p.89.

[4] *Ibid.*, p.101, emphasis added.

[5] *Ibid.*, p.83, note 1.

[6] See, *e.g.*, the list of such instruments in the Court's *Yearbook (op.cit.* in note 2, at pp.125-142). They include the Optional Protocol to the Vienna Convention on Diplomatic Relations concerning the Compulsory Settlement of Disputes of 18 April 1961 (500 UNTS 7312) and the similar Optional Protocol to the Vienna Convention on Consular Relations of 24 April 1963 (596 UNTS 8640) on a pattern similar to the Optional Protocol to the 1958 Geneva Conventions on the Law of the Sea referred to below.

352   *Chapter 9*

Geneva Conventions on the Law of the Sea.[7] Nor, in cases before the Court, did the attitudes of Iceland in the *Fisheries Jurisdiction* cases, of France in the *Nuclear Tests* cases, or of Turkey in the *Aegean Continental Shelf* case reflect a very positive attitude to international adjudication.[8] More recently, in 1994, Canada revised its optional clause declaration to ensure that any action taken against foreign vessels under its amended fishery legislation should not be challenged before the Court.[9]

Does this background have any relevance to the provision now made in the UN Convention for the settlement of disputes? It is submitted that it does. The very fact that the attitude of States to dispute settlement has apparently been radically transformed overnight by the UN Convention must at least suggest the need for caution in assessing the prospects for the successful implementation of the new scheme. A more positive attitude will clearly be called for if the new dispute settlement provisions are to be successful. However, the prospects for an effective dispute settlement system are much better in relation to sea-bed mining than in relation to the law of the sea more generally. The treaty regime of sea-bed

---

[7] United Nations, *Multilateral Treaties Deposited with the Secretary-General. Status as at 31 December 1999*, 2000 (UN, *Multilateral Treaties 1999*), Vol II, at p.207. Moreover, not all of these States were States Parties to all four of the Geneva Conventions.

[8] In *Fisheries Jurisdiction (U.K v. Iceland), Jurisdiction of the Court, ICJ Reports 1973*, p.3, Iceland simply declared that the Court lacked jurisdiction and declined to be represented in the proceedings or to file pleadings. The Court found that it possessed jurisdiction and gave judgment in 1974 (*ICJ Reports 1974*, p.3). In the *Nuclear Tests* cases *(Australia v. France; New Zealand v. France), ICJ Reports 1974*, pp.253 and 457, France stated that it considered the Court manifestly to lack jurisdiction and refrained from appearing at the public hearings or filing any pleadings. The Court indicated interim measures of protection in 1973 but found in 1974 that, as the application no longer had any object, it was not called upon to give a decision. Nor was New Zealand any more successful in attempting to re-open the case in 1995 (*ICJ Reports 1995*, p. 288). Finally, in the *Aegean Sea Continental Shelf Case (Greece v. Turkey), ICJ Reports 1978*, p.3, Turkey informed the Court on 20 April 1978 that it did not accept its jurisdiction and was not represented before the Court. The Court found that it lacked jurisdiction.

[9] The Canadian declaration of 10 May 1994 (*ICJ Yearbook 1997-1998*, No.52, 1998, p.89) replaced a Declaration of 10 September 1985 (ICJ *Yearbook 1992-1993*, No.47, 1993, p.79) and further reserved from the Court's jurisdiction: 'disputes arising out of or concerning conservation and management measures taken by Canada with respect to vessels fishing in the NAFO Regulatory Area, as defined in the Convention on Future Multilateral Cooperation in the Northwest Atlantic Fisheries, 1978, and the enforcement of such measures'. The reservation was clearly designed to prevent the submission to the Court of any dispute over amendments to the Coastal Fisheries Protection Act (text in *LOS Bull.* No.26, 1994, pp.20-23). The amendments made it an offence for foreign fishing vessels, in the NAFO Regulatory Area, to fish for a straddling stock in contravention of any of the prescribed conservation and management measures and gave protection officers wide ranging powers of enforcement, including the use of force to disable a foreign fishing vessel. In March 1995, Canada arrested the Spanish trawler *Estai* for alleged illegal fishing at a point on the high seas reported to be 45 nautical miles outside Canada's 200-mile fisheries zone after bursts of machinegun fire across its bows and cut the nets of another Spanish trawler (*The Times*, London, 14 and 28 March 1995). Spain nonetheless instituted proceedings against Canada on 28 March 1995. In 1998, the Court found that the dispute fell within the terms of the Canadian reservation and, consequently, it had no jurisdiction to adjudicate upon the dispute (*Fisheries Jurisdiction Case (Spain v. Canada), Jurisdiction of the Court, ICJ Reports 1998*, para. 87). There are echoes in this latest Canadian declaration of the policy adopted in 1970, when, under a declaration dated 7 April 1970 (ICJ *Yearbook 1984-1985*, pp.71-72), Canada ensured that its Arctic Waters legislation would not be tested in the International Court (for the Arctic Waters Pollution Prevention Act 1970 and related documents, see *International Legal Materials*, Vol. IX, 1970, pp.543 and 598-615).

mining is much more detailed than other parts of the UN Convention and parties to sea-bed mining disputes do not have the same freedom to choose from a wide range of different dispute-settlement mechanisms as they enjoy in relation to other law of the sea disputes.[10]

2. The UN Convention Model in Outline

The general scheme for the settlement of disputes is laid down in Part XV of the Convention and falls into three Sections dealing with: (1) the general obligation to settle disputes by peaceful means and preliminary steps to which all disputes are subject[11]: (2) compulsory procedures entailing binding decisions[12]; and (3) limitations and optional exceptions to such compulsory procedures.[13]

Article 279 of Section 1 is simply a restatement of the obligation upon members of the United Nations under Articles 2(3) and 33(1) of the Charter of the United Nations to settle disputes by peaceful means. It may be marginally useful in that it binds non-Members of the United Nations to undertake the same obligations. It is followed by Article 280, which preserves unimpaired the right of States Parties to agree to settle a dispute between them relating to the interpretation or application of the Convention by any peaceful means of their choice. If, however, no settlement is reached by such means, then, under Article 286, the dispute must be submitted, at the request of any party to it, to the court or tribunal which has jurisdiction under Section 2. Article 287(1) of this Section allows States Parties to make a written declaration choosing one or more of the four procedures specified: the International Tribunal for the Law of the Sea; the International Court of Justice (ICJ); an arbitral tribunal under Annex VII; or a special arbitral tribunal under Annex VIII. Where a party or parties to a dispute have made no such declaration or have not accepted the same procedure in their declarations, the dispute must be referred to arbitration under Annex VII.

Several other Parts of the Convention make special additional provision for the settlement of disputes in relation to particular matters, including the regime of the Area. So far as sea-bed mining is concerned, Section 5 of Part XI makes provision for 'settlement of disputes and advisory opinions'.[14] The principal forum is the Sea-bed Disputes Chamber of the International Tribunal for the Law of the Sea but, as will be seen below, certain types of dispute may, alternatively, be submitted to a special chamber of the International Tribunal for the Law of the Sea, to an *ad hoc* chamber of the Sea-Bed Disputes Chamber or to binding commercial arbitration. The extent to which the particular dispute settlement provisions of Part XI exclude the right of parties to settle their sea-bed dispute peacefully by means of their own choice under Article 280 is a matter of some doubt which will be considered further below.[15]

---

[10] See further E.D. Brown, 'Dispute settlement and the law of the sea: the UN Convention regime', 21 *Marine Policy* (No. 1, 1997), pp.17-43, and E.D. Brown 'The Law of the Sea at the Millennium: the status of UNCLOS and its dispute settlement system', 25 *Marine Policy* (No. 1, 2001).

[11] Part XV, Section 1 (Articles 279-285).

[12] Part XV, Section 2 (Articles 286-296).

[13] Part XV, Section 3 (Articles 297-299).

[14] Title of Section 5.

[15] See below, section IV, at note 61.

354   *Chapter 9*

II. THE INSTITUTIONS CONCERNED

1. International Tribunal for the Law of the Sea

Provision is made for the establishment of the International Tribunal for the Law of the Sea (ITLOS) in Article 287(1)(a) of the UN Convention, and its Statute, which in many respects has clearly been modelled on the Statute of the International Court of Justice, is to be found in Annex VI to the Convention.

1.1 Composition of Tribunal

The new Tribunal has its seat in Hamburg[16] and consists of 21 independent members,[17] no two of whom may have the same nationality.[18] It must include not less than three members from each of the five United Nations regional groups[19] and the representation of the principal legal systems must be assured, as must be equitable geographical distribution.[20] Each State Party may nominate not more than two persons[21] and election is by secret ballot at a meeting of States Parties on the basis of a list of such nominees.[22] Those nominees are declared elected who obtain the largest number of votes and a two-thirds majority of the States Parties present and voting, provided that such majority includes a majority of the States Parties.[23]

Given the preponderant voting strength of the developing States, it was thought unlikely that the Group of Western European and Other Countries would ever have more than three of their nationals on the tribunal and some of these States regarded this as a less than satisfactory 'representation' of their interests. It was suggested during UNCLOS III that greater recognition of these interests might be gained if the voting requirements were raised from two-thirds to four-fifths.[24] The Group of 77, voting together, could easily muster two-thirds but would be hard pushed to raise four-fifths without allies. It was also suggested that minority interests would be better protected by a system of elections which required that judges should be nominated by a Council, itself so designed as to assure protection of minority interests.[25] However neither proposal persuaded the Conference to change the formula and, indeed, the results of the first elections showed that the fears of the Group of Western European and Other Countries were groundless; four of their nationals were elected.[26]

In accordance with Annex VI, Article 4(3), the election of judges was supposed to have taken place within six months of the entry into force of the UN Convention, that is, by 16 May 1995. However, at a meeting of States Parties to

---

[16] In accordance with Annex VI, Art.1(2).

[17] Annex VI, Art.2(1).

[18] Annex VI, Art.3(1).

[19] Annex VI, Art.3(2).

[20] Annex VI, Art.2(2).

[21] Annex VI, Art.4(1).

[22] Annex VI, Art.4(4).

[23] *Ibid.*

[24] *Report of the Committee on Law of the Sea of the American Branch of the International Law Association,* March 1978, p.15.

[25] *Ibid.,* p.42 ('Separate statement of Luke W. Finlay').

[26] For details of the elections, see E D Brown, *loc cit.* in note 10, at pp.34-37.

Dispute settlement 355

the UN Convention on 22 November 1994, it was decided to defer the first election of judges until 1 August 1996. This allowed time for more States to become parties to the UN Convention and thus qualify to take part in the election. Judges are elected for 9 years and may be re-elected. However, a system of rotation operates under which the terms of office of one third of the 21 judges expires every three years.[27] The first elections duly took place on 1 August 1996 and, on 24 May 1999, at the first triennial election of 7 judges, 6 of the original judges were re-elected, together with 1 new judge. [28]

1.2 Special Chambers

As will be seen below, the Tribunal has to establish a Sea-Bed Disputes Chamber but it is also empowered to form special chambers of various kinds:

1.2.1 Summary Procedure Chamber

First, it is required annually to form a special chamber for the speedy dispatch of business by summary procedure.[29] This chamber consists of five members of the Tribunal, with two alternates.[30] National members retain their right of participation in cases involving their home States[31] and, as in the full Tribunal, an *ad hoc* member may be substituted for a regular member if one of the parties to the case does not have a member of its nationality in the chamber.[32] Such an *ad hoc* member will be drawn from the membership of the Tribunal if it includes a member of the required nationality. Failing this, or if such member is unable to be present, a non-member of the Tribunal may be specially chosen by the parties.[33] It follows that a judgment may be given by a five-member summary procedure chamber on which only three regular members of the Tribunal are sitting.[34] The Chamber was first constituted in 1996 and has been reconstituted annually.

1.2.2 Particular Category Chambers

Secondly, the Tribunal may form such special chambers, composed of three or more of its members, as it considers necessary for dealing with particular categories of disputes.[35] Given the fact that such a chamber might consist of only three members and that two of them might in certain circumstances be *ad hoc* judges,[36] it is possible that a judgment might be given by a chamber having only one regular member of the Tribunal among its members.

---

[27] UN Convention, Annex VI, Art. 5(1).
[28] UNCLOS, *Report of the Ninth Meeting of States Parties*, SPLOS/48, 15 June 1999, paras. 31-34.
[29] Annex VI, Art.15(3).
[30] *Ibid.*
[31] Annex VI, Art.17(1) and (4).
[32] Annex VI, Art.17(2)-(6).
[33] Annex VI, Art.17(4).
[34] The other two being *ad hoc* judges not regular members of the Tribunal.
[35] Annex VI, Art.15(1). So far, two such chambers have been constituted, the Chamber for Fisheries Disputes and the Chamber for Marine Environment Disputes.
[36] Annex VI, Art.17(2)-(6).

356   *Chapter 9*

1.2.3 Ad hoc Chambers
Finally, the Tribunal may form a special chamber to deal with a particular dispute if the parties so request.[37] The composition of such a chamber would be determined by the Tribunal with the approval of the parties.[38] Here too there is a possibility of having a three-man chamber including only one regular member of the Tribunal.

It is provided that the judgment of a special chamber is to be considered as rendered by the Tribunal itself.[39] Needless to say, the safeguards concerning representation of the principal legal systems and equitable geographical distribution are unlikely to be operative in these circumstances; and yet, certain disputes must be heard by this chamber if the parties so request.[40] Such a system seems ill designed to produce a consistent and uniform jurisprudence.

2. Sea-Bed Disputes Chamber
As has been seen, the principal forum for the settlement of sea-bed mining disputes is to be the Sea-Bed Disputes Chamber, established in accordance with Annex VI, Section 4.[41] Its jurisdiction, powers and functions, as provided for in Part XI, Section 5 of the Convention and the Implementation Agreement of 28 July 1994, are considered further below.[42]

2.1 Composition
The Chamber consists of 11 members of ITLOS selected by a majority of the members of ITLOS[43] to serve for a three-year term, renewable for a second term.[44] The first Chamber was constituted in February 1997 and reconstituted in October 1999. As was the case with the parent tribunal, in the selection of members of the Chamber the representation of the principal legal systems of the world and equitable geographical distribution must be assured.[45] Given the fact that the Chamber will decide all questions by a simple majority vote, there have been doubts raised here too about the adequacy of the 'representation' of the industrially advanced States.

As in the case of the special chambers referred to above, provision is made for the appointment of *ad hoc* judges[46] and judgments given by the Chamber are to be considered as rendered by the Tribunal.[47]

2.2 Ad hoc Chambers
Not content with having a Tribunal, a Sea-Bed Disputes Chamber and a variety of special chambers, including an *ad hoc* special chamber of the Tribunal, the

---

[37] Annex VI, Art.15(2).
[38] *Ibid.*
[39] Annex VI, Art.15(5).
[40] See Art.188(1)(a).
[41] Annex VI, Art.14.
[42] For overview, see Table below, and for details see sections which follow it.
[43] Annex VI, Art.35(1).
[44] Annex VI, Art.35(3).
[45] Annex VI, Art.35(2).
[46] Annex VI, Art.17.
[47] Annex VI, Art.15(5).

Dispute settlement 357

fathers of the Convention heaped complexity upon complexity by providing for one more sub-organ - an *ad hoc* chamber of the Sea-Bed Disputes Chamber. While the temptation to solve political problems through institutional proliferation may be understandable, it was nevertheless a temptation which should have been firmly rejected. In the interests of simplicity, and of certainty and of uniformity of interpretation, it is to be hoped that common sense in the employment of these various organs will establish the Sea-Bed Disputes Chamber itself as the pre-eminent forum.

The provision for *ad hoc* chambers of the Sea-Bed Disputes Chamber is made in Annex VI, Article 36. An *ad hoc* chamber of three members of the Chamber may be formed to deal with a particular dispute submitted to the Chamber in accordance with Article 188(1)(b). The composition of the *ad hoc* chamber is to be determined by the Chamber with the approval of the parties, though provision is made for cases of disagreement. That *ad hoc* judges may not be appointed to such *ad hoc* chambers seems to be implied by the exclusion of nationals of the parties to the dispute.[48]

3. Commercial Arbitral Tribunal

Finally, brief reference has to be made to the provision made in Article 188 for the submission, in certain circumstances, of disputes concerning the interpretation or application of a contract to binding commercial arbitration. No single commercial arbitral tribunal is established but it is provided that:

> In the absence of a provision in the contract on the arbitration procedure to be applied in the dispute, the arbitration shall be conducted in accordance with the UNCITRAL Arbitration Rules or such other arbitration rules as may be prescribed in the rules, regulations and procedures of the Authority, unless the parties to the dispute otherwise agree.[49]

III. THE RANGE OF DISPUTES

The range of issues which may be submitted to the above institutions for settlement is very wide, reflecting the complex nature of the regime established by the Convention to govern activities in the Area. Perhaps befitting an attempt to embody the 'common heritage of mankind' in precise treaty form, the legal regime belongs exclusively neither to public international law nor to the municipal legal orders of the States Parties. It is better regarded as a legal regime *sui generis*, founded on a convention governed by international law but extending also to cover the rights and remedies of persons natural or juridical which, though lacking international personality, have entered into contractual or other arrangements with the Authority. The law applicable by the Tribunal and its chambers is correspondingly varied. Thus, not only may they apply the Convention, as modified by the Implementation Agreement, and other rules of international law not incompatible with the Convention[50] and rules, regulations

---

[48] Annex VI, Art.36(3).
[49] UN Convention, Art.188(2)(c).
[50] Art.293(1).

358   *Chapter 9*

and procedures of the Authority,[51] but also the terms of any contracts concerning activities in the Area in any matter related to such contracts.[52] The ambivalence of the regime is similarly reflected in the rule concerning the enforceability of decisions of the Sea-Bed Disputes Chamber: they may be enforced in the territories of States Parties in the same manner as judgments or orders of the highest court of the State concerned.[53]

The range of disputes which may be generated by this *sui generis* legal regime is indicated in the table which follows and, in sections IV-XIII of this chapter, each of the categories identified in the table is considered in more detail. In reading this analysis, it should be borne in mind that, as has been seen, Part XI has been modified by the Implementation Agreement and the two instruments are to be interpreted and applied as a single instrument.[54] Accordingly, where general reference is made below to Part XI, it should be understood to extend also to the provisions of the Implementation Agreement.

Table 9.1
The Legal Regime of Activities in the Area:
Classification of Disputes

All references to the UN Convention are to the Convention as modified by the Implementation Agreement

	Type of Dispute	**Forum**	**UN Convention**
1.1	Disputes between States Parties concerning the interpretation or application of Part XI and related Annexes.	Sea-Bed Disputes Chamber (SBDC)	Art. 187(a)
		Special chamber of Tribunal	Art. 188(1)(a)
		Ad hoc chamber of SBDC	Art. 188(1)(b)
1.2	Disputes concerning the interpretation or application of the Mining Code	See text below, section IV	Part XI, section 5
2.1	Disputes between a State Party and the Authority concerning acts or omissions of a State Party alleged to be in violation of Part XI or related Annexes or rules, regulations and procedures of the Authority.	SBDC	Art.187(b)

---

[51] Annex VI, Art.38(a).
[52] Annex VI, Art.38(b).
[53] Annex VI, Art.39.
[54] Implementation Agreement, Art.2(1).

Dispute settlement 359

2.2	Disputes over allegations that a State Party has grossly and persistently violated Part XI.	SBDC	Art.185(2)
2.3	Disputes over obligations of States Parties in relation to transfer of technology	SBDC	Art.187(b)
3	Disputes concerning the production policy of the Authority.	See text below, section VI	See text below, section VI
4	Disputes between a State Party and the Authority concerning:		Arts.187(b) and 189
4.1	Acts or omissions of the Authority alleged to be in violation of Part XI or related Annexes or rules, regulations and procedures of the Authority;	SBDC	
4.2	Acts of the Authority alleged to be in excess of jurisdiction;	SBDC	
4.3	Acts of the Authority alleged to be a misuse of power.	SBDC	
5	Disputes concerning conformity with Convention of proposal before Assembly.	SBDC	Art.159(10)
6.1	Disputes between parties to a contract concerning the interpretation or application of a relevant contract or a plan of work	SBDC Commercial arbitral tribunal unless the parties otherwise agree	Art.187(c)(i) Art.188(2) Mining Code, Annex 4, Section 25
6.2	Disputes over the interpretation or application of the rules and regulations for financial terms of contracts; and disputes	SBDC Commercial arbitral tribunal unless the parties agree on 'other means'	Art. 187(c)(i) Annex III, Art.13(15) and Art.188(2)

360   *Chapter 9*

	between the Authority and a contractor over the interpretation or application of the financial terms of a contract.		
6.3	Disputes between parties to a contract concerning acts or omissions of a party to the contract relating to activities in the Area and directed to the other party or directly affecting its legitimate interests.	SBDC	Art.187(c)(ii)
6.4	Disputes between the Authority and a prospective contractor concerning the refusal of a contract or a legal issue arising in the negotiation of the contract.	SBDC	Art.187(d) Implementation Agreement, Annex, Section 3(12)
6.5	Disputes between the Authority and a State Party, State enterprise or natural or juridical person, where alleged that Authority is liable for damage arising out of wrongful acts including disclosure of industrial secrets etc.	SBDC	Art.187(e) (and (c)?) Annex III, Art.22 and Art.168(2)
7.1	Disputes concerning alleged violations of responsibilities by Secretary-General of Authority or a staff member.	Appropriate administrative tribunal	Art.168(1)
7.2	Disputes concerning alleged disclosure by Secretary-General of Authority or a staff member of industrial secrets etc.	A tribunal designated by the rules, regulations and procedures of the Authority	Art.168(3)
8	Disputes concerning the limits of the Area between:	See text below	See text below
8.1	States Parties;		

8.2	A State Party and the Authority.		
9	Disputes concerning overlapping pioneer area claims.	See text below	See text below
10	Disputes concerning the Enterprise.	See text below	See text below

IV. DISPUTES BETWEEN STATES PARTIES CONCERNING (1) THE INTERPRETATION OR APPLICATION OF PART XI AND RELATED ANNEXES, AS MODIFIED BY THE IMPLEMENTATION AGREEMENT AND (2) THE MINING CODE

1. Part XI and Related Annexes, as Modified by the Implementation Agreement
As the above table shows, resort may be had to any one of three fora to settle disputes between States Parties over the interpretation or application of Part XI and its related Annexes, as modified by the Implementation Agreement.

First, under Article 187(a) of the UN Convention, the Sea-Bed Disputes Chamber has jurisdiction over such disputes. However, at the request of any party to the dispute, the case may be submitted to an *ad hoc* chamber of the Sea-Bed Disputes Chamber.[55] As noted above,[56] the three-member *ad hoc* chamber may not include nationals of any of the parties to the dispute. Alternatively, if the parties agree, the dispute may be referred to a special chamber of the Tribunal under Article 188(1)(a). As was noted above,[57] it would be possible to have the case decided by a special chamber of three members, only one of whom was a member of the Tribunal.

The law to be applied will be the UN Convention, as modified by the Implementation Agreement, and other rules of international law not incompatible with it, and the rules, regulations and procedures of the Authority adopted in accordance with the Convention.[58]

The interpretation of the Convention given by the chamber in question will be binding upon the parties to the case[59] and also upon any State Party exercising its right to intervene in cases of interpretation or application under Annex VI, Article 32(3).[60]

It was noted above[61] that there is some doubt about the extent to which the particular dispute-settlement provisions of Part XI exclude the right of parties to settle their sea-bed disputes peacefully by means of their own choice under Article 280. According to Article 285, Section 1 of Part XV, which includes Article 280, applies to any dispute which, pursuant to Part XI, Section 5, is to be

---

[55] UN Convention, Art.188(1)(b).
[56] Text above at note 48.
[57] In sections II.1.2.2 and II.1.2.3.
[58] UN Convention, Art.293 and Annex VI, Art.38(a).
[59] UN Convention, Art.296 and Annex VI, Arts.33 and 40.
[60] Annex VI, Art.33(3).
[61] Text, at note 15.

362   *Chapter 9*

settled in accordance with procedures provided for in Part XV; and, if an entity other than a State Party is a party to such a dispute, then Section 1 applies *mutatis mutandis*. The first article of Part XI, Section 5, namely Article 186, provides that, 'The establishment of the Sea-Bed Disputes Chamber and the manner in which it shall exercise its jurisdiction shall be governed by the provisions of this section, of Part XV and of Annex VI'. It would seem to follow that the freedom of choice under Article 280 is thus preserved.

Caflisch implies that this is not so, arguing that the 'complex solution which was finally worked out' ensures 'that the settlement of every dispute concerning the interpretation or application of Part XI takes place within the general framework of the Law of the Sea Tribunal,'[62] that is, by reference to a special chamber of the Tribunal, or the Sea-Bed Disputes Chamber, or an *ad hoc* chamber of the Sea-Bed Disputes Chamber, as discussed above. It is certainly true, under Article 287(2), that the obligation to accept the jurisdiction of the Sea-Bed Disputes Chamber under Part XI, Section 5, prevails over any general declaration made under Article 287(1), choosing another means for the settlement of disputes concerning the interpretation or application of the Convention. However, the obligation to accept the jurisdiction of the Sea-Bed Disputes Chamber is only 'to the extent and in the manner provided for in Part XI, section 5' and it does not follow, therefore, that Articles 187(a) and 188(1) exclude the freedom of the parties under Article 280 to agree to refer the dispute to another means of pacific settlement. Any other conclusion would appear to render Article 285 meaningless.

It is true also that the Conference rejected a proposal that Article 187(a) should be deleted, leaving disputes covered by it to be settled under Part XV procedures, and that the opposition was said to be based on the ground that a uniform legal order must be maintained for all sea-bed questions.[63] The fact remains that the Convention does not seem to have excluded the right of States to act otherwise on the basis of Article 280. This does not, of course, mean that the retention of Article 187(a) is without important effect. Read with Article 188(1), it means that the jurisdiction of the Sea-Bed Disputes Chamber or an *ad hoc* chamber of the Sea-Bed Disputes Chamber will be compulsory in the absence of agreement by the parties to either settle the dispute by reference to another forum of their choice under Article 280 or to agree to submit it to a special chamber of the Tribunal under Article 188(1)(a).

---

[62] L.C. Caflisch, 'The Settlement of Disputes Relating to the Seabed', in C.L. Rozakis and C.A. Stephanou (eds.), *The New Law of the Sea*, 1983, pp. 303-344, at p.309.

[63] See further *UNCLOS III Off. Rec.*, Vol. XI, p. 117 and Vol. XII, p. 91. If 'the need to preserve the unity and continuity of jurisprudence with respect to activities in the area' (Vol. XI, p. 117) was so important, it would of course have been more sensible to have given exclusive jurisdiction to the Sea-Bed Disputes Chamber. However, as Caflisch notes *(loc.* cit. in note 62) the solution adopted reflected a compromise between those who favoured this course and a number of industrialised States who advocated a wider choice of fora.

Dispute settlement 363

2. The Mining Code
Part VIII of the Mining Code, adopted in July 2000, [64] consists of the single Regulation 39, under which disputes concerning the interpretation or application of the Regulations 'shall be settled in accordance with Part XI, section 5, of the Convention'. The absence of any more specific reference to the provisions of section 5 may well reflect uncertainty as to exactly which of those provisions applies. In fact, no reference is made in section 5 to the interpretation or application of the regulations adopted by the Authority. It is true that the Sea-Bed Disputes Chamber may well have to rule on the interpretation or application of the Mining Code in the course of exercising its exclusive jurisdiction over disputes between a State Party and the Authority concerning acts or omissions of a State Party, or acts or omissions of the Authority, alleged to be in violation of the rules, regulations and procedures of the Authority. [65] However, in the case of disputes more directly concerned with the interpretation or application of the Mining Code, the position is less clear. It seems likely that such disputes would be treated in the same way as those concerning the interpretation or application of Part XI and related Annexes, as discussed in section IV.1 above.

V. DISPUTES BETWEEN A STATE PARTY AND THE AUTHORITY CONCERNING ACTS OR OMISSIONS OF A STATE PARTY ALLEGED TO BE IN VIOLATION OF PART XI OR RELATED ANNEXES, AS MODIFIED BY THE IMPLEMENTATION AGREEMENT, OR RULES, REGULATIONS AND PROCEDURES OF THE AUTHORITY; AND DISPUTES OVER ALLEGATIONS THAT A STATE PARTY HAS GROSSLY AND PERSISTENTLY VIOLATED PART XI, AS MODIFIED

1. The Exclusive Jurisdiction of the Sea-Bed Disputes Chamber
Under Article 187(b), the Sea-Bed Disputes Chamber has exclusive jurisdiction over actions by the Authority against a State concerning an alleged violation of Part XI or related Annexes, as modified by the Implementation Agreement, or rules, regulations and procedures of the Authority. Proceedings will be instituted by the Council on behalf of the Authority.[66] Where the Chamber finds that a violation has occurred, the defaulting State will be under an obligation to comply.[67] Where the State's failure to carry out its responsibilities under Part XI has caused damage, an award of compensation may be made against it.[68] Moreover, the Council has to notify the Assembly of the findings of the Chamber in non-compliance proceedings instituted by the Council and 'make any recommendations which it may find appropriate with respect to measures to be taken'.[69]

---

[64] Regulations on Prospecting and Exploration for Polymetallic Nodules in the Area, ISBA/6/A/18, July 2000.
[65] See further below, section V.1 (acts or omissions of a State Party) and section VII.2 (acts or omissions of the Authority).
[66] UN Convention, Art.162(2)(u).
[67] Art.296(1).
[68] Art.139.
[69] Art. 162(2)(v).

364   *Chapter 9*

Where the decision relates to a gross and persistent violation, it will also be open to the Council to recommend to the Assembly that the State should be suspended from the exercise of the rights and privileges of membership.[70] Any such Council recommendation must be arrived at by consensus, or, if efforts to achieve a consensus have been exhausted, by a two-thirds majority of members present and voting, provided that the recommendation is not opposed by a majority in any one of the four chambers or groups of States into which the Council is divided.[71]   Naturally, the Council may only make such a recommendation following a finding by the Chamber that there has been a gross and persistent violation.[72] The final decision is taken by the Assembly,[73] acting by consensus, or, if efforts to achieve a consensus have been exhausted, by a two-thirds majority of the members present and voting, including the majority of the members participating in the session of the Assembly.[74]

2. Disputes over Transfer of Technology

'Transfer of technology' remains one of the 'principles governing the Area'[75] but it is now governed not only by Article 144 of the UN Convention but also by a set of three principles laid down in the Implementation Agreement[76]. However, the highly detailed rules incorporated in Annex III, Article 5 of the UN Convention, which required undertakings to transfer technology to be included as a term of the contract, have been rendered inapplicable by the Implementation Agreement.[77] One consequence of this is that the specific provision made in Article 5(4) for the settlement of contractual disputes over undertakings to transfer technology has also now disappeared. Accordingly, it would appear that such disputes are now subject to the general rules governing Part XI disputes between the Authority and States Parties. The much-reduced obligation now imposed upon States Parties is to 'co-operate fully and effectively with the Authority' to facilitate the acquisition of technology on fair and reasonable terms and conditions consistent with the effective protection of intellectual property rights; and to ensure that contractors sponsored by them also co-operate fully with the Authority.[78] Any dispute between a State Party and the Authority concerning such obligations falls within the jurisdiction of the Sea-Bed Disputes Chamber under Article 187(b)(i) of the UN Convention.

---

[70] Art.185(1) and 162(2)(t).

[71] The original voting rule in Art.161(8)(c) was rendered inapplicable by the Implementation Agreement, Annex, Section 3(8) and the new rule 11 in Section 3(2) and (5).

[72] UN Convention, Art.185(2).

[73] UN Convention, Art.160(2)(m).

[74] Implementation Agreement, Annex, Section 3(2)-(3), read with UN Convention, Art.159(8).

[75] UN Convention, Art.144, preserved by Implementation Agreement, Annex, Section 5(1), chapeau.

[76] Implementation Agreement, Annex, Section 5(1).

[77] *Ibid.,* Section 5(2).

[78] *Ibid.,* Section 5(1)(b).

Dispute settlement 365

VI. DISPUTES CONCERNING THE PRODUCTION POLICY OF THE AUTHORITY

As has been seen[79] the elaborate production control system embodied in Article 151 of the UN Convention has been replaced by a set of principles set out in Section 6 of the Annex to the Implementation Agreement. Specific provision is made in Section 6 for the settlement of disputes arising from the breach of the requirements of these provisions.

It may be recalled that the principles on which the Authority's production policy is to be based include the following:

(i)   the application to activities in the Area of the provisions of GATT and its relevant codes and successor or superseding agreements, including the World Trade Organisation (WTO) rules which emerged from the Uruguay Round;

(ii) prohibition of subsidisation of activities in the Area except as permitted by the said provisions of GATT and its successors;

(iii) prohibition of discrimination between minerals derived from the Area and those derived from other sources.[80]

The dispute settlement provisions of Section 6 are drafted in a somewhat fragmentary fashion but the position seems to be as follows. Any State Party which has reason to believe that there has been a breach of the requirements of (i)-(iii) above may initiate dispute settlement procedures.[81] The appropriate procedure depends upon the nature of the dispute:

(a) *disputes concerning the provisions of GATT or WTO.* If the States Parties concerned are parties to these agreements, the dispute will be resolved by reference to the procedures laid down in these agreements.[82] If, however, one or more States Parties are not parties to such agreements, they must have recourse to the dispute settlement procedures set out in the UN Convention.[83] In this latter case, the dispute would be disposed of in the manner considered above in section IV of this chapter.

(b) *disputes concerning any breach of the requirements of (i)-(iii) above other than those concerning the provisions of GATT/WTO.* It is open to any State Party at any time to bring to the attention of the Council activities which in its view are inconsistent with the requirements of (i)-(iii) above.[84] The Council may also become involved following a determination made under the GATT/WTO agreements that a State Party has engaged in subsidisation which is prohibited or has resulted in adverse effects on the interests of another State Party. If, in these circumstances, appropriate steps have not been taken by the defaulting State Party, the Council may be requested by a State Party to take appropriate measures.[85] Irrespective of how it has become involved, the Council may find that there are grounds for proceeding

---

[79] See above Chap.4, section VI.
[80] Implementation Agreement, Annex, Section 6(1)(b)-(d). See further Chap.4, section VI(1).
[81] Implementation Agreement, Annex, Section 6(4).
[82] Section 6(1)(f)(i).
[83] Section 6(1)(f)(ii).
[84] Section 6(5).
[85] Section 6(1)(g).

366   *Chapter 9*

against a State Party in the manner considered above in section V of this chapter.

(c) disputes concerning the acceptance by a contractor of forbidden subsidies. It is expressly provided in the Implementation Agreement that the acceptance by a contractor of subsidies other than those which may be permitted under the GATT/WTO rules shall constitute a violation of the fundamental terms of the contract forming a plan of work for the carrying out of activities in the Area.[86] The Council may be requested to take appropriate measures in response to such violations[87] and may decide to institute proceedings in the manner considered below in section IX(1) of this chapter.

VII. DISPUTES BETWEEN A STATE PARTY AND THE AUTHORITY CONCERNING:
(1) ACTS OR OMISSIONS OF THE AUTHORITY ALLEGED TO BE IN VIOLATION OF PART XI OR RELATED ANNEXES, AS MODIFIED BY THE IMPLEMENTATION AGREEMENT, OR RULES, REGULATIONS AND PROCEDURES OF THE AUTHORITY; (2) ACTS OF THE AUTHORITY ALLEGED TO BE IN EXCESS OF JURISDICTION; OR (3) ACTS OF THE AUTHORITY ALLEGED TO BE A MISUSE OF POWER

1. Exclusive Jurisdiction of Sea-Bed Disputes Chamber
In relation to this category of disputes, the Sea-Bed Disputes Chamber has exclusive jurisdiction.[88] In determining the scope of the Chamber's jurisdiction, it is clear that the draftsmen of the Convention were heavily influenced by the model provided by the treaties establishing the European Communities, which also provide for judicial review of administrative action in a legal regime *sui generis* extending to embrace the relations of States, Community institutions and individuals and companies.[89]

2. Acts or Omissions of the Authority Alleged to be in Violation of Part XI, as modified by the Implementation Agreement, or Rules, Regulations and Procedures of the Authority
Looked at chronologically, it would seem that the first rules, regulations and procedures which might have been subject to such alleged violations would be those prepared by the Preparatory Commission, 'as necessary, to enable the Authority to commence its functions, including draft regulations concerning the financial management and the internal administration of the Authority.'[90] Under Article 308(4) of the Convention, they were to apply provisionally pending their formal adoption by the Authority in accordance with Part XI.

Now that the Authority has commenced its functions, the rules, regulations and procedures are those formulated by the Legal and Technical Commission[91] and submitted to the Council. Those relating to prospecting, exploration and

---

[86] Section 6(3).
[87] Section 6(4) and 6(1)(g).
[88] UN Convention, Art.187(b).
[89] For a useful, brief account of the Court of Justice of the Communities, see Lasok & Bridge, *Law & Institutions of the EuropeanUnion.* 6th ed., 1994, Chap.12.
[90] UNCLOS III Resolution I on the Establishment of the Preparatory Commission, para.5(g).
[91] UN Convention, Art.165(2)(f).

Dispute settlement 367

exploitation in the Area and the financial management and internal administration of the Authority have to be adopted by the Council by consensus[92] and applied provisionally[93], pending approval by the Assembly.[94] Those concerned with the equitable sharing of financial and other economic benefits derived from activities in the Area and the payments and contributions with respect to exploitation of the continental shelf beyond 200 miles, under Article 82, have to be recommended by the Council, acting by consensus,[95] to the Assembly, and adopted by the Assembly.[96]

3. Acts of the Authority Alleged to be in Excess of Jurisdiction

It would appear that two types of lack of capacity are covered under this head. The first is akin to the French notion of *vice de forme* and the English concept of procedural *ultra vires*.[97] If, for example, the Council were to take a decision on a matter in relation to which its powers have to be exercised on the basis of advice or recommendations from one of its commissions, without receiving such advice or recommendations, such a decision would clearly be invalid because the correct procedure had not been followed, even though the matter was substantively *intra vires*. Under the European Community treaties, such defects were covered by a separate ground of illegality: infringement of an essential procedural requirement.[98] It may be assumed that the Sea-Bed Chamber, like the European Court, would not concern itself with trifling procedural irregularities and would apply the maxim *de minimis praetor non curat*.

The second kind of lack of competence is akin to the French *excès de pouvoir* or *incompétence* and the English doctrine of substantive *ultra vires*[99] and would invalidate decisions taken on matters not within the substantive competence of the Authority at all.

4. Acts of the Authority Alleged to be a Misuse of Power

This third ground of illegality is again found in the European Community treaties under the same name (*détournement de pouvoir*.)[100] Decisions or measures will be illegal on this ground if it can be shown that the organ in question exercised a power to achieve an object other than that for which the power was granted. The Chamber will of course have to build up its own jurisprudence on this concept but it is clear from the experience of the Community Court that it is seldom easy to prove this ground. Moreover, the Chamber will have to proceed with care because, as will be seen below, the Chamber is not permitted to substitute its own discretion for that of the Authority.

---

[92] Art. 161(8)(d).
[93] Art.162(2)(o)(ii), as developed by the Implementation Agreement, Annex, Sect 1(15).
[94] Art.160(2)(f)(ii).
[95] Art. 161(8)(d).
[96] Art. 160(2)(f)(i).
[97] See Lasok & Bridge, *op. cit.* in note 89, at p.263.
[98] EEC Treaty, Art.173.
[99] Lasok & Bridge, *op. cit.* in note 89, at p.263.
[100] EEC Treaty, Art.173.

368   *Chapter 9*

5. Limitations on Jurisdiction of Chamber
Article 189 of the Convention, another of the fruits of political compromise, places far-reaching, if ambiguous, limitations upon the jurisdiction of the Chamber with regard to decisions of the Authority. It provides that:

> The Sea-Bed Disputes Chamber shall have no jurisdiction with regard to the exercise by the Authority of its discretionary powers in accordance with this Part; in no case shall it substitute its discretion for that of the Authority. Without prejudice to article 191, in exercising its jurisdiction pursuant to article 187, the Sea-Bed Disputes Chamber shall not pronounce itself on the question of whether any rules, regulations and procedures of the Authority are in conformity with this Convention, nor declare invalid any such rules, regulations and procedures. Its jurisdiction in this regard shall be confined to deciding claims that the application of any rules, regulations and procedures of the Authority in individual cases would be in conflict with the contractual obligations of the parties to the dispute or their obligations under this Convention, claims concerning excess of jurisdiction or misuse of power, and to claims for damages to be paid or other remedy to be given to the party concerned for the failure of the other party to comply with its contractual obligations or its obligations under this Convention.

Accordingly, the Chamber's jurisdiction is confined to the following three types of claim:
(1) claims that application of the Authority's rules, regulations and procedures in individual cases would be in conflict with the contractual or Conventional obligations of the parties;
(2) claims concerning excess of jurisdiction or misuse of power; and
(3) claims for damages to be paid or other remedy to be given for the failure to comply with contractual or Conventional obligations.

While it is clear that the Chamber may not expressly 'pronounce itself' on the conformity with the Convention of the Authority's rules, regulations and procedures or declare them invalid, it is equally clear that in exercising jurisdiction in these three types of claim, it must have the competence to consider the legal validity of these rules, regulations and procedures as part of its judicial reasoning.

So far as remedies are concerned, Article 189 is equally vague. It is, of course, clear that damages may be awarded for failure of the Authority to comply with its obligations under the Convention.[101] Beyond that, there is very little that is certain.

What, for example, is the effect in this context of the rule in Article 296(1) of the Convention that the decisions of the Chamber are final and must be complied with by all the parties to the dispute? In the light of this provision, what 'other remedy' is available in respect of a finding by the Chamber that a decision or measure of the Authority, applying a rule, regulation or procedure considered by the Chamber to be invalid, is in conflict with the obligations of the Authority

---

[101] UN Convention, Art.189.

Dispute settlement   369

under the Convention?; or in respect of a finding of excess of jurisdiction or misuse of power? It would seem to follow from Article 296(1) that the effect of any such finding would be the annulment of the decision or measure in question. But, of course, the Chamber could neither substitute its own decision or measure for that of the Authority nor annul any underlying rule, regulation or procedure. On the other hand, 'other remedy' might well embrace the grant of an injunction to prevent the similar application of the suspect rule, regulation or procedure in other individual cases.[102]

VIII. DISPUTES CONCERNING CONFORMITY WITH THE CONVENTION OF PROPOSAL BEFORE ASSEMBLY

Proceedings under this head offer a further means of judicial review of the Authority's acts by way of the advisory jurisdiction of the Sea-Bed Disputes Chamber. Provided it is supported by at least one fourth of the members of the Authority, a request may be addressed by the Assembly to the Chamber for an advisory opinion on the conformity with the Convention of a proposal before the Assembly on any matter.[103] Voting must be deferred on the proposal until the advisory opinion has been received.[104] It may be assumed that the Assembly would not proceed to adopt any rules, regulations or procedures in the face of an opinion of the Chamber that they would not be in conformity with the Convention.

IX. CONTRACTUAL DISPUTES

As the above table on classification of disputes shows, five types of contractual dispute may be distinguished and they are considered in turn below.

1. Disputes between Parties to a Contract Concerning the Interpretation or Application of a Relevant Contract or Plan of Work
The parties to a contract may be States Parties, the Authority or the Enterprise, State enterprises, or natural or juridical persons. All such parties have a right of access to the dispute settlement procedures established for this type of dispute.
[105]Where, however, a 'natural or juridical person' is a party to a dispute, note has to be taken of the provisions of Article 190:

1. If a natural or juridical person is a party to a dispute referred to in article 187, the sponsoring State shall be given notice thereof and shall have the right to participate in the proceedings by submitting written or oral statements.
2. If an action is brought against a State Party by a natural or juridical person sponsored by another State Party in a dispute referred to in article 187, subparagraph (c), the respondent State may request the State sponsoring

---

[102] Suggested by Caflisch, *op.cit. in* note 62, at p.314.
[103] UN Convention, Arts.159(10) and 191.
[104] Art.159(10).
[105] UN Convention, Arts. 187(c)(1) and 188(2), and Mining Code, Annex 4, Section 25.

370　Chapter 9

that person to appear in the proceedings on behalf of that person. Failing such appearance, the respondent State may arrange to be represented by a juridical person of its nationality.

This distinctly odd provision is the result of a compromise necessitated by the reluctance of the socialist group in UNCLOS III to allow proceedings to be instituted against sovereign States by natural or juridical persons sponsored by another sovereign State.[106] It seems unlikely to present any problems in practice.

Alternative means of settlement are open to the parties to such disputes:- the Sea-Bed Disputes Chamber under Article 187(c)(i); a commercial arbitral tribunal under Article 188(2); or, arguably, any other means 'otherwise agreed'.[107] Reading Articles 187(c)(i) and 188(2) together, it would appear that there is a presumption that the dispute will be settled by recourse to binding commercial arbitration unless the parties agree to submit it either to the Chamber or, arguably, to another means of their choice. It may be submitted to commercial arbitration at the request of any party to the dispute.[108]　Caflisch contends that, in the absence of agreement, the claimant may have unilateral recourse to either the Chamber or commercial arbitration.[109] This would certainly be so if the respondent accepted the Chamber's jurisdiction following the claimant's unilateral application. Since, however, Article 188(2) seems to require submission to commercial arbitration at the request of any party to the dispute, 'unless the parties otherwise agree', it would always be open to the respondent to opt for commercial arbitration.

As regards the arbitration procedure to be applied, Article 188(2)(c) provides that:

> In the absence of a provision in the contract on the arbitration procedure to be applied in the dispute, the arbitration shall be conducted in accordance with the UNCITRAL Arbitration Rules or such other arbitration rules as may be prescribed in the rules, regulations and procedures of the Authority, unless the parties to the dispute otherwise agree.

While the advantages of commercial arbitration for the settlement of contractual disputes are self-evident, there is one major disadvantage. It would clearly be undesirable to have questions of interpretation of the Convention decided by commercial arbitration. It is accordingly provided that when the contractual dispute 'also involves a question of the interpretation of Part XI and the Annexes

---

[106] See for full explanation, the *Report of the Chairman of the Group of Legal Experts on the Settlement of Disputes relating to Part XI*, in *UNCLOS III Off. Rec.*, Vol. XII, p.90, at p.92 and M.H. Nordquist and Choon-ho Park (eds.), *Reports of the United States Delegation to the Third United Nations Conference on the Law of the Sea* (Law of the Sea Institute Occasional Paper No.33, 1983), at p.331.

[107] Art.188(2)(a). This interpretation assumes that the phrase 'unless the parties otherwise agree', which is not expressly restricted to the Chamber, is intended to grant such freedom in the choice of a means of settlement. See also the similar position, discussed below, in relation to Annex III, Art.13(15).

[108] Art. 188(2)(a) .

[109] *Loc.cit.* in note 62 at p.320.

Dispute settlement   371

relating thereto', that question has to be referred to the Chamber for a ruling.[110] The arbitral tribunal then has to render its award in conformity with that ruling.[111]

While it may be true that this dual system may involve the danger of delays in those cases where a reference has to be made to the Chamber for a ruling, it does nonetheless offer two principal advantages: uniformity of interpretation of the Convention and the speed and convenience of commercial arbitration in most cases.

2. Disputes over the Interpretation or Application of the Rules and Regulations for Financial Terms of Contracts; and Disputes between the Authority and a Contractor over the Interpretation or Application of the Financial Terms of a Contract

Under the original UN Convention, highly complex rules on the financial terms of contracts were laid down in Annex III, Article 13. The great bulk of these rules were rendered inapplicable by the Implementation Agreement[112] which substituted for them a set of six general principles which were to 'provide the basis for establishing rules, regulations and procedures ...'[113]. Disputes concerning the interpretation or application of such rules and regulations are to be 'subject to the dispute settlement procedures set out in the [United Nations] Convention [on the Law of the Sea].'[114]

Such disputes are most likely to arise in connection with disputes between the Authority and a contractor over the interpretation or application of the financial terms of a particular contract. In such cases the parties are offered various options. As in the case of disputes over the interpretation or application of contracts more generally, discussed above, these disputes too are covered by Article 187(c)(i), which gives the Sea-Bed Disputes Chamber jurisdiction over them. However, Annex III, Article 13(15) adds that:

> In the event of a dispute between the Authority and a contractor over the interpretation or application of the financial terms of a contract, either party may submit the dispute to binding commercial arbitration, unless both parties agree to settle the dispute by other means, in accordance with article 188, paragraph 2.

It would seem, therefore, that the parties may agree to submit the dispute to (1) the Chamber, (2) commercial arbitration, or (3) 'other means' of their own choice. In the absence of agreement, however, the claimant may unilaterally refer the dispute to binding commercial arbitration.

---

[110] Art.188(2)(a) and (b). If, as suggested above, the dispute may be referred by agreement to a means other than the Chamber or a commercial arbitral tribunal, questions of interpretation of the Convention would have to be referred to the Chamber in this case also.

[111] Art. 188(2)(b).

[112] Implementation Agreement, Annex, Section 8(2).

[113] *Ibid.*, Section 8(1).

[114] *Ibid.*, Section 8(1)(f).

372   *Chapter 9*

3. Disputes between Parties to a Contract Concerning Acts or Omissions of a Party to the Contract Relating to Activities in the Area, and Directed to the Other Party or Directly Affecting its Legitimate Interests

The Sea-Bed Disputes Chamber has exclusive jurisdiction over disputes under Article 187(c)(ii). Why this should be so when disputes over the interpretation or application of a contract may also be submitted to commercial arbitration is by no means clear.[115] As Caflisch has pointed out, this artificial distinction between the two types of dispute may well give rise to difficulties. 'What', he asks, 'will happen if one party has recourse to binding commercial arbitration, arguing that the dispute is one of interpretation or application of the contract, while the other party simultaneously seizes the Sea-Bed Disputes Chamber on the ground that the dispute relates to the performance of the contract?'[116]

4. Disputes between the Authority and a Prospective Contractor Concerning the Refusal of a Contract or a Legal Issue Arising in the Negotiation of the Contract

Under Article 187(d), the Sea-Bed Disputes Chamber has exclusive jurisdiction over disputes concerning the refusal of a contract, or a legal issue arising in the negotiation of the contract, between the Authority and a prospective contractor who has been sponsored by a State under Article 153(2)(b) and has duly fulfilled the conditions referred to in Annex III, Article 4(6)[117] and Article 13(2) (as 'implemented' by the Implementation Agreement, Annex, Section 8(3)).[118]

As was seen in Chapter 4, the procedure for the approval of plans of work, originally prescribed in Article 162(2)(j) of the UN Convention, has been modified by the Implementation Agreement, Annex, Section 3(11).[119] In this context, the Implementation Agreement adds that, 'Where a dispute arises relating to the disapproval of a plan of work, such dispute shall be submitted to the dispute settlement procedures set out in the Convention'.[120] It would seem to follow from Article 187(d) of the UN Convention that the Sea-Bed Disputes Chamber would have exclusive jurisdiction over such disputes.

5. Disputes between the Authority and a State Party, State Enterprise or Natural or Juridical Person, Where Alleged that Authority is Liable for Damage Arising out of Wrongful Acts, Including Disclosure of Industrial Secrets etc.

The liability of the Authority for any damage arising out of wrongful acts in the exercise of its powers and functions and for disclosure of industrial secrets under Annex III, Article 22 and Article 168(2) of the Convention has been examined above in Chapter 4.[121] As was seen, the Sea-Bed Disputes Chamber has exclusive jurisdiction over claims arising from this liability, though there was some doubt as to the position of aggrieved third parties outside the contractual nexus.

---

[115] See section IX.1 above.
[116] *Loc.cit.* in note 62, at pp.323-324.
[117] On the qualifications of applicants for contracts, see further Chap.4, section V.3.1.
[118] See further on the financial terms of contracts, Chap 4, section VIII, especially at VIII.2.1.1.
[119] See Chap.4, section V.4.2.
[120] Implementation Agreement, Annex, Section 3(12).
[121] Chap.4, section XIV.2.

X. ADMINISTRATIVE DISPUTES

Two types of administrative dispute are identified in Article 168 of the Convention. 'So-called classical disciplinary violations'[122] are dealt with in Article 168(1), while disputes relating to the disclosure of industrial secrets or information are covered by Article 168(3).

1. Disputes Concerning Alleged Violations of Responsibilities by Secretary-General of Authority or a Staff Member

Such disputes have to be submitted to 'an appropriate administrative tribunal as provided in the rules, regulations and procedures of the Authority'. [123] Under the Authority's Staff Regulation, the Secretary-General must establish administrative machinery with staff participation to advise him or her in disciplinary cases, and the Secretary-General is empowered to impose disciplinary measures for unsatisfactory conduct and to summarily dismiss a members of staff for serious misconduct. [124]

Appeals by staff members against administrative decisions – where staff members allege non-observance of their terms of appointment, including all pertinent regulations and rules – will be dealt with first by the Secretary-General, advised by 'administrative machinery with staff participation'. [125] Staff making such allegations may also apply to the United Nations Administrative Tribunal which, under conditions prescribed by its statute, may hear and pass judgment on such applications. [126]

2. Disputes concerning Alleged Disclosure by the Secretary-General of the Authority or a Staff Member of Industrial Secrets etc.

The question of the liability of the Authority and of the delinquent member of staff of the Authority for such disclosures has been considered above in Chapter 4.[127]

XI. DISPUTES CONCERNING THE LIMITS OF THE AREA

1. Disputes between States Parties

The rules governing the establishment of the outer limit of the continental shelf, which is also of course the inner limit of the Area beyond the limits of national jurisdiction,[128] have been fully analysed in Chapter 4 of Volume 1 of this work.[129]

---

[122] The phrase employed by the Chairman of the group of legal experts which developed these provisions. See *UNCLOS III Off. Rec.*, Vol. XI, at p.110.

[123] Art. 168(1).

[124] Staff Regulations of the International Seabed Authority (Annex to Decision of the Council of the International Seabed Authority Concerning the Staff Regulations of the Authority, ISBA/6/C/10, 13 July 2000), Regs. 10.1 – 10.3

[125] *Ibid.*, Reg. 11.1.

[126] *Ibid.*, Reg. 11.2.

[127] Chap.4, section XIV.2.1.

[128] See Arts. 1(1)(1), 76, 84(2) and 134(3)-(4) of the UN Convention.

[129] E.D. Brown, *Sea-Bed Energy and Minerals: The International Legal Regime*, Vol.1.The *Continental Shelf*, 1992, Chap.4, section I.

374   *Chapter 9*

In the section devoted to dispute settlement,[130] the possibility was explored of proceedings being instituted against State A, the coastal State, by State B, which challenged the legality of State A's outer limit, established unilaterally by State A contrary to the recommendations of the Commission on the Limits of the Continental Shelf. It was concluded that, in the absence of any more specific provisions in Part VI ('Continental Shelf') of the Convention or in Annex II, it must be presumed that there would be an obligation upon States A and B to settle the dispute in accordance with Part XV of the Convention. Under Part XV, the two States would be under an obligation to refer the dispute to one of the forms of binding settlement there specified (there being no exception provided for outer limit disputes, but only for disputes over delimitation between opposite or adjacent States under Article 298(1)(a)(i)).[131] It would of course be necessary for State B to demonstrate a legal interest in the location of State A's limit. Even then, it should be recognised that the absence of specific provision for the settlement of such disputes was by no means accidental and there are many States which would decline to accept that they were bound by a third-party decision on this question.[132]

2. Disputes between a State Party and the Authority

Under Article 84(2) of the Convention, coastal States are required to deposit with the Secretary-General of the Authority a copy of the charts, or a list of the geographical co-ordinates of points, showing the outer limit of their continental shelves and this duty is referred to again in Article 134(3) in the context of the limits of the Area. These provisions are simply a reflection of the self-evident truth that the Authority, as the representative of 'mankind as a whole' in whom 'all rights in the resources of the Area are vested',[133] has a legal interest in the boundary between the areas within the limits of national jurisdiction and the Area beyond.

However, it is less clear how the Authority could challenge any boundary line. Like third States, it would apparently be bound to accept any limit established by the coastal State on the basis of the recommendations of the Commission on the Limits of the Continental Shelf.[134] Even if the limit were established unilaterally and contrary to those recommendations, it is less than certain that there is any forum with compulsory jurisdiction over such a dispute between the coastal State and the Authority. Since the Authority does not in general have access to the range of procedures established in Part XV, it would probably have to rely on Article 187(b)(i) to found the jurisdiction of the Sea-Bed Disputes Chamber. The argument would be that State A, by extending the limits of its continental shelf to include a part of the sea-bed considered by the Authority to form part of the Area, had acted in violation of Part XI.

---

[130] *Ibid.*, at pp.31-32.

[131] *Ibid.*, at p.32

[132] *Ibid.*, at p.32, following note 56.

[133] Art.137(2).

[134] Under Art.76(8), 'The limits of the shelf established by a coastal State on the basis of these recommendations [of the Commission] shall be final and binding'.

Dispute settlement   375

XII. Disputes Concerning Overlapping Pioneer Area Claims

Such disputes are considered above, in Chapter 6.[135]

XIII. Disputes Concerning The Enterprise

Disputes concerning the Enterprise are dealt with above, in Chapter 8.[136]

XIV. Conclusion

In examining the scheme for the settlement of sea-bed disputes in Section 5 of Part XI of the Convention, one is reminded of the old adage that a camel is a horse designed by a committee. It may well be contended that some of the less pleasing aspects of this scheme, particularly its complexity and its ambiguities, are the inevitable product of a committee - UNCLOS III - representing many and diverse interests and plagued by an anxiety to ensure that the interests of their particular constituency in the regime for the exploitation of the Area should be fully safeguarded by adequate provision for compulsory, binding, third party settlement of disputes. The radical novelty of the regime and the emotional attachment to the new doctrines it embodies simply served to aggravate the anxieties. That the product is an ungainly beast is undeniable; the more important question, however, is whether, like the camel, it will confound its critics by proving to be functionally effective in the difficult environment in which it will have to operate.

Although the complexity of the scheme has been the object of much criticism, it is possible to take the view that this criticism has been greatly exaggerated. Even leaving aside the conviction of one influential school of thought, that compulsory adjudication may be made more palatable by presenting potential litigants with a multiplicity of alternative fora, the fundamental fact is that Part XI embodies a very complex regime extending well beyond the normal bounds of international law. The institutions of judicial settlement have accordingly to be designed to accommodate the interests of States, various organs of international institutions and a variety of other natural or judicial persons. Nor are the types of dispute lacking in variety, as is shown by the table of disputes presented above. There is thus a good case for saying that the basic tribunal, a Sea-Bed Disputes Chamber, needs to be supplemented by other organs better designed to deal with commercial, administrative and boundary disputes, not forgetting that there are also issues better dealt with by municipal courts. However, few would deny that a modicum of pruning would be advantageous and it may well be that practice will cut through the unnecessary layers and enhance the already dominant role of the Sea-Bed Disputes Chamber.

The positive side of the complexity is that it reflects the endeavours of the Conference to provide a dispute settlement system which would at once offer comprehensiveness and specialised fora to decide specialised issues. Given the

---

[135] See Chap.6, section III.
[136] See Chap.8, sections II.2.2, II.2.6 and II.2.7.

difficulties of negotiation, the Conference has succeeded in this to a remarkable degree.

PART 3

SEA-BED MINING AND THE MARINE ENVIRONMENT

CHAPTER 10

Protection and Preservation of the Marine Environment

I. Introduction

Prior to the adoption in 1994 of the Implementation Agreement, which opened the way for most of the principal industrialised powers to become parties to the UN Convention, a real possibility existed that deep-sea mining would take place under either the UN Conventional regime, or a Reciprocating States regime – coordinating the municipal legislation of leading industrialised States – or both. [1] Reflecting that situation, detailed rules were prepared on two levels to provide safeguards against pollution of the marine environment by sea-bed mining.

On the international level, the UN Convention itself provided a framework for the establishment of an environmental regime for sea-bed mining and a leading role was assigned to the Preparatory Commission in the preparation of detailed rules, regulations and procedures as part of a comprehensive Mining Code. At the same time, on the national level, some of the principal industrialised powers were drafting sea-bed mining legislation which included rules designed to protect the marine environment. By far the most far-reaching and sophisticated of this legislation was that adopted by the United States and it has had a marked influence upon the corresponding provisions of both the UN regime and the legislation of other States.

As has been seen, the Authority has adopted part of the Mining Code in the form of 'Regulations on Prospecting and Exploration for Polymetallic Nodules in the Area' and, in due course, States Parties to the UN Convention will have to bring their national legislation into line with it. In the meantime, the American regime in particular offers a useful basis for a critique of the UN Convention regime. For this reason, this chapter falls into two main parts, dealing respectively with the provisions of the UN Conventional regime and national legislation. First, however, it is necessary to review briefly what is known of the nature and scale of the threat to the marine environment posed by the plans to explore and exploit the mineral resources of the Area.

---

[1] On the Reciprocating States regime, see further Chap. 7 above.

380   *Chapter 10*

II. Assessment of Environmental Implications of Sea-Bed Mining

Perhaps the most striking fact which emerges from a review of the scientific literature[2], the proceedings of the Preparatory Commission's Special Commission 3 (SCN.3)[3] and the further work undertaken by the Authority [4] is that the environmental impact which sea-bed mining will have is largely unknown. Given the fact that no commercial recovery has yet taken place and that there has been only a limited opportunity to monitor pilot-scale mining tests and measure the impact of simulated mining disturbances, this is hardly surprising.   On the other hand, valuable pioneer work has already been done in a number of countries, increasingly, in recent years, on an international co-operative basis. Indeed, as has been noted, '…it is apparent that deep ocean seafloor mining will not be economically attractive for some time.   Much research effort is hence shifting from the development of technologies to harvest the minerals to studies of environmental impact associated with their future exploitation'.[5]   It is the purpose of this section to present a brief review of this research, conducted or planned for the future by the United States, Germany and a number of the pioneer investor countries – Russia, Japan, the Eastern European States members of Interoceanmetal (IOM), India, China and Korea.

1. United States Research
The United States National Oceanic and Atmospheric Administration (NOAA)

---

[2] See S. Berge, J. M. Markussen and G. Vigerust, *Environmental Consequences of Deep Seabed Mining*, 1991, especially Chap. 2 and Bibliography (pp. 124-135); C.L. Morgan, N.A. Odunton and A.T. Jones, *Synthesis of Environmental Impacts of Deep Seabed Mining*, 17 *Marine Georesources & Geotechnology* (No. 4, 1999), pp. 307-356; and   Metal Mining Agency of Japan (MMAJ), *International Symposium on Environmental Studies for Deep-Sea Mining   Proceedings*, Tokyo, November 1997 (*MMAJ Symposium Proceedings 1997*), including extensive bibliographical references in the various contributions. See also Proceedings of the Sanya Workshop referred to in note 4 below and the NOAA literature listed in note 6 below.

[3] See below, sections III.3.3.4 and IV.

[4] The Secretariat of the Authority held a workshop in China in June 1998. Its main purpose was to discuss common standards for the collection of environmental data and information for the purpose of progressively building up a database. See *Deep-Seabed Polymetallic Nodule Exploration: Development of Environmental Guidelines.   Proceedings of the International Seabed Authority's Workshop held in Sanya, Hainan Island, People's Republic of China, 1-5 June 1998* (ISBA/99/02,1999) (*Sanya Workshop Proceedings 1999*). The Proceedings include specialist contributions on the biological, chemical, phsyical and geochemical impacts of nodule exploration and offer a useful review of the state of current scientific knowledge. The Legal and Technical Commission considered Recommendations from the Workshop (ISBA/5/LTC/1, 21 June 1999) at its August 1999 session and recommended to the Council that, 'for the sixth session, the Secretariat should prepare a study that would, *inter alia*, identify international data repositories that collected environmental data required to monitor the impact of activities in the Area, identify gaps in their data coverage, formulate a plan for the retrieval of appropriate data from such sources and make recommendations for the development of a database for the analysis and synthesis of such data' (*Report of the Legal and Technical Commission on the Work of the Commission during the Fifth Session*, ISBA/5/C/6, 17 August 1999, para. 4).

[5] B.G. Barnett and T. Suzuki, 'The Use of Kriging to Estimate Resedimentation in the JET Experiment', *MMAJ Symposium Proceedings 1997*, pp. 143-151, at p. 143.

Protection of environment 381

began its research programme[6] some five years before the Deep Seabed Hard Mineral Resources Act was adopted in 1980, recognising the importance of acquiring an environmental database against which the impacts of manganese nodule recovery could be measured.[7] NOAA's Deep Ocean Mining Environmental Study (DOMES) was conceived as a comprehensive five-year research programme and had two phases, both undertaken in what has come to be called the DOMES area – an area of 13 million km^2 (3.8 million nm^2) of the equatorial Pacific Ocean lying between Central America and Hawaii, commonly known as the Clarion-Clipperton Fracture Zone.[8] The objectives of the study were described as follows in NOAA's *Report to Congress* in December 1981:

[6] The writer is indebted to Mr. J.P. Flanagan and Mr. M. Karl Jugel of NOAA's Ocean Minerals and Energy Division, for supplying copies of the following documentation on NOAA's work:

(i)   E. Ozturgut *et al., Deep Ocean Mining of Manganese Nodules in the North Pacific: Pre-Mining Environmental Conditions and Anticipated Mining Effects,* NOAA Technical Memorandum ERL MESA-33, 1978 (relating to DOMES I)

(ii)   R.E. Burns *et al., Observations and Measurements During the Monitoring of Deep Ocean Manganese Nodule Mining Tests in the North Pacific, March-May 1978,* NOAA Technical Memorandum ERL MESA-47, 1980 (relating to DOMES II).

(iii)   E. Ozturgut *et al., Environmental Investigation During Manganese Nodule Mining Tests in the North Equatorial Pacific in November 1978,* NOAA Technical Memorandum ERL MESA-48, 1980 (relating to DOMES II).

(iv)   NOAA, *Deep Seabed Mining. Final Programmatic Environmental Impact Statement,* Vols. I and II, 1981.

(v)   NOAA, *Deep Seabed Mining. Final Technical Guidance Document,* 1981.

(vi)   NOAA, *Deep Seabed Mining. Report to Congress,* December 1981.

(vii)   NOAA, *Deep Seabed Mining. Marine Environmental Research Plan 1981-85,* 1982.

(viii) NOAA, *Deep Seabed Mining. Final Regulations (with revisions),* June 1982.

(ix)   NOAA, *Deep Seabed Mining. Report to Congress,* December 1983.

(x)   NOAA, *Deep Seabed Mining. Draft Environmental Impact Statement on Issuing an Exploration License to Ocean Minerals Company,* May 1984.

(xi)   NOAA, *Final Environmental Impact Statement on Issuing an Exploration License to Ocean Minerals Company,* July 1984.

(xii)   NOAA, *Summary of Ocean Minerals Activities and Related Research,* June 1985.

(xiii) NOAA, *Deep Seabed Mining. Report to Congress,* December 1985.

(xiv)   NOAA, *Deep Seabed Mining. Report to Congress,* December 1987.

(xv)   NOAA, *Deep Seabed Mining. An Updated Environmental Assessment of NOAA Deep Seabed Mining Licensees' Exploration Plans,* January 1989.

(xvi)   NOAA, *Deep Seabed Mining. Report to Congress,* December 1989.

(xvii) NOAA, *Deep Seabed Mining. Final Regulations for Commercial Recovery Permits,* January 1990.

(xviii) NOAA, *Deep Seabed Mining. Report to Congress,* December 1991.

(xix)   NOAA, *Deep Seabed Mining. Report to Congress,* December 1993.

(xx)   NOAA, *Deep Seabed Mining. Final Environmental Impact Statement on Issuing an Exploration License to Ocean Minerals Company,* November 1994.

(xxi)   NOAA, *Deep Seabed Mining. A Report to Congress,* December 1995. No funds were appropriated under the Deep Seabed Hard Mineral Resources Act for fiscal year 1995 and NOAA, referring to the low level of industrial and NOAA activity under the Act, indicated that no further biennial reports would be issued until the level of activity increased (letters of submittal of 1995 Report to Senate and House attached to Report).

[7] NOAA, *loc. cit.* in note 6(vi), at p. 26.

[8] NOAA, *loc. cit.* in note 6(iv), Vol. 1, at p. xiii.

382   *Chapter 10*

The objectives of DOMES I were to establish environmental baselines at three sites typical of the environmental conditions likely to be encountered during mining, to develop a first-order predictive capability for determining potential environmental effects of nodule recovery, and to help develop an information base for the preparation of environmental regulations for industry and government. Domes II involved the monitoring of industrial, at-sea, pilot-scale mining tests conducted in 1978. The objectives here were to observe actual environmental effects to improve the ability to predict impacts, and to refine or modify the information base on which subsequent environmental regulations would be based.[9]

The data produced by this research is fully analysed in NOAA's Final Programmatic Environmental Impact Statement (PEIS) filed with the Environmental Protection Agency in September 1981, pursuant to section 109(c)(2) of the Deep Seabed Hard Mineral Resources Act.[10] Reference must be made to PEIS for detailed information but it may be helpful to review briefly, in the light of both PEIS and subsequent research:
  (i) the four principal phases of sea-bed mining which have a potential for impacts on the marine environment;
  (ii) the *modus operandi* of the hydraulic system of sea-bed mining; and
  (iii) the conclusions drawn from NOAA research.

1.1 Principal Phases of Sea-Bed Mining
Impacts upon the marine environment may arise during any one of four phases. The principal potential impact is that of the actual mining process itself, as described below. A second important potential impact is that which would be associated with offshore processing, that is, refining nodules and disposing of waste at sea rather than on land. For technical reasons this is considered impractical at present and is not expected to occur during first generation mining.[11] The third potential impact, therefore, is that arising from transfer of nodules from the mining ship to ore carriers and transport to port. It will suffice to say that no significant impact is expected to arise from these processes.[12] Finally, there is the potential impact of offshore waste disposal either through ocean dumping or discharge through an ocean outfall. It is thought likely that waste disposal will in fact take place onshore. If not, the problems of regulating disposal at sea will not differ essentially from those encountered and dealt with in relation to other forms of dumping and discharge. In any event, regulations must await further knowledge of the characteristics of nodule-processing waste.[13]

---

[9] NOAA, *loc. cit.* in note 6(vi), at p. 26.
[10] NOAA, *loc. cit.* in note 6(iv).
[11] *Ibid.*, Vol. I, p. xix.
[12] *Ibid.*, pp. xix-xxi.
[13] *Ibid.*, p. xix. See also NOAA's 1995 *Report to Congress, loc. cit.* in note 6(xxi), at p. 12, for indication that post-processing remains would not harm the environment.

Protection of environment 383

1.2 Modus Operandi of Sea-Bed Mining [14]

There are two main types of mining systems, the continuous line bucket (CLB) system favoured originally by the Japanese and French operators and the hydraulic system developed by the other consortia, including those with American participation. NOAA research has concentrated mainly on the hydraulic system. Using this system, nodules will be recovered by a collector up to 20 metres (66 feet) wide, pulled or driven along the sea-bed in nearly adjacent swathes. The nodules are then pumped in a seawater slurry through a pipeline to the mining ship. During collection, bottom water, sediments and macerated biota are drawn into the collector. Although most of this extraneous material is ejected near the sea-floor, some is pumped up the pipeline and discharged at the surface.

1.3 Conclusions Drawn From NOAA Research

The range of potential environmental impacts considered by NOAA and the tentative conclusions drawn from their research are summarised in a table which, though published in 1984,[15] is still of interest and is reproduced here. Since that time, NOAA has been conducting further research, increasingly on an international, co-operative basis. As will be seen, NOAA's investigations have concentrated on three potentially adverse impacts of sea-bed mining:

- the destruction of benthos in and near the collector track;
- the impact of the benthos plume or 'rain of fines'; and
- the effect of the surface plume.

The first two may be referred to together as the 'benthic impact' and the third as the 'surface discharge impact'.

Destruction of benthos in and near collector track. As the collector moves across the sea-bed, organisms living in its path (benthic biota) will be destroyed and those living between swathes will be smothered by heavy sediment. NOAA's worst case estimate in 1981 was that the benthic biota in about 1 per cent (130,000 square kilometres or 38,000 square nautical miles) of the DOMES area might be killed in first generation mining activities. No effect on the water column food chain was expected, however. NOAA regarded this impact to be both adverse and unavoidable and considered it unlikely that any mitigation measures would be available to reduce it. They were, however, 'unable at this time [September 1981] ... to conclude that the impact is *significant*'.[16] In a paper published in 1997, NOAA investigators, referring to this judgment, added that it would probably 'not be significant due to the fact that mining will occur in a very small percentage of the mine sites.'[17]

---

[14] See further NOAA, *loc. cit.* in note 6(iv), Vol. I, p. xviii, section II and App. 3. The CLB system is described briefly in App. 3, at pp. 226-227 and in H.Thiel, 'Exploration Techniques and Potential Mining Systems', *Sanya Workshop Proceedings 1999*, pp. 29-39, at pp. 33-35.

[15] NOAA, *loc. cit.* in note 6(x), p. 78.

[16] NOAA, *loc. cit.* in note 6(iv), Vol. I, p. xviii, emphasis added.

[17] E. Ozturgut, D.D. Trueblood and J.J. Lawless, 'An Overview of the United States' Benthic Impact Experiment', *MMAJ Symposium Proceedings 1997*, pp. 23-31, at p. 26. See also D.D. Trueblood *et al.*, 'The Ecological Impacts of the Joint U.S.-Russian Benthic Impact Experiment'. *MMAJ Symposium Proceedings 1997*, pp. 237-243.

TABLE 10.1: Deep seabed mining perturbations and environmental impact concerns**

		MINING PERTURBATIONS			
		BENTHIC IMPACT		SURFACE DISCHARGE	
	Status of Concerns*	**Collector Contact**	**Benthic Plume**	**Particulates**	**Dissolved Substances**
CONCERNS WITHOUT POTENTIAL FOR SIGNIFICANT OR ADVERSE IMPACTS	Low probability of impacts	Light from collector	Nutrient or trace metal increase	Bacteria growth deplete oxygen	Trace metals effects on phytoplankton
			Oxygen demand	Alter phytoplankton species composition	Nutrient increase cause phytoplankton blooms
				Affect fish	Airlift caused embolisms
				Zooplankton mortality and species composition and abundance changes in plume	
				Trace metals entry into food web	
				Pycnocline accumulation	
				Affect fish larvae	
	Potentially beneficial effects	Additional food supply for bottom scavengers	Not applicable	Bacteria increase food supply for zooplankton	Not applicable
				Filterfeeding zooplankton fecal pellets clean up plume	
	Certain impact without significant adverse effects	Not applicable	Not applicable	Increased turbidity reduce productivity	Not applicable
CONCERNS WITH POTENTIAL FOR SIGNIFICANT OR ADVERSE IMPACTS	Certain impacts	Destroy benthos in and near track	Not applicable	Not applicable	Not applicable
	Unresolved impacts	Not applicable	Blanket benthos; dilute food supply away from mine-site sub-areas	Not applicable	Not applicable

*   Note: Status of concerns is to be verified during demonstration-scale mining system tests and during commercial mining.
** Reproduced from National Oceanic & Atmospheric Administration, *Deep Seabed Mining. Draft Environmental Impact Statement on Issuing an Exploration License to Ocean Minerals Company, May 1984, p78.*

Protection of environment   385

Benthic plume ('rain of fines') impact. The collector's action on the sea floor raises a benthic plume of fine sedimentary particulates which moves with bottom currents away from the mine site. This 'rain of fines', which can extend tens of kilometres from the collector and last for several weeks, falls as a sedimentary blanket which may smother bottom feeders and interfere with their food supply. NOAA concluded in 1981 that 'interference with the food supply for the bottom-feeding animals ... and clogging of the respiratory surfaces of filter feeding benthic biota may have the potential for significant adverse impacts involving the biota in an estimated additional 0.5 per cent (65,000 km^2 or 19,000 nmi^2) of the DOMES area'.[18] Much of their research since that time has been designed to gain more information on this impact. Further details about this research will be found in NOAA's biennial reports to Congress [19] but a brief indication of some of its principal components may be given here.

In 1988 NOAA designated as a Provisional Interim Preservational Reference Area (PIPRA) a site contributed from their licence areas by three United States licensees, OMA, OMCO and KCON and was still evaluating its suitability as a control area for measuring environmental impacts when it reported to Congress in 1993 [20]. The existence of such a PRA will allow comparisons to be made with a corresponding Impact Reference Area (IRA) which will be used to monitor benthic impact during commercial operations. NOAA has designated an area within OMA's mine site as a proposed Provisional Impact Reference Area (PIRA)[21].

In recent years NOAA has been able to share the costs of its researches with other countries. For example, co-operative research agreements were signed with the Yuzhmorgeologiya Association of Russia's Ministry of Geology in 1989, 1990 and 1991[22]. A notable example of this co-ordinated research is the Benthic Impact Experiment (BIE), designed to assess the environmental impact of deep sea mining on the organisms living in and on the seafloor. The project used the Russian research vessel *Yuzhmorgeologiya* which employed NOAA's Deep Sea Sediment Resuspension System (DSSRS) to simulate large scale mining disturbances. As described in a NOAA report:

> The experiment consists of blanketing an area of the seafloor with sediments in a manner simulating the mining of manganese nodules. The response of the benthic organisms to different levels of sediment burial will be indicative of the impacts to be associated with commercial mining[23]

Following tests off the Californian coast, the main phase of BIE-I took place in the near-equatorial North Pacific, with participation by German and Japanese

---

[18] *Ibid.*, p. xviii.

[19] See NOAA, *loc. cit.* in note 6, item ix, at pp. 13-20; item xiii, at pp. 19-26; item xiv, at pp. 24-28; item xvi, at pp. 7-10; item xviii, at pp. 11-14; item xix, at pp. 11-13; and item xxi, at pp. 12-14.

[20] See NOAA, *loc. cit.* in note 6(xix), p. 11. However, as is made clear in the 1995 Report to Congress (*loc. cit.* in note 6 (xxi), at p. ii), 'activities were virtually terminated when no funds were appropriated for the program in Fiscal Year 1995'.

[21] *Ibid.*

[22] *Ibid.*

[23] *Ibid.*, at p. 12.

386   *Chapter 10*

scientists[24]. A further BIE-II research cruise took place in 1993 with a redesigned DSSRS-II blanketing the study area with sediment in the course of 49 tows and the area was revisited in 1994 to collect samples[25].

As will be seen below, similar BIE's were subsequently conducted by other countries, often with American collaboration. Referring to this series of BIE's, Barnett and Suzuki have recently noted that :

> The essence of these studies is the creation of an artificial seafloor sediment disturbance similar to that which may be expected from a seafloor mining machine. Careful monitoring of biological seafloor activity before during and after such a disturbance is then used to identify and quantify environmental impacts on benthic communities in the mining areas.[26]

Such studies always consist of three stages: baselines studies prior to the disturbance; disturbance of the seafloor by a DSSRS or similar 'disturber'; and post-disturbance monitoring.

While the exact impact of the benthic plume on the benthic fauna in the mining area of the Clarion-Clipper Fracture Zone is not fully known at present,[27] it has been reported that the results from NOAA's BIE (and DOMES) have indicated that 'the far field effects of sediment redeposition may have been overestimated'.[28] It was emphasised, however, that 'the Disturber used in the BIE [was] not a commercial miner, and until a full scale mining test [was] monitored, the plume dispersal and redeposition impact on the deep-sea benthos [would] remain open to scientific debate'.[29] Nonetheless, it was recognised that a comparison of the results of NOAA's BIE with those conducted by other countries, and with information from other studies such as Germany's DISCOL project, would improve predictive capabilities in evaluating the benthic impact of deep ocean mining.[30]

Effect of surface plume. The plume caused by the surface discharge of seafloor sediment and bottom water may adversely affect the larvae of those fish, such as tuna, which spawn in the open ocean. NOAA believes that, in the exploratory phase of sea-bed mining, the surface plume should not cause any significant adverse effects on the eggs and larvae of commercially important fish[31]. Similarly, experiments indicate a low probability of adverse effects from

---

[24] *Ibid.*
[25] *Ibid.*, at p. 13 and NOAA, *loc. cit.* in note 6(xxi), pp. ii and 13.
[26] B.G. Barnett and T. Suzuki, 'The Use of Kriging to Estimate Resedimentation in the JET Experiment', *MMAJ Symposium Proceedings 1997*, pp. 143-151, at p. 143.
[27] E. Ozturgut *et al.*, *loc. cit.* in note 17 above, at p. 26.
[28] *Ibid.*, at p. 30.
[29] *Ibid.* On the design of the 'Disturber' (DSSRS), see further K. Tsurusaki, 'Concept and Basic Design of the Plume Discharge', *MMAJ Symposium Proceedings 1997*, pp. 127-132.
[30] E. Ozturgut *et al.*, *loc. cit.* in note 17 above, at p. 30. On Germany's DISCOL project, see further section 7 below.
[31] See NOAA, *loc. cit.* in note 6(iv), Vol. I, p.xix and *loc. cit.* in note 6(xiii), at pp. 20-22.

Protection of environment 387

the surface plume which will result from the commercial recovery of manganese nodules[32].

2. Japanese Research

In Japan, the Metal Mining Agency of Japan (MMAJ) has undertaken investigations on the effect of manganese nodule mining in the marine environment. An 8-year study entitled 'Environmental Impact Research for Manganese Nodule Mining' began in 1989 and there was close collaboration with NOAA from 1990. In 1994, the Japan Deep Sea Impact Experiment (JET), fundamentally the same as the United States BIE, was conducted in the Japanese pioneer area in the north-east Pacific. Monitoring surveys were carried out following the artificial disturbance in 1994, 1995 and 1996.[33] In 1997, a nodule-collector test was performed.[34]

3. Research by Interoceanmetal (IOM)

The registered pioneer investor co-sponsored by a number of Eastern European States, Interoceanmetal (IOM), conducted a Benthic Impact Experiment (BIE) in 1995 in the eastern part of the Clarion-Clipperton zone, thus complementing the Japanese JET project and the joint United States-Russian BIE carried out in the western and central parts of the zone.[35] It was reported that the project produced data demonstrating the absence of particularly harmful consequences immediately after the disturbance was created. No immediate deleterious changes due to sediment resettlement, as opposed to changes in the sediment affected by the Disturber itself, were visible in the meiobenthic communities. It was noted, however, that further monitoring would be necessary to check if any longer-term effects would ensue.[36]

4. Indian Research

The Indian Deepsea Experiment (INDEX), initiated in the Central Indian Basin in 1995, involved the same three phases of baseline studies, disturbance and monitoring as the other BIE's conducted by NOAA-Russia, Japan and IOM and, indeed, used the same type of disturber. Monitoring cruises were scheduled for 1998 and 1999 with annual observations from 2000 to 2002.[37]

---

[32] NOAA, *loc. cit.* in note 6(xiii), p. 21.

[33] See further Y. Kajitani, 'Summary of the Japanese Environmental Study for Manganese Nodules Development', *MMAJ Symposium Proceedings 1997*, pp. 11-21.

[34] See further Prof. Y. Shirayama's report on Japanese research in *Sanya Workshop Proceedings 1999*, at pp. 161-163 and 171-174, and H. Yamada and T. Yamazaki, 'Japan's Ocean Test of the Nodule Mining System', *Proceedings of the 8th (1998) International Offshore and Polar Engineering Conference*, 1998.

[35] See further R.Kotlinski and G. Tkatchenko, 'Preliminary Results of IOM Environmental Research', *MMAJ Symposium Proceedings 1997*, pp. 35-44. For a useful sketch map showing the locations of major areas of environmental research, see *ibid.,* at p. 38. It shows the positions of (1) US DOMES stations; (2) the NOAA-Russian BIE; (3) the Japanese JET; (4) the German DISCOL; and (5) the IOM BIE.

[36] *Ibid.,* at p. 43. See also R. Kotlinski's report on IOM's environmental programme in *Sanya Workshop Proceedings 1999*, at pp. 159-161 and 173-174, with literature cited at p. 202, note 4.

[37] See further E. Desa and INDEX project group, 'Initial Results of India's Environmental Impact Assessment of Nodule Mining, *MMAJ Symposium Proceedings 1997*, pp. 49-63; and R. Sharma *et al.,* 'Seafloor and Sediment Characteristics in INDEX Area', *ibid.*, pp. 83-90.

388 *Chapter 10*

5. Korean Research
Korea's 'Plan of Work for Exploration' also includes a three-phase programme to be conducted in Korea's pioneer area in the eastern Pacific between 1998 and 2012 and preliminary results of the Korean Deep Ocean Study (KODOS) have recently been reported.[38]

6. Chinese Research
COMRA, the Chinese Registered Pioneer Investor, has included in its second 5-year plan (1996-2000) a Natural Variability of Baseline study (NaVaBa), designed to contribute to the understanding of the natural variabilities of the deep sea environment which will help with the assessment of impacts when deep seabed mining begins.[39]

7. German Research
The German ATESWPP project ('Impacts of potential technical interventions on the deep-sea ecosystem of the south-east Pacific off Peru') consists of 7 co-operating sub-projects. It includes the DISCOL project (DISturbance and reCOLonisation), a long-term, large-scale disturbance and recolonisation experiment conducted in the south-eastern Pacific Ocean off Peru. This 5-year (1988-93) project was succeeded by the ECOBENT investigations ('Benthic investigations in the Abyssal ecosystem in the south-east Pacific'). [40] The disturbance experiment was initiated during a two-month cruise of the *R/V Sonne* in 1989 with four re-investigations in the course of the following seven years.[41]

German scientists have emphasised the difference between the DISCOL/ECOBENT investigations and BIE experiments such as the Japanese JET project.[42] It has been pointed out that DISCOL focussed on the recolonisation of a large scale physical sea-bed disturbance, comparable to mining collector tracks, whereas JET investigated the impact of a resettled sediment plume on the fauna. Again, whereas the DISCOL disturbance modified the structure of the benthic environment, in JET the sediment structure in

---

[38] See further Kyeong-Yong Lee *et al.*, 'Korea Deepsea Environmental Research Program for the Deep Seabed Mining', *MMAJ Symposium Proceedings 1997*, pp. 65-72; Jung-Ho Hyun *et al.*, 'Some Results from Environmental Baseline Study at KODOS (Korea Deep Ocean Study) Area', *ibid.*, pp. 91-108; and Jung-Ho Hyun's report in *Sanya Workshop Proceedings 1999*, at pp. 163-165 and 189-194.

[39] See further Liu Feng, 'NaVaBa – A New Initiative of COMRA's Environmental Program', *MMAJ Symposium Proceedings 1997*, pp. 73-81; and Liu Feng *et al.*, 'Basic Research on Characteristics of Deep-Sea Sediment Clouds Produced by Marine Mining', *ibid.*, pp. 109-126. For further reports, see *Sanya Workshop Proceedings 1999*, at pp. 156-157 and 166-167.

[40] See H. Thiel, 'Report on German Studies on the Environmental Impact of Manganese Nodule Mining (Abstract)', *MMAJ Symposium Proceedings 1997*, p. 33. It was expected that a final report summarising all the work on DISCOL/ECOBENT would be delivered to the German Government at the end of 1998. See Prof. Thiel's report in *Sanya Workshop Proceedings 1999*, at pp. 157-159.

[41] This account is based on G. Schriever *et al.*, 'Results of the large scale deep-sea environmental impact study DISCOL during eight years of investigation', *MMAJ Symposium Proceedings 1997*, pp. 197-208.

[42] *Ibid.*, at p. 206.

principle remained unchanged, except that a few millimetre thick, resedimented soft layer was added on top.[43] Thus, the German research contribution may be regarded as complementary to that made by the various BIE projects.[44]

8. Russian Research

Reference was made above to the collaboration between NOAA and Yuzhmorgeologiya.[45] Professor Glumov has recently reported on this and other aspects of the environmental investigations conducted by Yuzhmorgeologiya at the ISBA Workshop held in China in 1998. [46]

III. THE UN CONVENTION REGIME

The UN Convention regime includes the relevant provisions of the UN Convention and the Implementation Agreement – which are considered here in section III – and of the Mining Code, analysed in section IV of this chapter.

Dealing first with the UN Convention itself, the relevant provisions may be considered under three heads. First, there are a number of provisions which feature among the Convention's 'Principles Governing the Area' or its 'Policies Relating to Activities in the Area'. Secondly, there are the substantive environmental rules concerning the Area incorporated in Part XII of the Convention. Thirdly, there are the provisions calling for the establishment of the detailed environmental rules, regulations and procedures which will be required to give effect to the more general norms prescribed in the Convention.

1. Principles and Policies

1.1 Common Heritage of Mankind

The most fundamental principle governing the Area is, of course, the principle laid down in Article 136 that 'The Area and its resources are the common heritage of mankind'. The specifically environmental rules which follow are designed to safeguard mankind's heritage from the pollution which its exploitation may threaten.

1.2 International Responsibility and Liability for Damage

Article 139 places a responsibility upon States and international organisations to ensure that activities in the Area take place in conformity with the regime established by the Convention. Failure to take all necessary and appropriate measures to secure effective compliance might render the State or international organisation liable for pollution damage caused by such activities.[47]

1.3 Rights and Legitimate Interests of Coastal States

Article 142 preserves the rights of coastal States to take such measures, consistent with Part XII, as may be necessary to prevent, mitigate or eliminate grave and

---

[43] *Ibid.*
[44] *Ibid.*
[45] See above, section II.1.3.
[46] I.F. Glumov, *Sanya Workshop Proceedings 1999*, at pp. 195-201.
[47] See also Art. 235. See further, on the question of liability, below section IV.6.4.8.

390   *Chapter 10*

imminent danger to their coastline, or related interests from pollution or threat of pollution, or from other hazardous occurrences resulting from or caused by any activities in the Area.

1.4 Protection of the Marine Environment
Article 145, embodying the Convention's fundamental principle on the protection of the environment of the Area, deserves reproduction *in extenso*:

> Necessary measures shall be taken in accordance with this Convention with respect to activities in the Area to ensure effective protection for the marine environment from harmful effects which may arise from such activities. To this end the Authority shall adopt appropriate rules, regulations and procedures for *inter alia*:
> (a) the prevention, reduction and control of pollution and other hazards to the marine environment, including the coastline, and of interference with the ecological balance of the marine environment, particular attention being paid to the need for protection from harmful effects of such activities as drilling, dredging, excavation, disposal of waste, construction and operation or maintenance of installations, pipelines and other devices related to such activities;
> (b) the protection and conservation of the natural resources of the Area and the prevention of damage to the flora and fauna of the marine environment.

1.5 Accommodation of Activities in the Area and in the Marine Environment
The principle laid down in Article 147, requiring, on a basis of reciprocity, reasonable regard for one another's activities among operators in the Area and other users of the seas, clearly has implications for the preservation of the marine environment.

1.6 Policies Relating to Activities in the Area
Article 150 includes among the policy objectives of sea-bed mining the 'orderly, safe and rational management of the Area, including the efficient conduct of activities in the Area and, in accordance with sound principles of conservation, the avoidance of unnecessary waste'.

1.7 Principles Entrenched Against Review
The provision made in Article 155 of the UN Convention for a review of the sea-bed mining regime to be undertaken fifteen years after the commencement of commercial production was rendered inapplicable by the Implementation Agreement of 28 July 1994 which now permits a review to be undertaken by the Assembly of the Authority at any time[48]. However the Assembly is required to

---

[48] Agreement relating to the Implementation of Part XI of the United Nations Convention on the Law of the Sea of 10 December 1982, 28 July 1994 ('Implementation Agreement'), *LOS Bull.*, Special Issue IV, 1994, p. 10; reproduced in Vol. 3 as Doc. No. 23.

Protection of environment 391

ensure the maintenance of a number of essential features of the Conventional regime and, specifically, the principles laid down in Part XI with regard to protection of the marine environment, rights of coastal States and accommodation between activities in the Area and other activities in the marine environment[49].

2. Part XII: Environmental Rules
2.1 General Obligation
The fundamental rule in Part XII ('Protection and Preservation of the Marine Environment') is laid down in Article 192:

States have the obligation to protect and preserve the marine environment.

2.2 Best Practicable Means
Under Article 194, States have the obligation, moreover, to take all measures necessary to prevent, reduce and control pollution of the marine environment *from any source.* In so doing, they must use 'the best practicable means at their disposal and in accordance with their capabilities'. Article 194 goes on to itemise various sources of marine pollution, referring to dumping, pollution from ships and pollution from installations and devices used in exploration or exploitation of the natural resources of the sea-bed and subsoil. Special mention is made too of the need to take the measures necessary to 'protect and preserve rare or fragile ecosystems as well as the habitat of depleted, threatened or endangered species and other forms of marine life'.

2.3 Duty Not to Transfer Pollution
Article 195 seeks to ensure that anti-pollution measures in one area should not cause the transfer of damage or hazards to another area or transform one type of pollution into another. This might apply, for example, to the dumping of spoils or to pollution caused by the transport of minerals or their processing in another area.

2.4 Use of Technologies
Article 196(1) requires States to 'take all measures necessary to prevent, reduce and control pollution ... resulting from the use of technologies under their jurisdiction or control'. It would seem to follow that, given a choice of alternative sea-bed mining devices, the State might be under a duty to require use of the technology posing the least threat to the environment.

2.5 Alien or New Species
Article 196 also requires States to take the measures necessary to prevent, reduce and control the intentional or accidental introduction of species, alien or new, to a particular part of the marine environment, which may cause significant and harmful danger thereto.[50]

---

[49] *Ibid.*
[50] On the possibility of causing changes in species composition of phytoplankton by surface discharge of deep-sea microbes or resting spores, see NOAA, *loc. cit.* in note 6(iv), Vol. I, pp. 84-85. No significant change is anticipated.

392　　*Chapter 10*

2.6 Notification of Imminent or Actual Damage and Contingency Plans
When a State becomes aware that the marine environment has been damaged or is in imminent danger of being damaged by pollution, it is required, under Article 198, immediately to notify other States deemed likely to be affected, as well as competent international organisations. Article 199 goes on to place the obligation upon States to jointly develop contingency plans to enable them to respond to such damage or threat of damage.

2.7 Monitoring and Environmental Assessment
Given the lack of experience of sea-bed mining and the paucity of knowledge on its environmental effects, it is clearly essential that adequate provision should be made to monitor the exploration and exploitation of the mineral resources of the Area and to assess their impact on the marine environment. Articles 204-206 provide the framework:

Article 204
Monitoring of the risks or effects of pollution

1. States shall, consistent with the rights of other States, endeavour, as far as practicable, directly or through the competent international organisations, to observe, measure, evaluate and analyse, by recognised scientific methods, the risks or effects of pollution of the marine environment.
2. In particular, States shall keep under surveillance the effects of any activities which they permit or in which they engage in order to determine whether these activities are likely to pollute the marine environment.

Article 205
Publication of Reports

States shall publish reports of the results pursuant to article 204 or provide such reports at appropriate intervals to the competent international organisations, which should make them available to all States.

Article 206
Assessment of potential effects of activities

When States have reasonable grounds for believing that planned activities under their jurisdiction or control may cause substantial pollution of or significant and harmful changes to the marine environment, they shall, as far as practicable, assess the potential effects of such activities on the marine environment and shall communicate reports of the results of such assessments in the manner provided in article 205.

Protection of environment 393

3. The Setting and Enforcement of Environmental Standards
3.1 Setting Environmental Standards
The principal provision is to be found in Article 209:

Article 209
Pollution from activities in the Area

1. International rules, regulations and procedures shall be established in accordance with Part XI to prevent, reduce and control pollution of the marine environment from activities in the Area. Such rules, regulations and procedures shall be re-examined from time to time as necessary.

2. Subject to the relevant provisions of this section, States shall adopt laws and regulations to prevent, reduce and control pollution of the marine environment from activities in the Area undertaken by vessels, installations, structures and other devices flying their flag or of their registry or operating under their authority, as the case may be. The requirements of such laws and regulations shall be no less effective than the international rules, regulations and procedures referred to in paragraph 1.

Paragraph 1 is followed up by Article 17(1)(b)(xii) of Annex III,[51] which provides for the adoption and uniform application by the Authority of rules, regulations and procedures on 'mining standards and practices, including those relating to operational safety, conservation of the resources and the protection of the marine environment.' Under Paragraph (2)(f) of the same Article, the rules regulations and procedures on the protection of the marine environment must 'fully reflect' the following 'objective criteria':

Rules, regulations and procedures shall be drawn up in order to secure effective protection of the marine environment from harmful effects directly resulting from activities in the Area or from shipboard processing immediately above a mine site of minerals derived from that mine site, taking into account the extent to which such harmful effects may directly result from drilling, dredging, coring and excavation and from disposal, dumping and discharge into the marine environment of sediment, wastes or other effluents.

Prior to the entry into force of the UN Convention, the Preparatory Commission was responsible for the preparation of these rules, regulations and procedures. Following the entry into force of the Convention, a number of the organs of the International Seabed Authority have been involved in their further preparation, adoption and enforcement. The rôles played by the Preparatory Commission and the various organs of the Authority are outlined below in sections III.3.3 and IV.1 and the relevant rules, regulations and procedures of the Mining Code are considered in section IV.

---

[51] UN Convention, Annex III: Basic Conditions of Prospecting, Exploration and Exploitation.

394   *Chapter 10*

3.2 Enforcing Environmental Standards
The principal provision is contained in Article 215:

Article 215
Enforcement with respect to pollution from activities in the Area

Enforcement of international rules, regulations and procedures established in accordance with Part XI to prevent, reduce and control pollution of the marine environment from activities in the Area shall be governed by that Part.

Of the provisions of Part XI referred to in Article 215, the most important are Article 185 and Annex III, Article 18. Under Article 185, a State which has grossly and persistently violated the provisions of Part XI may be suspended from the exercise of the rights and privileges of membership of the Authority by the Assembly upon the recommendation of the Council. No such action may be taken, however, until the Seabed Disputes Chamber has found that there has indeed been such a gross and persistent violation.

Article 18 of Annex III makes provision for the imposition of penalties on contractors for violation of the terms of contracts. They range from suspension or termination of rights under the contract to monetary penalties.

The functions of the organs of the Authority in the supervision and enforcement of the rules designed to protect the environment are outlined in section 3.3 below.

3.3 Rôle of Authority Organs and Preparatory Commission
Although in earlier years the Preparatory Commission played an important rôle in the preparation of rules, regulations and procedures, it is perhaps appropriate to give an account first of the functions of the more permanent organs of the Authority, before passing to the task allocated to the Preparatory Commission.

3.3.1 Rôle of Assembly[52]
Under Article 160(2)(f)(ii) of the UN Convention, the Assembly is empowered to consider and approve the rules, regulations and procedures of the Authority provisionally adopted by the Council under Article 162(2)(o)(ii). As will be seen below, this latter provision has been modified by the Implementation Agreement.[53]

3.3.2 Rôle of Council
As was seen in Chapter 8,[54] the original provisions of Article 162(2)(o)(ii), under which the Council is empowered to adopt and provisionally apply the rules,

---

[52] See further on the powers and functions of the Assembly, Chap. 8, section II.1.1.3.
[53] See Implementation Agreement, Annex, Section 1, paras 15 and 17 and further below in section 3.3.2.
[54] See further Chap. 8, section II.1.2.2.

Protection of environment 395

recommendations and procedures of the Authority relating to prospecting, exploration and exploitation in the Area, were modified by the Implementation Agreement and the Council now has to undertake this task in accordance with the revised rules laid down in Paragraphs 15-17 of Section 1 of the Annex to the Agreement. As previously, in adopting such rules, regulations and procedures, the Council has to take into account the recommendations of its subsidiary organ, the Legal and Technical Commission, and the rules, regulations and procedures will 'remain in effect on a provisional basis until approved by the Assembly or until amended by the Council in the light of any views expressed by the Assembly'.[55]

The Council's powers also enable it to:

- institute proceedings on behalf of the Authority before the Seabed Disputes Chamber in cases of non-compliance (Article 162(2)(u)); and notify the Assembly upon a decision by the Chamber on such a case and recommend appropriate measures (Article 162(2)(v));
- issue emergency orders, including orders for the suspension or adjustment of operations, to prevent serious harm to the marine environment arising out of activities in the Area (Article 162(2)(w));
- disapprove areas for exploitation by contractors or the Enterprise in cases where substantial evidence indicates the risk of serious harm to the marine environment (Article 162(2)(x));
- establish an inspectorate to determine that activities in the Area are in compliance with the rules, regulations and procedures of the Authority and the terms of the contract concerned (Article 162(2)(z)).

3.3.3 Rôle of Legal and Technical Commission

The Council has to endeavour to ensure that this Commission includes a member or members qualified in the protection of the marine environment (Article 165(1)). The functions of the Commission include the formulation and submission to the Council of the rules, regulations and procedures referred to in Article 162(2)(o), 'taking into account all relevant factors including assessments of the environmental implications of activities in the Area'; and keeping such rules etc. under review (Article 165(2)(f)-(g)). In addition, the Commission is entrusted with the following environmentally relevant tasks:

- preparation of assessments of the environmental implications of activities in the Area (Article 165(2)(d));
- the making of recommendations to the Council on the protection of the marine environment, taking into account the views of recognised experts in that field (Article 165(2)(e));
- the making of recommendations to the Council regarding the establishment of a monitoring programme to observe, measure, evaluate and analyse, by recognised scientific methods, on a regular basis, the risks

---

[55] UN Convention, Art. 162 (2)(o)(ii).

396 Chapter 10

or effects of pollution of the marine environment resulting from activities in the Area, ensure that existing regulations are adequate and are complied with and co-ordinate the implementation of the monitoring programme approved by the Council (Article 165(2)(h));

- the making of recommendations to the Council that proceedings be instituted on behalf of the Authority before the Seabed Disputes Chamber (Article 165(2)(i));
- the making of recommendations to the Council with respect to measures to be taken, upon a decision by the Seabed Disputes Chamber in such proceedings (Article 165(2)(j));
- the making of recommendations to the Council to issue emergency orders, which may include orders for the suspension or adjustment of operations, to prevent serious harm to the marine environment arising out of activities in the Area. Such recommendations have to be taken up by the Council on a priority basis (Article 165(2)(k));
- the making of recommendations to the Council to disapprove areas for exploitation by contractors or the Enterprise in cases where substantial evidence indicates the risk of serious harm to the marine environment (Article 165(2)(1));
- and, finally, the making of recommendations to the Council regarding the direction and supervision of the above-mentioned inspectorate (Article 165(2)(m)).

3.3.4 Rôle of Preparatory Commission

The organs of the Authority could not of course act until the Convention entered into force. In the interim, it was left to the Preparatory Commission, established by Conference Resolution I, to 'prepare draft rules, regulations and procedures, as necessary to enable the Authority to commence its functions ....'.[56] Under Article 308(4) of the Convention, these draft rules etc. were to apply provisionally pending their formal adoption by the Authority in the manner described above. An account of the Preparatory Commission's wok in preparing a set of draft regulations is given below in section IV.

4. The Implementation Agreement

As has been seen, the Implementation Agreement of 28 July 1994 was very much the product of the series of Informal Consultations sponsored by the UN Secretary-General between 1990 and 1994.[57] During the first phase of the

---

[56] Resolution I of UNCLOS III on Establishment of the Preparatory Commission for the International Sea-Bed Authority and for the International Tribunal for the Law of the Sea, para. 5(g). For details of Preparatory Commission and role in relation to pioneer investor scheme, see further Chap. 6, section III and Chap. 8, section III.

[57] See further Chap. 1 above. For a brief account of the Informal Consultations, see E D Brown, ' "Neither necessary nor prudent at this stage": the regime of seabed mining and its impact on the universality of the UN Convention on the Law of the Sea', 17 *Marine Policy* (1993), pp. 81-107 and 'The 1994 Agreement on the Implementation of Part XI of the UN Convention on the Law of the Sea; breakthrough to universality', 19 *ibid.* (1995), pp. 5-20; or E.D. Brown, *The International Law of the Sea*, Vol. I, 1994, Chap. 17, section IV.

Protection of environment 397

Informal Consultations in 1990-91, delegates had little difficulty in reaching agreement on the least contentious of the nine issues under consideration: 'environmental considerations'. They agreed that '....a comprehensive set of rules for the protection and preservation of the marine environment from deep seabed mining activities should be developed on the basis of the work done by the Preparatory Commission'.[58] In the course of the 1992 Consultations, it was generally agreed that this issue could be removed from the list of hard core issues, partly because it was not an obstacle to ratification and partly because it was recognised that a response to the accepted need for the provision of safeguards must await the outcome of further research. However, the Implementation Agreement did make some further progress.

The importance of the issue was acknowledged first in a preambular paragraph in which States Parties declared themselves to be 'Mindful of the importance of the [UN] Convention for the protection and preservation of the marine environment and of the growing concern for the global environment.'[59] That concern was further reflected in a series of substantive provisions relating to the protection of the marine environment from the impact of seabed mining:-

Rôle of Authority. The Agreement lists a number of tasks on which the Authority was to concentrate during the period between the entry into force of the UN Convention and the approval of the first plan of work for exploitation. Three of the eleven tasks relate to the environment. First, the Authority was to concentrate on the adoption of rules, regulations and procedures incorporating applicable standards for the protection and preservation of the marine environment.[60] Secondly, in promoting and encouraging the conduct of marine scientific research and disseminating its results, the Authority was to place 'particular emphasis' on research relevant to the environmental impact of activities in the Area'.[61] Thirdly, the Authority was to concentrate on the timely elaboration of rules, regulations and procedures for exploitation, '*including those relating to the protection and preservation of the marine environment.*'[62]

Environmental component of applications for approval of a plan of work. Such applications must be:

> ...accompanied by an assessment of the potential environmental impacts of the proposed activities and by a description of a programme for oceanographic and baseline environmental studies in accordance with the rules, regulations and procedures adopted by the Authority.[63]

---

[58] *Information Note concerning the Secretary-General's Informal Consultations on outstanding issues relating to the deep seabed mining provisions of the UN Convention on the Law of the Sea,* 26 May 1992, at p. 12, para. 33.
[59] Implementation Agreement, Preamble.
[60] Implementation Agreement, Annex, Section 1, para. 5(g).
[61] *Ibid.,* para. 5(h).
[62] *Ibid.,* para. 5(k), emphasis added.
[63] *Ibid.,* para. 7.

398 *Chapter 10*

Enterprise functions. The Agreement makes provision for certain functions of the Enterprise to be performed during a transitional period by the Secretariat of the Authority. These functions include assessment of the results of marine scientific research, 'with particular emphasis on research related to the environmental impact of activities in the Area'[64]; and assessment of technological developments relevant to activities in the Area, 'in particular technology relating to the protection and preservation of the marine environment.'[65]

Entrenched provisions. In making provision for future amendment of the UN Convention and the Implementation Agreement, the Agreement includes a proviso to the effect that 'the principles, regime and other terms referred to' in Article 155(2) of the UN Convention 'shall be maintained'. The principles so safeguarded include 'protection of the marine environment'.[66]

International technical and scientific co-operation. In a section of the Implementation Agreement dealing with transfer of technology, provision is made for the promotion of international technical and scientific co-operation by, *inter alia*, developing programmes in marine science and technology and the protection and preservation of the marine environment.[67]

IV. THE MINING CODE:
REGULATIONS ON PROSPECTING AND EXPLORATION FOR POLYMETALLIC
NODULES IN THE AREA

1. Introduction: Drafting History

At the Spring 1990 session of the Preparatory Commission, Mr. Satya Nandan introduced the Secretariat's draft of Part VIII of the Mining Code, containing regulations for the 'Protection and Preservation of the Marine Environment from Activities in the Area'.[68] He noted[69] that the draft regulations drew upon a number of sources: the relevant provisions of the UN Convention, the legislation of States concerned with deep-sea mining and the provisions of other multilateral conventions such as the 1988 Convention on the Regulation of Antarctic Mineral Resource Activities (CRAMRA).[70]

Mr. Nandan indicated that the most difficult problem faced by the draftsman had been to strike a fair balance between the need to preserve and protect the marine environment and the objective of developing the resources of the Area. In this context, an attempt had been made to define 'serious harm to the marine environment'. By excluding from its scope certain effects judged to be

---

[64] Implementation Agreement, Annex, Section 2, para. 1(b).
[65] *Ibid.,* para. 1(d).
[66] Implementation Agreement, Annex, Section 4, referring to UN Convention, Art. 155(2).
[67] Implementation Agreement, Annex, Section 5, para. 1(c).
[68] Draft Regulations on Prospecting, Exploration and Exploitation of Polymetallic Nodules in the Area ['Mining Code'], *Addendum*: Part VIII. Protection and Preservation of the Marine Environment from Activities in the Area. *Working Paper by the Secretariat,* LOS/PCN/SCN.3/WP.6/Add.5, 8 February 1990 (reproduced in *Draft Final Report of Special Commission 3*, LOS/PCN/SCN.3/1992/CRP.17, 22 July 1992, p. 170; and in XI *Platzöder (PrepCom),* p. 352).
[69] LOS/PCN/L.79, 28 March 1990 (XI *Platzöder (PrepCom),* p. 38(9))
[70] XXVII ILM (1988), p. 859.

Protection of environment 399

acceptable by the Authority according to the relevant rules and regulations, the regulations sought to ensure that deep-sea mining would not be unreasonably restricted.[71]

Mr. Nandan went on to explain that, 'In order to assess the effect of each contractor's activities in the Area, the draft regulations made provision for the establishment of environmental reference zones' and the submission of environmental impact statements to the Legal and Technical Commission prior to approval of plans of work, at both the exploration stage and the exploitation stage. It was envisaged in the draft that the Authority would monitor the contractor's compliance with his contract and related rules and regulations on the basis of annual reports submitted by the contractor and inspection by Authority inspectors on board ships and installations.[72]

It was explained that the liability article (Article 122) in the draft regulations was based on CRAMRA, described as 'the first important multilateral instrument to recognise the value of the marine environment, particularly that part of it constituting the global commons'.[73]

During the Spring 1990 session of Special Commission 3 (SCN.3), there was a preliminary first reading of the draft regulations. In the course of the debate, the need was stressed by many delegations for further environmental studies of the marine environment of the Area[74] and the Secretary-General was asked to organise a seminar on the environmental impact of deep sea-bed mining and the means of assessing it.[75] Such a seminar was held during the Summer 1990 session of SCN.3. In making brief reference to the seminar proceedings, the Chairman of SCN.3 noted that 'its predominant theme was that very little was known at present regarding the consequences of deep sea-bed mining and that it was clear that more substantial research would have to be conducted before any concrete conclusions could be reached.'[76] Nonetheless, the information and data provided by the experts would be very useful when dealing with the draft regulations of the Mining Code.[77] Further information on the current state of

---

[71] *Loc. cit.* in note 69, at p. 38 (10).

[72] *Ibid.*, at p. 39(12).

[73] *Ibid.*, at p. 39(13). It is now generally accepted that CRAMRA is unlikely ever to enter into force, having in effect been replaced by the Protocol on Environmental Protection to the Antarctic Treaty, 1991 (text in XXX ILM (1991), p.1461).

[74] *Loc. cit.* in note 69, at p. 39(14).

[75] *Ibid.*, at p.40(17).

[76] Statement to the Plenary by the Chairman of Special Commission 3 on the Progress of Work in that Commission, LOS/PCN/L.84, 29 August 1990 (XI *Platzöder (Prepcom)*, p. 89, at p. 90(6)).

[77] *Ibid.* For further information on the proceedings of the seminar, see the following Press Releases: SEA/1158-1165, 14-16 August 1990. Notable points emerging from the Press Releases include: a report by B. Haynes (USA) on study on the environmental impact of wastes resulting from the processing of manganese nodules (SEA/1162 p. 3); Japanese report on a large-scale Ocean Mining Test planned by Japan for 1994 (*ibid.*); a report by E Ozturgut (USA) on DOMES I and DOMES II (SEA/1164, p.2); an account by G. Wilson (Scripps Institution of Oceanography) of their nodule mining impact research (*ibid.*); discussion of the role of stable environmental reference areas by E. Ozturgut (USA) (SEA/1165, p. 2); advocacy of application of the 'precautionary principle' in the impact assessment of deep-sea mining (H. Thiel, University of Hamburg (*ibid.*, p.3)).

400   Chapter 10

research and the requirements for future environmental impact studies was given by two German experts who addressed the Special Commission in August 1992.[78]

No further formal discussion of the draft regulations took place in SCN.3 but the working paper was revised by the Chairman, 'following several sessions of informal consultations', and issued on 27 August 1991 under a new title: 'Protection and Preservation of the Marine Environment from Unacceptable Changes Resulting from Activities in the Area'.[79] The new draft was to provide 'a basis for further discussion' [80] and significant parts of it were 'the preliminary proposals of the Chairman' of SCN.3.[81] The issue of this working paper marked the end of the Preparatory Commission's substantive concern with this question and the burden then passed to the Authority.

Further work on the draft Seabed Mining Code commenced at the March 1997 meetings of the Legal and Technical Commission which had before it a new draft of 41 regulations prepared by the Secretariat of the Authority, taking account of the work done by the Preparatory Commission,[82] as well as the provisions of the 1994 Implementation Agreement. A revised version of the draft text [83] was circulated to members of the Authority following the March 1997 meetings [84] and was considered further by the Legal and Technical Commission at the August 1997 session of the Authority. Although the Commission was unable to prepare a final text during this session, it did produce a third revision of the draft Mining Code [85] and, following a brief discussion of the Commission's work, the Council agreed to invite its members to submit written comments and suggestions on the text to the Commission no later than 31 December 1997. Following further work during the first week of its March 1998 session, the Commission presented a revised draft to the Council on 23 March 1998.[86] Comments made during the Council's debate on the draft Mining Code indicated that there were still matters of concern to some Council members [87] and the text was considered further at the resumed fourth session of the Council in August

---

[78] For a summary, see Statement to the Plenary by the Chairman of Special Commission 3 on the Progress of Work in that Commission, LOS/PCN/L.106, 19 August 1992, at pp. 2-5.

[79] Draft Regulations on Prospecting, Exploration and Exploitation of Polymetallic Nodules in the Area, Part VIII. Protection and Preservation of the Marine Environment from Unacceptable Changes Resulting from Activities in the Area. Addendum. Preliminary redraft by the Chairman of Special Commission 3 intended to facilitate further consultations, which should provide the basis for a further revision of the working paper,LOS/PCN/SCN.3/WP.6/Add.5/Rev.1, 27 August 1991 (reproduced in *Draft Final Report of Special Commission 3*, LOS/PCN/SCN.3/1992/CRP.17, 22 July 1992, at pp. 187-201).

[80] Preparatory Commission, *Consolidated Provisional Final Report*, LOS/PCN/130, 17 November 1993, at p. 95.

[81] See Chairman's note to this effect in *loc. cit.* in note 79, at p. 188.

[82] ISBA/3/LTC/WP.1. See also Press Release SB/3/13, 27 March 1997.

[83] ISBA/3/LTC/WP.1/Rev. 1, 27 March 1997.

[84] Press Release SB/3/14, 14 August 1997, p. 2.

[85] ISBA/3/LTC/WP.1/Rev. 3, 25 August 1997.

[86] Draft Regulations on Prospecting and Exploration for Polymetallic Nodules in the Area Proposed by the Legal and Technical Commission, ISBA/4/C/4, 2 April 1998. See further Statement of the President on the Work of the Council During the First Part of the Fourth Session, ISBA/4/C/5, 31 March 1998, paras. 5 and 9-10, and Press Release SB/4/6, 23 March 1998.

[87] See Press Releases SB/4/6-9, 11 and 13, 23-26 March 1998.

Protection of environment 401

1998. [88] Following this examination of the text, an informal review of the Preamble and Regulations 2 to 21 was prepared by the Secretariat together with the President of the Council. [89] Discussions resumed at the fifth session of the Authority in August 1999 and led to the issue of a further revised text. [90] Yet a further version emerged from the first part of the sixth session of the Authority in March 2000. [91] Finally, at the resumed sixth session in July 2000, the final text of the Mining Code was adopted by the Council and approved by the Assembly. [92]

2. Scope and Structure of the Regulations
Although the Mining Code was drafted by the Authority, 'taking account of' the draft prepared by the Preparatory Commission, it is significantly different from it in both scope and structure.

As regards scope, the Authority version of the Mining Code covers the prospecting and exploration phases of seabed mining,[93] whereas the Preparatory Commission's draft dealt with 'activities in the Area',[94] defined as 'all activities of exploration for, and exploitation of the resources of the Area'. [95] Moreover, the new text refers to only polymetallic nodules,[96] whereas the earlier draft covered 'resources', [97] defined as 'all solid, liquid or gaseous mineral resources *in situ* in the Area at or beneath the sea-bed, including polymetallic nodules'.[98] It will of course be necessary for the Authority to prepare further regulations dealing with exploitation and with resources other than polymetallic nodules in due course.[99]

As regards the structure of the Mining Code, as it relates to environmental questions, the new text is again different from the earlier Preparatory Commission draft. In the earlier version, the bulk of the environmental provisions were embodied in a single Part VIII of the Mining Code on 'Protection and Preservation of the Marine Environment from Unacceptable Changes

---

[88] On the basis of ISBA/4/C/4/Rev. 1 of 29 April 1998.

[89] ISBA/4/C/CRP.1, 1 October 1998.

[90] Originally issued as ISBA/5/C/4, 16 August 1999 and Corr. 1, 18 August 1999; reissued with minor technical amendments as Draft Regulations on Prospecting and Exploration for Polymetallic Nodules in the Area, Revision of ISBA/4/C/4/Rev. 1 of 29 April 1998, prepared by the Secretariat together with the President of the Council, ISBA/5/C/4/Rev. 1, 14 October 1999.

[91] ISBA/6/C/2, 3 April 2000.

[92] Regulations on Prospecting and Exploration for Polymetallic Nodules in the Area, ISBA/6/A/18, adopted by the Council and approved by the Assembly on 13 July 2000 (hereafter cited as 'Mining Code').

[93] The title of the Mining Code (*loc. cit.* in note 92) refers to 'Prospecting' and 'Exploration'. Part II deals with prospecting and Parts III and IV deal respectively with applications for approval of plans of work for exploration in the form of contracts, and contracts for exploration.

[94] Art. 1(1) of the Draft of 27 August 1991 (*loc. cit.* in note 79 above) refers to 'activities in the Area'.

[95] UN Convention, Art. 1(1)(3).

[96] The title of the Mining Code (*loc. cit.* in note 92) refers to 'polymetallic nodules'.

[97] Art. 1(1) of the draft of 27 August 1991 (*loc. cit.* in note 79 above) referred to 'activities in the Area' which Art. 1(3) of the Convention defines as relating to the 'resources of the Area'.

[98] UN Convention, Art. 133(a).

[99] See further UN Convention Art. 162(2)(o)(ii) and Implementation Agreement, Annex, Section 1, paras. 15 and 16. On mineral resources other than polymetallic nodules, see further Chap. 4, section XVIII and Chap. 5, section II.1.3.

402   *Chapter 10*

Resulting from Activities in the Area'. The new text adopts a quite different approach and environmentally relevant regulations are to be found in:

- Part I, on 'use of terms and scope';
- Part II, on prospecting, and the related Annex 1 specifying the form of the notification of prospecting;
- Part III, on applications for approval of plans of work, and the related Annex 2 prescribing the form of the application;
- Part IV, on the contract for exploration, and the related Annexes 3 and 4 embodying a model contract and standard clauses;
- Part V, entitled 'Protection and Preservation of the Marine Environment', now a relatively brief 'Part'; and
- Part VII, Regulation 38, on the Legal and Technical Commission's powers to issue recommendations for the guidance of contractors.

3. Key Environmental Terms Defined

Regulation 1 includes definitions of two key environmental terms, 'marine environment' and 'serious harm to the marine environment'. An earlier draft of Regulation 1 referred to the concept of 'precautionary measures'[100] but it hardly amounted to a definition and the notion of precautionary measures, or, rather, 'a precautionary approach', is now dealt with in Regulation 31. [101]

3.1 'Marine Environment' Defined

Regulation 1(3)(c) embodies the following definition of the marine environment:

> 'marine environment' includes the physical, chemical, geological and biological components, conditions and factors which interact and determine the productivity, state, condition and quality of the marine ecosystem, the waters of the seas and oceans and the airspace above those waters, as well as the seabed and ocean floor and subsoil thereof.

While it is true that this definition is all-embracing, it is also, inevitably perhaps, drawn in very vague and general language and some delegations questioned the wisdom of attempting to provide a legal definition of this concept. [102] The view appears to have prevailed, however, that, in the absence of such a definition, it would be difficult to understand the meaning of 'serious harm to the marine environment'. [103]

3.2 'Serious Harm to the Marine Environment' Defined

The concept of 'serious harm to the marine environment' is one of the central environmental concepts of the Regulations. The term is employed in the UN

---

[100] ISBA/5/C/4/Rev. 1, 14 October 1999, Reg. 1(3)(e).
[101] Mining Code , Reg. 31(2). See further below section 6.1.
[102] ISBA, Fifth Session, Press Release SB/5/11, 13 August 1999.
[103] *Ibid.*

Protection of environment 403

Convention without definition[104] and has been variously defined in successive versions of the draft Mining Code.

As was noted above,[105] in drafting Part VIII of the 1990 version of the Preparatory Commission's draft Mining Code, [106] an attempt was made to define 'serious harm to the marine environment'. By excluding from its scope certain effects judged to be acceptable by the Authority according to the relevant rules and regulations, the draft Code sought to ensure that deep-sea mining would not be unnecessarily restricted. Under Article 1, the regulations were to 'apply to the protection and preservation of the marine environment from activities in the Area'. A general obligation was imposed upon States by Article 104(1) to protect and preserve the marine environment from activities in the Area and, under Article 105(1), it was a principal condition of such activities that they should take place only 'if they do not cause serious harm to the marine environment'.

Article 2(2) defined 'serious harm to the marine environment' as follows:-

> 'serious harm to the marine environment' means any effect from activities in the Area on the living or non-living components of the marine environment and associated ecosystems beyond that which is negligible or which has been assessed and judged to be acceptable by the Authority pursuant to these regulations and the relevant rules and regulations adopted by the Authority and which represent:
> (a) significant adverse changes in the living and non-living components of the marine and atmospheric environment;
> (b) significant adverse changes in the ecosystem diversity, productivity and stability of the biological communities within the environment; or
> (c) loss of scientific or economic values which is unreasonable in relation to the benefit derived from the activity in question.[107]

It was also noted earlier that a revised version of Part VIII was issued by the Chairman of SCN.3 in 1991. [108] The title of the revised version reflected a real change of emphasis from the concept of 'serious harm' to the notion of 'unacceptable change'. Whereas the original 1990 version of Part VIII contained regulations for the 'Protection and Preservation of the Marine Environment from Activities in the Area',[109] the revised 1991 version was concerned with 'Protection and Preservation of the Marine Environment from Unacceptable Changes Resulting from Activities in the Area.'[110]

The substitution of this same concept of 'unacceptable change' for that of 'serious harm' was the main revision introduced by the Chairman of SCN.3 in the 1991 version of Articles 104-106. Under the revised version of Article 104, States were to have a general obligation to protect and preserve the marine

---

[104] UN Convention, Arts. 162(2)(w) and (x) and 165(2)(k) and (l).
[105] See text above at note 71.
[106] *Loc. cit.* in note 68 above.
[107] *Ibid.*
[108] See text above, following note 78.
[109] *Loc. cit.* in note 68 above.
[110] *Loc. cit.* in note 79 above.

404   *Chapter 10*

environment from unacceptable changes resulting from activities in the Area. 'Unacceptable changes' were defined in Article 2(2) as meaning 'changes to the marine environment which will result or are resulting from activities in the Area and which are judged unacceptable according to environmental standards recommended by the Legal and Technical Commission and adopted by the Council'. Such regulations would have been only a half-way house between the UN Convention and the final detailed standards still to be adopted in the future by Authority organs. Article 125(1) accordingly provided for the adoption by the Council, upon the recommendation of the Legal and Technical Commission, of rules and regulations which would elaborate 'the principles' in Article 2(2).

That these changes were simply preliminary proposals of the Chairman was emphasised in a footnote to the draft:

> It should be noted that the textual changes appearing in the present document, including the introduction of the term 'unacceptable changes' in the title and in article 1 and the replacement of the terms 'harmful effects' and 'serious harm' in subsequent articles as well as the replacement in article 2 of the definition of 'serious harm' by a definition of 'unacceptable changes', are the preliminary proposals of the Chairman. These changes and all others appearing in the document will be considered in depth during the consultations to be conducted by the Chairman.[111]

When the organs of the Authority resumed consideration of the draft mining Code in 1997, it soon became clear that the notion of 'serious harm to the marine environment' had returned to centre stage and, in the August 1997 draft, it was defined as follows:

> … any effect from activities in the Area on the living or non-living components of the marine environment and associated ecosystems which represent significant adverse changes in the living and non-living components of the marine and atmospheric environment, ecosystem diversity, or productivity and stability of the biological communities within the marine environment, and which has been assessed and judged to be unacceptable by the Authority on the basis of internationally recognized standards and the rules, regulations, procedures and guidelines adopted by the Authority.[112]

Thus, under this definition, to amount to serious harm to the marine environment, an effect from activities in the Area would have to:

- represent 'significant adverse changes', a term which was undefined; *and*
- have been assessed and judged to be unacceptable by the Authority on the basis of two sets of criteria: (1) internationally recognised standards, which

---

[111] *Loc. cit.* in note 79 above, at p. 188.

[112] *Loc. cit.*, in note 85 above, Reg. 1(1)(s).

Protection of environment 405

are undefined, and (2) the rules, regulations, procedures and guidelines adopted by the Authority. Once again, this indicated that yet a further tier of norms, including 'standards' and 'guidelines', would be required before the Authority might 'assess and judge' particular effects of seabed activities as being unacceptable.

The term 'guidelines' appeared for the first time in this version of the Mining Code and was not defined. However, the Chairman of the Legal and Technical Commission explained that, 'it had been found useful to introduce the concept of "guidelines" – to be issued with the Commission's approval – which would complete the provisions of the code and guide the conduct of seabed contractors.' [113] In Part V of the Code, on 'Protection and Preservation of the Marine Environment', provision was made for the Authority to 'establish and keep under review *environmental guidelines* in order to ensure the protection and preservation of the marine environment.' [114] Apparently, the Commission was proposing to draft a list of environmentally appropriate technologies for exploration. [115]

Although the term 'guidelines' was not defined, Annex 4 of the Code defined 'Regulations' to include 'guidelines':

'Regulations' means the rules, regulations, procedures, standards *and guidelines* adopted by the Authority from time to time and which are in effect at the date of entry into force of this contract or which are anticipated thereunder or which may be incorporated into this contract by written agreement or which may apply to this contract as a consequence of a revision thereof. [116]

The Authority was also to develop procedures for the establishment of environmental baselines against which to assess the likely effects on the marine environment of activities in the Area'. [117] Like 'guidelines', 'procedures' were also included in the definition of 'Regulations' in Annex 4. [118] Contractors were to be required to report on the implementation and results of a monitoring programme and to submit data and information in accordance with the 'guidelines and procedures established by the Authority'. [119]

Yet another definition of 'serious harm to the marine environment' appeared in the April 1998 draft of the Mining Code. It was now defined as:

…any effect from activities in the Area on the living or non-living components of the marine environment and associated ecosystems which represents a significant adverse change in the marine environment determined according to the rules, regulations and procedures adopted by the

---

[113] Press Release Council (AM) SR/4/6, 23 March 1998, p. 1.
[114] Reg. 28(1), emphasis added.
[115] *Loc. cit.* in note 113 above.
[116] Annex 4, section 1.1(k), emphasis added.
[117] Reg. 28(1).
[118] See definition quoted above in text at note 116.
[119] Reg. 28(3).

406   *Chapter 10*

Authority on the basis of internationally recognized standards and practices.[120]

Although this definition was less complex than its predecessor, it was clear that there was still an intention to elaborate more detailed norms in the form of further procedures and guidelines once more was known about the impact of seabed mining activities on the environment. Thus, the Chairman of the Council reported, at the close of the March 1998 session of the Authority, that:

> The Council was also informed that the [Legal and Technical] Commission considered it important for the Authority to begin to elaborate procedures and guidelines for the protection of the marine environment as soon as possible. The Commission had recommended to the Secretariat, as a priority activity within its substantive work programme, the organization of two workshops: the first covering the available knowledge on the environment, the second on the technologies envisaged for the exploration and exploitation and for the protection of the environment. Such workshops would help to elaborate the guidelines that are necessary for the conduct of activities in the Area and should also address the question of mineral resources other than polymetallic nodules.[121]

It will be noted that, unlike the earlier draft, this revised definition of 'serious harm to the marine environment' did not refer to 'guidelines'. As the above quotation indicates, however, they still featured in the new scheme of things and, indeed, 'guidelines' were defined for the first time in this draft as:

> ...technical or administrative guidelines for the implementation of the rules, regulations and procedures of the Authority which may be issued from time to time with the approval of the Legal and Technical Commission.[122]

This draft also defined 'Regulations' to include 'guidelines':

> 'Regulations' means the rules, regulations and procedures, standards and guidelines adopted by the Authority from time to time and which are in effect at the date of entry into force of this contract or which may be incorporated into this contract by written agreement or which may apply to this contract as a consequence of a revision thereof. [123]

---

[120] *Loc. cit.* in note 86, Reg. 1(1)(x).

[121] Statement of the President on the Work of the Council During the First Part of the Fourth Session, ISBA/4/C/5, 31 March 1998, para. 7. The first workshop, devoted to the development of environmental guidelines for polymetallic nodule exploration, was held in China in June 1998 (see note 4 above) and a second, on mineral resources other than polymetallic nodules, met in Jamaica in June 2000.

[122] Reg. 1(1)(o).

[123] Annex 4, section 1.1(f).

Some indication of the function of such guidelines was given in Part V of the draft Code (on 'Protection and preservation of the marine environment') which required that:

> The Authority shall establish and keep under periodic review environmental regulations and procedures to ensure the protection and preservation of the marine environment. The Commission may from time to time issue guidelines listing activities which may be considered to have no potential for causing harmful effects on the marine environment. The Authority shall also develop procedures and guidelines for the establishment of environmental baselines against which to assess the likely effects on the marine environment of activities in the Area. [124]

The precise status of such guidelines was not clear and, in the course of the March 1998 session of the Authority, one delegation referred to them as 'mere guidelines' [125], and another considered that they should be mandatory. [126] It is true that they were to be issued by the Legal and Technical Commission which may normally only recommend rules, regulations and procedures to the Council. [127] Yet, the above-quoted Regulation 1(1)(o), in defining 'guidelines', spoke of them being 'for the implementation of the rules, regulations and procedures of the Authority...' and, under one of the standard clauses embodied in Annex 4 of the draft Code, the Contractor was to be required to give an undertaking 'to observe, as far as practicable, any guidelines which may be issued from time to time by the Authority'.[128]

The final formulation of the definition of 'serious harm to the marine environment' first appeared in the revised draft of the Mining Code issued following the fifth session of the Authority held in August 1999 [129] and survived unchanged in the final version of the Mining Code adopted in July 2000:

> 'serious harm to the marine environment' means any effect from activities in the Area on the marine environment which represents a significant adverse change in the marine environment determined according to the rules, regulations and procedures adopted by the Authority on the basis of internationally recognised standards and practices. [130]

At first sight, the new definition is essentially the same as the earlier, April 1998 version, though it simplifies the reference to the marine environment. On closer inspection, however, it becomes evident that a new approach has been adopted. As has been seen, the earlier draft defined 'guidelines' in Regulation 1(1)(o); defined 'Regulations' in Annex 4, section 1.1(f) to include 'procedures, standards

---

[124] Reg. 28(2).
[125] Peru (Authority Press Release SB/4/7, 24 March 1998).
[126] Tunisia (*ibid.*).
[127] See further above, section III.3.3.3.
[128] Annex 4, section 12(2)(e).
[129] ISBA/5/C/4/Rev/1, 14 October 1999, Reg. 1(3)(e).
[130] Mining Code, Reg. 1(3)(f).

408   *Chapter 10*

and guidelines'; and, in the standard contractual clause embodied in Annex 4, section 12(2)(e), required the contractor to undertake to observe guidelines issued by the Authority. [131] The new draft is quite different. There is no definition of 'guidelines' in Regulation 1; the definition of 'Regulations' in Annex 4, section 1.1(c) makes no mention of 'guidelines' – or indeed of 'procedures' or 'standards'; nor do the standard undertakings to be given by the contractor under Annex 4, section 13.2 make any reference to 'guidelines'.

In fact, these changes reflect the new Regulation 38, introduced in August 1999 as part of 'Part VII – General Procedures' of the draft Mining Code, which is unchanged in the final version of the Mining Code:

Regulation 38
Recommendations for the guidance of contractors

1. The Legal and Technical Commission may from time to time issue recommendations of a technical or administrative nature for the guidance of contractors to assist them in the implementation of the rules, regulations and procedures of the Authority.
2. The full text of such recommendations shall be reported to the Council. Should the Council find that a recommendation is inconsistent with the intent and purpose of these Regulations, it may request that the recommendation be modified or withdrawn. [132]

As was seen above, the Commission is empowered to make recommendations to the Council on a number of environmental issues, including the establishment of a monitoring programme. [133] Although Regulation 38 envisages the issue of recommendations 'for the guidance of contractors', rather than 'to the Council', as provided for in Article 165(2) of the Convention, the Council still has the ultimate control over such recommendations, since they must be reported to it, and it may 'request' their modification or withdrawal if found to be inconsistent with the intent and purpose of the Regulations. [134]

The Standard Clauses for Exploration Contracts in Annex 4 to the Mining Code now reflect this new approach and the contractor is required to undertake:

to observe, as far as reasonably practicable, any recommendations which may be issued from time to time by the Legal and Technical Commission. [135]

The fact that recommendations are to be issued 'for the guidance of contractors to assist them', [136] and the qualified nature of the obligation to observe them, are of

---

[131] The references are to ISBA/4/C/4, 2 April 1998, considered above.
[132] ISBA/5/C/4 and Corr. 1, 16-18 August 1999; unchanged in subsequent drafts and in the final version of the Mining Code.
[133] Under UN Convention, Art. 165(2). See further above, section III.3.3.3.
[134] Reg. 38(2).
[135] Annex 4, section 13.2(e).
[136] Reg. 38(1).

course consistent with the normal meaning of recommendation, that is, that it lacks the binding legal effect of a decision or a regulation.

One of the principal contexts in which the recommendations of the Commission are likely to be important is that of the establishment and implementation of environmental monitoring programmes. Thus, Regulation 31(4) provides that:

> Each contract shall require the contractor to gather environmental baseline data and to establish environmental baselines, taking into account any recommendations issued by the Legal and Technical Commission pursuant to regulation 38, against which to assess the likely effects of its programme of activities under the plan of work for exploration on the marine environment and a programme to monitor and report on such effects. The recommendations issued by the Commission may, *inter alia*, list those exploration activities which may be considered to have no potential for causing harmful effects on the marine environment. The contractor shall cooperate with the Authority and the sponsoring State or States in the establishment and implementation of such monitoring programme. [137]

The contractor has also to 'take into account' any recommendations issued by the Commission under Regulation 38 when submitting the annual report on the implementation and results of the monitoring programme which is called for by Regulation 31(5). [138]

Finally, it has to be recalled that the definition of 'serious harm to the marine environment, in Regulation 1(3)(f) provides that 'a significant adverse change in the marine environment' is to be determined 'according to the rules, regulations and procedures adopted by the Authority *on the basis of internationally recognised standards and practices*'. [139]

It may be noted in this context that Regulation 1(5) provides that, 'These Regulations may be supplemented by further rules, regulations and procedures, in particular on the protection and preservation of the marine environment'. The inclusion of such a clause would have been prudent in any event to provide a ready means of updating the Regulations from time to time; it is all the more necessary at this stage in the development of the new regime when so little is known about the impact of activities in the Area on the marine environment. However, a start has been made in filling this knowledge gap. As has been seen, the Secretariat of the Authority organised a Workshop in China in June 1998, [140] the major output of which was a set of draft guidelines for the assessment of environmental impacts of exploration in the Area. [141]

---

[137]Mining Code, Reg. 31(4).

[138] On environmental monitoring, see also Annex 4, section 5, dealt with below in section 6.4.1.

[139]Mining Code , Reg. 1(3)(f), emphasis added.

[140] See above, note 4.

[141] *Recommendations from the Workshop to Develop Guidelines for the Assessment of the Possible Environmental Impacts Arising from Exploration for Polymetallic Nodules in the Area. Report of the Secretary-General*, ISBA/5/LTC/1, 21 June 1999. The *Sanya Workshop Proceedings* were published in full in 1999 – see above note 4.

410   *Chapter 10*

The Legal and Technical Commission undertook a first reading of the draft guidelines at the Authority's fifth session in August 1999. [142] The Commission took the view that the emphasis in the recommendations on fundamental research (some of which was being requested of potential contractors) did not reflect the objective of the Authority's environmental monitoring programme and it reformulated the proposed guidelines accordingly. [143]

The Commission also discussed the purpose of the guidelines and:

> It was reiterated that the guidelines were not to be given the status of regulations but were to be seen as *recommendations* that contractors could follow depending upon their own circumstances and in consultation with the Authority. [144]

Thus, once again the emphasis has been put on the non-binding nature of the Commission's *recommended* guidelines.

A revised version of the guidelines was produced following further work undertaken by the Commission at the sixth session of the Authority in July 2000 and work will continue at the seventh session in July 2001. [145] The Commission intends to provide an explanatory commentary on the technical recommendations which, 'while not part of the main document, will be a useful tool for the contractor'. [146]

One further outcome of the Commission's proceedings deserves mention. Responding to the recommendations of the Sanya Workshop concerning international co-operation in research on common themes in relation to the protection of the environment from activities in the Area, the Commission recommended at the fifth session that:

> ... for the sixth session, the Secretariat should prepare a study that would, *inter alia*, identify international data repositories that collected environmental data required to monitor the impact of activities in the Area, identify gaps in their data coverage, formulate a plan for the retrieval of appropriate data from such sources and make recommendations for the development of a database for the analysis and synthesis of such data. The Commission also recommended that all registered pioneer investors should make their environmental data on claim sites available to the Authority for that purpose.[147]

---

[142] *Report of the Legal and Technical Commission on the Work of the Commission during the fifth session*, ISBA/5/C/6, 17 August 1999.

[143] *Ibid.*, para. 2. For informal revision of ISBA/5/LTC/1, see ISBA/5/LTC/CRP.1, 13 August 1999.

[144] ISBA/5/C/6, para 3, emphasis added.

[145] See *Report of the Chairman of the Legal and Technical Commission on the Work of the Commission during the Resumed Sixth Session*, ISBA/6/C/11, 11 July 2000, paras. 3-6.

[146] *Ibid.*, para. 6.

[147] *Ibid.*, para. 4.

In his annual Report to the Assembly in July 2000, the Secretary-General outlined the work which the Authority intended to carry out over the next two years. It included the development of:

>...environmental databases containing, *inter alia*, information on the basic biology of the deep sea benthos in the Clarion-Clipperton fracture zone, such as the distribution of fauna, faunal densities and spatial distribution of oceanographic parameters. Such databases will assist in the evaluation of data and information received from monitoring programmes established by contractors for the purpose of observing and measuring the effects of exploration activities on the marine environment. [148]

4. Prospecting and the Marine Environment

'Prospecting' is defined in the draft Regulations as:

>...the search for deposits of polymetallic nodules in the Area, including estimation of the composition, sizes and distributions of polymetallic nodule deposits and their economic values, without any exclusive rights. [149]

Part II of the Code, on 'Prospecting', contains a number of provisions designed to protect the environment.

Prospecting must not be undertaken in an area which the Council has disapproved for exploitation because of the risk of 'serious harm to the marine environment'.[150] The proposed prospector has to be informed by the Secretary-General of the Authority, within 45 days of receipt of its notification of prospecting, if the notification includes any part of such an area, and it may then, within 90 days, submit an amended notification. [151]

Nor may prospecting be undertaken if 'substantial evidence' indicates the risk of serious harm to the marine environment. [152] In this case, however, the role of the Authority is less clear. There is no reference to such circumstances in Regulation 4 ('Consideration of notifications' by the Secretary-General). It is true that, under Regulation 2(1), prospecting may commence only after the prospector has been informed by the Secretary-General that its notification has been recorded pursuant to Regulation 4(2) and it must be presumed that the Secretary-General, in reviewing the notification under that provision, could decline to record the notification on the ground that it did not conform with the prohibition in Regulation 2(2). However, this still leaves open the question of which organ of the Authority is empowered to determine the existence of the

---

[148] ISBA/6/A/9, 6 June 2000, section XI.E.3. See also *Report of the Secretary-General* on proposed budget for the Authority for the period 2001-2002 (ISBA/6/A/7 and ISBA/6/C/4, 31 May 2000, at para. 15) for further information on the development of environmental databases for the Clarion-Clipperton fracture zone and the Central Indian Ocean basin.

[149] Reg. 1(3)(e).

[150] Reg. 2(3).

[151] Reg. 4(3).

[152] Reg. 2(2).

412   *Chapter 10*

required 'substantial evidence', unless it is considered that the Secretary-General enjoys implied powers to make such a determination.[153]

It is also possible, of course, that serious harm may be caused to the marine environment in the course of prospecting. Regulation 7 covers this contingency and provides that:

Regulation 7
Notification of incidents causing serious harm to the marine environment

A prospector shall immediately notify the Secretary-General in writing, using the most effective means, of any incident arising from prospecting which causes serious harm to the marine environment. Upon receipt of such notification the Secretary-General shall act in a manner consistent with regulation 32.

On receipt of such a notification from the prospector, the Secretary-General must 'act in a manner consistent with regulation 32'. Regulation 32, on 'Emergency orders',[154] empowers the Secretary-General, Commission and Council to take measures to prevent, contain and minimise serious harm to the marine environment, including the issue of emergency orders by the Council. Although the Regulation is addressed to incidents 'resulting from or caused by a contractor's activities in the Area', the facts that a prospector is not a 'contractor' and prospecting is not strictly speaking 'activities in the Area' would probably not affect the application of Regulation 32 in such circumstances, given the clear intention of Regulation 7 and the fact that it enjoins the Secretary-General not to act under Regulation 32 but only in a manner consistent with that Regulation.

Every notification of prospecting has to be in the form prescribed in Annex 1 to the Mining Code.[155] Accordingly, it must have attached to it a written undertaking that the prospector will comply with the Convention and the relevant rules, regulations and procedures of the Authority concerning protection and preservation of the marine environment, and that the prospector will accept verification by the Authority of such compliance.[156] Information on compliance has to be included in the report which a prospector has to submit within 90 days of the end of each calendar year.[157]

---

[153] See also above, section III.3.2 and III.3.3.3, where the functions and powers of the Council and the Legal and Technical Commission are listed. The Commission's powers of recommendation under Art. 165(2)(e) of the UN Convention may be relevant.

[154] On emergency orders, see further above, sections III.3.3.3 and III.3.3.2, and below, section IV.6.4.2.

[155] Reg. 3(2).

[156] Annex 1, para. 17(a)(ii) and (b). Reg. 3(4)(d)(i)(b) and (ii), based on UN Convention Annex III, Art. 2(1)(b), is to the same effect.

[157] Reg. 5(1)(b).

Protection of environment 413

5. Applications for Approval of Plans of Work
Part III of the Mining Code regulates 'Applications for Approval of Plans of Work for Exploration in the Form of Contracts'.

As has been seen, every application has to cover an area sufficiently large and of sufficient estimated commercial value to support two mining operations and the Council has to designate one part of the total area as a reserved area.[158] Part III of the mining Code deals in turn with the data and information to be submitted before and after the designation of the reserved area.

5.1 Data and Information Required before Designation of Reserved Area
Applications have to be in the form prescribed in Annex 2. [159] Accordingly, the application must have an attachment giving information relating to the area under application, including:

> ... information concerning environmental parameters (seasonal and during test period) including, *inter alia*, wind speed and direction, wave height, period and direction, current speed and direction, water salinity, temperature and biological communities.[160]

Information has also to be attached relating to the programme of work for exploration, including:

(a) a general description and a schedule of the proposed exploration programme, including the programme of activities for the immediate five-year period, such as studies to be undertaken in respect of the environmental, technical, economic and other appropriate factors which must be taken into account in exploration;

(b) a description of a programme for oceanographic and environmental baseline studies in accordance with the Regulations and any environmental rules, regulations and procedures established by the Authority that would enable an assessment of the potential environmental impact of the proposed exploration activities, taking into account any recommendations issued by the Legal and Technical Commission.

(c) a preliminary assessment of the possible impact of the proposed exploration activities on the marine environment;

(d) a description of the proposed measures for the prevention, reduction and control of pollution and other hazards, as well as possible impacts, to the marine environment. [161]

It is of course important that the contractor should have the 'financial and technical capability to respond to any incident or activity which causes serious

---

[158] See Chap. 4, section VII.
[159] Reg. 10(1).
[160] Annex 2, para. 19(b).
[161] Annex 2, para. 24(a)-(d).

414   *Chapter 10*

harm to the marine environment' [162] and Regulation 12, which calls for the application to contain information on the applicant's financial and technical capabilities, requires the applicant to include a general description of such capability. [163]

5.2 Data and Information Required after Designation of Reserved Area
Regulation 18 provides, in part, that:

> After the Council has designated the reserved area, the applicant, if it has not already done so, shall submit, with a view to receiving approval of the plan of work for exploration in the form of a contract, the following information:
> (a) a general description and a schedule of the proposed exploration programme, including the programme of activities for the immediate five-year period, such as studies to be undertaken in respect of the environmental, technical, economic and other appropriate factors that must be taken into account in exploration;
> (b) a description of the programme for oceanographic and environmental baseline studies in accordance with these Regulations and any environmental rules, regulations and procedures established by the Authority that would enable an assessment of the potential environmental impact of the proposed exploration activities, taking into account any recommendations issued by the Legal and Technical Commission.
> (c) a preliminary assessment of the possible impact of the proposed exploration activities on the marine environment;
> (d) a description of proposed measures for the prevention, reduction and control of pollution and other hazards, as well as possible impacts, to the marine environment;
> (e) data necessary for the Council to make the determination it is required to make in accordance with regulation 12, paragraph 1. [164]

The latter item relates to the contractor's financial and technical capabilities to respond to any incident or activity which causes serious harm to the marine environment and such information would be required at this stage only if not already submitted – as discussed in section 5.1 above.

5.3 The Position of Registered Pioneer Investors
The position of the registered pioneer investor is dealt with in the Mining Code in a series of nine footnotes. [165] A footnote to Regulation 18 provides that:

---

[162] On responsibility and liability for damage to the marine environment, see below section 6.4.8.

[163] Reg. 12(7)(c). This requirement was added to the draft Mining Code following the August 1998 Session of the Authority. See ISBA/4/C/CRP.1, October 1998, Reg. 10(7)(c). See also Press Release SB/4/30, 28 August 1998, pp. 2-3.

[164] Reg. 18(a)-(e).

[165] In the August 1997 draft of the Mining Code, Reg. 1(3) specified that, 'The footnotes to those regulations shall be read and interpreted as part of the regulations'. Although this provision is absent

Protection of environment 415

In the case of a request by a registered pioneer investor for approval of a plan of work for exploration under paragraph 6(a)(ii) of section 1 of the annex to the [Implementation] Agreement, this Regulation shall be implemented in the light of Regulation 10. [166]

A footnote to Regulation 10 specifies the data and information to be supplied by the registered pioneer investor when applying for approval of a plan of work. *Inter alia*, it provides that:

The registered pioneer investor shall, where such information has not already been provided, update the information, using, as far as possible, the provisions of regulation 18 as a guide, and submit its programme of activities for the immediate future, including a general assessment of the potential environmental impacts of the proposed activities. [167]

This unusual way of dealing with the position of the registered pioneer investor would appear simply to reflect the fact that requests by registered pioneer investors for approval of plans of work for exploration had to be submitted within 36 months of the entry into force of the UN Convention, [168] that is, by 16 November 1997. Their situation is thus exceptional. In fact, all seven pioneer investors submitted such requests on 19 August 1997[169] and on 21 August 1997 the Secretary-General of the Authority informed the Legal and Technical Commission, *inter alia*, that:

...[each] registered pioneer investor has updated the information provided in the documents, reports and other data submitted to the Preparatory Commission both before and after registration and has submitted its programme of work for the immediate future, *including a general assessment of the potential environmental impacts of the proposed activities* ... [170]

He confirmed too that each pioneer investor had given a written undertaking that it would:

Accept as enforceable and comply with the applicable obligations created by the provisions of the Convention and the rules, regulations and procedures of the Authority *in force as at the date the application is submitted*, the

---

from the final text of the Mining Code, there is no reason to suppose that this reflects any change in the status of the footnotes.

[166]Mining Code, Reg. 18, footnote 6.

[167] Reg. 10, footnote 2.

[168] Implementation Agreement, Annex, Sec. 1, para. 6(a)(ii). See further above, Chap. 6, section IV.1.1.

[169] *Plans of Work for Exploration of the [seven Registered Pioneer Investors]. Report of the Secretary-General*, ISBA/4/A/1/Rev.1, 2 April 1998, para. 2.

[170] *Ibid.*, para. 5(c), emphasis added.

416 *Chapter 10*

decisions of the organs of the Authority and the terms of its contracts with the Authority.[171]

Since, obviously, the Mining Code was not in force on 19 August 1997, the date of submission of the applications, its terms were not embraced within such undertakings. However, on 28 August 1997, the Council, in requesting the Secretary-General to take the necessary steps to issue the plans of work in the form of contracts, specified that the contracts should incorporate:

> ...the applicable obligations under the provisions of the Convention, the [Implementation] Agreement and resolution II, and in accordance with the regulations on prospecting and exploration for polymetallic nodules in the Area and a standard form of contract to be approved by the Council.[172]

This will ensure that the activities of the pioneer investors will be subject to the same environmental obligations as those of other contractors.[173]

5.4 Consideration of Applications by the Legal and Technical Commission
In considering applications, the Legal and Technical Commission is required to determine, *inter alia*, whether the proposed plan of work will 'provide for effective protection and preservation of the marine environment'. [174] It 'shall not recommend approval of the plan of work for exploration if ':

> ...part or all of the area covered by the proposed plan of work for exploration is included in .... an area disapproved for exploitation by the Council in cases where substantial evidence indicates the risk of serious harm to the marine environment.[175]

6. The Contract for Exploration: Environmental Aspects
6.1 The Precautionary Principle and Best Available Technology
Rather surprisingly, given its recent ubiquitous appearance in international environmental law, the precautionary principle was not incorporated in earlier drafts of the Mining Code. This may simply have reflected the fact that there is no mention of the principle as such in the UN Convention or the Implementation Agreement. However, Article 145 of the UN Convention, embodying the Convention's fundamental principle on the protection of the environment of the Area,[176] is in sufficiently broad terms to justify the Authority in adopting a regulation based on the precautionary principle and, prompted by the South

---

[171] *Ibid.*, para. 5(d)(i).
[172] *Ibid.*, para. 6.
[173] On which see section 6 below.
[174] Reg. 21(4)(b).
[175] Reg. 21(6)(chapeau) and (c).
[176] See further above, section III.1.4.

Protection of environment 417

African delegation, [177] the Legal and Technical Commission included a new Regulation 28(1) in Part V of the March 1998 version of the draft Mining Code:

> Each contractor shall ensure the effective protection of the marine environment from serious harm which may arise from its activities in the Area and shall take precautionary measures to anticipate, prevent or minimise any adverse impacts on the marine environment in the Area as far as reasonably possible using the best available technology. [178]

This formulation does of course fall some way short of the demand for the incorporation of the 'precautionary principle' in the Code, especially as no definition was provided of the term 'precautionary measures'.

At the fifth session of the Authority, in August 1999, responding to the call from some delegations for a definition of the term 'precautionary measures', [179] a revised text added the following definition:

> 'precautionary measures' means that where there are threats of serious or irreversible damage to the marine environment, lack of full scientific certainty shall not be used as a reason for postponing cost-effective measures to prevent environmental degradation. [180]

This so-called definition was linked to a revised version of the above-noted draft Regulation 28(1). The revised formulation in Regulation 32(2) of the new draft was as follows:

> Pursuant to article 145 of the Convention, each contractor shall take precautionary measures to anticipate, prevent or minimise adverse impacts on the marine environment arising from its activities in the Area as far as reasonably possible using the best available technology. [181]

During the first part of the sixth session in March 2000, debate first centred upon a Netherlands proposal which emerged from informal consultations during the fifth session [182] and was said to be based on Principle 15 of the Rio Declaration, adopted at the Earth Summit in 1992. [183] The main paragraph read as follows:

---

[177] Press Release SB/4/8, 24 March 1998.

[178] ISBA/4/C/4, 2 April 1998, Reg. 28(1).

[179] ISBA/5/C/L.8, 25 August 1999. See also Press Release SB/5/11, 13 August 1999, p.2.

[180] ISBA/5/C/4/Rev.1, 14 October 1999, Reg. 1(3)(e).

[181] *Ibid.*, Reg. 32(2). For reports on extensive discussion during the fifth session, see Press Releases SB/5/22, 23 August 1999, pp. 4-5 and SB/5/24, 24 August 1999, pp. 5-6.

[182] ISBA/5/C/L.8, 25 August 1999.

[183] Rio Declaration on Environment and Development adopted at UN Conference on Environment and Development, June 1992 (A/CONF.151/26 (Vol. 1)). Principle 15 reads as follows: 'In order to protect the environment, the precautionary approach shall be widely applied by States according to their capabilities. Where there are threats of serious or irreversible damage, lack of scientific certainty shall not be used as a reason for postponing cost-effective measures to prevent environmental degradation'.

418   *Chapter 10*

> In the conduct of activities in the Area, the precautionary principle shall be applied to protect and preserve the marine environment, by virtue of which cost-effective preventive measures are to be taken when there are reasonable grounds for concern that these activities may cause serious harm to the marine environment, even where there is lack of full scientific certainty. [184]

The debate revealed that there were still widely diverging views on the wisdom or practicality of incorporating the precautionary principle in the Mining Code and, in an effort to reach a compromise solution, the Secretary-General of the Authority suggested that the Council might consider the term 'precautionary approach' [185] instead of 'precautionary principle'. [186] Mr. Nandan recommended 'marrying' the substance of Articles 204, 205 and 206 of the UN Convention (which deal with monitoring and environmental assessment) with the precautionary approach. The revised text, first circulated at the end of the March 2000 session [187] and now incorporated in the Mining Code as Regulation 31(2), provides that:

> In order to ensure effective protection for the marine environment from harmful effects which may arise from activities in the Area, the Authority and sponsoring States shall apply a precautionary approach, as reflected in Principle 15 of the Rio Declaration, to such activities. The Legal and Technical Commission shall make recommendations to the Council on the implementation of this paragraph. [188]

This paragraph is followed by a revised version of the former Regulation 32(2). The new version, Regulation 31(3), provides that:

> Pursuant to article 145 of the Convention and paragraph 2 of this regulation, each contractor shall take necessary measures to prevent, reduce and control pollution and other hazards to the marine environment arising from its activities in the Area as far as reasonably possible using the best technology available to it.

---

[184] *Proposal by the delegation of the Netherlands on the precautionary principle*, ISBA/5/C/L.8, 25 August 1999, Annex, draft Reg. 32(1).

[185] A good example of the adoption of the precautionary approach is provided by Resolution LDC.44(14), adopted in 1991, and recording the agreement that, in implementing the London Dumping Convention, the Contracting Parties should be '... guided by a precautionary approach to environmental protection whereby appropriate measures are taken when there is reason to believe that substances or energy introduced in the marine environment are likely to cause harm even when there is no conclusive evidence to prove a causal relation between inputs and their effects' (Report of 14 LDC Meeting 1991 (LDC 14/16, 30 December 1991), Annex 2, para. 1).

[186] Press Release SB/6/6, 21 March 2000.

[187] ISBA/6/C/2, 3 April 2000, Reg. 31(2).

[188] Mining Code, Reg. 31(2), footnote omitted. For the text of Principle 15 of the Rio Declaration, see note 183 above.

Protection of environment 419

Given the substitution of the 'precautionary approach' for the 'precautionary principle', the definition of the latter became redundant and no longer appears in Regulation 1 of the Mining Code. Nor was it replaced by a definition of 'precautionary approach'. It appears to have been thought that the reference to Principle 15 of the Rio Declaration in Regulation 31(2) would suffice and, indeed, it would have been at odds with the new approach, with its emphasis on the rôle of the Commission to make recommendations on the implementation of the precautionary approach, to have attempted to provide a more detailed formulation at this stage.

Thus, under the new formulation, the contractor will no longer have to take 'precautionary measures to anticipate, prevent or minimise adverse impacts....' ; instead, the contractor will have to 'take necessary measures to prevent, reduce and control pollution and other hazards to the marine environment....'. This is, of course, an exceedingly vague provision. However, the cross-reference in it to paragraph 2 suggests that its scope and meaning will be clarified in due course once the Legal and Technical Commission, acting under Regulation 31(2), makes recommendations to the Council on the implementation of the precautionary approach. It will be noted, however, that such recommendations are to be made to the Council rather than to contractors and it is not clear what connection there is, if any, between this power and the Commission's power to issue recommendations under Regulation 38 for the guidance of contractors and the related Standard Clause in Annex 4, section 13(2)(e), requiring contractors to undertake to observe, as far as reasonably practicable, recommendations issued by the Commission. [189]

6.2 The Contract

After a plan of work is approved by the Council, it has to be prepared in the form of a contract. Part IV of the Mining Code deals with such 'Contracts for Exploration' and includes a number of provisions concerning the environment.

Contracts have to be prepared in the form prescribed in Annex 3 of the Code and every contract must incorporate, as terms and conditions of the contract, the standard clauses set out in Annex 4 which are in effect at the date of entry into force of the contract. [190] A number of clauses refer to environmental matters.

6.3 'Exploration' Defined

'Exploration' is defined to include 'the carrying out of studies of the environmental ....factors that must be taken into account in exploitation'. [191]

6.4 Standard Clauses

From the environmental point of view, the main 'standard clauses' are those in Section 5 of Annex 4 on 'Environmental monitoring' and those in Section 6 on 'Contingency plans and emergencies'. Following a review of these sections,

---

[189] See further above, section 3.2, text following note 130. The Commission is 'mindful of the need to distinguish between the recommendations falling within regulation 31 (for approval by Council) and regulation 38 (for reveiw by the Commission)' (ISBA/6/C/11, 11 July 2000, para. 5).
[190] Reg. 23(1). Under Annex 4, section 3.1, contracts enter into force on signature by both parties.
[191] Reg. 1(3)(b).

420   *Chapter 10*

reference will also be made to other provisions of Annex 4 which are relevant to the protection of the marine environment.

6.4.1 Environmental Monitoring

Provision for the establishment of environmental baselines and procedures for monitoring and reporting on the effects on the environment of seabed mining activities is to be found at every level from the UN Convention to the Mining Code and beyond.

In earlier parts of this Chapter, reference has been made to the provision embodied in Articles 204-206 of the Convention for monitoring and environmental assessment[192], and to the role to be played by the Legal and Technical Commission under Article 165(2) in formulating and submitting to the Council rules, regulations and procedures.[193] It has been seen too that the Implementation Agreement made provision for an environmental component to be included in applications for plans of work, including a description of a programme for baseline studies in accordance with the rules, regulations and procedures adopted by the Authority.[194]

The Mining Code develops these provisions further in Part V (on 'Protection and Preservation of the Marine Environment') and Annex 4.

First, Regulation 31(4) specifies that:

> Each contract shall require the contractor to gather environmental baseline data and to establish environmental baselines, taking into account any recommendations issued by the Legal and Technical Commission pursuant to regulation 38, against which to assess the likely effects of its programme of activities under the plan of work for exploration on the marine environment and a programme to monitor and report on such effects. The recommendations issued by the Commission may, *inter alia*, list those exploration activities which may be considered to have no potential for causing harmful effects on the marine environment. The contractor shall cooperate with the Authority and the sponsoring State or States in the establishment and implementation of such monitoring programme.[195]

Thus, the Contractor will have three objectives:

- To gather environmental data and establish environmental baselines against which to assess the likely effects on the marine environment of its programme of activities under the plan of work. In so doing, the Contractor must take into account any recommendations issued by the Commission under Regulation 38. As was seen above, Regulation 38, embodying a relatively recent addition to the Mining Code, empowered

---

[192] See further above, section III.2.7.
[193] See further above, section III.3.3.3.
[194] See further above, section III.4, text, at note 63.
[195] See also above, section III.3.2, text, at note 137, where Reg. 31(4) is considered in the context of the definition of 'serious harm to the marine environment'.

Protection of environment 421

the Commission, from time to time, to issue *recommendations* for the *guidance* of Contractors, though Contractors had nonetheless to undertake to observe them 'as far as reasonably practicable'. [196] Such recommendations may, *inter alia*, list those exploration activities which may be considered to have no potential for causing harmful effects on the marine environment. As noted earlier in this chapter, at the March 2000 session of the Authority, the Commission began a review of recommendations which emerged from the ISBA Workshop held in China in 1998. [197] The proceedings of that Workshop included a set of Guidelines, including a first attempt to identify 'activities not expected to cause serious environmental harm'. [198]

- To establish a programme to monitor and report on such effects on the marine environment; and, in doing so:
- To co-operate with the Authority and the sponsoring State or States.

Regulation 31(5) goes on to impose a reporting obligation upon the contractor:

The contractor shall report annually in writing to the Secretary-General on the implementation and results of the monitoring programme referred to in paragraph 4 and shall submit data and information, taking into account any recommendations issued by the Commission pursuant to regulation 38. The Secretary-General shall transmit such reports to the Commission for its consideration pursuant to article 165 of the Convention.

Under Regulation 31(6), a duty of co-operation is placed upon the various actors involved:

Contractors, sponsoring States and other interested States or entities shall cooperate with the Authority in the establishment and implementation of programmes for monitoring and evaluating the impacts of deep seabed mining on the marine environment.

Finally, under Regulation 31(7), provision is made for the establishment of pre-exploitation reference zones: [199]

If the Contractor applies for exploitation rights, it shall propose areas to be set aside and used exclusively as impact reference zones and preservation reference zones. 'Impact reference zones' means areas to be used for assessing the effect of each contractor's activities in the Area on the marine environment and which are representative of the environmental characteristics of the Area. 'Preservation reference zones' means areas in

---

[196] See further above, section IV.3.2, text, at note 132 and following, referring to Reg. 38 and Annex 4, section 13(2)(e).
[197] See above, section IV.3.2, text, at note 140 and following.
[198] *Sanya Workshop Proceedings* (cited in note 4 above), at p. 221 *et seq.*
[199] See also below, section V.2.2.3 and 2.3.3, where reference is made to the provision made in US legislation for impact reference areas and interim preservational areas.

422   *Chapter 10*

which no mining shall occur to ensure representative and stable biota of the seabed in order to assess any changes in the flora and fauna of the marine environment.

The implications of those provisions of Regulation 31 for the substance of the contract are then detailed in Section 5 of Annex 4 of the Mining Code, which imposes two sets of obligations upon the Contractor. They relate to environmental baselines and monitoring, and environmental impact assessment and monitoring in relation to testing of collecting systems and processing operations. Logically enough (since the contract covers only *exploration*), the standard clauses do not include any clause reflecting the requirement in Regulation 31(7) that the Contractor, if it applies for *exploitation* rights, must propose areas to be set aside and used exclusively as impact reference zones and preservation reference zones.

Environmental baselines and monitoring: sections 5.2 - 5.4.   First, the Contractor has to *establish environmental baselines* against which to assess the likely effects of its exploration activities on the marine environment and to *establish, carry out and report on a programme to monitor such effects.* The text of sections 5.2 - 5.4 is as follows:

> 5.2 The Contractor shall, in accordance with the Regulations, gather environmental baseline data as exploration activities progress and develop and shall establish environmental baselines against which to assess the likely effects of the Contractor's activities on the marine environment.
> 5.3 The Contractor shall, in accordance with the Regulations, establish and carry out a programme to monitor and report on such effects on the marine environment. The Contractor shall cooperate with the Authority in the implementation of such monitoring.
> 5.4 The Contractor shall, within 90 days of the end of each calendar year, report to the Secretary-General on the implementation and results of the monitoring programme referred to in section 5.3 hereof and shall submit data and information in accordance with the Regulations.[200]

Environmental impact assessment and monitoring in relation to testing of collecting systems and processing operations: section 5.5.   Secondly, there is a series of obligations which have to be carried out prior to the commencement of testing of collecting systems and processing operations. They include the submission of:

- a site-specific environmental impact statement with data which could be used to establish an environmental baseline;
- an assessment of the effects on the marine environment of the proposed tests of collecting systems; and

---

[200] Annex 4, sections 5.2-5.4.

Protection of environment 423

- a proposal for a monitoring programme to determine the effect of the equipment to be used during the proposed mining tests. The text of section 5.5 is as follows:

Prior to the commencement of testing of collecting systems and processing operations, the Contractor shall submit to the Authority:
(a) a site-specific environmental impact assessment based on available meteorological, oceanographic and environmental data collected during the preceding phases of exploration and containing data that could be used to establish an environmental baseline against which to assess the likely effect of the mining tests;
(b) an assessment of the effects on the marine environment of the proposed tests of collecting systems;
(c) a proposal for a monitoring programme to determine the effect on the marine environment of the equipment that will be used during the proposed mining tests.[201]

6.4.2 Contingency Plans and Emergencies

The standard clauses dealing with contingency plans and emergencies have to be read with the related provisions of the UN Convention and Regulations 32 and 33 of the Mining Code.

Reference has been made earlier in this chapter to the rôles of the Legal and Technical Commission and the Council in the issue of emergency orders.[202] As was seen, the Commission is empowered to make recommendations to the Council to issue emergency orders, including orders for the suspension or adjustment of operations, to prevent serious harm to the marine environment arising out of activities in the Area. Such recommendations have to be taken up by the Council on a priority basis.[203]

6.4.2.1 'Emergency Orders' and 'Immediate Measures of a Temporary Nature' – Regulation 32

Under Standard Clause 6.2, the Contractor is obliged to promptly report to the Secretary-General any incident arising from its activities that has caused or is likely to cause serious harm to the marine environment.[204] When the Secretary-General has been notified of such an incident, or otherwise becomes aware of it, he has to set in train a process which may result in the issue by the Council of emergency orders and, pending such action by the Council, the Secretary-General is required to take immediate measures of a temporary nature. The process is prescribed by Regulation 32, under which the Secretary-General, the Legal and Technical Commission, the Council and the Contractor all have a part to play.

---

[201] Annex 4, section 5.5.
[202] See further above, sections III.3.3.3 and III.3.3.2.
[203] The Commission is so empowered under Art. 165(2)(k) of the UN Convention and the Council's corresponding powers are in Art. 162(2)(w).
[204] Standard Clauses, Mining Code, Annex 4, Section 6.2.

424   *Chapter 10*

The Secretary-General has duties of *notification, reporting, monitoring* and *taking immediate measures.* First he must:

- issue a general *notification* of the incident and *notify* in writing the Contractor and the sponsoring State or States; [205] and
- *report* immediately to the Commission and the Council, with copies to all members of the Authority, to competent international organisations and to concerned subregional, regional and global organisations and bodies. [206]

He has then to:

- *monitor* developments with respect to all such incidents and *report* on them as appropriate to the Commission and the Council. [207]

Finally, pending any action by the Council, the Secretary-General:

- must take such immediate measures of a temporary nature as are practical and reasonable in the circumstances to prevent, contain and minimise serious harm to the marine environment. [208] Such measures may remain in effect for a period of 90 days but will be terminated earlier if the Council decides within that time what measures, if any, to take. [209]

The Legal and Technical Commission's rôle, following receipt of the Secretary-General's report, is to determine on the basis of the evidence provided to it and taking into account the measures already taken by the Contractor, which measures are necessary to respond effectively to the incident in order to prevent, contain and minimise the serious harm. It makes recommendations to the Council accordingly. [210]

The Rules of Procedure of the Legal and Technical Commission [211] provide another basis on which the Commission may consider an environmental emergency and make recommendations to the Council. Rule 53(4) provides that:

Any member of the Authority may make a request to the Secretary-General to convene a meeting of the Commission in order to consider a matter of particular concern to that member involving an environmental emergency. The Secretary-General shall convene the Commission which shall give urgent consideration to such matter and report to the Council as soon as possible with its findings and recommendations. Any member concerned with such matter has the right to send a representative to the meeting of the Commission to express its views on the matter without participation in decision-making,

---

[205] Reg. 32(1).

[206] *Ibid.*

[207] *Ibid.*

[208] Reg. 32(2). The discretionary phrase 'may take such immediate measures' in the penultimate draft was replaced by the mandatory phrase 'shall take such immediate measures' in the final version of Reg. 32(2).

[209] *Ibid.*

[210] Reg. 32(3).

[211] Decision of the Council of the Authority Concerning the Rules of Procedure of the Legal and Technical Commission, ISBA/6/C/9, 13 July 2000, Annex.

although the Commission may determine that such presence be limited at certain stages when confidential information is being discussed.

The Council has to consider the Commission's recommendations [212] and, taking account of those recommendations and of any information provided by the Contractor, it may issue emergency orders. Such orders 'may include orders for the suspension or adjustment of operations, as may be reasonably necessary to prevent, contain and minimise serious harm to the marine environment arising out of activities in the Area'. [213]

If the Contractor fails to comply with an emergency order, the *Council* may take, or arrange for others to take on its behalf, such practical measures as are necessary to prevent, contain and minimise any such serious harm to the marine environment. [214] At the last moment, just before the Mining Code was approved at the sixth session of the Authority in July 2000, a final paragraph was added to Regulation 32, designed to respond to the need, felt by some States, for 'appropriate forms of guarantee to enable the Council to take immediately the necessary measures to implement an emergency order in the event of failure or inability on the part of the contractor to comply with such orders'. [215] Regulation 32(7) provides that:

> In order to enable the Council, when necessary, to take immediately the practical measures to prevent, contain and minimise serious harm to the marine environment referred to in paragraph 6, the contractor, prior to the commencement of testing of collecting systems and processing operations, will provide the Council with a guarantee of its financial and technical capability to comply promptly with emergency orders or to assure that the Council can take such emergency measures. If the contractor does not provide the Council with such a guarantee, the sponsoring State or States shall, in response to a request by the Secretary-General and pursuant to articles 139 and 235 of the Convention, take necessary measures to ensure that the contractor provides such a guarantee or shall take measures to ensure that assistance is provided to the Authority in the discharge of its responsibilities under paragraph 6. [216]

The origins of this provision are to be found in a proposal submitted by the Chilean delegation, under which applicants for exploration contracts would have been required to provide an 'environmental surety' when signing the contract in an amount to be assessed by the Legal and Technical Commission. [217] The new paragraph differs in two significant respects from the original Chilean proposal. The 'environmental surety' has become a 'guarantee' backed by sponsoring

---

[212] Reg. 32(4).

[213] Reg. 32(5).

[214] Reg. 32(6).

[215] Decision of the Council of 13 July 2000, ISBA/6/C/12, 13 July 2000, Part II, preamble.

[216] Mining Code, Reg. 32(7), footnote omitted.

[217] *Proposal submitted by the delegation of Chile concerning document ISBA/5/C/4/Rev.1 of 14 October 1999*, ISBA/6/C/L.3, 29 March 2000.

426   *Chapter 10*

States; and unlike the environmental surety, which was required 'up front', the guarantee will not be required until the contractor is about the begin the testing of collecting systems and processing operations. Regulation 32(7) does not determine the form which the guarantee will take. It does, however, make a footnote reference to the Council's Decision of 13 July 2000 which includes the following passages:

> 1. *Decides* to consider the matter of such a guarantee prior to the phase of testing of collecting systems and processing operations for the exploitation of polymetallic nodules with a view to adopting appropriate forms of guarantee to ensure compliance with emergency orders and the effective protection of the marine environment in accordance with article 145 and other relevant provisions of the Convention; and
>
> 2. *Requests* the secretariat to carry out studies of appropriate instruments or arrangements which may be available for this purpose and to report to the Council on the outcome of such studies prior to consideration of the matter pursuant to paragraph 1. [218]

The Contractor's obligations. The Contractor's obligations are prescribed   in standard contractual clauses relating to:

- the submission of a contingency plan to respond effectively to incidents likely to cause serious harm to the marine environment;
- the reporting of any incident that has caused or is likely to cause such harm;
- the duty to comply with emergency orders issued by the Council and immediate measures of a temporary nature 'issued' by the Secretary General; and
- the monetary consequences of failure to comply.

The contingency plan. [219] Prior to the commencement of activities under the contract, the Contractor must submit to the Secretary-General a contingency plan 'to respond effectively to incidents that are likely to cause serious harm to the marine environment arising from the Contractor's activities at sea in the exploration area.' The plan must 'establish special procedures and provide for adequate and appropriate equipment to deal with such incidents and, in particular, shall include arrangements for':

> (a)   the immediate raising of a general alarm in the area of the exploration activities;
>
> (b)   immediate notification to the Secretary-General;
>
> (c)   the warning of ships which might be about to enter the immediate vicinity;

---

[218] *Loc. cit..* in note 215, Part II, paras. 1-2.

[219] Mining Code, Annex 4, section 6.1.

Protection of environment 427

(d) a continuing flow of full information to the Secretary-General relating to particulars of the contingency measures already taken and further actions required;
(e) the removal, as appropriate, of polluting substances;
(f) the reduction and, so far as reasonably possible, prevention of serious harm to the marine environment, as well as mitigation of such effects;
(g) as appropriate, co-operation with other contractors with the Authority to respond to an emergency; and
(h) periodic emergency response exercises. [220]

The reporting of incidents. As has been seen, the Contractor must promptly report to the Secretary-General any incident arising from its activities that has caused or is likely to cause serious harm to the marine environment. The report has to give details of the incident, 'including, *inter alia*':

(a) the co-ordinates of the area affected or which can reasonably be anticipated to be affected;
(b) the description of the action being taken by the Contractor to prevent, contain, minimise and repair the serious harm to the marine environment;
(c) a description of the action being taken by the Contractor to monitor the effects of the incident on the marine environment; and
(d) such supplementary information as may reasonably be required by the Secretary-General. [221]

The duty to comply with 'emergency orders' and 'immediate measures' and the consequences of failure so to do. The Contractor's obligation to comply is prescribed in Standard Clause 6.3. Failure to comply may have financial consequences of two kinds. First, in the absence of compliance by the Contractor, the Council may take such reasonable measures as are necessary to prevent, contain, minimise or repair serious harm to the marine environment at the contractor's expense, and the Contractor must promptly reimburse the Authority. [222] Secondly, monetary penalties may be imposed on the Contractor pursuant to the term of the contract or the Regulations. [223]

As was seen above, the Contractor is also required, prior to the start of testing of collecting systems and processing operations, to provide the Council with a guarantee of its financial and technical capability to comply.

6.4.2.2 Rights of Coastal States – Regulation 33
The UN Convention recognises that activities in the Area may cause

---

[220] *Ibid.*
[221] Mining Code, Annex 4, section 6.2.
[222] Mining Code, Annex 4, section 6.4. See also, on the liability of the Contractor, Annex 4, section 16, considered below in section 6.4.8.
[223] *Ibid.* See also, on monetary penalties, Annex 4, section 21.5-21.6, considered below in section 6.4.9.

428   *Chapter 10*

environmental damage to coastlines or related interests of coastal States. Thus, Article 142(3) provides that:

> Neither this Part [XI of the Convention] nor any rights granted or exercised pursuant thereto shall affect the rights of coastal States to take such measures consistent with the relevant provisions of Part XII [on Protection and Preservation of the Marine Environment] as may be necessary to prevent, mitigate or eliminate grave and imminent damage to their coastline, or related interests from pollution or threat thereof or from other hazardous occurrences resulting from or caused by any activities in the Area.

Regulation 33, on the 'Rights of coastal States' develops this provision further and first ensures that the Mining Code will not affect the rights of coastal States in accordance with Article 142 and other relevant provisions of the Convention. [224] It then goes on to deal with the situation where the coastal State has grounds for believing that, 'any activity in the Area by a contractor is likely to cause serious harm to the marine environment under its jurisdiction or sovereignty' [225] – which would appear to mean the marine environment landward of the outer limit of the continental shelf. [226] Any such coastal State may notify the Secretary-General of the grounds on which such belief is based. [227] The Contractor and its sponsoring State or States are then to be given 'a reasonable opportunity to examine the evidence, if any, provided' and may submit their observations to the Secretary-General within a reasonable time. [228] The way would then be clear for the Secretary-General to decide if there are clear grounds for believing that serious harm to the marine environment is likely to occur. If so, he may take action in accordance with Regulation 32 [229] which, as seen above, may in appropriate cases result in the issue by the Council of emergency orders; [230] and, if necessary he may also take immediate measures of a temporary nature as provided for in Regulation 32(2), also considered above. [231]

6.4.3 Contractor's Annual Report

The Contractor must include in its annual report, *inter alia*, 'the results obtained from environmental monitoring programmes, including observations, measurements, evaluations and analyses of environmental parameters'.[232]

---

[224] Mining Code, Reg. 33(1).

[225] Reg. 33(2).

[226] The outer limit of the continental shelf marks the dividing line between 'the Area beyond the limits of national jurisdiction' and the offshore areas, including the territorial sea and any EEZ claimed by the coastal State, lying within the limits of national jurisdiction.

[227] Reg. 33(2).

[228] *Ibid.*

[229] Reg. 33(3).

[230] See above, section 6.4.2.1.

[231] *Ibid.*

[232] Annex 4, section 10.2(a). Under section 10.3, the Secretary-General may also 'reasonably require' additional information from time to time.

Protection of environment 429

6.4.4 Data and Information to be Submitted on Expiration of the Contract
The Contractor is required, upon expiration or termination of the contract, to submit to the Authority various data and information, including copies of environmental data acquired in the course of carrying out the programme of activities.[233]

6.4.5 Confidentiality of Data versus Environmental Protection
As has been seen, the UN Convention makes provision for the confidentiality of data transferred to the Authority by prospectors, applicants for contracts or contractors which is 'deemed proprietary'[234] and the rules are developed further in the Regulations of the Mining Code. [235] The Regulations reflect the need for a balance between the commercial need for confidentiality and the need to protect the marine environment from the serious harm which may be caused by activities in the Area.

6.4.6 Due Regard Undertaking
The undertakings required of the Contractor include the obligation to actively carry out the programme of activities with due regard to the impact of its activities on the marine environment.[236]

6.4.7 Inspection
One of the purposes for which the Contractor is obliged to permit the Authority to send its inspectors on board vessels and installations used to carry out activities in the exploration area is to monitor the effects of such activities on the marine environment.[237]

6.4.8 Responsibility and Liability
The Contractor's liability for damage to the marine environment is specified in the following clause:

> The Contractor shall be liable for the actual amount of any damage, including damage to the marine environment, arising out of its wrongful acts or omissions, and those of its employees, subcontractors, agents and all persons engaged in working or acting for them in the conduct of its operations under this contract, including the costs of reasonable measures to prevent or limit damage to the marine environment, account being taken of any contributory acts or omissions by the Authority.[238]

---

[233] Annex 4, section 11.2(a).
[234] See above, Chap. 4, section IX.
[235] See above, Chap. 4, section IV.3(Reg.6), as regards prospecting, and Chap. 5, section IV, as regards exploration.
[236] Annex 4, section 13.3(b).
[237] Annex 4, section 14.1(b).
[238] Annex 4, section 16.1. On the question of responsibility and liability, see further Chap. 3, section V and Chap. 4, sections XIII and XIV.

430   *Chapter 10*

6.4.9 Suspension and Termination of Contract and Penalties
Contracts may be suspended or terminated by the Council if, in spite of written warnings, the Contractor has conducted its activities in such a way as to result in serious, persistent and wilful violation of the fundamental terms of the contract, Part XI of the UN Convention, the 1994 Implementation Agreement and the rules, regulations and procedures of the Authority.[239] In the event of termination or expiration of the contract, the Contractor must comply with the Regulations and remove all installations, plant, equipment and materials in the exploration area, and must make the area safe so as not to constitute a danger to persons, shipping or to the marine environment.[240]

V. THE PROVISIONS OF NATIONAL LEGISLATION

As has been seen,[241] Article 209, Paragraph 2 of the UN Convention requires States to supplement the international rules, regulations and procedures called for in Paragraph 1 by adopting national laws and regulations, the requirements of which must be no less effective than those of their international counterpart. Given the delay in adopting that part of the Mining Code which will regulate prospecting and exploration in the Area, the expected further delay in the commencement of the commercial recovery of sea-bed minerals, and the acknowledged need for more research on the environmental effects of sea-bed mining, States Parties will not be in any great hurry to adopt detailed rules and regulations. Some indication of the likely content of such national legislation may be gleaned from an examination of the interim legislation adopted by leading industrialised States in the early 1980's. It has to be remembered, however, that the legislation was indeed 'interim'. Some of it has already been superseded by later legislation and further changes can be expected to be made by other States when they reconsider their legislation nearer to the time of actual exploitation. The current position is reviewed in this section.

1. Overview
As was seen in Chapter 7, seven States adopted interim national legislation to govern sea-bed mining, pending the entry into force for them of an agreed and acceptable international regime. The United States took the initiative in 1980 and was followed over the next five years by, in chronological order, Germany, the United Kingdom, France, the Soviet Union, Japan and Italy.

In this section an overview is given of the provision made in this national legislation for the protection of the environment and in the next section a more detailed analysis will be found of the United States legislation.

---

[239] Annex 4, section 21.1(a).
[240] Annex 4, section 21.7.
[241] In section III.3.1.

Protection of environment 431

1.1 United States

The American law is contained in the Deep Seabed Hard Mineral Resources Act 1980 and in Regulations adopted under the Act. As will be seen in section V.2 below, the United States has not only included extensive environmental provisions in the Act but has also produced very detailed subordinate legislation.

1.2 Germany

Sea-bed mining was originally regulated by the Act of Interim Regulation of Deep Seabed Mining 1980, as amended by the Act of 12 February 1982.[242] However, following Germany's accession to the UN Convention in 1994, new provision was made for sea-bed mining in a more comprehensive Law for the implementation of the UN Convention and the Implementation Agreement of 29 July 1994.[243]

Only very rudimentary provision was made for the protection of the environment in the earlier legislation.[244] The environmental provisions of the new Law are similarly brief and general but they will in due course be developed by regulations which will discharge Germany's obligation to implement the UN Convention, the Implementation Agreement and regulations adopted under these instruments.[245]

One of the purposes of the new Act is to guarantee the protection of the marine environment.[246] The Federal Ministry of Economics is authorised to issue ordinances for the implementation of UN regime of seabed mining. In so far as they relate to environmental protection, they have to be issued in agreement with the Federal Ministry for the Environment, Nature Conservation and Nuclear Safety.[247]

Applicants for seabed mining licences have to secure both the sponsorship of the Federal Government (in the form of the organ charged with the implementation of the Law, the 'Oberbergamt'[248]) and a contract with the Authority.[249] In considering the applicant's draft plan of work, the Oberbergamt has to take account of an assessment by the Federal Office for Sea Navigation and Hydrography (Bundesamt für Seeschiffart und Hydrographie) of the plan of

---

[242] Act dated 16 August 1980 (BGBl.I, p. 1457) as amended by Act of 12 February 1982 (BGBl.I, p. 136). English translations are in XX ILM(1981), p. 393 and XXI ILM (1982), p. 832 and in Vol. III of the first edition of this work at pp. III.3 115-121.

[243] Ausführungsgesetz Seerechtsübereinkommen 1982/1994 of 6 June 1995 (BGBl.I 778 9510-23). Section 2 of this Law for the Implementation of the UN Convention 1982/1994 deals with Seabed Mining and the Law Governing Deep Seabed Mining is contained in Art. 9. The writer is obliged to Prof. Dr. Rainer Lagoni for supplying a copy of an unofficial English translation of Art. 9 made by the Sprachendienst des Auswärtigen Amtes and entitled 'Act Governing Deep Seabed Mining of 6 June 1995 (Deep Seabed Mining Act)'. This text is reproduced in Vol. 3 as Doc. No. 27.1. The translation takes the form of a self-contained Act with renumbered sections and it is to this version that reference is made below.

[244] See further Vol. 2 of the first edition of this work (1986), at pp. II.9 20-21.

[245] Section 1(1) of the Act provides that its purpose is, *inter alia,* 'to guarantee fulfilment of the obligations of ... Germany deriving from Part XI of the Convention, its Annex III, the Implementation Agreement, and the rules issued by the Authority.

[246] Deep Seabed Mining Act, Section 1(1)(2).

[247] Section 7.

[248] 'Oberbergamt' is defined in Section 2(7) and its role is specified in Section 3.

[249] Section 4(2).

432　*Chapter 10*

work as regards navigation and environmental protection.[250]　One of the conditions which an applicant for sponsorship must satisfy is that it possesses the required reliability and can guarantee that activities in the Area will be carried out in a manner which is both orderly and serves the interests of environmental protection.[251]

Prospectors and contractors operating in the Area are made responsible for, *inter alia*, the protection of the environment.[252]

Special transitional provision had to be made for contractors holding licences issued under the original 1980 legislation.[253]　They had to make applications to the Oberbergamt for sponsorship and for a contract with the Authority immediately after the entry into force of the Implementation Agreement for Germany on 28 July 1996.[254]　The old licences were to expire after the conclusion of a contract with the Authority, at latest two years after the entry into force of the Agreement, that is, on 28 July 1998.[255]　However, if an international consortium was involved, licences could remain valid beyond that point, though not beyond 16 November 1998.[256] Once the last of the licences issued under the 1980 Act expired, the earlier legislation ceased to have effect.[257]

1.3 United Kingdom

The Deep Sea Mining (Temporary Provisions) Act 1981 provides framework rules for the protection of the marine environment and they are further elaborated in subordinate legislation. [258]

The principal provision is embodied in section 5(1) of the Act:

> In determining whether to grant an exploration or exploitation licence the Secretary of State shall have regard to the need to protect (so far as reasonably practicable) marine creatures, plants and other organisms and their habitat from any harmful effects which might result from any activities to be authorised by the licence; and the Secretary of State shall consider any representations made to him concerning such effects.

---

[250] Section 4(4), which also specifies that, in matters concerning environmental protection, the Bundesamt für Seeschiffahrt und Hydrographie must prepare its assessment in co-operation with the Umweltbundesamt.

[251] Section 4(6)(2)(a).

[252] Section 5(3).

[253] Section 13.

[254] Section 13(1).

[255] *Ibid.*

[256] Section 13(2).

[257] Section 13(3).

[258] Under s. 18(3) of the Act, it may be repealed by order if it appears to the Secretary of State that an international agreement on the law of the sea which has been adopted by a UN Conference on the Law of the Sea is to be given effect within the United Kingdom. The United Kingdom acceded to the UN Convention on 25 July 1997 but seems to have taken the view that, for the time being, it would suffice to extend the prohibition of unlicensed deep sea mining in s.1 to overseas territories. See the Deep Sea Mining (Temporary Provisions) Act 1981 (Guernsey) Order 1997 (S.I. 1997/2978) and the corresponding Orders for Jersey (S.I. 1997/2979) and the Isle of Man (S.I. 2000/1112).

Protection of environment 433

It is supplemented by a number of other provisions:

Under section 2(2), one of the relevant factors to which the Secretary of State must have regard in deciding whether or not to grant a licence is 'the desirability of keeping an area or areas of the deep sea bed free from deep sea bed mining operations so as to provide an area or areas for comparison with licensed areas in assessing the effects of such operations'. As has been seen, provision for environmental reference zones is made in the Mining Code[259] and, as will be seen below, provision for international negotiations on such 'stable reference areas' is made in the United States law.[260]

Under section 2(3)(c), the terms and conditions to be inserted in a licence may include those 'relating to the disposal of any waste material resulting from such processing or other treatment [of hard mineral resources]'. *Section 5(2)* adds that, without prejudice to this provision, licences shall contain such terms and conditions as the Secretary of State considers necessary or expedient to avoid or minimise any harmful effects upon marine creatures, plants and other organisms and their habitat. Moreover, under *section 6(1)*, licences may be varied or revoked where, in the opinion of the Secretary of State, it is required to provide such protection. Finally, it may be noted that, under *section 12*, read with the Schedule, the Secretary of State may include among the regulations made under the Act, 'The prohibition of any method of working which in the opinion of the Secretary of State is or is likely to be harmful to any marine creatures, plants or other organisms or their habitat'.

Regulations came into operation at the same time as the Act, on 25 January 1982, and prescribe the form and content of applications for exploration licences. So far as the environment is concerned, however, they simply require the applicant to provide a description of 'the proposed measures to investigate and protect the marine environment and to monitor the effectiveness of environmental safeguards'.[261]

More important are the environmental safeguards incorporated in the Deep Sea Mining (Exploration Licences) Regulations adopted in 1984.[262]

Under these Regulations, the licensee is licensed to explore in accordance with an exploration plan[263] submitted by him, accepted by the Secretary of State and more particularly described in Annex 2 to the licence.[264] In applying for an amendment, alteration or variation of the exploration plan, the licensee is required to set out details of all proposed changes and the likely effect thereof, *with particular reference to any environmental effects*.[265] These general provisions are supplemented by the following more particular provisions.

Model Clause 7 imposes various obligations upon the licensee in relation to safety, health and welfare, including compliance with ship construction standards and conduct of operations in the exploration area 'in a proper manner using all

---

[259] See above, section IV.6.4.1.
[260] See below, section V.2.2.3.
[261] Deep Sea Mining (Exploration Licences) (Applications) Regulations 1982, S.I. 1982/58, reg. 2(1) and Schedule, Part I, para. 8(c); reproduced in Vol. 3, as Doc. No. 28.2.
[262] S.I. 1984/1230; reproduced in Vol. 3 as Doc. No. 28.3.
[263] *Ibid.*, Schedule (Model Clauses for Exploration Licences), Model Clause 2(1).
[264] Model Clause 1(1), defining 'the exploration plan'.
[265] Model Clause 2(3).

434 Chapter 10

due skill and care.'[266] The required compliance with international conventions relating to safety, oil pollution and training of seafarers[267] will also help to ensure that the shipping phase of sea-bed mining operations will not cause significant environmental damage.

Model Clause 9 follows up section 5(1) of the Act by requiring the licensee to take all practicable steps to protect marine creatures, plants and other organisms and their habitats from any harmful effects that might result from activities in the exploration area.

Model Clause10 obliges the licensee to monitor and record environmental conditions in the exploration area in accordance with specified notes for guidance.[268]

Model Clause 11 seeks to ensure that no damage should be caused by the at-sea testing of mining systems or any equipment liable to be harmful to the environment. The licensee requires the consent of the Secretary of State and must comply with any conditions attached to such consent as may be granted.

Model Clause 12 places similar restraints on processing or dumping of mineral resources and waste arising from exploration activities.

Model Clause 13 specifies the detailed records to be kept by the licensee and, *inter alia*, requires the licensee to notify the Secretary of State three months in advance of the placing and position of any structure (either fixed or floating), light or buoy within the exploration area, and the timing and nature of any exploratory activities.

Model Clause 16 enables the Secretary of State to appoint inspectors with far-reaching powers to ensure compliance with licence conditions.

Model Clause 19, in providing for the protection of the various freedoms of the high seas, forbids the licensee from carrying out exploration activities in such a way 'as to interfere unjustifiably with navigation or fishing in the waters of the exploration area or with the observation of marine creatures, plants and other organisms and their habitats'.

Finally, *Model Clause 22* follows up section 6(1) of the Act by providing for the revocation or variation of a licence if, *inter alia*, there has been a breach of, or failure to observe, any of the terms or conditions of the licence, or it is necessary for the protection of marine creatures, plants and other organisms and their habitat.

1.4 France

France ratified the UN Convention and the Implementation Agreement on 11 April 1996[269] but has not yet amended or repealed the instruments adopted in 1981 and 1982 to govern seabed mining and ensure that it should not damage the marine environment.

---

[266] Model Clause 7(3)(a).
[267] Model Clause 7(3)(b) and Annex 4.
[268] The notes for guidance are set out in Annex 5.
[269] Ratification was authorised by Law No. 95-1311 of 21 December 1995, *Journal officiel*, 22 December 1995, p. 18543.

Under Article 9 of the French Law on the Exploration and Exploitation of Mineral Resources of the Deep Seabed 1981,[270] the holder of a permit for exploration or exploitation is required to respect the obligations which may be imposed on him by the French authorities in order to ensure the protection of the marine environment.

Under Article 14, one of the grounds on which permits may be withdrawn is 'grave infractions of the security, hygiene and police regulations, in particular those which ensure the protection of the marine fauna and flora'.

Article 15 provides for the imposition of fines upon permit holders violating Article 9 or implementing subordinate legislation.

These statutory provisions are developed further in the Decree of 29 January 1982,[271] and the Arrêté of the same date.[272] Under these instruments permit applications must be accompanied by a notice of impact indicating how the proposed general work programme will satisfy environmental requirements[273] and by an undertaking to adopt exploration or exploitation techniques appropriate to safeguard the environment.[274] In addition, permit applicants are required to indicate in a plan of work the measures to be adopted for the protection and surveillance of the marine environment.[275] Before granting a permit, the Minister of Mines must consult, *inter alia*, the Minister of the Environment.[276] An application for extension of a permit has to be accompanied by a detailed account of work completed and of its eventual consequences for the marine environment.[277] Before a permit holder may commence work, he must submit a work programme to the Minister of Mines, together with a notice of impact on the environment in the case of exploration work and an impact study, as prescribed in Article 2 of the Law for the Protection of Nature of 10 July 1976, in the case of exploitation work. Such work programmes are examined by an inter-Ministry commission which may advise the Minister of Mines to forbid the works in whole or in part or to allow them subject to certain conditions, if necessary to safeguard the environment.[278]

1.5 Russia (formerly the Soviet Union)

The Edict of 17 April 1982[279] of the Supreme Soviet of the former Soviet Union contained only outline provisions on the protection of the environment, with

---

[270] Law No. 81-1135 of 23 December 1981, *Journal officiel*, 24 December 1981, pp. 3499-3500. English translation in XXI ILM (1982), p. 808; reproduced in Vol. 3 as Doc. No. 29.1.

[271] Decree no. 82-111 of 29 January 1982 passed in application of the law of 23 December 1981 in respect of the exploration and exploitation of mineral resources of the deep seabed, *Journal officiel*, 31 January 1982, p. 431; English translation in Vol. 3 as Doc. No.29.2 .

[272] Arrêté of 29 January 1982 determining the contents of applications for permits for the exploration and exploitation of the deep seabed, *Journal officiel*, 31 January 1982; English translation in Vol. 3 as Doc. No. 29.3.

[273] Decree, Art. 3; Arrêté, Art. 2(4).

[274] Arrêté, Art. 2(6).

[275] Decree, Arts. 4 and 5.

[276] Decree, Art. 8.

[277] Decree, Art. 11.

[278] Decree, Arts. 15 and 16.

[279] Edict on Provisional Measures to Regulate the Activity of Soviet Enterprises Relating to the Exploration and Exploitation of Mineral Resources of Seabed Areas beyond the Limits of the

436 Chapter 10

responsibility being assigned to the Council of Ministers to establish detailed procedures and regulations. The principal provision in Article 14 required Soviet enterprises engaged in prospecting for or development of deep sea-bed mineral resources to take the necessary measures to ensure an effective protection of the natural environment from harmful consequences. Article 8, dealing with co-operation with treaty partners, envisaged the grant of Soviet assistance in carrying out measures to prevent pollution.

More recently, following the breakup of the Soviet Union, the President of the Russian Federation issued a decree 'to provide a legal basis for the activities of Russian national and juridical persons in the exploration and exploitation of the mineral resources of the seabed'.[280] Under Paragraph 3, the Government issued a further Order to regulate such activities in April 1995.[281] They are to take place in accordance with the universally recognised principles and norms of international law, international treaties and the legislation of the Russian Federation.[282] Provision is made for regulation by Federal executive organs but no particular reference is made to protection of the environment.

1.6 Japan

Although Japan acceded to the UN Convention in June 1996, seabed mining is still governed by legislation adopted in 1982.[283] The Law on Interim Measures for Deep Seabed Mining, 1982 contains scarcely any direct reference to the prevention of environmental damage threatened by sea-bed mining and, indeed, the language of the Law looks as if it has been borrowed from earlier legislation designed to regulate mining on land.

Article 27, which is concerned with 'compensation for damages', refers in particular to damage caused by the discharge of waste water, the accumulation of rubbish or slag or the release of mineral smoke accompanying deep sea-bed mining in Japan.

Article 33 enables the authorities, in granting permits, to impose and subsequently alter conditions to be observed by permittees and Article 35 establishes a system of reporting and inspection.

Continental Shelf, 17 April 1982, *Izvestia*, 18 April 1982, pp. 1-2; English translation in XXI ILM (1982), pp. 551.

[280] Decree by the President of the Russian Federation on the activities of Russian natural and juridical persons in the exploration and exploitation of the mineral resources of the seabed beyond the limits of the continental shelf, Decree No. 2099 of 22 November 1994 *(Collected Laws of the Russian Federation*, 1994, No. 31, p.3252); English translation in *LOS Bull.*, No. 28, 1995, pp. 28-30; reproduced in Vol. 3 as Doc. No. 30.1.

[281] Order No. 410, 25 April 1995 concerning the way in which activities are to be carried out by Russian natural and juridical persons for exploration and exploitation of the mineral resources of the seabed beyond the limits of the continental shelf *(Collected Laws of the Russian Federation*, 1995, No. 18, p. 1675); English translation by Ivan Tashev, reproduced in Vol. 3 as Doc. No.30.2.

[282] Para. 1.

[283] Law on Interim Measures for Deep Seabed Mining, 1982 (entered into force 20 July 1982), XXII ILM (1983), pp. 102-122; reproduced in Vol. 3 as Doc. No. 31.1. Regulations to enforce the Law have also been issued *(Official Register of Ministry of International Finance and Trade*, No. 9770, 26 July 1982) but no English translation has been traced.

Finally, Article 39, to ensure the safety of sea-bed mining, applies the provisions of the Mine Safety Law *mutatis mutandis.*

It is understood that a review of this Law will not be undertaken until nearer the time when seabed mining becomes economically viable.[284]

1.7 Italy

Originally, provision was made for the protection of the environment from sea-bed mining in Law No.41 of 20 February 1985[285] and in implementing regulations issued in 1988.[286] However, these instruments were repealed by Law No.689 of 2 December 1994[287] which authorised ratification by Italy of the UN Convention and the Implementation Agreement of 28 July 1994. Article 3(1) of this Law makes provision for the adoption of regulations which will establish conditions for sponsorship by Italy of sea-bed mining contractors, as envisaged in Article 153 of the UN Convention and Article 4 of its Annex III. Given the fact that Italian participation in the OMA consortium has been terminated,[288] it is unlikely that regulations will be adopted in the foreseeable future.[289] In the meantime, there is no specific reference to the marine environment in Law No. 689.

2. Analysis of United States Law

The United States law is laid down in the Deep Seabed Hard Mineral Resources Act 1980,[290] the Deep Seabed Mining Regulations for Exploration Licenses, which became effective on 15 October 1981[291] and the Deep Seabed Mining Regulations for Commercial Recovery Permits, issued in 1989.[292]

---

[284] The writer is indebted to Prof. Moritaka Hayashi for this information.

[285] Law No. 41 of 20 February 1985; Regulations on the Exploration and Exploitation of the Mineral Resources of the Deep Seabed, *Gazzetta Ufficiale*, No. 52, 3 March 1985, pp. 1593-1596; English translation in XXIV ILM (1985), pp. 983-996.

[286] Presidential Decree No. 200 of 11 March 1988, *Gazzetta Ufficiale*, No. 139 of 13 June 1988.

[287] Law No. 689 of 2 December 1994 authorising ratification and implementation of the United Nations Convention on the Law of the Sea of 10 December 1982 and the Agreement of 29 July 1994 on the Implementation of Part XI of the United Nations Convention, *Gazzetta Ufficiale*, No. 295 of 19 December 1994, Supplement No. 164; English translation in Vol. 3, Doc. No. 32.1.

[288] On the composition of the consortia with sea-bed mining interests, see Chap. 7, section V.

[289] The writer is obliged to Prof. Tullio Treves for this opinion. See further his work on *Il diritto del mare e l'Italia*, Milano, Giuffré, 1995.

[290] Public Law 96-283 of 28 June 1980; 94 Stat. 553; 30 USC 1401 *et seq.*, as amended to 1 July 2000; reproduced in Vol. 3 as Doc. No. 26.1.

[291] US *Federal Register*, Vol. 46, No. 178, 15 September 1981, pp. 45890-45920; 15 CFR Part 970; XX ILM (1981), pp. 1228-1258, as amended to 1 July 2000. Subpart C of the Regulations, relating to licence applications based on exploration commenced before 28 June 1980 and to resolution of conflicts among overlapping applications, was issued separately in 1982 and became effective as from 9 February 1982 (*Federal Register*, Vol. 47, No. 27, 9 February 1982, pp. 5966-5971; 15 CFR Part 970). Reference must also be made to the interim Deep Seabed Mining Regulations Affecting Pre-Enactment Explorers which became effective on 20 November 1980 (*Federal Register*, Vol. 45, No. 226, 20 November 1980, pp. 76661-76663; XIX ILM (1980), pp. 1475-1477) and enabled NOAA to ensure that the activities of pre-enactment explorers, temporarily exempted from the Act's prohibition of unlicensed exploration, should not have a significant adverse effect on the environment.

[292] *Federal Register*, Vol. 54, No. 525, 6 January 1989; 15 CFR Part 971.

438   *Chapter 10*

2.1 Purpose and Strategy of Legislation

The Act is based, *inter alia*, on the 'finding' that, pending the entry into force of a Law of the Sea Treaty acceptable to the United States, 'the protection of the marine environment from damage caused by exploration or recovery of hard mineral resources of the deep seabed depends upon the enactment of suitable interim national legislation'.[293]

The protection of the environment features among both the domestic 'purposes' of the Act and its 'international objectives'. Thus, one of the purposes of the Act is:

> to accelerate the program of environmental assessment of exploration for and commercial recovery of hard mineral resources of the deep seabed and assure that such exploration and recovery activities are conducted in a manner which will encourage the conservation of such resources, protect the quality of the environment, and promote the safety of life and property at sea;[294]

Similarly, one of the specified international objectives was to be provision in the Law of the Sea Treaty 'for the establishment of requirements for the protection of the quality of the environment as stringent as those promulgated pursuant to this Act.' [295] Moreover, pending conclusion of such a treaty, the Secretary of State was encouraged to promote 'any international actions necessary to adequately protect the environment from adverse impacts' caused by the sea-bed activities of persons not subject to the Act.[296]

It will be noted that the first set of Regulations, published in 1981, related only to the exploratory phase of sea-bed mining. In part, this reflected NOAA's regulatory approach,[297] somewhat inelegantly described by one commentator as its 'evolving combination strategy'.[298] In other words, NOAA recognised that the sea-bed mining industry was still evolving and that knowledge of the marine environment and of the likely impact on it of sea-bed mining was still limited. Since current knowledge indicated that *exploration* would probably have no *significant* adverse impact on the environment, the strategy was to allow exploration under a relatively liberal and flexible regime, imposing few restraints and allowing for initiatives in the development of technology. At the same time, however, current understanding of the environmental impact of exploration activities was to be tested and updated by a combination of further Government research and self-monitoring by industry. Ample powers were reserved to enable NOAA to modify licence terms or issue emergency orders suspending a licence or suspending or modifying particular activities, where necessary to prevent a significant adverse impact upon the environment.

---

[293] Act, § 2(a)(14); 30 USC § 1401(a)(14).

[294] Act, § 2(b)(4); 30 USC § 1401(b)(4).

[295] Act, § 3(b)(1); 30 USC § 1402(b)(1).

[296] Act, § 3(b)(2); 30 USC § 1402(b)(2). See too below, section V.2.2.3 on liaison with Reciprocating States and section V.3 on the co-ordination of national legislation.

[297] NOAA's 'evolving strategy' is discussed in NOAA, *loc. cit.* in note 6(iv), Vol. 1, section II.c.4.

[298] See NOAA, *loc. cit.* in note 6(iv), Vol. II, p. 63.

Under the Act, commercial recovery was prohibited before 1 January 1988[299] and, when the Regulations governing the exploration phase were published in 1981, it was recognised that the commercial recovery phase of mining might present quite a different threat and that separate regulations would have to be issued later in the light of further research and experience.[300] Similarly, in keeping with its gradualist, pragmatic approach, NOAA, in its 1981 *Report to Congress*, took the view that, since applications for commercial recovery permits were not expected to be filed until 1984 at the earliest, it could afford to await the results of the further research already under way before finalising the commercial recovery regulations.[301] The expected date of commencement of commercial recovery has of course been pushed back considerably further since that time. Nonetheless, NOAA came to recognise the need to proceed more expeditiously. As it was put in its 1989 *Report to Congress*:

> The regulations are designed to encourage orderly preparation for the development of technology necessary to recover deep seabed manganese nodules by providing a clear regime now, for industry and government planning purposes, while allowing for changes in regulations, if needed, and deferring detailed decisions on permit-specific terms, conditions and restrictions until the time of permit issuance.[302]

Accordingly, the preparation of the regulations was brought forward and NOAA was able to publish final Deep Seabed Mining Regulations for Commercial Recovery Permits on 6 January 1989.[303]

2.2 Environmental Safeguards in the Exploration Phase
The shape of the environmental provisions of the Act and Regulations, and the strategy underlying them, can perhaps be most easily perceived if they are considered as falling into three categories:
(i) regulatory safeguards prior to the issue of the exploration licence;
(ii) regulatory safeguards incorporated in the licence; and
(iii) regulatory safeguards provided by NOAA.

2.2.1 Safeguards Prior to the Issue of Licence
The most central provision of all is the requirement laid down in section 105(a)(4) of the Act that the Administrator, before issuing a licence, must find that the proposed exploration 'cannot reasonably be expected to result in a significant adverse effect on the quality of the environment, taking into account the analyses and information in any applicable environmental impact statement prepared pursuant to section 109(c) or 109(d)'. Section 970.506 of the Regulations adds that 'This finding also will be based upon the considerations and approach in § 970.701', a section of the Regulations which summarises the

---

[299] Act, § 102(c)(1)(D); 30 USC § 1412(c)(1)(D).
[300] This regulatory approach is described in the Regulations (*loc. cit.* in note 291, § 970.100(c)(1)-(2).
[301] *Loc. cit.* in note 6(vi), at p. 15.
[302] *Loc. cit.* in note 6(xvi), at p. 11.
[303] For analysis, see below, section 2.3

440   Chapter 10

conclusions drawn by NOAA from the DOMES project on the identification of activities with a potential for adverse environmental impacts.

Thus, in making his finding, the Administrator will consider:

(i) NOAA's Final Programmatic Environmental Impact Statement,[304] drawn up largely on the basis of DOMES,[305] (ii) a site-specific environmental impact statement (EIS) and (iii) the provisions of section 970.701 of the Regulations, summarising NOAA's conclusions on the likelihood of significant adverse effects arising from exploration. Of these three elements, only number (ii) relates specifically to the particular application and, in preparing this site-specific EIS, the Administrator will rely upon information from several sources.

Much of the data will be supplied by the applicant in its application and exploration plan. The environmental information which applicants are bound to supply is detailed in section 970.204(a) of the Regulations which refers applicants to NOAA's Technical Guidance Document[306] but also relieves applicants of any need to duplicate information already available from the DOMES project. Applicants are also required to provide a description of the environmental monitoring equipment to be used and of their experience in using such equipment.[307] The applicant's exploration plan must provide information on measures to protect the environment and to monitor the effectiveness of environmental safeguards and monitoring systems for commercial recovery.[308]

Other elements which will contribute to the site-specific EIS and the Administrator's eventual finding include his assessment of the environmental relevance of the size and location of the area of the exploration plan,[309] the results of consultations with the various other Federal agencies having responsibilities for interests which may be affected by the proposed exploration[310] and the results of public hearings on applications.[311]

Under section 109(e) of the Act, any discharge of a pollutant from a vessel engaged in exploration is made subject to the Clean Water Act and, as a result, each licensee must obtain a National Pollutant Discharge Elimination System (NPDES) permit. However, NOAA worked closely with the Environmental Protection Agency (EPA) to assist the EPA with the development of a general NPDES permit.[312] The general permit was issued in 1984 for a period of five years. It covers only the discharges associated with the operation of survey ships engaged in exploration activities prior to at-sea testing.[313] The general permit

---

[304] NOAA, *loc. cit.* in note 6(iv). On this, see section II of this chapter.

[305] See reports cited in note 6(i)-(iii).

[306] NOAA, *loc. cit.* in note 6(v).

[307] Act, § 103; Regulations, § 970.202.

[308] Act, § 103; Regulations, § 970.203.

[309] Act, § 103(D).

[310] Regulations, §§ 970.211 and 970.502.

[311] Regulations, § 970.212.

[312] See further Regulations, 'Summary of Comments and Responses', reference to *NPDES requirements (loc. cit.* in note 291 at p. 45892 of *Federal Register*, p. 1230 of ILM); NOAA's *Report to Congress*, 1981 (*loc. cit.* in note 6(vi)), pp. 3-4; NOAA's *Report to Congress*, 1983 (*loc. cit.* in note 6(ix)), p. 12; and NOAA's *Report to Congress*, 1985 (*loc. cit.* in note 6(xiii)), p. 1.

[313] NOAA, *loc. cit.* in note 6(xiii), p. 11. See also NOAA, *Draft Environmental Impact Statement on Issuing an Exploration License to Ocean Minerals Co.*, May 1984, p. 50, section VI.A, as amended by

Protection of environment   441

will have to be amended or re-issued to cover at-sea mining systems tests if industry conducts these tests under a licence.[314] The EPA was called upon to review Draft Environmental Impact Statements prepared by NOAA in relation to the four exploration licences issued in 1984.[315] In all cases EPA had no objections to the proposed issue of the licence.[316]

In the site-specific EISs prepared in 1984, the need for confidentiality prevented NOAA from giving the location of the areas for which the four American exploration licences were issued.   However, following the revocation of this confidentiality requirement late in 1984, the publication of the location of foreign licence areas in 1988, and the amendment of the licensed areas in three of the American licences, following the international resolution of area conflicts, NOAA felt that a supplemental document incorporating this information should be prepared.[317]   Since the licence site information did not change any analysis in the EISs, NOAA decided that there was no need for a supplemental EIS[318] (which would have been necessary if the information reported had indicated an environmental impact) and that an 'environmental assessment' (EA) would suffice.   National Environmental Policy Act (NEPA) regulations[319] allow an agency to prepare an EA on any action, at any time, in order to assist agency planning and decisionmaking.   Accordingly, an *Updated Environmental Assessment of NOAA Deep Seabed Mining Licensees' Exploration Plans* [320] was published in January 1989 and declared to be 'a finding of no significant impact'.[321]

In 1993 the Kennecott Consortium surrendered its licence area (USA-4) and NOAA received an application from Ocean Minerals Company (OMCO) for an exploration licence for the surrendered area.   Although OMCO's proposed activities were recognised as having no potential for significant environmental impact, NOAA was nonetheless required by the Act to prepare an EIS before issuing the licence on 22 December 1994.[322]

2.2.2 Safeguards Incorporated in the Licence

The Administrator is required to include in each exploration licence Terms, Conditions and Restrictions (TCR) which might, *inter alia*, prescribe the actions

---

'Errata Sheet for Ocean Minerals Company' published as part of NOAA, *Final Environmental Impact Statement on Issuing an Exploration License to Ocean Minerals Company*, July 1984.

[314] NOAA, *loc. cit.* in note 6(xiii), p. 11. Such tests were again prohibited under the licence granted to OMCO in 1994. See further NOAA, *loc. cit.* in note 6(xx), at p. 3.

[315] In August 1984 exploration licences were issued to Ocean Minerals Company (OMCO), Ocean Mining Associates (OMA) and Ocean Management Inc. (OMI) (*Federal Register*, Vol. 49, No. 179, 13 September 1984) and in October 1984 a licence was issued to Kennecott Consortium (KCON) (*ibid.,* No. 218, 8 November 1984).   The geographic co-ordinates of the areas were published in the *Federal Register* later in the year (OMA –No. 220, 13 November 1984; OMCO and KCON – No. 232, 30 November 1984; OMI – No. 239, 11 December 1984). See also on these consortia Chap. 7, section V.

[316] NOAA, *loc. cit.* in note 6(xi), at pp. 6, 8, 10 and 12.

[317] NOAA, *loc. cit.* in note 6(xv), at pp. 5-7.

[318] *Ibid.*, at p. 7.

[319] 40 CFR 1501-3.

[320] NOAA, *loc. cit.* in note 6(xv).

[321] *Ibid.*, at p. 9.

[322] NOAA, *loc.cit.* in note 6(xxi), p. i. For the final EIS, see NOAA, *loc cit.* in note 6(xx).

442   *Chapter 10*

the licensee has to take to assure protection of the environment.[323] The TCR are to be uniform in all licences, except to the extent that differing physical and environmental conditions require the establishment of special TCR for, among other things, the protection of the environment.[324]

Before establishing TCR, the Administrator is required to consult and co-operate with a wide range of federal agencies which are responsible for marine interests which may be adversely affected by sea-bed mining. These agencies include the Environmental Protection Agency, the Secretary of State and the Secretary of the Department in which the coast guard is operating. *Inter alia,* consultation is designed to ensure compliance with, for example, the Endangered Species Act of 1973, the Marine Mammal Protection Act 1972 and the Fish and Wildlife Co-ordination Act.[325]

One term which was considered for inclusion in licences was a requirement that licensees should use the best available technology (BAT). As will be seen below, BAT is required by the Regulations for Commercial Recovery Permits but it is not required for exploration licences. The distinction was justified by NOAA as follows:

> Assuming that NOAA has identified a significant impact on the environment, a technology proven to be less damaging than others must be considered for mandatory use for commercial recovery permits under the BAT provisions of § 109(b) of the Act. Regarding exploration, NOAA currently has no finding of significant impact. NOAA also has no evidence of a technology with an order of magnitude difference in adverse impact. Accordingly, it is premature to specify BAT based on present findings and state of technology.[326]

As has been seen, NOAA's strategy is to allow exploration to proceed with relatively few constraints. An essential corollary to this approach, however, is provision for careful monitoring. Accordingly, a standard term of all licences requires the licensee to allow the Administrator to place federal observers aboard exploration vessels.[327] Their duties include assessment of the effectiveness of the licence TCR and reporting any failure to comply with such TCR. The Administrator is also required to develop for inclusion among TCR an environmental monitoring plan.[328] Licensees will be called upon to submit such information as the Administrator finds necessary 'to assess environmental impacts and to develop and evaluate possible methods of mitigating adverse

---

[323] Act, §§ 105 and 109(b); 30 USC §§ 1415 and 1419(b); Regulations, § 970.500. For an example of such TCR, see NOAA, *loc. cit.* in note 6(xx), App. 4, which embodies those proposed for one licensee, Ocean Minerals Company (OMCO).

[324] Act, § 105; 30 USC § 1415; Regulations, §§ 970.500 and 970.523.

[325] Act, § 109(b); 30 USC § 1419(b); Regulations, §§ 970.211 and 970.502.

[326] NOAA, *loc. cit.* in note 6(iv), Vol. II, p. 61.

[327] Act, § 114; 30 USC § 1424; Regulations, § 970.522. See, *e.g.,* para 6 of the TCR prescribed for OMCO (*loc. cit.* in note 323, at p. 71).

[328] Regulations, § 970.522(c). See, *e.g.,* para. 2 of TCR prescribed for OMCO (*loc. cit.* in note 323, at p. 68).

Protection of environment 443

environmental effects.'[329] Reflecting NOAA's gradualist, flexible strategy, it is provided that:

> The monitoring plan, among other things, will include monitoring environmental parameters relating to verification of NOAA's findings concerning potential impacts, but relating mainly to the three unresolved concerns with the potential for significant environmental effect, [as described earlier] ...[330]

Again reflecting NOAA's flexible, pragmatic approach, far-reaching powers are reserved to amend TCR if relevant data and other information (including, but not limited to, data resulting from exploration activities under the licence) indicate that modification is required to protect the quality of the environment.[331] Moreover, if monitoring and continued research produce information on future needs for mitigating environmental effects, TCR can be modified accordingly.[332]

2.2.3 Safeguards Provided by NOAA
The duties assigned to NOAA under the Act include a number of tasks which will provide further safeguards. Mention has already been made of NOAA's *Marine Environmental Research Plan 1981-85* [333] and of NOAA's role in placing observers aboard exploration vessels[334] and supervising industry's self-monitoring[335]. It remains to refer to NOAA's duties in relation to liaison with Reciprocating States, the establishment of stable reference areas, enforcement and biennial reports.

Liaison with Reciprocating States. Pursuant to section 118 of the Act, NOAA, in consultation with the State Department and other agencies, actively pursued negotiations with other States which had adopted unilateral sea-bed mining legislation. The objective was to bring about reciprocal designation as Reciprocating States, co-operation and consultation in developing compatible sea-bed mining legislation and the conclusion of an agreement to co-ordinate national legislation and avoid or resolve conflicting sea-bed claims.[336] In particular, the discussions dealt with co-operation in the development of regulatory requirements and research projects on the environmental effects of deep sea-bed mining and the establishment of international stable reference areas.[337] It is noteworthy that section 118(f) of the Act authorises the Administrator to:

---

[329] Act, §114(3); 30 USC § 1424(3); Regulations, § 970.522(c).
[330] Regulations, § 970.702.
[331] Act, § 105(c); 30 USC § 1415(c); Regulations, § 970.512(a)(2).
[332] Regulations, § 970.702(b).
[333] NOAA, *loc. cit.* in note 6(vii).
[334] Text above, at note 327.
[335] Text above, at note 328 and following.
[336] See further section V.3 below.
[337] See further Act, § 118 (30 USC § 1428), NOAA's *Report to Congress*, 1981 (*loc. cit.* in note 6(vi), at pp. 3, 19 and 31-33, NOAA's *Report to Congress*, 1983 (*loc. cit.* in note 6(ix)), at pp. 23-24,and NOAA's *Report to Congress, 1985* (*loc. cit.* in note 6(xiii)), at pp. 30-31. NOAA's *Report to Congress, 1987* (*loc. cit.* in note 6(xiv)), at pp. 31-32, NOAA's *Report to Congress, 1989* (*loc. cit.* in note 6(xvi)), at pp. ii and 10, NOAA's *Report to Congress, 1991* (*loc. cit.* in note 6(xviii)), at pp. 12-

444   *Chapter 10*

provide such foreign nations with information on environmental impacts of exploration and commercial recovery activities, and [to] ... provide any technical assistance requested in designing regulatory measures to protect the environment.

Stable reference areas. 'Stable reference areas' (SRAs) are defined in the Act[338] as:

an area or areas of the deep seabed to be used as a reference zone or zones for purposes of resource evaluation and environmental assessment of deep seabed mining in which no mining will occur.

Such areas are to be identified in negotiations with Reciprocating States and it is specifically provided that they may not be established unilaterally.[339] Within four years after 28 June 1980, NOAA was required to make a progress report to Congress on the establishment of such areas, 'including the designation of appropriate zones to insure a representative and stable biota of the seabed'.[340]

The report was duly submitted in June 1984 and indicated that, although talks had taken place with other potential deep sea-bed mining countries, 'in-depth discussion of SRAs [had] been deferred pending completion of a thorough study of the scientific requirements for meaningful implementation of the SRA concept.'[341] The Ocean Policy Board of the National Academy of Sciences' National Research Council (NRC) was accordingly requested to evaluate the scientific validity of the SRA concept and to design a cost effective means to implement it. The NRC report determined that the concept was scientifically valid and recommended a research programme to provide the scientific basis for designating such areas and effectively assessing impact.[342] It was further recommended that international consultation 'should be undertaken immediately to maximise the collection of complementary field data and to minimise potential conflicts between reference and mining areas'.[343] Such consultation would also help to promote the acceptance of the SRA concept and refine the characteristics and locations of such areas.[344]

On the basis of the NRC report, NOAA decided that SRAs did not need to be established during the exploration phase but planned to draft regulations for the

---

14, NOAA's *Report to Congress*, 1993 (*loc. cit.* in note 6(xix)), pp. 11-13, and NOAA's *Report to Congress*, 1995 (*loc. cit.* in note 6(xxi)), at pp. 12-14.

[338] § 109(f)(4); 30 USC § 1419(f)(4).

[339] § 109(f)(2); 30 USC § 1419(f)(2).

[340] § 109(f)(3); 30 USC § 1419(f)(3).

[341] US Department of State, *Stable Reference Areas. Report to Congress*, 29 June 1984, at p. i.

[342] *Deep Seabed Stable Reference Areas. Report of a Study* (Board on Ocean Science and Policy, Commission on Physical Sciences, Mathematics, and Resources, National Research Council), 1984, at p. 2.

[343] *Ibid.*, at p. 3.

[344] *Ibid.*

Protection of environment 445

commercial recovery of deep sea-bed nodules 'which would allow for the inclusion of a strategy for implementing the SRA concept'.[345]

Enforcement. A range of enforcement measures is provided for in the Act and Regulations. Briefly,[346] they include, in addition to the placement of federal observers, already referred to, the assessment by the administrator of a civil penalty; the imposition of a fine; forfeiture of vessel and other property; and suspension or revocation of a licence or suspension or modification of activities under a licence. Provision is also made for the institution of civil proceedings against the Administrator by a person whose interests have been adversely affected by the failure of the Administrator to perform a non-discretionary duty under the Act.

Biennial reports. Finally, reference must be made to section 309 of the Act which provides for the submission by the Administrator to Congress of biennial reports on the administration of the Act, including:

> An assessment of the environmental impacts, including a description and estimate of any damage caused by any adverse effects on the quality of the environment resulting from such activities.[347]

2.3 Environmental Safeguards in the Commercial Recovery Phase

As was noted above, NOAA's earlier, gradualist approach to the preparation of regulations governing the environmental impact of commercial recovery gave way more recently to an acknowledgement by NOAA of the need to proceed more expeditiously and final Deep Seabed Mining Regulations for Commercial Recovery permits were published on 6 January 1989.[348]

As was the case with the earlier Regulations for Exploration Licenses,[349] the environmental provisions of the Commercial Recovery Regulations can best be understood if they are considered as falling into three categories:
(i) regulatory safeguards prior to the issue of the commercial recovery permit;
(ii) regulatory safeguards incorporated in the permit; and
(iii) regulatory safeguards provided by NOAA.

2.3.1 Safeguards Prior to the Issue of the Commercial Recovery Permit

No significant adverse effect

Under section 105(a)(4) of the Act, before issuing a permit for commercial recovery, the NOAA Administrator must make a finding that the proposed commercial recovery 'cannot reasonably be expected to result in a significant

---

[345] *Loc. cit.* in note 341 at p. 11. On the provision made for 'impact reference areas' and 'interim preservational reference areas' in the 1989 Regulations for Commercial Recovery, see further below, section V.2.3.3.

[346] For further details, see Act, §§ 117 and 302-304; 30 USC §§ 1427 and 1462-1464, and Regulations, §§ 970.1100-970.1107.

[347] Act, § 309(b)(3); 30 USC § 1469(b)(3). For reference to reports made between 1981 and 1995, see *loc. cit.* in note 6(vi), (ix), (xiii), (xiv), (xvi), (xviii), (xix) and (xxi). As noted in note 6(xxi), further reports have been suspended pending an increased level of activity.

[348] *Loc. cit.* in note 292.

[349] See above, section V.2.2.

446 *Chapter 10*

adverse effect on the quality of the environment, taking into account the analyses and information in any applicable environmental impact statement prepared pursuant to section 109(c) or 109(d)'. The term 'significant adverse environmental effect' is defined in the Regulations to mean:

(1) important adverse changes in ecosystem diversity, productivity, or stability of the biological communities within the environment; (2) threat to human health through direct exposure to pollutants or through consumption of exposed aquatic organisms; or (3) important loss of aesthetic, recreational, scientific or economic values.[350]

The manner in which such a determination is made is considered further below.

Applications to contain environmental information
To assist the Administrator in performing his duties in relation to applications for recovery permits, the applicant is required by the Regulations to include specified environmental information in the application.
Applications must include:

- sufficient marine environmental information to allow the Administrator to prepare an Environmental Impact Statement and to determine appropriate permit TCRs;[351]
- a description of the technology or equipment and methods to be used in carrying out environmental monitoring;[352]
- a proposed commercial recovery plan referring, *inter alia*, to environmental safeguards and monitoring systems which must take into account the requirements of Subpart F of the Regulations ('Environmental Effects'), including use of best available technologies (BAT)[353] and at-sea monitoring;[354] and to the methods to be used for disposal of wastes from recovery and processing;[355]
- onshore information to enable NOAA to prepare a site-specific EIS. The detailed information required includes: (1) The location and affected environment of port, transport, processing and waste disposal facilities and associated facilities (for example, maps, land use and layout); and (2) A description of the environmental consequences and socio-economic effects of construction and operation of the facilities, including waste characteristics and toxicity;[356]

---

[350] § 971.101(s).
[351] § 971.204(a).
[352] § 971.202(b)(1).
[353] §§ 971.203(b)(3) and 971.604.
[354] § 971.603.
[355] § 971.203(b)(7).
[356] § 971.606(a).

Protection of environment 447

- a monitoring plan for test-mining and at-sea commercial recovery activities which meets the objectives and requirements laid down in section 971.603 of the Regulations ('At-sea monitoring').

Public notice, hearing and comment

In preparing the EIS, the Administrator has to attempt 'to characterise the environment in such a way as to provide a basis for judging the potential for significant adverse effects or irreparable harm triggered by commercial mining'.[357] 'Irreparable harm' is defined to mean 'significant undesirable effects to the environment occurring after the date of the permit issuance which will not be reversed after cessation or modification of the activities authorised under the permit.'[358]

After preparing the draft EIS on an application, the Administrator is required to hold a public hearing on the application and the draft EIS.[359] He has also to publish notice that the application has been received and interested persons may then submit written comments.[360]

Certification of applications: required findings

'Certification' in this context is the process, intermediate between receipt of the application and issue of the recovery permit, whereby the Administrator has to make a determination focusing on the eligibility of the applicant.[361] One of the 'findings' which he is required to make is approval of the size and location of the commercial recovery area selected by the applicant and such approval 'will occur' unless the Administrator determines that, *inter alia*, 'commercial recovery activities in the proposed area would result in a significant adverse environmental effect which cannot be avoided by imposition of reasonable restrictions'.[362]

Significant adverse environmental effects

As was seen above, section 105(a)(4) of the Act, the central environmental provision of this statute, requires the Administrator, before issuing a recovery permit, to find that the proposed commercial recovery cannot reasonably be expected to result in a significant adverse effect on the quality of the environment. This provision is developed further in the somewhat repetitious sections 971.406 and 971.601 of the Regulations.

Section 971.406 provides that:

Before issuing or transferring a commercial recovery permit, the Administrator must find that the commercial recovery proposed in the application cannot reasonably be expected to result in a significant adverse environmental effect, taking into account the analyses and information in any applicable EIS and any TCRs associated with the permit. This finding also

---

[357] § 971.204(b)(1).
[358] § 971.101(l).
[359] § 971.212(b).
[360] § 971.212(a).
[361] § 971.300(a).
[362] § 971.301(a).

448 Chapter 10

will be based upon the requirements in Subpart F. However, as also noted in Subpart F, if a determination on this question cannot be made on the basis of available information, and it is found that irreparable harm will not occur during a period when an approved monitoring program is undertaken to further examine the significant adverse environmental effect issue, a permit may be granted, subject to modification or suspension and, if necessary and appropriate, revocation pursuant to § 971.417(a), or subject to emergency suspension pursuant to § 971.417(h).

Section 971.601, which is part of the Subpart F referred to above, repeats the substance of this provision but then goes on to add that, in examining this issue, NOAA has to give consideration to specified Ocean Discharge Criteria laid down in the Clean Water Act, as they may pertain to discharges and other environmental perturbations related to the commercial recovery operations.

Section 971.602 throws further light on the process of determination of adverse environmental effects. The Administrator is to make the determination on a case-by-case basis. The determination is to be based on the best information available, including relevant environmental impact statements, NOAA-collected data, monitoring results, and other data provided by the applicant, as well as consideration of the criteria in the Clean Water Act, already referred to. The Administrator may also take into account any TCRs or other mitigation measures. The nature of such 'related terms, conditions and restrictions' is further specified in section 971.602(f) which refers to 'TCRs containing environmental requirements with respect to protection (pursuant to section 971.419), mitigation (pursuant to section 971.419), or best available technology requirements (pursuant to section 971.423), as appropriate, and monitoring requirements (pursuant to section 971.424) to acquire more information on the environmental effects of deep seabed mining.'

Section 971.602(d)-(e) records the NOAA research findings, referred to above,[363] to the effect that NOAA believes that exploration-type activities require no further environmental assessment. On the other hand, NOAA research has identified at-sea testing of recovery equipment, the recovery of manganese nodules in commercial quantities from the deep seabed, and the construction and operation of commercial-scale processing facilities as activities which may have some potential for significant adverse environmental effects.[364]

TCRs, public hearings and consultations with Federal and State agencies

TCRs. After certification of an application,[365] the Administrator has to propose terms, conditions and restrictions for the proposed permit which have to be uniform in all permits except to the extent that differing physical and environmental conditions and/or mining methods require the establishment of special TCRs for, *inter alia*, protection of the environment.[366]

---

[363] See above, sections II and V.2.2.1 of this chapter.
[364] See above, section II of this chapter.
[365] See text above following note 360.
[366] § 971.400(a)-(b).

Public hearings. Reference is again made to the provision for the submission by interested persons of written comments on draft EISs and proposed terms, conditions and restrictions; and for public hearings.[367]

Consultations with Federal and State agencies. Provision is made in sections 971.200(g) and 971.211 for pre-application consultations between the applicant and NOAA or the applicant and affected States; and for consultations and co-operation between NOAA and Federal agencies or departments. It is subsequently provided in section 971.402 that, before issue of a recovery permit, the Administrator must conclude any such consultations or co-operation with other Federal and State agencies and it is indicated that:

> These consultations will be held to assure compliance with, as applicable and among other statutes, the Endangered Species Act of 1973, as amended, the Marine Mammal Protection Act of 1972, as amended, the Fish and Wildlife Coordination Act, and the Coastal Zone Management Act of 1972, as amended. The Administrator also will consult, before any issuance, transfer, modification or renewal of a permit, with any affected Regional Fishery Management Council established pursuant to section 302 of the Magnuson Fishery Conservation and Management Act of 1976 (16 U.S.C. 1852) if the activities undertaken pursuant to the permit could adversely affect any fishery within the Fishery Conservation Zone (now known as the Exclusive Economic Zone), or any anadromous species or Continental Shelf fishery resource subject to the exclusive management authority of the United States beyond that zone.[368]

2.3.2 Safeguards Incorporated in Commercial Recovery Permit

Environmental protection TCRs
Each commercial recovery permit must contain TCRs which prescribe actions the permittee must take to assure protection of the environment.[369] Reference is made to sections 971.601 and 971.602, considered above,[370] for an indication of the factors to be taken into account regarding the potential for significant adverse environmental effects.[371] Before establishing such TCRs, the Administrator has to consult the Administrator of the Environmental Protection Agency, the Secretary of State and the Secretary of the department in which the Coast Guard is operating. He has also to take into account and give due consideration to formal comments received from the public, including those from the State agency, and to the information contained in the final site-specific EIS prepared with respect to the proposed permit.[372]

---

[367] § 971.401(a) and (b).
[368] § 971.402.
[369] § 971.419(a).
[370] See above, section 2.3.1, under 'Significant adverse environmental effects'.
[371] § 971.419(a).
[372] § 971.419(b).

450   *Chapter 10*

TCRs on best available technologies (BAT) and mitigation
The use of BAT will be required for the protection of the environment wherever activities under a permit would have a significant adverse effect on the environment, except where the Administrator determines that the incremental benefits would clearly be insufficient to justify the incremental costs of using such technologies.[373]   However, given the embryonic nature of the industry, NOAA is not in a position to specify particular equipment and, pending the accumulation of experience, places the onus on the applicant to submit such information as is necessary to indicate that it is using BAT.   Similarly, the permittee is required to report any proposed technological or operational changes that will increase or have unknown environmental effects and, again, to submit information indicating the use of BAT.   If proposed changes have a high potential for increasing adverse environmental effects, the Administrator may disapprove or require modification of the changes.[374]

In the same vein, NOAA is not yet in a position to specify particular mitigation methodologies or techniques but requires applicants to submit plans describing how they would mitigate a problem.[375]

Monitoring TCRs
Permittees will be required to allow the Administrator to place Federal observers aboard vessels used in commercial recovery.[376]   Monitoring of the environmental effects of recovery activities will be carried out in accordance with a monitoring plan submitted by the applicant and approved and issued by NOAA as permit TCRs.   The detailed information to be included in monitoring plans is specified in section 971.603.   It is indicated in section 971.603(j) that the Administrator intends to place observers on board mining vessels, 'not only to ensure that permit TCRs are followed, but also to evaluate the effectiveness of monitoring strategies, both in terms of protecting the environment and in being cost-effective ..., and if necessary, to develop potential mitigation measures.   If modification of permit TCRs or regulations is required to protect the quality of the environment, the Administrator may modify TCRs pursuant to section 971.414, or the regulations pursuant to section 971.804'.

Special TCRs
Under section 971.429, the Administrator may impose special TCRs for the protection of the environment when required by differing physical and environmental conditions.

---

[373] §§ 971.423 and 971.604.
[374] § 971.604(a) and (c).
[375] § 971.604(b).
[376] §§ 971.424 and 971.603.

Protection of environment 451

Changes of circumstances

Permittees are required to advise the Administrator of any changes of circumstances which might constitute a revision which would be a major change as defined in section 971.412(c).[377]

Annual reports and records

Permittees will be required to submit information on their recovery activities to the Administrator upon request. At a minimum, they must submit annual reports. *Inter alia*, the reports must cover commercial recovery activities and expenditures and the implementation of approved monitoring plans.[378]

2.3.3. Safeguards Provided by NOAA

Sanctions

To ensure compliance with the Act, Regulations and TCRs, a range of sanctions is available. Subpart J of the Regulations provides uniform rules and procedures for their application by the Administrator.

(i) *Fines.* Section 303 of the Act provides for the imposition of fines for violations of any provision of the Act, regulations issued under it or permit issued under it.[379]

(ii) *Civil penalties.* Section 302 of the Act provides for civil penalties up to $25,000 per violation.[380]

(iii) *Suspension or revocation of permit or suspension or modification of activities.* Under section 106 of the Act and sections 971.1000(a)(2) and 971.1003 of the Regulations, the Administrator is empowered to suspend or revoke a permit or suspend or modify any particular activity/ies if the permittee 'substantially fails to comply with any provision of the Act, any regulation or order issued under' it or any TCRs in the permit. The effective date of the sanction is 30 days after the date of the prescribed notice of sanction unless it is made effective earlier, following the issue by the Administrator of an emergency order indicating that earlier application is necessary, *inter alia,* to prevent a significant adverse environmental effect.

(iv) *Seizure and forfeiture of vessels.* Section 304 of the Act and section 971.1004 of the Regulations, make provision for seizure and possible forfeiture of vessels involved in a violation of the Act.

Observers and monitoring

Section 114 of the Act authorised the Administrator to place observers on vessels used by the licensee or permitee in exploration or commercial recovery activities in order to monitor the environmental effects of such activities. Section 971.1005 of the Regulations provides details of the procedure to be followed. Such observers may 'board and accompany' any such vessel 'for the purpose of

---

[377] § 971.425.
[378] §§ 971.426 and 971.801.
[379] Also referred to briefly in §§ 971.417(a)(1) and 971.1003(a).
[380] § 971.1000(a).

452   Chapter 10

observing, evaluating and reporting on', *inter alia,* the environmental effects of the licesee's or permittee's activities.[381]

Under section 971.603(d), the monitoring of benthic impact is to involve the study of two types of areas: (1) an *impact reference area,* located in a portion of a permit area tentatively scheduled to be mined early in a commercial recovery plan; and (2) an *interim preservational reference area,* located in a portion of a permit area tentatively determined to be non-mineable, not to be scheduled for mining during the commercial recovery plan, or to be scheduled for mining late in the plan.   Reference areas have to be selected by the permittee in consultation with NOAA, have to be representative of the environmental characteristics of the permittee's site and may be selected provisionally, prior to application for a commercial recovery permit.[382]

In 1988 NOAA designated a site within the Clarion-Clipperton Fracture Zone as a potential Provisional Interim Preservational Reference Area (PIPRA).   The proposed site totals 15,157 km^2 in area and is made up of adjacent areas contributed from the licensed exploration areas held by Ocean Mining Associates (OMA, licence USA-3) and Ocean Minerals Co. (OMCO - licences USA-1 and USA-4).[383]   NOAA has continued to evaluate its suitability as a Preservational Reference Area (PRA).[384] The use of the term 'interim' in this context apparently indicates that the area may serve the purpose of a preservational area 'until areas are designated internationally.'[385]

Also in 1988, OMA requested consultations with NOAA for the early designation of a Provisional Impact Reference Area (PIRA), an area of about 4,629 km^2 within its licence site and NOAA designated it as a proposed PIRA.[386]

Modification of TCRs and amendment of Regulations
The Administrator is empowered, after consultation with appropriate Federal agencies and the permittee, to modify TCRs in a permit if 'relevant data and information (including, but not limited to, data resulting from activities under a permit) indicate that modification is required to protect the quality of the environment ...'.[387]

The Administrator is empowered also to amend the Regulations for Commercial Recovery Permits at any time if he determines it to be necessary and appropriate for the protection of the environment.[388]

---

[381] § 971.1005(a).
[382] On Stable Reference Areas during the exploration phase, see above, section V.2.2.3. On the impact reference zones and preservation reference zones envisaged in the Mining Code, see above, section IV.6.4.1.
[383] As noted above in section V.2.2.1, licence USA-4, surrendered by KCON in 1993, was issued to OMCO in 1994.
[384] See further NOAA, *loc. cit.* in note 6(xvi), at pp. 13-14, *loc. cit.* in note 6(xviii), at p. 11 and *loc. cit.* in note 6(xix), at p. 11.
[385] NOAA, *loc. cit.* in note 6(xvi), at p. 13.
[386] NOAA, *loc. cit.* in note 6(xvi), at pp. 15-16, *loc. cit.* in note 6(xviii), at p. 11 and *loc. cit.* in note 6(xix), at p. 11.
[387] § 971.414(a)(2).
[388] § 971.804.

Protection of environment 453

2.4 Environmental Safeguards for Pre-Enactment Exploration

The Deep Seabed Mining Regulations Affecting Pre-Enactment Explorers[389] were designed to enable NOAA to identify the pre-enactment explorers who, under the Act, were granted a temporary exemption from the prohibition of unlicensed exploration, and to assist NOAA in carrying out its statutory duty to issue emergency orders, where necessary to prevent a significant adverse effect on the environment. Accordingly, the Regulations required notice to be given to NOAA of each future pre-licence exploration voyage[390] and a report to be submitted to NOAA of any environmental data acquired on a future exploration voyage.[391] In addition, the Administrator was fully authorised to issue an emergency order requiring the immediate suspension of exploration activities.[392]

2.5 Polymetallic Sulphide Ores

As has been seen in Chapter 4, ores containing such valuable metals as copper, zinc and silver have been discovered at the spreading edges of tectonic plates and are thought to result from 'hydro-thermal activity'. In its 1981 *Report to Congress*, NOAA declared its intention to evaluate their potential and to consider the need to establish an additional legal regime for their commercial exploitation.[393]

3. The Co-ordination of National Legislation

As was seen above,[394] one of the objects of NOAA's negotiations with other States was the conclusion of an agreement to co-ordinate national legislation and avoid or resolve conflicting sea-bed claims. The earlier results of these negotiations, the two agreements concluded in 1982 and 1984, have been considered in detail in Chapter 7.[395] The first of them, the Agreement Concerning Interim Arrangements Relating to Polymetallic Nodules of the Deep Sea Bed, 1982,[396] made no reference to environmental matters. The second agreement, however, concluded between eight States in 1984, contained several provisions dealing with the protection of the environment.

The Provisional Understanding Regarding Deep Seabed Matters and the related Memorandum on the Implementation of the Understanding, both signed on 3 August 1984, not only provided for the co-ordination of national legislation; they also prescribed common standards.[397] Under Paragraph 1 of the Memorandum on Implementation, authorisations were to be issued only to applicants whose operations would be carried out in accordance with prescribed

---

[389] *Loc. cit.* in note 291.
[390] § 970.2501.
[391] § 970.2502.
[392] § 970.2503.
[393] NOAA, *loc. cit.* in note 6(vi), pp. 4 and 36. The Deep Seabed Hard Mineral Resources Act 1980, section 4(6), defines 'hard mineral resource' as referring only to nodules. For developments at the international level on non-nodule minerals, see Chap. 4, section XVIII.
[394] See above, section V.2.2.3, under 'Liaison with Reciprocating States'.
[395] See Chap. 7, section III.
[396] See further Chap. 7, section III.1.
[397] See further Chap. 7, section III.2.

454 Chapter 10

standards and States parties had to ensure that sea-bed operations under their control included efforts to protect the quality of the environment and did not result in significant adverse effects on the environment. To this end, operations had to be monitored.[398]

VI. CONCLUSIONS

Reviewing the above record of what has been achieved so far, there would appear to be grounds for cautious optimism that deep-sea mining may prove to be one area of industrial activity where the attendant threat to the environment has been identified and guarded against before it actually materialised.

It is fortunate that the whole question of sea-bed mining arose at a time in history when the international community had been fully alerted to the dangers of pollution generally and to the threat to the marine environment in particular. It has been helpful too that the technical problems posed by sea-bed mining and the consequent lengthy period of research and development preceding commercial recovery have presented international and domestic legislators with ample time and opportunity to investigate the environmental threat and devise adequate safeguards; and, of course, the moratorium will continue until commercial recovery is considered to be economically viable. It seems fair to say that good use has been made and is continuing to be made of the breathing space so afforded, both on the domestic and international levels.

As has been seen, on the domestic level, the United States Government has adopted a regulatory approach which reflects the nature of the problem. Thus, the still uncertain nature of the threat to the environment is mirrored in the flexible, evolving strategy described above, under which the adequacy of the regulatory safeguards are constantly tested in the light of continuing research on the impact of deep-sea mining on the environment. At the same time, care has been taken to arm the administration with adequate powers to act speedily and effectively as soon as the programme of research, monitoring and inspection identifies a threat. There can be little doubt that policy makers in other States have been greatly influenced by this regulatory approach, as well as by the results of the scientific work undertaken by NOAA and the legislative models developed by the United States authorities. It is noteworthy that, in recent years, much of the continuing research has been conducted by the United States in collaboration with other States.

On the international level too, commendable progress has been made by incorporating in the UN Convention extensive provision for the protection of the environment of the Area. In developing these provisions further in the Mining Code, it seems fair to say that the Legal and Technical Commission and the Council of the Authority have struck a sensible balance between the need to protect the environment and the need not to place unreasonable burdens upon sea-bed miners.

---

[398] For further details of the environmentally-relevant provisions of the Provisional Understanding and the Memorandum, see Chap. 7, section III.2.3.2.

Index of Persons

Amerasinghe, H.S., 30
Anderson, D.H., 16
Arangio-Ruiz, G., 24
Archer, A.A., 278
Arend, A.C., 93
Auburn, F.M., 93
Barnett, B.G., 380, 386
Berge, S., 380
Beurier, J.-P., xxvii
Birnie, P.W., 149
Bond, M., xxvii
Bowett, D.W., 317
Bridge, J.W., 366, 367
Broad, W.J., 149
Brown, E.D., 3, 4, 15, 18, 40, 73,
    74, 83, 93, 94, 99, 295, 353, 354,
    373, 396, 397
Burke, W.T., 149
Burns, R.E. 381
Caflisch, L., 93, 147, 362, 369
Cheng, B., 24, 26
Couper, A., 93
Deeley, L., xxvii
Desa, E., 387
Engo, P.B., 111, 189
Evensen, J., 111
Feng, L., 388
Finlay, L.W., 354
Flanagan, J.P., xxvii, 381
Galindo Pohl, Mr., 29
Glowka, L., 149
Glumov, I.F., 389
Hamad, Mr., 69

Hayashi, M., xxvii, 8, 437
Haynes, B., 399
Higgins, R., 24
Hyun, J.-H., 388
Jesus, J.L., 40
Jones, A.T., 380
Jugel, K., 381
Kajitani, Y., 387
Kateka J.L., 217
Koch, J., xxvii
Koh, T., 189, 192, 255
Kotlinski, R., 387
Kovalev, Mr., 62
Lagoni, R., xxvii, 431
Lasok, D., 366, 367
Lauterpacht, H., 24, 25
Lawless, J., xxvii, 383
Lee, K.-Y., 388
Lodge, M., xxvii
Lowe, A.V., 255
MacGibbon, I.C., 24, 25, 26
MacGregor, Mr., 261, 262, 263, 266
Markussen, J.M., 380
Miller, H. Crane, 93
Morgan, C.L., 380
Nandan, S., 103, 398, 399, 418
Nordquist, M.H., 60, 101, 115, 116,
    121, 133, 138, 293, 318, 323,
    331, 370
Njenga, Mr., 66, 69, 111
Nyhart, J.D., 20
Odunton, N.A., 380
O'Keefe, P.J., 93

456 *Index of persons*

Ozturgut, E., 381, 383, 386, 399
Papadakis, N., 21
Pardo, A., 3, 23, 350
Park, Choon-ho, 60, 101, 115, 116,
  121, 133, 138, 293, 318, 323,
  331, 370
Perisic, Mr., 57
Platzöder, R., xxvii
Prott, L.V., 93
Ratiner, L., 102
Riesenfeld, S.A., 217
Rogers, A., xxvii
Rosenboom, A., xxviii
Rosenne, S., 62
Rozakis, C.L., 147, 362
Schricke, Mr., 214
Schriever, G., 388
Schwarzenberger, G., 18, 57, 74
Sharma, R., 387
Shirayama, Y., 387

Sinclair, I.M., 57
Stephanou, C.A., 147, 362
Stevenson, G.R., 27, 28
Strati, A., 93
Thiel, H., 383, 388
Tkatchenko, G., 387
Treves, T., xxvii, 437
Trueblood, D.D., 383
Truman, H., 3
Tsurusaki, K., 386
van Lanschot, Mr., 218
van Meurs, L.H., 93
Verhoosel, G., 149
Verdross, A., 57
Vigerust G., 380
Warioba, J.S., 217, 218, 220
Wilson, G., 399
Wolfrum, R., 40
Yamada, H., 387
Yamazaki, T., 387

Subject Index

Abuse of rights, 74
'Activities in the Area', 53
  accommodation of with activities
    in marine environment, 86-88
  policies relating to, 100-104
  who may carry out, 109-120
Administrative disputes, 373
Advisory Opinion of ICJ,
  possibility of on sea-bed mining,
    255
Agreement Concerning Interim
  Arrangements Relating to
  Polymetallic Nodules of the
  Deep Sea Bed, 1982, 268-270
  compatibility with UN regime,
    270
  identification and resolution of
    conflicts, 269-270
  material scope, 269
  personal scope, 268
  temporal scope, 269
Archaeological and historical
  objects, 53, 54, 92-95, 109
'Area' beyond limits of national
  jurisdiction,
  development of resources of,
    96-151
  legal status of, 72-73
  limits of, disputes concerning,
    373-374
  Pardo proposal (1967), 3
  position of in 1967, 3
  principles of regime governing,
    49-95

'Area' beyond limits of national
  jurisdiction *cont.*
  use for peaceful purposes, 73
'Area', defined 52-53
Arusha Understanding (1986), 221-
  226
Assembly of the Authority, 295-297
  composition, 295
  decision-making, 295-296
  powers and functions, 296-297
Authority,
  establishment and purpose, 293
  organs, 293-342
    Enterprise, the, *q.v.*
    principal organs, 295-317
      Assembly, *q.v.*
      Council, *q.v.*
      Secretariat, 317
  provisional membership,11-12

'Banking' system, 131
Benefit of mankind, 65-71, 75
  beneficiaries 65-71
  distribution of, 70-71
  principle governing the Area, 75

Coastal States,
  rights and legitimate interests in
    sea-bed resources, 78
Cobalt crusts, 53, 149-151
Commercial arbitral tribunal, 357
Commodity arrangements, 134

458 *Subject index*

Common heritage of mankind, 3-46
  beneficiaries, 65-71
  distribution of benefits, 70-71
  freedom of the seas, conflict
    with, 14-46
  fundamental principle and
    alternative models
    distinguished, 43
  fundamental principle of UN
    regime, 49-71
  ideology or reality?, 5
  new species of *res communis*, 15
  versus unilateralism, 248-249
  view of industrialised States, 4
Compensatory economic assistance,
  124,127-131
Contractual disputes, 369-372
Contractual liability, 144-147
  of Authority, 145-146
    disclosure of industrial secrets,
      146-147
  of contractor, 144-145
Cook Islands, 59,60
Council of the Authority, 297-317
  composition, 297-307
  decision-making, 308-311
  powers and functions, 307-311
  subsidiary organs, 311-317

Declaration of PrepCom
  condemning Provisional
  Understanding regarding Deep
  Seabed Matters, 1984 (1985),
  31-32, 39, 210-212
Declaration of Principles Resolution
  (1970),
  States' comments on status of,
  28-32. *See also under* Table of
  UN and UNCLOS Resolutions.
Developing States,
  beneficiaries of common
    heritage, 65-71
  economic assistance to, 127-131
  marine scientific research, 79
  participation of in activities in
    the Area, 88-92

Developing States *cont.*
  positive discrimination in favour
    of, 74, 328
  transfer of technology to, 81-84
Development of resources of the
  Area, 96-151
Dispute settlement. *See* Settlement
  of disputes.
DOMES, 381-382, 440

Economic assistance fund, 130-131
Economic assistance to developing
  countries, 124, 127-131
Emergency orders, 423-427
Enterprise, the,
  disputes concerning, 322-323,
    332-333, 335, 375
  immunities and privileges,
    332-333
  legal personality, 322-323
  liability, 333-335
  operations, 324-328
    capacity to carry out,
      324-325
    commercial basis of, 328
    financial arrangements,
      328-332
    non-discrimination, 328
    outside reserved sites,
      327
    plans of work, 325
    reserved areas, 326-327
  relationship to Authority,
    317-318
  responsibility of, 333
  role of, 317-318
  structure, 323-324
  title to minerals and processed
    substances, 328
  transfer of technology to,
    81-84, 327
European Economic Community,
  Declarations on signature of
    UN Convention, 61
  participation in UN Convention,
    61

Subject index   459

Exploitation of resources of Area, who may carry our activities?, 109-123. *See also under* Exploration and Exploitation.

Exploration, Mining Code, 152-186. *See also under* Mining Code.

Exploration and Exploitation, the system of, 109-123
background, 109-112
plans of work, 117-123
role of Authority, 112-113
security of tenure for contractors, 123
who may carry out activities, 113-117

Finance Committee, 313-317
Financial Regulations, 90, 130, 140
Financial terms of contracts, 134-140
accounting and audit, 140
currency of payments or payments in kind, 140
disputes, 140
objectives, 136-137
pioneer investor financial arrangements, 193-194, 236-237
profit-sharing, 139-140
royalty system, 139-140
types of payments, 137-140
annual fixed fee, 138-139
application fee, 138
Freedom of the high seas, principle of, 3,4
artificial islands, freedom to construct, 21
as basis of Reciprocating States Regime, 4
as fundamental principle of international law, 18-19
cables and pipelines, freedom to lay, 21
deep sea mining as a freedom, any rule prohibiting?, 19-22

Freedom of the high seas *cont.*
dumping of toxic materials, as a freedom, 21
earlier State practice, 18
essential character of, 18-19
legal presumptions in favour of, 15
versus Common Heritage of Mankind, 14-46
versus Sovereignty, 14-15
weapons testing, as a freedom, 21
Fundamental principles in conflict, 14-46
freedom of the seas *v.* common heritage of mankind, 15-17, 17-22
freedom of the seas *v.* sovereignty, 14-15
legal presumptions, 15. *See also under* Common heritage of mankind *and* Freedom of high seas.

General Assembly Resolutions, legal effect of, 24-27
Good faith, 74
Group of 77, 4, 31-41
extreme view on common heritage principle, 72
Group of Legal Experts' letter on unilateral legislation on sea-bed (1979), 31, 34-38, 248
significance of 'practice' of, 31-32, 46
speech of Chairman, 15 September 1978, 38-39
statement declaring position on unilateral legislation on sea-bed (1978), 31, 38
who may exploit Area, view of on, 109
Group of Legal Experts of Group of 77, 31
Letter on unilateral legislation on sea-bed (1979), 31, 34-38, 248

460 *Subject index*

Human Life, protection of, as
  principle of the Area, 85-86

Implementation Agreement.
  status, 6-13. *See also under*
  Table of Treaties and
  International Regulations.
Industrial secrets, disclosure of,
  146-147
  disputes over liability for,   372,
  373
Industrialised States,
  practice of on sea-bed mining,
  41-45
  significance of practice of, 43-45,
  46
Installations for activities in
  the Area, 86-88
International Law Commission,
  on freedom to exploit sea-bed,
  21-22
International organisations,
  participation in UN Convention,
  59, 60-62
International Tribunal for the Law
  of the Sea, 354-357
  ad hoc chambers, 356-357
  composition, 354-355
  particular category chambers, 355
  seat of, 354
  special chambers, 355-356
  summary procedure chamber,
    355.   *See also under*
    Settlement of Disputes.

Jus cogens,
  UN Convention, common
    heritage regime as, 45, 57-59

Legal and Technical Commission,
  312-313
Legal effect of General Assembly
  Resolutions, 24-27

Legislation of Western States on
  sea-bed mining,187-188, 244-291
  anti-monopoly provisions?, 257-
  260
  benefits of operating under, 252-
  256
  common heritage versus
    unilateralism, 248-249
  diligence provisions, 257-260
  financial provisions, 261-266
  land-based mineral producers,
    protection of, 260
  legal basis of, 246-248
  licences, who may apply for,
    251-252
  personal scope, 249-251
  reasons for, 246-248
  reservation of sites, 256-257
  technology transfer, 266-267
  temporal scope, 249. *See also*
    under Reciprocating States
    Regime.
Maltese initiative, 3, 22-23
Maltese Memorandum, 3, 22
Mare clausum, 14
Mare liberum, 15
Marine environment. *See under*
  Pollution.
Marine scientific research, 53
  in the Area,79-81
'Mini-treaties', 39
Mining Code, 96-100,152-186. *See*
also Table of Contents, Chap. 5.
  exploration, 152-186
  confidentiality of data, 182-
    186
  contract for, 165-182
  marine environment, protection
    of, 182. *See also under*
    Pollution.
  pioneer investors, 153-154.
    See also under Pioneer
    investors.
  plan of work, applications for,
    153-165
  settlement of disputes, 186

Mining Code *cont.*
  prospecting, 104-109. *See also
  under* Prospecting.
Moratorium Resolution, 23, 27
  US attitude to, 27-28

NOAA,
  environmental research, 380-387
  evolving strategy, 438
  Marine Environmental Research
    Plan 1981-85, 443
  role under US legislation, 438-
    454
National legislation on sea-bed
  mining. *See under* Legislation of
  Western States.
National liberation movements,
  beneficiaries of common
    heritage, 66, 67
  participation in UN Convention,
    59, 62-64
Niue, 59, 60
Non-discrimination by Authority,
  104
Non-nodule minerals, 53, 149-151,
  453
Non-self-governing territories,
  beneficiaries of common
    heritage, 67-68
  participation in UN Convention,
    59, 64-65

Ocean Mining Associates (OMA),
  Exchange of letters with
    Yuzhmorgeologiya, 211
Optional clause declarations, 255
  US declaration, 255
Overlapping areas, obligation to
  avoid, 196-198

PLO, 62-64
'Parallel' system, 110
Pardo, A., historic speech (1967), 3

Peaceful purposes, 53
  use of Area for, 73
Penalties, 143
'Pioneer Areas',
  dimensions of, 19
  disputes concerning overlapping,
    197-198. *See also under*
    Pioneer Investor Regime.
Pioneer Investor Regime, 6, 187-
  243
  original scheme, 190-195
    development and adaptation,
      195-232
    Implementation Agreement,
      impact of, 232-243
  origins and raison d'être, 187-190
Pioneer Investors,
  categories of, 190-193
  protection of, 5
  registration of,
    Chinese, 230
    East European States and
      Cuba, 231-232
    French, Japanese and Russian,
      228
    Indian, 226
    Korean, 232
  obligations of,
    monitoring of fulfilment of,
      240-243
    understandings on, 229-230,
      231, 232
  plans of work,
    applications, 233-236
    approval of, 238-240
    fee, 236-237
Plans of work, 117-123, 233-240
Policies relating to activities in the
  Area, 100-104
Pollution from sea-bed mining, 379-
  454
  awareness of risks, 6
  environmental implications of sea
    bed mining, 380-389
  Implementation Agreement, 396-
    398

462   Subject index

Pollution from sea-bed mining *cont.*
  Mining Code, environmental
    regulations, 398-430. *See also*
    Table of Contents, Chap. 10,
    IV.
  national legislation, 430-454
    co-ordination of, 453-454
    France, 434-435
    Germany, 431-432
    Italy, 437
    Japan, 436-437
    overview, 430-437
    Russia, 435-436
    United Kingdom, 432-434
    United States, 431, 437-453
  protection of marine
    environment, as principle
    governing the Area, 53 84-85
  UN regime, 389-430
    Part XII: environmental rules,
      391-392
    principles and policies, 398-
      391
    setting and enforcement of
      environmental standards,
      393-396
Polymetallic sulphides, 53, 149-
  151, 453
Preparatory Commission,
  Arusha Understanding (1986),
    221-226
  Consensus Statement of
    Understanding, 345
  decision-making, 345, 346
  Declaration (1985) condemning
    Provisional Understanding on
    Deep Seabed Matters (1984),
    31-32, 39
  duration, 344
  functions, 344-345
  funding, 344
  General Committee, 347
  Group of Technical Experts, 347
  heavy burden upon, 5
  institutional aspects, 346-348
  membership, 343-344
  observers, 343-344

Preparatory Commission *cont.*
  organs and functions, 346-348
  Plenary, 346-347
  Resolution I, 343-345
  Rules of Procedure, 343
  Special Commissions I-IV, 347,
    348-349
  subsidiary bodies, 345
  'technical body', 347
  Training Panel, 348
Principles of UN regime, 49-95
  fundamental principle: common
    heritage of mankind, 49-71
  ideological milieu, 50-52
  scope *ratione loci*, 52-53
  scope *ratione materiae,* 53-54
  scope *ratione personae,* 56-71
  scope *ratione temporis*, 54-56
Production policy, 124-131
  economic assistance to
    developing countries, 127-131
  Implementation Agreement,
    impact of, 125
  unfair economic practices, 125-
    127
Prohibition of deep sea mining as
  freedom of seas, alleged
  existence of rule, 19-22
Prospecting, 104-109
  annual reports, 107-108
  archaeological objects, 109
  confidentiality, 107, 108-109
  defined, 104
  duration, 105
  environment, and, 109
  Mining Code, 105-109
  no right to resources, 106
  not exclusive, 105
  notification of, 106-107
  where undertaken, 105-106
Provisional membership of
  Authority, 11-13
Provisional Understanding
  Regarding Deep Seabed Matters,
  1984, 207-212, 271-275
  compatibility with UN regime,
    275

Subject index 463

Provisional Understanding *cont.*
 co-ordination of national
  legislation, 271-275
 Declaration of PrepCom
  condemning, 31-32, 39
 material scope, 271-275
 operating standards, prescription
  of, 272-275
 personal scope, 271
 prohibition of conflicting
  authorisations, 271
 temporal scope, 271

Reasonable regard rule, 86
Reciprocating States Regime,
 4, 6, 244-291
 compatibility with UN regime,
  270
 co-ordination of national
  legislation, 272-275
  Agreement Concerning Interim
   Arrangements Relating to
   Polymetallic Nodules of the
   Deep Sea Bed, 1982, *q.v.*
  Provisional Understanding
   Regarding Deep Seabed
   Matters, 1984, *q.v.*
 freedom of the high seas as basis
  of, 4
 impact of Implementation
  Agreement, 289-291
 legislation of Western States, *q.v.*
 UN Conventional regime
  compared, 244-268
Res communis,
 common heritage of mankind as
  new species of, 15
 status of sea-bed as, 37
Reservation of sites. *See under*
 Reserved areas.
Reserved areas, 91
 rights of operators other than
  Enterprise in, 131-134, 156-
  158. *See also under*
  Enterprise.

Reserved areas *cont.*
 under pioneer investor scheme,
  238
 unilateral legislation, position
  under, 256-257
Resources other than polymetallic
 nodules, 53, 149-151, 453
Responsibility to ensure compliance
 with UN regime and liability for
 damage, 75-78
 responsibility of international
  organisations, 77-78
 State responsibility, 75-77. *See
  also* Contractual Liability.
Review Conference, 54-56
Rio Tinto Zinc,
 statement on sea-bed mining, 257

St. Christopher-Nevis, 60
Scientific research. *See under*
 Marine scientific research.
Sea-bed mining,
 two alternative regimes, 4
 Reciprocating States Regime, *q.v.*
 United Nations Regime, *q.v.*
Sea-bed Disputes Chamber, 356-
 357
 ad hoc chambers, 356-357
 composition, 356. *See also*
  Settlement of disputes.
Security of tenure, 123
Self-governing associated States
 and territories,
 beneficiaries of common
  heritage, 66
 participation in UN
  Convention, 59-60
'Serious harm to the marine
 environment' defined, 402
Settlement of disputes, 6, 350-376
 classification of disputes, 357-
  361
 historical perspective, 350-353
 institutions concerned, 354-357
  commercial arbitral tribunal,
   357

464 *Subject index*

Settlement of disputes *cont.*
    International Tribunal for the
      Law of the Sea, *q.v.*
    Sea-bed Disputes Chamber,
      356-357
    optional clause declarations, 351
    range of disputes, 357-361
    UN Convention model in outline,
      353
'Site banking'. *See under* Reserved
    areas.
Sovereignty, fundamental principle
    of, 14-15. *See also under*
    Freedom of the high seas *and*
    Fundamental principles
    in conflict.
      legal presumptions in favour
      of, 15
'States Parties' defined, 66
State practice,
    earlier sea-bed claims, 18
    industrialised States, 41-45
Status of UN Convention, 6-13
Sui generis, EEZ as a zone, 15
Sulphides, 53, 149-151, 453

Technology transfer. *See under*
    Transfer of technology.
Territories under colonial
    domination,
    beneficiaries of common
      heritage, 66, 67-68
    participation in UN Convention,
      59, 64-65

Third parties,
    benefit of mankind, 65-66
    UN Convention effect on, 56-59
Title to minerals, 104
Transfer of data to Authority, 140-
    141
Transfer of technology, 81-84, 116
    joint ventures, 83-84
    mechanisms for, 82-84
    principle stated, 81-82
Truman Proclamation (1945), 3
Trust Territory of Pacific Islands,
    60

UN Convention
    parties to, capacity to become,
      59-65
    status of, 6-13
    third-party effect of, 56-59
UN Convention Regime,
    Principles of UN Regime, *q.v.*
Understanding on Resolution of
    Conflicts among Applicants for
    Registration as Pioneer Investors
    (1984), 213-220
Unfair economic practices, 125-127
Unilateral legislation on sea-bed
    mining, 187-188, 244-291
    alleged compatibility with UN
      regime, 42
    alleged interim character, 42
    embodiment of common heritage
      elements, 43-45
    Group of 77 position on, 31,33,
      37.

Printed in the United States
by Baker & Taylor Publisher Services